Lecture Notes in Computer Science 11869

More information about this series at http://www.springer.com/series/7409

Rogelio E. Cardona-Rivera ·
Anne Sullivan · R. Michael Young (Eds.)

Interactive Storytelling

12th International Conference
on Interactive Digital Storytelling, ICIDS 2019
Little Cottonwood Canyon, UT, USA, November 19–22, 2019
Proceedings

 Springer

Editors
Rogelio E. Cardona-Rivera ⓘ
University of Utah
Salt Lake City, UT, USA

Anne Sullivan
Georgia Institute of Technology
Atlanta, GA, USA

R. Michael Young
University of Utah
Salt Lake City, UT, USA

ISSN 0302-9743   ISSN 1611-3349   (electronic)
Lecture Notes in Computer Science
ISBN 978-3-030-33893-0   ISBN 978-3-030-33894-7   (eBook)
https://doi.org/10.1007/978-3-030-33894-7

LNCS Sublibrary: SL3 – Information Systems and Applications, incl. Internet/Web, and HCI

This Springer imprint is published by the registered company Springer Nature Switzerland AG
The registered company address is: Gewerbestrasse 11, 6330 Cham, Switzerland

Preface

It is our pleasure to present the proceedings of the 12th International Conference on Interactive Digital Entertainment (ICIDS 2019). This is a unique event formed at the intersection of many scholarly communities, ranging from core technologies to critical analysis, to the study of interactive narratives as cultural systems. The conference program reflects a discipline that has formed around interactive narrative research, drawing ideas and methods from many sub-disciplines to increase our understanding of interactive narratives as technical, cultural, and social artifacts.

With this 12th edition of the conference, ICIDS continues into its second decade as a recognizable entity at the forefront of interactive narrative research. As organizers, we took this opportunity to expand on mainstay topics within the community through the introduction of our theme "Design Foundations, Innovations, and Practices." Through this theme, we specifically encouraged submissions that focused on principles of design, advancements in the design lifecycle, and design process case studies for interactive storytelling.

For ICIDS 2019, 66 papers were submitted. Papers underwent a rigorous double-blind review, with each paper receiving a minimum of three reviews. Of the 66 submissions, 49 were submitted as full papers and 14 (14/49 = 29%) were accepted in that category. 6 papers from this submission category (or 12%) were accepted as short papers and 14 (29%) as posters. The conference received 14 short paper submissions, and 5 (5/14 = 36%) were accepted for presentation during the conference. 7 of the papers submitted in this category (7/14 = 50%) were accepted as posters. The ICIDS 2019 conference received 3 proposals for posters on preliminary work and 2 (2/3 = 66%) of these were selected as posters for inclusion in the poster session. All three types (full papers, short papers, and posters) appear in the conference proceedings (allotted 12 pages, 8 pages, and 4 pages plus references, respectively), as well as doctoral consortium and demo papers.

This year, we implemented detailed review guidelines, building upon those developed last year in collaboration with the ICIDS Steering Committee. Specifically, we modified the review form to require detailed written feedback from the Program Committee across several categories and developed a more structured area co-chair meta-review process. We are extremely grateful to all the Program Committee members for their dedication, hard work, and thoughtful reviews. In particular, we thank the area co-chairs for helping steward the papers in their respective tracks and ensuring that the conference remains competitive and collegial: Joshua Fisher, Hartmut Koenitz, Sandy Louchart, Chris Martens, Alex Mitchell, John Murray, Mark Nelson, Justus Robertson, Christian Roth, Rebecca Rouse, James Ryan, Nicolas Szilas, and Theresa Tanenbaum, thank you all!

ICIDS 2019 was held at the Snowbird Ski & Summer Resort in Little Cottonwood Canyon near Salt Lake City, UT, USA. The program ran during November 19–22, 2019, and included one day of workshops (including three workshop sessions) and three days of paper presentations. The program for ICIDS 2019 also included a peer-reviewed demonstration session and an art exhibit.

ICIDS is organized and operated by ARDIN, The Association for Research on Interactive Digital Narrative, a scientific society that oversees the conference and expands research activities in the area of interactive narrative. The conference gratefully acknowledges its very generous corporate sponsor, Springer. Their continued engagement with the conference reflects a clear commitment to leadership in support of the academic community working to create new knowledge around interactive narrative.

November 2019   Rogelio E. Cardona-Rivera
                                                                        Anne Sullivan
                                                                     R. Michael Young

ARDIN, the Association for Research in Digital Narratives

ARDIN's purpose is to support research in Interactive Digital Narratives (IDN), in all kinds of forms, be that video and computer games, interactive documentaries and fiction, journalistic interactives, art projects, educational titles, transmedia, virtual reality and augmented reality titles, or any emerging novel forms of IDN.

ARDIN is the next step of development after a decade of the ICIDS conferences. ARDIN provides a home for an interdisciplinary community and for various activities that connect, support, grow, and validate said community. These activities include membership services like a community platform, newsletters, job postings, and support for local gatherings, but also conferences, publication opportunities, research fellowships, and academic/professional awards. It is understood that not all of these activities can be supported right from the start, but they describe the ambition of the association.

ICIDS is the main academic conference of ARDIN. Additional international and local conferences are welcome to join the organization. The Zip-Scene conference, focused on eastern Europe, is the first associated conference.

Diversity is important to ARDIN. The organization will strive towards gender balance and the representation of different people from different origins. Diversity also means to represent scholars at different levels of their careers.

No ARDIN member shall discriminate against any other ARDIN member or others outside of the organization on basis of gender, nationality, race, or religion. Discrimination against these principles will not be tolerated and membership in ARDIN can be withdrawn based on evidence of such behavior.

The association is incorporated as a legal entity in Amsterdam, the Netherlands. During its foundational year, members of the former ICIDS Steering Committee continue to serve as the ARDIN board as approved by the first general assembly at ICIDS 2018 in Dublin, Ireland.

Organization

Organization Committee

General Chair

R. Michael Young   University of Utah, USA

Program Committee Chairs

Rogelio E. Cardona-Rivera University of Utah, USA
Anne Sullivan   Georgia Institute of Technology, USA

Workshop Chair

Jichen Zhu   Drexel University, USA

Local Arrangements Chair

Corrinne Lewis   University of Utah, USA

Art Exhibit Co-chairs

Ryan Bown   University of Utah, USA
Brian Salisbury   University of Utah, USA

Doctoral Consortium Chair

Ben Samuel   University of New Orleans, USA

Communication Chair

Rushit Sanghrajka   University of Utah, USA

Demonstrations Chair

Max Kreminski   University of California, Santa Cruz, USA

ARDIN Officers and Board

Founding Chair of the Board

Hartmut Koenitz   University of the Arts Utrecht, The Netherlands

Founding Treasurer

Frank Nack   University of Amsterdam, The Netherlands

Board Members

Luis Emilio Bruni	Aalborg University, Denmark
Andrew Gordon	University of Southern California, USA
Mads Haahr	Trinity College Dublin, Ireland
Lissa Holloway-Attaway	University of Skövde, Sweden
Alex Mitchell	National University of Singapore, Singapore
Valentina Nisi	University of Madeira, Portugal
David Thue	Carleton University, Canada
Rebecca Rouse	Rensselaer Polytechnic Institute, USA

Program Committee Area Chairs

Creating the Discipline: Interactive Digital Narrative Studies

Hartmut Koenitz	University of the Arts Utrecht, The Netherlands
Alex Mitchell	National University of Singapore, Singapore

Impacting Culture and Society

Joshua Fisher	Columbia University, USA
Rebecca Rouse	Rensselaer Polytechnic Institute, USA

Interactive Digital Narrative Practices and Applications

Sandy Louchart	Glasgow School of Art, UK
Theresa Jean Tanenbaum	University of California, Irvine, USA

Investigating Our History

Mark J. Nelson	American University, USA
James Ryan	Raytheon BBN Technologies, USA

Theoretical Foundations

John Murray	University of Central Florida, USA

Technologies

Chris Martens	North Carolina State University, USA
Justus Robertson	North Carolina State University, USA

Human Factors

Christian Roth	University of the Arts Utrecht, The Netherlands
Nicolas Szilas	University of Geneva, Switzerland

Program Committee

Devi Acharya	University of California, Santa Cruz, USA
Giacomo Albert	Università degli Studi di Pavia, Italy

Kasper Ingdahl Andkjær	Université de Genève, Switzerland
Ruth Aylett	Heriot-Watt University, UK
Sasha Azad	North Carolina State University, USA
Byung-Chull Bae	Hongik University, South Korea
Julio Bahamon	UNC Charlotte, USA
Sojung Bahng	Monash University, Australia
Alok Baikadi	Pearson, USA
Ágnes Karolina Bakk	Moholy-Nagy University of Art and Design, Hungary, and Sapientia Hungarian University of Transylvania, Romania
René Bakker	HAN University of Applied Sciences, The Netherlands
Paulo Bala	ITI-Larsys, Universidade Nova de Lisboa, Portugal
Jonathan Barbara	Saint Martin's Institute of Higher Education, Malta
Dan Barnard	London South Bank University, UK
Nicole Basaraba	Trinity College Dublin, Ireland
Mark Bernstein	Eastgate Systems, Inc., USA
Leonid Berov	University of Osnabrück, Germany
Kevin Bowden	University of California, Santa Cruz, USA
Alice Bowman	Abertay University, UK
Wolfgang Broll	Ilmenau University of Technology, Germany
Luis Emilio Bruni	Aalborg University, Denmark
Beth Cardier	Sirius-Beta, USA
Rogelio E. Cardona-Rivera	University of Utah, USA
Elin Carstensdottir	Northeastern University, USA
Miguel Carvalhais	INESC TEC, Universidade do Porto, Portugal
Marc Cavazza	University of Greenwich, UK
Vanessa Cesário	Madeira Interactive Technologies Institute, Portugal
Fred Charles	Bournemouth University, UK
Fanfan Chen	National Taiwan University, Taiwan
Yun-Gyung Cheong	SKKU, South Korea
Grant Christman	Children's Hospital Los Angeles, USC Keck School of Medicine, USA
Chris Crawford	Storytron, USA
Colette Daiute	City University of New York, USA
Rossana Damiano	Università di Torino, Italy
Mara Dionisio	ITI/LARSYS, Portugal
Esther Doorly	Trinity College Dublin, Ireland
Teun Dubbelman	HKU University of the Arts Utrecht, The Netherlands
Maria Engberg	Malmö University, Sweden
Sergio Estupiñán	University of Geneva, Switzerland
Rachelyn Farrell	University of New Orleans, USA
Dan Feng	Northeastern University, USA
Gabriele Ferri	Amsterdam University of Applied Sciences, The Netherlands
Mark Finlayson	Florida International University, USA
Joshua Fisher	Columbia University, USA

John Murray   University of Central Florida, USA
Frank Nack   University of Amsterdam, The Netherlands
Mark J. Nelson   American University, USA
Valentina Nisi   Madeira Interactive Technologies Institute, Portugal
Michael Nitsche   Georgia Institute of Technology, USA
Nuno Nunes   Madeira Interactive Technologies Institute, Portugal
David Olsen   Aeiouy, USA
Ethel Ong   De La Salle University, The Philippines
Luca Papale   IUDAV, Italy
Federico Peinado   Universidad Complutense de Madrid, Spain
Andrew Perkis   Norwegian University of Science and Technology,
                               Norway
Antonio Pizzo   Università di Torino, Italy
Marko Radeta   Madeira Interactive Technologies Institute, Portugal
Annalisa Raffone   L'Orientale University of Naples, Italy
María Cecilia Reyes   Università degli Studi di Genova, Italy
Jessica Rivera Villicana   Deakin University, Australia
Justus Robertson   North Carolina State University, USA
Raquel Robinson   University of Saskatchewan, Canada
Melissa Roemmele   SDL Research, USA
Christian Roth   University of the Arts Utrecht, The Netherlands
Sylvia Rothe   Ludwig Maximilian University of Munich, Germany
Rebecca Rouse   Rensselaer Polytechnic Institute, USA
Maria Roussou   National and Kapodistrian University of Athens,
                               Greece
Jonathan Rowe   North Carolina State University, USA
Carolina Beniamina Rutta   University of Trento, Italy
James Ryan   Raytheon BBN Technologies, USA
Anastasia Salter   University of Central Florida, USA
Sytze Schalk   Hogeschool voor de Kunsten Utrecht, The Netherlands
Henrik Schoenau-Fog   Aalborg University, Denmark
Digdem Sezen   Istanbul University, Turkey
Tonguc Ibrahim Sezen   Rhine-Waal University of Applied Sciences, Germany
Yotam Shibolet   Utrecht University, The Netherlands
Emily Short   Freelance, USA
Cláudia Silva   Madeira Interactive Technologies Institute, Portugal
Callum Spawforth   University of Southampton, UK
Ulrike Spierling   RheinMain University of Applied Sciences, Germany
Anne Sullivan   Georgia Institute of Technology, USA
Torbjörn Svensson   University of Skövde, Sweden
Nicolas Szilas   University of Geneva, Switzerland
Theresa Jean Tanenbaum   University of California, Irvine, USA
Mariet Theune   University of Twente, The Netherlands
David Thue   Reykjavik University, Iceland
Emmett Tomai   University of Texas Rio Grande Valley, USA
Clark Verbrugge   McGill University, Canada

Mirjam Vosmeer	Hogeschool van Amsterdam, The Netherlands
Eric Walsh	Rensselaer Polytechnic Institute, USA
Pengcheng Wang	North Carolina State University, USA
Stephen Ware	University of Kentucky, USA
Nelson Zagalo	University of Aveiro, Portugal

Additional Reviewers

Hameed, Asim
Irshad, Shafaq
Katifori, Akrivi

Contents

Technologies

Demonstrations

Creating the Discipline: Interactive Digital Narrative Studies

Experimental Analysis of Spatial Sound for Storytelling in Virtual Reality

Saylee Bhide[(✉)], Elizabeth Goins, and Joe Geigel

Rochester Institute of Technology, Rochester, NY 14623, USA
{smb6390, esggsh}@rit.edu, jmg@cs.rit.edu

Abstract. Spatial sound is useful in enhancing immersion and presence of the user in a virtual world. The spatial audio design allows the game designer to place audio cues that appropriately match with the visual cues in a virtual game environment. These localized audio cues placed in a story based game environment also help to evoke an emotional response from the user and construct the narrative of the game by directing the user's attention towards the guiding action events in the game. Our paper explores the usefulness of spatial sound for improving the performance and experience of a user in a virtual game environment. Additionally, with the help of the relevant subjective and objective inferences collected from a user study conducted on three different test cases, the paper also analyzes and establishes the potential of spatial sound as a powerful storytelling tool in a virtual game environment designed for Virtual Reality.

Keywords: Spatial sound · Storytelling · Virtual Reality

1 Introduction

Virtual Reality (VR) is a powerful platform for conveying narratives through games and films. In a story based virtual environment, badly designed environment may cause confusion and break the flow of the experience to negatively affect immersion. In a well-designed environment, appropriate visual and audio cues may be embedded in the game space to evoke emotional response, construct the underlying narrative, and contribute to presence and immersion while still preserving game interactivity [4]. The current discussions in game design posit that VR sound design should mimic real sound environments by employing fully spatialized sound so that spatial immersion and presence are supported by the audio components [2]. However, it is an ongoing debate on the usefulness of spatial sound in achieving total immersion [7]. Furthermore, although the idea of using visuals and audio as a storytelling tool in a game environment has been suggested, little has been discussed about spatial sound as an influence in conveying narrative [3]. This is a preliminary study that contributes to the field of spatial storytelling by studying the influence of audio cues on player experience. The goals of this study are to (1) Evaluate the impact of spatial sound on a user in a virtual environment and its contribution to immersion; and (2) Analyze the significance of spatial sound as a storytelling tool in a virtual game environment.

© Springer Nature Switzerland AG 2019
R. E. Cardona-Rivera et al. (Eds.): ICIDS 2019, LNCS 11869, pp. 3–7, 2019.
https://doi.org/10.1007/978-3-030-33894-7_1

2   Background and Related Work

The guidelines for interactivity and narrative in a virtual game environment are often conflicting [6]. Jenkins established a relationship between games and stories by introducing a spatial aspect to merge narrative and interactivity into game design. Besides visual cues [3], spatial sound cues embedded in the space can also evoke an emotional response and construct the narrative. The influence of spatial audio on immersion has been implied in a general context but the parameters of incorporating spatial audio in a virtual environment remain unclear. On the face of it, employing spatial audio, with its higher fidelity to the natural world, seems an obvious choice. However, spatial audio is vulnerable to creating the "Uncanny Aural Valley" in VR, an audio equivalent of "Uncanny Valley" [7]. Also, sound, like graphical components, demand processing resources which can result in competition for allocation of resources between audio and video at run-time [5]. These insights lead to questioning the need of sonic realism for VR storytelling thereby, offering a designer an audio-related choice for the development of immersive worlds [7].

3   Experimental Design and Implementation

Charlotte, is a VR door puzzle set in a haunted mansion wherein the narrative is to pass through multiple rooms via doors that can be operated with the help of switches [1]. Each door has a spatial sound cue that indicates the opening or closing action accordingly. *Charlotte* was modified to rid the game of all narrative game object interactions and enrich the soundscape exclusively. Three sound cue categories were introduced which were moderated as required. *Door sounds* are the sound cues for the doors in the puzzle. *In-place triggers* activate the sound cue at the player's location when the player overlaps the location within the radius of the trigger. These are intended to evoke fear in the player in form of a jump scare. *Far-place Triggers* activate the sound cue at a distant location when the player overlaps the location within the radius of the trigger. These are intended to influence the player's direction by capturing his attention towards the direction of the next room.

4   User Study

Three separate test cases which differ only with respect to the soundscape were introduced. A no-sound test case was setup for one participant at the end of the study as a control. For the Spatial Audio test case, door sounds, in-place triggers and far-place triggers were rendered spatial. For the Ambient Audio test case, door sounds, in-place triggers and far-place triggers were rendered ambient. For the Mixed Audio test case, door sounds, in-place triggers and far-place triggers were moderated depending on how each sound category would potentially impact the gameplay. The user-study was conducted with 34 participants wherein equal number of participants were assigned a single soundscape test case. The user-study was conducted individually, starting with a pre-experiment questionnaire, participating in an introductory test environment, participating in the VR puzzle and then the post-experiment questionnaire. The time to finish the complete experiment was estimated to be around 45 min. The main measures in this experiment is the time to solve the puzzle and the subjective experience measured by the 24 questions on engagement, engrossment, participation and immersion in the post-experiment questionnaire.

5 Results

All the participants are equally Engaged with the environment irrespective of the sound condition. There are slight differences between the Engrossment levels, however, consistently, spatial and mixed case results have no significant differences. The same applies to both the Participation and Immersion levels, where in there is a significant difference between spatial case and ambient case, and mixed case and ambient case, but no significant difference between the spatial and mixed tests case results. *Therefore, we conclude by saying that both spatial and mixed audio helped to achieve total immersion and provided the best experience.* The inferences from the post-experiment questionnaire results for spatial audio test case gave us evidence that spatial audio helped the participants to construct the narrative in the environment. The participants agreed that the spatial sound cues helped them understand the genre of the game and also conveyed the emotion of the environment. *To conclude, since spatial audio was successful in constructing the narrative and evoking fear, it could potentially be a powerful storytelling tool.*

6 Discussion

Finding 1: The results do not statistically prove that spatial audio helped to improve the player performance. Ambient sound performed better than spatial and mixed audio. In our opinion, in the ambient sound test case, the player learned the spatial map of the environment instead of relying on sound cues. In the spatial audio test case, the player most likely followed the direction of the sound and overlooked the spatial mapping of the environment. However, in the mixed sound test case, it is unclear whether the participants were following the sound or learning the spatial map, therefore, the average time taken to solve the puzzle lay between the average time taken for ambient audio and spatial audio. Additionally, in the no sound test case condition, the participant solved the puzzle in the average time. This gave us evidence that, in the absence of sound, the participant relied on the spatial map of the environment. Due to the small area of the environment, it was easy to memorize the spatial map. This served as evidence that learning the spatial map in the absence of persuasive sound helped the participants to solve the puzzle faster. Alongside varying participant knowledge and familiarity with VR games, another reason for not having significant performance time differences between the test cases could be the genre and nature of the game itself. Many participants mentioned that fear dominated their sense of direction while some stated that they were too focused on the task to notice the sounds.

Finding 2: Ambient sound evoked more fear with respect to spatial sound. Ambient sounds were more jarring to the participants thereby startling them and triggering the "fear of unknown" phenomenon due to the absence of directional audio information.

Finding 3: Environment exploration pattern varied with test case. In the ambient sound scenario, we assume that on the first non-directional door sound, the participants knew that they had to rely on visuals and memory to locate the door. The sound gave away the occurrence of the event but not the location. Therefore, the participant was observed to explore the environment piece by piece in search of the door. Since there were multiple sound triggers placed in different parts of the room, the ambient sound scenario participant was successful in activating almost all the triggers in the environment. Conversely, in the spatial audio scenario, we assume that the first door sound hinted to the player that they had to follow the sound. Therefore, on our visual observation, we found that their movement initially was very quick and focused towards the sound of the door. We also observed that since the participant did not try to explore the environment thoroughly, the triggers that were located away from the doors were not activated.

7 Conclusion

The results indicate that spatial audio did not help to improve the performance of the player. This could have been due to the failure of the spatial sound cues, thereby, allowing memorization of the spatial map of environment to aid in solving the task. Nevertheless, spatial audio did positively affect the immersion and experience of the player. However, the mixed sound test case performed almost on par with the spatial audio test case. The equivalent performance of both indicates that the sound in the environment can be optimized by rendering some parts as ambient and some as spatial, thereby making the environment relatively computationally inexpensive. Therefore, sonic realism although desired, can be compensated by appropriately designing the sound cues. When creating narrative rich VR environments, the results indicate that designers should consider what is needed, story wise, from the sound. Ambient sound was interpreted by the players, the lack of directional information did not break immersion but rather supported the thematic aspects of the environment. Ambient sound also did not hinder player performance, rather players employed different strategies to progress. The strategy employed for the ambient scenario encouraged exploration and slower pacing. On the other hand, the spatial sound scenario encouraged focus on task and quicker pacing.

References

1. Goins, E., et al.: Charlotte. Game, MAGIC (2016)
2. Goins, E.: Personal communication. GDC VR discussion (2018)
3. Jenkins, H.: Game design as narrative. Computer **44**(53), 118–130 (2004)
4. Altman, R.: Tackling VR storytelling challenges with spatial audio. https://postperspective.com/tackling-vr-storytelling-challenges-spatial-audio/. Accessed 16 July 2019

5. Superpowered: How 3D Spatialized Audio Bottlenecks Virtual Reality Video. https:// superpowered.com/3d-spatialized-audio-virtual-reality. Accessed 18 July 2019
6. The Designer's Notebook: Three Problems for Interactive Storytellers, Resolved. https:// www.gamasutra.com/view/feature/189364/the_designers_notebook_three_.php. Accessed 16 July 2019
7. Video Game Composers: The Art of Music in Virtual Reality (GDC 2018) (2018). https:// www.gamasutra.com/blogs/WinifredPhillips/20180213/314609/Video_Game_Composers_ The_Art_of_Music_in_Virtual_Reality_GDC_2018.php. Accessed 16 July 2019

A Model for Analyzing Diegesis in Digital Narrative Games

Erica Kleinman[✉], Elin Carstensdottir, and Magy Seif El-Nasr

Khoury College of Computer Sciences, Northeastern University,
Boston, MA 02115, USA
kleinman.e@husky.neu.edu, elin@ccs.neu.edu,
m.seifel-nasr@northeastern.edu

Abstract. Effectively communicating information about the diegetic boundary of a story world is critical to interactive narratives in games. It is crucial to the player's ability to reason about how the game establishes and limits their options for interaction. However, games have proven difficult to apply traditional models of diegesis to, due to their interactive nature. Having a model for analyzing diegesis in interactive storytelling games could prove beneficial for the examination of communication between designer and player. In this paper, we present possible foundations of such a model, using film theory and the Interaction Model for Interactive Narratives as a lens. We define constructs and components that can be used to identify, isolate, and examine elements of a narrative game that define its diegetic experience and, through four case studies, demonstrate the utility of the model in analyzing the effects of diegesis and include observations on how to improve communication about diegetic boundaries between designer and player.

Keywords: Diegesis · Interactive Narrative · User experience · Communication · Interaction design · Narrative design

1 Introduction

Establishment of story world is of crucial concern to any interactive narrative endeavor regardless of format. Whether it is through establishing a common ground for live action role play, a set of rules for a card game, or constraining the range of action relevant to an ARG, the player needs to have a clear sense of where the story world begins and where it ends. The player's awareness of the story world boundary allows them to reason about what knowledge they can apply to their interaction within the world. Players will approach a story world, and formulate hypotheses about its boundary, from multiple points of view, depending on what inferences they have access to as a result of previous experiences, whether that be from other games or the real world. If a story world boundary is not well established or blurred, the player will rely on previous experience to guide them. Previous work has established that players can transfer

© Springer Nature Switzerland AG 2019
R. E. Cardona-Rivera et al. (Eds.): ICIDS 2019, LNCS 11869, pp. 8–21, 2019.
https://doi.org/10.1007/978-3-030-33894-7_2

inferences from a game to the real world [38], making the study of how story world boundaries are established and maintained through design of significant importance in the study of not only interactive narratives, but broadly for how people transfer and apply knowledge between games and the real world.

For digital games, such boundaries are often blurred. Menus, interfaces, and in-game systems, elements outside the defined frame of the story world, are often used to facilitate narrative interaction and communication, while simultaneously acting as a gateway between the player and the story world [18]. While interacting with them, the player will try to understand and reason about which actions will impact narrative progression [4]. For the player, differentiating between elements within and outside the frame of the story world becomes even more complex when elements outside the conventional frame of the game world, such as the file system of the computer, are used to progress the narrative. Designers need to be able to communicate to the player where the boundaries of the story world lie and what actions exist within it.

In non-interactive media, specifically film, such boundaries, and the navigation thereof, are discussed and defined in relation to *diegesis*. There are multiple definitions of diegesis in different mediums. Theater, as far back as ancient Greece, used the terms "diegetic" and "mimetic" to refer to narrated and enacted stories, respectively [1,31,43]. By contrast, previous work in literature and film discusses diegesis in a manner similar to theories of fabula, where there is a distinct separation of the world of the story as it exists, and the events of the story as they are presented [3,15]. Within the medium of film, specifically, the concept of diegesis is concerned with establishing a universe within which the events of the story occur [15,31,42,46].

Borrowing from film, for the purpose of this paper, diegesis will be defined as the frame and contents of the story world that is presented to a player, confined within the software window that the interactive narrative and/or game is presented within. A diegetic boundary, like film, denotes that there exists a conceptual story world frame that distinguishes it from the apparatus. Diegetic elements exist, or originate from sources, within the story world, while non-diegetic elements come from outside of it.

While there has been much work by the community to generate a formal understanding of how diegetic boundaries are established and interacted with by players [6,11,18,26,40], currently, there is no fully developed, generalizable model of diegesis in digital games. This results in situations where games that try to blur the boundaries of the storyworld can confuse and frustrate players. If the means they have to navigate them are not clearly communicated, players may encounter unexpected narrative ramifications. For example, characters in Undertale [12] will frequently inform the player that they should not perform violent actions, such as killing the enemies they encounter. However, due to the existing conventions of role playing games, Undertale's genre, many players fail to recognize these as actual instructions and do not understand that ignoring or defying them will have plot-relevant consequences. While this confusion might be part of authorial intent, it is important to acknowledge that this will violate the expectations of many players that want to play the game in a manner aligned with their own goals. This violation of expectations may then lead to player frustration and loss of interest. This is becoming a more pressing concern as designers explore these diegetic boundaries more frequently, for example through 4th wall breaking and rewind mechanics [22,23]. A formal understanding of diegesis in games can help designers conventionalize how the boundaries of a story world can be communicated to the player. Which can, in turn, help control for player expectations as well as minimize frustration and confusion.

Previous work in games and diegesis have shown the potential of the film studies approach in which the focus is on the division and relationship between the audience and the storyworld [6,24,39,40]. However, existing work has also illustrated that the film studies approach on its own is not enough to account for the interactive nature of games [11,19,40]. In addition, it's important to note that diegesis does not have an agreed upon definition in the literature for interactive storytelling. It is not the intent of the authors that the work presented here provide such a definitive definition of diegesis, but rather, a point of view to consider when analyzing diegesis in any form for interactive stories. Building on film studies, we expand the existing understanding of diegesis to account for interactivity. Using previous work and the Interaction Model for Interactive Narratives [4,5], we develop an initial model for analyzing diegesis in games, from the perspective of how players perceive what their diegetic action set is and how the narrative can be progressed. We illustrate the use of the model through four case studies. In each case study we analyze a single game, OneShot [27], The Stanley Parable [13], The Wolf Among Us [45], and Harry Potter: Wizards Unite [32] in terms of its diegetic experience.

2   Related Work

2.1   Diegesis in Non-interactive Media

In ancient Greek theater, the term diegetic was conceived to refer to theatrical narratives that were delivered through the speech of a narrator. It was used in contrast to the term mimetic, which referred to narratives delivered through the actions or speech of an actor, spoken as the character they are imitating [1,31,43]. Unlike theater, literature has only text at its disposal, thus, mimesis, in the traditional sense where it means storytelling through imitation [1], does not exist. Instead, literature focuses on diegesis in terms of layers [1,3,29] and as a way of identifying where the boundaries of the story world lie [3,15].

Like theater, film contains visual, enacted elements. However, as a medium, film is more concerned with the establishment of the story space, rather than exploring the difference between different modes of storytelling [21,34,42,46]. As a result, similar to literature, film also considers diegesis in terms of marking the separation between the universe in which the events of the story occur, and the universe that exists beyond that [8,15,31,42,46]. In this context, diegetic refers to the represented world of the story that is displayed on the screen, while anything beyond that world, such as background music, title screens, or even the audience, is non-diegetic [31]. The screen, as a window or a frame [8], acts as a border between the worlds, granting the audience a view of the story world on the other side. However, a film only shows parts of the world within the screen, communicated to the audience by the filmmaker. It is the role of the film viewer, informed by conventions of the art, to piece the fragments together into a perception of the diegetic world within [7]. To further enhance this interpretive process, the film maker uses various tools for communicating details regarding the diegetic world to the viewer [8,15].

Film sound is one of the most commonly used tools for diegetic communication, to the point where it is almost ambiguous with conventional storytelling methods in film [8,15]. Diegetic sounds, those that originate from an on-screen source, are those that the characters within the storyworld can observe or be affected by, while non-diegetic sounds, those with no source, exist for the sake of the viewer [8,35]. To the audience, non-diegetic sounds, such as soundtracks and audio effects, set the mood of a scene, foretell events to come, and convey meaning that may not be explicitly shown or stated [8,15,31,35,46]. Further, non-diegetic sounds were used often, in early film, to mask the presence of the film projector, also referred to as "apparatus" [34,42]. Diegesis in film is an understanding of the boundary between the world of the film's events and the world in which the audience resides, and the positioning of said boundary is an established convention of the medium [7,8]. This clear boundary allows for filmmakers to rely on conventions of their craft to leverage both diegetic and non-diegetic elements to clearly communicate narrative information to their audience.

2.2 Diegesis in Games

Unlike film, in games the boundary between the diegetic world of the game and the non-diegetic world of the player becomes permeable. For example, non-diegetic sound, such as a soundtrack or audio effects, will influence the way the player perceives events and influence the actions they take. These actions are diegetic and have diegetic consequences, but are informed and enacted by non-diegetic entities [17,19,25]. In this sense, games are a medium where the diegetic world can be dynamically influenced and manipulated by the non-diegetic world, effectively blurring the boundary between the two spaces.

Despite these differences, games, like film, rely on visuals, text, sound effects, and music to create the illusion of a world beyond the events framed by the game window [18,39]. As such, film theory has been successfully used to discuss games, how they establish diegetic story worlds, and how the player relates to and navigates such worlds [6,7,20,24,39]. One example, is Crick's use of Sobchack's theory of a "film body" to analyze camera perspectives in games in order to better reason about how players are able to simultaneously exist in multiple spaces [6]. However, existing work that utilizes film theory to examine games has not focused on the synthesis of a model that can be used, specifically, to analyze diegesis in games as a unique medium.

Much of the existing work on diegesis in digital game environments concerns itself with the idea of a story world, the diegetic space of that world, the maintenance of the illusion of that world's reality [10, 26, 37, 44], the analysis of how players interact with and understand that world [6, 11, 18], and how diegesis is constructed between participants of role playing games [28, 30]. The positioning of the player within the diegetic storyworld, and the ways in which the player can manipulate both character and view, are believed to impact the ways in which the player perceives their interaction with the diegesis [6, 39, 40]. Unlike film, where the director has complete control over what is on the screen at any moment, games allow the player to manipulate their field of view, meaning that there is no guarantee that they will see what the designer intends them to [7]. Similarly, the control of game progression that is allowed by interactivity means that a gameplay experience may not be the same every time or for everyone [11]. Such freedom of action can make it difficult for designers to establish a diegetic world through the same conventions as film. This makes framing and presentation of information about the diegesis a significant design concern. Games have developed their own conventions for establishing such a diegesis, often using non-interactive elements, such as cutscenes, as a form of narration that establishes a diegetic playground in which the player can take action [10, 24]. Another tool for this purpose is sound, which, like film sound, is closely linked to the discussion of diegesis. Horror games, for instance, take advantage of trans-diegetic sounds, which cross the barrier between the diegetic world and the player's world, to put the player in a state of discomfort, or alert them of incoming action they must prepare for [17, 19, 25].

Although film theory has informed existing analysis of game diegesis, film theory alone cannot properly account for the interactive nature of games, for reasons similar to why Ferri argues that a pure literary analysis is not adequate [11]. Interaction is the defining characteristic that distinguishes games as a unique medium. However, interaction is an element so at odds with the maintenance of a diegetic world that games often go to great lengths to mask their interface elements behind narrative explanations [7, 44]. Further, because the player's actions can, and often will, impact the progression of the narrative, it is important to communicate to the player what actions are available to them, and which of those will have a diegetic impact.

3   The Model

For this initial model, we analyze diegesis in games through the lens of a user experience (UX) feedback loop. In this context, a UX feedback loop is when the player observes the story world, considers the information available, and builds a plan of action. The player attempts to take action, in accordance with the plan, and once their action has been performed, the player observes the impact on the story world, and the loop repeats. Analyzing diegesis in this way allows for distinguishing between what information is available to the player and what is presented, and how that relates to what kind of diegetic impact a particular action might have. Distinguishing between these steps is necessary in order to reason about and design narrative progression, which is foundational to interactive narrative games. To guide our analysis, we used the Interaction Model for Interactive Narratives [4,5], which builds upon the same UX feedback loop, and we augment the analysis using film theory, borrowing the idea of a diegetic story world that is separate from the non-diegetic world of the audience and the apparatus. We add additional variables to the model, specifically, to presentation and feedback, sub-components of the Interaction construct, to describe, analyze, and categorize what the designer communicates to the player about the boundary between the diegetic and non-diegetic elements of the game. The new sub-components are meant to be used either independently or within the context of the interaction model as a whole. While we recognize that the constructs and components included in this paper are not exhaustive, we argue that these present foundational concepts that are needed to analyze and differentiate diegetic and non-diegetic elements in single player interactive narratives.

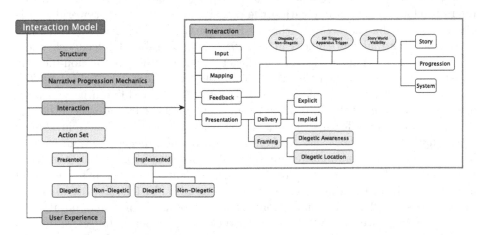

Fig. 1. An illustration of how the diegesis model (whose elements are highlighted in blue) fits into the Interaction Model for Interactive Narratives [4,5] (Color figure online)

To presentation, we add a new sub-component, "Framing", referring to the story information that the designer builds into the experience, that contains two sub-categories: diegetic awareness and diegetic location. Diegetic awareness refers to the extent to which characters that exist within the game narrative are aware of the boundary between the diegetic (story world) and non-diegetic spaces. For example, Noctis in *Final Fantasy 15* [9] is not aware of the non-diegetic world beyond the story, nor that the story world exists as a diegetic space within that world. Thus, he has no diegetic awareness. By contrast, the Pods in *Nier: Automata* [14] are aware of the player and speak with them directly. As such, they do have diegetic awareness. Diegetic location refers to the metaphorical positioning of narrative entities in relation to the boundary between the diegetic and non-diegetic spaces. In other words, whether the entity is located inside or outside the fiction of the game. The people you interact with in *Papers Please* [36] are positioned strictly within the diegetic world of the story, thus they have a diegetic location. By contrast Monika, in *Doki Doki Literature Club* (DDLC) [41], and Flowey, in *Undertale* [12], are both able to manipulate elements of the apparatus that support their games, such as editing files or closing windows. At the same time, both characters exist and are able to interact within the diegetic world of the narrative. Thus, both characters can be categorized as having a trans-diegetic location, or a location that exists both in the diegetic and non-diegetic. Notably, a character's awareness does not necessarily correspond with their location. Despite their diegetic awareness, the previously mentioned pods from *Nier* [14] exist exclusively within the story world and are unable to cross the boundary. This means that their location is strictly diegetic.

To feedback, we add distinctions between diegetic and non-diegetic feedback, whether the feedback is triggered by diegetic or non-diegetic (apparatus) inter-action, and whether the feedback is visible to diegetic entities. Diegetic feedback refers to changes that occur within the diegetic space of the storyworld and is observable by the characters within it. For example, the characters' responses to the player's dialogue choices in *Oxenfree* [33]. Non-diegetic feedback refers to changes that occur outside of the diegetic space, either in the non-diegetic interface or in the apparatus itself. For example, notifications in *Long Live The Queen* [16] that notify the player of failed stat checks. We differentiate between feedback in response to actions taken within or beyond the boundaries of the storyworld. Most games feature diegetic action, such as dialogue choices in *Dragon Age: Inquisition* [2], however, *DDLC* [41] requires non-diegetic action, such as having the player manipulate computer files in order to progress the narrative. Feedback visibility is the extent to which the residents of the game's storyworld are aware of the feedback or actions that triggered it. In DDLC [41], when the player takes non-diegetic action, Monika is aware of, and comments on, it.

Additionally, we define the new construct "Action Set": the set of actions available to the player. It contains two components: *presented action set*, the action set that can be inferred from the affordances of the interface and infor-mation from the story world, and *implemented action set*, the "actual" set of actions that the player has access to in relation to what can progress the narra-tive. Both have sub-components that refer to the set of actions available to the player within the story world, the diegetic action set, and the set available to the player outside of the story world, the non-diegetic action set, which could be within the apparatus or outside of it. If the mapping between the presented and implemented action sets is sufficiently overlapping, the player is more likely to perceive their set of actions to be the same as, or close to, the "actual" set of available actions, which allows them to more accurately reason about the narra-tive and their place in it. This is especially important in games that transcend the diegetic boundaries, and allow interaction with the apparatus to influence and progress the narrative. For example, DDLC [41] invites the player to manipulate files in order to progress the narrative, but the game does not explicitly articu-late the exact limitations it poses on file manipulation and how that potentially impacts narrative progression. As a result, many players continuously manipulate irrelevant files in the hopes of finding new outcomes. While this may be a deliberate design choice, clear communication about available action is the key to allowing players to reason about how they can pursue their goals in game.

Combining all of these components into the UX loop: the player is presented (see Fig. 1 for the Presentation construct) with information by observing the story world. When the player formalizes their plan, they consider what actions are afforded by the presented action set. The player then tries to take that action, and if that action exists within the implemented action set, the action will succeed and the player will be able to observe the consequences of their action on the story world, and the loop continues.

4 Case Studies

To demonstrate the model's use, we conducted four case studies on commercial games that showcase different approaches to the diegetic experience for interactive narratives. *The Wolf Among Us* presents an isolated diegetic world. *The Stanley Parable* makes reference to the non-diegetic world, but the available actions in this space are limited. *OneShot*, embraces the non-diegetic to the furthest degree by both acknowledging and establishing a non-diegetic action set. *Harry Potter: Wizards Unite*, an alternate reality game, overlays a diegetic world on top of the player's non-diegetic world, creating the illusion of a merged space.

4.1 The Wolf Among Us

The Wolf Among Us [45] (TWAU) is an interactive adventure game in which the player controls the character of Bigby Wolf as he attempts to solve a murder mystery in a fantastical version of New York City. The player's interaction options consist of dialogue and action choices selected through menus, quick-time events, and searching for clues in a 3D space. The game has a clearly defined diegetic space, none of the characters are aware of the non-diegetic space beyond the boundaries of the story world, and all story world entities are diegetically located. Feedback occurs both within the diegesis, in the form of dialogue and narrative events, and in the non-diegetic space in the form of notifications. While the interface menus used to take action are not, themselves, diegetic, they are presented such that they act as a mediation tool connecting the player to Bigby through a mapping, allowing them to take diegetic action. Thus, all feedback in TWAU is triggered by diegetic action. The game features no presented nor implemented non-diegetic action set, only an implemented diegetic action set within the story world, one which is clearly presented to the player.

4.2 The Stanley Parable

The Stanley Parable [13] is a interactive environmental narrative game, in which the player influences progression by deciding where to go and what buttons to press via a first person view. During this process, a disembodied narrator will direct the player and comment on their ability to follow or defy his instructions. The narrator is diegetically located, but implies a degree of non-diegetic awareness. Feedback, always in the form of dialogue and environmental events, and most interaction, primarily through navigation, are diegetic. However, the game relies on rewind to allow the player to explore the entire story [22,23]. This is an example of a non-diegetic interaction (restarting the game) triggering diegetic feedback (the narrator comments on the player doing this). The implemented diegetic action set is clearly presented both visually and through the narrator's spoken instructions, however the non-diegetic action set within the apparatus (the ability to experience more by restarting the game) is only implied through context clues and the narrator's dialogue.

4.3   One Shot

OneShot [27] is a role playing game in which the player must aid the character Niko on their quest to restore light to the world. The game expresses explicit self awareness of its existence as a game, acknowledges the player as an entity separate and unique from Niko, and requires the player to perform actions within their computer in order to progress. Numerous characters posses non-diegetic awareness, and diegetic location also varies depending on the character. Despite being aware, the Author's followers are strictly diegetically located. Niko, mostly diegetically located, is able to cross the boundary into the non-diegetic at the end of the game, placing them in a trans-diegetic location along with The Entity, who is able to manipulate and speak through the player's computer, but also appears within the story world. Finally, The Author, who never appears inside the story world, only communicates with the player via their computer, and thus, is strictly non-diegetically located. Both the story world and apparatus action sets are presented through dialogue with various characters, and feedback is both diegetic, character dialogue and story world updates, and non-diegetic, changes to the computer. Feedback can be triggered by interactions both within the storyworld, such as traveling to a location, or the apparatus, such as rewinding [22,23] and moving or deleting files. Non-diegetic feedback is only explicitly visible to The Entity and The Author.

4.4   Harry Potter: Wizards Unite

Harry Potter: Wizards Unite [32] is a narrative driven, location based, augmented reality game where players assume the role of a wizarding world resident charged with retrieving wayward magical artifacts. The game was analyzed soon after launch (version 2.0.1.). The goal of the player is to collect diegetic elements that are scattered about the physical, non-diegetic world. The player does this by walking around, a non-diegetic interaction, while tracking their location diegetically on an in-game map. The player is physically located in a non-diegetic space, and performing non-diegetic interaction that results in diegetic feedback. Simultaneously, the player is narratively located in a diegetic space. The player engages with the non-diegetic action set until they encounter a diegetic element, at which point they transition from the non-diegetic space to the diegetic space, in order to do battle, mix potions, or collect items. Because the game is dependent on the apparatus to function, it attempts to mask it through diegetic explanations, such as referring to it as a magical map. However, when the player transitions from the non-diegetic interaction to the diegetic, the mask slips away as the apparatus becomes the controller through which the player is able to see and interact with the diegetic action set. A notable exception is the portkey interaction, which incorporates both non-diegetic and diegetic interaction simultaneously. Elements of the diegetic world are framed as being embedded within the non-diegetic world, but can only be observed and interacted with by the player through the phone screen. Thus, the diegetic world exists in an overlay that sits atop the non-diegetic, creating the illusion of a merged space.

4.5   Discussion and Comparison

Using the model, we are able to identify how the four games differed in their approaches to the diegetic experience. *The Wolf Among Us* has the least amount of non-diegetic elements in its experience. Its characters have no non-diegetic awareness or location, and are unable to see non-diegetic feedback. The same is true for *Wizards Unite* where characters possess only diegetic awareness and location. Further, feedback is never triggered by apparatus interaction in either game. By contrast, both *The Stanley Parable* and *OneShot* contain some amount of non-diegetic awareness and apparatus interaction. *OneShot* embraces the non-diegetic experience to the furthest degree by also including characters who are non-diegetically, and trans-diegetically, located, and including non-diegetic feedback. There is disparity in how the games establish and present their action sets. *The World Among Us* and has no apparatus action set, and instead focuses entirely on clearly presenting its story world action set. *The Stanley Parable* has a limited apparatus action set, the player can only affect narrative progression through rewinding, and presents this through implications in dialogue, menus, and loading screens. *OneShot* has a much larger apparatus action set, though still limited, and presents it much more explicitly, through direct instructions and non-diegetic feedback. *Wizards Unite* does not have a non-diegetic action set within the apparatus but does present a limited non-diegetic action set within the physical world in allowing the player to walk around. Despite their differences, all games contained diegetic feedback, feedback triggered by diegetic interaction, and diegetically located characters. We argue that these elements are conventional to narrative games.

OneShot and The Stanley Parable are notably similar in that both have at least one diegetically located character that possesses non-diegetic awareness. In both cases they are used to instruct and guide the player in relation to their diegetic and non-diegetic action sets. For The Stanley Parable, this non-diegetic awareness is not diegetically framed as part of the game story, which is very explicitly about the relationship between the player and the designer, and the nature of free will in digital games. As such, the framing of the non-diegetic awareness is non-diegetic. OneShot has a different, diegetic justification for the non-diegetic awareness of its characters, related to how the story world exists within a game, framing the non-diegetic awareness diegetically. Both games had diegetic feedback triggered by non-diegetic interaction. For The Stanley Parable, more branches of the story can be explored if the player restarts the game, and the narrator comments on this action. In OneShot, rewinding, file manipulation, and manipulation of program windows can all trigger narrative progression, change the state of the game world, and trigger responses from characters.

A mapping that is close to being one to one between presented and implemented action sets allows the player to reason about what actions are available to them. A failure to establish such a mapping is likely to lead to confusion and frustration. This is especially true for games that involve non-diegetic action sets, as they must communicate the availability and limitations of actions in said space to the player. Failure in doing so results in players who repeatedly attempt to perform irrelevant actions within the apparatus under the assumption that they may trigger narrative progression. This was observed as a possible issue in both *The Stanley Parable* and *OneShot*. As an illustrative example, in The Stanley Parable, the player may continuously restart the game believing it'd be possible to find new story content by combining different sets of choices.

We observed that there needs to be diegetic feedback in response to non-diegetic action to inform the player that their non-diegetic actions can have story ramifications. Non-diegetic awareness seems to be used as an indicator of there being the possibility of non-diegetic interaction having an effect on the diegetic space. Further, establishing the non-diegetic awareness of a character early on can ensure that the player understands when instructions are being given diegetically, and avoid frustration as a result of misinterpretation, see the *Undertale* [12] example discussed in the introduction. In both *The Stanley Parable* and *OneShot*, diegetically located characters with non-diegetic awareness are used to encourage and guide the player to the non-diegetic actions they can take that will have diegetic consequences. However, non-diegetic awareness is not necessary. *Wizards Unite* establishes a non-diegetic action set through diegetic feedback alone. We acknowledge that these are only four case studies and that it is likely that the current form of the model may not be sufficient to analyze the diegetic experience in all types of interactive narrative games. However, we argue that this model is a tool containing foundational concepts necessary for understanding diegesis in the context of the player experience, and that this foundation can be built upon in future work. Further, we argue that the games selected, while not representative of all games, are suitable examples of the types of approaches to diegesis that are exhibited in contemporary narrative games.

5   Conclusion

In this paper we proposed a model for analyzing diegesis in interactive narratives in digital games, using film theory and the Interaction model for Interactive Narratives as theoretical lenses and grounding. Diegesis is a term used to discuss the boundary and relationship that exists between a story world and its audience. In the context of film studies, diegetic refers to what is contained within the story as it exists and is presented to the audience with the assistance of an apparatus (i.e. a projector). Non-diegetic, in contrast, refers to what is outside the story, but presented to the audience in some form, such as a soundtrack that the characters in the story world do not hear. Interactive storytelling media, such as digital games, frequently explore these diegetic boundaries with interesting and widely popular results. However, this traversal of diegetic boundaries can result in player frustration and confusion, often in relation to narrative progression, when the nature of the diegetic boundaries and the means provided to successfully traverse them are not successfully communicated to the player.

Previous work for diegesis in games and interactive narrative has not focused on developing models to analyze diegesis from the perspective of how it is communicated to and experienced by the player. This is important for identifying usability and narrative understanding issues, especially for games that push diegetic boundaries. In this paper we presented a theoretical grounding for such a model, and demonstrated how the diegetic content and design of four different types of interactive storytelling games could be compared and discussed using the model. We found the model suitable for isolating the properties of each game that defined its diegetic experience, and were able to compare these properties across games in order to sufficiently describe the ways in which they differed. We argue the model is beneficial in analyzing the ways in which games communicate the boundaries of the story world and the range of actions available to the player. In addition to analysis, we argue that the proposed model can aid in designing diegetic and non-diegetic elements that allow developers to better predict how their players reason about narrative progression.

One example of the usefulness of this model is being able to identify and analyze the elements that might cause player confusion and frustration. In the Undertale [12] example discussed in the introduction, the game intentionally subverts conventional diegetic boundaries. However, the characters', non-diegetic locations and awareness are established too late for many players to recognize critical instructions that establish their diegetic and non-diegetic action sets. As a result, many players are confused and frustrated when conventionally non-diegetic interaction has diegetic consequences. While this was authorial intent, in this particular case, it defies player expectations and can result in a negative reaction that has put many players off playing the rest of the game. Using this model during the design of interactive narrative games, especially those that attempt to push the conventional boundaries of diegesis, can help ensure that the players can understand the scope and impact of their actions and how it affects their progression and experience with the story.

Going forward, we would like to further refine the model, and use it to analyze diegetic and non-diegetic communication between characters and other elements of the game and player in order to design such interaction more effectively. We hope that proposing this model for the analysis of diegesis for interactive narrative in games will help in future discussions about the various considerations that diegesis impacts in game design and interactive storytelling.

References

1. Berger, K.: Diegesis and mimesis: the poetic modes and the matter of artistic presentation. J. Musicol. **12**(4), 407–433 (1994)
2. Bioware: Dragon Age: Inquisition. [Playstation 4] (2014)
3. Bunia, R.: Diegesis and representation: beyond the fictional world, on the margins of story and narrative. Poet. Today **31**(4), 679–720 (2010)
4. Carstensdottir, E., Kleinman, E., El-Nasr, M.S.: Player interaction in narrative games: structure and narrative progression mechanics. In: Proceedings of the 14th International Conference on the Foundations of Digital Games, p. 23. ACM (2019)
5. Carstensdottir, E., Kleinman, E., Seif El-Nasr, M.: Towards an interaction model for interactive narratives. In: Nunes, N., Oakley, I., Nisi, V. (eds.) ICIDS 2017. LNCS, vol. 10690, pp. 274–277. Springer, Cham (2017). https://doi.org/10.1007/978-3-319-71027-3_24
6. Crick, T.: The game body: toward a phenomenology of contemporary video gaming. Games Cult. **6**(3), 259–269 (2011)
7. Davis, S.B.: Interacting with pictures: film, narrative and interaction. Digit. Creat. **13**(2), 71–84 (2002)
8. Elsaesser, T., Hagener, M.: Film Theory: An Introduction Through the Senses. Routledge, New York (2015)
9. Enix, S.: Final Fantasy 15. [Play Station 4] (2016)
10. Fernández Vara, C.: The tribulations of adventure games: integrating story into simulation through performance. Ph.D. thesis, Georgia Institute of Technology (2009)
11. Ferri, G.: Interpretive cooperation and procedurality. Computer Games Between Text and Practice, E|C 5 (2009)
12. Fox, T.: Undertale. [Digital Game] (2015)
13. Galactic Cafe: The Stanley Parable. [Digital Game] (2013)
14. PC Games: Nier: Automata. [Digital Game] (2017)
15. Gorbman, C.: Narrative film music. Yale French Stud. **60**, 183–203 (1980)
16. Games, H., Caterpillar, S.: Long Live the Queen. [Digital Game] (2012)
17. Jørgensen, K.: Time for new terminology? Diegetic and non-diegetic sounds in computer games revisited. In: Game Sound Technology and Player Interaction: Concepts and Developments, pp. 78–97. IGI Global (2011)
18. Jørgensen, K.: Between the game system and the fictional world: a study of computer game interfaces. Games Cult. **7**(2), 142–163 (2012)
19. Jørgensen, K.: On transdiegetic sounds in computer games. North. Lights Film Media Stud. Yearb. **5**(1), 105–117 (2007)
20. Juul, J.: Introduction to game time/time to play: an examination of game temporality. In: First Person: New Media As Story, Performance and Game, pp. 131–142 (2004)
21. Kerins, M.: Constructing the diegesis in a multi-channel world. In: Forum 2: Discourses on Diegesis-On the Relevance of Terminology. Offscreen, vol. 11, pp. 8–9 (2007)
22. Kleinman, E., Carstensdottir, E., El-Nasr, M.S.: Going forward by going back: redefining rewind mechanics in narrative games. In: Proceedings of the 13th International Conference on the Foundations of Digital Games, p. 32. ACM (2018)
23. Kleinman, E., Fox, V., Zhu, J.: Rough draft: towards a framework for metagaming mechanics of rewinding in interactive storytelling. In: Nack, F., Gordon, A.S. (eds.) ICIDS 2016. LNCS, vol. 10045, pp. 363–374. Springer, Cham (2016). https://doi.org/10.1007/978-3-319-48279-8_32

24. Klevjer, R.: In defense of cutscenes. In: Computer Games and Digital Cultures Conference (2002)
25. Kromand, D.: Sound and the diegesis in survival-horror games. Audio Mostly 2008 (2008)
26. Lindley, C.A.: Game space design foundations for trans-reality games. In: Proceedings of the 2005 ACM SIGCHI International Conference on Advances in Computer Entertainment Technology, pp. 397–404. ACM (2005)
27. Little Cat Feed: OneShot. [Digital Game] (2016)
28. Loponen, M., Montola, M.: A semiotic view on diegesis construction. In: Beyond Role and Play, pp. 39–51 (2004)
29. Mackey, M.: At play on the borders of the diegetic: story boundaries and narrative interpretation. J. Lit. Res. **35**(1), 591–632 (2003)
30. Montola, M.: Role-playing as interactive construction of subjective diegeses. In: As Larp Grows Up, pp. 82–89 (2003)
31. Neumeyer, D.: Diegetic/nondiegetic: a theoretical model. Music Mov. Image **2**(1), 26–39 (2009)
32. Niantic: Harry Potter: Wizards Unite. [Digital Game] (2019)
33. Night School Studio: Oxenfree. [Digital Game] (2016)
34. Paul, W.: Breaking the fourth wall: 'Belascoism', modernism, and a 3-D "Kiss Me Kate". Film Hist. **16**, 229–242 (2004)
35. Percheron, D., Butzel, M.: Sound in cinema and its relationship to image and diegesis. Yale French Stud. **60**, 16–23 (1980)
36. Pope, L.: Papers, Please. [Digital Game] (2013)
37. Prestopnik, N.R., Tang, J.: Points, stories, worlds, and diegesis: comparing player experiences in two citizen science games. Comput. Hum. Behav. **52**, 492–506 (2015)
38. Rosenberg, R.S., Baughman, S.L., Bailenson, J.N.: Virtual superheroes: using superpowers in virtual reality to encourage prosocial behavior. PLoS ONE **8**(1), e55003 (2013)
39. Rutter, J., Bryce, J.: Understanding Digital Games. Sage, London (2006)
40. Ryan, M.L.: Beyond myth and metaphor. Consultant 1983, p. 91 (2001)
41. Salvato, D.: Doki doki literature club. [Digital Game] (2017)
42. Sandifer, P.: Out of the screen and into the theater: 3-D film as demo. Cinema J. **50**, 62–78 (2011)
43. Segre, C., Meddemmen, J.: A contribution to the semiotics of theater. Poet. Today **1**(3), 39–48 (1980)
44. Stern, E.: A touch of medieval: narrative, magic and computer technology in massively multiplayer computer role-playing games. In: Computer Games and Digital Cultures Conference (2002)
45. Telltale Games: The Wolf Among Us. [Digital Game] (2013)
46. Winters, B.: The non-diegetic fallacy: film, music, and narrative space. Music Lett. **91**(2), 224–244 (2010)

An Educational Program in Interactive Narrative Design

Hartmut Koenitz[✉], Teun Dubbelman, and Christian Roth

Professorship Interactive Narrative Design, HKU University of the Arts Utrecht,
Nieuwekade 1, 3511 RV Utrecht, The Netherlands
{hartmut.koenitz, teun.dubbelman,
christian.roth}@hku.nl

Abstract. In recent years, interactive narrative design has become the main activity of a diverse group professionals working in video games, agencies, museums, at broadcasters, and online newspapers. At the same time, there has been no degree program in interactive narrative design, which indicates that many narrative designers are self-trained. By starting an educational program we aim to address this problem, using the opportunity to also include perspectives outside of games.

Keywords: IDN pedagogy · Game design education · Interactive digital narrative

1 Introduction

A key missing piece in the further development of the field of interactive narrative studies and practice is an educational program. So far, interactive narrative designers are mostly self-trained. Many programs in game design offer only rudimentary education, mostly a single class. The exception are a handful of programs in game writing.

Thus, any professional interactive narrative project can create a challenge, as there are few trained designers to hire when it comes to games and none as soon as any non-game project is concerned. Consequently, companies needing new recruits in this position often have no choice but to engage in in-house training.

Yet, interactive narrative design is a growing area. In recent years, a growing number of narrative-focused games (e.g. Telltale Games' productions like The Walking Dead [1], Firewatch [2] and Detroit: Become Human [3]) have gained critical acclaim and commercial success. Additional forms such as interactive documentaries [4, 5], exhibition pieces and journalistic interactives have alerted us to the possibilities of narrative expressions that embrace the affordances and unique possibilities of digital interactivity. This development needs to be reflected in education. So far, however, a full degree program is elusive. Our approach is a first step - to offer a minor within a game design program, yet with a clear cross-cutting perspective, integrating views on works other than games.

© Springer Nature Switzerland AG 2019
R. E. Cardona-Rivera et al. (Eds.): ICIDS 2019, LNCS 11869, pp. 22–25, 2019.
https://doi.org/10.1007/978-3-030-33894-7_3

2   Minor Interactive Narrative Design

The minor Interactive Narrative Design has been developed because the game industry in the Netherlands expressed the need for skilled interactive narrative designers. When developing the narrative content for games, such as dialogues or storylines, game studios often rely on scriptwriters. While these master the art of creating traditional, fixed forms of storytelling, and understand the appeal of narrative experiences, scriptwriters often cannot apply their mastery in an interactive context. In contrast, game designers understand the art of interaction design, and see the appeal of inter-active experiences, but often lack a deep understanding of narrative. On this profes-sional backdrop, the minor targets game design students with an interest in designing interactive narrative experiences.

2.1   Two Approaches: Unlearn and Reuse

The challenge for us as educators in the minor is to first help game design students "unlearn" linear and static ways of storytelling, which still dominate school education and public discourse about narrative [6]. We do this by expanding students' under-standing of narrative and raising awareness for alternatives to the dominant euro-centric forms (e.g. multi-climactic and cyclical Africa oral storytelling forms or the 'conflict-less' Asian form of Kishetenketsu).

Secondly, we train students to "reuse" their game design skills for narrative pur-poses. Students first need to develop a new understanding of narrative; one that is not based on established notions of storytelling, but one that understands narrative as a cognitive meaning-making process [7, 8]. When they have acquired this alternative understanding of narrative, they can start using their skillset in a new way. For example, we ask students to design interesting narrative game mechanics [9], which invite the player to perform actions that support the construction of engaging stories and fictional worlds in the imagination of the player.

2.2   Trained Skillset

Our conversation partners in the games industry are well aware of the limitations of auto-didactic knowledge in interactive narrative design, especially when it comes to recruitment, teamwork, professional development and communication with clients. Therefore, they see professional development programs as an important aspect for the development of the field, which should run parallel to the training of new recruits. In our conversations, a specific profile and skillset emerged. The interactive narrative designer is the combination of a narrative artist, an interactive system designer, and a vision holder. First, we consider interactive narrative designers to be artists, working with interactive technologies as their medium of (self-)expression. The skills pertaining to this narrative sensibility are, amongst others, the ability to imagine and express engaging and believable characters, worlds, events and conflicts. Although they do not necessarily have to been trained scriptwriters or visual artists, they do need to be able to understand and apply the basic principles of writing and visualizing for an interactive context. Second, they are system designers who need to be deeply aware that their

Table 1. Skillset of the interactive narrative designer

Skills	Basic	Advanced	Expert
(1) IDN design conventions	Student is able to recognize IDN design conventions in existing interactive narratives	Student is able to apply existing IDN design conventions in her own work	Student is able to develop new (potential) IDN design conventions
(2) Narrative sensibility	Student understands the appeal of (interactive) narrative experiences and the basic components of (interactive) narrative	Student is able to apply her insight in the appeal of (interactive) narrative experiences in her own work	Student is able to apply her insight in the appeal of (interactive) narrative experiences in her own work, creating works with emotional impact
(3) Ideation and concepting	Student has worked incidentally with existing tools and methods for ideation and concepting (e.g. IDN design canvas/IDN design lenses/IDN design branching cards)	Student has worked regularly with existing methods for ideation and concepting (e.g. IDN design canvas/IDN design lenses/IDN design branching cards)	Student develops new tools and methods for ideation and concepting Student develops unexpected ideas and concepts
(4) Testing	Student is able to conduct existing user experience tests	Student is able to combine existing user experience tests	Student is able to develop new user experience tests
(5) Prototyping	Student masters three methods for physical prototyping (e.g. paper prototyping, play prototyping, preja vu prototyping)	Student masters three tools for simple digital prototyping (e.g. Twine, Construct 3, Ren'Py)	Student masters three tools for complex digital prototyping (e.g. Unity, Unreal, Godot)
(6) Writing (for interaction)	Student is able to recognize 'writing for interaction' techniques	Student is able to apply 'writing for interaction' techniques in her own work	Student is able to develop new 'writing for interaction' techniques
(7) Audio-visualizing (for interaction)	Student is able to recognize the power of audiovisual (and haptic) stimulus for narrative expression	Student is able to design the audiovisual (and haptic) stimulus for narrative expression (in concept)	Student is able to develop the audiovisual (and haptic) stimulus (e.g. illustration, modelling, animation, UI, etc.)
(8) Communication	Student is able to share ideas internally, supported by basic communication tools (e.g. pitch, slides)	Student is able to share ideas internally, supported by advanced communication tools (e.g. video, prototypes)	Student is able to share ideas externally (offline/online), supported by advanced communication tools (e.g. video, prototypes)
(9) Creative leadership	Student is able to integrate the various elements of her own work, supporting an overall vision	Student is able to integrate the various elements of a small team production, supporting an overall vision	Student is able to integrate the various elements of a large team production, supporting an overall vision

creation is a dynamic artefact that already by itself at runtime can show intricate and even unintended behaviors. Once interactors enter the picture, the complexity only grows. The role of the designer is to plan for these effects and embrace a role of "narrative architect" [10] who sets boundaries, and offers opportunities for meaningful interaction. Third, as vision holder, it is the responsibility of the interactive narrative designer to facilitate the vision of an interactive narrative project and communicate about it internally with clients. This is a considerable responsibility due to the lack of standardized procedures. Equally, interactive narrative is often little understood by clients and the lack of an established lingo means that a considerable effort is needed to prevent misunderstandings and ensure successful communication.

The multiple roles of the designer translate to an expanded skillset (Table 1) in eight areas: interactive narrative design conventions, narrative sensibility, ideation and concepting, testing, prototyping, writing (for interaction), audio-visualizing (for interaction), communication, and creative leadership. In each area we define three different skill levels with expected knowledge/abilities at that level. In this way both educators and students have a clear understanding where they stand and what they need to accomplish to reach the next level.

3   Conclusion

In this paper, we have described the context of our educational efforts in IDN education and outlined our approach in creating a minor in interactive narrative design. We invite the community's feedback and plan to report on the results after the program has first run its course in early 2020.

References

1. Telltale Games: The Walking Dead [Video game] (2012)
2. Campo Santo: Firewatch (2016)
3. Quantic Dream: Detroit: Become Human (2018)
4. Dufresne, D.: Fort McMoney (2013). http://www.fortmcmoney.com
5. Duijn, M.: The Industry (2018). https://theindustryinteractive.com/
6. Koenitz, H., Dubbelman, T., Knoller, N., Roth, C.: An integrated and iterative research direction for interactive digital narrative. In: Nack, F., Gordon, A.S. (eds.) ICIDS 2016. LNCS, vol. 10045, pp. 51–60. Springer, Cham (2016). https://doi.org/10.1007/978-3-319-48279-8_5
7. Herman, D.: Story Logic. University of Nebraska Press, Lincoln (2002)
8. Ryan, M.-L.: Avatars of Story. University of Minnesota Press, Minneapolis (2006)
9. Dubbelman, T.: Narrative game mechanics. In: Nack, F., Gordon, A.S. (eds.) ICIDS 2016. LNCS, vol. 10045, pp. 39–50. Springer, Cham (2016). https://doi.org/10.1007/978-3-319-48279-8_4
10. Jenkins, B.H.: Game design as narrative architecture, pp. 1–14 (2009)

Challenges of IDN Research and Teaching

Hartmut Koenitz[1]([✉]) [iD] and Mirjam Palosaari Eladhari[2] [iD]

[1] HKU University of the Arts Utrecht,
Postbus 1520, 3500 BM Utrecht, The Netherlands
hartmut.koenitz@hku.nl
[2] Södertörn University, Alfred Nobels allé 7, 141 89 Huddinge, Sweden
mirjam.palosaari.eladhari@sh.se

Abstract. In this paper, we react to developments that frame research in interactive digital narrative (IDN) as a field of study and potential future academic discipline. We take stock of the current situation, identify issues with perception and point out achievements. On that basis we identify five critical challenges, areas in need of attention in order to move the research field forward. In particular we discuss the dependency on legacy analytical frameworks (Groundhog Day), the lack of a shared vocabulary (Babylonian Confusion), the missing institutional memory of the field (Amnesia), the absence of established benchmarks (No Yardstick) and the overproduction of uncoordinated and quickly abandoned tools (Sisyphus). For each challenge area, we propose ways to address these challenges and enable increased collaboration in the field. Our paper has the aim to both provide orientation for newcomers to the field of IDN and to offer a basis for a discussion of future shared work.

1 Introduction

Nearly 35 years have passed since Buckles' 1985 PhD thesis on the Computer Storygame 'Adventure', and even more time since the early experiments in interactive narrative systems James Ryan has documented [51]. At this point, research in Interactive Digital Narrative (IDN) is maturing into an academic field [32,41]. This means there is an opportunity to consider achievements and ongoing challenges in order to take stock and identify areas for future research. Our paper thus is directed at the community engaged in research and practice of IDN with two aims: 1. to provide orientation for newcomers and 2. to offer a basis for a discussion of future shared work.

2 Achievements and Difficulties of Perception

As for achievements in the field of IDN, we are faced with a situation that mirrors the one the field of AI (artificial intelligence) faced - an initial 'hype' with the associated large claims, followed by a period of disappointment and adjustment.

© Springer Nature Switzerland AG 2019
R. E. Cardona-Rivera et al. (Eds.): ICIDS 2019, LNCS 11869, pp. 26–39, 2019.
https://doi.org/10.1007/978-3-030-33894-7_4

Examples are the "The end of books" article in the New York Times Literary Review [15] in which Coover claimed that hyperfiction works in such as Afternoon, A Story [29], spelled the end of traditional books and heralded a new era of narrative expression. Another example is Chris Crawford's famous "Dragon Speech" [16] with which he announced his exit from the games industry in order to pursue the more promising area of interactive narratives. These claims created overblown expectations which both scholars and practitioners still struggle to fulfill, as most any actual work falls short in comparison and is no longer seen for its own merits which becomes clear when judged within a more realistic framework of expectations. Just as with AI, progress and successes exist, but the pace is slower than originally anticipated and setbacks occur on the way. In the case of AI, that field had to survive several "AI winters" (cf. [26]) - periods when the term alone was considered detrimental to an academic career and funding had dried up considerably. Similarly, when it comes to IDN, many setbacks and an 'IDN winter' period can be identified. Indeed, even the current period might be interpreted as an extended winter. In terms of critical success we have not seen a work with the same level of recognition than *Façade* [34] since 2005 and in terms of funded research there has not been anything the size of the EU IRIS project [14] since 2009. These setbacks do not only exist in the academic realm, but also on the industry side - several systems have been developed but never 'released' or were available only for a short time. These include Versu [22] and StoryBricks [50]. A more recent example is that of TellTale Games, which had started a team to work on a title applying narrative generation [25] led by Stacey Mason, which was shut down due to economic problems. Nonetheless, these and similar efforts have brought the field forward. The fact that progress is made that goes unrecognized, e.g. because it is not published, is a considerable challenge for the field, that has definitely increased negative perceptions.

The problem with perception is magnified by the visionary nature of IDN. This vision–of a novel form of narrative and its associated expressive potential– are not immediately accessible, even to scholars and professionals in related fields and thus a considerable effort is needed to explain it. The relation to the well-known category of narrative adds a further layer of complication. A new field without such legacy connections – for instance AI – is understood as novel automatically and thus can explain itself without regard for established legacy frameworks. In contrast, IDN scholars and practitioners are frequently challenged to motivate the relation to more established practices of narrative and storytelling.

Janet Murray's published books can be seen as a tacit recognition of this struggle. Her initial groundbreaking volume *Hamlet on the Holodeck* [39], a work specifically on interactive narrative was followed up by *Inventing the Medium* [40], a more fundamental and general discussion of design in the digital medium in which Murray explicitly motivates the novelty of the digital medium: "The digital designer is more often inventing something for which there is no standard model, like word processing in the age of the typewriter, or video games in the age of pinball" [40].

However, even if we accept the metaphor of an IDN winter, its actual temperature and severity can be debated and might change in the eye of the respective beholder. The Wikipedia entry (see Fig. 1) on Interactive Storytelling paints a rather dark and cold picture in 2016 (23rd of May 2016), stating "Like many closely related AI research areas, interactive storytelling has largely failed to deliver on its promises over its forty year history. By the early 2010s, most research efforts in this area had failed, stalled, or been abandoned, including Chris Crawford's own Storytron project." Yet, the Wikipedia entry on Interactive Storytelling as accessed on July 13 2019 instead paints a more positive picture and presents a table of sophisticated IDN systems, not mentioning the perceived failure of the research field anymore [4].

Fig. 1. Screenshot of the Wikipedia entry "Interactive storytelling" from the 23rd of May 2016

Indeed, despite the challenges of the field, a number of substantial achievements have been made. Consider for example *Blood and Laurels* by Emily Short [53]. Not only was this an IDN work that gained critical acclaim, it was also made possible by an innovative system, *Versu*, authored by Richard Evans [22], who had previously build systems that also enabled story construction and narration (Black and White [21], Sims 3 [61]). Other important works include *Nothing for Dinner*, using the underlying IDTension [56] system, and *PromWeek*

[35], that utilizes the Comme Il Faut [36] system that helps simulating "social physics". In the area of video games, a range of commercial and critical successes have shown the aesthetic potential and mass-market appeal of narrative-focused works. Examples are *Dear Esther*[59], *Gone Home* [60], *Firewatch* [13], *80 Days* [28], *Night in the Woods* [27], *Papers, Please*[45], *Oxenfree* [43], *The Return of the Obra Dinn* [46], several of the TellTale games (*The Walking Dead* [57], *The Wolf Among Us* [58]), and the productions by Quantic Dream (*Heavy Rain* [47], *Detroit Become Human* [48]). In the field of interactive documentaries, works such as *The Last Hijack Interactive* (an interactive documentary about piracy at the Horn of Africa) [19], *Fort McMoney* (on a environmental issues and urban planning challenges of a small town overtaken by the oil industry) [17] and *The Industry* (about the illegal drug industry in the Netherlands) [18] have won critical acclaim and a considerable audience. Outside these more established forms, experimental works exist such as *IceBound* [23], a combination visual novel and puzzle game or Karen [11], a virtual life coach who brings her own problems to the sessions. All the works mentioned in this section have won critical acclaim in one form or other, reaching from "best in narrative design" and "game of the year" awards to an International Emmy and a Peabody award. Thus, there is a considerable (and growing) list of IDN achievements.

If the issue is not actually with the lack of achievements, but rather with perception and the lack of recognition, there might be an additional factor at play - that these works are simply not understood as various representations of the same underlying category of interactive digital narratives. Instead they often appear as marginal cases in their respective field - the interactive variant of documentaries, the subfield of AI and interactive computing concerned with narrative, the a small group of games that focus on narrative instead of action (as exemplified by the derogatory term 'walking simulator'). Consequently, many IDN works essentially drown in the noise of their existing disciplinary context. This is another important aspect of the lack of a disciplinary context and consequently another reason why the move towards a discipline is beneficial and overdue.

3 Ongoing Challenges

3.1 Groundhog Day: Legacy Dependencies

Practice of and research in Interactive Digital Narrative does not have a 'foundational moment' which can be clearly identified. Instead, it has grown out of earlier academic and professional practices and thus has inherited vocabulary and methods from these earlier practices and research. The coming of age of IDN as a field thus is also a moment of divorce and distinction, in which the dependency on legacy frameworks needs to be considered carefully. We need to ask what price we pay if we continue to use terminology created to describe print literature and to analyze artifacts that differ from books in important ways. Espen Aarseht's warning about the dangers of inherited terminology is still as valid as it was in 2012: "Do theoretical concepts such as "story", "fiction", "character", "narration" or "rhetoric" remain meaningful when transposed to a new field, or do they turn into empty, misleading catchphrases, blinding us to the empirical differences and effectively puncturing our chances of producing theoretical innovation?" [6]. Additionally, we need to be aware that the instrument of measurement influences and even determines the results, as we can learn for example from the wave-particle dualism in quantum physics: depending on the experimental setup, light will appear as either particles or waves. The danger here is to forget that any instrument - analytical methods are instruments, too - can only show us what they are intended to detect. As long as we are not prepared to consider changing the instrument, we might be in a Ground Hog day cycle, destined to forever repeat a discussion that is not aware of the limitations on insights imposed by the shortcomings of analytical tools inherited from earlier mediated forms of narrative.

At the very least, if we want to continue to use analytic units like 'text' in the sense used by narratology, we need to have a proper discussion of the pros and cons of doing so. For example, does the term 'text' in the sense of literary studies and the associated method of textual analysis (as for example used by Clara Fernandez-Vara [24]) need to be used differently, adjusted and modified, or is it useful at all when software code is considered? Does its use effectively prevent us from recognizing what is specific about IDN as for example Koenitz [31] suggests or is it still useful when applied, for example, to the code layer as for example in Eladhari's model [20].

Arguments for both of these positions can be found. Koenitz for instance focuses on the systemic nature of IDN works and reiterates argument originating in the discourse around cybernetic art [7] that foreground the need for novel models to understand novel phenomena - a position that Koenitz also relates to film studies [12]. Eladhari, on the other hand, considers the term as useful for decreasing misunderstanding in the context of IDN development, describing in her model the code as a specific text-layer, which proceeds the artifact an interactor encounters. In the area of software studies it is indeed the code which is the analytical object, such as in the anthology 10 PRINT [37] where a small number of code lines are studied from multiple perspective, each chapter focusing on the different effects the code has.

As the examples above show, there are ways to break the Groundhog Day cycle and gain fresh viewpoints outside of long established analytical frameworks. At the beginning of an emerging discipline we should seize the opportunity to not only change the object of inquiry, but also our instruments to measure them in order to understand specific characteristics and enable novel insights.

3.2 Babylonian Confusion: The Lack of a Shared Vocabulary

In a recent (2019) workshop about "benchmarking" for interactive digital narrative systems, the topic of a shared vocabulary was a one of the main foci. The workshop members[1] agreed that, despite many efforts, a shared language for describing narrative systems is not in place. The consequences of this are dire; it is common to have misunderstandings in the development process, and it is unfeasible to conduct comparisons between systems, since there is no common understanding of what type of metrics would be useful in order to compare and evaluate IN systems. The reasons for this state of affairs is multifaceted, a major one being that researchers and practitioners have their academic "homes" in very different fields – fields that may not share foundational norms about what are worthy avenues of questions, nor success criteria for conducted work. Indeed, such analysis of the problem are not new, when we look for example at a description from a workshop at ICIDS 2010 entitled "Towards a Shared Vocabulary for Interactive Digital Storytelling" which states [33]:

> Scholars and practitioners in the interdisciplinary area of Interactive Digital Storytelling come from many different academic backgrounds, each of which has developed its own critical vocabulary with specific definitions. Researchers originally trained in a specific field often continue to use the terminology they are familiar with, sometimes unaware of the potential misunderstandings that may arise.

It is disconcerting, if not outright frustrating to realize that nearly a decade later, nothing much has changed. Is thus the Babylonian confusion of vocabulary the celestial punishment for the hubris of creating interactive digital narratives? We might be tempted to feel so when we consider that the issue is not confined to the scholarly discourse. The question of a missing "lingo" for communication among professionals and with clients is a topic brought up frequently in conversations with practitioners which means any approach considered to address the problem also has to have the needs of the practice in mind.

So what are promising strategies for approaching the topic? In the conversation of the above mentioned benchmarking workshop, by courtesy of Professor Ruth Aylett, the area of robotics emerged as an example of a field where a common language has been established. Consequently, there was a common ground to build upon, which helped researchers to collaborate, compare approaches and move the field forward. Therefore, the developments in robotics might serve as an example for the IDN community and one which shows that a shared vocabulary is an attainable goal. Studying that field's successful approach, combined with a shared effort (including the professional field) to create an accessible repository of terms hosted by ARDIN, the new professional association of the field, are promising avenues that the community should pursue.

---

[1] List of participants in Benchmarking Interactive Narrative Systems (BEINS) - 13 June 2019: Ruth Aylett, Rogelio E. Cardona-Rivera, Mirjam P. Eladhari, Hartmut Koenitz, Vincenzo Lombardo, Sandy Louchart, Michael Mateas, Josh McCoy, Henrik Schoenau-Fog, Nicolas Szilas, Mariët Theune, David Thue, Sergio Estupinan Vesga, Stephen G. Ware, and Michael Young.

3.3 Amnesia: The Missing Foundational Canon for Teaching and Research

So far, there is no established canon of literature and works for the study of interactive digital narratives. Curricula vary widely and are often made from scratch, which points to the constant danger of memory loss, of forgetting what has already been addressed. This also means there is always a looming danger of a wasteful cycle of "re-inventing the wheel". More than twenty years after Janet Murray's paper on teaching IDN, "The pedagogy of cyberfiction: teaching a course on reading and writing interactive narrative" [38], this should no longer be the case. It is high time to address this issue and work on the creation of a shared canon of essential scholarly and artistic works. The question is less where to start, and more how to organize a consensus in the community. In Fig. 2 we make a start by proposing an initial list. For the sake of keeping within the limits of the allowable paper length, we present here only an abridged version, selecting harbingers to IDNs, early scholarly work on the topic, and early liminal IDNs. Even in this abridged state, it will be tentative and most likely missing important entries and even categories. Yet, this is exactly our intent - to provide a foundation in order to start a discussion.

And What About Tools? A foundational canon for IDN without authoring tools would be incomplete. Yet to define such a list of IDN authoring systems for educational purposes is yet another daunting challenge. On the one hand, few courses would have the space to allow an in-depth exploration of systems such as TADS [49] or Inform 7 [42], on the other hand, using more limited systems such as Twine [30] or HyperCard [8] might not be representative of the possibility space. When it comes to narratives for games, there is a rich field to draw upon, however, most of associated systems (e.g. level editors) lock designers into very specific narrative structures and interaction modes. For instance, when using the Aurora Engine [9] each resulting work would follow the same formulae as other narratives in Neverwinter Nights [10]. Another important question is that of scope - how broadly to cover authoring systems. Currently each educator needs to decide whether to include systems for the generation of narrative, and whether to include systems enabling the creation of conversational agents in the tradition of ELIZA [64], using for example ALICE [62], a tool to create chatbots. Likewise, it is up to each educator whether to cover analog systems that have been and can be used as inspiration for digital authoring tools, such as table top story making games, ideation tools framed as card games, live action role play, commedia dell'arte, or tarot card reading practices.

A Critical History of the IDN Field. Syllabi are only the beginning in an effort to combat the amnesia of the field. An important task for the coming years is to write a critical history of the field, to pool the knowledge of the building of our field, to bring it forth from the anecdotal crannies and into a well-preserved

Early Scholarly Publications (until Hamlet on the Holodeck)
Buckles, M. A. (1985). Interactive Fiction: The Computer Storygame "Adventure." PhD Thesis, University of California, San Diego.
Laurel, B. (1986). Toward the Design of a Computer-Based Interactive Fantasy System. PhD Thesis, Ohio State University.
Bolter, J. D. & Joyce, M. (1987). Hypertext and creative writing (pp. 41–50). Presented at the conference on Computational Semiotics for Games and New Media, New York, New York, USA: ACM. http://doi.org/10.1145/317426.317431
Laurel, B. (1991). Computers As Theatre. Boston, MA: Addison-Wesley.
Coover, R, (1992, June 21). The End of Books. New York Times Book Review, pp. 1, 23-25.
Landow, G. P. (1992). Hypertext. Baltimore : Johns Hopkins University Press.
Murray, J. H. (1995). The pedagogy of cyberfiction: teaching a course on reading and writing interactive narrative. In E. Barrett & M. Redmond (Eds.), Contextual Media: Multimedia and Interpretation (pp. 129–162). Cambridge, MA: MIT Press.
Jennings, P. (1996). Narrative Structures for New Media. Leonardo, 29(5), 345–350.
Aarseth, E. J. (1997). Cybertext. JHU Press.
Davenport, G. (1997). Extending the documentary tradition (Speech at the Oberhausen International Film Festival) [PDF document]. http://mf.media.mit.edu/pubs/conference/OberhausenExtending.pdf
Murray, J. H. (1997). Hamlet on the Holodeck: the Future of Narrative in Cyberspace. New York: Free Press.
Works: Harbingers (selection)
Kurosawa, A (1950) Rashomon
Raymond Queneau, R. (1961) Cent mille milliards de poèmes.
Cortazar, J. (1963) Rayuela.
Borges, J. L. (1964). The garden of forking paths. In Labyrinths: Selected stories and other writings. New Directions, New York. http://www.american- buddha.com/garden.fork.htm
Naimark, M. (1977). [Video of Aspen Movie map demonstration] http://www.naimark.net/projects/aspen/aspen_v1.html
Crowther, W., and Woods, D., (1976) Adventure
Infocom, (1977) Zork
Works: IDN (selection)
Joyce, M. (1991). Afternoon, a story. [Hypertext fiction]. Watertown: Eastgate Systems
Mateas, M., & Stern, A. (2005). Façade, Interactivestory.net
Paperdino (2013) Save the Date http://paperdino.com/save-the-date/

Fig. 2. An abridged list of foundational IDN works (Addressing challenge 3: Amnesia)

and accessible archive. Out of necessity, this should mean an effort into digital preservation in addition to scholarly publications, of which [51] and [63] are first examples.

3.4   No Yardstick: The Absence of Benchmarking

The field is crucially missing the yardstick of benchmarking, which is necessary in order to better understand the progress being made, to enable comparisons between different approaches, and to identify specific areas needing attention. At one point, a significant effort at benchmarking was made. In the IRIS project [14] the "Little Red Riding Hood" format was developed as a method to compare different IDN authoring tools. The idea behind the concept was to develop interactive variants of the Grimm's fairy tale of the same name, enabling comparisons between different systems. Members of the IRIS project used the approach in a series of workshops at the TIDSE and ICIDS conferences in 2006, 2008 and 2009 [2].

Ever since, larger collaborative efforts have not had a similar platform. In the years after the end of the IRIS project, numerous ambitious projects have been in the working, both realized ones (as noted in Sect. 2) and those who, despite extensive work, has not reached their audiences nor been published in a way that ensures the legacy of the progress that was made. In order to preserve the memory of such efforts, it is particularly important for the current and future state of the art to create metrics that build upon the work done in the IRIS project. A first necessary step is to update the design space to reflect the current state of affairs in terms of large commercial games that have reached market, and in terms of ongoing research projects in the field of IDN. In addition, it is important to recognize different needs associated with different interactor roles in IDN systems.

The following is a tentative list of categories, focusing on two aspects: why the comparison would be needed, and who it would be useful for:

- **Affordances for an author designing a narrative for an interactor.** A crucial question could be: *What kind of a narrative experience and realized story can the INS enable me to make?*
- **Affordances for a system designer.** The system designer might be working with designers/authors, and may have several roles as developer, author and designer. A question can be: *How can I use a particular IDN system to afford both artistic vision as well as combine the IDN System in question with my existing system(s)? Do I need to build additional systems to realize an artistic vision, and if so, how can they be intergrated?*
- **Evaluation of the interactor's experience.** During or the production of an IDN, and after it's release, developers/designers/researchers may want to know what impacts or effects their work has for the intended audience. This also concerns IDNs produced over time, releasing new content in episodes. The questions asked will depend on the vision for the particular game or narrative, closely tied to the success criteria of the production. These questions can include:
    - **Critique/Aesthetics.** *How is the IDN received by its audience in terms of critical and public acclaim?*
    - **Effects.** Success criteria can also be focused on what type of effects a production has had on their users, for instance if it is a 'serious game',

intended to educate the users, or to have an impact on behavior or afford an attitude change. Potential Question: *Does the IDN have the effects on users that it was designed to?*

- **Market.** It is not uncommon that the purpose of an IDN is to market something. For example, this was the case with, the alternate reality game I Love Bees [5] that promoted the game Halo 2, and the time limited tweet-based text adventure Ultimate Quest [54] that was released to promote an NVIDIA graphics card. Potential question: *Does the INS increase sales of, or positively impact the attitude to a certain product or brand?*

A challenging task in evaluating the interactors' experiences is how to determine causes and effects of IDNs: in most cases there are multiple other contextual factors that affect the interactors' experiences, both in terms of aesthetic values and terms of potential effects and impacts on the users. For instance, prior experience with interactive works impact the appreciation of and engagement with IDNs. Another factor to take into the account is the dependency between the artifact (or narrative experience given to the interactor), and the underlying systems, the tools that enable the creation of artifacts in the first place.

3.5   Sisyphonian Tool Production

Authoring tools play a crucial role in the creation of IDN works. This insight has led many researchers and practitioners to focus on the creation of authoring tools. Indeed, Shibolet et al. have identified 300 tools in a survey conducted 2018 [52]. This is an astonishing number that speaks of high interest, but also of a problematic division of effort. Unfortunately – as shown by Shibolet et al. – the majority of them go to waste in the long run, becoming being either dormant or abandoned. Most authoring tools seem to suffer the fate of carefully crafted instruments that are used a handful of times at best before they are abandoned - an effort reminiscent of Sisyphus. One reason for this wasteful practice is the scarcity of knowledge about earlier efforts - Shibolet et al.'s paper appears to be a first comprehensive survey in more than 30 years, surpassing earlier efforts, e.g. of the IRIS project (25 tools) [3] by a significant margin.

The absence of exchange standards amplifies the problem: so far it is not possible for one tool to simply enhance an existing one. A proposal for such a standard exists but so far has had little impact [55]. One reason for this state of affairs might be in the lack of shared vocabulary - without it is difficult to enable any kind of coordination.

In the field of authoring tools for IDN, it is not the end user - or in Murray's term the "interactor" - who are the primary audiences. Instead, these systems are intended for authors who in turn are producing IDN works of all kinds, from narrative fiction to interactive documentaries to video game systems. Further, it can be argued that such an IDN authoring system is more than a tool - it might also be an artistic work in its own right, creating opportunities and affordances for the very creation of interactive narratives. Thus, producing a "tool" is also an act of authorial creation, and as such, an art practice. Therefore, identifying the intended audience of a work and the affordances that come with it are important factors in evaluating a work.

Towards Critical Tool Studies. So far, very little effort has been spent on developing critical perspectives for authoring tools. One might say that scholars and practitioners have developed tools, used them and described them, but so far hardly ever studied them. Shibolet et al.'s paper, proposing a methodology for categorizing IDN tools, is a case in point as it can claim a number of firsts in 2018, including a first effort at a critical vocabulary. The lack of critical perspectives is even more problematic when we consider how tools organize and influence the creative process. Indeed, Simon Penny in 1997 describes the relationship between digital tools and artists as "implicit and rarely discussed" [44]. For example, the Twine [30] authoring tool has become very popular in recent years, for both stand-alone works and for prototyping. Yet, the way Twine influences creators through its foundational concepts, UI and technical affordances has hardly been discussed so far. In the strictest sense, our use of Twine thus qualifies as naive, since we are unable to assess whether it is the right tool for a given project. Easy accessibility and popularity thus are most likely the main reasons to use that tool rather than a critical assessment.

Studying, categorising and critiquing IDN tools is an essential aspect of a field that wants to understand the process of creating interactive narrative works. It is surprising how little effort has been made to improve this important aspect. The development of tools studies - of which tools criticism would be an important subcategory - is therefore a challenge that the community needs to address.

4   Conclusion

In this paper, we have considered the state of the field of IDN research, its achievements and ongoing challenges. More concretely, we have identified an issue with perception that obscures progress in research and milestones of artistic achievements.

We have identified five major challenges for the field of IDN research: the dependency on legacy analytical frameworks (Groundhog Day), the lack of a shared vocabulary (Babylonian Confusion), the missing institutional memory of the field (Amnesia), the absence of established benchmarks (No Yardstick) and the overproduction of uncoordinated and quickly abandoned tools (Sisyphonian Tool Production).

We like to end this paper with a proposal for concrete actions. To address the dependency on legacy frameworks (Groundhog Day), we propose to investigate the limitations of existing analytical instrument and seize the opportunity to introduce specific frameworks. For the lack of shared vocabulary (Babylonian Confusion) a potential way forward could be to look at examples from other fields, such as robotics, for successful ways of creating a sustainable shared vocabulary. To address the lack of institutional memory (Amnesia) we propose to build a library of pointers to a shared canon. For the fourth challenge, the lack of a yardstick and benchmarking, we propose to examine possible comparison strategies according to how the comparisons and their metrics would be useful: for whom, in what contexts and for what types of purposes. Finally, for the challenge of the Sisyphonian tool production, we propose a communal effort towards critical (authoring) tools studies.

As a hub of the community, the website and communication platform of ARDIN (Association for Research in Digital Interactive Narratives) [1] could host several of these efforts as open access community-driven projects, formalized as special interest groups (SIGs). We see these proposals as contributions to help move the field forward and lay the foundations for future work and an eventual discipline of IDN research. We are looking forward to implement them together with the community.

References

1. Ardin website. http://ardin.online
2. Little Red Riding Hood Workshop: The Authoring Process in Interactive Storytelling. http://redcap.interactive-storytelling.de/
3. Iris authoring tool descriptions (2008). http://iris.interactive-storytelling.de/AuthoringToolDescriptions
4. Interactive storytelling, Wikipedia, page version id: 906128942, July 2019. https://en.wikipedia.org
5. 42 Entertainment: I Love Bees. [Alternate Reality Game] (2004)
6. Aarseth, E.: A narrative theory of games. In: Proceedings of the International Conference on the Foundations of Digital Games - FDG 2012, p. 129. ACM Press, New York, May 2012. https://doi.org/10.1145/2282338.2282365
7. Ascott, R.: The Construction of Change. Cambridge Opinion (1964)
8. Atkinson, B.: HyperCard (1987)
9. Bioware: Aurora Engine (2002)
10. Bioware: Neverwinter Nights. Infogrames/Atari MacSoft [Computer Game-Role Playing Game] (2002)
11. Blast Theory: Karen (2014)
12. Bordwell, D.: Three dimensions of film narrative. In: Poetics of Cinema (2007)
13. Santo, C.: Firewatch (2016)
14. Cavazza, M., et al.: The IRIS network of excellence: integrating research in interactive storytelling. In: Spierling, U., Szilas, N. (eds.) ICIDS 2008. LNCS, vol. 5334, pp. 14–19. Springer, Heidelberg (2008). https://doi.org/10.1007/978-3-540-89454-4_3. http://iris.scm.tees.ac.uk/
15. Coover, R.: The End of Books. New York Times Literary Review (1992)
16. Crawford, C.: The Dragon Speech (1993). http://www.erasmatazz.com/personal/videos/the-dragon-speech-1993.html
17. Dufresne, D.: Fort McMoney (2013)
18. Duijn, M.: The Industry (2018)
19. Duijn, M., Wolting, F., Pallotta, T.: Last Hijack Interactive (2014)
20. Eladhari, M.P.: Re-tellings: the fourth layer of narrative as an instrument for critique. In: Rouse, R., Koenitz, H., Haahr, M. (eds.) ICIDS 2018. LNCS, vol. 11318, pp. 65–78. Springer, Cham (2018). https://doi.org/10.1007/978-3-030-04028-4_5
21. Electronic Arts: Black & White. Lionhead Studios [Computer Game] (2001)

22. Evans, R., Short, E.: Versu—a simulationist storytelling system. IEEE Trans. Comput. Intell. AI Games **6**(2), 113–130 (2014). https://doi.org/10.1109/TCIAIG. 2013.2287297. http://ieeexplore.ieee.org/document/6648395/
23. Fastermind Games: Icebound (2013)
24. Fernández-Vara, C.: Introduction to Game Analysis. Routledge, New York (2014)
25. Garrett, E.: Telltale Games' Cancelled Zombie Project Details Revealed by Former Employee, September 2018. https://dontfeedthegamers.com/telltale-games-cancelled-zombie-project/
26. Hendler, J.A.: Avoiding another AI winter. IEEE Intell. Syst. **23**(2), 2–4 (2008)
27. Infinite Fall: Night in the Woods (2017)
28. Inkle: 80 Days (2014)
29. Joyce, M.: Afternoon: a story. Eastgate Systems (1999)
30. Klimas, C.: TWINE (2009). https://twinery.org
31. Koenitz, H.: Towards a specific theory of interactive digital narrative. In: Interactive Digital Narrative: History, Theory and Practice (2015)
32. Koenitz, H.: Thoughts on a discipline for the study of interactive digital narratives. In: Rouse, R., Koenitz, H., Haahr, M. (eds.) ICIDS 2018. LNCS, vol. 11318, pp. 36–49. Springer, Cham (2018). https://doi.org/10.1007/978-3-030-04028-4_3
33. Koenitz, H., Haahr, M., Ferri, G., Sezen, T.I.: Towards a shared vocabulary for interactive digital storytelling. In: Technologies for Interactive Digital Storytelling and Entertainment, pp. 293–294. Springer, Heidelberg (2010)
34. Mateas, M., Stern, A.: Façade: an experiment in building a fully-realized interactive drama. In: Game Developers Conference, vol. 2, pp. 4–8 (2003)
35. McCoy, J., Treanor, M., Samuel, B., Mateas, M., Wardrip-Fruin, N.: Prom Week: social physics as gameplay. In: Proceedings of the 6th International Conference on Foundations of Digital Games, pp. 319–321. ACM (2011)
36. McCoy, J., Treanor, M., Samuel, B., Wardrip, N., Mateas, M.: Comme il Faut: a system for authoring playable social models, pp. 158–163 (2010)
37. Montfort, N., et al.: 10 PRINT CHR $(205.5+ RND (1));: GOTO 10. MIT Press (2012)
38. Murray, J.H.: The pedagogy of cyberfiction: teaching a course on reading and writing interactive narrative. In: Barrett, E., Redmond, M. (eds.) Contextual Media, pp. 129–162. MIT Press, Cambridge (1995). http://dl.acm.org/citation.cfm?id=212279.212296
39. Murray, J.H.: Hamlet on the Holodeck. The Free Press (1997)
40. Murray, J.H.: Inventing the Medium: Principles of Interaction Design as a Cultural Practice. MIT Press, Cambridge (2011)
41. Murray, J.H.: Research into interactive digital narrative: a kaleidoscopic view. In: Rouse, R., Koenitz, H., Haahr, M. (eds.) ICIDS 2018. LNCS, vol. 11318, pp. 3–17. Springer, Cham (2018). https://doi.org/10.1007/978-3-030-04028-4_1
42. Nelson, G.: Inform 7 (1993)
43. Night School Studio: Oxenfree (2016)
44. Penny, S.: The virtualization of art practice: body knowledge and the engineering worldview. Art J. **56**(3), 30 (1997)
45. Pope, L.: Papers, Please (2013)
46. Pope, L.: The Return of the Obra Dinn (2018)
47. Quantic Dream: Heavy Rain [Video game] (2010)
48. Quantic Dream: Detroit: Become Human (2018)
49. Roberts, M.: Text Adventure Development System (TADS) (1988)
50. Rosini, R.: Storybricks is no more - Rodolfo Rosini, May 2015. https://medium.com/@rodolfor/storybricks-is-no-more-f26b0980e62e

51. Ryan, J.: Grimes' fairy tales: a 1960s story generator. In: Nunes, N., Oakley, I., Nisi, V. (eds.) ICIDS 2017. LNCS, vol. 10690, pp. 89–103. Springer, Cham (2017). https://doi.org/10.1007/978-3-319-71027-3_8

52. Shibolet, Y., Knoller, N., Koenitz, H.: A framework for classifying and describing authoring tools for interactive digital narrative. In: Rouse, R., Koenitz, H., Haahr, M. (eds.) ICIDS 2018. LNCS, vol. 11318, pp. 523–533. Springer, Cham (2018). https://doi.org/10.1007/978-3-030-04028-4_61

53. Short, E.: Blood & Laurels. Linden Lab (2014)

54. Short, E.: Ultimate Quest. AKQA [Tweet-based text adventure] (2014)

55. Szilas, N., Boggini, T., Axelrad, M., Petta, P., Rank, S.: Specification of an open architecture for interactive storytelling. In: Si, M., Thue, D., André, E., Lester, J.C., Tanenbaum, J., Zammitto, V. (eds.) ICIDS 2011. LNCS, vol. 7069, pp. 330–333. Springer, Heidelberg (2011). https://doi.org/10.1007/978-3-642-25289-1_41

56. Szilas, N., Couronnes, T.: IDtension: the simulation of narrative. In: 3rd Conference on Computational Semiotics for Games, pp. 106–107 (2003)

57. Telltale Games: The Walking Dead [Video game] (2012)

58. Telltale Games: The Wolf Among Us (2013)

59. The Chinese Room: Dear Esther (2008)

60. The Fullbright Company: Gone Home (2013)

61. The Sims Studio: The Sims 3. Electronic Arts [Computer Game] (2009)

62. Wallace, R.: A.L.I.C.E. (Artificial Linguistic Internet Computer Entity) (1995)

63. Wardrip-Fruin, N.: Digital media archaeology: interpreting computational processes. In: Huhtamo, E., Parikka, J. (eds.) Media Archaeology: Approaches, Applications, and Implications, pp. 302–322. University of California Press, Berkeley (2011)

64. Weizenbaum, J.: ELIZA—a computer program for the study of natural language communication between man and machine. Commun. ACM 9(1), 36–45 (1966). https://doi.org/10.1145/365153.365168. http://portal.acm.org/citation.cfm?doid=365153.365168

Is "Citizen Kane" Moment Coming?
- A Research on Chinese VR Documentary
Practice and Storytelling

Chanjun Mu[✉]

School of Creative Media, City University of Hong Kong, Kowloon, China
Chanjunmu2-c@my.cityu.edu.hk

Abstract. "Citizen Kane" moment is the occasion when a work achieves mastery of the form, defining a language of storytelling for future creators. [1] As a newborn genre, VR documentary is currently somewhere in that intermediate phase. 2016 is the first year of Chinese VR documentary. Over the past three years, more than 100 artworks have emerged, besides, some of them has been exhibited in famous international film festival such as Cannas. The embryonic Chinese VR content industry also serves this fresh genre with a favorable environment and support. With the advent of 5G era, will the creation of VR documentaries in China usher in a new Kane moment, or encounter more cruel challenges? Through investigating the main distribution platforms and the storytelling characteristics of existing artworks, this research aims to analyze and discuss the practice environment, creation development and potential storytelling strategies of Chinese VR documentaries.

Keywords: VR Documentary · VR storytelling · Chinese VR industry

1 Chinese VR Documentary: Definition and Situation

The year of 2016 is called the first year of Chinese VR industry. The virtual reality technology changes panoramic game and video, becoming more and more popular in people's daily lives and mass media reports. 2016 is the first year of Chinese VR Documentary as well. Since the birth of the first VR documentary *Kindergarten in Village*, there were over 100 works in the past three years. Among them, the first domestic religious theme VR documentary produced by Huarong Road Media *Greetings! Little Master* showing the real life of Buddhist monks and nuns, won the 2016 CHINA VR New Image Award "Best Humanistic Documentary Award", and was invited to participate in the documentary exhibition by the 70th Cannes Film Festival in France, so that the world can re-understand the religious culture in China. The Tibet theme VR documentary *Polar*, produced independently by Microwhale VR and co-produced with Beijing Five-star Legend, won a documentary short film award at the Accolade International Film Festival. Documentary distribution platforms such as iQiyi VR, SoVR, VeeR have also sprung up, which shows the creation of VR documentary in China has a satisfactory beginning.

R. E. Cardona-Rivera et al. (Eds.): ICIDS 2019, LNCS 11869, pp. 40–44, 2019.
https://doi.org/10.1007/978-3-030-33894-7_5

The upcoming 5G communication technology will also bring the creation of Chinese VR documentary into a new era. 5G is a set of technical basic rules, which defines the working mode of bee network, including the rate of non-connected computer and the number of components such as computer chip and antenna. 5G speed is especially noticeable in high volume streaming media films. According to the median speed of Qualcomm (Qualcomm), it takes only 17 s to load a regular 5 GB film, while 4G takes 6 min. 5G technology will inevitably will bring opportunities and cruel challenges to the Chinese VR documentary industry, especially the distribution platform.

We can again look to history to glean some lessons from earlier revolutions in media. It took a long time for motion picture creators to figure out how to tell stories with film. Arguably half a century passed before the grammar of filmmaking was fully defined. [2] Just like the traditional film, the storytelling of the newly born VR documentary is still in the exploratory stage, and it is urgent to form its own systematic narrative theory and creative methods to define a new grammar of storytelling in the next generation of 5G.

2   Chinese VR Content Distribution Platforms

The VR industry in the world experienced both prosperous and bubble period from 2015 to 2017. According to research statistics, as the first year of VR in China, there were hundreds of VR enterprises in the Chinese market in the first quarter of 2016, but fewer than 10 brand enterprises still exist now. The elimination rate of VR start-up enterprises is close to 99%, [3] among which there are many reasons, such as maturing of capital market, imperfect supply chain and ecology, etc. However, the core reason is that VR cannot provide users with the expected good experience, which involves the integrity and maturity of the whole ecology such as hardware, system and content, etc., and is the fundamental problem of the whole VR industry for a long time.

In such an environment, VR content websites, the main distribution platforms of VR documentaries in China, has also experienced a round of elimination. In 2016, a large number of VR content platforms have sprung up in a blowout way. Up to now, there are only less than 10 mainstream VR platforms, and the competition is very fierce. Fortunately, several influential VR content platforms, such as iQiyi VR, CCTV VR, SoVR, VeeR and UtoVR, which have won both opportunities and challenges, are still continuously enhancing their capabilities in content production and supporting hardware, forming unique content distribution mechanisms and industry chains. The upcoming 5G era is a huge change not only for major distribution platforms but also for the entire VR industry. With the change and rise of the dissemination platform, the creation and industry of VR documentaries will usher in a new stage.

3   Chinese VR Documentary Storytelling

3.1   Theme: Mainstream and Marginal

From 2016 to 2018, an overall of more than 100 VR documentaries have been produced in China, among which, 24 are of the humanistic and natural geography theme, 12 the biography, 23 the social humanity, and more than 50 are the other themes. In terms of the theme, it extends the consistent style of Chinese documentaries: a co-existence of mainstream and independent documentaries. The mainstream documentary refers to those invested and shot by official TV stations, large film studios or institutions and organizations. The concept of China's independent documentary was formed in the early 90 s. It stands for the "independent system", and works discard in-system units like TV stations and film studios, which are instead, filmed by individuals.

Therefore, the classification and style of the themes of China's VR documentaries follow the features of the two categories of creators. China's VR documentaries enjoy mainstream themes, including the works that record China's traditional folk custom and religious culture, such as *Eye of the Terra-Cotta Warriors of the Qin Dynasty*, *The Great Wall*, *The Shrine at the Penpoint*; Chinese military and history like *August 1st Nanchang Revolution, Conquer! China's Marine Corps*; as well as China's particular natural wonders like *Beautiful Xinjiang* and *Beautiful China*. In the meantime, it concentrates on special social issues and groups, for example, the problem of domestic violence in *Survivors*, the special religious phenomenon of the female ascetic in *An Audience with the Little Master*, and the left behind children in *Jialu*. In addition, a series of campus-related themes shot by university teams, such as *A Touch of THU* and *Special Tactics Exercise* are impressive as well.

3.2   Space: Breaking Through the Fourth Wall

Though little breakthrough has been made in the narrative time of China's VR documentary, the narrative space is entirely different from the traditional documentary. The storytelling of China's VR documentary has broken "the fourth wall", facilitating the audience to personally step into the story.

In terms of spatial narrative, the works are endowed with more freedom, which has also enhanced the authenticity. The theory of "the fourth wall" is originated from the drama field, which indicates an intangible wall that separates the stage from the audience. [4] This wall isolates the "narrative time and space" on the stage from the "viewing time and space" off the stage. Yet, in the VR realm, the audience leave from their original space, and is invited onto the stage, then into the story.

In the space of VR documentaries, the activities of all the present objects are recorded, including the director and the whole staff, which has caused many troubles for mise-en-scene. However, such peculiarity can be applied appropriately for the shooting of natural landscape, architectures, etc., which is also the reason why the geographic theme accounts for a vast majority of VR documentaries. When filming the protagonist, the biography type of VR documentary displays the character's surrounding comprehensively, its sense of space and the powerful storytelling impact far surpasses than that of the traditional documentary. Despite of that, the excessively open space brings challenges to the storytelling: since the average field of view only reaches one third of the full view, which unavoidably leads to the omission of key plots or information in other scenes. In most Chinese VR documentary works, it is common that they lack screen guides or prompts. Since the film is short with a relatively simple story, and the viewing experience is slightly weakened.

3.3 Structure: Linear Storytelling

Although VR documentaries greatly enhance the audience's immersion and interactive experience compared with traditional documentaries, the storytelling structure is still monotonous. The narrative time and viewing time basically coincide, the plot clues are relatively single, and even filled with a large number of long shots. There are also some experimental works in Chinese VR documentaries that have multi-perspective and multi-clue parallel storytelling structures, even use some scattered cultural and montage narrative techniques, which break through the continuity of time and space to a certain extent. For example, *Survivor* is a 360° VR film, which combines the interview content of the victims and their memory video clips into a complete film in a unique form of 180° interviews and 180° documentary, bringing the audience an immersive viewing experience. However, this kind of documentary is still a linear storytelling in essence, because the audience's participation has not changed the plot direction, story plot or narrative time-space sequence. The story itself is still set by the creator: a goal-oriented protagonist situated within a discrete spatiotemporal reality, actively making attempts to reach a goal, with these attempts resulting in causally linked plot points. [5] Therefore, Chinese VR documentaries are still exploring the possibility of non-linear storytelling in narrative structure.

4   Conclusion

Compared with foreign countries, although the creation of VR documentaries in China started relatively late, the timing for its growth is favorable: VR technology has undergone a long period of research and development innovation and has become relatively mature. The cost of VR broadcasting and production equipment has been reduced, and the advent of 5G era has raised the possibility of VR popularization. Documentary authors have accumulated creative experience in several Chinese experimental periods such as Internet+ documentaries, network interactive documentaries and device interactive documentaries. Therefore, the practice of VR documentary creation in China improves rapidly and has gained many awards both domestic and abroad. China has a large number of VR documentary distribution platforms with abundant capital and pays attention to both content creation and promotion. Many platforms have independently developed VR equipment and creation tools, providing a very healthy and viable distribution mechanism, environment and communication carrier for the creation of VR documentaries in China. The creators of VR documentaries in China include mainstream organizations such as television stations and media, as well as independent documentary authors. Therefore, the works are abundant in themes and varied in styles, with large number of geographic, social and humanistic works. Based on the inherent advantages of VR technology, the immersive experience of VR documentary content is indisputable, but the relatively simple linear storytelling, single narrative technique and structure are still regarded as its storytelling defects, which need further exploration.

This is also one of the core problems currently encountered in VR documentary practice in China. Immersion and interaction two most prominent characteristics of digital media storytelling: interaction and immersion, which are almost permeated in all the elements of digital media narrative. Murray describes that immersion as derived from our "fantasy" brought by digital media narrative. Whatever the fantasy is, the personal experience of the simulation is pleasant, and this experience is called "immersion". [6] Correspondingly, interaction is "a key additional value of new media technology". [7] It is not only the feature of digital media technology", but also the characteristic of the user. Users play the role of an agency in digital media works, just like the agent of a certain character or action in the narrative. Different behavior and languages can lead to different results. [6] Immersion and interaction are contradictory while closely connected features.

On the basis of the natural immersive essence of VR technology, VR documentary creators should make best use of immersive and interactive experience to design appropriate plots. And then viewers can really enter the story world to generate story through physical participation, enhancing the immersive experience of storytelling. Specific interactive methods can draw lessons from the increasingly mature creation of interactive movie and interactive documentaries such as *Heavy Rain, Prison Valley* and even some narrative methods in interactive games. Only in this way can Chinese VR documentaries embrace the real "Citizen Kane" moment and enter the interactive era.

References

1. Salz, P.A.: VR: From Storytelling to Story Living. EContent Magazine, Autumn 2018 Issue, p. 9 (2018)
2. Bosworth, M.: Lakshmi Sarah, Crafting Stories for Virtual Reality, p. 2. Routledge, New York (2019)
3. Xiong, W.: Triple Ox Principle: The Three Ox Carts Motivating Strategy of IQiyi, IT Home (2019). https://www.ithome.com/0/423/756.htm. Accessed 18 July 2019
4. Liao, K.: The History of Western European Drama, p. 105. China Drama Press, Beijing (2002)
5. Fox, B.: Documentary Media: History, Theory, Practice, p. 96. Routledge, New York (2017)
6. Murray, J.H.: Hamlet on the Holodeck: The Future of Narrative in Cyberspace, p. 98. The MIT Press, Cambridge (1998)
7. Lister, M., et al. (eds.): New Media: A Critical Introduction, p. 212. Routledge, London (2003)

Impacting Culture and Society

Someone Else's Story: An Ethical Approach to Interactive Narrative Design for Cultural Heritage

Rebecca Rouse[✉]

Rensselaer Polytechnic Institute, Troy, NY 12180, USA
`rouser@rpi.edu`

Abstract. This paper outlines an approach to community based co-design of interactive narrative (IN) cultural heritage experiences, based on the author's development of an advanced-level project course on the topic over the past six years. Several projects are discussed as case studies, including projects that address the history of Irish immigrants working as domestic laborers in Troy NY in the 1850s; urban renewal in Albany NY and Troy NY in the 1960s and 1970s; the Native American nations' Iroquois Confederacy in present-day Cohoes NY; and the upstate New York history of Harriet Tubman, the legendary African American liberator of hundreds of enslaved people during the 1850s and 1860s. Issues highlighted include the ethics of telling other people's stories in the IN medium, the myth of the designer as impartial facilitator, the power structures of different types of design processes, and complexities of large scale projects that incorporate emergent technology, contested histories, and a wide range of stakeholders and participants. Lessons learned are shared in the form of a set of guidelines to help shape design and development of interactive narrative projects in educational, museum, and heritage settings.

Keywords: Co-design · Pedagogy · Digital heritage · Interactive narrative

1 Introduction

1.1 New Technologies Telling the Past

What does it mean to tell someone else's story? Actors in a play, for example, encounter this dynamic as a regular condition of their profession. There is often discussion of identification with the character one portrays, and even the need for research to best be able to do justice to the portrayal. Theatre is often neatly framed for the audience, to acknowledge this distance between portrayal and reality [1]. Even in documentary theatre, program notes explain the origin of the work and delineate the lines between the real and the fictionalized or interpreted. In the cultural heritage sphere, however, there is sometimes less demarcation or acknowledgement of the distance between those whose stories are told, and those who are the tellers. Some notable exceptions exist, and there is a trend toward the inclusion of more critical reflection on the presentation of history and heritage in the museum and at historic

© Springer Nature Switzerland AG 2019
R. E. Cardona-Rivera et al. (Eds.): ICIDS 2019, LNCS 11869, pp. 47–60, 2019.
https://doi.org/10.1007/978-3-030-33894-7_6

sites, such as the Swedish History Museum's recent "History Unfolds - A Reflection" exhibit in Stockholm.

The inclusion of digital technologies in museum and heritage settings, however, has further impacts for representations of authenticity, voice, and power. As museum scholar Ross Parry has described, the museum field has entered a new phase in its relationship with technology that can be understood as post-digital [2]. Parry's contention is that digital technologies have become anticipated and even demanded by museum audiences, which opens up an opportunity for the designer to be freed from the constraints of novelty. The digital can become de-spectacularized, and possibilities for more critical engagements with works that incorporate digital technologies can begin. While the 'post' of the post-digital does not mean we are done or through with the digital, or that we have finished sorting out our cultural and social entanglements with the technology, it does recognize the emergence of a new phase of our relationship with the digital.

Displays of heritage and public history have long been associated with new technologies, and today this trend continues. From the innovation of the 360-degree painted panorama to tell military history and simulate foreign travel from the 1790's through the early twentieth century [3], to the use of the stereoscope from the mid-1800's to dazzle with 3D views of historic locations [4], the telling of history has a long tradition of engagement with emerging technologies. In the more recent development of cultural heritage applications with digital technologies, there is a long history of work with audio guides, interactive mapping, and immersive visualization [5]. The inclusion of game technologies and mixed or augmented reality capabilities in the field has led to even more complex interactions between user, machine, designer, site, and heritage experience. Complexity can be represented in new ways, through branching storylines, multiple or shifting perspectives, and even procedurally generated narratives [6].

Interactive narrative (IN) technologies are yet another emergent component in the heritage sphere. At first glance, it may seem an unlikely fit to combine IN and history; once can't change what has happened in the past, so what role could IN possibly play? However, when it is acknowledged that the act of storytelling itself, the act of narra-tivizing, which is necessarily a part of any museum or heritage experience, is con-structivist, we can see that the storytelling of history has always been interactive. Traditionally this interactivity has been reserved for the curator and exhibit designer, not the museum visitor. Incorporating IN in the museum or heritage site results in further layers of complexity, yet to be fully understood, regarding authorship in this new medium. Scholars such as Koenitz have acknowledged the role of system level architectures in IN authorship [7], and more work should be contributed in this area to help illuminate the embedded politics of the designs of IN systems. As IN technologies become more seamless and easier to use, an ironic secondary effect of this democra-tization is the accompanying black-boxing of system architectures and their embedded politics from authors and users.

Claims for the impacts of IN in heritage and museums have not yet been solidified, but some practitioners and scholars place emphasis on the promise of the medium to evoke empathy as a tool for social justice [8–10]. However, as Shuman has noted, claims for empathy in non-interactive narratives are at best fraught and at worst entirely uncritical [11]. The IN field is still in the early stages of grappling with the ethical implications of empathy claims for the medium, particularly in the heritage field. Recent scholarship from Engberg on the concept of care as a design approach [12] and Fisher and Schoemann [13] on the ethics of IN in dark tourism both represent an important beginning.

Non-interactive forms already exhibit a complex relationship between the promises claimed for their narratives regarding empathy and justice, and issues of power and entitlement in the manner of their telling. Think for example of the many recent discussions in the popular press and social media regarding which actor is entitled to play a marginalized character in a film, when the actor in question does not share this marginalized identity in everyday life. As Phelan has noted [14], mere representation or increased visibility does not equate to power, and can in fact be a trap resulting in commodification and sublimation. In terms of the strategy of 'giving voice' or practices of speaking for others, Alcoff has provided incisive analyses of these impulses as too often glory-seeking, exploitive, and colonizing, and urged instead dialogic approaches that seek to open spaces for critique, and push back against Western conceptions of complete individuality and total agency [15]. So while the promise of empathy or justice as an outcome of narrative in general, and IN in particular, is exciting, it must be tempered with careful and critical consideration.

IN may have qualities that allow for the possibility to contribute in this space in ways that differ from less interactive narrative forms. For example, the IN form is ontologically always incomplete, in a sense. The narrative is understood as mutable, and even if all branches of a narrative have been explored, the reader has a model of the IN form as able to encompass or engender further possibilities. In this way, the IN form is more mutable, or at least potentially mutable, than traditional forms, and therefore always less complete. This always-already incompleteness is a step toward better representations of complexity, and may point a way toward a remedy for what Cavarero has discussed as the human propensity to conceive of the self as narratable, which is a fictionalization or streamlining of lived reality at best, and a reification of oppressive structures at worst [16]. IN's incompleteness may also allow for a shift away from mythic Western notions of completeness. These ideas of completeness show up in concepts like self-reliance, individualism, and retreat away from dialogue into monologue. Nyamnjoh has warned against completeness as "an illusion that can only unleash sterile ambitions of conquest and zero sum games of superiority," inviting scholars instead to embrace the ontology of incompleteness by more forcefully acknowledging borrowings, collaborations, sources of inspiration, multiplicities, and fragments in our work [17]. In the context of IN digital cultural heritage, this means acknowledging the messiness of the nature of the work, and staying open to dialogic processes and the criticisms that will inevitably arise. It also means tempering claims to 'correct' or even 'erase' dominant histories, and work instead toward continuing to add to the collaborative accretion of humanity's understanding of itself. This paper works to add to the growing field of research in this design space developing a range of methods and approaches for creating work with and in communities, particularly when the project at hand concerns difficult or contested histories.

Design Methods and Approaches to Working with People and Machines. While the museum and heritage fields have over the past several decades shifted into postdigitality, the design field has also advanced through the development of a variety of approaches and perspectives on the role and relationships of the designer and user in the design process. Scholarly approaches have shifted away from a machine-focused approach toward early human computer interaction and later human-centered design [18, 19] toward user experience or UX, and user-centered design [20–23] as well as the moves toward participatory design in urban planning [24] to more contemporary research in feminist design and co-design methods [25, 26].

Parvin's recent paper [27] provides a much-needed critical examination of the claims made for digital storytelling as a medium for social justice, and makes a similar call to designers to recognize that "what matters most is not giving voice but rather a renewed attentiveness to the act of listening" and that we "(re)consider the practices of storytelling and listening as dialogic." Listening, however, doesn't erase the designer. Just as the theatre actor can never fully disappear into a character, so too the designer is *always* present. Some design rhetoric from the HCI or UX traditions can imply the designer becomes, or at least strives to become, a neutral facilitator or pseudo-anthropological observer of the user's needs and wishes. For example, the IDEO design firm's "Method Cards" list many strategies such as "Shadowing," "Rapid Ethnography", and "Fly on the Wall" that all involve close and rather invasive observation of users without any reflexive examination of the designer's own social and political positioning [28].

There's something disingenuous here, a lack of acknowledgement of the power relations between designer and user, and disregard for the inevitable fingerprint of the designer. As Helguera has pointed out, a stance of detachment can make communities "feel like they are being used instead of like true partners in a dialogue or collaboration." Indeed, Helguera continues, the trait of genuine openness and curiosity to engage with, learn from, and bring oneself into a community is a likely pre-requisite to determining a designer's or artist's capability for community-based work, and cannot be "created artificially." Curiosity alone, however, is not a strategy for successful community engagement, and Helguera acknowledges the "delicate negotiation" that is the nature of the ongoing process of community-based, or as he terms it, socially engaged art [29]. Acknowledging the delicate, messy, and incomplete nature of the work at hand, how to move from theory to practice and develop works with IN for cultural heritage? In the following section I will share lessons learned, processes tried out, and tips gleaned from experiences developing an AR Design for Cultural Heritage course.

2 AR Design for Cultural Heritage

2.1 Course Design and Development

Over the past six years through a series of collaborations with local and regional organizations, community members, colleagues, and approximately 45 of my own undergraduate and graduate students, I have developed a course in Augmented Reality (AR) Design for Cultural Heritage, as well as a method or approach for creating these types of projects. Over time and iteration, it has become clear that a deeply collaborative, co-design approach best supports this particular kind of work for a variety of reasons. Ethically, the tensions inherit in telling other people's stories are best navigated in a maximally transparent and collaborative process with all stakeholders. Practically, to ensure the uptake of projects beyond the duration of the course, this type of truly collaborative process also ensures community members and other stakeholders have ownership of the project, and genuine interest and desire in pursuing it to completion.

To provide an overview of the course, starting in the classroom at the beginning of the semester students are introduced to core concepts in critical history [30, 31], co-design and community engagement [26, 29, 32], and issues specific to design with mixed or augmented reality [33–35]. (This core background is necessary, as Rensselaer has no history department, so history pre-requisites can be set for the course, and this also happens to be the only mobile development or mixed reality course regularly offered on the campus, at the time of writing this paper.) Following this initial period with core readings, students develop mini-projects using a range of AR tools (see Fig. 1), depending on availability of the tools, and the skill level of the students involved. At the same time, while students get their feet wet in AR, they also get to know the client, community, and general history the project will focus on. Through a series of conversations, co-design workshops, and community connections, students develop design sketching, then paper prototypes, and finally a digital prototype plus detailed design document. These final projects are discussed below.

PROJECT	TOOLS	TAKE-AWAYS
Below Stairs (2015)	Prototyped in Wikitude, Processing, and ARToolKit; Final made first in Junaio then Argon	The client and the user may not want the same story/experience. Be in for the long haul if the client wants to complete the project.
The Foerster File (2016)	Prototyped in Argon	If the client does not know who the audience would be, and if you do not define the audience, there won't be one!
Finding Roebling (2017)	Prototyped and made in Unity + Vuforia	Intensive user testing can help lead to insights on overcoming hardware shortcomings.
Rapp Road (2018)	Prototyped and made in Blippar	Multiple workshops with client and community greatly aid uptake, ownership, and success of project.
Discover Cohoes (2018)	Prototyped in Apple's ARKit and Unity + Vuforia	Sometimes neither the client nor the user knows the story they will be interested in before-hand. Some digging may be required.
Harriet Tubman: Guided by the Night (2019)	Prototyped in Unity + Vuforia	Sometimes circumstances are beyond your control, such as client-side leadership turnover.

Fig. 1. Distillation of lessons learned from each project over the past six years regarding design process, and the range of AR tools that have been used.

Example Projects. Over the past six years the course has been offered four times, and has spawned two independent study courses as well, resulting in a total of six projects. Three of the six projects have been fully developed and implemented for the public, and a fourth is still in progress. Two have not yet progressed past the prototype phase. Each project is described here in brief:

- *Below Stairs: AR History Adventure* (Completed 2015)
  Below Stairs was developed for the Rensselaer County Historic Society's house museum, The Hart Cluett Mansion. After visiting the museum as a patron myself, and taking part in several of the curator's historic walking tours, the possibility of collaboration on a project through my course was discussed. The museum was interested in attracting younger patrons, and saw the use of new technologies like AR as a possible way to accomplish this. The project we developed centered on the Hart Cluett Mansion, which is a marble townhouse in downtown Troy, NY dating from the 1800's. The house museum includes exhibits that mostly focus on the wealthy owners of the home. The AR role-playing game *Below Stairs* instead tells the story of recent Irish immigrants working as domestic laborers in the house in the 1850's. While the museum leadership at the time originally wanted a story about the wealthy owners of the home, descendants of whom are still on the board of the museum, through workshops with museum visitors we were able to identify that younger people in their twenties and under (the group the museum most wanted to attract) were far more interested in the lives of the workers in the house. In the AR game, the user interacts with virtual characters by scanning codes with a phone or tablet, listening to character audio, and selecting their character's text responses. The virtual characters include a cook who runs the household and sends the user throughout the house to complete tasks. But the cook does not give precise instructions, so the user is compelled to explore the house, collecting virtual versions of historic objects onto the phone, like a platter, teacup, and even a chamber pot. If the user completes all the tasks, the cook will offer the user the job … if they still want it! The experience of exploration and physical exertion gives visitors to the house a more embodied relationship to the history and space, and ignites their curiosity to talk with curators or docents in more depth, or even take a traditional tour.
- *The Foerster Files* (Prototype 2016)
  The Foerster Files was developed for the New York State Office of Historic Preservation, to look at the relatively recent history of urban renewal in our area from the 1960's-1980's. Researching this topic, the students came across the papers of Bernd Foerster, former Architecture professor at Rensselaer, filmmaker, author, and pioneer of the preservation movement pushing back against urban renewal in Albany and Troy NY. Students found a copy of Foerster's 1960 book, *Man and Masonry*, which includes a vinyl LP with a commissioned orchestral work designed to accompany the reading experience. Discovering this analogue 'augmented book' inspired the students to develop an AR book experience to tell the story of urban renewal in Troy and Foerster's involvement to save historic architecture. The prototype is a fictionalized 'lost file' of Foerster's that uses archival film, audio, and object reproductions plus an interactive map for use with phones and tablets. The

project was developed to the prototype level, and received well by the client, but not selected for further development to completion or presentation for the public. In this iteration of the course, we did not use a community-based or co-design approach. I believe this omission hampered the project's success, and is in part what resulted in the client's disinterest in continuing the work.

- *Finding Roebling* (Completed 2017)
  Finding Roebling is a multi-modal AR experience that was developed as a spin-off from the AR class for our campus Library and Archives, with a former student from the AR class, Noah Zucker. Our Director of Libraries had seen the *The Foerster Files* prototype and approached me about a collaboration to develop something similar for a library exhibition. The project centers on the history of Washington Roebling, builder of the Brooklyn Bridge and Rensselaer alum. Traditional exhibit cases, filled with original and reproduced artifacts are augmented by providing additional imagery, animations, 3D models and text accessed via the Microsoft HoloLens head mounted display. A second part of the exhibit simulates author Erica Wagner's research journey through the Rensselaer archives, which holds many of Roebling's papers and artifacts, to develop her new biography of Washington Roebling, "Chief Engineer: The Man Who Built the Brooklyn Bridge." Erica's desk is playfully re-created, strewn with reproductions of manuscripts and objects from the Rensselaer archives that were instrumental in her research. Using a phone or tablet, the user accesses AR content tied to each physical object, including videos, animations, and images that illustrate Erica's story. While most exhibits, books, and documentaries on Roebling focus on the bridge and his engineering prowess, Erica's research unearthed the more personal history of Roebling from his childhood living with an abusive father, to struggles during his time as a student at Rensselaer, to his unconventional relationship with his wife Emily, who became a key collaborator on the bridge project when he was stricken with caisson poisoning from involvement in the underwater construction. This project was commissioned by our school Library and Archives for their own exhibit series, and like the *Foerster Files* (above) did not include a community-based or co-design process, but rather a more traditional HCI user-testing iterative approach.
- *Rapp Road Family Album* (Completed 2018)
  The *Rapp Road Family Album* project was an independent study spin-off from the AR class with a former student from the class, Kyle Ring. The project was developed for the Rapp Road Historical Society, led by Stephanie Woodard, who had approached me after learning about the AR course to discuss possibilities for collaboration. The Rapp Road community is a group of African-American families that came to Albany NY during the period of Great Migration in the 1920's and '30s, leaving their homes in Mississippi due to increasing racist violence in the region. Coming to Albany NY with few material resources the community relied on the engineering, architectural, entrepreneurial, and agricultural knowledge of its members to build an entire neighborhood of homes by hand, plant extensive gardens, build a community smokehouse, start businesses, and thrive. The community has continued to grow today, also preserving many of the original family ties. The AR project is an augmented book, for use with phones and tablets. The book is designed

in the style of a family photograph album, but combines documentary footage from Todd Ferguson's film *Crossroads: The History of Rapp Road* with oral histories of residents and photographic imagery and maps of the community through the years. The album is used by the Rapp Road Historical Association as a public education tool at heritage events in the region. Like the *Below Stairs* project above, this project was again developed with community involvement and co-design workshops.

- *Discover Cohoes* (In Progress since 2018)
  Discover Cohoes was developed to the prototype level for the City of Cohoes, a small municipality close to campus. Town leadership had circulated a call for proposals for the development of a technologically enhanced mural that would celebrate the town's heyday during the 19th century industrial revolution. Through our own research as well as workshops with the community center and middle school, we discovered that most people in the town already knew the story of industrial history in Cohoes, but they were unaware of the rich Native American history prior to the town's establishment. The town has a large waterfall, Cohoes Falls, which is second in size only to Niagara Falls in New York State. The falls are often highlighted for their hydropower role in industrial history, but this waterfall is the site of the Iroquois Confederacy, which still persists, bringing together six previously warring Native American nations in 1722. The Confederacy was one of the first examples of participatory democracy, and directly inspired Benjamin Franklin and others for the structure of the US Constitution. Middle School social studies teachers we collaborated with were eager to bring this history into the classroom through the AR app as a low-cost local field trip, so we used grant funding to hire local expert, Mohawk storyteller, and retired schoolteacher, Kay Olan (Ionataiewas). Kay worked as a consultant with us and taught us, and provided feedback to the artist developing the mural so that Native American iconography could be incorporated in meaningful, appropriate, and respectful ways in both the mural and the AR application. Working with middle school students and teachers in a co-design process, *Discover Cohoes* was developed as an AR scavenger hunt game. The game interacts with the planned mural as well as other sites of interest in downtown Cohoes to compliment existing public school curriculum. Four learning modules were developed in the prototype, with plans for a further three sketched out to the concept level. After completing each module, the player receives a 3D model on the phone or tablet of a local animal that also has cultural significance for Native American nations in the area. After collecting the 3D models, players can bring their phones to the public library nearby to receive a prize of a set of cut-and-fold cardstock models of the animals that are printed with more information about the role they play in Native American culture, and can be built and decorated by the player. The city has expressed interest in bringing the project to completion, and is currently working to implement the physical component of the project, the mural, which the AR application is designed to interact with.

- *Harriet Tubman: Guided By The Night* (Prototype 2019)
  Harriet Tubman: Guided By The Night was developed in collaboration with Prof. Janell Hobson at University at Albany for the MiSci: Museum of Innovation and Science in Schenectady, NY. The project includes both a mixed reality interactive planetarium show and take-home AR kit for local middle school students that tells

the fuller history of American hero Harriet Tubman through the lens of her STEM expertise in astronomy. The interactive planetarium show uses an infrared pointer system to allow students to collectively make choices about following stars and moving a compass as they learn the story of Tubman's early life, escape from slavery, and work helping hundreds of enslaved people to escape to freedom on the underground railroad and during the Civil War. The show includes silhouetted animatics to illustrate the story, an animated 3D model of Tubman with actor voiceover, and narrative teaching about the history of slavery, constellations, and way-finding. An AR 3D-printed kit with map is designed to go home with students after the planetarium experience, or for use in the classroom prior to a field trip to the museum, to tell the story of Tubman's activities in our local area, such as her role in the rescue of escaped slave Charles Nalle in 1859. This project was developed with community involvement through a series of co-design workshops with a local middle school and a Girls Who Code community group in our area. Due to large-scale leadership changes at the MiSci museum, the project will not be developed to completion at their facility. However, Hobson and I are currently pursuing a potential partnership with the recently commissioned Harriet Tubman National Historical Park in Auburn NY as a future venue.

3 An Ethical Approach for Telling Other People's Stories

3.1 Generalizing Diverse Processes

While every project developed in the AR Design for Cultural Heritage course has focused on very different aspects of local history, included collaborations with diverse groups, and progressed via different methods, by stepping back to reflect I can see a generalized process (see Fig. 2) that seems to work best in navigating the delicate and shifting balance of the needs of all involved. In this section, lessons learned are presented as one possible approach (among many) for the ethical telling of other people's stories in digital heritage IN projects.

Building on the now traditional iterative (as opposed to waterfall) design process of creation, feedback, and revision, I have developed a process specific to the AR cultural heritage area that prioritizes community teaching and learning, historical research, and collaboration. This process takes direct inspiration from Helguera's scholarship on socially engaged art [29] and Sanders' and Stappers' scholarship on co-design methods [26]. I have combined elements from each of these, along with elements more specific to the heritage and mixed reality design spaces.

Prior to the semester beginning, I work with the client to understand their desires and ideas for the project, and explain what is possible for students to develop in the span of one course. We settle on a schedule of interaction, in terms of how many times my students will meet with the client, where, and for how long. I also ask the client for help in identifying resources, other collaborators like local experts, relevant archives, and connection to end users - in other words, community members. At the start of the semester early community workshops taught by my students include demystifying the AR technology for community members, and teaching them some of the basic skills of

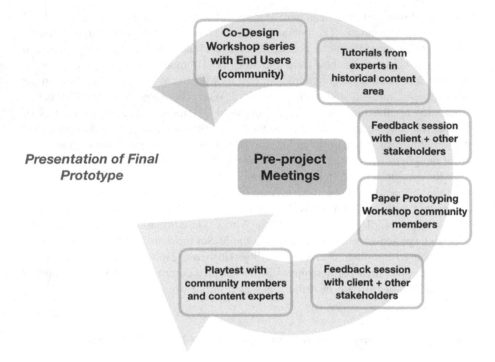

Fig. 2. Generalized process for project development during the span of one semester.

design with AR. The core concept for the project is introduced in a open ended manner, and through design sketching activities community members share their ideas for what should be included in the project. Sketching activities could include asking community members to draw psychogeographic maps of their town, to help share what spaces are important to them and what spaces they already move through or visit on a regular basis. Another activity could be asking community members to write a postcard from the future of the town, sketching an image that shows what spaces, places, objects, animals, or people the town is proud of or claims as an identity in the future, to help understand community members' aspirations for the town.

At the same time as these initial workshops are facilitated, students and I are also doing our own research to educate ourselves on the topic at hand, and networking with community experts, to identify threads in the story that may be misunderstood, over-looked, or simply absent. Students are learning the basics of storytelling with AR/MR technologies, as well as the practicalities of working with these systems. Assignments during this time include written reflections on initial readings assigned, a journal-type reflection on a site visit outside of class time, and AR 'exercises' downloading existing applications and critiquing them, making a simple AR panorama that includes audio or other interactions, and deploying a basic AR object at a GPS location and testing it.

As students reflect on what they are learning through these first meetings, work-shops, assignments, and readings, they are led through a structured brainstorming process to develop initial concept sketches to take to the client and other experts for feedback. Students assimilate this feedback and identify what is needed in terms of further research to bring their ideas into more concrete form as rough paper prototypes. Following this, a second set of community workshops are set up to try out the paper prototypes and invite community members into the process again. Paper prototypes are ideal in terms of flexibility, since community members can write on, tear, tape together, etc. as they engage in co-design instead of only giving written or oral feedback or only being observed as they interact as in more traditional user testing protocols. Following paper prototyping in this second round of workshops, students develop a digital prototype, which they then playtest with community members and the client in a final round of workshops. Then at the end of the semester as the final exam, students formally present to the client and community members the finished working digital prototype, video trailer, and accompanying design document that details the larger vision for the project, and what resources would be needed to develop the project to completion.

Again, this process is just one way to approach IN for digital cultural heritage and the complex ethics of telling other people's stories. I hope that others will take this as a point of inspiration and critique, revise, and build other methods and approaches. In the name of practicality, I have also drawn out a set of tips for instructors interested in developing a course of this kind, listed in Fig. 3.

- Develop community partners well in **advance** of the course; **network** (attend local meet-ups and regional conferences; invite press to cover initial work to get the word out to more potential contacts; visit heritage sites, museums, and galleries regularly)

- Create a course **structure** that benefits all stakeholders; the students, the community partners, the faculty member

- Implement a participatory or **co-design** process

- Make time for formal **reflection** throughout the process

- Use digital tools for **project management** (Slack, GitHub)

- Over the course of the semester the faculty member should **fade into the background** (when your students can demo for the community and the client without you taking the lead, you've succeeded)

- Be prepared to be **in for the long haul**, such as possible multi-year collaborations. If the community partner wants to move ahead do not leave them hanging. This may mean multi-semester course structures are ideal

- **Pair** tech skill-building assignments with critical readings

- Teach to an interdisciplinary **'one-room schoolhouse'** with students working in one large team to maximize peer learning + serendipity

Fig. 3. Tips for developing a community engaged course in digital cultural heritage

4 Conclusion

As the students move through the semester, they take more ownership over the process. Emphasis is placed on centering the community members and client, and approximately half of class meetings take place at community locations, not on campus. By the second round of workshops, students are leading the process more fully, not the instructor. By the end of the semester, students are able to present to the client and community members without any assistance from the instructor. Throughout the process, students are prompted to write reflections, which are then brought into dialogue in the classroom, thinking about their contributions to the team, the shifting roles they have played, and how the process is going for them and others.

At times, students find the course frustrating, as it has no guaranteed outcomes in the same way that a textbook-based course does. The path every semester is different, and always an adventure. But once students reach the paper prototype phase, and begin to see how their multiplicity of ideas and the ideas of community members and the client can coalesce, they often become energized, working well above and beyond expectation, choosing to take over liaison communication responsibilities from the instructor (although communication lines with the instructor must always remain open), spend more time in the community, and see the value of their work beyond the walls of campus. Student feedback has been positive to the course, including comments on evaluations indicating how much the students enjoyed using their skills from Game Design and Computer Science for communities, and how much they valued the experience of working in a large, complex team, as well as their hopes to continue to contribute to community-based work in their careers following graduation.

In reflecting on this process, I claim it as neither fully original (see the many sources of inspiration above) or complete. Building on Nyamnjoh's call for a new valuation of the incomplete in the digital humanities [17], I feel that unlike the common HCI practice of conceptualizing users through "personas" or other designer-centered processes, the co-design process structure reflects the necessary incompleteness underlying the task - no one person or group has complete knowledge of history, and in addition, history is never complete in its telling or representation. In its incompleteness, history is an ideal match for the ontological incompleteness or mutability of IN. As I continue to develop this course in future iterations, I will continue to strive to enact teaching as a "practice of freedom," as discussed by hooks [36], in the hopes that all involved, myself included, learn new ways of being in the world as storytellers and listeners of history for the future.

Acknowledgements. Some of the activities described in this paper were supported by an NEH Humanities Connections Grant. The author also wishes to acknowledge and thank the many community organizations and individuals who welcomed her and her students into collaboration with incredible grace and generosity: The Rensselaer County Historical Society, Ilene Frank, Stacey Pomeroy Draper, Kathy Sheehan, The New York State Office of Historic Preservation, Mary Paley, Tony Opalka, Jenifer Monger, Tammy Gobert, Andrew White, Erica Wagner, The Rapp Road Historical Association, Stephanie Woodard, Beverly Bardequez, Todd Ferguson, The City of Cohoes, Ken Ragsdale, Melissa Cherubino, Michael Jacobson, Kay Olan (Ionetaiwas), Cohoes Middle School, Judith Pingelski, Jennifer Sangiacomo, Steve Lackmann, Mickey Smith, MiSci Museum of Science and Innovation, Janell Hobson, Marc Destefano, Megan Norris, Troy Middle School, Kathy Fuller, Girls Who Code, Chris Sohn, and all the wonderful students of the AR Design for Cultural Heritage course.

References

1. Goffman, E.: Frame Analysis: An Essay on the Organization of Experience. Harvard UP, Cambridge, MA (1974)
2. Parry, R.: The end of the beginning: normatively in the postdigital museum. Mus. Worlds **1** (1), 24–39 (2013)
3. Rouse, R.: VR and Media of attraction: design lessons from history. In: Sherman, W. (ed.) Virtual Reality Programming Gems. Taylor and Francis CRC Press (2019)
4. Schiavo, L.B.: From phantom image to perfect vision: physiological optics, commercial photography, and the popularization of the stereoscope. In: Gitelman, L., Pingree, G.B. (eds.) New Media 1740-1915, pp. 113–137. MIT Press, Cambridge MA (2003)
5. Parry, R. (ed.): Museums in a Digital Age. Routledge, New York (2013)
6. Knoller, N.: Complexity and the Userly Text. In: Grishakova, M., Poulaki, M. (eds.) Narrative Complexity: Cognition, Embodiment, Evolution, pp. 98–122. University of Nebraska Press, Lincoln (2019)
7. Koenitz, H.: Towards a Specific Theory of Interactive Narrative. In: Koenitz, H., Ferri, G., Haahr, M., Sezen, D., Sezen, T.I. (eds.) Interactive Digital Narrative: History, Theory, and Practice, pp. 91–105. Routledge, New York (2015)
8. de la Pena, N., et al.: Immersive Journalism: immersive virtual reality for the first-person experience of news. In: Presence: Teleoperators and Virtual Environments **19**(4), pp. 291–301 (2010)
9. Milk, C.: How virtual reality can create the ultimate empathy machine. TED Talk (2015)
10. Fisher, J.A.: Empathic actualities: toward a taxonomy of empathy in virtual reality. In: Nunes, N., Oakley, I., Nisi, V. (eds.) ICIDS 2017. LNCS, vol. 10690, pp. 233–244. Springer, Cham (2017). https://doi.org/10.1007/978-3-319-71027-3_19
11. Shuman, A.: Other People's Stories: Entitlement Claims and the Critique of Empathy. University of Illinois Press, Urbana, Chicago (2005)
12. Engberg, M.: Augmented and mixed reality design for contested and challenging histories. MW17: Museums and the Web Published, 30 January 2017. Consulted 17 July 2019. https://mw17.mwconf.org/paper/augmented-and-mixed-reality-design-for-contested-and-challenging-histories-postcolonial-approaches-to-site-specific-storytelling/
13. Fisher, J.A., Schoemann, S.: Toward an ethics of interactive storytelling at dark tourism sites in virtual reality. In: Rouse, R., Koenitz, H., Haahr, M. (eds.) ICIDS 2018. LNCS, vol. 11318, pp. 577–590. Springer, Cham (2018). https://doi.org/10.1007/978-3-030-04028-4_68
14. Phelan, P.: Unmarked: The Politics of Performance. Routledge, London (1993)
15. Alcoff, L.: The problem of speaking for others. Cult. Crit. J. (20) 5–32 (1991–1992). https://www.jstor.org/stable/1354221
16. Cavarero, A.: Relating Narratives: Storytelling and Selfhood. Routledge, Abingdon (2014)
17. Nyamnjoh, F.B.: ICTs as Juju: African inspiration for understanding the compositeness of being human through digital technologies. In: Keynote address at the 2019 Digital Humanities Conference, Utrecht University, Netherlands (2019)
18. Rouse, W.B.: Design for Success: A Human-Centered Approach to Designing Successful Products and Systems. Wiley, Hoboken (1991)
19. Rouse, W.B.: People and Organizations: Explorations of Human-Centered Design. Wiley, Hoboken (2007)
20. Kelley, T., Littman, J.: The Art of Innovation: Lessons in Creativity from IDEO. America's Leading Design Firm. Doubleday, New York (2000)
21. Moggeridge, B., Atkinson, B.: Designing Interactions. MIT Press, Cambridge (2007)

22. Hench, J., Van Pelt, P.: Designing Disney: Imagineering and the Art of the Show. Disney Editions (2003)
23. Verplank, B.: Interaction Design Sketchbook: Frameworks for Designing Interactive Products and Systems. Unpublished paper posted, 1 December 2009. Consulted 17 July 2019. http://www.billverplank.com/IxDSketchBook.pdf
24. King, S., Conley, M., Latimer, B., Ferrari, D.: Co-Design: a Process in Design Participation. Van Nostrand Reinhold Company (1989)
25. Bardzell, D., Bardzell, S.: Towards a feminist HCI methodology: social science, feminism, and HCI. In: Proceedings of the SIGCHI Conference on Human Factors in Computing Systems, pp. 675–684. ACM (2011)
26. Sanders, E.B.-N., Stappers, P.J.: Probes, Toolkits, and Prototypes: three approaches to making in codesigning. CoDesign 10(1), 5–14 (2014)
27. Parvin, N.: Doing justice to stories: on ethics and politics of digital storytelling. Engag. Sci. Technol. Soc. 4, 515–534 (2018)
28. Stout, W.F.: IDEO Method Cards: 51 Ways to Inspire Design. IDEO (2003)
29. Helguera, P.: Education for Socially Engaged Art: A Materials and Techniques Handbook. Jorge Pinto Books, New York (2011)
30. Baldwin, J.: Unnameable objects, unspeakable crimes. In: The White Problem in America, pp. 170–180. Johnson, Chicago (1966)
31. Bennett, T.: The exhibitionary complex. In: New Formations (4) Spring, pp. 73–102 (1988)
32. Dunne, A., Raby, F.: Speculative Everything: Design, Fiction, and Social Dreaming. MIT Press, Cambridge (2013)
33. Packer, H.S., Hargood, C., Howard, Y., Papadopoulos, P., Millard, D.E.: Developing a Writer's Toolkit for Interactive Locative Storytelling. In: Nunes, N., Oakley, I., Nisi, V. (eds.) ICIDS 2017. LNCS, vol. 10690, pp. 63–74. Springer, Cham (2017). https://doi.org/10.1007/978-3-319-71027-3_6
34. Rouse, R., Engberg, M., Parvin, N., Bolter, J.D.: Understanding mixed reality. Digit. Creat. 26(3–4), 175–227 (2015)
35. Rouse, R., Barba, E.: Design for emerging media: how MR designers think about storytelling, process, and defining the field. In: Nunes, N., Oakley, I., Nisi, V. (eds.) ICIDS 2017. LNCS, vol. 10690, pp. 245–258. Springer, Cham (2017). https://doi.org/10.1007/978-3-319-71027-3_20
36. hooks, B.: Teaching to Transgress: Education as the Practice of Freedom. Routledge, London (1994)

Interactive Digital Narrative Practices
and Applications

Practical Insights for XR Devised Performances

Joshua A. Fisher[1]([⊠]) [iD], Melissa Foulger[2], and Jennifer Edwards[3]

[1] Columbia College Chicago, Chicago, IL 60605, USA
jofisher@colum.edu
[2] Georgia Institute of Technology, Atlanta, GA 30332, USA
melissa.foulger@lmc.gatech.edu
[3] JenEd, Philadelphia, PA 19125, USA
jenedproductions@gmail.com

Abstract. Devised performances are produced through improvisations and theater games in order to develop a story. Devising has a tradition of using supplementary media. However, its collaborative storytelling process presents design challenges when using Reality Media (XR). We present a series of challenges and design insights derived from the production of a devised performance with XR, *The Safety Show*. This novel performance utilized 20 mobile devices networked to a stage manager running a shared XR experience with live actors. The work sketches a rich space for research and creative expression.

Keywords: Augmented reality · Devised performance · Interactive non-fiction

1   Introduction to XR Devising Through the Safety Show

Devised performances engage a group of committed actors to develop a story through improvisational games and creative exercises. The production is developed in a participatory culture [1]. Increasingly, ensembles are supporting their work with computational media. Augmented, mixed, and virtual reality—referred to as Reality Media (XR) [2]—can now be integrated into the devising process [3]. To aid practitioners, we present design solutions to issues that arise during the production of XR devised performances. These insights are derived from a devised XR performance called *The Safety Show*. Additional inspiration came from scenographic theory [4]. The production, practice-based design research, was an experimental step in an emerging creative practice.

The Safety Show was performed in February 2019 at DramaTech, a theater at the Georgia Institute of Technology. It was part of a campus-wide collective art project entitled *I Feel Safe When* created and lead by resident artist Jennifer Edwards (2015–2018). For the show, six student actors devised stories about feeling safe. They included losing a friend, losing a grandfather, witnessing a birth, body shaming and empowerment, religious disillusionment, non-binary empowerment, mental health, self-discovery, friendship, and the campus police's fatal shooting of Scout Schultz, a nonbinary engineering student in their senior year [5].

© Springer Nature Switzerland AG 2019
R. E. Cardona-Rivera et al. (Eds.): ICIDS 2019, LNCS 11869, pp. 63–67, 2019.
https://doi.org/10.1007/978-3-030-33894-7_7

The performance was directed by Melissa Foulger and the ensemble. In total, 34 students participated [6]. The show was performed over two weekends with two performances per night. With the support of a grant, 20 iPhone 7 devices were rented and shared between audience members. Over the show's run, 78 people attended. Their reactions varied depending on the night, their familiarity with XR, and how well the technology worked. The university wrote a news article heralding the work as innovative. A short video on social networks garnered thousands of views [7–9].

2 XR in the Production Process

The devising process is dynamic. Its variability can make implementing XR an obstacle to improvisation. While human factors can change quickly to suit a performance's new direction, computational factors are procedural and cannot be altered with ease. Nonetheless, XR designers and developers need to be committed to the devising process.

In pre-production, actors practice engaging with XR that is invisible to them but visible to an audience. Once learned, the actor can use their movements to bridge the physical experience and the XR. The actor can become "a form of living scenery", as scenography scholar Pamela Howard has written, "the human body may be considered as the primary plastic element for the scenographer to work with in creating the unity between space, object, light and performer" [10]. We challenge actors to create dramatic tension between their bodies, XR, and members of the audience.

In early production, an aesthetic play between the XR, actors, and set should be established. For example, an audience's suspension of disbelief can be tickled by considering the physical space and its tension with the invisible yet present XR. In the show, this play occurred through a real-time multi-user network that enforced the XR's social presence even when an audience member wasn't using their device. Accordingly, XR designers should consider ways in which XR can create interactive, spatial, and visual tension [11]. The media should enhance the spatial presence of a story that develops from the actors' gestures and the audience's movement.

In mid production, rehearsals begin, the crew begins working out technical aspects, and actors solidify their script and choreography. XR designers focus on elevating details for dramatic effect through the creation of digital assets and prototypes. In *The Safety Show*, this process changed two physical platforms, meant to represent a mountain, into an XR forest with trees, clouds, and rocks—animated birds flit about as an actor told their story. As part of creating these and other assets, actors had their motions captured with the Orion iKinema system and an HTC Vive. Actors' movements were rehearsed while practicing monologues aloud. Once satisfied, actors' motions were captured. If necessary, they were re-recorded. The process lasted one hour per actor.

Audience placement is established during mid production and can be a challenge. The XR and actors looked best from certain angles, but *The Safety Show* allowed the audience to move freely. Actors gestured audiences toward these better viewpoints. We also considered stationary iPads for the XR. This could have been an effective primary setup for spectatorship or a secondary support to improve the XR's accessibility for people with reduced mobility.

In late production, technical rehearsals are underway in preparation for the performance. The ensemble should look for ways to elevate aspects of established XR. In the show, the petals of a cherry blossom tree fall to the ground as an actor relates his grandfather's death. He gestures toward petals to create a shared dramatic moment through the XR. The petals were added in late production to enhance the existing XR tree. Another example: it became clear that actors' motion-captured models were stuck in the uncanny valley. Since the models' faces did not move, their monologues seemed disembodied. Accordingly, a ghost shader was applied to the models. This spoke to the biographical nature of the actors' monologues and improved their presence.

During late production, procedures for stage management should be finalized. This includes how the XR will be managed and how devices to access the XR will be deployed. For *The Safety Show*, XR was synched asymmetrically between the audience members' devices and the stage manager. Two apps were developed: one for stage management and the other for the audience. They were synched using the Photon Pun Network solution for Unity. The audience app provided only a screen to look through.

The stage management app was designed for an iPad screen. Each act had a screen of buttons to cue XR. These were deactivated after they were pressed to avoid repeated instantiations. When this method didn't work, it caused a cascade of failures as the stage manager would attempt to synch the performance. It is suggested that a fail-safe button that clears the XR while maintaining tracking be included to re-synch the performance.

Regarding device distribution, if the ensemble lets their XR experience run on their audience's personal devices, the app needs to be downloaded. Once downloaded, the ensemble needs to confirm that the app is working before the show. If providing devices, a procedure needs be developed for their distribution and set up. In our show, a docking bay with fast-charging stations that accommodated 20 iPhone 7 devices was constructed. Before the performance, members of the crew would check the phones to ensure their volume was up, battery was charged, and app was running. The phones had Guided Access turned on to keep the audience locked into the app. The crew would then detect features with the application to track the XR. Once all of this was confirmed, the devices were handed off to audience members who were instructed to raise their hands should they run into any issue. The crew then practiced running phones out to audience members having difficulties. This was an imperfect process.

During tech rehearsals, the apps and the Wi-Fi network need to be put under a stress test. Using one or two devices is not enough. The performance space needs to be filled with people. We were informed by IT staff that the water in humans can interfere with Wi-Fi signals. If a theater is small and has an aging Wi-Fi network, a packed audience moving about the performance space can cause issues. Placing Wi-Fi repeaters and network boosters throughout the space can and did dramatically help connectivity.

3   XR in the Performance: Maintaining the Illusion

Keeping the audience engaged with the XR can be a challenge and even an obstacle to the performance. This challenge is caused by the weight of the devices, how hot they get, unfamiliarity with XR devices, technical issues, and how easy the experience is to enjoy. The cumulative effect of these challenges is a listless audience.

Stage management can be a challenge depending on the XR platform used and the performance space's connectivity. Timing the instantiation of XR material requires not just responding to rehearsed cues but also the audience's participation and an actor's impromptu gesture. Achieving these moments to dramatic effect takes practice. The person controlling the XR needs a small crew to help them distribute devices, achieve tracking with the app, and collect devices. During the show, there was only one person managing the XR. This proved untenable. The show's XR ran best when there were at least three other crew members. It became easier to respond to the actors and audience.

The final challenge comes when the devices need to be collected, charged, and set up for the next show. Over an hour, devices running XR will lose a substantial amount of power. If the devices are to be used again, they need to be recharged and sanitized. There were two shows per night with about 30 min between them. Depending on the audience, there were only eight to 12 phones available for the second performance.

4   Challenges and Insights for the Set and Digital App

Hiding technical elements, maintaining a safe space for the audience to move, and facilitating stable tracking for XR can be difficult. Masking can be used to hide pieces such as charging stations and Wi-Fi boosters, but it can obscure trackable features. We learned that the efficacy of tracking will be impacted by lighting cues, the stage's texture, and a device's allocated memory for the experience. In terms of lighting, as cues change so too will features. This alteration will influence the effectiveness of the tracking algorithms. During *The Safety Show*, lighting cues were removed in order to keep lighting stable. Additionally, between scenes, the performance space's light was cued to its originally tracked setting to aid feature detection. Both solutions were imperfect.

Mapping the space for features will be difficult if the stage's texture is uniform. While minimalism can be pleasing to the human eye, computer vision has a difficult time ascertaining differences in symmetrical designs scattered across a stage with shifting lighting conditions. This applies similarly to props' textures and dimensions.

ARkit provides memory-efficient affordances for object, plane, and light detection. However, the complexity of models' textures and polygon counts for XR can use a lot of an app's allotted memory [12]. For our show, we learned that iOS devices released from 2017 to 2019 running iOS 12.1 only allow an application a 1.4 GB memory footprint. Passing that threshold causes an experience to crash. The current AR services will utilize about half that amount and do not leave much space for complex models.

5   Conclusion: A Call to Create

The Safety Show was a highly experimental project and provided insight into the potential challenges for XR in devised performance. Multi-user XR performances are a rich creative space in need of exploration. We hope this paper encourages others to devise their own XR performances.

References

1. Jenkins, H., Ito, M.: Participatory Culture in a Networked Era: A Conversation on Youth, Learning, Commerce, and Politics. Wiley, Hoboken (2015)
2. Engberg, M., Bolter, J., MacIntyre, B.: RealityMedia: an experimental digital book in WebXR. In: 2018 IEEE International Symposium on Mixed and Augmented Reality Adjunct (ISMAR-Adjunct), Munich, pp. 324–327 (2018)
3. Rouse, R.: MRx as a performative and theatrical stage, pp. 193–206 (2015)
4. Watson, I.: Levels of Visuality: Integrated Scenography for Devised Theatre (2008)
5. McCausland, P., Rosenblatt, K.: NBC news. In: Georgia Tech Student-Activist Shot Dead by Campus Police. https://www.nbcnews.com/news/us-news/georgia-tech-student-activist-shot-dead-campus-police-n802146
6. Friends of Dramatech: Friends of DramaTech. In: DramaTech Theatre Cast and Crew Database. http://imdt.friendsofdt.org/index.php?action=show_detail&show_id=457
7. Atkinson, E.: Georgia tech news center. In: DramaTech Theatre Uses Augmented Reality in "The Safety Show. https://www.news.gatech.edu/2019/02/22/dramatech-theatre-uses-augmented-reality-safety-show
8. Georgia Institute of Technology: YouTube. In: DramaTech performance uses augmented reality to engage audience. https://www.youtube.com/watch?v=wOaZST8gBt8
9. Georgia Institute of Technology: Instagram. In: Georgia Tech. https://www.instagram.com/p/BuMnXFrB-ka/?utm_source=ig_web_copy_link
10. Howard, P.: Actors as Scenography, pp. 1–10 (2008)
11. Schlemmer, O., Moholy-Nagy, L., Molnar, F., Gropius, W.: The Theater of the Bauhaus, 1st (edn.). Wesleyan University Press, Middletown (1961)
12. Apple: Apple Developer. In: Reducing the Memory Footprint of Metal Apps. https://developer.apple.com/documentation/metal/reducing_the_memory_footprint_of_metal_apps

Using Ink and Interactive Fiction
to Teach Interactive Design

Kenton Taylor Howard[(✉)] and Rachel Donley

University of Central Florida, Orlando, USA
{Khowar12, RDonley}@knights.ucf.edu

Abstract. Fundamentals of Interactive Design is a large, mixed-mode, entry level course in the Games and Interactive Media program at the University of Central Florida. In the course we use Inky, an interactive fiction scripting engine created by Inkle Studios, to teach interactive design by having students create a choice-based interactive fiction story as a major course project. In this paper, we provide a brief overview of our approach to teaching the course that others can build upon. We discuss the class itself, previous research related to teaching interactive fiction, and some of the assignments we created. We argue that interactive fiction is an effective framework for teaching interactive design and suggest that Inky facilitates teaching those concepts through code in an entry-level course very well.

Keywords: Interactive fiction · Interactive design · Inkle

1 Introduction

This paper discusses our experiences with teaching interactive fiction in an interactive design course using Ink, a scripting language created by Inkle Studios that creates choice-based interactive fiction. First, we provide some background on the ways that interactive fiction has been used in educational settings in the past. We then offer an overview of the course and the approaches we used in the class. After that, we discuss the assignments we used in the course and the kinds of feedback we gave students to show how interactive fiction-based assignments were integrated into the course. Overall, we argue that interactive fiction is an effective framework for teaching interactive design and suggest that the Inky editor facilitates teaching those concepts through code in an entry-level course.

2 Background

Interactive fiction has been used in the classroom in many ways, suggesting that it can be an effective framework for students to learn about a variety of concepts. Approaches to teaching with interactive fiction have been quite diverse: for example, IF has been used by Lester [1] to teach students about the Hebrew Bible in college-level religious studies classes, by Flynn and Hardman [2] to generate interest in physics in high school science courses, and by Lundberg and Lyons [3] to help students with literacy in

© Springer Nature Switzerland AG 2019
R. E. Cardona-Rivera et al. (Eds.): ICIDS 2019, LNCS 11869, pp. 68–72, 2019.
https://doi.org/10.1007/978-3-030-33894-7_8

grammar and creative writing in intermediate level English as a Second Language classes. IF is particularly common in creative writing contexts, and many classes and programs use it to bridge game design and English: Skains [4] has used it in this way in a Game Design and Professional Writing program. In this paper, we expand on such research by describing how we used interactive fiction to teach an interactive design course focused on introducing students to basic programming and design concepts.

3 Course Overview

Fundamentals of Interactive Design is an entry-level course in the University of Central Florida's Games and Interactive Media undergraduate program. The course has an average of about 130 students per semester. The class is a 16-week mixed-mode course; students complete most of their work online and attend class for lectures, demonstrations, and other face-to-face activities once a week for two hours. Because most of the students in the program focus on either web design or game design, the course is divided in half and focuses on two major projects: the first half centers on having the students create a personal website using HTML and CSS, while the second centers on having the students create an interactive story using Ink, which this paper will discuss.

Because it is an entry-level course, students enter Fundamentals of Interactive Design with a variety of backgrounds in terms of their experience with interactive fiction and coding. Students in the Games and Interactive Media program are typically going on to either game design or web design courses, so the course emphasizes development of students' coding skills so that they can be successful in future courses in the program. Students who are not in the program sometimes take the course as an elective, especially those who are in other digitally focused programs, such as Computer Science. These factors mean that students are very diverse in terms of their previous coding experience: some have never written code before, while others have experience as professional coders or have developed interactive products already.

The main goals of the course are to introduce students to coding skills and design concepts. Students also develop entry-level interactive projects that prepare them for later web design or game design courses in the Games and Interactive Media program. Ink code can also be integrated into the popular Unity game design engine through a plugin and has been used by Inkle Studios to make well-received games like *80 Days* (2014) and *Heaven's Vault* (2019), so it introduces students to software that has been used in the industry for professionally released products, another major goal of the course.

4 Scaffolding Assignments and Projects

While Fundamentals of Interactive Design uses quizzes, exams, and participation grades like many other college-level classes, much of the course focuses on two types of linked assignments: scaffolding assignments that are made up of small, incremental objectives that students receive weekly feedback on, and major projects that bring together the scaffolding assignments by asking students to create an interactive product. Scaffolding assignments are graded on a pass/half/fail basis and build upon each other: each one asks students to create one or more components of an upcoming major project.

The first half of the course has assignments that build up to having the students create a short personal website, the first major project in the course. The second half of the course has assignments that build up to a full interactive story created in Ink, the final project of the course. These assignments begin with short brainstorming and storyboarding assignments that ask students to plan out the content and structure of their story, then move on to Ink-related assignments that ask them to implement that content in code. This paper will review the basic structure of the Ink-related scaffolding assignments below; while these are not the full assignment prompts given to students, these prompts give a brief idea of what each assignment asks students to do and how we gave feedback on each assignment. We have also provided an overview of the final project assignment.

4.1   Scaffolding Assignment 4: Basic Ink

Assignment prompt: In Ink, create the majority of the content for your story. Create the 2 main decision points that will make up the structure of your story. Finally, create 2 endings for your story. Note that this assignment is a draft, which means that some elements of your story can be a bit "rough," but you should complete all the content described above.

The goal of this assignment is to introduce students to Ink by having them implement all of the story content that they have created in previous assignments in the Inky editor itself. The scaffolding assignment approach is effective here because it allows the students to focus on the code needed to create the story that they have already written instead of creating new story content. This structure is particularly useful for beginning coders who often have trouble with the coding concepts and need time to work through them. Ink is relatively easy to learn, but this point in the scaffolding assignment sequence is also where students usually start to struggle since it requires them to write code. Since many story problems have been addressed on the previous planning assignments, most of our feedback focuses on programming mistakes or other design problems, and we usually try to be very clear about what was not working so that students can fix coding errors before the next assignment.

4.2   Scaffolding Assignment 5: Advanced Ink

Assignment prompt: In Ink, create all of your story content. Create the main decision points and both of the endings for your story. Create a conditional within your story and one instance of alternative text. In addition, since this is a second draft, you should have made some changes from your first draft; some elements of the story can still be rough, but if your story shows little to no change whatsoever, you will not receive ANY points for this assignment.

This assignment asks students to create most Ink content that is required on the final project. By structuring the final assignment before the project in this way, students complete almost all required code and story elements before the final project, allowing us to check these key components early and helping the students to focus on revision and refinement. Students also learn some more advanced interactive design concepts that are useful in other classes in the Games and Interactive Media program since many of Ink's advanced features employ traditional programming concepts. Students who are new to coding sometimes have trouble with this assignment, and one of the biggest challenges when giving feedback is ensuring that students have a conceptual understanding of how elements like variables and conditionals work and, more importantly, why they are used. Some students struggle with the idea that while their code is functional, it does not actually do anything because it serves no purpose in the story and does not change the user's experience in any significant way. We focus on pointing out those kinds of issues so that students can address them before the final project.

4.3   Final Project: Ink Story

Assignment Prompt: In Ink, finalize all of your story content. Finalize the main decision points and both of the endings for your story. Use a conditional within your story and an instance of alternative text. Use HTML/CSS to modify at least two significant elements of your story, such as the background color or font. Note that this is your final version of the story, so your writing and code should be well-polished and error-free.

This final project asks students to make use of all the interactive design skills they have learned in the class - the HTML/CSS visual styling they add comes from the web design skills that they learned in the first half of the course, and the required Ink content uses what they learned in the second half. The main focus of the project is on polish so that students can create an interactive product that they would be proud to put in a portfolio or use as a demonstration piece. This assignment does not ask students to add new narrative or code content to their story so they can focus on revision and finalizing the content they have created. Students who struggle do so for a reason that many educators might expect: they simply have not reviewed their feedback or spent time revising their work to address concerns that were raised on previous assignments. Because students have ample opportunities to plan their story and receive incremental feedback on it, such situations are rare.

5   Conclusion

In this paper, we suggest that Ink is a powerful tool for creating interactive fiction as well as for learning about interactive design. In particular, the affordances of Inky as a simple code-based tool that can be integrated into Unity make it an ideal platform for teaching students new to coding while allowing students with advanced coding to take advantage of those. Our approach to teaching students interactive design skills through a code-based interactive fiction scripting engine helps them prepare for future courses in web or game design. We believe that our work provides an effective framework for using interactive fiction and Inky to teach interactive design.

References

1. Lester, G.B.: What IF? Building interactive fiction for teaching and learning religious studies. Teach. Theol. Relig. **21**(4), 260–273 (2018)
2. Flynn, S., Hardman, M.: The use of interactive fiction to promote conceptual change in science: a forceful adventure. Sci. Educ. **28**(1–2), 127–152 (2019)
3. Lundberg, K., Lyons, K.: Using twine to deliver a grammar-linked creative writing assignment in a hybrid ESL course. HETS Online J. **9**, 98–112 (2019)
4. Skains, R.L.: Teaching digital fiction: integrating experimental writing and current technologies. Palgrave Commun. **5**(1), 1–10 (2019)

How Relevant Is Your Choice?
User Engagement and Perceived Agency in Interactive Digital Narratives on Video Streaming Platforms

Lobke Kolhoff[✉] and Frank Nack

Informatics Institute, University of Amsterdam,
Science Park 904, 1098 XH Amsterdam, The Netherlands
lobkekolhoff@gmail.com, f.m.nack@uva.nl

Abstract. With the release of the film *Black Mirror: Bandersnatch* Netflix entered the area of interactive streamed narratives. We performed a qualitative analysis with 169 Netflix subscribers that had watched the episode. The key findings show (1) participants are initially engaged because of curiosity and the novelty value, and desire to explore the narrative regardless of satisfaction, (2) perceived agency is limited due to arbitrary choices and the lack of meaningful consequences, (3) the overall experience is satisfactory but adaptions are desirable in future design to make full use of the potential of the format.

Keywords: Interactive Digital Narrative (IDN) · User engagement · Agency · Streamed interactive fiction · Netflix · Bandersnatch

1 Introduction

In December 2018, Netflix extended its offer on interactive films, so far only aiming at programmes for children, to adult customers by launching *Bandersnatch*[1]. This film is part of the science fiction anthology series *Black Mirror*[2] and this particular episode was released as a 'Choose Your Own Adventure' story. The interactive decision-making allows users to choose between two options of narrative development at multiple times during the episode, hereby determining the course of events in the film. *Bandersnatch* is a streaming endeavour with the aim to get subscribers more engaged and give them a feeling of control in the story.

Yet, interactive storytelling is not a novel technology as it has already been applied from as early as the 80s of the last century in stand-alone pc-based narrative environments, or more recently in games [1,2]. However, the application to the domain of video streaming services is new and poses some exciting possibilities, with respect to story design in the context of streamed fictional content

---

[1] https://www.netflix.com/title/80988062. The film is officially named *'Black Mirror: Bandersnatch'*, in this study we will refer to it as *'Bandersnatch'*.

[2] https://www.netflix.com/title/70264888.

© Springer Nature Switzerland AG 2019
R. E. Cardona-Rivera et al. (Eds.): ICIDS 2019, LNCS 11869, pp. 73–85, 2019.
https://doi.org/10.1007/978-3-030-33894-7_9

as well as towards the critical analysis of customer perception behaviour and hence the influence of decision-making on this behaviour.

In this article, we address the issue of what effect choice-based interactive digital narrative has on user engagement and perceived agency in a streamed interactive narrative environment, where the goal is to better understand if those aspects trigger the wish for interactive content and/or to explore the content in depth.

2   Related Work and Definitions

In our analysis we see Interactive Digital Narrative (IDN) as 'digital interactive entertainment media in which users are able to intentionally influence a multi-sequential narrative, mediated by an interactive storytelling system' [3,4]. We chose for this view based on earlier work on visual media branching narratives and technical developments that make the application of interactivity available to a larger audience.

Already in the 1960s systems like *Kinoautomat* [5] experimented with breaking up film inherent linearity by giving the cinema audience decision-points to alter the story flow. The introduction of computers in private households in the 1980s also introduced first attempts to establish interactive narratives in the form of classical hypertexts, such as *Afternoon, a story* [2], and much later, more enhanced examples such as *Lucy Hardin's Missing Period* [6]. The latter is of interest due to the impossibility to revoke a decision, so that frustration over the plot is deliberately evoked by the author. In parallel, we also observed the transition from film as a public medium, to be presented at cinemas, into a private medium, where film is presented via cassette recorders on the home tv. The company Blockbuster built on this home-video revolution by establishing a rental video tape service that allowed the customer to freely choose content to be watched at home [7]. At the same time, we saw developments in research that used the access liberation of first VCRs and then later laserdiscs and DVDs for methods to manipulate mixed media in a personalised manner. Examples of this type of work are:

- *New Orleans in Transition* [8], which is a linear video with explorative text-elements.
- *Terminal Time* [9], which is, in the tradition of *Kinoautomat*, an interactive, ideologically-based documentary generator where the cinema audience answers questions about it's view on historical events, expressed by clapping. As the narrative progresses it exaggerates ideas and, while maintaining a coherent story, it reflects biases present in the audience.
- *Façade* is an interactive drama, which is described as a hybrid entertainment form, with elements of a game and storytelling [10]. It is an open-ended narrative about a married couple, with multiple possible outcomes. The interactive experience is enabled by artificial intelligence and users are allowed an active role in the conversations of the story, determining the direction of the drama.

Around the turn of the century, developments in network technology and computing resulted in streaming and video-on-demand services, which personalised the access to media even further as any media could be accessed anytime and anywhere. Gaming made use of streaming to introduce interactivity in form of massively multiplayer online role-playing games such as World of Warcraft [11]. Digital video first mainly focused on streaming media for the use of video-on-demand. One of the first companies here was Netflix [12], which entered the market as a postal start-up delivery service for DVDs but then changed into a streaming-based video-on-demand service for the young and web-literate part of society, where the service offers professionally designed fictional content, in comparison to YouTube[3] and related services, which provide mainly privately generated content. Currently, several service providers in the field of professionally produced fictional content approach the market, such as Hulu[4], Amazon Prime[5], Apple TV Plus[6] and Disney Plus[7]. They all compete for a broad spectrum of the cloud audience. So obviously we have reached the end of the transition of presenting visual linear fictional content in pure public and location-fixed settings to individualised access anywhere and anytime. In the competitive field, where content and its access are the driver, the next step is to investigate different ways to handle content - where one option is to provide IDN.

Netflix has taken the first step for enhancing the experience of fictional material by introducing simple interactive storytelling in the area of online streaming services with interactive shows for children. The company believes that kids who grow up in today's digital era request interactivity and agency not only with respect to their use of technology but also in the use of content[8]. With the release of *Bandersnatch* the adult audience is now addressed. The goal is to foster engagement by creating a connection with the viewers by letting them participate in the process of storytelling. User engagement is here defined as a type of user experience which is characterised by elements of interactivity, positive affect, challenge, sensory appeal, aesthetics, attention, endurability, perceived user control, and novelty [13]. Thus, engagement stimulates cognitive, emotional and behavioural aspects of perception, which shape the connection between a user and a resource [14]. It relies on the positive aspects of interaction with an application, and consequently, the desire to interact more frequently and for a longer time [15, 16]. Hence, engagement is about a user's involvement and interest in an experience [10], which in this context refers to being captivated by a narrative and motivated to interact with it and continue to do so. The ability to influence the plot of the story as an effect of interactivity can positively influence the experience of entertainment for the user [17]. Interactive content could be

---

[3] https://www.youtube.com/.

[4] https://www.hulu.com/.

[5] https://www.primevideo.com/.

[6] https://www.apple.com/apple-tv-plus/.

[7] https://preview.disneyplus.com/.

[8] https://www.theverge.com/2017/6/20/15834858/netflix-interactive-shows-puss-in-boots-buddy-thunderstruck.

the means to get the user to engage, but can also result in distraction and disruption of the experience instead of sustained engagement [18]. The interaction can become complex due to branching narratives, resulting in choices that may lead to undesirable consequences or endings, and the experience may become lengthy, which can negatively affect the users' engagement as well.

Agency is described in research as the experience of control over one's body and the external environment [19]. According to Bandura [20], the core features of human agency include the notion of intentionality, forethought, self-reactiveness, and self-reflectiveness. Therefore agency refers to intentional acts and anticipation of the consequences, and includes taking actual action and reflecting on oneself and one's actions. In relation, Murray [21] identifies the concept of 'dramatic agency' as the most important term to evaluate the success of any IDN. The ability to make "meaningful choices" and see their effects differentiates it from terms like participation and activity. As agency is the actual ability to influence deliberately through actions, perceived agency includes how much of this agency is perceived by a user. It is this sense of control, that is essential for meaningful interaction in interactive narratives [22].

The question remains, with respect to a reflective audience, how far the wish for well-designed storytelling can be integrated with the wish to be served on a personalised level that addresses the individual perceptional, reflective and emotional preferences. That is what this paper addresses. Roth and Koenitz [23] already took a first step in exploring the reception of interactive narratives in a streaming environment. They also analysed *Bandersnatch*, with a user study of 32 participants that were asked to watch the episode in a university course setting. The study found global effectance, perceived meaningfulness, and positive affect to be significant indicators of user enjoyment. Also, transformational power and agency of the users appeared relevant for the experience. Coherence of the story was perceived high and confusion about it proved lower than expected. The possible influence of the novelty value of an interactive experience is touched upon but not further elaborated.

3   Bandersnatch - An Introduction

Before we introduce our analysis we provide a short introduction to the content and structure of *Bandersnatch*. The interactive film is released as part of the series *Black Mirror*, which is a dystopian science-fiction series about a dark future shaped by technology, that addresses philosophical issues, paradoxical tensions and twisted endings [24]. *Bandersnatch* is framed as part of the *Black Mirror* series. The series consists of non-interactive, stand-alone episodes, that last between 41 and 89 min each[9]. *Bandersnatch* is not part of any season of *Black Mirror* but released separately. However, the film may profit from the reputation of an established and successful series. This might encourage the audience to interact with the film. This audience is presumed to be interested in

---

[9] https://www.netflix.com/title/70264888. Before *Bandersnatch*, four seasons have been introduced where each has three to five episodes.

technology, may it be in the possibilities or the downsides of it. Because of these properties, the *Black Mirror* audience seems like a proper fit when considering the interactive format and the content of *Bandersnatch*.

Bandersnatch is set in the year 1984 and tells the story of Stefan Butler, a young British programmer and game designer. In his quest to design a video game based on a Choose Your Own Adventure fantasy novel, he is facing several challenges and starts to question his reality. During the film, he struggles with losing the feeling of control over his actions and decisions. The different storylines can result in different outcomes based on decisions of the viewer, and as is almost characteristic for *Black Mirror* productions these endings focus on the gloomy side for the main character.

The film can be watched on an iOS or Android device, smart TV, streaming media player, or game console,[10] as these devices allow the viewer to participate by making decisions. If the film is viewed on a device that does not support interactive content, the viewer is not able to select any choices and the system selects a default option.

The narrative does not follow a structured pattern and choices in one 'timeline' can affect other timelines. Thus, the architecture of *Bandersnatch* has characteristics of a 'Directed Network' structure, the standard structure of literary hypertexts [25]. As circuits are allowed there is limited control over the duration of the experience of the user. The film has five main endings, and 30 decision points throughout the entire experience, where decision points can establish crosses of storylines. Each time a choice is presented to the viewer, the 'pause', 'rewind' and 'forward' buttons disappear from the screen and are replaced by a black beam containing two options of story development. In a time frame of 10 seconds one of the options can be selected, while the scene continues. If no choice is made a default mode is played in which the system selects the way to proceed. The film lasts 90 min if no choices are made and the minimal duration is 30 min. There are several dead ends in the film, in which the story ends but there is no option to go to credits. The viewer can only go back to an earlier point in the film, and is sometimes offered a choice between two moments in the past. After a dead end a recapitulation of past events is shown, saving the user from experiencing long sequences all over again. It is important to note that in case the user approaches the story without interaction and also does not stop after the first story end is reached, the system automatically branches back to a crosspoint and follows from there the path to another ending. It is doing so until four endings are covered and then it proceeds to credits. This means a passive user has by accident (as only a basic version is advertised for passive mode) the best chance to see most of the endings, with still an incentive to start again to see the one that he or she missed. We interpret this mechanism that Netflix does not fully trust in it's audience desire to interact with a story.

Concerning the choices, a few of these at the beginning of film are merely of an aesthetic nature or introduce the user to the story. For example, the user can decide which cereal the main character should have for breakfast or which song

---

[10] https://help.netflix.com/nl/node/62526.

to play at the time of choice. These decisions only partially affect what happens the next moment and we interpret those as means to familiarise the user with the interaction process and choice making. The local agency is emphasised over global agency here. As the film progresses, global agency increases as the choices have more of influence on the story overall.

4   Methodology

We studied the film *Bandersnatch* to gain insights into the relevance of engagement and perceived agency for the experience of users of a streamed IDN. We are interested in those concepts as they are always named as the reason why people want to use IDN. We also investigate them in this context as we now can see in a broad setting if the assumption is valid. We define user engagement as the experience of a user in which one is captivated by the experience and motivated to interact with it and continue to do so. Perceived agency is defined here as the idea that users can make meaningful choices in the interactive narrative and observe and evaluate the consequences of the choices.

The target group of the study are Netflix users who interacted with the film *Bandersnatch*. As the interaction takes place in an online environment, we figured potential participants could be reached online as well. We chose to develop and use a questionnaire to measure engagement and agency because this is a form of self-report that allows for sizeable simultaneous distribution. *Bandersnatch* is available to Netflix users worldwide, which is why the study should not be limited to one geographic location.

Questionnaire. We designed an interactive and adaptive questionnaire that focused on gathering information on the interaction with the medium, evaluation of the content, levels of engagement and the amount of agency perceived by users.

The questionnaire starts with demographic questions (3), after which the participants are asked to confirm to have watched *Bandersnatch*. If this has not been the case, the only question that remains for a participant concerns the reason he or she did not watch it. In all other cases, participants are asked when and with whom the interaction took place and how traversal decisions were made with multiple people (2 or 3 questions depending on answers). Next, participants were asked about the first ending that was encountered, their satisfaction with it and if they continued the exploration after the ending to encounter further storylines (3 or 4 questions depending on answers). The next questions concern satisfaction about elements of the experience (6 questions), such as the overall story, being able to make decisions, the existence of multiple endings and dead ends. Participants were asked to provide an overall rating of the *Bandersnatch* environment and they state and explain if they would recommend the film. The set of questions about engagement (7 questions) is based on the attributes of engagement, as stated by O'Brien et al. [13]: novelty, perceived usability, focused attention, felt involvement, aesthetics, and endurability.

The final questions on perceived agency (9 questions) are based on the control heuristic of Thompson in which perceived agency over outcomes is judged based on the intention and connection between actions and consequences [26]. All multiple-choice questions about satisfaction, engagement ad agency use a five-point Likert scale, ranging from *very unsatisfied* or *strongly disagree* (at a value of 1) to *very satisfied* or *strongly agree* (at a value of 5).

The most crucial prerequisite for participants is to have interacted with *Bandersnatch*. Because of this specific property, we distributed the questionnaire in our own social networks and online communities with the theme '*Bandersnatch*' on Facebook and Reddit. Snowball sampling was used to reach more potential participants, because virtual snowball sampling is effective to increase the sample size and representative of "hard-to-reach" populations [27]. In this respect, the population used for this analysis is considered more representative than the one described in Roth & Koentiz [23], as we assume that the participants had already an intrinsic interest in watching the content and experiencing the interaction without being asked to do so in an educational setting. The questionnaire was distributed on May 18th 2019, five months after the release of *Bandersnatch*. We closed the form ten days later, on May 28th, as the incoming responses had been decreasing over the preceding days.

Participants. From all participants (N = 187) of this study, the majority (N = 169; 90.4%) watched *Bandersnatch*.[11] As the viewers of *Bandersnatch* belong to the main target group, we will refer to this group (N = 169) when discussing the sample, unless stated otherwise. In the sample of 169, 51% of the participants were female and 48% male. The remaining 1% did not disclose their gender. The age of the participants ranged from 13 to 61 years (M = 24.26, SD = 7.28). People from 29 different countries worldwide participated, and 40% of the sample are from the Netherlands. Other countries participants are from include, but are not limited to, the United States (21%), United Kingdom (8%) and Canada (5%). The continents that were represented most were Europe and Northern America.

5   Findings and Evaluation

In this section the results from the questionnaire will be described. For answers to multiple-choice questions, we present answers in the following way: SA (Strongly Agree) - A (Agree) - NA (Neither Agree Nor Disagree) - D (Disagree) - SD (Strongly Disagree). When asked about satisfaction, the range of answers is: VS (Very Satisfied) - S (Satisfied) - NS (Neither Satisfied Nor Unsatisfied) - U (Unsatisfied), VU (Very Unsatisfied).

5.1   Reasons for Not Watching

Responses from the participants who did not watch the film (N = 18) show that 72% did not know the film, 22% had not enough time to watch but were aiming at watching it later, and 6% simply had no interest in the content.

---

[11] The results of the questionnaire can be viewed at http://bit.ly/InteractiveStory telling2019.

5.2   Interaction

At the time of the study, in May 2019, the duration of last having seen the film has been distributed as: five months before (53%) four months (17%), three months (14%), two months (7%), less than a months ago (3%), and less than a week ago (7%). Thus, the majority watched the film short after its release, which indicates interest.

The amount of people that watched the film in a setting ranged from: alone (43.8%), two people (47.3%), three (5%), four (1.2%), five (1.2%), or more (1.2%). From those who did not watch alone (N = 95), 82.1% made decisions by attempting to reach a consensus in the provided time frame of 10 seconds. This behaviour we see in all group constellations. It seems agency (reflection and discussion) is a driver in group decision-making within IDN.

For participants who watched the film alone (N = 74) it is more difficult to state how decisions are formed. Thirteen of them finished in the first go at the end of the default path, which could mean they did not interact. However, all of them stated later that they reached several endings. It is unclear what drove them to start exploring the interactive feature, but it can be stated that they made the decisions all by themselves. Thus, we can conclude that both groups made active choices which indicates performed agency. We also conclude that streamed interactive fictional content needs to be designed so that a group decision process is possible. This requires that the decision points need to be set so that a discussion about various opinions is possible, but not so complicated that a decision in the given decision time frame is not feasible.

Table 1 shows which ending was encountered first by participants, the average satisfaction with this ending and the part that continued the experience to explore alternative endings. It shows that 89.6% of participants continued the experience after the first ending encountered. Most participants continued after this ending, regardless of their satisfaction with it. This is illustrated by the fact that there is a minimal difference in the percentages that continue, when looking at satisfaction about the first ending. From the participants satisfied with the first ending (45.4%), 90.5% continued the experience, and 88.8% of those who were dissatisfied (54.6%) continued. Thus, we clearly see that a good choice, thus positive agency (influential actions and anticipated consequences), relates to positiveness and interactivity and hence engagement. We also observe that unsatisfied agency still can generate engagement but then rather based on aspects such as challenge. In both cases the result is to interact more and to experiment with the experience of choice. The average number of endings found is four (M = 4.1, Median = 4) out of five possible endings.

5.3   Experiences

We have already established that overall participants appreciated that they can choose but showed an irritation with the choice environment in general. We investigated how they perceived their agency and the results of that investigation are presented in Tables 2 and 3. The overall distribution of responses

Table 1. Satisfaction and continuation after first ending encountered. Five main endings: Collins daughter works on *Bandersnatch* years later (A), Young Stefan goes with his mother and dies in the present (B), Stefan discovers he is on a film set (C), Stefan is arrested for killing his father (D), and Stefan fights therapist and father (E).

Ending	Encountered first (N)	Satisfied	Continued
A	30	80%	93.3%
B	32	65.6%	71.9%
C	23	39.1%	95.7%
D	49	26.5%	98%
E	29	24.1%	86.2%
	163	45.4%	89.6%

related to agency is rather diverse. In line with this, the participants think they are provided with the right amount of choices and seem to be adequately in control of those. However, they are in particular unhappy with the predictability and desirability of the consequences. This complaint is also visible in the fact that 41% felt that they were confronted with unnecessary choices, and that 44% had anticipated choice options of which no were provided. There were also complains about dead-ends, thus paths with no real story ending. In summary, these observations result in the finding that the participants wish to alter the content but consider the design of the choice space as poorly performed. We face the interesting fact that though the perceived agency was lower evaluated as the actual performed agency, the participants still continue exploring. An answer to this effect can be found in the results of our elucidation of the participants engagement.

When looking at user engagement we found that, on a scale from 1 to 10, participants rated the overall interaction experience with a mean of 7.76 (Median = 8). We consider this a clear indication of high engagement. However, we were also interested in which of the engagement elements as outlined in our definition contributes at all, and if so most. For the findings, see Table 4. The results manifest that all engagement attributes contribute to the overall highly perceived engagement, yet not all of them similarly. Two aspects we found in particular interesting. It seems to be that there is a correlation between the novelty aspect and focused attention as this type of storytelling is novel for most of the participants, they need to concentrate more and therefore are aware of passing time (Table 3 also supports this). This means that high levels on concentration are not considered a downsizing effect in this context. Second, novelty also influenced the interest in the future use of other interactive storytelling videos. In line with this, we also see that 89% would recommend the film, which indicates that the novelty paired with the made experiences is considered positive.

However, the free answers in the questionnaire indicate that this does not mean necessarily that participants were satisfied with the content. For example, participant 39 stated: *"Probably only for the interactive feature, not because*

Table 2. Participant responses on statements related to agency

	SA	A	NA	D	SD
Content frequency choices	20%	47%	20%	11%	4%
In control experience	21%	33%	24%	15%	7%
Desirable consequences	5%	26%	46%	20%	4%
Foreseeable consequences	5%	14%	33%	36%	11%
No choice while preferred	14%	30%	27%	20%	9%
Unnecessary choices	17%	24%	22%	28%	8%

Table 3. Participant responses to the influence of decision-making on the experience

Decision-making	SA	A	NA	D	SD
Was demanding	5%	22%	21%	33%	20%
Caused annoyance	4%	11%	10%	31%	44%
Disrupted experience	5%	14%	14%	35%	33%

Table 4. Participant responses on statements related to engagement. Concepts in () are added here for clarity, they were not part of the questions asked

	SA	A	NA	D	SD
Interface is clear (usability)	72%	17%	8%	4%	0%
Watched out of curiosity (novelty)	60%	25%	9%	4%	1%
Watching was worthwhile (endurability)	48%	24%	9%	6%	4%
Interest in IDN afterwards (endurability)	58%	24%	9%	5%	4%
Visually appealing layout (aesthetics)	49%	33%	16%	2%	1%
Involved in experience (felt involvement)	43%	34%	14%	9%	1%
Lost track of time (focused attention)	34%	32%	19%	13%	2%

the film is good." Participant 110: *"Yes, but more because this is the first film where you can choose how the storyline goes. I feel like there are better, more intriguing, films possible with this technology."* This is also in line with the fact that merely 72% found watching the film worthwhile. In some of the endings the initial level of satisfaction is not perceived highly, e.g. 24.1% for ending E (see Table 1). Thus, the free exploration generates a large deviation on how content is perceived. Thus, engagement elements such as curiosity and challenge can be considered well approved, whereas sensory appeal and aesthetics are considered weaker. Those findings also explain why the participants continued looking for new endings even though they perceived the way to choose and the ability to forethought beyond optimal. This also means, however, that once the novelty wears off the problem of authoring such story spaces has to improve drastically as otherwise the interest will drop due to low levels of perceived control, positive effect and endurability.

6   Conclusions and Future Work

If we look at our findings and compare them with those of Roth & Koenitz [23], we would agree that positive affect, transformational power and agency are indeed relevant, not only for enjoyment, but also for engagement. However, our findings show a more diverse image with respect to engagement and agency, which is certainly also based on the fact that the population size is larger than in Roth & Koenitz' paper. What we can show is that the basic assumption of all IDN research, namely that people desire agency to alter story paths, is correct. That is not only substantiated by the fact that our participants rated the overall experience highly, they also showed a reasonable level of intentional acting and anticipation of the implications with their responses regarding decision-making, control of the experience, and desirable and foreseeable consequences. We also observed that all aspects of engagement contribute, only we are not sure to what extent, so more detailed and discriminating research is necessary. We also show that agency is more complex, as it is even less coherent than engagement, and hence additional research is necessary to establish under which circumstances the relation between the control experience, the desirable outcomes and the foreseeable outcomes have an influence on the desire to make choices. In any case, we have to investigate for both engagement and agency how they can stimulate curiosity in the context of streamed interactive fictional content.

We could also show that this awareness of potential agency is strongly related to the engagement but not so much on content level (aesthetics and sensory appeal), but in the *Bandersnatch* context mainly on novelty. In the context of story design of streamed fictional content, this opens up the need to look again in more detail to the problem of IDN authoring. The case of *Bandersnatch* clearly shows that problems in the content and more relevantly, in the underlying navigation engine, will only be tolerated as long as the experience of navigation is new. We do not know for how long this novelty will last in a streamed fictional context, but we can state that all aspects of engagement and agency need to be addressed to stimulate the desire to interact more frequently and for a longer time with the content (this aim is also followed in the domain of gaming and from a business point of view in streaming services, and from both the IDN community can learn). Thus, more research is needed to understand which relations between conceptual aspects of engagement and agency have an influence on the perception of story content and story structure, so that authoring environments can be designed that can support authors in the design of streamed interactive fiction. In this context it also needs to be mentioned that *Bandersnatch* is a particular type of story, and additional research is needed to see if different narrative styles and genres would establish similar findings as presented in this paper. Our assumption is that this is not the case. Another topic of research is to identify which of the aspects of engagement and agency support which type of genres or narrative styles to what extent.

Overall, it seems advisable for the interactive storytelling community to collaborate with companies like Netflix, as they can provide a test field in which critical analysis can be performed on the perception and the real-world behaviour of the interactive user. In that way, not only a better understanding of streaming communities and their preferences regarding content can be established but also the various theories, such as Murray's theory on 'dramatic agency' [21], can be empirically tested.

References

1. Solarski, C.: Interactive Stories and Video Game Art: A Storytelling Framework for Game Design. AK Peters/CRC Press, New York (2017)
2. Walker, J.: Piecing together and tearing apart: finding the story in afternoon. In: Proceedings of the Tenth ACM Conference on Hypertext and Hypermedia: Returning to Our Diverse Roots, pp. 111–117 (1999)
3. Roth, C.: Experiencing Interactive Storytelling (2016)
4. Murray, J.: Hamlet on the Holodeck: The Future of Narrative in Cyberspace. The Free Press, New York (1997)
5. Hales, C.: Cinematic interaction: from kinoautomat to cause and effect. Digit. Creat. **16**, 54–64 (2005)
6. Hammond, A.: Literature in the Digital Age: An Introduction. Cambridge University Press, Cambridge (2016)
7. Gomery, D.: The Hollywood blockbuster: industrial analysis and practice. In: Stringer, J. (ed.) Movie Blockbusters, pp. 84–95. Routledge, London (2013)
8. Davenport, G.: New Orleans in transition, 1983–1987: the interactive delivery of a cinematic case study. The International Congress for Design and Planning Theory, Education Group Conference Proceedings (1987)
9. Mateas, M., Stern, A.: Build it to understand it: ludology meets narratology in game design space. In: Proceedings of the 2005 Digital Games Research Association Conference (DiGRA), 3 (2005)
10. Dow, S., Mehta, M., Harmon, E., MacIntyre, B., Mateas, M.: Presence and engagement in an interactive drama. In: Proceedings of the SIGCHI Conference on Human Factors in Computing Systems, pp. 1475–1484 (2007)
11. Nardi, B., Harris, J.: Strangers and friends: collaborative play in World of Warcraft. In: Proceedings of the 2006 20th Anniversary Conference on Computer Supported Cooperative Work, pp. 149–158 (2006)
12. Burroughs, B.: House of Netflix: streaming media and digital lore. Popul. Commun. **17**, 1–17 (2018)
13. O'Brien, H., Toms, E.: What is user engagement? A conceptual framework for defining user engagement with technology. J. Am. Soc. Inf. Sci. Technol. **59**, 938–955 (2008)
14. Attfield, S., Kazai, G., Lalmas, M., Piwowarski, B.: Towards a science of user engagement (position paper). In: WSDM Workshop on User Modelling for Web Applications, pp. 9–12 (2011)
15. Lalmas, M., O'Brien, H., Yom-Tov, E.: Measuring User Engagement. Synth. Lect. Inf. Concepts Retr. Serv. **6**, 1–132 (2014)
16. Schoenau-Fog, H.: Hooked! Evaluating engagement as continuation desire in interactive narratives. In: International Conference on Interactive Digital Storytelling, pp. 219–230 (2011)
17. Vorderer, P., Knobloch, S., Schramm, H.: Does entertainment suffer from interactivity? The impact of watching an interactive TV movie on viewers' experience of entertainment. Media Psychol. **3**, 343–363 (2001)

18. Ben-Shaul, N.: Can narrative films go interactive? New Cine.: J. Contemp. Film **2**, 149–162 (2004)
19. Limerick, H., Coyle, D., Moore, J.: The experience of agency in human-computer interactions: a review. Front. Hum. Neurosci. **8**, 643 (2014)
20. Bandura, A.: Social cognitive theory: an agentic perspective. Annu. Rev. Psychol. **52**, 1–26 (2001)
21. Murray, J.: Research into interactive digital narrative: a kaleidoscopic view. In: International Conference on Interactive Digital Storytelling, pp. 3–17 (2018)
22. Roth, C., Vermeulen, I.: Real story interaction: the role of global agency in interactive storytelling. In: International Conference on Entertainment Computing, pp. 425–428 (2012)
23. Roth, C., Koenitz, H.: Bandersnatch, yea or nay? Reception and user experience of an interactive digital narrative video. In: Proceedings of the 2019 ACM International Conference on Interactive Experiences for TV and Online Video, pp. 247–254 (2019)
24. Cirucci, A., Vacker, B.: Black Mirror and Critical Media Theory. Rowman & Littlefield, Lanham (2018)
25. Egenfeldt-Nielsen, S., Smith, J., Tosca, S.: Understanding Video Games: The Essential Introduction. Routledge, New York (2013)
26. Thompson, S., Armstrong, W., Thomas, C.: Illusions of control, underestimations, and accuracy: a control heuristic explanation. Psychol. Bull. **123**, 143–161 (1998)
27. Baltar, F., Brunet, I.: Social research 2.0: virtual snowball sampling method using Facebook. Internet Res. **22**, 57–74 (2012)

Designing and Developing Interactive Narratives for Collaborative Problem-Based Learning

Bradford W. Mott[1(✉)], Robert G. Taylor[1], Seung Y. Lee[1],
Jonathan P. Rowe[1], Asmalina Saleh[2], Krista D. Glazewski[2],
Cindy E. Hmelo-Silver[2], and James C. Lester[1]

[1] North Carolina State University, Raleigh, NC 27695, USA
{bwmott,rgtaylor,sylee,jprowe,lester}@ncsu.edu
[2] Indiana University, Bloomington, IN 47405, USA
{asmsaleh,glaze,chmelosi}@indiana.edu

Abstract. Narrative and collaboration are two core features of rich interactive learning. Narrative-centered learning environments offer significant potential for supporting student learning. By contextualizing learning within interactive narratives, these environments leverage students' innate facilities for developing understandings through stories. Computer-supported collaborative learning environments offer students rich, collaborative learning experiences in which small groups of students engage in constructing artifacts, addressing disciplinary challenges, and solving problems. Narrative and collaboration have distinct affordances for learning, but combining them poses significant challenges. In this paper, we present initial work on solving this problem by introducing collaborative narrative-centered learning environments. These environments will enable small groups of students to collaboratively solve problems in rich multi-participant storyworlds. We propose a novel framework for designing and developing these environments, which we are using to create a collaborative narrative-centered learning environment for middle school ecosystems education. In the learning environment, students work on problem-solving scenarios centered on how to support optimal fish health in aquatic environments. Results from pilot testing the learning environment with 45 students suggest it supports the creation of engaging and effective collaborative narrative-centered learning experiences.

Keywords: Narrative-centered learning · Collaborative learning

1 Introduction

Recent years have seen significant growth in research on the role of narrative and collaboration in education. Narrative-centered learning environments contextualize learning within interactive narratives in which students actively participate in engaging story-based problem solving [1, 2]. These environments encourage students' active participation in learning, critical thinking, and analysis. Meanwhile, computer-supported collaborative learning environments offer students inquiry experiences that

© Springer Nature Switzerland AG 2019
R. E. Cardona-Rivera et al. (Eds.): ICIDS 2019, LNCS 11869, pp. 86–100, 2019.
https://doi.org/10.1007/978-3-030-33894-7_10

are deeply collaborative [3]. These environments engage students in investigating complex ill-structured problems, making use of authoritative resources, and constructing informed explanations. Leveraging the affordances of both narrative-centered learning environments and computer supported collaborative learning environments offers significant potential.

By integrating narrative-centered learning with collaborative learning, *collaborative narrative-centered learning environments* will enable small groups of students to collaboratively solve problems in rich multi-participant storyworlds. As opposed to traditional narrative-centered learning environments, in collaborative narrative-centered learning environments, students work in groups solving motivating problem-based learning scenarios that feature compelling plots, engaging characters, and inviting settings. These environments will dynamically generate narratives to be interactively experienced by a group of participants. (We use the term "participant" to emphasize the active role played by students experiencing and affecting the narrative that is unfolding in the multi-participant interactive environment). Here, computational models of narrative must craft global story arcs and dynamically direct storyworld events to create the most effective collective story-centric learning experience for all of the participants. For collaborative narrative-centered learning environments, these computations entail dynamically selecting and arranging plot elements that will engender group-based problem-solving activities so that participants can together achieve the resolution of the narrative, while developing flexible knowledge, critical reasoning skills, and collaboration skills.

2 Background

2.1 Narrative-Centered Learning

Computational models of narrative can serve as the foundation for learning environments that provide effective story-centered pedagogy that is both meaningful and motivated [4–8]. In narrative-centered learning environments, learning occurs in the context of interactive narratives [9–11]. Such learning environments leverage the power of dynamically generated narrative to create learning experiences that are both effective and engaging. Drawing on intelligent tutoring systems, intelligent virtual agents, and serious games, narrative-centered learning environments offer the promise of adaptive, situated learning experiences that are highly interactive and engaging for students. Narrative-centered learning environments have been investigated in a broad range of educational domains, including anti-bullying education [4], health intervention education [12], social issues [13], computational thinking [14], and science learning [9, 15]. In addition to education, narrative-centered learning environments have also been used effectively in training [16–18]. While significant progress is being made on narrative-centered learning environments, most of the work to date has focused primarily on single-learner scenarios.

2.2 Collaborative Learning

Contemporary approaches to inquiry learning are deeply collaborative [3]. Collaborative inquiry involves small groups of students engaging in constructing artifacts, addressing disciplinary challenges, and solving problems. These approaches rely on scaffolded student engagement, including different forms of learning cycles that help provide norms, routines, and teacher guidance [19, 20]. Problem-based learning (PBL) is an effective approach to enabling collaborative inquiry that challenges students with investigating and resolving complex, ill-defined problems [21, 22]. In PBL, students engage in self-directed learning as they collaboratively solve problems while co-constructing flexible knowledge through small group discussions and negotiations [22]. Story-centric scenarios often serve as an effective approach for structuring the problems that lie at the heart of problem-based learning for students [23]. Although originally developed as an instructional model for medical schools, there is significant interest in applying PBL within primary and secondary education [24], including science classrooms [23]. Although progress is being made to realize the potential of problem-based learning through computer-supported collaborative learning environments, limited work has explored the unique opportunity provided by the rich, dynamic problem contexts of narrative-centered learning to support deep collaborative inquiry at the classroom scale.

3   Designing Collaborative Interactive Narratives

Collaborative narrative-centered learning environments extend educational narratives into the social arena and call for the creation of *computational models of collaborative narrative generation*. Rather than generating narratives for a single participant, computational models of collaborative narrative generation create shared, collective narrative experiences to be interactively experienced by a group of participants [25–27]. In contrast to multiplayer online games in which a loosely formed sense of narrative may emerge from sandbox-style interactions or completed quests, computational models of collaborative narrative generation are concerned with explicitly reasoning about narratological elements (fabula, sjužet, and medium) to create engaging narrative experiences for groups of participants. The work presented in this paper focuses on computational models of collaborative narratives with an emphasis on collaborative learning in which students cooperate to solve ill-structured problems. Our work targets the generation of narratives for small multi-participant groups consistent with problem-based learning. Computational models of collaborative narrative generation must address two sets of design requirements: those stemming from interactive narrative generation, and those stemming from the multi-participant nature of collaborative narratives. Each of these is discussed in turn.

Computational models of interactive narrative generation construct stories in which an audience member plays an active role. In addition to crafting narratives that have many of the properties of traditional stories such as conflict, compelling characters, plot-driven storylines, and crisis decision points, computational models of interactive narrative should create narratives that exhibit three properties: (1) *participant agency*, which imparts the perception of control to the participant with respect to the short-term and long-term impact of her actions on the story [28, 29]; (2) *believable characters*, in which the participant's interactions with "non-player" characters are contextualized in the narrative's plot and setting [4, 30]; and (3) *participant-tailored experiences*, in which plot elements and character behaviors are customized to the individual participant [31, 32].

In addition to the requirements noted above for interactive narrative, computational models of collaborative narrative generation should address the following requirements. First, the models should support collaboration-centered plot generation, in which the narrative generator creates plot lines that require cooperative actions on the part of the participants. For example, they should introduce plot points requiring participants to devise plans leading to the achievement of a common goal, and they should encourage communication among participants. Second, the models should support role-based participant-character interactions. Endowing characters with specific expertise and abilities is an oft-used literary device from traditional narratives, and it can be effectively leveraged in collaborative narratives for both participant characters and synthetic characters (e.g., virtual agents). Third, the models should create stories that maximize the utility of the resulting narratives. In addition to being engaging for a single individual participant, collaborative narratives should be engaging for the group as a whole.

Our approach to organizing computational models of collaborative narrative generation employs the jigsaw methodology to create multi-participant groups for collaborative problem-based learning. In *jigsaw-based problem solving*, students become experts on different aspects of the problem under investigation and then share what they have learned with group members [33]. Effective collaborative work depends upon the presence of positive interdependence between participants, thereby requiring students to interact and rely upon contributions of others [34]. Most effective collaboration occurs when group members have both resource and goal interdependence. Jigsaw approaches used in science classrooms have led to increases in affective outcomes [35], and Aronson and Bridgeman (1979) argue that the jigsaw methodology reduces classroom competition and creates an environment that leads to goal attainment [36]. Jigsaw-based problem solving offers a practical and effective approach to organizing the design of collaborative problem-based learning narratives.

4   Developing Collaborative Interactive Narratives

While promising, integrating interactive narrative and collaboration to create effective group learning experiences poses significant challenges. To this end, we have designed STORYLOOM, a rapid prototyping tool for creating interactive narratives that enable students to work together to solve problem-based learning scenarios, while allowing researchers to investigate collaborative learning within the classroom.

4.1   Architecture

The STORYLOOM architecture defines key components of a collaborative interactive narrative that represent distinct groups of functionality and resources (Fig. 1). The primary purpose of STORYLOOM is to provide a blueprint for creating engaging interactive narratives that support effective group learning. To this end, the architecture defines two types of resources that when combined represent the narrative experienced by a group of students: *World Resources* and *Story Resources*.

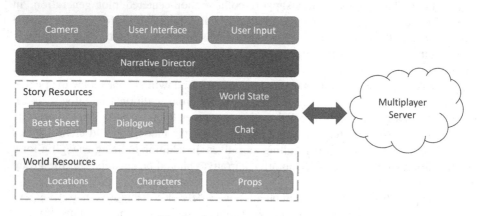

Fig. 1. STORYLOOM architecture.

World Resources are the building blocks for the storyworld that the students will experience while interacting with STORYLOOM: *Locations*, *Characters*, and *Props*. These resources represent the physical manifestation of the narrative. These are the objects that the students will see, hear, and interact with as they are transported into the storyworld. The Story Resources define how the World Resources interact with each other and with the students as they progress through the narrative. Story Resources are composed of *Dialogue* and *Beat Sheet* resources. Dialogue resources represent the conversations, narration, and dialogue choices presented to the students as they interact with characters, manipulate props, and visit locations within the storyworld. A Beat Sheet resource represents a complete story within the narrative environment from a particular student's perspective organized around the jigsaw methodology with the student becoming an expert on some aspect of the story. A story beat is an event within the narrative where something changes and the story advances [37]. For example, a young boy learns he is a wizard after receiving an acceptance letter to wizarding school. The Beat Sheet resource, as defined in the STORYLOOM architecture, is a collection of story beats that represent the entire narrative experienced by a student. A story may contain multiple character roles that can be assumed by students. Each beat sheet represents a different narrative experience within a larger collaborative story, and thus there may be multiple beat sheets in a story, each one describing the story from a particular student's perspective.

Another key requirement of STORYLOOM is to allow students to interact and collaborate within the storyworld as they experience the interactive narrative. This functionality is represented by three components within the architecture: *Multiplayer Server*, *World State*, and *Chat*. The Multiplayer Server is responsible for providing a real-time communication channel between each interactive story client that is participating in a shared narrative experience (Fig. 2). The Multiplayer Server allows multiple students to interact over a network connection. It also allows an optional tutor, perhaps a human serving in the role of a wizard within a Wizard-of-Oz data collection or an intelligent tutoring system, to participate in the learning experience by providing content and collaboration scaffolding as the students work together to solve the problem-based learning scenario. The World State component represents the functionality and data that must be replicated across all of the interactive story clients and the optional *Tutor Control Panel* in order to create a consistent and shared virtual world and narrative experience for all the students (Fig. 2). For example, if a student places a sticky note on a whiteboard in the virtual world, the same action must be replicated to all of the other students' interactive story clients. Lastly, the Chat component represents the functionality that allows students as well as the tutor to communicate across the network in real-time. This functionality is crucial for collaborative problem solving as students share what they have learned and discuss possible solutions to the problem scenario within the context of the interactive narrative.

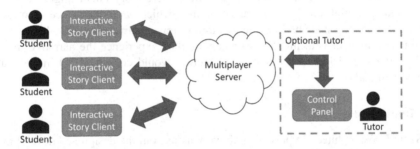

Fig. 2. Interactive story clients collaborating with a human tutor.

The *Narrative Director* is a central component within the STORYLOOM architecture that is responsible for orchestrating the interactions of all the other components within the interactive story clients to generate a collaborative, problem-based learning experience (Fig. 1). The Narrative Director loads narrative-specific Story and World Resources based on the role assumed by the student within the larger shared narrative. For example, a student may have assumed the role of a toxicologist in a team of scientists who have been asked to determine why farm animals are getting sick. The toxicologist Beat Sheet would contain individual beats that define a unique narrative in which the student (acting as the toxicologist) visits the farm, takes water samples from the pond, and then discovers that the water is contaminated with hazardous chemicals. This narrative experience will be unique to the student playing the toxicologist role. Likewise, the other students will experience their own unique narratives based on their roles as they gather evidence to be shared and discussed as part of the collaborative problem-solving learning experience within STORYLOOM. For example, two students playing the roles of a toxicologist and botanist might progress through a simple narrative in which each student experiences unique story beats that provide evidence and insights that are shared during collaboration sessions where they discuss and negotiate as they work together to determine why the farm animals are getting sick (Fig. 3).

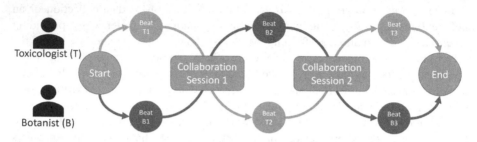

Fig. 3. Two-student progression through a shared collaborative learning experience.

The *Camera* and *User Interface* components in the architecture represent how the narrative is conveyed to the student, while the *User Input* component represents how the student interacts with the narrative. The interactive story client might be implemented using a high-fidelity 3D game engine, which would produce immersive experiences in which students have the freedom to travel between realistically rendered locations and interact with lifelike characters as they experience the narrative. In this situation, the World Resources in the architecture would consist of 3D models, animations, and audio.

4.2   Implementation

The STORYLOOM architecture presented above was used in the design and development of a 2D visual novel-style collaborative narrative-centered learning environment. The learning environment was developed using an agile development process in which the software was iteratively designed, implemented, and reviewed. This particular implementation of STORYLOOM supports rapid prototyping and deployment of 2D interactive narratives into classrooms. In this implementation, the Camera, User Interface, and User Input components were implemented using the Unity game engine. The Unity game engine is capable of rendering 3D environments and characters. However, we decided to create a 2D narrative experience to simplify art creation, while we focused our development efforts on refining the narrative and collaboration-specific functionalities. The Unity game engine is cross-platform and enables the learning environment to be deployed on a wide variety of platforms such as Windows, macOS, Android, iOS, and Chromebooks.

This version of STORYLOOM presents the storyworld to students as 2D representations of locations, characters, and props. Because students can choose to travel between locations, converse with characters, interact with props, and collect information as they progress through the problem-solving scenario, they are active participants within the narrative. For example, a student could be asked by a character in the learning environment to travel to a fish hatchery and measure the dissolved oxygen levels in a water tank as the student attempts to determine why the fish have become sick. This implementation of StoryLoom includes text-based chat that students can use at any time during the narrative to communicate with one another. In addition, a human tutor can also participate in the conversation to provide content or collaboration scaffolding.

This 2D version of StoryLoom provides a flexible framework for quickly developing and evaluating interactive narratives by allowing non-technical authors to create story beats in a Google Sheet and author dialogue in Google Documents. These documents are imported into the system as Beat Sheet and Dialogue resources that are combined with the 2D representations of locations, characters, and props to produce an interactive narrative. Using Google Docs as an authoring tool has several significant advantages for authors: (1) familiar and feature-rich word processor, (2) collaborative authoring, and (3) revision tracking and revert capability, and 4) readily available. These features allow content to be authored and easily revised, thus, enabling a tight iterative loop to quickly refine the narrative experience.

This version of StoryLoom fully supports the creation of jigsaw-based narratives where students acquire expert knowledge as they experience their own unique stories. This acquired knowledge can then be shared with their group through collaboration as they work together to solve a problem-based learning scenario. When using this version of StoryLoom to create a collaborative, narrative learning experience, the following high-level steps are used to structure the jigsaw-based narrative: (1) Create an overarching narrative that features the problem-based learning scenario, (2) Identify possible solutions including knowledge required to solve the problem, (3) Create individual narratives that correspond to roles within the larger overarching narrative wherein students acquire knowledge, (4) Define story beats in a Google Sheet that represent the significant events that move each individual narrative forward, (5) Identify characters and author dialogue in a Google Document for narration and conversation associated with the story beats (such interactions reveal expert knowledge to the students), (6) Create story beats that represent collaboration points in the overarching narrative, (7) Identify all of the locations, characters, and props necessary to tell the story and create art assets for them. The artifacts from the previous steps can then be combined with StoryLoom to create a deployable learning environment. Creating a collaborative interactive narrative is a creative endeavor and will likely require several passes through the above steps.

5   Crystal Island: EcoJourneys Testbed

To investigate how interactive narrative and collaboration can be combined to yield effective small group learning experiences in the classroom, we created Crystal Island: EcoJourneys to serve as a testbed for prototyping a collaborative narrative-centered learning environment to be deployed in classroom studies (Fig. 4). Chromebooks were selected as the lead development platform due to their availability for use at our partner schools as well as their widespread adoption by schools throughout the

United States. ECOJOURNEYS was developed using the 2D version of STORYLOOM described above. Locations, characters, and props are presented to students as 2D assets. The learning environment's look and feel closely resembles a genre of video games referred to as "visual novels".

Fig. 4. Interacting with characters and props in CRYSTAL ISLAND: ECOJOURNEYS.

The interactive narrative that was authored for ECOJOURNEYS tells the story of four students who are visiting Buglas Island in the Philippines as part of a cultural exchange program. While on the island, the students learn from local farmers that the fish in their fish farms are getting sick. Since fish farming is critical to the island economy, the local stakeholders ask the students for help in investigating why the fish are getting sick. The students' relationship with the local stakeholders follows an apprentice-based model [38]. The stakeholders provide the expertise and insight critical to solving the problem. As newcomers to the island, the students are tasked with "pitching in," to help with the investigation. The interactive narrative reveals a complex problem scenario that four students are asked to solve together as a group. Each student will experience a unique narrative within the context of the larger story as they visit different locations, have conversations with characters, and interact with props as they help solve the mystery.

In addition to text-based chat, ECOJOURNEYS includes a virtual whiteboard (Fig. 5) to support collaboration and the problem-based learning inquiry cycle [39]. During collaboration sessions within the context of the interactive narrative, students are asked to go to a virtual conference room in the storyworld. There, students place sticky notes on the virtual whiteboard. These notes were collected during students' unique explorations and contain information related to the aquatic problem.

The sticky notes can be associated with specific topics that help students support or rule out hypotheses. As students share their notes at the whiteboard, they discuss their findings and attempt to arrive at a hypothesis that is both supported by the evidence and that explains why the fish are getting sick. The virtual whiteboard was designed to support the following collaborative interactions between small groups of students: (1) sharing information, (2) selecting information to be used as evidence, and (3) evaluating whether evidence supports, does not support, or might support a specific hypothesis. Furthermore, to support sensemaking, students can vote on a sticky note which will cause it to change color to indicate whether students agree (green) or disagree (red) that the information on the note supports the hypothesis represented by the column. An orange sticky note indicates that not all the students have voted on

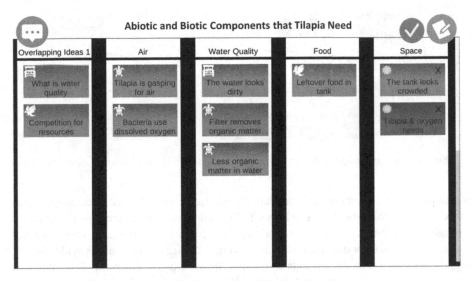

Fig. 5. Virtual whiteboard used by students during collaboration points.

whether the note supports a hypothesis or not. If students disagree on the placement of a sticky note, they must negotiate using the text-based chat to resolve their disagreement. This provides students with sense-making agency, since they are allowed the freedom to make mistakes as they collaborate and reason about the evidence and how it relates to the hypotheses.

Because ECOJOURNEYS is built upon STORYLOOM, the team was able to rapidly create a collaborative narrative-centered learning environment that was ready for deployment into the classroom. This left additional time for the team to focus on two elements that are key to the PBL inquiry cycle: the interactive narrative and scaffolded collaboration. STORYLOOM's Google Docs-based authoring allowed the four narratives that represent each student's role in the overarching narrative to be quickly written and easily refined through rapid iteration. This allowed the creation of the jigsaw-based problem scenario where students learn from experts as they experience the interactive narrative by talking to characters and collecting evidence. Likewise, STORYLOOM's data replication functionalities allowed for the creation of the shared virtual whiteboard, which, along with text-based chat, allowed students to share what they learned with group members. Figure 6 depicts a student's narrative experience as they collect jigsaw-based information through the interactive narrative and collaborate with the group through the virtual whiteboard. To ensure that students have access to critical information required to solve the mystery, key jigsaw-based information was provided to at least two students in their narrative experiences (i.e., similar facts or observations). Thus, the information was more likely to be discovered and shared by students during their collaboration.

Another important feature of STORYLOOM that was utilized in ECOJOURNEYS was the capability to have an expert human tutor join the group of four students in the chat and virtual whiteboard sessions. This facilitator provided scaffolding for both collaboration

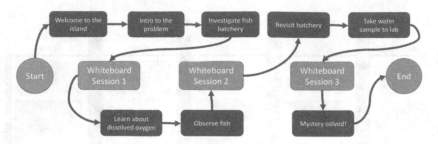

Fig. 6. Story beats and collaboration points of student's unique narrative experience.

and inquiry-based thinking. The facilitator was also responsible for checking the students' work in the whiteboard sessions before allowing the students to continue on through the narrative. If the virtual whiteboard contained hypotheses that were not correctly supported (or disproved) by the evidence, the facilitator could provide hints or suggest approaches to the students to resolve disagreements. Once the facilitator was convinced that the students had successfully completed a whiteboard session, she would use the STORYLOOM Control Panel to allow the students to exit the whiteboard and continue through the narrative.

6 Pilot Study

To evaluate the effectiveness of ECOJOURNEYS, we conducted a pilot study to understand if it supported productive collaboration and effective learning.

6.1 Participants and Procedure

A total of 11 groups of students (N = 45, 22 females, 23 males) ages 11 to 12 from the rural midwest in the United States participated in the classroom study for a total of nine 55-min sessions. Students worked in groups of four (except for one group of five). Each group was assigned a facilitator who provided prompts focused on supporting collaboration and inquiry thinking. On the first day of the study, students took a pre-test and were introduced to their groups. They also generated a group contract that allowed them to dictate the norms for collaborative inquiry learning that they wished to follow. On the second day, students started playing ECOJOURNEYS. Throughout the sessions, students collaborated with their group members via text chat and at the virtual whiteboard. Students evaluated the data that each student gathered and discussed possible explanations to the problem scenario. On the last day, students created an explanation as to why the fish were sick and took a post-test.

6.2 Data and Analysis

The pre-post test focused on ecosystem concepts, specifically the relationship between biotic and abiotic components and the impact that these components have on populations in an ecosystem. Students also took a survey from the Adaptive Instrument for

Regulation of Emotions survey [40]. Log data of students' chat and interaction within the learning environment were recorded and stored on a remote server. Group chat log data was coded according to accountable talk and PBL facilitation moves [41, 42]. Each conversational turn in the chat log was coded for one of the following turn-taking codes: *Collaboration* (five sub-codes), *Rigorous Thinking* (ten sub-codes), *Facilitation* (six sub-codes), and *Content* (eight sub-codes). Collaboration codes refer to utterances that focus on coordinating, goals, and content understanding whereas Rigorous Thinking codes highlight students' argumentation moves. Utterances made by facilitators were coded separately from students' talk (i.e., Facilitation) and all utterances were coded for the Content of the talk.

6.3   Results

A mixed ANOVA test with groups as between-subjects and time as within-subjects factor indicated a main effect of time. Students scored significantly better on their post-tests, $F(1, 49) = 17.919$, $p < .001$ (pre-test mean = 13.6, SD = 3.7; post-test mean = 15.8, SD = 3.7), indicating that students improved their ecosystem concept knowledge overall. Analysis of group chat data revealed that there was a positive strong relationship between the total Collaboration and students' Rigorous Thinking codes, $r(9) = .78$, $p = .004$ and a moderate relationship between the total Facilitation and Rigorous Thinking codes, $r(9) = .71$, $p = .015$. These results suggest that productive collaboration among students are critical in supporting robust argumentation. Students also remained engaged in the game, with 66% of student utterances coded for productive discussions.

7   Conclusion and Future Work

Collaborative narrative-centered learning environments, which integrate narrative-centered learning with collaborative learning, offer significant promise for creating effective and engaging learning experiences. These environments enable small groups of students to actively participate in collaborative problem solving featuring compelling plots, engaging characters, and inviting settings. In this paper, we have presented STORYLOOM, a novel framework for designing and developing collaborative narrative-centered learning environments. Using the framework, we developed a prototype learning environment, CRYSTAL ISLAND: ECOJOURNEYS. A classroom study with middle school students indicates that interactions with CRYSTAL ISLAND: ECOJOURNEYS yielded improved learning outcomes and evidence of productive collaboration. These results suggest that STORYLOOM holds promise for creating effective and engaging group-based narrative learning experiences.

Two directions for future work are particularly promising. First, since scaffolding is critical for supporting student teams, developing automated models to provide support during students' problem solving is key. In our pilot study, a human facilitator provided guidance via a text chat interface to help orchestrate student interactions. Devising adaptive conversational agents that use natural language dialogue capabilities to provide automated scaffolding functionalities for collaborative narrative-centered learning environments is a promising direction. Second, investigating computational models of collaborative narrative generation that leverage artificial intelligence-based techniques offers significant promise for creating learning experiences that feature dynamic collaboration-centered plots and adaptable role-based interactions that adapt to students' desires and behaviors.

Acknowledgements. This work is supported by the National Science Foundation through grants DRL-1561655, DUE-1561486, DRL-1934153, DRL-1934128, and DRL-1921495. Any opinions, findings, and conclusions or recommendations expressed in this material are those of the author(s) and do not necessarily reflect the views of the National Science Foundation.

References

1. Lester, J., Rowe, J., Mott, B.: Narrative-centered learning environments: a story-centric approach to educational games. In: Mouza, C., Lavigne, N. (eds.) Emerging Technologies for the Classroom: A Learning Sciences Perspective, pp. 223–238 (2013)
2. Lester, J., Spires, H., Nietfeld, J., Minogue, J., Mott, B., Lobene, E.: Designing game-based learning environments for elementary science education: a narrative-centered learning perspective. Inf. Sci. **264**, 4–18 (2014)
3. Hmelo-Silver, C.E., Chinn, C.A., Chan, C., O'Donnell, A.M.: The International Handbook of Collaborative Learning. Routledge, New York (2013)
4. Aylett, R.S., Louchart, S., Dias, J., Paiva, A., Vala, M.: FearNot!: an experiment in emergent narrative. In: Proceedings of the 5th International Conference on Intelligent Virtual Agents, pp. 305–316 (2005)
5. Mott, B., Lester, J.: U-director: a decision-theoretic narrative planning architecture for storytelling environments. In: Proceedings of the 5th International Conference on Autonomous Agents and Multiagent Systems, Hakodate, pp. 977–984 (2006)
6. Riedl, M.O., Lane, H., Hill, R., Swartout, W.: Automated story direction and intelligent tutoring: towards a unifying architecture. In: Proceedings of the Workshop on Narrative Learning Environments at the 12th International Conference on Artificial Intelligence in Education, pp. 23–30 (2005)
7. Lee, S., Rowe, J., Mott, B., Lester, J.: A supervised learning framework for modeling director agent strategies in educational interactive narrative. IEEE Trans. Comput. Intell. AI Games **6**, 203–215 (2014)
8. Wang, P., Rowe, J., Mott, B., Lester, J.: Decomposing drama management in educational interactive narrative: a modular reinforcement learning approach. In: 9th International Conference on Interactive Digital Storytelling, pp. 270–282 (2016)
9. Rowe, J., Shores, L., Mott, B., Lester, J.: Integrating learning, problem solving, and engagement in narrative-centered learning environments. Int. J. Artif. Intell. Educ. **21**(1–2), 115–133 (2011)
10. Wouters, P., van Nimwegen, C., van Oostendorp, H., van der Spek, E.: A meta-analysis of the cognitive and motivational effects of serious games. J. Educ. Psychol. **105**(2), 249–265 (2013)
11. Clark, D.B., Tanner-Smith, E., Killingsworth, S.: Digital games, design, and learning: a systematic review and meta-analysis. Rev. Educ. Res. **86**(1), 79–122 (2016)
12. Marsella, S.C., Johnson, W.L., LaBore, C.M.: Interactive pedagogical drama for health interventions. In: Proceedings of the 11th International Conference on Artificial Intelligence in Education, pp. 341–348 (2003)

13. Mitgutsch, K., Alvarado, N.: Purposeful by design? A serious game design assessment framework. In: El-Nasr, M., Consalvo, M., Feiner, S. (eds.) Proceedings of the 7th International Conference on Foundations of Digital Games, pp. 121–128 (2012)

14. Min, W., Frankosky, M., Mott, B., Wiebe, E., Boyer, K.E., Lester, J.: Inducing stealth assessors from game interaction data. In: Proceedings of the 8th International Conference on Artificial Intelligence in Education, pp. 212–223 (2017)

15. Ketelhut, D.J., Dede, C., Clarke, J., Nelson, B., Bowman, C.: Studying situated learning in a multiuser virtual environment. In: Baker, E., Dickieson, J., Wulfeck, W., O'Neil, H. (eds.) Assessment of Problem Solving Using Simulations, pp. 37–58 (2007)

16. Riedl, M.O., Stern, A., Dini, D., Alderman, J.: Dynamic experience management in virtual worlds for entertainment, education, and training. Int. Trans. Syst. Sci. Appl. 4(2), 23–42 (2008)

17. Johnson, W.L.: Serious use of a serious game for language learning. Int. J. Artif. Intell. Educ. 20(2), 175–195 (2010)

18. Pynadath, D.V., Wang, N., Yang, R.: Simulating collaborative learning through decision-theoretic agents. In: Proceedings of the AIED Workshop on Team Tutoring (2018)

19. Belland, B.R., Walker, A.E., Kim, N.J., Lefler, M.: Synthesizing results from empirical research on computer-based scaffolding in STEM education: a meta-analysis. Rev. Educ. Res. 87(2), 309–344 (2017)

20. Puntambekar, S.: Distributing scaffolding across multiple levels: individuals, small groups, and a class of students. In: Ertmer, P.A., Hmelo Silver, C., Walker, A., Leary, H. (eds.) Essential Readings in Problem-based Learning, pp. 207–222 (2015)

21. Barrows, H.S.: A taxonomy of problem-based learning methods. Med. Educ. 20(6), 481–486 (1986)

22. Hmelo-Silver, C.E.: Problem-based learning: What and how do students learn? Educ. Psychol. Rev. 16, 235–266 (2004)

23. McConnell, T., Parker, J., Eberhardt, J.: Problem-based learning in the life science classroom. K-12 (2016)

24. Torp, L. Sage, S: Problems as possibilities: Problem-based learning for K-16 education. ASCD (2002)

25. Riedl, M., Li, B., Ai, H., Ram, A.: Robust and authorable multiplayer storytelling experiences. In: Proceedings of the 7th Artificial Intelligence and Interactive Digital Entertainment Conference (2011)

26. Spawforth, C., Millard, D.E.: A framework for multi-participant narratives based on multiplayer game interactions. In: Proceedings of the 10th International Conference on Interactive Digital Storytelling, pp. 150–162 (2017)

27. Zhu, J., Ontañón, S.: Experience management in multi-player games. arXiv preprint arXiv: 1907.02349 (2019)

28. Riedl, M.O., Saretto, C.J., Young, R.M.: Managing interaction between users and agents in a multi-agent storytelling environment. In: Proceedings of the 2nd International Conference on Autonomous Agents and Multi-Agent Systems, pp. 186–193 (2003)

29. Young, R.M.: Story and discourse: a bipartite model of narrative generation in virtual worlds. Interact. Stud. 8(2), 177–208 (2007)

30. Traum, D., Marsella, S.C., Gratch, J., Lee, J., Hartholt, A.: Multi-party, multi-issue, multi-strategy negotiation for multi-modal virtual agents. In: Proceedings of the 8th International Conference on Intelligent Virtual Agents, pp. 117–130 (2008)

31. McQuiggan, S., Rowe, J., Lester, J.C.: The effects of empathetic virtual characters on presence in narrative-centered learning environments. In: Proceedings of the 2008 SIGCHI Conference on Human Factors in Computing Systems, pp. 1511–1520 (2008)

32. Thue, D., Bulitko, V., Spetch, M.: Making stories player-specific: delayed authoring in interactive storytelling. In: Proceedings of the 1st Joint International Conference on Interactive Digital Storytelling, pp. 230–241 (2008)
33. Aronson, E., Blaney, N., Stephin, C., Sikes, J., Snapp, M.: The Jigsaw Classroom. Sage Publishing Company, Beverly Hills (1978)
34. Cohen, E.G.: Restructuring the classroom: conditions for productive small groups. Rev. Educ. Res. **64**, 1–35 (1994)
35. Lazarowitz, R., Hertz-Lazarowitz, R., Baird, J.H.: Learning science in a cooperative setting: academic achievement and affective outcomes. J. Res. Sci. Teach. **31**, 1121–1131 (1994)
36. Aronson, E., Bridgeman, D.: Jigsaw groups and the desegregated classroom: in pursuit of common goals. Pers. Soc. Psychol. Bull. **5**, 438–446 (1979)
37. McKee, R.: Substance, structure, style, and the principles of screenwriting (1997)
38. Lave, J., Wenger, E.: Situated Learning: Legitimate Peripheral Participation. Cambridge University Press, Cambridge (1991)
39. Hmelo-Silver, C.E., Eberbach, C.: Learning theories and problem-based learning. In: Bridges, S., McGrath, C., Whitehill, T. (eds.) Problem-Based Learning in Clinical Education, pp. 3–17 (2012)
40. Järvenoja, H., Volet, S., Järvelä, S.: Regulation of emotions in socially challenging learning situations: an instrument to measure the adaptive and social nature of the regulation process. Educ. Psychol. **33**(1), 31–58 (2013)
41. Hmelo-Silver, C.E., Barrows, H.S.: Facilitating collaborative knowledge building. Cogn. Instr. **26**(1), 48–94 (2008)
42. Michaels, S., O'Connor, M.C., Hall, M.W., Resnick, L.B.: Accountable Talk Sourcebook: For Classroom Conversation that Works. University of Pittsburgh Institute for Learning, Pittsburgh (2010)

The 'Angstfabriek' Experience: Factoring Fear into Transformative Interactive Narrative Design

Christian Roth[✉]

University of the Arts Utrecht, P.O. Box 1520, 3500 BM Utrecht,
The Netherlands
christian.roth@hku.nl

Abstract. Interactive Narratives in the form of Interactive Theater have the potential to offer a transformational learning experience on societal and political topics. The purposive interactive installation Angstfabriek (Dutch for fear factory) lets visitors experience fear-mongering and the related safety industry, with the goal of eliciting reflection, insight and discussion. As a case study for a potentially transformative experience, the installation is described and evaluated by means of a focus group interview and a pilot user experience study (N = 32). Findings show the importance of sufficient scripting of interactors regarding their role and agency, highlighting the conceptual connection between interactive digital narrative design and interactive theater design.

Keywords: Transformative design · Interactive narrative design · Interactive theater · User experience evaluation

1 Transformative Learning Through Interactive Narratives

The Angstfabriek, the factory of fear, is a physical installation combining theatrical elements and insightful interactive exercises with the goal of raising awareness and stimulating dialogue on fear-mongering as instrumentalized by the safety industry. Communication strategies often make use of narrative as a means to engage audiences, drawing them in and inviting them to experience a story that illustrates a point rather than simply stating facts in order to convey a lesson. This communication style has the effect of eliciting an emotional and cognitive response from the audience, thus helping the message create a more significant impact, in some cases influencing transformation. Interactive narrative experiences take this one step further, changing the role of the audience from spectator to interactor, and increasing the potential for transformative learning [1, 2].

Murray postulated that interactive narratives should provide interactors with agency, "the satisfying power to take meaningful action and see the result of your decisions and choices" [1]. This gives audiences the ability to influence the course of a narrative to some degree, for instance by taking decisions of a main character or by choosing one of several perspectives to experience the narrative from. Interactive

© Springer Nature Switzerland AG 2019
R. E. Cardona-Rivera et al. (Eds.): ICIDS 2019, LNCS 11869, pp. 101–114, 2019.
https://doi.org/10.1007/978-3-030-33894-7_11

narratives allow for exploration, play, performance and experimentation with different actions and consequences [1, 3].

This is in line with the concept of *transformative learning* which, according to Mezirow [4], is an attempt to explain how cultural assumptions and presuppositions influence our expectations, in turn framing our perception and interpretation of our experiences. This concept explains a change in meaning structures within the domains of instrumental and communicative learning. *Instrumental learning* focuses on learning through activities designed to promote the discovery, analysis and understanding of cause-and-effect relationships. *Communicative learning*, on the other hand, involves the understanding of different perspectives concerning values, ideals, feelings, moral decisions, and concepts such as freedom, justice, love, labor, autonomy, commitment and democracy. Transformative learning occurs when communicative and instrumental learning involve a "reflective assessment of premises . . . [and] of movement through cognitive structures by identifying and judging presuppositions" [4].

The constructivist, inquiry-based approach by Bruner [5] introduced the concept of *discovery learning*, which implies that students construct their own knowledge for themselves, enabling them to find answers and solve problems on their own with minimal guidance. This encourages motivation, active involvement, and creativity, promoting autonomy and independence.

Interactive digital narratives offer such a learning environment, enabling interactors to derive meaning from active involvement and experience. This underscores the value of interactive narratives beyond entertainment, as applied in education, health awareness and the communication of ideas.

Only a few studies exist so far that evaluate the effectiveness of interactive (digital) narratives (e.g. [3, 6–8]). Findings of these studies suggest that interactive narratives may be effective tools in raising awareness and empathy, creating insight, and increasing pro-social behavior.

Similarly, *Interactive Theater* has been conceptualized and applied in education or to illustrate real life political and moral debates [9]. The roleplaying aspect of interactive theater, for instance, has been shown to be an effective tool in teaching medical students communication skills when breaking bad news to patients [10].

Saypol [11] defined interactive theater as "a theatrical form in which the audience participates, in varying degrees, in the creation of the drama on stage in real time, resulting in a combination of scripted and improvisational performance, with the goal of fostering critical dialogue designed to challenge attitudes and behaviors around a variety of social issues". Interactive theater can be understood as a non-digital implementation of interactive narrative design, where audiences shift from the role of observer to that of participant, immersing themselves through interaction with their surroundings, e.g. by conversing with actors.

For instance, the interactive installation or documentary theater *Situation Rooms* by art collective, Rimini Protokoll, allows participants to perceive several out of 20 different roles (weapon seller, soldier, ruler, refugee) by re-enacting the personal narratives told through a video device [12]. By following what they hear and see on the video equipment, participants are led through the installation, which takes them through sets depicting the world of weapons manufacturing, sales and war.

In a similar fashion, the installation *Angstfabriek*, uses an interactive narrative theatrical experience as a way to invite participants to reflect on the societal and political implications of fear-mongering.

2 Case Study: Angstfabriek

Fear, a ubiquitous experience among humans, has evolved over millions of years as an autonomous mechanism to aid safety and survival [13]. However, given the complexity of modern society and the factors that influence human interactions, fear – its fabrication and perpetuation – can be a threat in itself.

Fear is fueled by complex issues such as divisive politics, war, migration, climate change and health risks, but is equally propagated by seemingly ordinary everyday discussions about vaccination, dietary choices, or the excessive consumption of social media and games. People are increasingly driven towards an immense need to limit risks and dangers – idealizing a society with guaranteed safety, to which the safety industry responds by developing solutions. And while the world is safer and better than ever before in many ways [14], there is also the risk of fear leading to potentially harmful solutions.

Consider the dystopian scenarios featured by Black Mirror. The episode "Nosedive", for example, shows a social credit system similar to the one now being implemented in China, which – in an attempt to create an ideal society – rewards preferred social behaviors while penalizing undesirable ones. Such a premise is controversial not only because it creates a system that fosters a false sense of self-valuation, but because it normalizes the notion of surveillance and profiling. This demonstrates that people, perhaps in their need for the reassurance of safety, are willing to bend on otherwise inviolable democratic values and civil rights, raising the question of whether societies are at risk of falling victim to unchecked and unregulated safety measures.

Dutch NGO *Critical Mass* created the theatrical pop-up experience 'Angstfabriek' (Dutch for 'fear factory') intending to unmask the inner workings of the global fear industry and safety industry [15]. The Angstfabriek is a physical installation with theatrical elements, narration and interactive experiences that challenge visitors to reflect on their own attitude and behavior towards the topic.

With the goal of raising awareness, encouraging critical thinking, and stimulating dialogue, the Angstfabriek is based on the concept that fear can be manufactured to create a demand for safety as a product and as a service. As a fear factory – a place where fears are made – techniques to frighten us are designed, tested and thoroughly perfected for maximum impact and then marketed to companies, politicians, activists and lobbyists that require tailor-made fear campaigns for a variety of agendas.

This concept is inspired by *Securitization theory* and the so-called Copenhagen School of Security Studies, which asserts that security is about survival, and that an issue, when posed as an existential threat to a designated referent object, legitimizes the use of extraordinary measures to handle them [16].

2.1   The Angstfabriek Experience

Entrance. The fake fear factory welcomes visitors in groups of up to 6, at 15-minute intervals. As participants enter the building, they are asked to sign up with their real names. Personal information is used to create the illusion that the factory has background information on each participant. Information from online profiles etc. are used for short personal verbal interactions. At times, the demonstration is subtler, in the case of a visitor who suddenly hears music written by his band playing as the group enters the installation, causing him to react, "That's my music!".

Then participants are asked to stand behind a futuristic display to be scanned. The scan presumably searches for themes that they might be afraid of – terrorism, alt-right, climate change, food safety – and depicts these with percentages on the transparent screen in front of them. See Fig. 1.

Fig. 1. Entrance (left) and reception of the Angstfabriek with scanning platform (right)

Virtual Reality Lab. Participants are then guided into the VR lab where four members of the group are shown scenes through VR headsets. The remaining members act as test supervisors, selecting which topics, and at which intensity, to show to the testers. As the testers view the clips, their heart rate, perspiration and brain activity are monitored to measure their reaction to the visual stimuli. Finally, the results are shared with the participants, showing them their personal level of susceptibility to media messages. See Fig. 2.

Fig. 2. Conducting the fear response experiment in the VR lab (left) and discussing the results using the measurement graphs for each participant.

Corporate Video. A stack of boxes is used as a projection screen to show a corporate film featuring satisfied customers talking about their fears (e.g. of foreigners, of harmful ingredients in products, etc.) and how the Angstfabriek helped them. Visitors wait here for the director to pick them up. On a design level this also serves as a buffer to manage the flow of visitors. See Fig. 3.

Fig. 3. Angstfabriek corporate film (left) and director's speech in his office

Director's Office. Next, visitors listen to the Director deliver a speech. He is proud of his factory and emphasizes the usefulness for society as he needs public support. He asks visitors about their personal fears and then argues that fear is a natural instinct intended to keep people safe. He concludes by stating that fear creates the need for safety, hoping to turn some of the visitors into future clients. See Fig. 3.

Whistleblower. As the visitors prepare to leave, they suddenly encounter an employee, the cleaner, who offers to show them "what is really going on". While the work of the Angstfabriek sounds good at first, the reality is different. Former factory staff have therefore decided to leave without letting the director know. This allows visitors to step into their shoes and experience with their own eyes what is happening in the factory and to make this information public. The cleaner, part of the whistleblower team, therefore helps visitors to go undercover by wearing the uniforms of employees that have gone missing due to their moral reservations. As they go through the facility again, they are able to see behind the curtain and form their own opinion.

Fear Video Creation. The first stop is the creation of an impactful news clip on an important topic such as terrorism or climate change. This gives participants insight into how messages are combined in order to create fear. Through this exercise participants begin to see through fear as a business concept. Video clips, text, music and titles have to be combined to create a strong, fear inducing media message. The results are critiqued and rated by the CEO on the screen. Participants who complete this task become complicit in spreading fear. See Fig. 4.

Fig. 4. Following instructions at the media station (left) and creating an impactful fear video

Assembly Line. In their role as fear factory workers, participants have to order 4 out of 8 possible safety measures. They investigate boxes on a movable assembly line, by scanning QR codes using an augmented reality device to reveal the safety measure contained by each box (e.g. anti-riot drones, social credit systems, smart borders, 3D printed weapons, tracking devices). See Fig. 5.

Fig. 5. Following instructions at the assembly line (left) and choosing safety measures

Locker Room. The installation ends when visitors bring the coats back to the staff room, where they find the lockers of the employees that have left. Visitors are given the opportunity to look inside these lockers, where they find personal stories on the effects of fear-mongering and interactions to further convey the installation's message with an invitation to reflect.

3   Evaluation

In this paper, we discuss the results of two studies: a focus group interview (N = 7) conducted with docents from the Games & Interaction department at HKU University of the Arts Utrecht, with backgrounds in psychology, interaction and game design, game art, documentary making, and interactive narrative design; and a pilot study (N = 32) using a questionnaire, with qualitative and quantitative sections. A summary of the studies follows.

3.1   Focus Group

After experiencing the Angstfabriek for about 70 min, the focus group made suggestions on what they would improve to create a more meaningful and more impactful experience.

Overall, the focus group praised the installation in terms of concept, engagement and presentation. The experience flow was good. The more interactive parts, such as talking to the director and creating a fear video, were deemed engaging and valuable to the concept of raising awareness and giving insight. The locker design in the end felt overwhelming as it provided too much information, and not entirely related to the topic of fear and safety. This issue has since been improved and the subsequent pilot study already used the new design.

Other points of critique, however, concerned the visitors' role, agency and immersion. The focus group had been recruited without significant knowledge of the installation. While the tagline on the Angstfabriek website [15] clearly states "Go undercover in a fake fear factory", it was not clear to the focus group what this actually entailed. A number of group members pointed out that the introduction to the context and their role in it could have been better.

With regard to agency, the creation of a fear-inducing news item offered the most interaction, as the activity involved a process of content selection and feedback. This forced participants to think about which options would work best in creating fearful reactions, and then – in consultation with the group – to come to a choice that was morally reprehensible. The focus group participated in creating an impactful fear inducing news item without discussing rebellious alternatives.

Interactive narratives usually involve some level of influence on the story. At the Angstfabriek, agency was only possible on a local level, during certain scenes, without having any impact on subsequent scenes or the overall outcome.

Finally, the focus group pointed out that the narrative twist and their new role as undercover employee were not sufficiently convincing. The whistleblower cautions visitors to avoid eye contact with the director, and to put on employee uniforms. However, a lab coat passing off as a convincing disguise requires considerable suspension of disbelief, which was not helped by an unconvincing performance from the whistleblower. Ultimately, these issues contributed to a break in immersion.

One participant remarked that for interactive narratives, Murray [1] stresses the importance of active creation of belief and that allowing for more roleplaying is a way to achieve this.

3.2   User Experience Study

A total of 32 participants visited the Angstfabriek, after which they filled out a questionnaire comprised of qualitative (open questions) and quantitative sections (statements rated via 5-point Likert scales). The sample consisted of 20 women, 11 men, and 1 non-binary with ages ranging from 15 to 71 (Median = 37, M = 39, SD = 13), having moderate experience with virtual reality (M = 2.77, SD = 1.25) and interactive theater (M = 2.86, SD = 1.11) on a scale from 1, no experience, to 5, a lot of experience.

The open questions asked what participants liked and what they would improve, as well as what they think the installation was about and what their take-away message was. Overall, participants gave similar feedback to the focus group here, by praising the concept and presentation: "The overall concept was very impressive. In particular the start, where you are immediately confronted with questions, the sales pitch of the director, the fabrication of your own news item and the end with the various stories of 'employees'".

Based on participants' responses the intent of the experience was well understood. 23 participants understood that the topic of the installation was related to fear-mongering, specifically about the use of fear to influence people's opinion about social issues. Feedback from 6 other participants focused on the effects of fear.

Table 1. Rating of the experience sections; mean values and standard deviations (N = 32).

Section	M	SD
Entrance/reception	4.03	0.85
Virtual reality lab	4.23	0.77
Corporate film	3.33	0.88
Director's office	3.93	1.23
Whistleblower	3.43	1.16
Fear video creation	4.36	0.89
Assembly line	3.00	1.08
Lockers	3.20	1.29

When asked what could be improved, 6 participants stated that they expected a more frightening experience: "It remains too distant, does not create a sense of fear in me".

These expectations probably stem from the naming of the interactive installation: Angstfabriek (fear factory) and the entrance scene, that presumably detects personal fears, whereas the remainder of the experience focuses on given topics: climate change, terrorism and the safety industry.

The lack of a concretely defined role became apparent by statements of 5 participants: "I did not know who I am as a participant in the experience", "Improve the introduction to role and context: who am I, where am I, why am I here, what can I do?".

Participants were asked to rate their liking of the different Angstfabriek sections on a 5-point scale (1 – I did not like it at all, 2 – I disliked it, 3 – I neither liked nor disliked it, 4 – I liked it, 5 – I liked it a lot). Table 1 shows the results, with the creation of the fear news video being the most preferred part and the assembly line getting an overall neutral score (Table 2).

Curiosity and Expectation. Participants were intrigued by the installation and wanted to find out what it is about. Overall, they deemed it to be interesting, albeit it did not meet all of the expectations. Only a minority knew what the experience was about beforehand.

Insight. While participants stated that the installation triggered thoughts about fear-mongering, they did not state a strong impact on their critical perception of the safety industry. This seems to be connected to the mixed reactions towards the assembly line interaction. On average participants were not very well informed about the safety industry prior to the experience. Men rated their familiarity with existing safety products (M = 3.45, SD = .93) significantly higher than female visitors (M = 2.45, SD = 1.23), t(29) = 2.348, p = .026. Interestingly, participants did not state that their experience with the Angstfabriek resulted in an increased interest in learning more about the topic of fear-mongering and the safety industry. However, participants' takeaway messages in the qualitative part of the study indicate their insights on the importance of thinking for oneself, remaining objective, and being critical of information received from the media. It is possible that the participants found these insights

Table 2. Ratings of statements regarding the user experience via 5-point Likert scales; mean values and standard deviations (N = 32).

Statement	M	SD
Curiosity and expectation		
During the experience I felt curious and wanted to know more	3.87	0.82
The experience was interesting	4.00	0.87
The experience met my expectations	3.56	1.16
Before visiting, I already knew what the Angstfabriek is about, so I knew what to expect	2.03	1.06
Insight		
The experience got me thinking about the topic of fear-mongering	4.03	1.09
I had already a good insight into the topic of fear-mongering	3.36	1.03
The experience made me more critical about the safety industry	3.20	1.16
I was familiar with the products of the safety industry	2.93	1.20
Because of this experience I want to learn more about fear-mongering and the safety industry	2.93	1.17
Character believability		
I found the character of the director believable	3.80	0.96
I found the character of the whistleblower believable	3.06	1.14
Role-identification		
After meeting the whistleblower, I felt like I was actually going undercover in the Angstfabriek	2.30	1.15
I could identify with the 'undercover employee' character	2.63	1.13
I tried to sabotage the factory	2.67	1.51
Personal meaningfulness		
I was inspired by the experience	3.63	0.89
I was impressed by the experience	3.60	0.93
I found this experience to be very meaningful	3.80	1.09
I was moved by this experience	3.26	1.34
The experience was thought provoking	3.70	1.08
This experience will stick with me for quite a while	3.10	1.11
I was touched by the stories in the locker room	3.33	1.37

sufficiently transformative, which may explain their lack of interest in learning more about the topic.

Character Believability. The performance of the director was overall rated as more believable than the whistleblower's. That poses a problem for the experience, as the director is persuasive and in line with the messages of the corporate film. This finding supports the opinion of the focus group that felt underwhelmed by the whistleblower character. Interestingly, men found the character of the director (M = 4.37, SD = .65) significantly more believable than female visitors (M = 3.55, SD = .99), t(29) = 2.156, p = .040. This shows the importance of taking possible biases into account when designing characters.

Role-Identification. Identification with the new role of an undercover employee was rated low, which supports the result from the focus group interview. Many participants were not aware that it was possible to sabotage the experience. The analysis of the open question "If you tried to sabotage, how did you do it?" revealed that 13 out of 32 participants tried to actively sabotage the factory by not following the instructions. Most reported boycott strategies involved creating a neutral news clip instead of a fear inducing one, not sending the clip, or scanning an insufficient number of products at the assembly line. Other participants stated that they were not aware of this option. Two exceptions are worth noting. One participant stated that he was inspired by the director's speech and "[...] enthusiastically went along to spread fear". Another claimed that he did not sabotage on purpose: "I enjoyed playing the bad guy for once". We did not find significant differences when comparing the experience ratings of participants that claimed to have sabotaged with those who did not.

Personal Meaningfulness. The items of this category are based on Roth's measurement toolbox [17], which follows the taxonomy of Murray (Agency, Immersion and Transformation) and which locates personal meaningfulness (eudaimonic appraisal) under transformation [18]. The results indicate a clear trend of participants rating their experience as meaningful. More so on a cognitive than on an emotional level. The locker room stories were deemed touching by a minority. On average, participants gave a rather neutral rating when asked if the experience will stick with them for a while. These findings indicate that the emotional impact could be even stronger.

Furthermore, the study revealed that the participants' age plays a crucial role in the rating of the experience. Age correlates significantly negatively with evoked thinking about fear-mongering ($r = -.495, p = .004$), and personal meaningfulness, e.g. "I found this experience to be very meaningful" ($r = -.458, p = .008$), "I was moved by the experience" ($r = -.495, p = .004$), "The experience was thought provoking" ($r = -.527, p = .002$). A statement of the oldest participant (age 71) gives insight to why it was not meaningful to him: "It is not confrontational. It is too hasty and not interactive enough. There is not enough time to consult, especially if you do not know the others in your group". Older participants seemed to be knowledgeable with the concept of interactive theater as age correlates positively ($r = .434, p = .013$). However, visitors within the older age range encountered difficulties when using some technological parts of the installation, hampering a more meaningful experience.

4   Discussion and Conclusion

As a project that seeks to raise awareness of fear-mongering, the Angstfabriek is a cleverly thought-out interactive narrative experience that was well received by the focus group and our subsequent sample consisting of 32 participants. As a project that is defined in terms of encouraging a more critical attitude towards the media, raising awareness, and initiating dialogue on the topic of fear-mongering, Angstfabriek has already partly succeeded. In order to create a more impactful or *transformative* interactive narrative experience, it would benefit from better scripting of the role that the interactors play, including the level of agency and roleplaying as the focus group interviews revealed. Murray [1] refers to this design strategy as Scripting the Interactor (StI), which casts an interactor into her role by providing context, manages expectations and exposes opportunities for action. Roth and Koenitz [19] identified StI as a design convention for interactive digital narratives, where it is commonly used as introductory information.

The interactive installation seems to work better with a younger audience and the topic of fear-mongering and media literacy is both timely and relevant in an educational context. However, the limited number of 6 concurrent participants makes it more challenging for larger school classes to visit, as groups have to wait up to 15 min for their turn. Here, digital interactive narrative experiences have a clear advantage as they scale more easily.

For a transformative learning experience, it is crucial to allow for reflection and discussion [4]. Currently, this has to be self-organized by visitors. Inviting them to a discussion round directly after the visit could be a valuable addition.

If transformation is influenced by the level of interaction in the sense of the agency that participants experience, then one could argue that the Angstfabriek is mainly exploratory (cf. classification model of Ryan [20]). While it is possible to boycott certain tasks (create a video that is neutral instead of fear-inducing, pull out a power cord to stop the assembly line), these actions bear no clear dramatic agency [1] that significantly impacts how the plot plays out. And in the event that participants purposely or unwittingly break with this order, actors immediately intervene to inform them that this is not allowed. Usually, visitors of the Angstfabriek do not challenge the actors through off-beat behavior. Inviting more roleplaying could change this, though, which might become difficult for the experience designers to handle. In this regard, interactive theater installations face a similar challenge as interactive digital narratives. Aylett [21] describes this as the *narrative paradox* – the required moderation between interactor freedom and the structured experience, which was designed for maximum emotional impact. It is important to note that interactive narratives offer different levels of agency and that the granting of agency by itself does not automatically guarantee a richer user experience (cf. [22, 23]).

Dubbelman, Roth, and Koenitz [24] discuss the challenge of creating transformative interactive narratives from a pedagogical perspective. Following Janet Murray [1], the authors see one educational aspect of interactive digital narratives in the potential to revisit earlier decisions by replaying. This allows to explore a topic from additional perspectives which are not given by linear and static representations. While replaying interactive digital narratives is usually a matter of restarting the application, it becomes more difficult, in terms of cost, time and availability, when visiting interactive theater presentations and physical installations that only allow for a limited number of interactors at a time.

However, Boal [9] states that interactive theater is not meant to satisfy participants, and instead suggests that "these theatrical forms create a sort of uneasy sense of incompleteness that seeks fulfillment through real action" (p. 120).

Practitioners therefore often endeavor to measure the efficacy of interactive theater by asking about the medium and their long-term influence on a participant's tendency towards social activism [25]. This study is therefore only a first step in evaluating the potentially transformative effects of the Angstfabriek installation. When visitors start to engage with the topic, their personal experience triggers an interest in seeking more education on the subject. Whether this interest leads to action or results in nothing more than mild curiosity is unclear.

Perhaps further study could be dedicated to measuring transformation in the sense behavior and subsequent action, similar to the study by Steinemann et al. [6], which measured the amount of money participants donated out of their participation reward to a related cause.

Furthermore, future evaluation needs to aim at a younger, more coherent, group of visitors, like school classes, and could include a knowledge test to measure what was learned. The project is perfectly suited as part of an educational program, particularly one tackling the role of media and public perception.

Acknowledgments. Thanks to Hiske Arts, founder and creative brain of Critical Mass, for involving and supporting us in the critical evaluation of their Angstfabriek project. Thanks to the visitors for taking the time to give insights into their experience. Thanks to the focus group who gave their professional feedback and for approving the usage of pictures showing them.

References

1. Murray, J.H.: Hamlet on the Holodeck: The Future of Narrative in Cyberspace. Free Press, New York (1997)
2. Ritterfeld, U., Cody, M., Vorderer, P.A. (eds.): Serious Games: Mechanisms and Effects. Routledge, New York (2009)
3. Green, M.C., Jenkins, K.M.: Interactive narratives: Processes and outcomes in user-directed stories. J. Commun. **64**(3), 479–500 (2014)
4. Mezirow, J.: Transformative dimensions of adult learning. The Jossey-Bass Higher and Adult Education Series. Jossey-Bass, San Francisco (1991)
5. Bruner, J.S.: The act of discovery. Harv. Educ. Rev. **31**, 21–32 (1961)
6. Steinemann, S.T., Mekler, E.D., Opwis, K.: increasing donating behavior through a game for change. Presented at the 2015 Annual Symposium, New York, NY, USA (2015)
7. Steinemann, S.T., Iten, G.H., Opwis, K., Forde, S.F., Frasseck, L., Mekler, E.D.: Interactive narratives affecting social change. J. Media Psychol. **29**, 54–66 (2017)
8. Parrott, S., Carpentier, F.R.D., Northup, C.T.: A test of interactive narrative as a tool against prejudice. Howard J. Commun. **28**, 1–16 (2017)
9. Boal, A.: Theater of the Oppressed, 3rd edn. Pluto Press, London (2000)
10. Skye, E.P., Wagenschutz, H., Steiger, J.A., Kumagai, A.K.: Use of interactive theater and role play to develop medical students' skills in breaking bad news. J. Cancer Educ. **29**(4), 704–708 (2014)
11. Saypol, B.: Effective practices for establishing an interactive theatre program in a university community. Theatre and Dance Graduate Theses and Dissertations (2011)
12. Rimini Protokoll, Situation Rooms. https://www.rimini-protokoll.de/website/media/situationrooms/programmhefte/Situation_Rooms_englisch.pdf, last accessed 2019/08/19
13. Öhman, A.: Fear and anxiety. In: Handbook of Emotions, pp. 709–729 (2008)
14. Rosling, H., Rosling, O., Rönnlund, A.R.: Factfulness: Ten Reasons We're Wrong About the World – and Why Things Are Better Than You Think. Flatiron Books, New York (2018)
15. Critical Mass' Angstfabriek website. https://angstfabriek.nl. Accessed 19 Aug 2019

16. Buzan, B., Weaver, O., de Wilde, J.: Security – A New Framework for Analysis. Lynne Rinner Publishers, Inc., Colorado (1998)
17. Roth, C.: Experiencing interactive storytelling. Dissertation at Vrije Universiteit Amsterdam (2016). https://research.vu.nl/en/publications/experiencing-interactive-storytelling
18. Roth, C., Koenitz, H.: Evaluating the user experience of interactive digital narrative. In: Proceedings of the 1st International Workshop on Multimedia Alternate Realities, pp. 31–36. ACM (2016)
19. Roth, C., Koenitz, H.: Towards creating a body of evidence-based interactive digital narrative design knowledge: approaches and challenges. In: Proceedings of the 2nd International Workshop on Multimedia Alternate Realities, pp. 19–24. ACM (2017)
20. Ryan, M.-L.: Beyond myth and metaphor: narrative in digital media. Poet. Today **23**(4), 581–609 (2002)
21. Aylett, R.: Emergent narrative, social immersion and "storification". Presented at the 1st International Workshop on Narrative Interaction for Learning Environments, Edinburgh (2000)
22. Harrell, D.F., Zhu, J.: Agency play: dimensions of agency for interactive narrative design. In: AAAI Spring Symposium: Intelligent Narrative Technologies II, pp. 44–52 (2009)
23. Knoller, N.: Agency and the art of interactive digital storytelling. In: Aylett, R., Lim, M.Y., Louchart, S., Petta, P., Riedl, M. (eds.) ICIDS 2010. LNCS, vol. 6432, pp. 264–267. Springer, Heidelberg (2010). https://doi.org/10.1007/978-3-642-16638-9_38
24. Dubbelman, T., Roth, C., Koenitz, H.: Interactive digital narratives (IDN) for change. In: Rouse, R., Koenitz, H., Haahr, M. (eds.) ICIDS 2018. LNCS, vol. 11318, pp. 591–602. Springer, Cham (2018). https://doi.org/10.1007/978-3-030-04028-4_69
25. Hamel, S.: When theatre of the oppressed becomes theatre of the oppressor. Res. Drama Educ.: J. Appl. Theatre Perform. **18**(4), 403–416 (2013)

Spaceline: A Concept for Interaction in Cinematic Virtual Reality

Sylvia Rothe[✉] and Heinrich Hussmann

LMU Munich University, Munich, Germany
sylvia.rothe@ifi.lmu.de

Abstract. Watching omnidirectional movies via head-mounted displays places the viewer inside the scene. In this way, the viewer attends an immersive movie experience. However, due to the free choice of the viewing direction, it is possible to miss details which are important for the story. On the other hand, the additional space component gives the filmmakers new opportunities to construct non-linear interactive stories. To assist this, we introduce the concept of a *spaceline* which connects movie sequences via interactive regions. This work explains the terms of the spaceline concept and introduces methods that make it easier for the viewer to follow the story, at their own pace with their own focus. We present a design space that supports filmmakers in designing interactive CVR experiences.

Keywords: Cinematic Virtual Reality · 360° movie · Omnidirectional movies, timeline · Interactivity · Story structure, nonlinear storytelling

1   Introduction

Already the Russian filmmaker Sergei Eisenstein had the desire for non-linear movies and books, in which the story can go on in all directions [1]. Cinematic Virtual Reality (CVR), where omnidirectional movies are watched via head-mounted displays, brings us closer to this dream of spherical dramaturgy. The additional space component facilitates interactivity in a natural way. Comparing traditional movies with CVR, many parallels can be found. However, the narrative methods of traditional film production cannot simply be transferred. The transition of some activities from the filmmaker to the viewer and new interaction possibilities requires and enables new approaches.

Traditionally, a movie is arranged on a *timeline*. Beginning and end of a shot are determined by in- and out-points. Brillhart adapted these terms: "In VR, the *in-point* is where a visitor's experience is most likely to begin and the *out-point* is where it's most likely to end" [2]. However, it cannot be assumed that the viewer really looks to the out-point at the time when the shot changes and therefore the in-point might not be seen. Moving away from tools of traditional film production and taking advantage of the possibilities offered by VR, opens up new options. Since CVR adds a space component in addition to time, it is worth to consider that cuts not only depend on elapsed time, but also on the viewing direction.

R. E. Cardona-Rivera et al. (Eds.): ICIDS 2019, LNCS 11869, pp. 115–119, 2019.
https://doi.org/10.1007/978-3-030-33894-7_12

2 Spaceline Concept

Two fundamental terms of film montage are those of a shot and a scene. While a *shot* is a segment of a film between two cuts, a *scene* represents a unit of a movie at the same location and continuous in time, which in traditional film often consists of several shots. The number of cuts is reduced in CVR since the viewer himself selects different parts of the scenery for viewing. Often a scene has no further cuts. In a traditional film, the image of the camera and that of the viewer coincide. In CVR there are two perspectives: the around view of the camera and the smaller, self-selected *field of view (FoV)* of the viewer. The term shot is therefore not directly transferable, two terms are required for the film segment between two cuts. We distinguish between a space and a shot. A *space* is an omnidirectional movie segment that has been recorded without interruptions. The *shot* is the image sequence chosen by the viewer between the cuts, within this space. It is not omnidirectional, rather corresponds to the viewer's FoV in a space. A *spaceline* is a path through a structure of spaces. This structure is designed by the filmmaker. Based on it, the viewer determines the spaceline – a line through this construct consisting of several shots. In contrast to the timeline-based film, which is determined by the filmmaker alone, the spaceline is determined by the filmmaker and the viewer. Timeline and spaceline together set up the *storyline*.

Regions: The spaceline concept defines different types of regions: The *out-region* is the area whose activation ends a shot. From there, the switch to the next shot takes place, where the viewer first sees the *in-region,* from where the scenery then can be explored. The spaceline structure links out-regions with in-regions. In this way, shot changes become interactive, triggered by the viewer. For non-linear stories, more than one out-region can be defined in a space. In addition, we introduce *act-regions* which offer supplementary interaction options, such as enlarging details or retrieving additional visual information (embeddings) or sounds. One important characteristic of a region is the *size*: a large region is discovered faster than a small region. Regions can have different *priorities*: a region with high priority has to be discovered by the viewer before the story goes on, others are less important. A region can be activatable permanently, in a restricted time interval or just after another action was already activated.

Indicators: To make it easier for the viewer to recognize out- and act-regions, we introduce *indicators*. It is important that their visualizations do not disturb the viewing experience. *On-screen indicators* can be used for regions in the viewer's current FoV. To make the regions recognizable they can, e.g., be highlighted or framed. On the other hand, *off-screen indicators* point to regions out-of-display to make the discovery easier [3]. *Screen-referenced* items are connected to the display and move along with it in case the viewer is turning the head (e.g. arrows, buttons). *World-referenced* items are connected to the virtual world, in our case to the movie. They stay fixed at their place in the movie world, even if the viewer turns the head (e.g. lights, signs). Indicators can inform about the direction of the target, the distance, the relevance and the type of the regions, e.g., by using different colors or sizes. Also, unmarked regions are conceivable, e.g. where the out-region is indiscernible for the viewer, but when looking at it for a certain time interval, the next shot starts.

Pointer/Activation: For selecting the out-region, *eye* or *head* tracking methods are most natural. However, also a *controller* or hand *gestures* are possible. A selection process consists of two parts: the *pointing* and the *activation* [4]. Both processes can go unnoticed by the viewer or be triggered actively. If head or eye tracking is used, the head/gaze direction is the pointer (cursor), which can be invisible for the viewer. Using *dwell-time* (looking for a certain time interval at a target) for activating the out-region, no additional devices are needed. If there is no feedback, the user does not notice why a space changes or any other action was activated. However, with this technique, it can happen that the viewer was not ready for the next space and would prefer to see more in the current space. Activation after a dwell-time interval could be randomly triggered but desired in certain constructions. It depends on the story if the selection and activation process should be unnoticeable or triggered actively by the viewer.

Table 1 shows the elements of the spaceline concept as a design space with four dimensions: region, indicator, pointer and activation. Each of these dimensions has several subdimensions. The values for the subdimensions which were discussed in the previous sections are listed and added by options which resulted from talks with VR and CVR experts. This design space is intended for support in designing applications for the spaceline concept, e.g. interactive CVR movies.

Table 1. Dimensions of the design space for the spaceline concept. The table shows for every dimension the subdimensions and options for the subdimensions

		Option 1	Option 2	Option 3	Option 4
Region	Type	In-region	Out-region	Act-region	
	Size	Small	Middle	Big	
	Priority	High	Medium	Low	
	Duration	Permanent	Restricted	Sequence	
Indicator	Type	On-screen	Off-screen		
	Reference	World-referenced	Screen-referenced		
	Visibility	Clear	Unobtrusive	Invisible	
	Notification	Direction	Distance	Relevance	Type
Pointer	Mount	Head	Eye	Controller	Hand
	Visibility	Clear	Unobtrusive	Invisible	
	Feedback	Cursor change	Target change	Sound	None
Activation	Mount	Head	Eye	Controller	Hand
	Trigger	Nod/dwell	Dwell/blink	Click	Gesture
	Feedback	Visual	Auditive	Haptic	None

2.1 Examples of Indicators and Pointers

There are several opportunities to draw the viewer's attention to regions on the screen, e.g. movements, arrows, lights, or colors. Examples for world-referenced, on-screen indicators are framed targets. The frame colors can be used for indicating different region types. The frame can be highlighted if the viewer's view is inside the region. It depends on the story how obvious such a frame should be. Since the viewer only sees a small part of the omnidirectional image in the HMD, regions can also be outside of the FoV. There are various possibilities for indicating off-screen objects on flat devices [5–8], in 3D environments [9] and augmented reality [10, 11] which can be partly adapted to CVR. Examples for screen-referenced off-screen indicators are signs on the edge of the display towards the off-screen region.

The easiest possibility for pointing in CVR is using the head direction, which is connected to the center of the display. Other examples are eye gaze, controller techniques or gestures. Pointers can also support the viewer's awareness of a region, e.g. by changing the color when it enters an act-region.

The visualization of the indicators and the pointer depends on the story content. The filmmaker has to decide how subtle or how obvious they should be. Different indicator types can be selected and customized in their appearance to the film project, similar to film transitions in timelines of traditional films.

3   Conclusion

In this conceptual paper, we introduced the novel concept of a spaceline for CVR, in analogy and addition to the traditional timeline. Film terms such as shot and sequence were transferred to CVR and explained in the new context. New terms as spaces, spaceline, in-, out- and act-regions were introduced and on-screen and off-screen indicators were presented.

We described the relation of the spaceline concept to traditional filmmaking. Our concept should encourage filmmakers to create CVR movies with dynamic non-linear story plots where scene changes depend on interactive regions defined by the filmmaker and selected by the viewer.

Reflecting on the overall concept in the CVR context, we highlight that spaceline and timeline are both needed to realize interactive storylines in CVR. Even when using the spaceline concept, filmmakers should be able to define the time limit of a shot.

We conclude that the spaceline is a valuable concept to support filmmakers in the process of designing interactive, non-linear CVR experiences. We presented first indicator designs and described their potential in guiding the viewer.

As a broader outlook, these methods are not only relevant for CVR but can also be adapted to virtual and augmented reality applications and motivate further research. It is important to know how viewers feel in different scenarios for developing a film language for Cinematic Virtual Reality. To support this process is the long-term goal of our research.

References

1. Tikka, P.: (Interactive) cinema as a model of mind. Digit. Creat. **15**(1), 14–17 (2004)
2. In the Blink of a Mind—Attention – The Language of VR – Medium. https://medium.com/the-language-of-vr/in-the-blink-of-a-mind-attention-1fdff60fa045. Accessed 30 June 2018
3. Rothe, S., Buschek, D., Hußmann, H.: Guidance in cinematic virtual reality-taxonomy, research status and challenges. Multimodal Technol. Interact. **3**(1), 19 (2019)

4. Rothe, S., Pothmann, P., Drewe, H., Hussmann, H.: Interaction techniques for cinematic virtual reality. In: 2019 IEEE Conference on Virtual Reality and 3D User Interfaces (VR), pp. 1733–1737 (2019)
5. Gustafson, S., Baudisch, P., Gutwin, C., Irani, P.: Wedge: clutter-free visualization of off-screen locations. In: Proceedings of the SIGCHI Conference on Human Factors in Computing Systems, pp. 787–796 (2008)
6. Gustafson, S.G., Irani, P.P.: Comparing visualizations for tracking off-screen moving targets. In: CHI 2007 Extended Abstracts on Human Factors in Computing Systems, pp. 2399–2404 (2007)
7. Zellweger, P.T., Mackinlay, J.D., Good, L., Stefik, M., Baudisch, P.: City lights. In: CHI 2003 Extended Abstracts on Human Factors in Computing Systems - CHI 2003, p. 838 (2003)
8. Hossain, Z. Hasan, K., Liang, H.-N., Irani, P.: EdgeSplit. In: Proceedings of the 14th international conference on Human-computer interaction with mobile devices and services - MobileHCI 2012, p. 79 (2012)
9. Jo, H., Hwang, S., Park, H., Ryu, J.: Aroundplot: focus+context interface for off-screen objects in 3D environments. Comput. Graph. 35(4), 841–853 (2011)
10. Gruenefeld, U., El Ali, A., Heuten, W., Boll, S.: Visualizing out-of-view objects in head-mounted augmented reality. In: Proceedings of the 19th International Conference on Human-Computer Interaction with Mobile Devices and Services - MobileHCI 2017, pp. 1–7 (2017)
11. Gruenefeld, U., Ennenga, D., El Ali, A., Heuten, W., Boll, S.: EyeSee360. In: Proceedings of the 5th Symposium on Spatial User Interaction - SUI 2017, pp. 109–118 (2017)

Facilitating Information Exploration of Archival Library Materials Through Multi-modal Storytelling

Zev Battad$^{(\boxtimes)}$, Andrew White, and Mei Si

Rensselaer Polytechnic Institute, 110 8th Street, Troy, NY 12180, USA
{battaz,whitea9,sim}@rpi.edu

Abstract. This project aims to help people explore, understand, and rediscover the many-to-many relationships of content within library archives using multi-modal storytelling. This project builds upon an existing multi-modal storytelling system which is designed to help people explore large knowledge graphs by actively constructing narratives using information from the knowledge graphs. We present this system and a case study of how the process of creating the knowledge graph from existing archives becomes an iterative hypothesis testing process and triggers new knowledge discovery.

Keywords: Library achieves · Knowledge graph · Multi-modal presentation

1 Introduction

Evolution, innovation, and history are typically documented in a chronological manner, with their associated processes set sequentially through a series of highlighted events filtered from a myriad of interactions that ultimately lead to the culminating event. But the reality of history and culture exists within a broader context of those relationships across multiple dimensions that are filtered out because they appear to be lesser influencers in the historical universe. Depending upon perspective and focus, the accepted seminal events in a narrative of history and culture represent a distillation of other smaller tangential narratives. Yet it is the role of archivists to "employ as broad a definition as possible of what records are and of what events and phenomena are worth documenting" [7].

Rebuilding these inter-relationships and piecing together the various interactions in history from archival collections of primary sources is typically a labor-intensive endeavor. In many cases, archival library collections are comprised of various donations or acquisitions, some with questionable provenance and completeness. One may consider that portions of such collections are analogous to fossils or ancient artifacts [6,8,14]. Like incomplete buried skeletons, some sections of an archival collection are distributed across various archives and processed with varying degrees of descriptive detail. The frequent archival approach

R. E. Cardona-Rivera et al. (Eds.): ICIDS 2019, LNCS 11869, pp. 120–127, 2019.
https://doi.org/10.1007/978-3-030-33894-7_13

to such disjuncts and variety of information formats (i.e. photographs, drawings, manuscripts, and physical artifacts) is to sort and catalog materials using a combination of chronological, donor-specific, or subject-affinity methodologies. As a consequence, research with primary archival sources is a time-consuming manual process where the various relationships among archival collections are uncovered through happenstance.

This work aims to help people explore, understand, and rediscover the many-to-many relationships of content within library archives using multi-modal narrative agents. Over the last several decades, the scale of accessible information has grown, both in the volume in which information is being gathered and the openness by which information has been shared and made available. This has lead to incredible opportunities for knowledge and discovery. For example, the English Wikipedia alone has more than five million entries. As the oldest technological university in the US, Rensselaer Polytechnic Institutes archival collections document the evolution and impact of technology and engineering from the Industrial Revolution through the Space Age. Our digital collections alone consume 1.5 TB of storage.

As the scale and complexity of available information grows, the ease by which individuals may reasonably be expected to traverse and explore said information unassisted wanes. Furthermore, ones ability to ascertain the veracity of information sources becomes challenged. The amount of information can easily overwhelm a person and prevent one from seeing the underlying relationships among facts and data. We believe that with new digital mediums, people can benefit from machine-assisted methods of data exploration.

In this project, we describe and define digital objects, curated within library archives via a semantic web, with a focused group of individuals composed of librarians and graduate and undergraduate students. The project uses a narrative agent to help people explore the semantic web by actively constructing narratives using information from the semantic web, and to help trigger new information discoveries by posing questions based upon previously undiscovered relationships. In the next sections, we will discuss related work, present our system and report preliminary findings.

2   Narrative as the Basis for Making Sense of the History

Storytelling is ubiquitous with the human cultural experience. To see how prevalent narrative is and has been, one has to look not only at the widespread existence in the past of oral storytelling traditions in many of the worlds oldest cultures, but also observe the success of modern forms of entertainment with underlying narrative, such as cinema and video games. However, besides its apparent utility as a method of entertainment, narrative is also one of the oldest methods by which humans have traditionally exchanged information.

Narrative is concerned with how information is structured in a story: what information is included, how it is ordered, and how it is connected. We use narrative to share the happenings in our lives, to sway each others opinions, and to pass knowledge between one another. Narrative may also have a more basic connection with human knowledge.

Narrative is thought to be intuitive to how humans think about and organize information. Narrative has been posited as one of the general fundamental ways that humans organize knowledge [9]. More specifically, experiences and memories are said to be organized in a narrative fashion, with the various facts of our personal experiences being cast as a series of events and their narrative connections [5]. So too is our understanding of time cast in a narrative light, as a temporal sequence of linked events [2]. Through narrative storytelling, there exist methods for ordering and presenting information that are related to how humans intuitively organize knowledge.

American cognitive scientist Jerome Bruner pointed out that there are two modes of how people make sense of their environment [4]. Bruner calls the two modes the paradigmatic or logico-scientific mode and the narrative mode. The paradigmatic or logico-scientific mode collects facts from ones experience and the narrative mode tries to make sense of the experience. In other words, the narrative process aims at endowing experience with meaning, which is often composed of causal and temporal relationships of events – the core components of narrative. For people, these two modes are used as means for convincing one another: facts convince one of their truths, while stories support their likeness. Our multi-modal visualization and narrative system works in a similar way, by making the relationships among information more visible and thus inspiring people to discover new relationships. To our knowledge, there has not been an interactive storytelling system that is specifically designed to help people discover new information centered and based on library archives.

3   System Architecture

In our previous work, we have applied narrative and storytelling strategies to qualitative information presentation, developing a system to automatically generate narratives from topic-relationship information networks [10,11], as well as techniques for using multiple interweaving story lines [3], topic anchor points, and analogies [12].

We have also created an automated narration system that takes structured open domain information and tailors the presentation to a user using storytelling techniques [3,10,11]. It aimed at presenting the information as an interesting and meaningful story by taking into consideration a combination of factors, ranging from topic consistency and novelty to learned user interests.

Starting from any point in a knowledge graph, such as the subset shown in Fig. 1 (left) with part of its XML representation (right), the agent can talk about the knowledge graph by introducing the topics one by one. Note that, while not shown, each directed edge in Fig. 1 has an edge in the other direction with a reciprocal relationship. A diagram of the systems architecture is shown in Fig. 2. When deciding what to talk about next, the agent strives to form a piece of narrative rather than simply listing the facts. It does so in two steps: sequencing and connection.

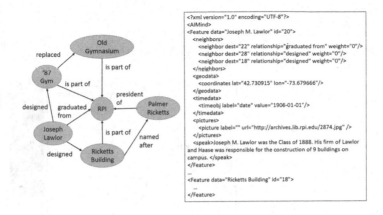

Fig. 1. An example of a subset of a knowledge graph.

First, the Topic Sequencer creates an initial sequence of topics to present. Starting from an initial topic, it adds topics to the end of the sequence iteratively. The next topic of the sequence is chosen by balancing multiple objectives related to narrative and user experience, such as suggesting novel content or maintaining spatial and temporal consistency. These objectives form a set of constraints, which are used to score each potential next topic. The best-scoring topic is added to the end of the sequence. The Topic Sequencer is derived from previous work on automatic narrative generation from information networks [10, 11].

Next, the Topic Connector creates connections between topics in the sequence based on pairwise relationships between topics in the knowledge graph. The Topic Connector marks when in the sequence to allude to a future topic in the sequence and when in the sequence to refer back to past topics in the sequence. Examples of both can be seen in Fig. 4. In this example, relationships with the topic directly prior to the current one (blue text), reminders of topics visited several topics ago (yellow text), and allusions to future topics (purple text) can be seen.

The Topic Connector also marks the most appropriate places in the sequence to pause narration of the sequence and explicitly give the user a turn to interact. Places in the sequence to pause narration are selected based on the connectivity between topics in the sequence that have already been presented and topics in the sequence that have yet to be presented. The Topic Connector is derived from previous work on analogies [12] and using multiple interleaving storylines in narrative generation [3].

Once a connected topic sequence is created, the Narration Manager presents the sequence one topic at a time through the interactive visualization. The interactive visualization consists of three panels, as can be seen in Fig. 3. The left panel shows a map displaying the location of each topic. The center panel shows a timeline with topics represented as nodes, with category lanes and lines connecting topics that are related in the knowledge base. The right panel shows

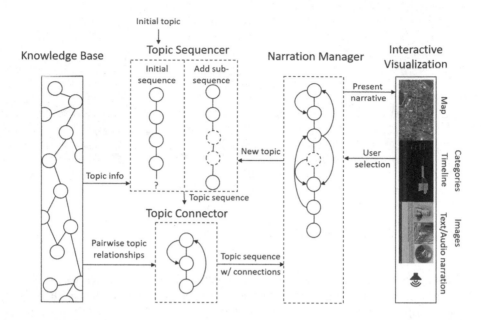

Fig. 2. System diagram.

a set of images and the text narration for the topic the Narration Manager is currently presenting. The agent gives an audio narration of the text as well.

At any point in the narration, the user can select a topic in the center panel that they wish for the agent to discuss. The Narration Manager also explicitly asks the user to select a topic at points deemed most appropriate by the Topic Connector. When the user selects a topic, it interrupts the current sequence with a short, new subsequence calculated from the selected topic.

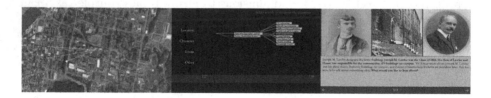

Fig. 3. Screen shots from existing system.

The Topic Sequencer creates a new subsequence, taking into consideration the topics that have been presented in the initial sequence and the new topic selected by the user. The subsequence is inserted after the point where the initial sequence was paused. Then, the rest of the initial sequence is placed after it. Connections between the subsequence and the initial sequence are formed by the Topic Connector. The Narration Manager then continues narration with the new combined sequence, starting with the user's selected topic. Thus, the storytelling agent is able to both react to the user and maintain a consistent narrative plan.

In the top text in Fig. 4, which shows the text from the right panel in Fig. 3, the system can be seen pausing narration of the sequence and alluding to future topics in the sequence which have yet to be presented and which are related to topics that have been presented. In the bottom text in Fig. 4, the system can be seen describing the user-selected topic later in the same narration.

Joseph M. Lawlor designed Ricketts Building. Joseph M. Lawlor was the Class of 1888. His firm of Lawlor and Haase was responsible for the construction of 9 buildings on campus We'll hear more about Joseph M. Lawlor and his alma mater, Ricketts Building on campus, and Palmer Chamberlain Ricketts as president later. But for now, let's talk about something else. What would you like to hear about?

'87 Gymnasium replaced Old Gymnasium. Once the campus was established on the hill, students began to complain about the location and inadequacy of the old gymnasium. The Alumni Association led a movement to raise money to build a new building near the athletic field. The Class of 1887 took up the cause and presented $150,000 to the Institute in 1911 to build and equip a new gymnasium. The building was designed by Lawlor & Haase of New York and built of Harvard brick and Indiana limestone. The Class of 1887 formally presented the building to the Board of Trustees on Alumni Day, June 11, 1912. Do you remember Joseph M. Lawlor? Well, '87 Gymnasium designed by Joseph M. Lawlor.

Fig. 4. Example text from two topics in the same narration. (Color figure online)

4   New Knowledge Discovery While Constructing a Knowledge Graph

We performed a preliminary study of using this interactive narrative system to organize and describe Rensselaer Polytechnic Institute's library archives. The details of the study and our main findings are included below.

We experimented with creating new knowledge graphs based on archival library content and with a focused group comprised of four librarians, one graduate student and one undergraduate student. When working with the interactive storytelling system, we need to represent the network of archival information as topics and their relationships. More specifically, each topic is treated as a node in a knowledge graph, which has a description and links to other nodes. For example, the node "Alumni Building" and the node "Rensselaer Polytechnic Institute" are linked by the "is part of" relationship.

Prototyping of this project revealed a need for librarians and archivists to move beyond sets of simple format conversion tasks towards the development of new methodologies in controlled vocabularies, metadata, and cataloging. As librarians worked to migrate the institutional archives, which are stored in a hierarchical data structure, e.g. Dublin Core to the new graphical structure associated used by the multi-modal storytelling system, we found that the difference between the two representations of data can often inspire the librarians to form new hypotheses and discover new information. The new information, in turn, becomes part of the knowledge graph and may inspire new discoveries.

For example, a previously known relationship between two topics (a campus president and an architect) had only one type of connection (contractual) – President Ricketts contracted with architect Joseph Lawlor on several building construction projects. While working through the structural migration, librarians began to question if other types of additional connections existed. One building contracted to Joseph Lawlor is the fraternity house for Theta Xi. Librarians began to wonder if both Lawlor and Ricketts were members of the fraternity. After researching the Theta Xi yearbooks, librarians confirmed that both Lawlor and Ricketts were members of the same fraternity, and that Ricketts had predated Lawlor as a fraternity brother. The newly uncovered relationship helped to add greater context to the facts and the narrative constructed by the system.

Thus, the process of creating the knowledge graph from existing archives becomes an iterative hypothesis testing process. In this work, we observed how the same focus group of librarians and archivists went through these iterations multiple times in order to establish appropriate metadata needed to document relationships between data points.

5   Discussion and Future Work

While the Rensselaer Polytechnic Institute librarians searched for information to encode into a knowledge graph for the system, the process of exploration was valuable and revealing. However, despite the value of the process, building the knowledge graph was performed with minimal machine assistance by web-browsing online resources, reading physical archives, and writing the XML file for the knowledge graph by hand. As the librarians' discoveries were made from the connections they found while building the knowledge graph, and the narrative generation system reveals connections between topics while exploring the knowledge graph, a natural enhancement to the process would be to integrate knowledge base authoring with the narrative system. While exploring the existing knowledge base using the system, new incidental connections, like the relationship between Joseph Lawlor and President Ricketts, can be hypothesized, confirmed with additional external resources, and included into the knowledge base. There are two main directions in pursuit of this. The first is the integration of a knowledge graph authoring tool with the system, such as Jambalaya for Protégé [13] or Lucidchart for the creation of mindmaps [1], to alter knowledge graphs in real-time without directly handling an XML representation. The second is the integration of external resource access and exploration to directly browse and display digital archives.

References

1. Lucidchart.https://www.lucidchart.com/pages/examples/mind_mapping_software
2. Abbott, H.P.: The Cambridge Introduction to Narrative. Cambridge University Press, Cambridge (2008)
3. Battad, Z., Si, M.: Using multiple storylines for presenting large information networks. In: Traum, D., Swartout, W., Khooshabeh, P., Kopp, S., Scherer, S., Leuski, A. (eds.) IVA 2016. LNCS (LNAI), vol. 10011, pp. 141–153. Springer, Cham (2016). https://doi.org/10.1007/978-3-319-47665-0_13
4. Bruner, J.: Two modes of thought. In: Actual Minds, Possible Worlds, pp. 11–43 (1986)
5. Bruner, J.: Self-making and world-making. In: Narrative and Identity: Studies in Autobiography, Self, and Culture, pp. 25–37 (2001)
6. Forster, N.: The use of company documentation. In: Cassell, C., Symon, G. (eds.) Qualitative Methods in Organizational Research: A Practical Guide. Sage, London (1994)
7. Hickerson, H.: Ten challenges for the archival profession. Am. Arch. **64**(1), 6–16 (2001)
8. Hill, M.R.: Archival Strategies and Techniques, vol. 31. Sage Publications, London (1993)
9. Neumann, B., Nünning, A.: An Introduction to the Study of Narrative Fiction. Klett, Stuttgart (2008)
10. Si, M.: Tell a story about anything. In: Schoenau-Fog, H., Bruni, L.E., Louchart, S., Baceviciute, S. (eds.) ICIDS 2015. LNCS, vol. 9445, pp. 361–365. Springer, Cham (2015). https://doi.org/10.1007/978-3-319-27036-4_37
11. Si, M.: Facilitate knowledge exploration with storytelling. Proc. Comput. Sci. **88**, 224–231 (2016)
12. Si, M., Carlson, C.: A data-driven approach for making analogies. In: CogSci (2017)
13. Storey, M.A., et al.: Jambalaya: interactive visualization to enhance ontology authoring and knowledge acquisition in Protégé. In: Workshop on interactive tools for knowledge capture, vol. 73 (2001)
14. Welch, C.: The archaeology of business networks: the use of archival records in case study research. J. Strateg. Mark. **8**(2), 197–208 (2000)

The Impact of Multi-character Story Distribution and Gesture on Children's Engagement

Harrison Jesse Smith[1]([✉]), Brian K. Riley[1], Lena Reed[2], Vrindavan Harrison[2], Marilyn Walker[2], and Michael Neff[1]

[1] University of California, Davis, Davis, CA 95616, USA
{hjsmith,bkriley,mpneff}@ucdavis.edu
[2] University of California, Santa Cruz, Santa Cruz, CA 95064, USA
{lireed,vharriso,mawalker}@ucsc.edu

Abstract. Effective storytelling relies on engagement and interaction. This work develops an automated software platform for telling stories to children and investigates the impact of two design choices on children's engagement and willingness to interact with the system: story distribution and the use of complex gesture. A storyteller condition compares stories told in a third person, narrator voice with those distributed between a narrator and first-person story characters. Basic gestures are used in all our storytellings, but, in a second factor, some are augmented with gestures that indicate conversational turn changes, references to other characters and prompt children to ask questions. An analysis of eye gaze indicates that children attend more to the story when a distributed storytelling model is used. Gesture prompts appear to encourage children to ask questions, something that children did, but at a relatively low rate. Interestingly, the children most frequently asked "why" questions. Gaze switching happened more quickly when the story characters began to speak than for narrator turns. These results have implications for future agent-based storytelling system research.

Keywords: Embodied storyteller · Listening comprehension · Primary school · Case study

1 Introduction

For many, being read a bedtime story is a fond childhood memory. This comforting experience also creates excitement as the the new world of the story unfolds. While enjoyable, such storytelling also provides the foundation for developing listening comprehension and later reading comprehension skills [16,19,20,28,38,48,59,63] which are critical to educational attainment.

While the levels of quality home language input low socioeconomic status (SES) children receive is debated [25,57], it is clear that the absence of such language input can negatively affect a child's early language development

R. E. Cardona-Rivera et al. (Eds.): ICIDS 2019, LNCS 11869, pp. 128–143, 2019.
https://doi.org/10.1007/978-3-030-33894-7_14

skills [4,8,14,26,27,31,35,44,56,64,67]. If children do not have adequate language skills in the primary grades, they are likely to have persistent academic difficulties [30,56,62], leading to long lasting consequences [52].

Computer storytelling apps may provide a way to address this early exposure gap and remediate, at least in part, the early educational deficit by providing high quality language exposure at home or in the classroom. They can be displayed on phones or tablets and deployed at low cost. It remains unclear, however, how to effectively design these apps in order to maximize child engagement.

To help answer this question, we present the results of experiment that looks at two factors in story presentation. The first compares narrator-only storytellings (third-person) with tellings that distribute the text between a narrator and story characters (first and third-person). The second factor varies the amount of nonverbal behavior present in the characters, comparing a condition that only uses beat gestures and subtle head nods with a condition that includes character deixis gestures, turn taking cues, and interaction prompts (see 2.3 for gesture type definitions).

To investigate these factors, we used a custom-built Unity application and cloud-based text-to-speech software to present four Aesop's fables in a repeatable, controlled fashion. The storytelling application is shown in Fig. 1. During the story presentation, we recorded participants' gaze locations. After each story concluded, the system solicited and recorded questions asked by the participant.

The experiment was run as a 2 × 2, within-subjects study focused on children aged 5–8. Results indicate that a multi-character, distributed telling of the story is more engaging than a narrator-only telling, based on gaze behavior. The impact of nonverbal communication appears complicated, as the additional animation of a conversational turn handover can hold student attention, rather than directing it at the intended target. However, there is some evidence that question prompting gestures can help elicit feedback from children. Question elicitation at the end of the story resulted in questions 20% of the time, most of which (70%) where different types of *why* questions.

The results reported in this paper have implications for future automated and/or interactive storytelling applications. They suggest that presenting stories from multiple characters' first-person points of view is an effective way to increase student engagement. While question-prompting gestures may be a useful way to ellicit questions from students, it is unclear whether nonverbal turn-over gestures are an effective method for signalling the next speaker to children aged 5–8. The frequency and types of questions asked is useful for developing a conversational storytelling framework, which is a long-term aim of this project.

The contributions of this work are as follow:

- We show that a distributed storytelling model results in significantly higher engagement than a narrator-only model.
- We present data suggesting that question-prompting gestures may be effective for eliciting questions from children.
- We present the frequency and types of questions asked by children to an automated storytelling application.

- We present data showing that nonverbal turnover gestures may not be an effective method of signalling the next speaker to children aged 5–8.
- We demonstrate a webcam-based method for collecting gaze data, useful in certain experimental settings.

Fig. 1. Left: the laptop and camera placement used to collect video footage of the participants. Right: the video footage used to extract gaze targets. Inverted screen capture overlays are added in a post-processing step to provide additional context for the annotators.

2 Background

2.1 Automated Storytelling and Editing

Recognizing the importance of reading and storytelling for children's development, related work has also focused on improving children's reading skills. Project LISTEN was one of the first systems in this area: it aimed at computer tutors that could listen to a child read aloud and provide help where needed with pronunciation and other types of reading aloud errors [2,47]. Other work has focused on virtual peers for pedagogical purposes, and tested the effect of having the peer model more advanced storytelling behaviors [10,15,55]. Storytelling agents have also been explored with robots as reading companions and tutors [17,36,49,65], including studies placing robots in classrooms over extended period of time [32].

An automated storyteller could potentially tailor the text of a story based on the needs of the current user. Adjusting vocabulary level or narration point-of-view could result in a more effective and rewarding storytelling session. Due to the complexities of natural language, however, it is challenging to create robust methods for automatically editing text in non-trivial ways. Several researchers in the field of natural language processing have focused efforts on this problem. One set of researchers presented methods for automatically generating dialogues from monologues [51]. In another work, the author presented methods for generating full virtual-agent based performances, given only input text [50].

2.2 Eye Tracking in Multimedia Learning

Multimedia learning materials, which distribute conveyed information across multiple visual and/or audio channels, are widely used and are an effective way to foster meaningful learning outcomes in students [42]. In the past, the efficacy of such materials were commonly assessed using post-intervention interviews and behavioral assessments [53]. While such techniques are useful to measure the overall learning outcomes induced by the materials, they do not provide the resolution necessary to link detailed behaviors of a participant to on-screen causal elements [43]. Such linkages, and the insights they can provide, may aid in the creation of valuable design principles for different categories of multimedia applications.

An alternative to post-assessments is tracking participant gaze behavior. It is a useful measure for understanding how a viewer allocates their visual attention and how this engagement temporally fluctuates as a function of on-screen events [29]. Analyzing such engagement is particularly useful when developing design guidelines for interactive storytelling applications, whose primary purpose is fostering listening comprehension in the viewer. Such applications should engage the viewer without resorting to seductive details (motions or other stimuli that are pleasant but distracting, and which do not further comprehension).

While interest in eye tracking has increased rapidly in recent years [3], relatively few researchers have studied the eye movement of early grade school students interacting with multimedia stimuli [46,60]. Neither study reported eye tracking movement of students observing the stimuli in an in-use classroom. This may be due to the chaotic nature of such classroom, the expense and sensitivity of eye-tracking software, and the difficulty of properly calibrating and controlling the behaviors of a young child during a sedentary experiment. In contrast, the current study focuses on engagement and attention of early grade school students within in-use classrooms and makes use of multiple web cameras to record gaze behaviors.

2.3 Gesture

To further engage the child, we will endow the child-like narrator with nonverbal communication behaviors, as endorsed by the PAL framework [34] and other related work on pedagogical agents and agent personality [11,37,41]. Studies of teacher communication have found a cluster of nonverbal behaviors that are particularly effective in the teaching context. Termed "immediacy", these factors generate positive affect and include eye contact, smiling, vocal expressiveness, physical proximity, leaning towards a person, using appropriate gestures and being relaxed [5,6,33,58]. They are consistently shown to impact affective learning [7,18,54], which impacts students predisposition towards material and motivation to use knowledge [6,9]. Their impact on cognitive learning is less clear, with mixed findings [18,54]. Deictic (or pointing) gestures help ground the conversation by establishing shared reference [45] and can help children distinguish ambiguous speech sounds [61]. Speech that is accompanied by gesture leads to better recall than the same speech without gesture [13]. In teaching settings, gesture can provide a second representation, and multiple representations are known to enhance learning [23].

Beat gestures [45] are small, downward movements of the arms and hands that accompany the cadence of the speech and may add emphasis, but do not convey clear meaning. They are used in this work to make the characters appear more alive. Deictic gestures [45] are used to create reference, such as by pointing. Backchanneling, such as head nods and affirmative utterances, are used by the listener to signal their agreement with the speaker [66]. Conversational turn management in human dialog is largely nonverbal [66], motivating its use here.

3   Method

Participants. Participants from four K-2 classrooms in two schools in the United States participated in this experiment. Consent from school administration, classroom teachers, parents, and an institutional review board was obtained prior to the study. All participants spoke English and had normal or corrected-to-normal vision. In total, 33 participants, 12 girls and 21 boys, were included in the final analysis. Their ages ranged from 5–8 years old (M = 6.4, SD = 1.05).

Design. The study used a 2×2 experimental design in which every participant observed all four stimuli combinations. A within-subjects design was used to minimize sources of non task-related variance, such as participant's base attention spans or moods on the day of the experiment. The first factor was **Storytelling Perspective**, which employed a **Narrator Only** level and a **Distributed** level. The second factor was **Gesture Types**, which employed a **Complex Gesture** level and a **Simple Gesture** level. A single story was used for each condition combination (see Fig. 2).

Materials. Four Aesop's Fables were selected for use in the experiment. Aesop's Fables are commonly used in studies on (oral) narrative comprehension and are often used in teaching materials for the K-2 age group. We selected four fables that could be animated using Narrator, Fox and Crow characters. These were *The Fox and the Grapes*, *The Fox and the Crow*, *The Dog and His Shadow* and *The Crow and the Pitcher*. The fable *The Dog and his Shadow* was converted to *The Fox and his Shadow* in order to use the Fox's character model and gestures.

The original text of the stories came from the versions of Aesop's Fables distributed as part of Elson's Drama Bank [1, 21]. For each story we produced (by hand) a version of the story with simpler sentences and simpler vocabulary: these story versions were double-checked by a learning scientist for their age appropriateness. Because all the original stories are presented in third person by a narrator, we used the Fabula tales natural language generation engine to generate first person direct versions of story sentences for half of the stories [39, 40].

Figure 2 provides examples of how each story was told and how the content was distributed amongst the characters. In the **Narrator Only** condition the

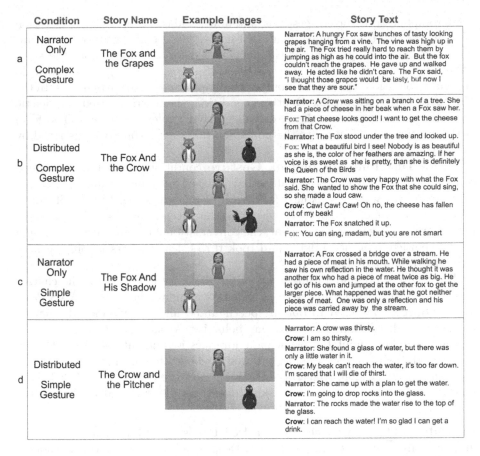

Condition	Story Name	Example Images	Story Text
a Narrator Only / Complex Gesture	The Fox and the Grapes		**Narrator**: A hungry Fox saw bunches of tasty looking grapes hanging from a vine. The vine was high up in the air. The Fox tried really hard to reach them by jumping as high as he could into the air. But the fox couldn't reach the grapes. He gave up and walked away. He acted like he didn't care. The Fox said, "I thought those grapes would be tasty, but now I see that they are sour."
b Distributed / Complex Gesture	The Fox And the Crow		**Narrator**: A Crow was sitting on a branch of a tree. She had a piece of cheese in her beak when a Fox saw her. **Fox**: That cheese looks good! I want to get the cheese from that Crow. **Narrator**: The Fox stood under the tree and looked up. **Fox**: What a beautiful bird I see! Nobody is as beautiful as she is, the color of her feathers are amazing. If her voice is as sweet as she is pretty, than she is definitely the Queen of the Birds **Narrator**: The Crow was very happy with what the Fox said. She wanted to show the Fox that she could sing, so she made a loud caw. **Crow**: Caw! Caw! Caw! Oh no, the cheese has fallen out of my beak! **Narrator**: The Fox snatched it up. **Fox**: You can sing, madam, but you are not smart
c Narrator Only / Simple Gesture	The Fox And His Shadow		**Narrator**: A Fox crossed a bridge over a stream. He had a piece of meat in his mouth. While walking he saw his own reflection in the water. He thought it was another fox who had a piece of meat twice as big. He let go of his own and jumped at the other fox to get the larger piece. What happened was that he got neither pieces of meat. One was only a reflection and his piece was carried away by the stream.
d Distributed / Simple Gesture	The Crow and the Pitcher		**Narrator**: A crow was thirsty. **Crow**: I am so thirsty. **Narrator**: She found a glass of water, but there was only a little water in it. **Crow**: My beak can't reach the water, it's too far down. I'm scared that I will die of thirst. **Narrator**: She came up with a plan to get the water. **Crow**: I'm going to drop rocks into the glass. **Narrator**: The rocks made the water rise to the top of the glass. **Crow**: I can reach the water! I'm so glad I can get a drink.

Fig. 2. Overview of the conditions, along with story names, example images, and story text. Example image in row A shows the *Question Gesture* and example images in row B show *Nonverbal Turnover Gestures*.

Narrator recounted the entire story (see Rows a and c of Fig. 2). The Narrator refers to the story characters in third person, and all utterances and gestures are produced by the Narrator. The story characters appear on the screen but do not speak.

The first person, direct speech, versions of the stories are used in the **Distributed** condition, and thus the story telling is split between the onscreen characters (Rows b and d of Fig. 2). The Narrator only produces the utterances that describe actions. Utterances that provide content for character speech and thought are converted to first person direct speech and spoken by the character to whom the speech or thought is attributed, e.g. *What a beautiful bird I see! Nobody is as beautiful ...* in Row b of Fig. 2.

While all stories employed character blinks, idle breathing motions, and minor head/arm beat gestures, the **Complex Gesture** condition included three different types of gestures not present in the **Simple Gesture** condition: question prompt gestures, deictic gestures, and nonverbal turnover gestures. Question prompt gestures (see example image of Fig. 2-a) were performed by the Narrator while she verbally prompted the participants for questions about the story (*"Now tell me, do you have any questions about the story?"*); in the **Simple Gesture** condition, the Narrator only verbally prompted the participants. In the **Narrator Only, Complex Gesture** condition, the Narrator used two deictic gestures, pointing towards the Fox, while verbally referring to him. The form of this gesture was identical to the *nonverbal turnover gesture* demonstrated by the Narrator in Fig. 2-b.

In the **Distributed, Complex Gesture** condition, characters performed conversational turnover gestures after they finished speaking, visually indicating which character would speak next (see example images in Fig. 2-b). In all stories there was a pause of 1.2 s between when one character stopped speaking and the next character began. When present, the conversational turnover gestures began as the character finished talking and took 0.75 s, leaving 0.5 s before the next character began to speak.

Stories were presented using a custom-built Unity application. The characters, story text, and gestures were provided as input to the system. AWS Polly Text-to-Speech was used to obtain speech audio and the viseme information necessary to drive character lip syncing behavior. At the end of each story, the Narrator would prompt the participant for questions about the story. During this period, the researcher used an external keyboard to control the Narrator in a *Wizard of Oz* fashion, triggering verbal and nonverbal backchanneling behaviors. After the child was finished asking questions, the researcher initiated the next story.

Procedure. Stimuli were shown on a Dell Precision laptop with 17 in. screen in a partially secluded classroom corner. Despite this separation, other students would sometimes distract the participant with their presence, actions, and noises. This environment therefore contained the same types of distractions that a child would experience while reading or working in school.

Upon starting the experiment, each participant watched an introductory segment in which the Narrator introduced herself, explained that she would be telling stories, and invited the participant to ask questions at the end of each story. Then all four stories were shown sequentially. Order was randomized to control for ordering effects. At the end of each story, the Narrator prompted the participant to ask any questions they had about the story. The entire procedure took, on average, 3.5 min. For an example screen recording showing the experimental stimuli presented to participants, please visit the following link: https://youtu.be/HEeQica-xHY.

Measures. Due to the in-classroom nature of our experiment, expensive, sensitive eye-tracking hardware was avoided. Rather, two webcams were positioned around the perimeter of the laptop screen to record the gaze behaviors of the participant (see Fig. 1-Left) for post-hoc annotation. Simultaneously, Open Broadcast Studio was used to record the contents of the screen. Taken together, this information was sufficient to determine when a participant was looking at the stimuli and at which character they were looking. See Fig. 1-Right for an example of the resulting video. The webcams also captured the questions each participant asked at the conclusion of each story.

Gaze Annotation. Two undergraduate annotators were hired to annotate gaze behaviors and transcribe the utterances of each participant. Based on the synced screen recording and dual webcam footage, annotators identified the participant's area of focus throughout the duration of the experiment by labeling it with one of four categories: *Narrator, Fox, Crow,* and *Non-Task. Non-Task* was used when the participant was not looking at any of the characters on the screen.

The data from one participant was used to train the annotators; both annotators, along with the lead researcher, collectively discussed and annotated the gaze behavior. Next, data from six participants (21 min, 19% of the remaining data) was independently annotated by each annotator. Inter-rater reliability was very high (observed agreement was 97% and Cohen's kappa was 0.93), so data from the remaining 26 participants was split between the annotators.

4 Results

4.1 Visual Attention

Attention To Story. Using the gaze annotations, it was possible to determine the percentage of time participants were actively observing each story (viewing a character versus viewing a *Non-Task* category). These are shown in Fig. 3. Summary attention statistics are given in Table 1.

To assess whether attention differed significantly as a function of condition, we conducted a Friedman test of differences using the single factor of 'Condition' with four levels. While a repeated measures ANOVA is commonly used in 2×2 within-factors designs, the percentage values analyzed were not normally distributed, and thus the non-parametric Friedman test was used instead. The test rendered a Chi-square value of 9.13, which was significant (p = 0.02). Post-hoc analysis using multiple Wilcox signed-rank tests with Bonferroni correction revealed multiple significant differences (Fig. 2, left). **Distributed, Complex Gesture** was significantly higher than both **Narrator Only, Simple Gesture** ($p_{adj} < 0.01$) and **Narrator Only, Complex Gesture** ($p_{adj} = 0.02$). **Distributed, Simple Gesture** was significantly higher than **Narrator Only, Simple Gesture** ($p_{adj} < 0.01$) and almost significantly higher than **Narrator Only, Complex Gesture** ($p_{adj} = 0.09$). Other differences were not significant.

Using the same technique, we evaluated the effect of order on attention (Fig. 2, right). As might be expected, attention wanes over time. Attention to the first story was significantly higher than to the third ($p_{adj} = 0.008$) and fourth ($p_{adj} = 0.006$) story, and marginally higher than to the second story ($p_{adj} = 0.10$).

Table 1. Left: summary statistics on the amount of attention paid to each story as a function of condition. Right: summary statistics on the amount of attention paid to each story as a function of story order.

	Condition				Order			
	Narrator, Complex	Narrator, Simple	Distributed, Complex	Distributed, simple	1	2	3	4
Mean	78.6%	79.5%	91.7%	89.9%	91.4%	85.2%	82.6%	80.5%
Standard deviation	19.3	21.8	8.0	7.9	10.8%	13.5%	18.6%	19.9%

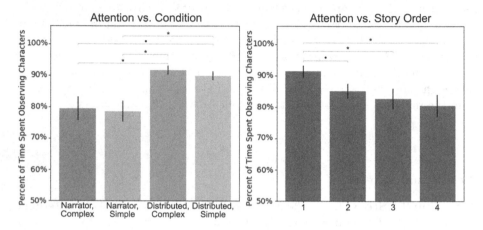

Fig. 3. The percentage of time students gazed at the *Narrator, Fox,* or *Crow* (as opposed to *Non-Task*) as a function of story condition. Error bars indicate standard error of the mean. Results significant at $p_{adj} < 0.05$ denoted by asterisk, result approaching significance at this level denoted by dot.

Gaze Behavior During Conversational Turnovers. We next used gaze information to evaluate differences in the amount of time it took participants to focus on the next speaker after a conversational turnover. Because these turnovers only occur when two or more characters take turns speaking, this analysis was conducted only on data obtained from the **Distributed** conditions.

For each conversational turnover, we determined the time at which the new character began to speak. We then calculated, relative to this point, the amount of time it took each participant to first glance at the new speaker. This value was positive if the speaker began talking before the participant looked to them and negative if the participant looked to the speaker before they began to speak.

Using these values, an independent samples t-test was conducted to compare the differences in gaze switching time between the **Distributed, Complex Gesture** condition and the **Distributed, Simple Gesture** condition. The results are shown in Table 2, top. There was a significant difference between these two conditions, with participants taking longer to switch their gaze to the new character in the **Distributed, Complex Gesture** condition.

Table 2. Summary statistics of the amount of time, in seconds, it took participants to switch their gaze to a new speaker after that speaker first began their conversational turn. The top row compares instances in which turnover gestures were present to instances in which the gesture was absent. The bottom row compares turnovers to the Narrator with turnovers to the Fox or the Crow.

	Mean	Standard deviation	P value	T statistic
Distributed, Complex Gesture	0.71	1.47	0.004	2.88
Distributed, Simple Gesture	0.19	1.86		
Turnover to Narrator	1.15	1.64	<0.001	7.72
Turnover to Fox or Crow	−0.08	1.55		

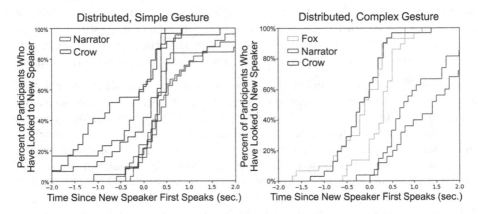

Fig. 4. Cumulative distributions functions showing the percentage of participants who looked to the next speaker relative to when the speaker began talking. Each line indicates a single conversational turnover from the story.

Table 3. Count of questions asked, separated by **Gesture** condition level.

	Question asked	No question asked	P value	Chi squared statistic
Complex gesture	18	48	0.052	3.77
Simple gesture	9	57		

After visual inspection of the cumulative distributions of gaze switching vs. time (as shown in Fig. 4), it appeared that, when the Narrator took over speaking, participants turned their gaze back to her more slowly and less frequently that with the other two characters. We therefore conducted a t-test to determine if this difference was significant. The results are shown in Table 2, bottom. Participants took significantly longer to turn their gaze back to the speaker when the new speaker was the Narrator ($p < 0.001$). This could be because the participants were less interested in the Narrator (as they see her in every story), participants were more intrigued by the animal characters, and/or participants were more interested in the story characters.

4.2   Question Analysis

Question Frequency. In this study, we only elicited questions from participants at the end of the story. This protocol created 132 possible question opportunities and resulted in 27 questions. 17 participants asked no questions, eight asked one, six asked two, one asked three, and one asked four. To assess whether the **Complex Gesture** condition (and the question prompt gesture it contained) influenced participant's tendency to ask questions, we performed a chi-squared independence test. The results are given in Table 3. While the $p = 0.05$ level of significance was narrowly missed, this could be due to the small total number of questions collected. A larger sampling may reveal that the question prompt gesture is a clear visual indicator encouraging children to interact with the system.

Question Type. We conducted an analysis of the types of questions the children asked in order to determine the needed future capabilities of a conversational storytelling system that can answer questions as the story unfolds. We expected questions about comprehension, and two main types: (1) questions based on understanding the meaning of sentences, based on vocabulary or syntax within a sentence; (2) questions based on inferring causality, since that is a key part of understanding narrative [12, 22, 24]. Our goal is to support these kind of questions from students in a future version of our system, as well as to add question categories based on these to the narrator's repertoire. Examples are shown in Table 4. Q1 illustrates a comprehension question. We expect these would be more frequent if we allowed questions as the story unfolds. There were 19 *why* questions of different types. Questions Q2, Q3 and Q4 illustrate the 12 *why* questions related to causal understanding about how the world works or failure to fill in implicit actions or state changes. Q2 illustrates a very simple causal inference: the Fox is described as *hungry* but two participants asked why the Fox wanted the grapes, while the others involve complex causal reasoning. The other question types target unexpected competencies that would be hard to support in our future conversational storyteller. Q5 and Q6 illustrate the 5 questions about the back-story, about how the situation came to be at the start of the narrative, which is not part of the story content. There were also 5 questions about what might happen in the story world after the end of the story (*What Next*): this is illustrated by questions Q7 and Q8. This could partly be due to the fact that we only asked questions at the end of the story. Finally, in Q9 and Q10 the participants question presuppositions of the story, i.e. that a Fox wouldn't recognize his reflection, and that birds can sing, rather than simply chirp.

Table 4. Example Questions from Participants

ID	N	Type	Example
Q1	1	Comprehension	What is a vine? (vocabulary)
Q2	12	Why,	Why did the Fox try to get the grapes? (hungry)
Q3		Causal chain	Why did the Fox get the cheese?
Q4			Why did she put rocks in the water? That sounds gross.
Q5	5	Why, BackStory	How did the Crow get the cheese?
Q6			Why was the Crow so thirsty?
Q7	5	What Next	Is he going to get the water?
Q8			The Fox will eat the bird?
Q9	2	Why, storyline	Why wouldn't the Fox know that it was his reflection?
Q10			How is the Fox able to listen to the bird sing when a bird can only chirp?

5 Conclusion

The greater visual attention children paid to stories presented in first-person by story characters, in addition to the narrator, suggest that such distribution of storytelling may be an effective approach for building engagement. Gaze analysis also showed that children switched attention more quickly to story characters than to the narrator. The use of intentional gestures presents a mixed picture. It appears that gestures to the child are helpful in eliciting questions. Gestures for conversational turn management appeared to hold children's interest, rather than directing them to the next character to speak.

Children did ask questions of the system some of the time and these were frequently *why* questions. In future work we plan to elicit questions and ask questions **during** the storytelling at particular story points, rather than simply at the end of the story. We expect this to increase children's engagement with the story, and hopefully increase their narrative comprehension. We also wish to study deixis in cases where it is non-redundant with the text.

References

1. Aesop, Jones, V.S.V., Rackham, A., Chesterton, G.K.: Aesop's Fables: A New Translation. W. Heinemann, Portsmouth (1933)
2. Aist, G., Kort, B., Reilly, R., Mostow, J., Picard, R.: Experimentally augmenting an intelligent tutoring system with human-supplied capabilities: adding human-provided emotional scaffolding to an automated reading tutor that listens. In: Proceedings of Fourth IEEE International Conference on Multimodal Interfaces, pp. 483–490. IEEE (2002)
3. Alemdag, E., Cagiltay, K.: A systematic review of eye tracking research on multimedia learning. Comput. Educ. **125**, 413–428 (2018)
4. Alexander, K.L., Entwisle, D.R., Dauber, S.L.: First-grade classroom behavior: its short-and long-term consequences for school performance. Child Dev. **64**(3), 801–814 (1993)

5. Andersen, J.F.: The relationship between teacher immediacy and teaching effectiveness. Ph.D. thesis, ProQuest Information & Learning (1979)
6. Andersen, J.F.: Instructor nonverbal communication: listening to our silent messages. New Direct. Teach. Learning **1986**(26), 41–49 (1986)
7. Andersen, J.F., Norton, R.W., Nussbaum, J.F.: Three investigations exploring relationships between perceived teacher communication behaviors and student learning. Commun. Educ. **30**(4), 377–392 (1981)
8. August, D., Hakuta, K.: Improving schooling for language minority students: a research agenda. A Research Agenda, Improving Schooling for Language Minority Students (1997)
9. Baylor, A.L.: Promoting motivation with virtual agents and avatars: role of visual presence and appearance. Philos. Trans. Roy. Soc. London B: Biol. Sci. **364**(1535), 3559–3565 (2009)
10. Baylor, A.L., Kim, Y.: Pedagogical agent design: the impact of agent realism, gender, ethnicity, and instructional role. In: Lester, J.C., Vicari, R.M., Paraguaçu, F. (eds.) ITS 2004. LNCS, vol. 3220, pp. 592–603. Springer, Heidelberg (2004). https://doi.org/10.1007/978-3-540-30139-4_56
11. Baylor, A.L., Ryu, J.: The effects of image and animation in enhancing pedagogical agent persona. J. Educ. Comput. Res. **28**(4), 373–394 (2003)
12. Bloom, C.P., Fletcher, C.R., Broek, P.V.D., Reitz, L., Shapiro, B.P.: An on-line assessment of causal reasoning during comprehension. J. Mem. Cogn. **18**, 65–71 (1990)
13. Breckinridge Church, R., Garber, P., Rogalski, K.: The role of gesture in memory and social communication. Gesture **7**(2), 137–158 (2007)
14. Brooks-Gunn, J., Duncan, G.J.: The effects of poverty on children. Future Child. **7**, 55–71 (1997)
15. Cassell, J.: Towards a model of technology and literacy development: story listening systems. J. Appl. Dev. Psychol. **25**(1), 75–105 (2004)
16. Catts, H.W., Adlof, S.M., Hogan, T.P., Weismer, S.E.: Are specific language impairment and dyslexia distinct disorders? J. Speech Lang. Hear. Res. **48**(6), 1378–1396 (2005)
17. Chang, A., Breazeal, C.: TinkRBook: shared reading interfaces for storytelling. In: Proceedings of the 10th International Conference on Interaction Design and Children, pp. 145–148. ACM (2011)
18. Chesebro, J.L.: Effects of teacher clarity and nonverbal immediacy on student learning, receiver apprehension, and affect. Commun. Educ. **52**(2), 135–147 (2003)
19. Cunningham, A.E., Stanovich, K.E.: Early reading acquisition and its relation to reading experience and ability 10 years later. Dev. Psychol. **33**(6), 934 (1997)
20. Duncan, G.J., et al.: School readiness and later achievement. Dev. Psychol. **43**(6), 1428 (2007)
21. Elson, D.: DramaBank: annotating agency in narrative discourse. In: LREC, pp. 2813–2819 (2012)
22. Fletcher, C.R., Hummel, J.E., Marsolek, C.J.: Causality and the allocation of attention during comprehension. J. Exp. Psychol. **16**(2), 233–240 (1990)
23. Goldin-Meadow, S., Singer, M.A.: From children's hands to adults' ears: gesture's role in the learning process. Dev. Psychol. **39**(3), 509 (2003)
24. Graesser, A.C., Singer, M., Trabasso, T.: Constructing inferences during narrative text comprehension. Psychol. Rev. **101**(3), 371 (1994)
25. Hart, B., Risley, T.R.: Meaningful Differences in the Everyday Experience of Young American Children. Paul H Brookes Publishing, Baltimore (1995)

26. Hoff, E.: Environmental supports for language acquisition. Handb. Early Lit. Res. **2**, 163–172 (2006)
27. Hoff, E., Naigles, L.: How children use input to acquire a lexicon. Child Dev. **73**(2), 418–433 (2002)
28. Hoover, W.A., Gough, P.B.: The simple view of reading. Read. Writ. **2**(2), 127–160 (1990)
29. Hyönä, J.: The use of eye movements in the study of multimedia learning. Learn. Instr. **20**(2), 172–176 (2010)
30. Juel, C.: Learning to read and write: a longitudinal study of 54 children from first through fourth grades. J. Educ. Psychol. **80**(4), 437 (1988)
31. Juel, C., Griffith, P.L., Gough, P.B.: Acquisition of literacy: a longitudinal study of children in first and second grade. J. Educ. Psychol. **78**(4), 243 (1986)
32. Kanda, T., Hirano, T., Eaton, D., Ishiguro, H.: Interactive robots as social partners and peer tutors for children: a field trial. Hum.-Comput. interact. **19**(1), 61–84 (2004)
33. Kennedy, J., Baxter, P., Belpaeme, T.: Nonverbal immediacy as a characterisation of social behaviour for human-robot interaction. Int. J. Social Robot. **9**(1), 109–128 (2017)
34. Kim, Y., Baylor, A.L.: A social-cognitive framework for pedagogical agents as learning companions. Educ. Tech. Research Dev. **54**(6), 569–596 (2006)
35. Korenman, S., Miller, J.E., Sjaastad, J.E.: Long-term poverty and child development in the united states: Results from the nlsy. Child Youth Serv. Rev. **17**(1–2), 127–155 (1995)
36. Kory, J., Breazeal, C.: Storytelling with robots: learning companions for preschool children's language development. In: The 23rd IEEE International Symposium on Robot and Human Interactive Communication, RO-MAN 2014, pp. 643–648. IEEE (2014)
37. Lee, K.M., Peng, W., Jin, S.A., Yan, C.: Can robots manifest personality?: An empirical test of personality recognition, social responses, and social presence in human-robot interaction. J. Commun. **56**(4), 754–772 (2006)
38. Literacy, D.E.: Report of the national early literacy panel Washington. DC National Institute for Literacy (2008)
39. Lukin, S.M., Reed, L.I., Walker, M.: Generating sentence planning variations for story telling. In: 16th Annual Meeting of the Special Interest Group on Discourse and Dialogue, p. 188 (2015)
40. Lukin, S.M., Walker, M.A.: A narrative sentence planner and structurer for domain independent, parameterizable storytelling. Dialogue Discourse **10**(1), 34–86 (2019)
41. Mairesse, F., Walker, M.A.: Towards personality-based user adaptation: psychologically informed stylistic language generation. User Model. User-Adapt. Interact. **20**(3), 227–278 (2010)
42. Mayer, R.E.: Cognitive theory of multimedia learning. Cambridge Handb. Multimed. Learn. **41**, 31–48 (2005)
43. Mayer, R.E.: Using multimedia for e-learning. J. Comput. Assist. Learn. **33**(5), 403–423 (2017)
44. McLoyd, V.C.: Socioeconomic disadvantage and child development. Am. Psychol. **53**(2), 185 (1998)
45. McNeill, D.: Hand and Mind: What Gestures Reveal about Thought. University of Chicago Press, Chicago (1992)
46. Molina, A.I., Navarro, S., Ortega, M., Lacruz, M.: Evaluating multimedia learning materials in primary education using eye tracking. Comput. Stand. Interfaces **59**(C), 45–60 (2018). https://doi.org/10.1016/j.csi.2018.02.004

47. Mostow, J., et al.: Evaluation of an automated reading tutor that listens: Comparison to human tutoring and classroom instruction. J. Educ. Comput. Res. **29**(1), 61–117 (2003)
48. NICHD Early Child Care Research Network, et al.: Child Care And Child Development: Results from the NICHD Study of Early Child Care and Youth Development. Guilford Press (2005)
49. Park, H.W., Gelsomini, M., Lee, J.J., Breazeal, C.: Telling stories to robots: the effect of backchanneling on a child's storytelling. In: Proceedings of the 2017 ACM/IEEE International Conference on Human-Robot Interaction, pp. 100–108. ACM (2017)
50. Piwek, P., Hernault, H., Prendinger, H., Ishizuka, M.: T2D: generating dialogues between virtual agents automatically from text. In: Pelachaud, C., Martin, J.-C., André, E., Chollet, G., Karpouzis, K., Pelé, D. (eds.) IVA 2007. LNCS (LNAI), vol. 4722, pp. 161–174. Springer, Heidelberg (2007). https://doi.org/10.1007/978-3-540-74997-4_16
51. Piwek, P., Stoyanchev, S.: Generating expository dialogue from monologue: motivation, corpus and preliminary rules. In: Human Language Technologies: The 2010 Annual Conference of the North American Chapter of the Association for Computational Linguistics, pp. 333–336. Association for Computational Linguistics (2010)
52. Ritchie, S.J., Bates, T.C.: Enduring links from childhood mathematics and reading achievement to adult socioeconomic status. Psychol. Sci. **24**(7), 1301–1308 (2013)
53. Rodrigues, P., Rosa, P.J.: Eye-tracking as a research methodology in educational context: a spanning framework. In: Eye-Tracking Technology Applications in Educational Research, pp. 1–26. IGI Global (2017)
54. Rodríguez, J.I., Plax, T.G., Kearney, P.: Clarifying the relationship between teacher nonverbal immediacy and student cognitive learning: affective learning as the central causal mediator. Commun. Educ. **45**(4), 293–305 (1996)
55. Ryokai, K., Vaucelle, C., Cassell, J.: Virtual peers as partners in storytelling and literacy learning. J. Comput. Assist. Learn. **19**(2), 195–208 (2003)
56. Snow, C.E., Burns, M.S., Griffin, P.: Preventing reading difficulties in young children committee on the prevention of reading difficulties in young children. National Research Council, Washington, DC (1998)
57. Sperry, D.E., Sperry, L.L., Miller, P.J.: Reexamining the verbal environments of children from different socioeconomic backgrounds. Child Dev. **90**(4), 1303–1318 (2019). https://doi.org/10.1111/cdev.13072. https://onlinelibrary.wiley.com/doi/abs/10.1111/cdev.13072
58. Staudte, M., Crocker, M.W., Heloir, A., Kipp, M.: The influence of speaker gaze on listener comprehension: contrasting visual versus intentional accounts. Cognition **133**(1), 317–328 (2014)
59. Storch, S.A., Whitehurst, G.J.: Oral language and code-related precursors to reading: evidence from a longitudinal structural model. Dev. Psychol. **38**(6), 934 (2002)
60. Takacs, Z.K., Bus, A.G.: Benefits of motion in animated storybooks for children visual attention and story comprehension. An eye-tracking study. Front. Psychol. **7**, 1591 (2016)
61. Thompson, L.A., Massaro, D.W.: Children's integration of speech and pointing gestures in comprehension. J. Exp. Child Psychol. **57**(3), 327–354 (1994)
62. Torgesen, J.K.: Avoiding the devastating downward spiral: the evidence that early intervention prevents reading failure. Am. Educat. **28**(3), 6–19 (2004)

63. Vellutino, F.R., Scanlon, D.M., Zhang, H.: Identifying reading disability based on response to intervention: evidence from early intervention research. In: Jimerson, S.R., Burns, M.K., VanDerHeyden, A.M. (eds.) Handbook of Response to Intervention, pp. 185–211. Springer, Boston (2007). https://doi.org/10.1007/978-0-387-49053-3_14

64. Wertheimer, R.F., Moore, K.A., Hair, E.C., Croan, T.: Attending kindergarten and already behind: a statistical portrait of vulnerable young children. Child Trends Washington, DC (2003)

65. Westlund, J.K., Breazeal, C.: The interplay of robot language level with children's language learning during storytelling. In: Proceedings of the Tenth Annual ACM/IEEE International Conference on Human-Robot Interaction Extended Abstracts, pp. 65–66. ACM (2015)

66. Whittaker, S.: Theories and methods in mediated communication: Steve Whittaker. In: Handbook of Discourse Processes, pp. 246–289. Routledge (2003)

67. Zill, N.: Promoting educational equity and excellence in kindergarten. Transit. Kindergart. 67–105 (1999)

Dungeon on the Move: A Case Study of a Procedurally Driven Narrative Project in Progress

Maurice Suckling(✉)

RPI, Troy, NY 12180, USA
Sucklm@rpi.edu

Abstract. *Dungeon on the Move* is a single-player casual mobile game dungeon crawler in development, in which the dungeon itself is in flux – rooms change, they disappear, and even the room the player is trying to reach won't stay still. This paper concerns a case study of an in-development project that seeks to explore the creative opportunities in blending a procedurally generated dungeon with a partially procedurally generated story. It explores the research question: *How might we design a simple digital dungeon crawler utilizing a procedurally driven narrative that offers some promise of innovation?* It provides a brief explanation of terms then explores details of the development, anticipated difficulties, with a view to next steps on the project.

Keywords: Dungeon crawler · Procedural storytelling

1 The Research Question

Late 2018 a small team was assembled at RPI, New York, to answer this question[1]:

How might we design a simple digital dungeon crawler utilizing a procedurally driven narrative that offers some promise of innovation?

Why? Dungeon crawlers are staple fare for gamers with well-worn tropes. Leveraging these tropes might offer opportunities in storytelling, perhaps beyond pastiche or parody, and, through the procedurally driven element, into a narrative experience that feels different to players. Rooting the research within such a familiar area for gamers, would, it was felt, ensure the architecture of the narrative wasn't being pushed too far too fast, so that a great deal was implicitly being promised which the research question ultimately could not deliver on. Procedurally driven stories offer a rich field of learning - the development of them, their execution, and player reception of them is still a relatively nascent field (Fig. 1).

2 Explanation of Terms

Dungeon Crawler: a game type where players control one or more characters with whom they explore a dungeon, or series of dungeons, fighting monsters, perhaps

---

[1] Maurice Suckling, Fanghong Dong, Rachel Mailhot, Kirsten Pilla, Samuel Gould, Yi Ning, Yizhe Wu, Leonardo Price, and Yueqing Dai.

R. E. Cardona-Rivera et al. (Eds.): ICIDS 2019, LNCS 11869, pp. 144–147, 2019.
https://doi.org/10.1007/978-3-030-33894-7_15

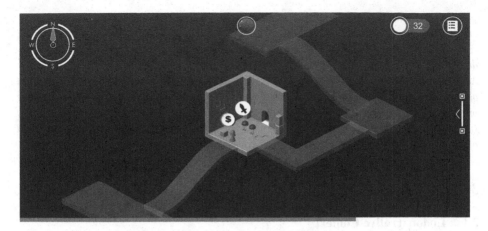

Fig. 1. Screenshot, work in progress

encountering other challenges, and collecting treasure (perhaps of various kinds) as a reward.

Video game examples: Wizardry (1981), Diablo II (2000), Bastion (2011), Baldur's Gate II (2013), The Binding of Isaac: Rebirth (2014), Darkest Dungeon (2016).

Board game examples: The Sorcerer's Cave (1978), The Tomb of Annihilation (2017).

Analog RPG examples: Four Against Darkness (2016), Labyrinth (2016).

Simple: *the team focused on a 'simple' dungeon crawler, meaning without deep character progression (leveling up, or skill trees), resource management, and without sophisticated action gameplay and 3D graphics. In addition, although its story promised to be partially procedurally driven, the team were not promising this element would be complex either. This was to be a small research project with a small team with modest and reachable goals.*

Procedurally Driven Narrative: *in this project, we would see a procedurally driven narrative as constituting one experienced by the player as a result of their actions in conjunction with probability-triggered systems [1]. The narrative would not be built by an artificial intelligence. Nor would an AI adapt in complex ways to game states. This is procedurally generated AI as a production system, built on probability triggers.*

Innovation: *dungeon crawlers have a tendency to culminate in predictable ways: having passed through a series of scripted challenges of escalating difficulty a final boss battle brings the adventure to an end; having accumulated sufficient experience points (EXP) a final battle is triggered bringing the adventure to an end; or some combination of those two. Unscripted digital dungeon crawlers can exist as near-infinite loops of monster > level-up > monster inside random dungeon creation algorithms but with questionable incentives to keep playing within them. Similarly, at least as far back as 1975, a year after D&D's first publication, unscripted solo play analog dungeon crawlers have had a known propensity to expend the surprises their systems self-circumscribe [2].*

It isn't essential for us to find solutions to all of these issues, or indeed any. But we are looking for something innovative to come from our enquiry, perhaps from novel combinations of design and narrative elements. In particular it's the sense of something innovative that we're pushing. Our game is still, at heart, an EXP trawl. Acquiring EXP is how game progress is still marked. Yet this will be masked from players and our intention is to misdirect them so they believe they are solving the puzzle of the dungeon pathing, which they are not. We're interested in learning if this subterfuge is quickly identified, and, for the duration its ruse is maintained, what kind of responses it provokes in players.

3   Development

3.1   Ludonarrative Context

The game opens with text on screen:

> *One thousand years ago Loco, a fearsome Mage was born - with powers so frightful they were interned in the highest security dungeon imaginable - a cube with magical properties.*

This mage has now managed to take control of this dungeon and can soon be expected to break out from it. The player, through their character Pita, is tasked with entering the dungeon to confront the mage before their powers are fully restored, and to re-imprison the mage.

Pita moves through a series of three linked dungeons, each with their own distinct identity as an environment with a related set of monsters. Different monsters reward players with different levels of EXP, and different kinds of rewards. Certain EXP thresholds trigger crystal ball (CB) interactions with a quest-giver character and trigger parts of a probability-built encounter story composed of four parts. Further EXP thresholds unlock target rooms, giving access to a new sub-section of a dungeon. Each dungeon culminates in a boss battle with the main antagonist. But the antagonist would remain alive, even in defeat, through various narrative means.

The dungeon is presented as a kind of maze, and the designated 'target rooms' are where the player is trying to direct Pita to. But a central design element we incorporated (indeed central to the entire ludonarrative theme, carried within the game's title) was of the dungeon being not just a conventional challenge - with monsters - but to be a kind of puzzle in its own right - presented as a kind of maze - but not actually a maze. It is not a pathing puzzle. There are no environmental challenges to overcome. Instead the dungeon is built - or appears to players to be built - through procedural generation, and not only do rooms seem to appear as they progress, but rooms change (from a swamp, to a grove, or cave to a desert, for example), and they may remain the same size but become flooded. More than that they also disappear entirely, and players are forced to navigate around them because even the room they are trying to get to doesn't stay in the same place - it moves - or at least appears to move - around the dungeon, as if aware it is being chased.

The core loop is:

MOVE > FIGHT/BRIBE/BUY > EXP > UNLOCK ENCOUNTER > MOVE

3.2 Anticipated Difficulties

Difficulties are expected in managing player frustration - the way the target room moves. Not enough and there is nothing new for the player to feel. Too much and the player will become frustrated by the game. A connected issue is that of pacing. To keep the game feeling engaging a balance will need to be struck between the speed of the overall game and the repetitive nature of the player actions. To (See game loop above.)

In addition, combinatorial growth while retaining narrative cohesion is a known issue. We intend to prevent it becoming unmanageable by limiting the number of encounters. Further, narrative cohesion is assisted by the tone of voice used, which is generally somewhat comic, and allows for a breadth of encounters working within known tropes. There are also known difficulties in screen space to communicate the story without voice over, and with reasonably minimal text, that still permits our tone of voice to come through.

3.3 Next Steps

There is clearly much more to be said. This poster has barely scratched the surface of the development process and the design elements being worked on.

The game is currently in early prototype form. The first third of the first dungeon will be playable as a proof of concept by late summer 2019. At this stage we can begin to gather findings to discover if we have found any answers to our initial research question, or to perhaps discern how far off acquiring answers we may be.

Following feedback and design iterations, research is intended to continue into late 2019 and into 2020.

References

1. Ryan, J.: UCSC, Curating Simulated Storyworlds, December 2018. https://escholarship.org/uc/item/1340j5h2. Accessed 10 Sept 2019
2. Gygax, G.: Solo dungeon adventures. The Strategic Review, vol. 1, no. 1. Spring (1975). https://annarchive.com/files/Strv101.pdf. Accessed 10 Sept 2019

Choose Your Permanent Adventure: Towards a Framework for Irreversible Storygames

Kenneth Tan[1,2] and Alex Mitchell[1(✉)]

[1] National University of Singapore, Singapore, Singapore
kennethetan@u.nus.edu, alexm@nus.edu.sg
[2] Nanyang Polytechnic, Singapore, Singapore
kenneth_tan@nyp.edu.sg

Abstract. The majority of interactive narrative games allow the player to save their progress as the game unfolds. These save game options are either automatically enforced or manual. However, there is an increasing trend for interactive narrative games to be 'irreversible'. In such cases, this makes it difficult for the player to load or access previous save games. As a result, the player's sense of agency changes within the game, as the stakes and consequences of their story decisions are more difficult to reverse, and thus take on a feeling of permanence. Through close readings of *The Walking Dead: Season One*, *Sorcery!* and *Undertale*, this paper aims to provide an initial framework for irreversible storygames by (i) defining the different types of irreversibility by analyzing three games in which the form of irreversibility differs, and (ii) exploring subjective factors of the user experience that may be impacted by the different types of irreversibility.

Keywords: Storygames · Irreversibility · Agency · Rereading · Replay

1 Introduction

As players exert agency in interactive narrative games and progress in the story, almost all games allow the player to save the game state for reloading or replay [1]. The option to save and load games can be considered a form of rereading since the reader has the option to re-experience the narrative and re-exert agency if they so choose.

However, recent trends in narrative games have seen the interval between save points in games extend into longer and longer space and time frames. As past save games and corresponding past story decisions become more difficult to access and change, the games become more "irreversible". This has a potential impact on agency, which Murray defines as "the satisfying power to take meaningful action and see the results of our decisions and choices" [2]. If the player finds it difficult, or even impossible, to change past choices, how does the player's perception of their choices change? Does the consideration of their choices change if they realize their decisions have permanent consequences? In this paper, we begin the process of classifying the types of irreversible narratives, and propose a preliminary framework for this classification, focusing specifically on single-player "storygames" [3].

© Springer Nature Switzerland AG 2019
R. E. Cardona-Rivera et al. (Eds.): ICIDS 2019, LNCS 11869, pp. 148–157, 2019.
https://doi.org/10.1007/978-3-030-33894-7_16

2   Related Work

Focusing on non-interactive stories, Călinescu [4] categorizes rereading into partial, simple and reflective rereading. Partial rereading involves trying to clarify details or understand information previously missed. In simple reading, the reader tries to recapture the experience of the story. In reflective rereading, the reader is stepping back to analyze the story or text. Mitchell explores rereading in interactive narratives [5], pointing out that "readers who are rereading to find closure are involved in what is equivalent to Călinescu's partial rereading. It is only when they achieve closure that they can potentially shift to either simple or reflective rereading". He also highlights that "rereading, rather than involving reading something again, instead involves reading anew."

Research has also been conducted on reader motivations to reread in interactive narratives. Academics such as Selig [6] and Peacock [7] assert that the multiple meanings and challenges encountered by the reader motivate rereading, while Murray [2, 8, 9] feels that the reader enjoys repeating the story from different perspectives. Ryan sees replayability as a key feature of interactive stories, as it is "only by replaying... several times, by seeing different story variants develop, and by receiving response to her input that the user will be convinced she exercises true agency" [10]. Douglas [11] points out that readers reread hypertext fiction, not to experience variation but to seek closure.

The concept of rewinding time in order to progress the narrative has been studied by Kleinman [12]. Kleinman has created a framework of the time rewind mechanic used in games, covering different ways game designers have implemented the concept. While irreversible games do not necessarily require the rewind of time to progress, two of the three games researched in this paper have implemented this mechanic.

3   Research Question

Loading a save game file in storygames is akin to rereading, as the player re-experiences the narrative. Research has been conducted on reader motivation and satisfaction in re-experiencing traditional text and interactive narratives, as well as the role of save games in the player experience. "Rewinding" has also been researched as a narrative mechanic within a storygame. However, what the player experiences by *not* having the option to go back, as well as what would constitute such an "irreversible" storygame, has not been studied. What factors would a storygame designer need to implement to make the player see the game as "irreversible? The objective of this paper is to develop a preliminary framework to characterize what constitutes an "irreversible" storygame.

4   Methodology

Bizzocchi and Tanenbaum's close reading approach [13] was used to analyze a set of games, namely: *The Walking Dead: Season One* [14], *Sorcery!* [15] and *Undertale* [16]. Close reading is a technique adapted from the humanities, one that provides for rich insights into a particular play experience. It involves the construction of analytical lenses, the performance of an imagined naïve player and the construction of performative player stereotypes. The approach does not, and we do not, attempt to claim that insights gained from close readings are immediately or directly generalizable. This paper is a preliminary attempt to establish a framework for irreversible storygames.

The games analyzed in this paper were selected as they each address a different aspect of irreversibility. *The Walking Dead* was chosen as it autosaves your progress and tries to simulate an interactive "TV series" experience. The *Sorcery!* Series was chosen as the game initially allows you to backtrack through your save checkpoints via a timeline, and gives the player the option to load his game all the way to the beginning of the current part or chapter of the series. This is possible until a crucial point in the story - the entrance to the fortress of Mampang in *Sorcery! Part 4: The Crown of Kings* [17]. *Undertale* was chosen because the game remembers every decision you made, and reminds you of your past story decisions even when you start a new playthrough.

The close readings were conducted by the first author, and are presented in the first person to reflect this. Tanenbaum proposed the notion of using "analytical lens" to create 'constrained close readings' for storygames [18]. The "analytical lens" used in this research would be in the field of 'irreversibility' – we define this as "a factor which discourages or prevents the player from loading a previous save game." Each playthrough was played until the point whereby the researcher found it "exceedingly difficult or frustrating" to access a previous save game. Despite this, the researcher attempted to access a previous save game and conduct at least one more playthrough. Questions focused on include: Do I want to access my previous save game or conduct another playthrough, despite my frustration in doing so? Why or why not? What are my experiences, emotions and attitude toward the game on the second playthrough with regards to the game choices I am making, in particular, regarding with my ability to influence what I perceive as diegetic choices? Are my choices meaningful? Is the story I am creating significant to me, or is it the game designer's story?

In the following sections, we discuss the results of these close readings.

5   *Undertale*: Restricted Saves and Limited Access to Saves

In *Undertale* there are two main ways that the game creates a sense of irreversibility: restricting the player to only a single, manual save game, and limiting the player's access to the save state. Both of these limit the player's ability to "go back" in the game.

Undertale only allows one save game at any point of time in the game, i.e. there are no multiple save games, and you can only play one character. There are checkpoints scattered throughout the game at regular intervals which give you the option to save your game. The player is only able to manually save the game at these checkpoints.

By following a "one save game" rule, the game does not allow you to revisit story decisions made before your last checkpoint save. This made me feel very cautious in actually saving the game when I came to a checkpoint. Once the game was saved, there was no option of reloading a previously played checkpoint, making it feel irreversible.

For example, in an encounter with Papyrus, a skeleton NPC who is determined to capture you in order to achieve his dream of joining the Underworld's Royal Guard, I spared Papyrus' life and chose the option of "Let's be friends." I wanted to know what would happen had I chosen the other option, which was "What a loser". Unfortunately, I had saved at the checkpoint shortly after, effectively making my choice permanent.

Undertale's irreversibility is aligned thematically with the metagame plot. When I try to reset *Undertale* at the title screen, the game states that "A name has already been chosen", and forces me to play the game with the name I chose in the previous playthrough. This was frustrating because I felt that the right I had to change my character's name, which is common when restarting RPG games, was being taken away from me.

In addition, when dying and then loading the save game in a fight with Asgore, the king of the Underworld, I realized the PC (player character) was aware he was being "resurrected", as he tells Asgore he had been killed before. The number of times killed is also stated in the dialogue, and Asgore displays a vague memory of having killing the PC. Events appear to be irreversible and persist even after loading the save game.

The dialogue is different when conducting a second playthrough, with the NPC (non-player character) Flowey implying that you already know him. The other NPCs such as Toriel also indicate they vaguely remember you. At this point, I wondered whether Flowey's threats (that the game between me and him would never end) were indeed true, and if I had taken a "non-peaceful" route in the game, would events be different? Researching online, I found that the game not only remembers your story choices, it also remembers whether you have killed certain NPCs or monsters. The game would then remind you of these choices in the next restart. Indeed, on such a restart Flowey said that "I know what you did" and that "you went back, because you regretted it."

While playing the game a second time and experiencing variations in dialogue with the NPCs such as Toriel, I felt all my decisions from the first playthrough were irreversible and the second playthrough's events and dialogues were changed based on the first playthrough's decisions. I wondered how I could get a "truly fresh start", and went online to research this. Other players complained they could not have a truly fresh restart even after re-installing the game, and had to wipe out all trace of *Undertale* from their registry or restart the game on a new computer [19]. I accepted that short of re-installing the game on another computer, my decisions were truly permanent, that I had only "one playthrough", and there was never a "true reset" available despite the fact that I could restart the game (albeit with the same character name). It was frustrating that I probably would never be able to re-experience the game "for the first time" again.

6 *Sorcery!*: Long and Selectively Removed Rewinding

Throughout most of the *Sorcery!* series, the game provides the ability to freely rewind to any previous checkpoint. However, the effort required to "go back" and replay from a much earlier checkpoint can create a sense of irreversibility. This sense of irreversibility becomes even stronger towards the start of *Part 4*, when beyond a certain point the ability to return to any subsequent checkpoints is removed.

Sorcery! allows only a single save game and one character or profile to be played at a time. As a result, the possibility of exploring the story space is restricted. The series uses a "rewinding checkpoint" mechanic which saves past checkpoints you have encountered in your journey, and allows you to load any point in the past in that particular chapter. Checkpoints are not far apart and it is easy to access recent and past events.

While I was able to freely rewind and "load" the game to any point in the past, even upon an unsatisfactory result in battle, the game created significant obstacles to changing story choices if there were significant benefits to be reaped. For example, in *Sorcery! Part 2* I discovered no matter what option I chose via rewinding, I was unable to obtain the patronage of the God of grace, Courga. Courga claimed the reason was because I had killed an innocent. I then recalled killing a temple guard six real-time hours ago. I did not think of this event as important at the time, as I wanted to get on with the story and the game did not highlight this as an important event. In fact, my past murderous action had elicited a very nondescript, matter-of-fact text description, so I progressed with the story, ignorant that this action would have disastrous consequences later. I had no wish to backtrack six hours of my time to change my choice of deity. In this respect, the game became "irreversible" because I did not want to spend the time and effort involved in "loading" a save game that was too far back in the timeline and then replaying the intervening events. I progressed into *Part 3* worshipping the evil deity Slangg. Until the end of the series in *Part 4*, there was no opportunity to obtain Courga's patronage. Even though the game did not mechanically prevent me changing my previous actions, the time and effort involved effectively made that earlier decision irreversible.

After playing about 10% of *Sorcery! Part 4*, the game declares, "You have entered the Citadel of Mampang. Here no decision can be rewound." From this point, the option to rewind is removed. The stakes are high, for the game has many choice paths which result in death, many of which are random, unpredictable and sudden, and will take you back to the entrance of Mampang. For example, towards the end of the game you are imprisoned in a cell with a tiny elf-like creature. You have three options, one of which is to throw the creature through an air grate, which would kill it. If you are "moral" and do not take that option, you starve to death. The game has many such situations where there is no way of knowing which choice will result in death. This annoyed me, since I would likely be forced to restart outside Mampang after hours of gameplay. While I was frustrated upon dying due to "randomness" and I felt that my moral choices did not matter, I also appreciated how the game made me feel frustrated if I made a wrong move and took my actions for granted. This made my choices feel more significant.

7   *The Walking Dead*: Fast Pace and Chapter-Based Saves

In *The Walking Dead*, the use of automatic checkpoint saving, time-limited choices, and a fast pace draw the player into the story and discourage any consideration of rewinding. In addition, chapter-based saving and limited save points impacted replay.

The game automatically saves at various checkpoints. When this happens, an asterisk-like indicator appears in the top right-hand corner. This is a common mechanism in console games. In addition, many of the story choices are time-based, with only a limited amount of time given to make a choice. The game also reminds you when you have made "significant" choices, telling you the characters you interact with remember your actions. As I was playing the game, I felt I was almost watching a dramatic TV episode unfolding in real time, particularly when I had to react or make decisions quickly.

The first time I played the first episode, I completed it in one sitting. When I did regret a decision, the TV drama-like pacing moved forward quickly enough for me to discard any thought of going back to change any decision. For example, in *Episode 1*, I chose to save Kenny's child, Duck, from the zombies instead of Shawn who had helped me earlier. I had no time to reflect on this decision. This time-sensitive decision was followed by a few other time-sensitive choices. After the intensity of the moment was over, I went along with the quickly moving story and did not think of rewinding.

There are five episodes in *Season One*. In each episode, which takes approximately 2 h to play, there are checkpoints which constitute chapters in the story. Loading to the start of the chapter is the main way to "rewind" to a past save game and replay past story decisions. During gameplay you can exit the game at any point. The game will remind you that any progress since the last autosave will be lost. There are also three save slots in *The Walking Dead*, and an existing game can be copied onto another slot. When you do so, you copy all progress and story decisions. Each slot can be used for a different story playthrough or to experiment with a different story choice for the same character profile. When I was playing the game, I found myself using the save slots to save alternate story choices and journeys, but the limitation of only three save slots compared to storygames like *Elder Scrolls V: Skyrim* [20], which can hold thousands of saves [21], limited exploration of alternate story possibilities.

One of the key choices the player faces regarding whether to "load" the game comes at the end of *Episode 4*, when the game reveals how many of the survivors came with you and compares it to other online players. Everybody came with me at the end of my first playthrough and I did not want to change that decision. I felt this was the closest to a "score" that the game had, since if Lee was a good leader, he would have convinced as many survivors as possible to come with him. Had I failed to convince all four survivors to come with me I would rewind and replay until I had a "perfect" score.

8   Proposed Framework of Irreversibility

Based on the above close readings, we propose a preliminary framework of factors that affect irreversibility: *save game design*, *game mechanics*, and *significance to the player*.

1. **Save Game Design:** This category involves how, when, and the frequency with which games are saved, which can impact the player's ability to reverse their choices or replay portions of a storygame.
   a. *Chapter:* The separation of the game into "chapters" is more relevant in more linear storygames such as *The Walking Dead*. A chapter end is established when the player is prevented from traversing backwards to previously visited environments or sections of the game. By increasing the time taken to complete a chapter and simultaneously preventing manual saves, the game designer makes it more difficult for the player to arbitrarily access a previous chapter in order to change his or her story decisions.
   b. *Autosave:* By implementing an autosave function and removing or restricting the "load saved game" option, a persistent world somewhat like a massively multiplayer online game is emulated. A sense of an irreversible, continuous narrative is established by frequent autosaves, particularly if combined with one save slot.
   c. *Limiting player access to save state:* Having to change the computer's registry to restart a game is considered an extreme type of irreversibility, as most players do not have the technical knowledge to safely remove the game's registry entry from their system. The player might even be forced to start the game on a new system.
   d. *Checkpoint/marker granularity:* The further apart the save game checkpoints are located spatially on the game map, the more time and effort it would take for the player to replay previous decisions.
   e. *Save slots:* A single save game creates one "bookmark" and a single timeline pertaining to past choices and events. Fewer save slots restrict the player's ability to experience story variation by restricting the ease of accessing past options.
2. **Game Mechanics:** This category involves ways the design of the gameplay can impact the player's sense of irreversibility.
   a. *Pace:* A quick story pace would discourage the player from accessing a save game, particularly if they are experiencing a flowing, continuous story without much time to reflect upon story decisions. This discourages the player from wanting to access a save game until there is a lull in the game.
3. **Significance to player:** This refers to factors impacting the player's experience of irreversibility through manipulation of the save game design or game mechanics.
   a. *Obstacle difficulty:* If the player thinks there is a low probability of success in overcoming a particularly difficult test of skill or luck, they could be deterred from loading a save game to explore an alternate story path after overcoming said obstacle. When combined with other factors such as checkpoints which are far apart, this can also deter the player from loading saves to explore alternate paths.
   b. *Character/story crafting:* In making story choices, the player may choose an option which they identify with personally. The player would not want to change the story decisions he or she made with his character thus far, and this would deter him or her from loading a previous save game, making the game more irreversible. However, this can go either way. If the outcome is

unsatisfactory, the player may invest time to load an earlier save game to stay true to "their story". In extreme circumstances, a player committed to crafting a particular character or plot may restart the game to obtain a particular outcome. They could also be motivated to load an earlier save game in an attempt to obtain a more favorable story ending.

c. *Time:* Significant cost of time to the player to change story decisions or to explore alternate story choices is a deterrent to reloading the game.

d. *Finances:* In extreme cases, it could even be possible that the player would have to invest money to, for example, pay someone to reset the computer's registry, or buy a new system or new copy of the game to have a fresh restart of the game.

e. *Emotions:* In *The Walking Dead*, some events can also be emotionally disturbing or frustrating. Such a situation may be too gruesome for players to re-experience, and they would avoid accessing the previous save game leading to that event.

9 Discussion

These games make it frustrating or difficult for players to access a past save game or restart the game. Murray argues that players enjoy repeating an interactive story from different perspectives [2, 8, 9, 22]. It is worth considering why, then, a player might enjoy these irreversible games since they deliberately restrict replay, and even prevent players from "rereading" and exploring alternate story possibilities? Spielberg claims that "Audiences don't want to be in control of a story. They want to be lost in your story. They come to hear you be the storyteller, but in gaming it's going to have a bit of both, a little bit of give and take" [23]. In contrast, Aarseth [24] believes the player desires control and choice, what he refers to as intervention. Aarseth postulates that the player "struggle[s] not merely for interpretative insight but also for narrative control: 'I want this text to tell my story; the story that could not be without me." While exploration may be pleasurable, the satisfaction of having created a story unique to the player can also be pleasurable, particularly when the player knows the story cannot be easily duplicated or experienced by another player.

Mateas discusses agency and its relationship to rereading, arguing that "On subsequent replays of the world, the player and the observer become the same person. The total interactive experience consists of both first-person engagement within the dramatic world and third-person reflection across multiple experiences in the world" [25]. Is this "total interactive experience" essential to fully appreciate storygames? If so, can irreversible games provide a more meaningful balance of first-person engagement and third-person reflection, since the number of "subsequent replays" can be restricted? Agency is an important topic in the study and design of interactive stories. There are many questions to be explored here, including assessing how we can position irreversible stories in relation to agency: as unique and personal story experiences as described by Aarseth, but also as giving latitude to the player to explore variation as suggested by Murray. These questions are worth exploring, building on the foundation provided by our preliminary, proposed framework for irreversible storygames.

10   Conclusion

The proposed irreversibility framework presented in this paper gives us a scaffolding on which we can review storygames and understand why some games seem to be more irreversible than others. Consideration of significant factors such as time, obstacle difficulty, emotions and finances are personal and relative to the player. On the other hand, the game designer is able to control the save game design as well as game mechanics to vary the state of irreversibility in the storygame. We hope the framework can establish a foundation upon which to conduct further research and discussion on other subjects of significant interest, such as agency, to irreversible storygames.

Acknowledgments. This research is funded in part under the Singapore Ministry of Education Academic Research Fund Tier 1 grant FY2018-FRC2-003, "Understanding Repeat Engagement with Dynamically Changing Computational Media".

References

1. Adams, E.W.: Fundamentals of Game Design. New Riders Games (2013)
2. Murray, J.H.: Hamlet on the Holodeck: The Future of Narrative in Cyberspace. The MIT Press (1998)
3. Reed, A.: Changeful Tales: Design-Driven Approaches Toward More Expressive Storygames (2017)
4. Calinescu, M.: Rereading. Yale University Press (1993)
5. Mitchell, A., McGee, K.: Reading again for the first time: a model of rereading in interactive stories. In: Oyarzun, D., Peinado, F., Young, R.M., Elizalde, A., Méndez, G. (eds.) ICIDS 2012. LNCS, vol. 7648, pp. 202–213. Springer, Heidelberg (2012). https://doi.org/10.1007/978-3-642-34851-8_20
6. Selig, R.L.: The endless reading of fiction: stuart Moulthrop's hypertext novel "victory garden". Contemp. Lit. **41**, 642–660 (2000)
7. Peacock, A.: Towards an aesthetic of 'the interactive'. Digit. Creat. **12**, 237–246 (2001)
8. Murray, J.: From game-story to cyberdrama. In: Wardrip-Fruin, N., Harrigan, P. (eds.) First person: New Media as Story, Performance, and Game, pp. 2–11. The MIT Press (2004)
9. Murray, J.H.: Why Paris needs hector and lancelot needs mordred: using traditional narrative roles and functions for dramatic compression in interactive narrative. In: Si, M., Thue, D., André, E., Lester, J.C., Tanenbaum, T.J., Zammitto, V. (eds.) ICIDS 2011. LNCS, vol. 7069, pp. 13–24. Springer, Heidelberg (2011). https://doi.org/10.1007/978-3-642-25289-1_2
10. Ryan, M.-L.: The interactive onion: layers of user participation in digital narrative texts. In: Page, R.E., Thomas, B. (eds.) New Narratives: Stories and Storytelling in the Digital Age, pp. 35–62. Lincoln, Bison (2012)
11. Douglas, J.Y.: The End of Books - or Books Without End? Reading Interactive Narratives. University of Michigan Press, Ann Arbor (2001)
12. Kleinman, E., Carstensdottir, E., El-Nasr, M.S.: Going forward by going back: re-defining rewind mechanics in narrative games. In: Proceedings of the 13th International Conference on the Foundations of Digital Games, pp. 32:1–32:6. ACM, New York (2018)
13. Bizzocchi, J., Tanenbaum, T.J.: Well read: applying close reading techniques to gameplay experiences. In: Davidson, D. (ed.) Well Played 3.0, pp. 262–290. ETC Press (2011)
14. Telltale Games: The Walking Dead: Season 1 (Computer Game) (2012)

15. Inkle: Sorcery! (Computer Game series)
16. Fox, T.: Undertale (Computer Game) (2015)
17. Inkle: Sorcery! Part 4: The Crown of Kings (Computer Game) (2016)
18. Tanenbaum, T.J.: Believability, adaptivity, and performativity: three lenses for the analysis of interactive storytelling (2008)
19. Dahpie: Selling your......is a PERMENANT DECISION. Spoilers. https://steamcommunity.com/app/391540/discussions/0/523897653304070081/
20. Bethesda Softworks: Elder Scrolls V: Skyrim (Computer Game) (2011)
21. Roak12: How many save files do you all have? Is there a limit? https://www.reddit.com/r/skyrimmods/comments/46uga9/how_many_save_files_do_you_all_have_is_there_a/
22. Murray, J.H.: Research into interactive digital narrative: a kaleidoscopic view. In: International Conference on Interactive Digital Storytelling, pp. 3–17 (2018)
23. Breznican, A.: Spielberg, Zemeckis say video games, film could become one (2004)
24. Aarseth, E.J.: Cybertext: Perspectives on Ergodic Literature. The Johns Hopkins University Press (1997)
25. Mateas, M.: A preliminary poetics for interactive drama and games. Digit. Creat. **12**, 140–152 (2001)

The Potential of Interactive Digital Narratives. Agency and Multiple Perspectives in *Last Hijack Interactive*

Renske van Enschot[1]([✉]), Iris Boogaard[1], Hartmut Koenitz[2],
and Christian Roth[2]

[1] Department of Communication and Cognition, Tilburg Center for Cognition
and Communication, Tilburg University, Warandelaan 2, 5037 AB Tilburg,
The Netherlands
r.vanenschot@tilburguniversity.edu,
info@irisboogaard.nl
[2] University of the Arts Utrecht, P.O. Box 1520, 3500 BM Utrecht,
The Netherlands
{hartmut.koenitz, christian.roth}@hku.nl

Abstract. Interactive Digital Narratives (IDN) have the capacity to represent multiple, even competing perspectives and to allow audiences to change between them. Such meaningful changes have been defined as agency by Murray [1] transforming the audience into interactors. These experiential qualities of interactive digital narrative (IDN) define the potential of the form to improve the representation and understanding of complex topics. In this paper, we present an initial study designed to evaluate this potential of IDN by means of the complex topic of piracy in the region of Somalia. To this end, we ran an experiment comparing interactive and non-interactive versions of *Last Hijack Interactive*, an award-winning Dutch interactive documentary. With this study, we contribute to the establishment of an evaluation framework that can be used to more clearly identify the potential of IDN in terms of representing and understanding complexity. We discuss the results and propose next steps.

Keywords: Narrative complexity · Interactive documentary · Interactive Digital Narrative · User experience evaluation

1 Introduction

If someone were to ask you to explain the piracy crisis off the coast of Somalia, would you be able to? At first, the situation might seem pretty clear. A failing state unable to enforce common law, little opportunities to make a living and a major international shipping route in plain sight of desperate people. All of these factors may serve as triggers for piracy. Yet, is this really the full picture? One aspect you might probably struggle with is how to account for the different perspectives of all the parties involved (e.g., the hijackers vs. the hijacked vs. the negotiators). It seems quite impossible to explore all these perspectives to the full extent in one comprehensive traditional narrative form such as a documentary or a newspaper article.

© Springer Nature Switzerland AG 2019
R. E. Cardona-Rivera et al. (Eds.): ICIDS 2019, LNCS 11869, pp. 158–169, 2019.
https://doi.org/10.1007/978-3-030-33894-7_17

In order to understand and represent these kinds of complex situations, we need to look beyond traditional, linear narratives. As Koenitz [2] suggests, "traditional narratives are no longer able to adequately represent our complex reality." Instead, interactive-digital narratives (IDN) – described by Roth and Koenitz [3] as an expressive form in the digital medium which "affords dramatic agency for interactors" allowing them "to intentionally influence salient aspects (character development, sequencing, outcome, etc.) of a narrative" – may be the better option, since IDN enables interactors to explore multi-sided narratives in greater detail. Yet, so far, the potential of IDN to represent and understand complex topics has not been evaluated. It is timely to address this question and develop an evaluation framework for this purpose. In this paper, we report on an initial study to investigate whether people's understanding of a complex situation benefits from having agency and being exposed to multiple perspectives in an interactive digital narrative, in this case the documentary *Last Hijack Interactive* (2014)[1].

2 Related Work

Interactive digital narratives have emerged as promising means for providing new ways to communicate with and engage us, in fields such as journalism, education and entertainment. IDN has the potential to represent complex topics and make them more easily understandable [2, 4–6]. However, up until today, no framework exists that is designed to empirically evaluate the understanding of complex topics through interactive digital narratives. The work presented here is a contribution towards the development of such a framework. The most closely related works so far are discussed here.

An early study by Vorderer, Knobloch and Schramm [7] indicated that interactive narratives might be more enjoyable for individuals with higher cognitive capacity. In this experiment, participants were randomly assigned to one of three groups differing in how much a participant could affect the narrative progression (high level of interactivity, low level of interactivity, and no interactivity) of a 30-minute TV program. It was found that individuals with less cognitive capacity rated the program more positively when they watched it without any interactivity whereas individuals with greater cognitive capacity felt more entertained when they were able to influence the plot of the TV program. Vorderer et al. suggested that providing users with the ability to interact with a narrative supported involvement and empathy towards characters. However, these benefits only applied to users with a high cognitive capacity.

A study conducted by Steinemann et al. [8] compared participant behavior after experiencing one of six versions of a story set in Darfur, each version having either interactive conditions (interactive text and game) or non-interactive conditions (non-interactive text and video). Participants were later asked to consider making a financial donation to aid Darfur refugees. Responses revealed that participants who had experienced the story through interactive conditions were willing to donate higher amounts

---

[1] https://lasthijack.submarinechannel.com.

(12%) than those who had experienced the story through non-interactive conditions. The different presentation modes had no impact on the percentage donated. However, in a follow-up study, Steinemann et al. [9] examined donating behavior comparing an interactive CYOA text about a single mom with three children becoming homeless versus a linear counterpart. In this study, interactivity did not affect the percentage donated as opposed to in their previous study.

Furthermore, in a study by Parrott, Dillman Carpentier and Northup [10], audience members adopted the perspective of an immigrant illegally entering the United States from Mexico by either being exposed to an interactive narrative or a different traditional narrative (in which participants adopted the perspective of an American athlete navigating the rules of the National Collegiate Athletic Association). It was found that participants experiencing the interactive narrative had more positive affect towards Mexicans in the U.S than participants who experienced the traditional narrative. So, putting audiences in the same position as members of a marginalized group and having them make choices as if they were walking in their shoes increased positive affect. Parrott et al. concluded that interactive narratives have great potential to help reduce prejudice towards marginalized social groups.

Moreover, van t' Riet, Meeuwes, van der Voorden and Jansz [11] (study 3) compared a narrative-focused video game with a recorded version of the gameplay (the 'non-interactive narrative') on the dimensions of immersion, identification, and willingness to help. In this game, players were faced with the challenges of arriving in a safe country after having fled from a country at war. It was found that the persuasive game did not provide a stronger sense of immersion and identification and did not increase willingness to help. However, participants did feel an increased sense of embodied presence in contrast to participants who were shown the recorded video.

The above-mentioned studies can be applauded for the promising steps they have taken towards empirical research on the potential of IDN. More research is needed to focus on the specific potential of IDN to increase the understanding of complex topics. In addition, it can be argued that some of the described studies lacked comparable control conditions. We address these issues in the current study, by creating different versions of one and the same interactive documentary and by focusing on the effects of IDN on understanding the complex topic of Somalian piracy.

3   A Study of Last Hijack Interactive

For our study we use the online interactive documentary *Last Hijack Interactive* (2014) created by interactive director Mirka Duijn and directed by Femke Wolting and Tommy Pallotta. Our aim is to address the following research question:

RQ: To what extent do agency and perspectives in an interactive narrative influence understanding of a complex situation?

Interactive digital narratives provide individuals with agency [1, 3] being defined as "the satisfying power to take meaningful action and see the result of your decisions and choices" [6], something that traditional narratives cannot offer. In interactive narratives, readers become interactors who have the ability to influence the course of the narrative to varying degrees, for example by choosing between different perspectives on the same subject. This aspect has been put into practice in the interactive documentary *Last Hijack Interactive* (2014) in which interactors can engage with different perspectives on piracy in Somalia, amongst them a ship captain and a pirate.

Learning theories about constructivist, discovery, inquiry-based teaching state that people learn best when constructing information themselves, with no or minimal guidance (e.g., [12–15]). Interactive digital narratives enable this very situation; interactors are given the agency to construct their own representation of the given information [16]. Based on these learning theories, we hypothesize that being given agency enables users to construct knowledge about a complex situation themselves, leading to a better understanding of this situation:

H1: Having the agency to influence a narrative provides a higher degree of understanding of a complex situation than having no agency to influence a narrative.

Furthermore, the present study also investigates the difference between being exposed to multiple perspectives versus a single perspective. Although traditional narratives also allow for multiple perspectives, the ability to choose from a multiplicity of perspectives can be recognized as an important characteristic of interactive narratives related to Murray's [1] participatory and encyclopedic affordances. In the case of *Last Hijack Interactive*, interactors are given a range of different perspectives, amongst which are the captain of the hijacked ship (the "good guy") having to endure a hijacking but also the hijacker (the "bad guy"); what made him decide to become a hijacker? Such a variety of perspectives invites interactors to experience the view of characters dissimilar to them, potentially enriching and nuancing their understanding of the characters (character models: [17, 18]) and - in this case – the intricate issue of Somalian piracy (the situation model: [17]). Accordingly, we hypothesize that being exposed to different perspectives provides for a richer understanding of a complex situation than being exposed to just a single perspective.

H2: Multiple perspectives provide a higher degree of understanding of a complex situation than a single perspective.

4 Method

4.1 Design

An experimental 3×2 factorial design was used to test the hypotheses. The independent variables were (a) Agency and (b) Perspectives. The independent variable Agency originally included three levels: Extended Agency, Limited Agency, and No Agency. The independent variable Perspectives included three levels: Multiple Perspectives, the Captain's Single Perspective and the Hijacker's Single Perspective.

4.2 Participants

This research focused on Dutch-speaking participants in order to keep cultural influences constant. The participants were recruited via both convenience sampling and the Human Subject Pool of the Department of Communication and Cognition and Department of Cognitive Science and Artificial Intelligence at Tilburg University. This resulted in a sample of bachelor, premaster and master students. Participants from the Human Subject Pool were compensated with one credit. The sample consisted of 96 participants, 45 males and 51 females with a mean age of 21 years.

4.3 Materials

In this experiment, the interactive documentary *Last Hijack Interactive* (2014) was used, focusing on the complex situation of Somalian piracy. One of the initial reasons to select this particular interactive documentary was the presence of a non-interactive version of this documentary. Both variants offer a similar narrative about piracy in Somalia, and introduce the same characters. However, we found that the two differ from each other in more aspects than just the presence or lack of interactivity, e.g., the storyline (the hijack of a ship versus a pirate's life) and the amount and kind of offered perspectives (seven different perspectives versus just the pirate's perspective). Therefore, a direct comparison was deemed not appropriate for our experimental study. Consequently, we decided to use the interactive documentary as a starting point, and leave the existing non-interactive documentary aside in the experiment.

Last Hijack Interactive is a web-based interactive documentary that is freely available and can be experienced from the documentary's website in three languages: German, English, and Dutch. The Dutch version was used for the experiment. The interactive documentary focused on the piracy industry in Somalia, and specifically the hijacking of a Western ship in the Arabian Sea that occurred in real life in 2008. The online interface allowed users to view this hijack event from seven different perspectives: a pirate, a captain, an ex-pirate, the captain's wife, a Somali journalist, a Somali lawyer, and a British security expert.

For the experiment, we created five different versions of the interactive documentary, differing in Agency (Extended, Limited, None) and Perspectives (Multiple versus Single Captain versus Single Hijacker). In Table 1, an overview of the different versions can be found. Participants in the Extended Agency condition (A) were instructed to "try to reach the end of the timeline of the interactive documentary twice

Table 1. Different versions/conditions of the Last Hijack interactive documentary

Version	Agency	Amount of perspectives
A	Extended	Multiple (captain, hijacker, journalist, etc.)
B	Limited	Multiple (captain and hijacker)
C	None	Multiple (captain and hijacker)
D	None	Single (captain)
E	None	Single (hijacker)

by experiencing as many character perspectives as possible". Participants in the Limited Agency condition (B) were instructed to focus solely on the main characters' perspectives (the captain and the hijacker): "try to reach the end of the timeline twice by focusing on the captain's and hijacker's perspectives". For conditions C, D and E, non-interactive versions of the documentary were created in which either the perspectives of both the captain and hijacker were shown (C) or just the perspective of the captain (D) or hijacker (E) was shown.

4.4   Instrumentation

First, we decided to split the dependent variable Understanding of Complex Situation into Perceived Understanding and Observed Understanding. For Perceived Understanding, seven statements (6-point scale) were used, partially adopted from Busselle and Bilandzic' Narrative Engagement Scale [19]:

1. At points, I had a hard time making sense of what was going on in the documentary.*
2. My understanding of how the characters in this story ended up in this situation is clear.
3. I had a hard time recognizing the thread of the story.*
4. After having watched the documentary, my understanding of the different sides to the problem of piracy in Somalia has grown.
5. After having watched the documentary, I am capable of explaining the situation of piracy in Somalia to a friend.
6. After having watched the documentary, I have an understanding of the complexity of the situation.
7. After having watched the documentary, I see that there are different sides to the piracy situation in Somalia.

For Observed Understanding, a small knowledge test was presented including three multiple choice questions and one open question regarding the Somali piracy situation in general.

How did piracy develop in Somalia?

(a) The Somali government has ordered the protection of the Arabian Sea against foreign ships.
(b) Somali fishermen were no longer able to earn money due to illegal fishing from foreign ships, which made them run into financial problems.
(c) The trade agreements between Somalia and the European Union were canceled in 2007, creating an economic crisis in Somalia.
(d) Piracy is a consequence of the unemployment that arose after the decolonization in the years following the Cold War.

Why do so many young Somali adult men decide to become pirates?

(a) Because they are forced by their family.
(b) Because the Somali government rewards piracy.

(c) Because piracy is a way to earn a lot of money.
(d) Because the Somali police doesn't combat piracy.

Why are pirates not being arrested by Western countries after being caught engaging in piracy?

(a) Because the pirates often have fake passports and cannot be prosecuted.
(b) Because piracy is not punishable in Somalia.
(c) Because piracy is punishable by death in Somalia.
(d) Because legislation on international waters is different from European law.

According to both Somali and European experts, Somali piracy is "organized crime in which pirates at sea are only pawns in a much bigger problem". Explain what these experts mean by this statement.

Various other measures of interactive narrative experience were embedded in the questionnaire as well: Eudaimonic Appraisal, Character Believability, Enjoyment, Curiosity, Suspense, and Affect (positive and negative), adopted from Roth's evaluation framework [20]. The participants were also asked to list the characteristics of the captain and the hijacker.

4.5 Procedure

Prior to the start of the experiment, participants signed a document of informed consent. Participants were randomly assigned to one of the five conditions. Depending on each condition, participants were instructed on how they were going to engage with the documentary. In the No Agency conditions, participants were instructed that they were going to watch a documentary. All participants were told that the aim was "to get a better understanding of the character perspective(s) and the situation of piracy in Somalia as a whole". In conditions A and B, screen recordings of the participants' interaction with the interface were made to investigate how many walkthroughs they had completed and which character perspectives were experienced. After experiencing the material, participants filled out a questionnaire. Furthermore, participants in the Agency conditions answered various questions about their interaction experience. The total duration of the experiment was approximately 50 min. Afterwards, participants were thanked for their time and effort and any remaining questions were answered via a short debriefing.

4.6 Data Analysis

A manipulation check was carried out based on the screen recordings in order to analyze whether participants in the Limited Agency condition (B) had followed the instructions (i.e., focused solely on the captain and the hijacker). For each participant in the Agency conditions, it was registered how many perspectives they had seen, how many times they switched perspectives and how much time they had spent watching each character in the documentary. Unfortunately, screen recording failed for five participants due to technical errors. Moreover, it was found that not all participants in the Limited Agency group had followed the provided instructions, and had focused on other perspectives as well, similar to the Extended Agency group. Reassigning these participants from the Low Agency to the Extended Agency group lead to such a small sample size in the Limited Agency group (N = 9) that it was decided to merge Extended and Limited Agency in the analysis.

To compute the scores for Observed Understanding, points were given for correct answers to the three multiple-choice questions (maximum 3 points in total) and maximum 2 points were given for a fully correct answer to the open question (the participant acknowledges that Somali piracy is an ongoing cycle with multiple agents), leading to a maximum of 5 points for Observed Understanding.

5 Results

5.1 Agency

A multivariate ANOVA was used to test for differences between Agency (AB) and No Agency (C) on the DV's. We hypothesized that having the agency to influence a narrative provides a higher degree of understanding of a complex situation than having no agency to influence a narrative (H1). On average, Perceived Understanding was indeed higher for participants who had the agency to influence a narrative (M = 4.55, SD = 0.46) than for participants who had no agency to influence a narrative (M = 4.38, SD = 0.89) but this difference was not significant (F < 1). On average, Observed Understanding was higher for Agency (M = 3.48, SD = 0.81) than for No Agency (M = 3.25, SD = 0.80), but this difference was not significant as well (F < 1).

As for the other variables, the only significant difference was found for Character Believability (F(1) = 4.86, p = .03, η^2 = .095), in that Character Believability was higher in the No Agency condition (M = 4.58, SD = 0.58) than in the Agency conditions (M = 4.20, SD = 0.56). A marginally significant difference was found for Perceived Similarity to the Captain F(1) = 3.17, p = .082, η^2 = .064): the participants who had agency perceived themselves as more similar to the captain (M = 4.06, SD = 1.19) than the participants who did not have agency (M = 3.38, SD = 1.39). No other differences were found (p's > .10).

5.2 Perspectives

Again, a multivariate ANOVA was used, to test for differences between Multiple Perspectives (C) and a Single Perspective (D: captain and E: hijacker separately), with Bonferroni for pairwise comparisons. We hypothesized that having access to multiple perspectives in a narrative provides a higher degree of understanding of a complex situation than having access to a single perspective. Perspectives did have an effect on Perceived Understanding (F(2) = 7.58, p = .001, η^2 = .252) as well as on Observed Understanding (marginally significant: F(2) = 3.21, p = .050, η^2 = .125). Perceived Understanding was lower when people only saw the hijacker's perspective (M = 3.70, SD = 0.79) in comparison to experiencing multiple perspectives (M = 4.38, SD = 0.89, p = .049) or the captain's perspective (M = 4.75, SD = 0.60, p = .001). However, no difference in Perceived Understanding was found between multiple perspectives and just the captain's perspective (p = .56). As for Observed Understanding, although the scores were higher for multiple perspectives (M = 3.25, SD = 0.80) than for both single perspective versions (captain: M = 2.66, SD = 0.75; hijacker: M = 2.59, SD = 0.88), just a marginally significant difference was found between multiple perspectives and the hijacker's single perspective (p = .08). No difference was found between multiple perspectives and the captain's single perspective (p = .13) and between the captain's single perspective and the hijacker's single perspective (p = 1.00).

As for the other variables, Perspectives had an effect on Eudaimonic Appraisal (marginally significant: F(2) = 2.80, p = .07, η^2 = .111; no pairwise differences), Character Believability (F(2) = 3.42, p = .04, η^2 = .132), Enjoyment (F(2) = 4.64, p = .015, η^2 = .171), Curiosity (F(2) = 6.15, p = .004, η^2 = .215), Suspense (F(2) = 11.84, p < .001, η^2 = .345) but not on Affect (F < 1). Character Believability was higher for multiple perspectives (M = 4.58, SD = 0.58) than for the hijacker's single perspective (M = 4.00, SD = 0.70; p = .036). Enjoyment was higher for the captain's single perspective (M = 4.73, SD = 0.95) than for the hijacker's single perspective (M = 3.67, SD = 1.00; p = .012). Curiosity was also higher for the captain's single perspective (M = 5.31, SD = 0.48) than for the hijacker's single perspective (M = 4.25, SD = 1.21; p = .003). Suspense was highest for the captain's single perspective (M = 4.44, SD = 0.48) as compared to the multiple perspectives (M = 3.69, SD = 0.54; p = .014) and the hijacker's single perspective (M = 3.22, SD = 1.00; p < .001). No other pairwise differences were found (p > .10) (Table 2).

Table 2. Results with mean values and standard deviations

	Cond. A + B Agency Mult. Persp. (N = 32)	Condition C No agency Mult. Persp. (N = 16)	Condition D No agency - Single Persp. (Captain) (N = 16)	Condition E No agency - Single Persp. (Hijacker) (N = 16)
Perceived understanding	4.55 (0.46)	4.38 (0.89)	4.75 (0.60)	3.70 (0.79)
Observed understanding	3.48 (0.81)	3.25 (0.80)	2.66 (0.75)	2.59 (0.88)
Eudaimonic appraisal	3.91 (0.69)	4.09 (0.82)	4.14 (0.75)	3.56 (0.74)
Character believability	4.20 (0.56)	4.58 (0.58)	4.28 (0.59)	4.00 (0.70)
Enjoyment	4.33 (0.53)	4.10 (1.02)	4.73 (0.95)	3.67 (1.00)
Curiosity	4.78 (0.61)	4.69 (0.73)	5.31 (0.48)	4.25 (1.21)
Suspense	3.47 (0.80)	3.69 (0.54)	4.44 (0.48)	3.22 (1.00)
Affect	3.72 (0.51)	3.44 (0.76)	3.65 (0.73)	3.49 (0.52)

A further qualitative analysis of the listed characteristics of the captain and the hijacker showed that the hijacker was characterized as someone who focuses on materialistic and short-term goals like "money", "cars" and "women" understood as items to gain through piracy. In addition, he is described as a "jerk" who "doesn't show remorse". In contrast, the captain was described as "empathetic", someone who "is able to see the bigger picture", who "can reflect on why this has happened to him" and who "changes his view on piracy".

6 Conclusion and Discussion

In this study, we took a first step to investigate whether and how the understanding of a complex situation might benefit from having agency and being exposed to multiple perspectives in an interactive narrative. We compared interactive and non-interactive versions of the same material, in our case the award-winning interactive documentary *Last Hijack Interactive*, on the topic of Somalian piracy.

In our study, agency lead to a higher degree of understanding, but this difference was not statistically significant, rejecting H1. Enabling users to construct a representation of the given information themselves did not foster a significantly better understanding of the complex situation than just presenting them a linear version of the documentary. Kirschner and colleagues [21, 22] provide a possible explanation for this result. Kirschner et al. state – in line with Cognitive Load Theory [23] – that giving novices an overly demanding learning task can overload working memory and hamper learning. Interactors in this experiment may have been novices with regard to IDN, especially interactive documentaries. They may not have known how to fully exploit the potential of this form and thus may even have gotten confused and lost track midway through the experience. This assumption is supported by screen-recording data that showed how some participants in the extended agency group did not watch any chapters of the main characters. Users could have felt overwhelmed by the choices of the interactive documentary negatively impacting their understanding of the topic. In follow-up research, we would therefore include the interactor's savviness with interactive forms as an important parameter. Participants who are experienced with IDNs or other interactive forms such as video games may exploit the potential of these works more fully than novices.

Furthermore, we originally made a distinction between extended and limited agency, which differed in the amount of guidance we offered on how to address the interactive documentary: no guidance versus minimal guidance ("focus on the perspectives of the captain and the hijacker"). However, due to small participant numbers in the Limited Agency group, we had to merge these two groups. More data needs to be collected to be able to investigate the differential effects of extended versus limited versus no agency, again related to the user's savviness with interactive digital narratives. This would also enable us to relate the findings to the other variables of our evaluation framework (e.g., enjoyment but also behavioral measures based on the screen-recording data).

With regard to the perspectives that the participants were exposed to, H2 was only partially supported. The multiple perspectives version did score higher on understanding than the version with just the hijacker's perspective but scored equally high as the version with just the captain's single perspective. The captain's single perspective version was also rated more enjoyable and created more curiosity and suspense for the participants than the hijacker's single perspective version. Our qualitative analysis revealed that the hijacker's storyline remained underdeveloped in the documentary, possibly explaining the absent effect. The opportunity to elucidate the hijacker's difficult situation and create a better understanding of his situation and motives wasn't taken advantage of enough in the work. The hijacker remained a flat character throughout the different versions of the documentary, being described by the participants as a "jerk" motivated by the lure of money and women – understood essentially as a good that can be acquired.

This finding demonstrates the importance of having fully developed building blocks in place (c.f. [24, 25]), in this case rich characters who are able to demonstrate the complexity of a situation. Further studies on other IDN with well-developed characters are much needed to better understand the potential effect of comprehending complex situations through exposure to differing perspectives [17, 18, 26].

With the rising number of available channels to provide us with all sorts of information and the growing speed of how this information reaches us, information overload has become almost inevitable. The unique affordances of the digital medium (e.g., agency) enable the creation of interactive narratives which are capable of representing our complex reality in great detail within a single work. This study is an encouragement to further investigate how these affordances can be used to our society's advantage.

References

1. Murray, J.H.: Hamlet on the Holodeck: The Future of Narrative in Cyberspace. Free Press, New York (1997)
2. Koenitz, H.: Representations of complexity - Interactive Digital Narratives enabling discourse for the 21st Century. In: Keynote at Zip-Scene Conference, Budapest, 11 November 2018 (2018). https://www.slideshare.net/HartmutKoenitz/representations-of-complexity-interactive-digital-narratives-enabling-discourse-for-the-21st-century
3. Roth, C., Koenitz, H.: Evaluating the user experience of interactive digital narrative. Presented at the 1st International Workshop on Multimedia Alternate Realities. ACM, New York (2016)
4. Downs, J.S., Murray, P.J., Bruine de Bruin, W., Penrose, J., Palmgren, C., Fischhoff, B.: Interactive video behavioral intervention to reduce adolescent females' STD risk: a randomized controlled trial. Soc. Sci. Med. 59, 1561–1572 (2004)
5. Baranowski, T., Buday, R., Thompson, D.I., Baranowski, J.: Playing for real: video games and stories for health-related behavior change. Am. J. Prev. Med. 34, 74–82. e10 (2008)
6. Murray, J.H.: Hamlet on the Holodeck. The Free Press, New York (2016)
7. Vorderer, P., Knobloch, S., Schramm, H.: Does entertainment suffer from interactivity? The impact of watching an interactive TV movie on viewers' experience of entertainment. Media Psychol. 3, 343–363 (2001)
8. Steinemann, S.T., Mekler, E.D., Opwis, K.: Increasing donating behavior through a game for change. Presented at the 2015 Annual Symposium, New York, USA (2015)
9. Steinemann, S.T., Iten, G.H., Opwis, K., Forde, S.F., Frasseck, L., Mekler, E.D.: Interactive narratives affecting social change. J. Media Psychol. 29, 54–66 (2017)

10. Parrott, S., Carpentier, F.R.D., Northup, C.T.: A test of interactive narrative as a tool against prejudice. Howard J. Commun. **28**, 1–16 (2017)
11. van't Riet, J., Meeuwes, A.C., van der Voorden, L., Jansz, J.: Investigating the effects of a persuasive digital game on immersion, identification, and willingness to help. Basic Appl. Soc. Psychol. **40**, 180–194 (2018)
12. Bruner, J.S.: The act of discovery. Harv. Educ. Rev. **31**, 21–32 (1961)
13. Freeman, S., Eddy, S.L., McDonough, M., Smith, M.K., Okoroafor, N., Jordt, H., Wenderoth, M.P.: Active learning increases student performance in science, engineering, and mathematics. PNAS **111**, 8410–8415 (2014)
14. Jonassen, D.H.: Objectivism versus constructivism: do we need a new philosophical paradigm? Educ. Technol. Res. Dev. **39**, 5–14 (1991)
15. Steffe, L.P., Gale, J.E.: Constructivism in Education. Lawrence Erlbaum, Hillsdale (1995)
16. Baldwin, S., Ching, Y.-H.: Interactive storytelling: opportunities for online course design. TechTrends **61**, 179–186 (2016)
17. Busselle, R., Bilandzic, H.: Fictionality and perceived realism in experiencing stories: a model of narrative comprehension and engagement. Commun. Theory **18**, 255–280 (2008)
18. Graesser, A.C., Olde, B., Klettke, B.: How does the mind construct and represent stories. In: Narrative Impact. Erlbaum, Mahwah, NJ (2012)
19. Busselle, R., Bilandzic, H.: Measuring narrative engagement. Media Psychol. **12**, 321–347 (2009)
20. Roth, C.: Experiencing interactive storytelling. Ph.D. thesis. Vrije Universiteit Amsterdam (2016). https://research.vu.nl/en/publications/experiencing-interactive-storytelling
21. Kirschner, P.A., Sweller, J., Clark, R.E.: Why minimal guidance during instruction does not work: an analysis of the failure of constructivist, discovery, problem-based, experiential, and inquiry-based teaching. Educ. Psychol. **41**, 75–86 (2010)
22. Kirschner, P.A., van Merriënboer, J.J.G.: Do learners really know best? Urban legends in education. Educ. Psychol. **48**, 169–183 (2013)
23. Sweller, J.: Cognitive load during problem solving: effects on learning. Cogn. Sci. **12**, 257–285 (1988)
24. Murray, J.H.: Inventing the Medium: Principles of Interaction Design as a Cultural Practice. MIT Press, Cambridge (2011)
25. Koenitz, Hartmut: Design approaches for interactive digital narrative. In: Schoenau-Fog, Henrik, Bruni, Luis Emilio, Louchart, Sandy, Baceviciute, Sarune (eds.) ICIDS 2015. LNCS, vol. 9445, pp. 50–57. Springer, Cham (2015). https://doi.org/10.1007/978-3-319-27036-4_5
26. Rapp, D.N., Gerrig, R.J., Prentice, D.A.: Readers' trait-based models of characters in narrative comprehension. J. Mem. Lang. **45**, 737–750 (2001)

Theoretical Foundations

Leveraging Machinima to Characterize Comprehension of Character Motivation

Kara Cassell[1] and R. Michael Young[2(✉)]

[1] 3C Institute, Durham, NC 08544, USA
`cassell@3cisd.com`
[2] University of Utah, Salt Lake City, UT 84112, USA
`young@eae.utah.edu`

Abstract. Deliberation-driven reflective sequences, or *DDRSs*, are cinematic idioms used by film makers to convey the motivations for characters adopting a particular course of action in a story. We report on an experiment where the cinematic generation system Ember was used to create a cinematic sequence with variants making different choices for DDRS use around a single decision point for a single character.

Keywords: Experimental evaluation · Cinematic generation · Machinima

1 Introduction

One important aspect of visual narrative is character development. Understanding the deliberations that a character undergoes when deciding between competing goals or courses of action is one key aspect of the insight viewers gain on a character's personality and growth. Conveying the mental processes involved in those deliberations is key to portraying character personality to a narrative consumer. In written narratives this can be done through the use of an internal monologue or by a narrator explicitly describing a character's internal thought processes. In film, storytellers typically use *internal shots*, close ups of characters, to signal to the viewer that characters are thinking. Cinematographers use specific shots, usually *cut-away shots* – shots that briefly cut to some other content and cut back to the previous context – to indicate what it is that the character is thinking about. Cut-away shots help to break up otherwise long static shots, make the sequence more interesting, and (most relevant to this paper) display relevant information to the viewer or audience [1].

The work described in this paper seeks to provide experimental insight into the ways that visual narrative making use of internal shot/cut-away filmic idioms may impact the comprehension of viewers. Previous work by Cassell [4] has developed a computational method for generating these types of idioms in the context of comic panels and machinima, but questions remain about when a generation system should make use of these idioms and what the likely cognitive consequences on viewers would be from their use.

© Springer Nature Switzerland AG 2019
R. E. Cardona-Rivera et al. (Eds.): ICIDS 2019, LNCS 11869, pp. 173–177, 2019.
https://doi.org/10.1007/978-3-030-33894-7_18

The system *Ember* [3], a visual discourse generator developed by Cassell, is a narrative discourse generation system that reasons about character decision making to construct a discourse that can communicate character decision-making to the viewer. Ember's generative capability was specifically developed to be able to create cinematic sequences that effectively convey these decision making processes using what they call a *reflective sequence*, the pattern of an internal shot, some number of cut-away shots, followed by another internal shot. When the internal shots occur during a deliberation by the character being filmed, and the content of each cut-away shows some aspects of the story world relevant to the deliberation, Cassell calls these shot sequences ***deliberation-driven reflective sequences*, or *DDRSs***. While Ember has demonstrated the ability to generate shot sequences that meet the structural definition of a DDRS, no clear empirical evidence exists that shows the impact on a viewer's comprehension of the story that results from the inclusion of DDRSs in Ember cinematics.

In order to better understand how DDRSs play a role in audience inferences around action choice, we designed an experiment that would compare viewer reports of their inferences across a range of similar machinima sequences, where each cinematic varied only by the presence/absence/content of a DDRS. As we describe below, that experiment showed little differentiation in effect between the various DDRSs that were generated. While the experiment does not shed light on the impact of DDRSs, it does (a) provide a methodology for leveraging machinima to explore narrative film comprehension and points to a number of specific revisions to needed follow-on experiments that will provide better experimental control.

2 Background and Related Work

Current cinematic generation research typically falls into one of two main categories: (1) work that focuses on the low-level problems of camera placement, direction, focus, and angle and (2) work that views cinematic generation as a narrative discourse construction problem. Systems that focus on the low level problems typically use constraint solvers or intelligent agents [2,6,8,13]. They make use of knowledge around film-making developed and articulated by cineamtographers (e.g., [11]), such as the rule of thirds or not crossing the line, to guide camera shot selection.

One such system is the one developed by Christianson et al. [6] that encodes cinematic idioms, or standard sequences of shots, into a declarative camera control language (DCCL). Christie and Normand [7] designed an interactive system which allows the viewer to see similar shots that are created based on cinematic principles. Lino [10] created a system that automatically generated cinematics by breaking a virtual space into what was called *director volumes*. The goal was to encode knowledge of cinematic principles into spaces in the world so the system would be able to place the camera accurately for low level shot manipulation. Work by Wu et al. [14] has created the *Film Editing Patterns* (FEP) language. This was designed to formalize standard cinematographic techniques and styles. The language specifies FEP constructs that constrain shot sequence features.

Systems that view cinematic generation as narrative discourse construction use methods similar to those in the natural language generation community. Darshak [9], for example, views cinematics as a hierarchical structure similar to how the work of Moore and Paris [12] views discourse. This hierarchical structure uses abstract and base shots to encode cinematic principles. Darshak then uses a decompositional planner to create a shot sequence using these abstract shots and their decompositions into base shots [5].

The Ember system [3,4] expands on ideas developed in Darshak, consisting of a partial-order, causal link planner [15] extended with the capability to reason about character decision making during cinematic generation. This reasoning leads to discourse structure intended to help maintain the salience of references to past events, characters or objects that can contribute to the explanation of characters' action-centered decision-making processes. In the experiment described below, we leverage Ember's ability to generate cinematics containing shot sequences that convey DDRSs. The shot specifications created by Ember make assumptions about the inferences drawn by human viewers, and the evaluation seeks to characterize those inferences as a means to further support Ember's expressivity.

3   Brief Summary of the Experiment

The experiment described here sought to gauge the extent to which inclusion of DDRSs in cinematic sequences can affect a viewer's comprehension of characters' decision-making processes. In this experiment, we showed viewers a cinematic sequence constructed by hand but whose story and discourse structure was created automatically by planning systems (In the case of the discourse, the structure was created by Ember). Subjects were divided into five treatment groups, and each treatment group viewed a cinematic story that differed from other groups only in the inclusion of a DDRS that focused on a decision made by the story's protagonist around his future plan for action. After viewing the cinematic, we asked subjects to characterize their judgment about why the protagonist decided on his course of actions. We then compared their judgments with the presence/absence/content of the DDRS they saw to gauge the DDRS impact.

Questions presented to subjects were written to specifically ask why actions had happened in the story. The possible answers were presented as still frames from the cinematic that conveyed specific actions, and subjects were asked to rank the set of still images in order of best answer to worst answer. Ten questions were asked. The first question was concerning the character decision. The next nine were a combination of three causal ancestor questions, three temporal questions, and three causal descendant questions.

87 paid participants were recruited on Amazon Turk and randomly assigned to one of five treatment groups. 25 recruited subjects were excluded due to incomplete surveys for a total of 62 participants.

Each participant viewed the cinematic assigned to their treatment group. After viewing the cinematic, participants were asked to complete a survey. The survey questions asked subjects to select actions that pertained to causal and/or motivational relationships between actions they had seen occur in the cinematics. These actions were presented as still frames showing a representative moment of each relevant action as portrayed previously in the cinematic they viewed.

In this study, we sought to evaluate whether the participants would rank answers that relate to the actions present in the conveyed decision sequences higher than the alternate actions that were not. To do this, we ran a Wilcoxon rank sum test between groups for the ranks of each relevant answer to the first question. We also wanted to evaluate whether the participants would rank answers that relate to the actions present in the conveyed decision sequences higher than their rankings for the same actions if no DDRS was conveyed. To do this, we ran a Wilcoxon rank sum test between groups for the ranks of the same answers.

Interestingly, for all but one of the comparison groups, the comparisons between groups resulted in no significant differences.

4 Discussion and Future Work

We found the lack of significant difference between groups surprising, as we felt in particular that the two of our treatment groups conformed to Hollywood conventions that clearly indicate distinct interpretations about the cause of characters' choices for action.

Two reasons why none of the different DDRS situations, including both control groups, resulted in any significant differences may be:

1. Uncontrolled structural or semantic aspects of the stories designed for the experiments may influence subjects' attribution of a character's motivation.
2. DDRS do not play the role in prompting inferences that we assumed they do.

It may be the case that there are underlying semantics around the sources for the knight's motivation that are uncontrolled for in our design. Also, it may be that DDRSs are not able to shift a viewer belief of a character's decision making.

References

1. Arijon, D.: Grammar of the Film Language. Silman-James Press (1976)
2. Bares, W., McDermott, S., Boudreaux, C., Thainimit, S.: Virtual 3D camera composition from frame constraints. In: Proceedings of the Eighth ACM International Conference on Multimedia, pp. 177–186 (2000)
3. Cassell, B.A., Young, R.M.: Ember, toward salience-based cinematic generation. In: Workshop on Intelligent Narrative Technologies at the Ninth Annual AAAI Conference of Artificial Intelligence and Interactive Digital Entertainment (2013)
4. Cassell, K.: Dynamic Generation of Narrative Discourse that Communicates Character Decision Making. North Carolina State University (2019)
5. Cheong, Y.G., Jhala, A., Bae, B.C., Young, R.M.: Automatically generating summary visualizations from game logs. In: AIIDE, pp. 167–172 (2008)

6. Christianson, D.B., Anderson, S.E., He, L.W., Salesin, D.H., Weld, D.S., Cohen, M.F.: Declarative camera control for automatic cinematography. In: Proceedings of the Thirteenth National Conference on Artificial Intelligence and the Eighth Innovative Applications of Artificial Intelligence Conference, pp. 148–155 (1996)
7. Christie, M., Normand, J.M.: A semantic space partitioning approach to virtual camera composition. Comput. Graph. Forum **24**(3), 247–256 (2005)
8. Elson, D.K., Riedl, M.O.: A lightweight intelligent virtual cinematography system for machinima production. In: Artificial Intelligence and Interactive Digital Entertainment (2007)
9. Jhala, A., Young, R.M.: Cinematic visual discourse: representation, generation, and evaluation. IEEE Trans. Comput. Intell. AI Games **2**(2), 69–81 (2010)
10. Lino, C.: Virtual camera control using dynamic spatial partitions. Ph.D. thesis, University Rennes 1 (2013)
11. Monaco, J.: How to Read a Film: The Art, Technology, Language, History, and Theory of Film and Media. Oxford University Press, New York (1981)
12. Moore, J.D., Paris, C.L.: Planning text for advisory dialogues: capturing intentional and rhetorical information. Comput. Linguist. **19**(4), 651–694 (1993)
13. Tomlinson, B., Blumberg, B., Nain, D.: Expressive autonomous cinematography for interactive virtual environments. In: Proceedings of the Fourth International Conference on Autonomous Agents, pp. 317–324. ACM (2000)
14. Wu, H.Y., Palù, F., Ranon, R., Christie, M.: Thinking like a director: film editing patterns for virtual cinematographic storytelling. ACM Trans. Multimedia Comput. Commun. Appl. **14**(4), 81:1–81:22 (Oct 2018). https://doi.org/10.1145/3241057, http://doi.acm.org.prox.lib.ncsu.edu/10.1145/3241057
15. Young, R.M., Pollack, M.E., Moore, J.D.: Decomposition and causality in partial order planning. In: Proceedings of the Second International Conference on AI and Planning Systems, pp. 188–193 (1994)

Narrative Urgency: Motivating Action in Interactive Digital Media

Bjørn Anker Gjøl, Niels Valentin Jørgensen, and Luis Emilio Bruni[✉]

Augmented Cognition Lab, Aalborg University Copenhagen,
A. C. Meyers Vænge 15, 2450 Copenhagen, Denmark
leb@create.aau.dk

Abstract. In this paper, we address specific problems related to the temporal development of narratives in games and interactive media in general. Game narratives can be inconsequential when they progress isolated from coherent temporal aspects, which in turn affects the possibility for pacing and experiencing a dramatic arc. The problem arises when the agency afforded to the players leads them to pursue non-narrative activities, which "put the story on hold".

We introduce the concept of *narrative urgency* in interactive narratives as a means of discussing and avoiding this issue. While 'agency' is the potential to act in interactive narratives, 'urgency' would be the desire to do so in the narrative context. This may serve as a starting point for designers to explore how players can be motivated to take actions that enable optimal narrative coherency and enhance suspension of disbelief.

Keywords: Interactive digital narratives · Narrative-driven games · Storytelling · Narrative time · Time frames · Temporality · Urgency · Agency

1 Introduction

Conflict is often regarded as the heart of drama [1], as it is used in narrative media to capture attention and evoke emotions. In film, directors are in complete control of these aspects, and use pacing to retain suspense and tension to keep viewers engaged to great effect [2], resulting in a condensed experience that blows an audience away in the span of a few hours.

What film and cinema does so well in terms of balanced storytelling is almost entirely lost on interactive narratives. Here, the idea of pacing is often rather vague, as plot and how it is told is only part of the experience, whereas *Agency* - the desire for certain actions, afforded by the system [3,4] - is usually considered the most important aspect of interactive experiences [5]. As a result of this, storytelling is easy to include (e.g. via *cutscenes* in games), but difficult to integrate [6], as user freedom negatively affects author control of the narrative - a problem often referred to as the *Interactive Paradox* [7] or the *Narrative Paradox* [8].

© Springer Nature Switzerland AG 2019
R. E. Cardona-Rivera et al. (Eds.): ICIDS 2019, LNCS 11869, pp. 178–182, 2019.
https://doi.org/10.1007/978-3-030-33894-7_19

A problem with interactive narratives is when they attempt to instill a sense of *urgency* in the player yet fail to deliver on it; nothing creates more dissonance than being tasked with saving the world from certain doom, and instead spending hours scavenging for ingredients for some old lady who wanted to have a bakesale, while doom waits. It is not suggested here that participants should necessarily be 'punished' for exerting their free will on a platform that allows them to do so. However, the narrative loses relevance when the urgency presented through the plot does not translate to any actual urgency when the user is in control. This 'pausing of time' is explained by Zagal et al. [9] as a *temporal bubble* - "If a game begins in temporal frame A, continues with B, and then goes back to A, there is a temporal bubble when, from the perspective of frame A, no time has passed during the activity in frame B". It is arguably detrimental to otherwise well-formed narrative arcs when *time itself* can be frozen indefinitely, awaiting the actions required of the user to 'restart' it.

2   Narrative Time

Usually, *time* is considered of utmost importance to how narratives are told, and at a very deep level, what narratives are [10]. *Change* is perhaps the most basic requirement of what constitutes *events* [7,11], more than one of which in a series might be considered a narrative, and change requires temporality: A *before* and an *after*. Traditional narratives operate in two different "temporalities", related to story and discourse - *story time*, the chronological time period covered by a story, and *discourse time*, the time taken by audiences to experience the narrative [12,13]. According to Juul [14], games operate on similar temporalities, namely "play time (the time the player takes to play) and event time (the time taken in the game world)". The only difference here is that event time also includes time taken in the game world *not* progressing narratives. Shown in Fig. 1 is Juul's mapping of these temporalities, in which he suggests that player actions (which take place in play/discourse time) are projected into the game world, and translated into the time frame that exists in the game.

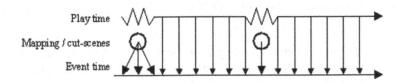

Fig. 1. Juul's depiction of how play time can be mapped to event time. The player takes actions in play time ("real" time), which are projected into the game world. Also shown in this model is how cutscenes create a break in play time, but are similarly mapped to event time. [14]

In Fig. 2 we present an updated version of Juul's mapping, featuring a temporal bubble as described in Sect. 1. This version contains four different temporalities, as opposed to the two in Juul's model. *Play time* constitutes the "real" time taken to play the game - similar to discourse time, but also featuring non-narrative activities. The second timeline, *Experienced time*, is a new addition; it indicates how players construct a linear timeline for their imagined storyworlds through their interaction with the game narrative. This experience of time relies on the player's perception of time by comparing the real-world play time with whichever representations of time are present in the game. *Gameworld time* signifies in general how time passes in the game world, including all of the events taking place - as such, it is more or less synonymous with 'story time' for traditional narratives. It may be implemented as the "intradiegetic clock" featured in most open-world-type games, or it may be more loosely defined. Finally, *Event time*, unlike Juul's single time frame, consists of all the separate event frames implemented in the game (three are shown in Fig. 2). As an event is experienced, the different 'steps' in the event time frame can be projected onto the *Gameworld time*, e.g. relating them to a specific in-game 'time of day' (if cues of this nature are present). After relating the event time to gameworld time, the event can then be mapped to the player's experienced time, as an event happening after what has previously been experienced.

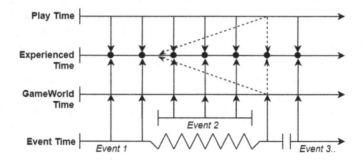

Fig. 2. An updated version of the game time diagram by Juul [14]. In this version, play time maps to experienced time, while the events played map to gameworld time, and from there, to experienced time, to the points where play time maps to as well. Shown in the figure is also a 'temporal bubble'.

Temporal bubbles, as shown in Fig. 2, occur when the first experienced frame of events (denoted in the figure as "event 1") is abandoned by the player before its completion, and another event frame (event 2) is instigated and played to completion instead. Following the conclusion of event frame 2, event frame 1 is then continued - but the time that has passed since it was abandoned plays no role in how the final events in the frame play out. The consequence of this is a 'break' in the player's experience of the game time, where the final part of event frame 1 is experienced both as happening at the time it is played, but also as something that happened immediately after the earlier events in the event frame. This conundrum could not possibly be explained by the original game time mapping by Juul, but the updated version presented in Fig. 2 considers cases like this. Furthermore, barring the game-specific terms, the model could apply to all forms of interactive narratives.

3   Narrative Urgency

The issues surrounding temporal bubbles could potentially be solved by having players act urgently towards narrative events that are supposedly urgent. Thus, we introduce the concept of *narrative urgency*: While "Agency" is the *potential* to act in interactive narratives [4], narrative urgency would be the *desire* to act in accordance with optimal narrative coherency - and create an appropriate outcome if the user failed to do so. Understanding and processing a narrative includes constructing a mental storyworld, based on the cues presented in the discourse (and in the case of games, presented in the game world) [15]. At its core, narrative urgency is linked to the construction of these storyworlds in the minds of players, as a process of determining what actions to pursue at a given moment, i.e. what actions are 'most necessary' in the player's perception of the world. Lack of narrative urgency is not always an issue - to some extent, urgency is something that can be imposed upon players by limiting their agency in certain situations, which at the present time is the standard approach for many applications. However, we argue that what is achieved through such an approach is simply an *illusion* of urgency. In addition to imagining a world in which the story takes place, immersing oneself in the narrative may also require that one 'allows' oneself to *believe in it* [16]. This act was first described more than 200 years ago by Samuel Taylor Coleridge as "the willing suspension of disbelief" [17], a term which has since been adopted and researched by scholars worldwide. What will be suggested here, is that a failure to "follow through" when the illusion of urgency is broken may negatively influence the believability, what is known in classical narratology as *verisimilitude* [12], of interactive narrative media, and consequently make it harder for users to suspend their disbelief and immerse themselves in the experience.

4   Conclusion

In our view, time in games has become lost in the medium. The aim of this paper has been to highlight and characterize the problem and its possible consequences when trying to find a balance between agency and narrative suspension of disbelief. It remains an open question what different kinds of "mechanisms" and rhetorical devices can contribute to incorporate the sense of urgency in order to achieve a suitable balance between gameplay and narrative. There are many conceivable different solutions for the problem in accordance with the specific requirements and characteristics of a given application. Combining narrative and storyworld in a more dynamic and complementary relationship - where the player is made aware of time and its consequences, but not constricted by it - can yield more coherent designs in which the interactor chooses the actions from the available response-repertoire in accordance to the narrative context, ensuring the continuity and the quality of his or her suspension of disbelief.

References

1. Szilas, N., Estupiñán, S., Richle, U.: Automatic detection of conflicts in complex narrative structures. In: Rouse, R., Koenitz, H., Haahr, M. (eds.) ICIDS 2018. LNCS, vol. 11318, pp. 415–427. Springer, Cham (2018). https://doi.org/10.1007/978-3-030-04028-4_49
2. Bizzocchi, J.: Games and narrative: an analytical framework. Loading **1**(1), 5–10 (2007)
3. Harrell, D.F., Zhu, J.: Agency play: dimensions of agency for interactive narrative design. In: Proceedings of the 2nd AAAI Spring Symposium on Intelligent Narrative Technologies, pp. 156–162 (2009)
4. Wardrip-Fruin, N., Mateas, M., Dow, S., Sali, S.: Agency reconsidered. In: DiGRA 2009 - Proceedings of the 2009 DiGRA International Conference. Brunel University (2009)
5. Stern, A.: Embracing the combinatorial explosion: a brief prescription for interactive story R&D. In: Spierling, U., Szilas, N. (eds.) ICIDS 2008, vol. 5334, pp. 1–5. Springer, Heidelberg (2008). https://doi.org/10.1007/978-3-540-89454-4_1
6. Domsch, S.: Storyplaying : Agency and Narrative in Video Games. Wordware Publishing (2013)
7. Ryan, M.L.: From narrative games to playable stories: toward a poetics of interactive narrative. Storyworlds: J. Narrat. Stud. **1**, 43–59 (2009)
8. Bruni, L.E., Baceviciute, S.: Narrative intelligibility and closure in interactive systems. In: Koenitz, H., Sezen, T.I., Ferri, G., Haahr, M., Sezen, D., Ç atak, G. (eds.) ICIDS 2013. LNCS, vol. 8230, pp. 13–24. Springer, Cham (2013). https://doi.org/10.1007/978-3-319-02756-2_2
9. Zagal, J.P., Mateas, M.: Temporal frames: a unifying framework for the analysis of game temporality. In: Proceedings of the 2007 DiGRA International Conference: Situated Play. The University of Tokyo (2007)
10. Ricoeur, P.: Time and Narrative, vol. 1, 1st edn. University of Chicago Press (1990)
11. Toolan, M.: Narrative: Linguistic and Structural Theories, 2 edn, pp. 459–473. Elsevier Science (2006)
12. Chatman, S.: Story and Discourse: Narrative Structure in Fiction and Film, 1st edn. Cornell University Press (1980)
13. Genette, G.: Narrative Discourse: An Essay in Method. Cornell University Press (1980)
14. Juul, J.: Introduction to game time. In: First Person: New Media as Story, Performance, and Game, pp. 131–142. MIT Press (2004)
15. Herman, D.: Basic Elements of Narrative, 1st edn. Wiley, Hoboken (2011)
16. Ryan, M.L.: Cambridge companions to literature. In: Toward a definition of narrative, pp. 22–36. Cambridge University Press (2007)
17. Coleridge, S.T.: Biographia Literaria (1817)

"What'chu Lookin' At?": Narrative, Spectatorship, and Ludic Constructivism in Variable State's *Virginia*

Ryan House[(✉)] [iD]

University of Wisconsin Milwaukee, Milwaukee, WI 53201, USA
rnhouse@uwm.edu

Abstract. This paper focuses on Variable State's 2016 game *Virginia*, a game that may have as much in common with film as it does traditional video games. One of the things that makes *Virginia* stand out is a complete lack of dialogue, either spoken or textual. Instead, interactions within the game are abstracted; players are asked to intuit character motivations through body language and other non-verbal cues. *Virginia* is an interesting marriage between film and game design that surpasses the legacy of interactive films – the game has only one story to tell; there are no branching narratives or multiple endings. Instead, I argue that the game makes literal David Bordwell's constructivist theory of narrative film in that the player must execute operations corresponding to filmic devices in order to frame narrative information within their point of view in the game.

Keywords: Narrative · Spectator · Point-of-view · Video game · Film · *Virginia*

1 Introduction

For the past several years, the medium of digital games has experienced an expansion of definition. Many game designers are moving past traditional expectations of games, particularly in terms of telling stories. Narrative games are becoming increasingly prevalent in the games market, and some even find high-profile, mainstream success. Campo Santo's *Firewatch*, for instance, sold half a million copies within its first month. But for every *Firewatch*, there are innumerable narrative games dismissed out of hand as "walking simulators," a derisive term that points to the absence of traditional markers of the medium, such as fail states, complex mechanics, or action sequences. This criticism ignores the fundamental similarities between narrative games and other games and undermines the innovation that these games bring to the medium.

To explore this idea, this paper focuses on Variable State's 2016 game *Virginia*, a game that may have as much in common with film as it does traditional video games. Inspired by the likes of *Twin Peaks* and *The X Files*, *Virginia* tells the story of two FBI agents investigating a missing person case in the rural setting of the titular state. One of the things that makes *Virginia* stand out is a complete lack of dialogue, either spoken or textual. Instead, interactions within the game are abstracted; players are asked to intuit

R. E. Cardona-Rivera et al. (Eds.): ICIDS 2019, LNCS 11869, pp. 183–189, 2019.
https://doi.org/10.1007/978-3-030-33894-7_20

character information through body language and other non-verbal cues. *Virginia* is an interesting marriage between film and game design that surpasses the legacy of interactive films – the game has only one story to tell; there are no branching narratives or multiple endings. Instead, the game makes literal David Bordwell's constructivist theory of narrative film in that it requires the player to execute filmic operations in order to frame narrative information within their point of view in the game.

To this end, *Virginia*'s designers employ many traditional techniques of game design as well, such as the use of lighting, contrasting colors, and sound in level design to direct player's attention to pertinent information. Narrative information is woven into the game's spaces, exemplifying Henry Jenkins' theory of narrative architecture. Through evoked, enacted, and embedded narratives, the players begin to construct the game's plot by virtue of moving through its spaces and gazing at its details. In this action is where the ludic activity lies; players are responsible for putting the pieces of the narrative together and may very well miss vital information. This paper argues that *Virginia* transcends traditional distinctions between film and video games, and in doing so, opens both mediums to new possibilities.

Virginia was released in 2016 by Variable State, a small developer out of London, who describe the game as a "first person interactive drama" [1]. The game is an experiment that introduces the vocabulary of film into the realm of videogames. Johnathan Burroughs, the writer and main creative force for the game, attributes the inspiration of this game to Brendon Chung's experimental short *Thirty Flights of Loving* and the ways it incorporates cuts into the context of real-time gameplay. While *Thirty Flights...* is a brief, 10-minute experience, Burroughs was interested in developing that idea into a feature-length narrative, particularly focused on characterization and emotional investment on the part of the player. The result is a game in which the player not only experiences the narrative from the point of view of a character but must also build that narrative – in part – by following cinematic and game design cues to frame relevant narrative information within that point of view in order to interpret the abstract and surreal story. Burroughs' insistence that these filmic narrative devices be deployed in real, game-time rather than in cutscenes underlines his intended experience: "We don't want the player to feel like they're witnessing a cinematic play out around them. They should always feel like they are the character they are embodying, existing in the moment they're experiencing" [2].

Placing this emphasis on a player's immersed experience means relinquishing some narrative control to them. Unnoticed details or paths not chosen could very well change a player's interpretation, thus creating a multitude of readings. In this way, *Virginia* exemplifies Roland Barthes' writerly text – a text that requires more from a "reader" than simply absorbing the words on the page or the images on the screen; the text must allow the reader to produce meaning through the interpretation of what is written/shown. As Barthes explains, "to interpret a text is not to give it a (more or less justified, more or less free) meaning, but on the contrary to appreciate what plural constitutes it" [3]. *Virginia*'s plurality of meaning is predicated upon its main ludic activity – looking. The game succeeds in its ambition of adapting cinematic techniques to the medium and, in doing so, transforms spectatorship into a ludic activity.

2 The Processes of Looking

To account for *Virginia*'s narrative requires a theory of narrative that considers the active participation of the spectator. In his seminal work Narration in the Fiction Film, David Bordwell provides an account of narration in which the viewer of film is involved in a dynamic process of executing assumptions, inferences, and hypotheses via cues derived from the film that he calls the Constructivist theory of narration. Bordwell's work represents a break from the theretofore traditional concepts of narration: mimetic and diegetic – theories that Bordwell claims favor mediums other than film, and neither account for the subjective spectator. He argues that mimetic and diegetic theories of narrative:

> ... have little to say about the spectator, except that he or she is relatively passive. Perspectival accounts tend to treat the viewer pointillistically, as the sum total of ideal vantage points shifting from shot to shot.... [M]imetic theories assign few mental properties to the spectator.... Diegetic theories... also tend to downplay the viewer's role.... The passivity of the spectator in diegetic theories generally is suggested not only by the extensive borrowing of mimetic concepts of narration but also by the use of terms like the 'position' or the 'place' of the subject. Such metaphors lead us to conceive of the perceiver as backed into a corner by conventions of perspective, editing, narrative point of view, and psychic unity [4].

Bordwell's Constructivist theory foregoes the preoccupation of the spectator's "position" of the mimetic and diegetic accounts to focus on how the text leads the viewer to "execute a definable variety of *operations*" that constitute their mental experience of the narrative [5]. This dynamic psychological process foregrounds three factors: perceptual capacities, the bottom-up processes of our perception, like flicker fusion and apparent motion; prior knowledge and experience, a drawing on "schemata derived from our transactions with the everyday world, with other artworks, and with other films;" and the material and structure of the text itself, or those "cues, patterns, and gaps that shape the viewer's application of schemata and the testing of hypotheses" [6]. Bordwell notes that while these factors can be isolated in theory, in practice they are intertwined and all but inseparable. For the purposes of this paper, I will focus on the latter two factors – prior knowledge/experience and the material and structure of the text – to build an argument for how *Virginia* remediates the Constructivist theory of film spectatorship to video games.

Before I begin a close reading of the game, I want to expand on Bordwell's classifications of the schemata drawn upon in a spectator's utilization of prior knowledge to comprehend a narrative. He identifies three major categories – the prototype schemata, the template schemata, and the procedural schemata – and each represents a larger structure that the previous schemata operate within. Prototype schemata are useful when trying to understand individual characters, settings, actions, goals, et cetera. Understanding the protagonists in *Virginia*, for instance, involves applying the protypes of 'partners' and 'law enforcement.' Next, template schemata function as a framework, or a "filling system" in Bordwell's terms, within which the viewer attempts to fit the protype schemata into a larger system based on other similar narratives. These schemata assist in filling in gaps of information. Template schemata apply to structural characteristics like temporality and causality, too. Finally, prototype and template schemata are subsumed by the procedural schemata, or "those operational protocols which dynamically acquire and organize information" [7]. These processes operate according to procedural rationales, such as compositional, or the justification of "material in terms of its relevance to story necessity;" realistic, or according to "notion [s] of plausibility derived from some conception of the way things work in the world;" transtextual, or according to established motifs of the genre or medium; and artistic, to justify material in terms of its own sake – its artistic merit [8]. These schemata account for the mental processes undergone by the spectator in their experience and interpretation of narrative elements presented to them. Understanding these processes allows filmmakers (and game designers) to develop and exploit them to deliver a range of intended experiences to the spectator through the structure and materials of the text.

3   Looking as Game Play

Now I will discuss a few scenes from *Virginia* to explicate how the game enacts these processes of Constructivist narration, and how the player actively contributes to the uncovering of the fabula (story) by participating in the divulgement of the syuzhet (discourse). Because the narrative is communicated without the aid of any dialogue whatsoever, players must ascertain the characters motivations, goals, and relationship by way of "reading" the environment of the game. In his work on "narrative architecture," Henry Jenkins suggests that we should view games "less as stories than as spaces ripe with narrative possibility" [9]. *Virginia*'s spaces imbed narrative information within their scenography – players are asked to interpret details of the world to intuit exposition, characterization, and themes. The living spaces of the two lead characters, Tarver and Halperin, illuminate aspects of their characters: The stacks of moving boxes and general disarray of Tarver's apartment reflects her (perhaps over) dedication to her job. She lives alone with few if any visitors and has yet to even take the time to fully unpack. She is living out of those boxes: the only things up and running are the computer she no doubt uses for work. A scene in which she imagines a fulfilling future highlights this through its opposite: this hypothetical apartment is bright, decorated, and even has a card table set up for a poker night with friends. Meanwhile, a tour of Halperin's living space midway through the game uncovers a trauma of her recent past – a lift on the stairs, bathroom modifications for a disabled person, and an empty hospital bed allow readers to infer the story of her mother, of whom we have seen a picture that Halperin wears in a charm around her neck. Thus, without stopping the action for scripted, emotional dialogue, *Virginia* shows us the story of these two women by asking us to fill in gaps of knowledge around these prototype schemata. But, I want to clarify, this is not the showing of mimetic narration – what is interesting about the way *Virginia* shows us this information is that it is all incidental. You need not even enter the bedroom with the hospital bed or the modified bathroom to advance the game – that information is there for players to find rather than being conspicuously paraded through the *mise-en-scene* as if to say, "I'm important! Pay attention!" In this way, *Virginia* involves the player in the responsibility of the unfurling of narrative information via the syuzhet, while simultaneously undergoing the operational protocols of interpretation.

This responsibility on the part of the player to uncover pertinent information is not to suggest that *Virginia* leaves players to their own devices. In fact, *Virginia* communicates to the player very specific modes of looking through its very structure and content. For instance, because the game uses a first-person perspective, the act of looking is already privileged through the very way the game is presented. Likewise, that the player character is an investigator for the FBI provides reason for the player to look closely at details. The game provides these sorts of template schemata to encourage players to respond as they have been conditioned to do through other, similar media and experiences. I have mentioned already the pop culture influences on the game from shows like *The X-Files* and *Twin Peaks*. These transtextual references invite players to make assumptions about characters and events in *Virginia* based on their knowledge of these similar texts. For instance, players can easily assume why Halperin's office is way down in the basement of the FBI office or why Tarver has been assigned to investigate her. Memories of Dale Cooper enjoying coffee infuses the diner in *Virginia* with an eerie familiarity. Moreover, *Virginia* presents itself much like a film – from the opening credits, to the editing, the musical score, and even its duration – and this communicates to its players how to interact with it, specifically through the act of looking, or framing the narrative information within the point of view of the "camera."

I will next discuss two scenes that showcase how *Virginia* guides player action into a cinematic aesthetic: one overtly, the other subtly. In the first example, the designers utilize techniques of level design often seen in game development to direct the player's gaze. In this case, light and sound are used to lead the player through the execution of filmic operations, namely the tilt and pan of the camera. In the first example, Tarver, ostensibly waking from a dream, jolts upright in bed, the camera focusing on the opposite wall of her bedroom. Around her in the bed are pieces of evidence, mirroring a scene from earlier where she is examining them in this very spot. By imitating that scene, the designers are betting that players will once again focus on those items, trying to figure out what object to click on and distracting them from looking elsewhere. Before long, a low guttural noise emanates from her immediate right. The player, now back in control of the camera, instinctively follows the sound to find a buffalo nonchalantly gazing at her from across the room. As the player focuses on the buffalo, beams of red light appear over its body, prompting the player to turn again to locate the source of this light, seemingly directly behind her. As the player frames the illuminated closet door within her point of view, the screen cuts to black and the scene closes. Using elements of level design normally deployed to guide players through a space, the game designers successfully orchestrate an act of cinematography through the player's action to create an atmospheric and tense dream sequence. I call this example overt in its utilization of these processes because the movement of the camera procedurally affects the state of the game. The duration of the scene will extend indefinitely until the player completes the movement of the camera to the closet door. However, other scenes are more discrete.

My second example comes from a scene earlier in the game when Halperin and Tarver first drive into town. The player is positioned in the passenger seat and is free to look around the interior of the car, read the case files in her lap, or stare out the window. These scenes are interspersed with cuts to signify the passage of time. After the last of these cuts, the score (which happens to be the game's main theme) swells as the town's "Welcome" sign passes by on the right. Halperin pulls the car over to the scenic overlook and the player has three choices of interesting things to look at. First, a sign with some information about the town of Kingdom; second, the town itself; and finally, Halperin in the driver's seat. Based on the position of the player's viewpoint from looking at the Welcome sign earlier, a logical order takes shape: first the sign, then the town, then Halperin. As the score builds to a crescendo, the remaining duration of the scene becomes linked to the music in the player's mind – there is a feeling that when the score reaches its conclusion, the scene is over regardless of what the player has missed. This causes, in my experience anyway, a desire to look at all three without lingering too long on any. The result of this action – the panning from right to left to frame Halperin before the end of the scene – is a match cut to the next scene of the diner where Halperin is seated in the booth across from the player, but still facing in the same direction as in the car. Thus, the game influences the player to create this artful camera movement apropos of nothing other than artistic motivation. The movement is not necessary to change the game state (as in the prior example) or to acquire narrative information (as in other scenes), but it does satisfy a cinematic aesthetic – one that is familiar to the player through her prior knowledge and experience with other media.

4   Conclusion

At the beginning of this paper, I made the claim that *Virginia* represents a potential shift in the ways we think about games and films – in how they are different, and how they are similar. The game proceduralizes the actions of the player, not through actual, literally procedural codes and rules, but through a co-option of the player's psychological processes – it uses suggestion and cues as much as affordances and constraints to lead them through the experience to a desired (albeit inherently plural due to the dependency on the player's inferences, etc.) outcome. This in turn creates not the forking paths in the vein of traditional notions of interactive films, but a multiplicity of reading possibilities in a way that explodes Barthes' writerly text into the 21st century.

Because *Virginia* requires the player to simultaneously take part in constructing the syuzhet while also interpreting the fabula, players undergo shifts in cognitive modes of interaction: an oscillation between deep and hyper attention. Deep and hyper attention are terms coined by Hayles to describe the contrasting ways that we engage with various media objects. Deep attention, Hayles writes, "is characterized by concentrating on a single object for long periods... ignoring outside stimuli while so engaged, preferring a single information stream, and having a high tolerance for long focus times. Hyper attention is characterized by switching focus rapidly among different streams, seeking a high level of stimulation, and having a low tolerance for boredom." [10] The two modes of attention highlight the phenomenological differences brought about in the user that is created through the interface of the game and underline the defining characteristic that narrative games like *Virginia* share: ludic Constructivist narration and its power of absorption.

In an article entitled "Games are Better Without Stories" for The Atlantic, Ian Bogost writes: "Think of a medium as the aesthetic form of common materials. Poetry aestheticizes language. Painting aestheticizes flatness and pigment. Photography does so for time. Film, for time and space" [11]. He goes on to say that "games are not a new, interactive medium for stories. Instead, games are the aesthetic form of everyday objects. Of ordinary life. Take a ball and a field: you get soccer. Take property-based wealth and the Depression: you get Monopoly" [12]. While I do not necessarily disagree with this observation, I feel that it is missing something. Games aestheticize *effort and attention*. They demand a form of engagement that television, film, theatre, and even novels do not: namely, a responsibility on the part of the player/reader to propel the narrative forward; to enable the text. I feel that Bogost's article is but a (somewhat) recent example of an ongoing attempt to further taxonomize games into neat, but narrow definitions; to further sequester them away from "serious" media like film. It can be helpful, of course, to have agreed upon meanings and definitions about what it is we consume, produce, and study, but, being overly concerned with what games are or are not may prevent us from ever seeing what they can be. And, furthermore, what they can lend to those other media.

References

1. Virginia. https://variablestate.com/projects/Virginia. Accessed 19 July 2019
2. Alexander, L.: Strange and Mundane Come Together in Variable State's *Virginia*. http://www.gamasutra.com/view/news/221585/Strange_and_mundane_come_together_in_Variable_States_Virginia.php. Accessed 19 July 2019
3. Barthes, R.: S/Z. Translated by R. Miller. Hill and Wang, New York (1974)
4. Bordwell, D.: Narration in the Fiction Film. University of Wisconsin Press, Madison (1985)
5. Ibid. emphasis in original
6. Ibid
7. Ibid
8. Ibid
9. Jenkins, H.: Game design as narrative architecture. In: First Person: New Media as Story, Performance, and Game, pp. 118–130. MIT Press, Cambridge (2004)
10. Hayles, N.K.: Hyper and deep attention: the generational divide in cognitive modes. In: Profession, no. 1, pp. 187–199 (2007)
11. Bogost, I.: Video Games are Better Without Stories." http://www.theatlantic.com/technology/archive/2017/04/video-games-stories/524148/
12. Ibid

The Story We Cannot See: On How a Retelling Relates to Its Afterstory

Bjarke Alexander Larsen[✉], Luis Emilio Bruni, and Henrik Schoenau-Fog

Aalborg University, Copenhagen, Denmark
bal@create.aau.dk

Abstract. The field of Emergent Narrative in digital narrative studies has seen a lot of research since its inception in 1999, and a lot of it is helpful, but also there has been confusion in terms and a lack of focus on the specifics of how the narrative is shaped in the mind of the player. The term itself has been used to both describe the ensuing field, the concept, the process, and the resulting narrative experience. This paper aims to clarify these misunderstandings by investigating the field and defining the term "afterstory" to help solidify the relationship between the differing aspects of Emergent Narrative. Afterstory is specifically defined as the virtual, mental story that exists in the player's mind after play and informed by the interactions and their perspective on them. Then, using previous work on retellings, the paper will relate afterstory to how people retell their afterstories, and what we can use those retellings for in relation to the system that helped form them. In conclusion, some examples will be brought forth that showcase the difficult nature of extrapolating a retelling's quality to its interactive narrative system's quality, but how it can still be done with careful, purposeful analysis.

Keywords: Emergent Narrative · Afterstory · Interactive Digital Narrative · Emergent storytelling · Storyworld · Retelling

1 Introduction

This paper looks into the field of emergent narratives, specifically focusing on the idea of (interactive) stories as experiences originating from the creative interaction between a storytelling system and a human subject. Over the years, this field has seen some inconsistent and ambiguous definitions and this paper hopes to clarify some of the confusion by reviewing several perspectives and introducing the concept "afterstory", to help clarify the differences between the storytelling system in play, the narrativization process, the resulting product and the possible retellings that occur later. Furthermore, the paper will look at the concept of retellings, as proposed by Eladhari [7], to discuss how it can be used and how it relates to the afterstory concept, thus providing use-cases and potential avenues for research on how to use retellings to assess the quality of interactive storytelling systems, as well as the potential pitfalls when doing so.

© Springer Nature Switzerland AG 2019
R. E. Cardona-Rivera et al. (Eds.): ICIDS 2019, LNCS 11869, pp. 190–203, 2019.
https://doi.org/10.1007/978-3-030-33894-7_21

2   The Ambiguity of the Emergent Narrative Field

The origin of Emergent Narrative in the field of interactive storytelling is often attributed to Aylett's paper [2] from 1999[1], and then further expanded in Aylett and Louchart et al.'s papers [16–19, 27], which demonstrates how narrative can "emerge" out of the events of an interactive experience. Their classic example is seeing narrative structures from a football match, like a late substitution scoring the winning goal etc. This ability for games and simulation-esque systems to create interactions and events that emerge into narratives, is a powerful idea that has since proliferated throughout both games, narrative studies, interactive storytelling etc. [2, 10, 11, 24, 28, 30]. However, when we look closer at how people talk about emergent narratives, we get a few different results. Outside Aylett and Louchart's definitions [2, 17], another often cited example is Koenitz' "System-Process-Product" model [11, 12], where a IDN (Interactive Digital Narrative) system can be described as a sum of potential narratives. Using Montfort [21], Koenitz distinguishes between the system and its output (and crucially, the relation between those). The output, relevant here, is similar to the notion of an emergent narrative, even if Koenitz does not use the term "emergent", but rather describes the system as a possibility space of different narratives that, through the user's actions and the opportunities given by the system, are instantiated into a single instantiated narrative [12]. This product of an IDN system, a "recording" of a single playthrough can be understood as a more traditional narrative, after the fact.

Ryan et al., in 2015 [25], made this definition: "by emergent narrative', we mean the application area characterized by digital, fundamentally interactive systems whose narratives emerge bottom-up". He is here more talking about the area of research (a turn Aylett and Louchart later also did [18]). Quickly, we see emergent narrative both as a research field, as a concept, and an emergent narrative by itself. This final distinction was one James Ryan included in his latest (to our knowledge) definition of the term in his PhD thesis [24]:

> "[Emergent narrative is] the methodology characterized by computational systems in which narrative emerges bottom-up from the interaction of processes in underlying simulations that typically feature autonomous characters (or, alternatively, the actual narrative material produced by this method)."

This definition is relevant for two reasons: Firstly, the mention of the term as meaning two different things in one, but also another: Ryan here has no inclusion, nor a need, for a user. Ryan does not require interaction, which is something Aylett and Louchart did. The user can be purely passive, while the system creates behaviour that we read narratives out of.

---

[1] We say often attributed because an older source is Galyean III, who coined the term in their PhD thesis on Narrative Guidance of Interactivity, from 1995 [8]. However, while their use and definition is interesting, they do not have a focus on emergence the same way Aylett had.

Walsh [30] takes a slightly different approach to his definition, and splits emergent narrative in two. The first one could be classified as the narrative sense-making process, which is making narrative out of non-narrative behaviour (the simulation), while the second is seen as a product of interaction between the user and the digital agent (or bot) within the simulated environment, more akin to improvisation. His key point is that in the first definition, the simulation itself is not a narrative product, but rather purely a simulation out of which can be read a narrative. Here, Ryan agrees with him. Every game generates events, but that is not enough to make an emergent narrative: Someone or something has to curate those events into a story [24], and therein lies the emergent narrative: The events themselves are not a narrative. What Walsh does not get to is Ryan's ideas of the system performing the curation (his word, roughly meaning storification, but focused on the idea that events are curated into story-sense rather than made) necessary to create a narrative artifact out of the simulation behaviour. Ryan sees the system as capable of presenting stories to an experiencer without the need for the experiencer to do the work to put that story together themselves. He acknowledges that most emergent storytelling up to this point has relied on what he calls mental curation, but his point highlights the difference between event generation and curation. Walsh's second definition, as he points out himself, has similarities with Aylett and Louchart's focus on RPG game systems and their improvisational narrative structure, as his focus here is on the emergence of new narrative events instigated by a user interacting with the system (his example is a player playing the Sims and actively role-playing within the system, an example Jenkins also used in his use of the term from 2004 [10]).

Swartjes [28], too, has another definition: *"Emergent narrative can be seen both as a theory of narrative in virtual environments, addressing the paradox between free-form interactivity from a first person perspective and narrative structure, and as a design approach"* [28]. Here is another element added, namely that of Emergent narrative as a design approach. The authoring and design of Emergent narrative is another topic, that Aylett and Louchart, along with Suttie and Lim also began focusing on [27]. This paper will not focus on that aspect, though, so please refer to those sources if interested.

So, we are left with several concepts within the field of emergent narrative: As the design of a simulation, as design process or approach, both through the designers (authors) themselves and the approach that guides them. There's the simulation itself, and the events that it produces, there's the curation (or storification) of those events into a single story, which can be experienced, or has been experienced, in the mind of a person, depending how you view it. There's the parts that happen inside the system and those that happen in the mind of the person experiencing them and there's different kinds of experiencing based on whether the user can interact or not. Wrapping all of this under one term is not inherently a bad thing, but it has led to confusion, as shown by Walsh, Ryan [25, 30] and others. Therefore we believe some clarification is in order, which we will do by ordering the events and proposing a new term in the place of story as outcome: The *afterstory*.

1. There's a world, a design, a system that can construct a large (but finite) amount of possible events and world states. This world (game/design) is designed by people who intentionally placed content and rules within the world to run with certain behaviours and with certain kinds of schemas, but ultimately, it is left to run by itself or in interaction with a user.
2. The world runs its simulation, with or without interaction as a self-contained emergent system wherein events occur, creating emergent behaviour[2].
3. Those events form what Ryan calls a chronicle: A series of events. This is *not* an emergent narrative, nor is it a story.
4. Those events are curated, sorted and accentuated into an experience akin to a story by the experiencer. This is a narrative experience. The system here has conveyed a narrative to the user, through its system. Vitally, this can happen *during* play or after play, and both are equally valid and, probably, happens in equal amounts. If it happens during, it has the possibility of feeding back into the events and thereby altering the chronicle real-time.
5. This experience ultimately leaves the player with what we will call an afterstory. It exists in the mind of the user and there alone. They can then choose to retell it to another person, at which point it will be relayed as a new (retold) narrative (more on this in Sect. 4).

This entire process is what we would call Emergent Narrative (see Fig. 1 for a visual representation). This is what the field of Emergent Narrative studies concerns itself with. It is thereby not the outcome as *that* is the narrative that did emerge, and it is, by definition, not emerging anymore; it is an afterstory.

3   Afterstory: A Definition

Afterstory is a term we first coined in a previous paper from 2016 about game mechanics and narrative [14], as a term to describe the specific, actual story that happened as a result of a play experience. It is specifically the (static) story itself, rather than the behaviour that creates it. It is, to use Koenitz' word, a "product" [12] of the systemic interaction *and* the player's perspective on it, but not to be compared with Koenitz' use of that word since it is not an instantiation in the sense that it is real; rather, an afterstory is purely in the mind of the player. Any game can produce an afterstory, and every game does when you play it. This is what you remember after you close the game down. It is what happened to you, with emphasis on the past tense. The afterstory can vary greatly from person to person in a more emergent game or be more similar in a linear game, but there will always be subtle nuances, since the player's interpretation, reading, and feeling of narrativity will be different, even in a completely scripted sequence (even in a movie). It is thus a product of both what happened in the simulation of the game (did you take path A or path B, etc.) but also, inherently, the player's reading and reasoning of those events. If they focused more on one part of the game than another, if they disliked a part, their afterstory will be coloured by

---

[2] This inherently assumes that the system is capable of creating emergent behaviour.

that read. A person will always keep their own idea of what happened, rather than what they actually did. As memories, the afterstory is paradoxically both virtual and actual. It exists both in the mind of the player and as something that has happened, but not as something that is measurable or real.

It is specifically called an after*story* and not a narrative because it is story-like in its nature. If we look at the traditional story/discourse split [1, 26] (or more relevant to this discussion, Ryan's reinterpretation of that split), a narrative is the *"textual actualization"* of a story when it is told through a discourse [26]. Marie-Laure Ryan says that a story is *"a mental image, a cognitive construct that concerns certain types of entities and relations between these entities"*, or, *"story is narrative in a virtual form."* [26, p. 7]. If we map that onto our previous distinctions, story is then the pre-actualized world, it is the designed world before it is run: The possible stories. Or what Ryan (James, this time, not Marie-Laure) (and others) calls the storyworld [24]. The discourse is then the simulation itself; both in how it simulates and how it conveys what is simulated. Those two together create a narrative (emergent) that the player experiences. But inside the mind of the player, after the experience, it once again becomes virtual. No longer actualized (despite the fact that it is actual), it is now a story and not a narrative, because it is not being told. In the instance that it is being told by the system, it is a narrative, but as we mentioned before, what the player is left with (in their mind) is a story. Thus, afterstory.

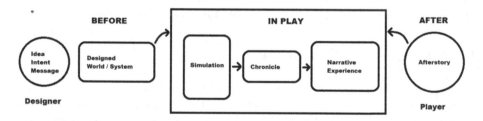

Fig. 1. A crude overview of the Emergent Narrative concept, as explained in the text. There exists three primary positions, one before play, one during and one after, and while they all affect each other, the distinction is useful. The circles represent people and the elements inside purely exist in the mind.

Now, the question is, what do we use this for? First, it helps us clarify the distinction between the simulation, the storification process and the outcome of the emergent narrative experience. By specifically separating the outcome from the experience, we can better understand them as two separate things, and see how one leads to the other, as well as how the system that created them is shaped. The second aspect of afterstory comes in what it is already used for in everyday scenarios: Retelling.

4   Retelling

Eladhari's paper from 2018 [7] discusses the possibility of retelling stories from the play of interactive storytelling experiences, and how that can be viewed as a potential avenue for critique and analysis of the system they came from. This is a relevant thesis that has some great potential, but to understand how, we can put it in relation to afterstory. Eladhari doesn't use the word afterstory, but her use of retelling touches on it: *"The narrative layer of re-tellings consists of tales told about events and actions in an INS or a game world."*. The "events and actions" that happened in the game, as viewed by the player, is the afterstory. What the retelling then is, is a new narrative that is formed with the afterstory as its story content: With a new discourse created by the reteller. To put it in traditional words, the relationship between afterstory and retelling is the same as the one between story and narrative. As any narrative, this retelling is coloured the moment it is told; there is an inherent degree of interpretation, projection, superimposition or formulation within it. Eladhari's example of a retelling of The Sims is a great example: Here, one of the characters has just earned a little bit of money and the first thing they want to do after is to give it to charity. This could've been viewed as the machinations of the system working, but the reteller shows that they are reading more into it: This act has meaning because of what happened before, and because of how the player views the characters. When these events are then retold, they are given meaning again by the discourse of the reteller: They are given dramatic weight, and they are even retold in a different order than they would have experienced them in game (as they would have known that it was money for a charity before performing the action, a fact we are only told as the letter is sent). These retellings are not exact copies of the afterstories they are coming from, as it is impossible to tell a story without, well, telling it, and thereby shading it through a discourse. This retelling, when it has been told, is then interpreted *again* by the new readers, who never experienced the events that led to the afterstory but only get the retelling, and then add their own layer of interpretation to it. Eladhari touches upon this as well when she quotes some of the comments that have different viewpoints of the retelling. A reader of this retelling could then take what they got from reading it and retell that again to someone else, and thereby have a new narrative created from a different type of afterstory, and like a great game of telephone, this chain could potentially go on forever, losing all resemblance and relevance to the story system and player who helped spawn it in the first place. This cycle, it should be mentioned, is no different than a regular retelling cycle of any kind of narrative, as is by no means a negative to the concept of retelling, but it is something to bear in mind.

Another type of retelling that functions a little differently is the automated retellings created runtime, such as log files or character-generated diaries. Eladhari mentions how this corresponds to Koenitz' notion of "product" from his framework [12]. And this is indeed an immediate retelling rather than an afterstory as it has a built-in discourse through its medium (and is not inside the player). A log file uses the structure and discourse of a log file. What it tells about, is in theory the same bones that make up the afterstory, but it is different from the afterstory of the player as this has none of the player's interpretation and is only a "series of actions and events"; or the chronicle. Other types of retellings Eladhari mentions are community generated ones (such as the ones in Second Life [15] or Eve [5,9], simultaneous ones such as livestreams and esports (as the one mentioned by Eladhari [23]), or stories written from the perspective of a character (see Murnane [22]). Others still could be pass-along stories like "Boatmurdered" [29] or comedic serials like "Breaking Madden" [3].

Eladhari's primary thesis with the paper is that we can use these retellings as an instrument for critique of the storytelling system that created them. The idea being that if we consider leaving a meaningful impact on the player a strong criteria for judging the story, this retelling is proof that a *"game or an INS - at its base level - has provided an experience that is significant or meaningful enough that it is worth telling someone else about."* And this is a powerful thing. Ryan mentions something similar: *"The greater our urge to tell stories about games, the stronger the suggestion that we experienced the game narratively."* [26, p. 193] This suggestion is obvious and straightforward at first: If we told a story from an experience it was powerful enough to retell, and that must mean there was something worth talking about, some narrative quality the player experienced as strong enough to want to talk about. However, if we delve a little deeper into it, this correlation is more nuanced. And here is where the afterstory/retelling split can help us. Because while the correlation at large might stick, there are several caveats to remember before we say that retellings show an inherently great system. It is possible to get bad stories (boring/meaningless stories) from good games. It also is possible to tell a great story of a mostly boring system. However, if it gave one great story, is it then not a great storytelling system for, if nothing else, one instance? Or was it just our interpretation as readers that formed a great story from something the system never intended as a story in the first place, in which case would be difficult to argue that it is a great storytelling *system*? Or maybe a system is great at giving experiences, but not the kind of experiences that are fun to retell? There's a lot to unpack there, so let's look at the fundamentals first.

If we assume that the fundamental goal of a storytelling system is to create a (great) narrative experience, any system that accomplishes this, must be a good storytelling system, even if it did so by accident (whether that was what the author intended will be looked at in Sect. 4.2). Thus, if it failed, it is not. Yet, what we're talking about here, is the afterstory, not the retelling. A retelling can be something else than the afterstory, and therefore it can become a great narrative, even if the story content it is made of is not. So while the hypothesized examples above all hold true, it is because we are always looking at the retelling of the afterstory, and not the afterstory itself. Since an afterstory, the moment it is told, becomes a retelling, we have to analyse the retelling. This retelling, and specifically, the discourse of it, can be good or bad, but has, potentially, little to do with the quality of the storytelling system[3]. The afterstory that created this could be interesting or not, and the discourse could as well, and while they are often correlated, it is dangerous to assume that a well-told story is inherently a good one—or one stemming from a good system. For example, we can hypothesize an example of a retelling where the purpose is to highlight how the system did not provide a meaningful narrative. In this, you could purposefully tell your story so it shows how the afterstory you had was lacklustre, and still manage to tell a great story of how that happened.

This is not to knock the entire idea of analysing retellings, but mostly to warn about the fact that the retelling is not the afterstory: It is a *new* narrative, and one that is different from the storytelling system that helped create it. However, we would still agree that the correlation is still valid enough to be useful, even by itself. However, we have to consider how we assess systems through retellings.

4.1 Assessing Storytelling Systems

If we want to assess the quality of the system, assuming that the greater the stories and the more the stories it tells, the better the storytelling system, is the most obvious approach. However, that loses a lot of nuance, and we all know how difficult it is to accurately measure the quality of a story. Eladhari offers two approaches. The first, being the, in her words, blunt option, namely to simply find the total amount of retellings and judge that the more, the better—but offer no reaction on the quality of those retellings. The other would be a deeper analysis of some retellings, that could help provide pointers to what aspects of the storytelling system in question is interesting, and why.

To start with the first and simpler of the options, its great advantage is that it is an easy measurement (assuming one can get the data, which admittedly can be tricky) and an easy comparison point across systems. However, what it loses is quality and variability. One can imagine a system that is able to create one really amazing story, that then gets retold a lot because it is worth retelling, but then fails to create any other kind of narrative. That system would succeed well in a query that only looks at occurrence. Therefore, we propose a two axis system for charting retellings of storytelling systems, where the first axis is occurrence and the second is variability. This axis is used to determine the range of afterstories that spring from a system, and can be used to analyse the robustness and range of a system: The more varying stories it can tell, the more robust that system must be at handling a wide variety of stories. A low variability is not necessarily a knock against a system, but it is a good measure of the type of storytelling system it is, and give a potential suggestion for the range of potential afterstories it can create. How to chart this variability is up to the individual research, as it can probably be done in many ways: By genre, by theme, by moment-to-moment content, to event-variance (how many events vary

---

[3] An argument can be made that a more involved (or elaborate, or deep) discourse shows an effort to want to tell a story well because it is an interesting story, but one can still tell a bad story well.

in between retellings), by word count, or even by medium of retelling (although this will provide different results), and probably others. This choice will greatly determine the kind of answers you will get and is therefore dependent on what you want to research.

The second approach Eladhari offers is a qualitative approach, looking at doing in-depth studies of retellings to understand the storytelling system behind this. Eladhari doesn't provide much analysis into what this means. And at first, this is a process similar to doing any literary analysis of a traditional narrative work (as Koenitz also mentions [12]), but we want to spend a second discussing how to look at retellings specifically to learn something about the storytelling system behind it. Because it is a different exercise to analyse a retelling for why it is a good story than to analyse why the storytelling system that helped create its foundational story is a good system. A good starting point would probably be to focus on where the system aided in interpretation and where it didn't. It is impossible to split the interpretation from the events that were interpreted, so instead it should be more fruitful to see where the system created events that were more easy to interpret into something meaningful (that was then told). To take the Sims example from her paper [7], that the system recognized that the character had money and thus wanted to spend that money on something that fit their character (as a good person)—donating to charity—was an action that was easy to interpret into meaning. It was a smart narrative move because it was a wish immediately caused by recent events and fuelled by the characterization that fit the already established fiction. This is naturally only a single event, and thus an analysis ought to go deeper and look for more, and potentially how it succeeds over different retellings, where the base content (the events and actions) and player interacting with it is different.

These two examples show different ways to use retellings, and there's almost certainly more possible venues, but each approach would have to harken back to the question of how do we use this inherently warped (not in a bad way) telling of a story to see how that (retold) story was created.

4.2   The Intent of the Teller

Finally, there's a point of intention. We phrased previously that even an accidental storytelling system was a successful one, and while we stand by that, there is another point of analysis which is about what the author intended with the system and whether *that* was successful. The concepts of narrative intelligibility and closure helps define that relationship, as defined by Bruni and Baceviciute [4]. Shortly: Closure is when a story feels closed and satisfying by itself, regardless what the author wanted to convey, and an intelligible story is when the reader understand the intent and design of the author. A storytelling system where the only intent is narrative closure, any accidental storytelling that happens is fine, as long as closure is achieved in the afterstory. If the intent is intelligibility, on the other hand, there is a degree to which the storytelling system must create the kinds of stories intended by the creator, or at least create stories that can be read as intelligibly the ideas formulated by the author—otherwise it fails as a system intending on narrative intelligibility.

Therefore, when looking at the retellings of narratives from storytelling systems, it is relevant to consider whether this retelling was an intended outcome, to determine the possible intent behind the system, and how it employed that intent (or accidental intent) in its design. And furthermore, like there is a level of discourse in the retelling that is not in the afterstory, there is also an intent with the retelling that might be different than the narrative given from the storytelling system. It is by looking at this intent we can identify whether the retelling wants to tell a story as it happened because it was a series of narratively interesting events that they just had to tell, or for some other purpose. And if this purpose defeats the use of this retelling as a viable analysis of the storytelling system, it shouldn't be looked at with that in mind (but can potentially still be used for other avenues of research). To bring back the previous example, if a retelling was told to showcase how awful a story this system produced, it (probably) isn't a retelling we can use to say it was a good storytelling system.

All this said, we believe it is clear how one should be mindful when looking at retellings as an avenue for critique of a system that helped create that retelling, but that does not mean that it shouldn't be done or that it isn't a valuable exercise. All of Eladhari's points about it still stand, these past points were just to provide caution and method before we draw conclusions from material that doesn't justify it. Retellings, like any avenue of research, has caveats and biases to keep in mind.

5   Examples of Retellings

An example of a retelling that is interesting in this context is Jon Bois' "Breaking Madden" [3] from 2015, where his intent from the outset is to "break" Madden (the american football game, not the person), by altering the in-game values and creating scenarios that couldn't possibly exist in a real game of football. For example, in an early story, he creates a character with a completely disproportionate physique to a real human being; gives him inhumanly strong abilities in some departments (like running, throwing, stamina) and inhumanly terrible abilities in others (vision, agility, elusiveness), and thus creating a caricature of a person rather than approximating a real human playing football. Here we see already a discrepancy in the intent of the storytelling system (Madden 25 [6]) and the retelling. Madden the game is interested in creating stories, as most sports games, but it is most likely stories of a different kind than the ones Jon Bois' wants to tell, and using different rules—even though Jon Bois technically always stays within the rules of the game (at least from what we can tell). We say this because, while we could argue that the intent of Madden is up for debate since these "breaks" are possible, it is likely that the intent behind the creation of the game was not to create unfair, impossible scenarios that almost do not resemble real american football. Jon Bois uses Madden to create comedic sports stories that feel familiar in topic and scope but are always slightly off-kilter by purposefully twisting the system to his design. And so, the idea of analyzing "Breaking Madden" is subverted by "Breaking Madden" itself. Jon Bois' intent with the play *is* retelling—not playing. He plays with the idea of creating an article about his play. So, already from the get-go, he subverts the system by making it do something he needs to write a feature, rather than play and tell only the interesting stories. He, in a way, forces the game to give him a retellable story, which could be argued is a knock against the idea that the retelling itself is enough to show a powerful storytelling system. Taken further, you could argue that any "Let's Play"-style content, where a person shows themselves playing a game with the intent of showing that playthrough to other people, is an inherent bias against the value of that retelling: As it is not necessarily interesting *because* the system is interesting. However, referring back to Walsh's second notion of Emergent Narrative [30], this can also just as well be read as an improvisational act with the player (Jon Bois) and the system as participators, through which we can still construe whether the system is capable of allowing this improvisation in meaningful ways.

Another example the first author has previously used (in his Master's Thesis [13]) was the game Loneliness [20]. It is a simple, affective game, about the experience of loneliness. You control a little square moving upwards, and every time you try to approach the other squares in the space, who are either standing around or playing or jumping or walking—they move away from you. You can never be close to anyone, until you finally move up to the very end, where there are no one else and you are all alone. This provides an interesting counterpoint as well because we cannot imagine most retellings or afterstories of this game to be terribly interesting or variant: There is no choice in the game, there is no point of difference between experiences (other than choosing to stop before the end), and the story itself retold (as we just did) is rather bland. Loneliness isn't designed to be an emergent storytelling system with a lot of options, so the analysis doesn't quite hold when taken to an extreme, but the point is still relevant: A retelling does not necessarily capture (even though, the existence of it might allude to) the emotional affect of the narrative experience as it happens. Emergent stories, unlike Loneliness, are probably inherently more fun to retell (Ryan touches on this [24]), but maybe it is possible to create an abstract emergent system that is *difficult* to retell, but still leaves the player with a meaningful experience and a powerful afterstory—but less retellings because it is simply a more challenging experience to convey. However that again illustrates Eladhari's point; that a person *chose* to tell about their experience with Loneliness is a valid, valuable point of data by itself.

Finally, we want to highlight is the work of Murnane [22], and his in-depth analysis of 400 player stories from Skyrim, from 2018. This is an excellent example of a thorough examination of retellings from a system and the types of stories it made. Here, he makes some key points about the nature of retellings as well, first by showing their blurred relationship with fanfiction, and more importantly to this topic, the existence of glitches as a part of the emergent narrative experience. His point on the matter can be summed up with this quote: *"Even when we know the system has failed, players want the story to make sense.*" [22] His examples include players weaving the breaking of the system into the story in their heads and making it a part of the world, supposing logic to it when they know there is none—a rather pure form of narrative sensemaking. It serves as a nice commentary to our points about "Breaking Madden", and highlights how the intent of a system can become secondary to the stories we tell with them. His conclusions on the nature of emergent narrative from this research is also interesting: "...*when I am talking about emergent narrative, I am describing a story told by a player about interacting with a game in which events occurred which are significant to the player but ignored by the system.*" [22]. Especially the last point, "*ignored by the system*", is fascinating, as this specifically focuses on events that were not intended by the system, in the sense that it did not react or use it in a meaningful way. Here, looking at Murnane's retellings is enlightening, as many of them enrich the narrative of the systemic events, by authoring more aspects, more details, showing the inner minds of characters, reflecting on off-screen events, pondering motivations etc. This "more" is generally ignored by the system, as the purpose of the retelling is often to fill in those exact missing parts (in the afterstory), and thereby enrich the story into something enjoyable outside the afterstory itself.

6   Conclusion

This paper started as a discussion of the ambiguity of emergent narrative, and introduced the term afterstory, the actual, mental story a player is left with after the experience, to help solidify the differences between the storytelling system as it simulates events, the narrativization process, and what the player is left with in their mind. Furthermore, the afterstory was then discussed in relation to retellings, when a player later retells their experience to other people, thus creating a new narrative of the story-material that shapes the afterstory— which originally came from their interaction with a storytelling system. This distinction was used to discuss how to use retellings as assessment of the quality of the storytelling system, by investigating the variability of those retellings, the ways the system influenced the retelling, and what the intent of both the system and the retelling was. Finally, a few examples were presented of different kinds of retellings, showcasing how varied and awkward these can be to analyse as directly as one would want.

We hope this paper shows the value of a concept like afterstory, to help bridge the gap between the narrative experience as it happens and the retellings afterwards. Defining clearly what is in the mind of the player and what is not helps us—as designers and scholars—focus on the only variable we can control before, the system, and the only artifact we can analyse after, the retelling, and not begin to confuse the two.

References

1. Abbott, H.P.: Story, plot, and narration. In: Herman, D. (ed.) The Cambridge Companion to Narrative. Cambridge Companions to Literature, p. 39–51. Cambridge University Press (2007). https://doi.org/10.1017/CCOL0521856965.003
2. Aylett, R.: Narrative in virtual environments-towards emergent narrative. In: Proceedings of the AAAI Fall Symposium on Narrative Intelligence, pp. 83–86 (1999)
3. Bois, J.: Breaking madden (2013–2015). https://www.sbnation.com/a/breaking-madden. Specific episode referenced is at https://www.sbnation.com/nfl/2013/9/5/4691010/breaking-madden-clarence-beeftank-jaguars
4. Bruni, L.E., Baceviciute, S.: Narrative intelligibility and closure in interactive systems. In: Koenitz, H., Sezen, T.I., Ferri, G., Haahr, M., Sezen, D., Ç atak, G. (eds.) ICIDS 2013. LNCS, vol. 8230, pp. 13–24. Springer, Cham (2013). https://doi.org/10.1007/978-3-319-02756-2_2
5. CCP Games: Eve Online (2008)
6. Tiburon, E.A., Sports, E.A.: NFL Madden 25 (2013)
7. Eladhari, M.P.: Re-Tellings: the fourth layer of narrative as an instrument for critique. In: Rouse, R., Koenitz, H., Haahr, M. (eds.) ICIDS 2018. LNCS, vol. 11318, pp. 65–78. Springer, Cham (2018). https://doi.org/10.1007/978-3-030-04028-4_5
8. Galyean III, T.A.: Narrative guidance of interactivity. Ph.D. thesis, Massachusetts Institute of Technology (1995)
9. Groen, A.: Empires of Eve. Self published (2016)
10. Jenkins, H.: Game design as narrative architecture. In: The Game Design Reader: A Rules of Play Anthology, chapter 4, pp. 118–130. MIT Press, Cambridge (2004)
11. Koenitz, H.: Towards a theoretical framework for interactive digital narrative. In: Aylett, R., Lim, M.Y., Louchart, S., Petta, P., Riedl, M. (eds.) ICIDS 2010. LNCS, vol. 6432, pp. 176–185. Springer, Heidelberg (2010). https://doi.org/10.1007/978-3-642-16638-9_22
12. Koenitz, H.: Towards a specific theory of interactive digital narrative. In: Interactive Digital Narrative, pp. 107–121. Routledge (2015)
13. Larsen, B.A.: The narrative quality of games and play. Master's thesis, Aalborg University, CPH (2017)
14. Larsen, B.A., Schoenau-Fog, H.: The narrative quality of game mechanics. In: Nack, F., Gordon, A.S. (eds.) ICIDS 2016. LNCS, vol. 10045, pp. 61–72. Springer, Cham (2016). https://doi.org/10.1007/978-3-319-48279-8_6
15. Linden Lab: Second Life (2003)
16. Louchart, S., Aylett, R.: The emergent narrative theoretical investigation. In: the 2004 Conference on Narrative and Interactive Learning Environments, pp. 21–28 (2004)
17. Louchart, S., Aylett, R.: Narrative theory and emergent interactive narrative. Int. J. Contin. Eng. Educ. Life Learn. 14(6), 506–518 (2004)
18. Louchart, S., Swartjes, I., Kriegel, M., Aylett, R.: Purposeful authoring for emergent narrative. In: Spierling, U., Szilas, N. (eds.) ICIDS 2008. LNCS, vol. 5334, pp. 273–284. Springer, Heidelberg (2008). https://doi.org/10.1007/978-3-540-89454-4_35
19. Louchart, S., Truesdale, J., Suttie, N., Aylett, R.: Emergent narrative, past, present and future of an interactive storytelling approach. In: Interactive Digital Narrative: History, Theory and Practice, pp. 185–199. Routledge (2015)
20. Magnuson, J.: Loneliness (2010). http://www.necessarygames.com/my-games/loneliness/flash

21. Montfort, N.: Twisty Little Passages: An Approach to Interactive Fiction. MIT Press (2005)
22. Murnane, E.: Emergent narrative: stories of play, playing with stories. Ph.D. thesis, University of Central Florida (2018)
23. Ringer, C., Nicolaou, M.A.: Deep unsupervised multi-view detection of video game stream highlights. In: Proceedings of the 13th International Conference on the Foundations of Digital Games, p. 15. ACM (2018)
24. Ryan, J.: Curating simulated storyworlds. Ph.D. thesis, UC Santa Cruz (2018)
25. Ryan, J.O., Mateas, M., Wardrip-Fruin, N.: Open design challenges for interactive emergent narrative. In: Schoenau-Fog, H., Bruni, L.E., Louchart, S., Baceviciute, S. (eds.) ICIDS 2015. LNCS, vol. 9445, pp. 14–26. Springer, Cham (2015). https://doi.org/10.1007/978-3-319-27036-4_2
26. Ryan, M.L.: Avatars of Story. University of Minnesota Press, Minneapolis (2006)
27. Suttie, N., Louchart, S., Aylett, R., Lim, T.: Theoretical considerations towards authoring emergent narrative. In: Koenitz, H., Sezen, T.I., Ferri, G., Haahr, M., Sezen, D., Ç atak, G. (eds.) ICIDS 2013. LNCS, vol. 8230, pp. 205–216. Springer, Cham (2013). https://doi.org/10.1007/978-3-319-02756-2_25
28. Swartjes, I.M.T.: Whose story is it anyway? How improv informs agency and authorship of emergent narrative. Ph.D. thesis, University of Twente, The Netherlands (2010)
29. Various: The Boatmurdered Let's Play Archive. all entries archived at (2006). https://lparchive.org/Dwarf-Fortress-Boatmurdered/
30. Walsh, R.: Emergent narrative in interactive media. Narrative 19(1), 72–85 (2011)

"Well, That was Quick" – Towards Storyworld Adaptivity that Reacts to Players as People

Bjarke Alexander Larsen[✉] and Henrik Schoenau-Fog

Aalborg University, Copenhagen, Denmark
bal@create.aau.dk

Abstract. This paper proposes an investigation into interactive story-world adaptivity, which is adapting the world in ways that do not necessarily alter the plot or narrative management of the story, but rather, purely change the world around the player. Using the game "Red Dead Redemption 2" as a case study, the paper discusses the possibilities of these kinds of adaptations and looks ahead to the future possibilities and what an interactive storyworld design might need to consider if it could change the entire world in real time, while letting the player roam free. It considers the types of interactions we should focus for more natural adaptations and what technology might help implement such a future, and why we would want to do so in the first place.

Keywords: Adaptivity · Storyworlds · Interactive storyworlds · Red Dead Redemption 2

1 Introduction

In the Old West of Red Dead Redemption 2 [16], Arthur Morgan needed to buy some supplies. So the player controlling him went into a store. The man behind the counter said "Hello, glad to have you here", and the player began browsing his catalogue. After they got what they thought they needed, they turned around and went out, only to remember that they forgot to buy some gun oil—the original reason for heading to the store. So they went back in and the shopkeeper looked up at them with a smile. "Well, that was quick?" he said. It took a second to notice that this was strange. At first, the reaction seemed so natural there was no reason to think about it. But this was a video game and the simulation needed to serve that line rather than another generic "Hello, there!" was staggering for such a small event. The player took a pause and looked at the man, almost forgetting to buy gun-oil again.

This example of a player's experience is one of many of Red Dead Redemption 2's adaptivity in motion, a game that was lauded for its ability to create natural-sounding interactions like this one. And it is a sign that the current standard in video games reacting to players have come a long way from the morality meters of

© Springer Nature Switzerland AG 2019
R. E. Cardona-Rivera et al. (Eds.): ICIDS 2019, LNCS 11869, pp. 204–213, 2019.
https://doi.org/10.1007/978-3-030-33894-7_22

Mass Effect [3] and the physics simulations of Half Life 2 [26]. And what is unique about this specific scenario is that it is not a grand-scale system that affects the entire fate of the world, nor is it an important branching point or a deep, systemic interaction, but is merely something that happened, and has no further consequence for the player, except that they remember it. This type of adaption, that is less focused on the narrative at large, less interested in altering the player's trajectory or providing meaningful consequence, is different than the types of adaptation and narrative management we typically focus on when we talk about interactive storytelling. However, this moment was memorable anyway, partly because it was novel, but also because of another reason: It treated the player like a person. This paper will look into how games use adaptivity, and, by using Red Dead Redemption 2 as a case, offer a preliminary analysis of how games and interactive digital storytelling can provide meaningful, interactive, adaptive storyworlds, today and in the future.

2   Defining Storyworld Adaptation

Before we begin to understand how adaptivity works, we must first define what we mean: The adaptivity definition we're using here is this: *Adaptivity is when a game changes the storytelling based on previous actions/behavior from the player, without telegraphing to the player that it has done or will do so when the action is performed.* Adaptivity is different from interactivity or choice (although it relies on interactivity) since it is not about intentional, direct actions and choices of a player, but rather adapting to a history of actions and/or behaviour, possibly unintentional, from the player. A game adapting to the user is everything from sports commentator providing a contextual voice-line based on the current game's impact on the season, to giving you a different ending because you killed people throughout the game you didn't have to. It is not a defined reward from a quest, or an enemy reacting to getting shot, as these are predefined and known—either for the player or the designer. It is more complex than a reaction: The fact that the player enters a store and the shopkeeper says hello is a reaction. The fact that the player enters the store a second time and the shopkeeper gives a different line, specifically reacting to the fact that they are there again, is adaptation. Said in another way, the fact that it reacts is merely a reaction, but that the reaction is changed by other events is adaptation.

Storyworld adaptivity is then when the storytelling the adaptation changes is not directly related to narrative management, but rather to storytelling in the world sense: Changing the place rather than the plot. It will still have storytelling relevance as the world is part of the story, but it does not have to affect the current or future actions of the player or the events they partake in. Instead, it will change the spaces they move through, the tone or the way they are perceived or acted against in those spaces (which might change the actions of the player, but it does not have to).

3   Red Dead Redemption 2: An Improbable Game

Before we delve into the possibilities of this type of adaptivity, we will spend
a few moments on Red Dead 2 (as it will be shortened to) to understand how
the game provides storyworld adaptivity. Red Dead 2 is not the only game to
deliver this kind of adaptivity, nor is it necessarily the one to do it best, but it
is a recent candidate that does it well, and with a high profile, and it does have
some advantages by being such a large game as it is, as adaptivity on a large
scale is still expensive. And Red Dead 2 was *expensive*[1]. So in a sense, it is unfair
to compare it to other games, as it vastly outperforms the scope of most other
AAA titles, but it is therefore also the kind of game that is useful to study for
adaptivity since it is able to do things most other projects are not. This will not
be an in-depth analysis of the entire game, but it will be used as a jumping off
point for a discussion of storyworld adaptivity and how it can be shaped in the
future.

At first glance, Red Dead 2 looks fairly similar to most big move-and-shoot
action games: You can run, shoot, ride a horse, use items, etc. However, one
key action stands out: The Focus action. With a hold of a button, the player
can focus attention on a character, an event or similar. This then allows them
to do contextual actions to or with that focused entity–for example, greeting
any character in the entire game. It is not a "sticky" lock-on like a 3d action
game (like Zelda [13] or Dark Souls, [8]) and it isn't so loose that it might as
well not be a targeting system. It is this sort of hybrid where it matters that
you do it, but there's not an immediate consequence to using it. This kind of
"squishy" interaction is a great affordance for reactivity since it is always done
intentionally by the player but it is not something that demands a reaction–and
therefore the game can react to it only when it has a meaningful reaction in
stock and the player won't feel cheated when it doesn't. And there are a lot of
great examples of this system being reacted to, as we will show later.

Red Dead 2 uses this, and a lot of information about the player's current
state, such as how clean they are, the length of their beard, etc. as well as
their position, their current or previous participation in crime etc. to inform
its reactions by the world. It is impossible to know everything the game tracks,
unfortunately, (barring Rockstar telling us) as the only way we can see a tracked
datapoint is through the game using it to react to us. It is also impossible to know
how they store the data and for how long, but we can make some inferences from
how it is used. Most of its usage is through reactions from other people, and that
is also the most interesting, from this paper's perspective, as it is here the world
comes alive in its adaptation. The usage of its data tracking is present through UI
or deliniated story events, and are not as relevant to this paper. There are many
examples of ways the game has reacted to actions the player took in believable,
adaptive ways. The store example from the intro is a great one, but there are

---

[1] The cost is unknown for certain as Rockstar (and other developers) keep costs private, but they credit around 2800 people on their website [15,24], who worked harder
than we probably should demand of anyone [22], working over 8 years.

many more. One time, three characters in camp were having a conversation that Arthur (the player's character) happened to stop by and listen in on. Later, he went to talk to a fourth person, and they asked about what Arthur had heard. If you have been away from camp long, another character will find you and ask how you've been, and people will comment on your beard, your horse, your cleanliness, etc. In larger systems, e.g. the Bounty system, the adaptivity also shows, but it is of a slightly different kind, and a more systemic approaches to adaptivity than we are focusing on here. An example worth mentioning is how other characters in town reacted to the fact that the player had done crime in that city previously, warning them to stay in line, etc.

However, there are plenty of things Red Dead 2 does not change or adapt to or just forget. That the player bumped into a man on his way to work is not remembered an hour later in any notable form. The character might use that for an action in the moment, but if you leave and come back later, it might as well not have happened. The world, while vast and lived in and detailed, does not alter itself much based on player actions, and the player doesn't have much influence over its development, outside scripted sequences and missions.

If we were to be reductive about much of this adaptivity, it is often a series of "remember that thing you did", events, where characters refer back to previous events. Yet, that is exactly reductive because it omits the point of doing that kind of memory. This type of adaptivity, as shown by Red Dead 2, has the potential to be as powerful as an emotional cutscene. The next section will look at how this might be possible, before we reach the ultimate discussion of why.

4   Looking Further into Time and Space

If we look further and think about what kinds of things we could change in the world, both using similar techniques and pondering what we might do with more powerful capabilities to alter the storyworld. If we look at the types of elements games typically react to, derived from the Red Dead 2 analysis, we can see three elements: (a) Values (numeric values in the system, e.g. a karma meter, a trait, or a statistic), (b) Events (triggered by certain action, placement, status or similar), and (c) Space-Time (the current and previous position in time of the player and other actors (the name is a reference to a previous paper [21])).

By far the most underused of them (and why the store example feels special) is Space-Time [21]. It is still rare for a game to continuously use the current position in space relative to their time there, and to adapt with events not only in place but also in time. As Meyer [11] mentions, games still rely much more heavily on where the player is rather than when. Federico [7] calls this, similarly, "player-centric time", that is, time only moves when the player calls for it, either by triggering an event or literally moving time forward (by e.g. resting in Skyrim [2]). There are reasons for this: Most games have not wanted to use time as a gating factor in their designs because it can be difficult for the player to deal with, and annoying when they can't. As a player who wants to do X, it can feel frustrating to have to wait to a certain time, or not be able to find a character because they happen to be in the shop at 5'o'clock and they didn't know. This is in large part due to conventions of commercial AAA games, where letting the player be in complete control at all times is an imperative. We can find plenty of examples of games intentionally not letting the player do what they want in the indie space, or in art games, poem games, vignette games, etc.

Nitsche's [14] approach to the topic, though, shows that the relation is a little more complicated. In their attempt to map time in video games, they distinguish between a formal approach and an experiential approach to time. The formal sees a difference in "event time" and "play time", that is similar to how Genette described "story time" and "narrative time" in traditional storytelling [9]—the first being the time it takes for the story to unfold in world and the second the time it takes to tell the story. The relations between these can give rise to dynamics such as flashbacks, slowed down time, fast-forwards, etc. which can all be used for dramatic effect. Experiential time, on the other hand, takes a different approach to time and focuses instead purely on the player's experience of it. Here Nitche borrows from linguists, saying how time has long been spatially mapped across cultures, and we almost always experience space over time: *"A visitor can experience a larger physical space, such as a house or a city, only over a period of time – usually in the form of movement"*. Contrary to "player-centric time", Nitche here highlights how time is actually moving forward still, for the player, always, as they move through space. And then the relationship between play and story time becomes clear: *"Space and spatial comprehension (e.g. through a camera) can be seen as the canvas through which the player understands time."* Seen through an experiential lens (pardon the mixed metaphor), time is player-centric in a much different way: Instead of relying on the player to move time, the player always experiences time as moving, regardless of whether it does or not in the world, because it is a necessity to them moving through space. Maybe the answer is to keep this in mind when designing time-based solutions, and not just tracking the current position of the player in time, but also considering that movement as a separate kind of time than the in-world, fictional time of the game, and adapt based on both. Correctly adapting based on the player's experience of time and position is one thing, though, but affecting change in the world is an entirely different, difficult problem. But if we take a leap in technology, and imagine a different way of creating worlds than we do now, that might become more feasible.

4.1   Technologies for Adaptive Storyworlds

Traditionally, video game worlds have been created either by hand-authoring (Skyrim [2], Mass Effect [3]), or by entirely procedural means (Dwarf Fortress [1], Minecraft [12]). However, in today's video game industry, it is pretty common procedure to generate parts of large open worlds procedurally [6,20]. In Spider-Man's case [20], this was done to assist human creators in creating the final city, and thus focused on shaping the first 80% of the city, which human artists could then go in and touch up.

And while a world on Red Dead 2's scale and fidelity might always be impossible procedurally, we don't have to imagine an entirely generated world to still see advantages of real-time procedurality. Instead of thinking of the entire world as a giant mutable space, we can perhaps imagine a world created by blocks (not unlike streaming "cells" used to stream current large environments, but on a more variable scale) but where each block has or can have its own adaptive, procedural behaviour and events. If we take the shop example from the beginning again, the shop here could not just adapt to the player's behaviour through a line of dialogue, but through altering the contents of the store itself, through spawning other characters in the store, through even changing the house itself, the shop could close down because it ran out of business or expand to a larger area in a different place. Those last examples still require a great deal of authored content (for now) but technologies like machine and deep learning could help begin make strides here, by (staying with the store example) find ways to mold stores depending on different parameters, which in turn is controlled at run-time in the game, adapting to behaviours around it. Instead of seeing the store as a fixed object, perhaps it can be viewed as an evolving space, that is continuously adapted to the algorithm's latest reasoning. This is said with an admittedly nascent understanding of machine- learning, but it is not the only option. "Simple" procedurality can also help great deals here, but done on a different scale.

Ryan in his PhD thesis [18] talks about curationist emergent narratives, where we instead of procedurally generating potential for a few outcomes and hoping it is an interesting narrative, we instead generate an overflowing wealth of content, and then curate the best parts. That curation, he poses, could be done automatically by machines, as long as we handle some key problems, namely that of "story sifting". For this example, it could be that an algorithm could simulate a thousand ways for the store to change, but only actuate the ones that work best for the narrative, and is feasible within the world. But this could also be taken on a much larger scale: Think of all the events that occur during a game of Red Dead 2. If we use a curationist approach to find those that have narrative structure and relevance, and can float those to the top and focus on adapting to them, rather than attempting to adapt to everything that wouldn't be interesting.

It is one of the more time-consuming parts of modern commercial video games to make several versions of the same environment, and most cases where that is done today (Spiderman [20], Red Dead 2, etc.), it is hand-crafted and scripted events that make such a change, and the change is often singular, immediate, and akin to a state-change. But if we instead approach the world creation procedurally (or parts of it, as mentioned), and base its elements on a range of factors, those factors can be influenced over time by events that happen in the game, and thus, the world will gradually change in small ways that are affected e.g. the player, and thus let the world help create itself. It could be something small like changing how a character greets you to something global like altering the amount of grass and flowers dependent on how much has been driven on it to something huge like shifting the power balance of the world based on how much a player helps some characters over others. What specifically can and should change largely depends on the project in question. The important point here is that these adaptations could help implement time-based worlds that don't operate on gates and states but rather use a procedural, adaptive measure that changes how things happen and offer more malleable, softer systems.

4.2 Affordances that Matter

As a final aside to the technology, we want to highlight the interaction of the player and, specifically, the importance of giving the player more abilities that do not alter the world with every button press. The Focus action from Red Dead 2 is a great example of the type of interaction that, as mentioned, shows intent but does not require reaction, and therefore can be used for meaningful adaptations when possible, without the player feeling cheated when it does not. Contrast this with the typical action of most violent games: Shooting a gun, which is the type of action that immediately feels off the moment someone does not react very violently to it. This puts a lot of constraints on the types of adaptive behaviour the other characters in the world can do. Therefore, by allowing the player to exist and act within the world in ways that more closely mimic an everyday interaction, with smaller, "squishier" gestures, that are nevertheless just as trackable as any other, gives us a much greater breadth of actions to adapt to.

But the final question you might be asking after all of this, is the simplest one: Why?

5   What's the Point?

With the technology, with adaptivity and interaction, comes the following question: What can we use it for? And for storytelling, for creating interactive, adaptive storyworlds, that question becomes what can we tell with that tool? Or, said in another way, what are the poetics of a changeable world? This is a question that is dependent on the project and therefore does not have one answer. Just like procedural rhetoric [4] uses mechanics and procedures to convey meaning through interaction, the world that the player interacts with is very relevant to that conversation[2]. By having a world that changes depending on time and space gives a world that is less controlled by the author, but it does not necessarily give more control over to the player—it will adapt to them but as long as they don't understand the mechanisms by which that adaptation is working, they will have to succumb to it as much as they will to rain when they walk to the bus. Oppositely, a changing world can give the player a sense that they can change things, that the world isn't an unstoppable force but that it does adapt

---

[2] Just see Bogost's focus on objects in his much-discussed article about stories in video games [5].

to them, that they can affect change, which is a powerful—and dare we say it, necessary—statement in this current time.

Even if we could alter the entire storyworld at runtime and grow moss on the rocks based on the player's actions, the clever designer must always ask themselves why. What's the use of changing the entire world if the player does not care? The player won't care that there's less moss on the rock, if the game is about checking people's passports. But they might be concerned if it is a game about the environment. Because the truth about any of these adaptations is that they fundamentally do not matter if the player does not feel impacted by them. To the question of why it mattered that a shopkeeper noticed the player had been in the shop moments before, the answer isn't that it drastically altered the player's perception of the world or changed their character. But what it did do was make the player feel seen. It gave them a sense of, not quite perceived agency [10], but something similar. They remembered that interaction long after it happened, partly because of the novelty of it, but also because an action like that helps place the player in the world. Instead of feeling like the player changed the world, it feels like the world acknowledged them, not as a player this NPC was meant to serve, but as a person entering their store. It was less consequential than "Clementine will remember that" (The Walking Dead [25]), but more consequential than the average hello, and therefore it was memorable.

If games will keep doing this kind of adaptivity, there will be a point where it is no longer mentioned for its novelty like we are here, but rather for what it achieves by itself. And that will be measured not by the technical prowess or the complexity of the system, but by the player's reaction to the game. That can be done with grand, sweeping changes that shake the world, which are expensive, difficult to realize and even more difficult to follow through, or it can be done in small, personal interactions and tiny changes that matter to the player. If a player likes picking flowers, the answer to a better game isn't just to spawn more flowers, but to find ways to change the world in ways that makes picking flowers worth it for them, and not leave them feeling like they lost two hours finding the red flower they can't actually use. That is not an easy problem and nor do we propose to have the solution, but if the technology truly does get to a point where the question isn't how but why, then we must begin to consider the implications of those choices. And the fundamental core there should be that you should make the changes that matter to the player. Which is done by smartly giving the player options that let them express what they want to express, and smartly adapt, using that information when relevant, and showing those changes in a way that feels natural and powerful to the player.

6 Future Work

This paper was a preliminary investigation into storyworld adaptivity and its possibilities, and there are many more avenues for research. A few notes were made here on a framework for how this kind of adaptation works and could be designed/analysed, focusing on the Space-Time dimension, but more work is required, also referencing other work on the topic of narrative adaptation (as [17] and [23], and microinteractions [19]). The relationship between adaptivity and time was mentioned here but warrants much more in-depth research, as well. Another avenue is looking into the relationship between agency and adaptation, and investigating how knowledge of storyworld adaptation plays a role in it working. Finally, Red Dead 2 is just one game, and looking how other games and interactive narrative experiences treat similar ideas is crucial to gaining a more holistic theory, in order to facilitate richer storyworld adaptation.

References

1. Adams, T., Adams, Z.: Dwarf Fortress (2006)
2. Bethesda Game Studios: The Elder Scrolls V: Skyrim (2011)
3. BioWare: Mass Effect (2007)
4. Bogost, I.: Persuasive Games: The Expressive Power of Videogames. MIT Press, Cambridge (2007)
5. Bogost, I.: Video games are better without stories, April 2017. https://www.theatlantic.com/technology/archive/2017/04/video-games-stories/524148/
6. Carrier, E.: Procedural world generation of 'far cry 5'. GDC Talk (2018). https://www.gdcvault.com/play/1025557/Procedural-World-Generation-of-Far
7. Federico, A.I.: Cause, effect, and player-centric time. In: DiGRA & rsquo18 & ndash Abstract Proceedings of the 2018 DiGRA International Conference: The Game is the Message. DiGRA, July 2018. http://www.digra.org/wp-content/uploads/digital-library/DIGRA_2018_paper_130.pdf
8. From Software: Dark Souls (2011)
9. Genette, G.: Narrative Discourse: An Essay in Method. Cornell University Press, Ithaca (1983)
10. Kway, L., Mitchell, A.: Perceived agency as meaningful expression of playable character personality traits in storygames. In: Rouse, R., Koenitz, H., Haahr, M. (eds.) ICIDS 2018. LNCS, vol. 11318, pp. 230–239. Springer, Cham (2018). https://doi.org/10.1007/978-3-030-04028-4_23
11. Meyer, S.R.: Right, left, high, low narrative strategies for non–linear storytelling. In: Nack, F., Gordon, A.S. (eds.) ICIDS 2016. LNCS, vol. 10045, pp. 325–335. Springer, Cham (2016). https://doi.org/10.1007/978-3-319-48279-8_29
12. Mojang: Minecraft (2011)
13. Nintendo: The Legend of Zelda: Breath of the Wild (2017)
14. Nitsche, M.: Mapping time in video games. In: DiGRA Conference (2007)
15. Rockstar: The Red Dead Redemption 2 thank you page (2018). https://www.rockstargames.com/reddeadredemption2/thankyou
16. Rockstar Studios: Red Dead Redemption 2 (2018)
17. Rowe, J.P., Shores, L.R., Mott, B.W., Lester, J.C.: A framework for narrative adaptation in interactive story-based learning environments. In: Proceedings of the Intelligent Narrative Technologies III Workshop, INT3 2010, pp. 14:1–14:8. ACM, New York (2010). http://doi.acm.org/10.1145/1822309.1822323
18. Ryan, J.: Curating simulated storyworlds. Ph.D. thesis, UC Santa Cruz (2018)
19. Saffer, D.: Microinteractions: Designing with Details. O'Reilly Media, Inc. (2013)
20. Santiago, D.: Procedurally Crafting Manhattan for Marvel's Spider-Man. GDC Talk (2019). https://www.youtube.com/watch?v=4aw9uyj9MAE

21. Schoenau-Fog, H.: Adaptive storyworlds. In: Schoenau-Fog, H., Bruni, L.E., Louchart, S., Baceviciute, S. (eds.) ICIDS 2015. LNCS, vol. 9445, pp. 58–65. Springer, Cham (2015). https://doi.org/10.1007/978-3-319-27036-4_6
22. Schreier, J.: Inside Rockstar Games' Culture Of Crunch (2018). https://kotaku.com/inside-rockstar-games-culture-of-crunch-1829936466
23. Steiner, K.E., Tomkins, J.: Narrative event adaptation in virtual environments. In: Proceedings of the 9th International Conference on Intelligent User Interfaces, pp. 46–53. ACM (2004)
24. Takahashi, D.: The DeanBeat: how much did Red Dead Redemption 2 cost to make? (Updated) (2018). https://venturebeat.com/2018/10/26/the-deanbeat-how-much-did-red-dead-redemption-2-cost-to-make/
25. Telltale Games: The Walking Dead: Season 1 (2012)
26. Valve: Half life 2 (2004)

A Spectrum of Audience Interactivity
for Entertainment Domains

Alina Striner[1(✉)], Sasha Azad[2], and Chris Martens[2]

[1] Centrum Wiskunde and Informatica (CWI), Amsterdam, Netherlands
alina.striner@gmail.com
[2] North Carolina State University, Raleigh, NC 27695, USA

Abstract. The concept of audience interactivity has been rediscovered across many domains of storytelling and entertainment—e.g. digital games, in-person role-playing, film, theater performance, music, and theme parks—that enrich the form with new idioms, language, and practices. In this paper, we introduce a *Spectrum of Audience Interactivity* that establishes a common vocabulary for the design space across entertainment domains. Our spectrum expands on an early vocabulary conceptualized through co-design sessions for interactive musical performances. We conduct a cross-disciplinary literature review to evaluate and iterate upon this vocabulary, using our findings to develop our validated spectrum.

Keywords: Audience interaction · Audience participation · Entertainment · Agency · Performance interaction · Immersion

1 Introduction

Interactivity has the power to immerse and empower audiences across divergent domains. Although these mediums use different terminology, sometimes describing interactive approaches as *participatory* or *immersive*, their desired outcome is to design fulfilling storytelling experiences. In Hamlet on the Holodeck, for instance, Murray argues that future science fiction authors will be challenged to define rules for narrative interaction that transform passive readers into audiences engaged in immersive and reactive narrative experiences [81].

In pursuit of this dream of the Holodeck, HCI research often designs novel technology to support immersive experiences [65,105]. However, generalizing and characterizing *rules for interaction* is as tricky for writers and designers as it is for practitioners [20]. Designing interactive experiences often means learning from previous work and building experiences using available tools. Since interactive audience experiences exist in a range of contexts, designers are often limited to learning from their area of expertise. We posit that in addition to new technology, the HCI community needs *conceptual* tools that help designers across performance mediums consider and compare how audiences can interact.

© Springer Nature Switzerland AG 2019
R. E. Cardona-Rivera et al. (Eds.): ICIDS 2019, LNCS 11869, pp. 214–232, 2019.
https://doi.org/10.1007/978-3-030-33894-7_23

To develop new forms of artistic expression, HCI practitioners require a common language to compare and learn from diverse experiences. Prior work defined models that broadly measure [119], and describe audience agency and participation [9,33,90,107,126], but literature suggests that more complicated relationships must be defined to address Murray's fully interactive world [81].

This paper expands on an early spectrum conceptualized through co-design sessions for interactive musical performances [108], using it to develop our *Common Spectrum of Audience Interactivity for Entertainment Domains*. Our approach explicitly allows designers across domains to discuss interactive experiences using a common taxonomy. First, we define audience interactivity, describe its benefits, and overview previous efforts to characterize interactivity. Then, we conduct an extensive review of interactive experiences across theater, theme parks, and games, three domains that represent diverse audiences, modes of interaction, and performance spaces. Our findings validate and expand on the early spectrum, refining it with additional levels, labels, and definitions. For clarity, the paper presents the literature review after introducing the new spectrum.

In summary, our work (1) overviews previous work on audience interactivity, (2) reviews literature across three entertainment domains, and (3) presents a new Spectrum of Audience Interactivity.

2   Related Work

In this section, we first describe how storytelling has evolved to include audiences, resulting in more immersive and engaging experiences. Then, we define interactivity as audience agency and participation in performance, and describe how it contributes to immersion and engagement. Finally, we overview previous efforts to characterize audience interactivity.

2.1   Storytelling

Throughout history, narratives have defined human culture and entertainment, *transporting* audiences [48] by creating "an experience of cognitive, emotional, and imagery involvement." In our research, we use Zimmerman's definition of narrative [126], building on Miller [78], who defines narrative as an initial state, a change in that state, and insight brought about by that change. We also adopt the term *transmedia* [27,44] to refer to interactive audience experiences.

In transmedia experiences, narratives invite audiences to interact with experiences. Theme parks fulfill audience needs to interact by creating a fantasy of another place and time [24,79]. Purposely designed to be isolated, theme parks invite guests to travel [29], to transport themselves to a new location. Leaving the real world at the parking lot, guests gain temporary "citizenship" to a fantasy world [17], escaping the rules and conventions of the outside world [118] for one with no clocks [24] or defined social barriers [12].

We see this model replicated in live theater. In audience-driven experiences like *Coffee! A Misunderstanding* [105], authors invite audiences to change the direction of an improvised narrative. Other examples include *The Night of January 16th* [91], in which audience members play the role of a courtroom jury, and *Drood* [89], a musical adaptation of a murder mystery. Games likewise offer players roles in predefined narratives, or allow narratives to naturally emerge from play [70,94], such as in the interactive drama *Façade* [69], where virtual characters respond to a player-performer narrative.

2.2   Defining Audience Interactivity

The role of the audience has changed. The capacity to alter and transform experiences has empowered audiences [75], leading to a dissolution of traditional audiencehood [16]. Previous work has described degrees of audience immersion in a narrative, however, the relationship between immersion, audience, and performers have not yet been explored. This paper extends current definitions to concretely classify the full breadth of audience experiences in entertainment.

For this reason, we define an audience member broadly; as a *bystander, spectator, customer, participant,* or *player*. Likewise, we define audience interactivity as a range of experiences that may allow audiences to participate or interact. These experiences may vary in:

- **Physical and Virtual Mediums.** Experiences can be *physical*, such as live theater, or *virtual*, such as VR or Twitch streams.
- **Location.** Experiences settings may vary in size and scale, from a single room (or virtual dungeon), to a university campus (or virtual world).
- **Formality and Setting.** Experiences can be private or public. For instance, an arcade simulator may be a individual experience, a murder mystery might include a group of friends, and a street performance may be public-facing.
- **Ratio of Participants to Performers.** Experiences may have varied ratios of audiences to performers. For instance, a massively-multiplayer role-playing game (MMORPG) may have thousands of players, while an interactive art installation may have no designated performers.
- **Audience Influence and Agency.** Experiences may afford audiences a range of influence or agency. For instance, a formal theater might designate when audiences should interact in performance, whereas a street performance might give them the freedom to join in when they feel comfortable.
- **Tools & Technology.** Interactive experiences use a range of tools to create interaction. Tools can range from physical props and costumes to smartphones, tablets, or wearables.

2.3   Supporting Engagement and Immersion

Entertainment literature supports the value of audience interaction to create engagement and immersion [111]. For instance, Green et al. found that narrative transportation can affect persuasion and belief change, as well as enjoyment [48].

Engagement refers to the intensity and emotional quality of user involvement [43]; engaged users exhibit positive emotion, and show sustained cognitive task involvement [41]. Engagement is often created through immersion [15], a feeling of "deep play" [26,32] that furthers emotional investment [111]. Several constructs [47] have been proposed to describe immersion. Ermi and Mayra [32] divide immersion into *sensory* immersion, *challenge-based* immersion, and *imaginative* immersion. Brockmyer [15] suggests that sensory immersion often creates a sense of presence or "being there," surrounded by another reality that takes over attention and perception [26,32,74]. Likewise, Csikszentmihalyi describes the pinnacle of challenge-based immersion as *flow* [25,31,58,99], a state of total task absorption and optimal performance [32].

2.4   Previous Efforts to Describe Interactivity

Previous research endeavored to characterize interactivity in media experiences. Relatively simple models include Everett's single-dimensional scale that rated the interactivity of communication technologies [33], and Rafaeli [90], who classified media based on audience responsiveness. Based on empirical data from questionnaires answered by 6700 players, Yee [124] added an "immersionist" factor to Bartle's classification of players into achievers, explorers, socializers and killers [7]. Zimmerman [126] identified four modes of audience interactivity that complement our goal of broadly defining a taxonomy; *Cognitive Interactivity*, a response to an internalization of a narrative, *Functional Interactivity*, interaction with physical text such as turning pages, *Explicit Interactivity*, participation in narrative flow by making choices and participating in narrative events, and *Meta-interactivity*, interaction that allows for narrative construction, deconstruction, and reconstruction.

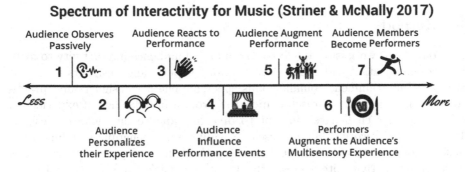

Fig. 1. Early spectrum of interactivity for musical performances [108]

Multiple models characterize interactivity by the choices and actions of audiences [45,61–63,103]. Lindley compared audience types, motivations, and play styles across current literature [88,121], and defined his own taxonomy [64] to describe three attitudes in narrative; the *audience*, the *performer*, and the *immersionist*. Steuer [107] expanded on Everett's characterization of interactivity with a two-dimensional model based on vividness, the richness of a mediated environment, and interactivity, a user's ability to modify the vividness of their experience. While Steuer's method is highly cited as a measure of immersion and engagement, it notably fails to provide explicit criteria to map new experiences onto his scale [55]. Laurel's three-dimensional model further characterizes interactivity by frequency, the range of choices available, and the extent to which choices affect experience [62]. Likewise, Goertz introduced a four dimension scale of interactivity using degrees, numbers, and flexibility of choice [45,55]. We extend these models, accounting for both audience engagement and agency.

Interactivity has also been discussed in great detail by researchers in HCI [61,101]. Zeltzer describes autonomy and interaction as a single dimension that encompasses all aspects of an audience's relationship to their environment [125]. Laurel further emphasizes the experiential nature of interaction with media technologies [61]. Both [61] and [107] describe media use in terms of *mimesis*, likening the relationship between users and technology to actions in a play, encouraging users to develop a first-person, not third-person, relationship with their environment. Engagement, which Laurel (1991) describes as a primarily emotional state with cognitive components [63], serves as a critical factor in arousing a feeling of "first-personness" [107].

Previous work by Striner and McNally [108] stewarded a first step toward understanding the many ways in which technology can allow audiences to interact with musical performances. Their work developed a spectrum of interactivity (Fig. 1) for musical performances from children's codesign sessions using Cooperative Inquiry (CI) derived from *Participatory Design* [28,50]. Using their spectrum as a starting point, we conducted an extensive, cross-disciplinary literature review to evaluate and iterate upon this vocabulary. This paper presents findings from the literature survey and a revised spectrum of interactivity.

3   Method

The goal of this work is to develop a taxonomy of audience interactivity to facilitate communication and collaboration among experts and designers in a wide variety of entertainment domains. This spectrum enables designers and practitioners across domains to discuss and learn from a broad range of experiences, and to consider challenges inherent to diverse audience interactivity designs. Building on prior work [108], this research evaluates and generalizes findings from music across various entertainment domains through a comprehensive review of audience interactivity literature in theater, theme parks, and games and introduces a common *Spectrum of Audience Interactivity* for entertainment. In this section, we first overview the underlying factors for our choice of theater, theme parks, and games as our three representative entertainment domains. Then, we describe our literature review process.

3.1   Choice of Entertainment Domains

Audience interactivity exists across a broad range of entertainment domains [40, 42,86,100]. To validate Striner's spectrum [108], we considered how well it

Table 1. Index of literature review organized by theory, storytelling, theater and music, theme parks, games, and transmedia topics.

Topic	Citation index
Theory	8, 9, 12, 13, 14, 15, 18, 21, 22, 25, 28, 31, 32, 33, 37, 41, 42, 45, 46, 49, 50, 52, 55, 60, 61, 64, 68, 74, 75, 78, 81, 90, 99, 101, 108, 109, 126
Storytelling	5, 9, 19, 20, 22, 43, 44, 48, 49, 54, 63, 67, 70, 76, 81, 84, 86, 91, 93, 114, 116, 120, 127
Theater, music	1, 8, 10, 11, 12, 16, 23, 30, 34, 38, 40, 54, 56, 57, 60, 62, 69, 71, 76, 80, 82, 83, 84, 88, 89, 92, 96, 105, 107, 109, 110,117, 121, 123
Theme parks	2, 17, 24, 29, 35, 51, 59, 65, 72, 79, 85, 95, 98, 103, 119
Games	3, 4, 5, 7, 8, 10, 15, 18, 32, 36, 39, 41, 47, 53, 58, 66, 70, 74, 94, 97, 100, 104, 111, 112, 113, 114, 115, 118, 125, 127
Transmedia	9, 18, 20, 27, 30, 39, 44, 73, 77, 87, 92, 102, 105, 107, 117, 122

reflected interactivity across three domains—theater, games, and theme parks—that embodied the range of audience interaction described above. Together, our review uncovers insights that inform our iteration on the spectrum.

The three domains vary greatly in form. Theater and music performances are primarily physical experiences that occur in dedicated venues. Conventional theatrical segregates audiences from performers, curbing feedback to pre-and-post show clapping and cheering [60], while contemporary theater allows audiences to contribute to performance, encouraging spontaneous [68] and structured participation [96,105]. In contrast, games exist in a range of physical and virtual forms, from tabletop games that build narrative through a shared imaginative fantasy [36], to video games that immerse audiences through integrated graphics, animation, and reward structures [104,111]. In juxtaposition to theater and games, theme parks created shared experiences for divergent audiences. Based on ancient and medieval religious festivals, trade fairs, and traditional amusement parks [79], themes parks assimilate storytelling [17,95], simulation, and interactivity [79,98] through blended physical and virtual experiences.

3.2 Literature Review Process

The primary goal of this work was to understand how the three representative domains describe audience interactivity. Our goal was to understand what interactions existed in those domains.

We extensively reviewed literature on interactive audience experiences across academic publications and in practitioner mediums. We systematically reviewed multiple databases (e.g. AAAI, ACM, PsycINFO, CiteSeerX, CogPrints Electronic Archive, ResearchGate, TRLN) for a range of topics (previous definitions and models of audience interactivity, engagement, immersion, agency, mediums of interaction, and roles), performing "related article" searches to identify model applications and limitations. Next, we shortlisted articles that defined interactivity or described interactive experiences in the three domains. In parallel, we came up with a list of synonymous phrases and keywords across the three domains, and searched websites and blog posts for descriptions of practitioner experiences. We analyzed domain publications to understand how the original spectrum levels were reflected in academic literature, and to identify gaps where literature did not fit the original spectrum. When domains were not evenly represented at a level, we performed a secondary Google Scholar search to identify any literature we may have missed. The literature we reviewed is indexed by topic in Table 1.

4   Summary of Results

This section summarizes our literature findings and introduces our *Spectrum of Audience Interactivity for Entertainment Domains*. First, we affirm the presence of a spectrum, describe modified levels, and present our validated spectrum.

4.1   Confirming the Existence of a Spectrum

The literature review affirmed the presence of the interactivity continuum, finding that interactivity ranged from passive to active experiences delineated by the agency of individual audience members. "Passive" and "personalized experiences" gave audiences agency over themselves, and "influencing," "augmenting," and "becoming a performer" levels gave audiences agency over other audience members, performers, and over the larger experience. Cross-domain literature supported the presence of these different levels, however we found that interactivity was more prominent in some domains; for instance, theater and music predominantly use interactivity to influence and augment performances [105,116,123], games employ audiences as performers [70,97], and theme parks create personalized and bidirectional experiences [95,118].

4.2   Modified Levels

Our review found that the spectrum required some modification. Shown in Fig. 2, the new spectrum introduces a new level of audience interactivity and modifies the name of an existing level.

Bidirectional Influence. The early spectrum included the level "Performers Augmenting the Audience's Multisensory Experience." This level was difficult to describe, however, we found that "Bidirectional Influence" clearly characterized the back-and-forth dynamic of interactive performance.

Take over Performance. The early spectrum described "Become Performers" as the highest level of interactivity. However, we found that interactivity extended beyond this; audience members could not only become performers, but fully control an experience. For instance, audience members invited into a drum circle could lead the music. Thus, we added a new level, "Take over the Performance," that describes this experience.

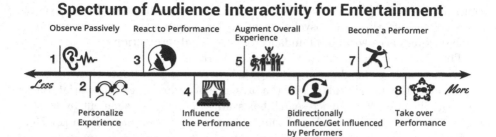

Fig. 2. The new Spectrum of Audience Interactivity for Entertainment Domains. We map audience interactivity from left to right; from least to most active.

4.3 Proposed Spectrum of Audience Interactivity

Presented in Fig. 2, the *Spectrum of Interactivity for Entertainment Domains* expands on Striner's *Spectrum of Interactivity* [108] using findings from the literature. Least interactive on the spectrum are (1) *observing passively*, referring to an audience member cognitively shaping their experience, and (2) *personalizing their experience*. More interactive is (3) *reacting to performance*, a level that describes how audience members react to performance and to one another, such as by clapping or responding to a comment on YouTube.

In (4) audience members influence the performance, exerting indirect control over the overall experience. For example, virtual audiences watching a Twitch stream could suggest a way for a streamer to solve a puzzle. Audience members in (5) *augment the overall performance experience* without explicitly becoming performers, for instance, dancing along at a rock concert. In (6) *bidirectional influence* between audience and performers, performers explicitly respond to the audience's influence or reactions, such as Mickey Mouse waving back at children.

Higher levels give audience members an explicit role in the performance, allowing them to (7) *become performers* and (8) *take over the performance*. In the former, performers are in control, for instance, audiences singing along with a choir, while in the latter, audiences take control. For example, an audience member invited to perform karaoke onstage would take over a performance.

5   Review of Interactivity Levels

The following section presents our review of the interactivity literature, organized from least to most interactive across the levels of our proposed Spectrum.

5.1 Interactivity in Passive Experiences

Traditional performances assume a clear distinction between the role of the audience and performers [16]: audiences do not interact with performers or have a role in the direction of performance or narrative. Forlizzi and others [37,57,126] contradict this assumption, suggesting that audiences can interact with experiences cognitively, through a psychological reader-response that imbues seemingly passive experiences with an abundance of emotional interaction.

The literature suggests that audiences participate in collective emotional experiences such as laughing or holding their breath that validate their personal experiences; this helps explain why the presence of an audience is essential to the sense of "liveness" [92]. HCI research has studied passive engagement by watching audience expressions and analyzing gestures using computer vision [14,73].

Research also argues that audience interaction is not always necessary or appropriate [108]. Green et al. [49] discuss how participants may simply wish to be distracted or passively entertained [14] by fiction. This outcome is further supported by literature on interactive film suggesting that passive experiences allow audiences to absorb, appreciate, and reflect on performance [14,48,120].

5.2   Interactivity Through Personalization

Personalization in interactivity describes the task of tailoring experiences to audience preferences, tastes, or capabilities. Theme parks fully embrace personalization in order to fully immerse audiences in fantastical worlds [72]; guests can meet characters [53], and personal experience narratives [24,95]. Paralleling these physical experiences, recent advances in narrative intelligence and augmented and mixed reality have likewise allowed for games to be personalized to player locations [4,66], abilities [97,113], and preferences [110].

Stapleton [106] describes how audiences personalize performances, discussing how a story originating in print (e.g. Harry Potter) can ignite a surge in new markets in games, theme parks, and costumes. Using dress to personalize experiences [108] is heavily paralleled in literature; Eicher's theory describes dressing up in fantasy costumes as a communication of the *secret self*, where the bulk of fantasy interactions takes place [30,39]. Similarly, Miller proposes a construct of fantastic socialization, where individuals play unrealized roles "constructed only with the cooperative help... and the contrasting foil provided by others" [46,78]. Fron et al. define such personalization as a co-performative act with other spectators, gaining pleasure from the ingenuity and artistry that go into creating one's persona and costume [8,39,53]. This style of personalization can be seen at American cultural festivals such as *DragonCon* [39], and also reflects Zimmerman's "meta-interactivity" mode [126].

5.3   Reacting to the Performance

Reacting to performance is a staple of traditional audience experience [60]. Literature suggests that audience members enhance the collective audience experience by influencing others' reactions [87]; Brignull and Rogers [13] explain that such interactions begin with peripheral awareness, transition to focal awareness, and culminate in direct interaction with the display. Their research observes the "honey pot" effect, in which bystanders are more likely to cross interaction thresholds when others do. For instance, audiences are likely to give a standing ovation (or throw rotten fruit) when others do the same [56]. An immersive interactive play, *Sleep No More* [116], extended this concept, allowing live and remote audiences to communicate through Internet-of-things (IoT) props.

Theme park literature characterizes this phenomenon as a learning tool. For instance, guests at the Wizarding World of Harry Potter watch others learn the mechanics of "casting a spell" [18,59]. Reeves describes this experience as an entertainment and teaching experience [92] that allows audiences to study interaction while waiting their turn. Magic Kingdom line experiences actively design for this affordance; guests in line for a Peter Pan ride view members ahead of them play with interactive shadow puppet displays, ringing bells, or even releasing Tinker Bell from inside a lantern [3,35]. This, in turn, prompts them to interact, mimicking scenes they have seen before, playing on each other's interactions and inventing new ones. Michelis [77] describes this phenomenon of the phases of interactions with gesture-based displays as an "audience funnel."

5.4   Influencing Performers

Interaction often allows audience members to indirectly influence the performance experience. Influencing performance includes visual voting systems [117], and audience input in improve [76]. While these types of interactions are popular, theater literature suggests that they are often asynchronous or inequitable [60], prioritizing audience members closer to the stage [23] or in positions of power [80].

Technical advancements have helped support democratic influence over voting. In an early example, audiences at the 1967 World's Fair in Montreal voted on alternative endings to a film [2]. Likewise, technology has allowed audiences to influence narratives [19], dialogues [105], or musical compositions [38]. Literature also found that designers wanted audiences to influence different sensory modalities, such as controlling gusts of wind onstage [108].

5.5   Augmenting the Experience

The literature suggests that audiences also want to augment experiences [108]. One way to do this is through multisensory design. For instance, child co-designers augmented music experiences with tangible "sound chips" [108]. Relatedly, Stapleton and Hughes [106] found that immersing movie-goers in multisensory mixed reality trailers created fond memories and positive associations.

Literature suggests that audiences can likewise augment experiences by adopting a composition role. Winkler notes that interactive computer music can "create new musical relationships" between audience and performers [123]; for instance, McAllister [71] allowed audience members to add to a digital score synced to a real-time display for musicians to read. Likewise, audiences can "compose" by dancing to music during performances [83,109].

This compositional relationship between audience and performers can also be asynchronous; for instance, van Troyer [115] introduced an interface for audiences to co-create asynchronously with composers by drawing "constellation" maps that synthesized new music from previous pieces. Similar examples exist in interactive fiction design. For instance, Machado [67] recounts a storytelling environment, *Once Upon A Time*, that developed characters, story themes, and narratives out of interactions with children.

5.6   Bidirectional Influence

Both physical and digital interactive performances lean heavily on the affordances of bidirectional interaction. For instance, gospel music uses call-and-response to nudge democratic audience participation [82], and computational narratives personalize player experiences by iteratively tracking and adapting narrative scheduling to player pacing [6]. Similar research has produced a virtual dance partner that improvises dance moves based on audience actions [54], and a narrative agent that responds to audience gestures with dialogue [84].

As well as responding to each other, some literature characterizes bidirectional interactions as "pushing and pulling" between audiences and performers. For instance, Rickman [93] described a text narrative mechanic that drives the narrative forward by using word selection to reveal additional information about an object or action [22]. Curiously, the research suggests that bidirectionality many not always be intentional. For instance, Van Maanen [118] describes how at Walt Disney World, guests and cast members cyclically affect each other; cast members are required to smile, but guests not smiling can ruin an operator's day.

5.7   Becoming Performers

All three domains allow audience members to take on performative roles, but differ in their approach. Games create immersion by giving players a sense of control [21], allowing users to select strategies, and affect outcomes [97]. Video games have an inherent performative experience, allowing audiences to dually function as players and audiences members [104], imbuing players with spectatorship in-between moments of play [112]. For instance, LARPS (Live-action-role-playing games) are considered performance-play experiences [102]. LARPS have no separate audience members, allowing audiences to extemporaneously create engaging narratives from limited preparatory materials [102].

Fantasy sports games further blend the roles of audiences and performers [100] by integrating the "activity of a virtual game and spectatorship of a real sport" [100]; Developments in large-scale streaming, tangible interfaces, and virtual and augmented reality have further changed the game viewer landscape. Twitch allows audiences to watch, and interact with streamers during games [114]. Similarly, augmented reality has given players and viewers a way to experience narratives in physical space [5, 51, 106].

Although less accessible than games [24], theme parks fully embrace audiences in performative roles, integrating storytelling [17,95], simulation, and interactivity [79,98], and emphasizing physical experiences. Theme park experiences often give audiences a chance to re-experience character roles and narratives. These firsthand narratives lean heavily on multisensory, spatial, and temporal experiences [79] to create a sense of presence [17,85].

5.8 Taking over Performance

Performance experiences also allow audiences to "take over" performances, building self-esteem [83] by allowing audiences to reshape existing experiences or co-create new ones. For instance, Boal [11] developed the *Theater of the Oppressed* to promote social and political change; audience members became "spect-actors," who used the medium to explore, and analyze their personal experiences. Likewise, home experiences like Guitar Hero [10] and Hyperscore [34] have contributed to music appreciation by bridging skill gaps.

Relatedly, music experiences help audiences make sense of and appreciate complex arts [82] by allowing them to co-create new experiences. For instance, Whitacre [122] developed a virtual choir that allowed singers all over the world to contribute to a performance, and Machover's *City Symphonies* [52] allowed audiences to contribute ambient sounds that made up their city.

Notably, in theater, the role of audiences as a performative agent is contested. In Hamlet on the Holodeck, Murray [81] suggests that audience participation may be "awkward" and potentially "destructive;" she describes a Woody Allen story, the *Kugelmass Episode* [1] where a literature professor jumps into the pages of Madame Bovary, only to confuse the narrative of the novel; "Who is this character on page 100? A bald Jew is Kissing Mme Bovary?" With this, Murray points out that "when we enter the enchanted world as our actual selves, we risk draining it of its delicious otherness" [81].

6   Conclusion

The goal of this work was to develop a taxonomy to explicitly characterize how audiences can interact and influence experiences across a range of entertainment domains. The spectrum aims to be a useful resource for researchers, designers, and artists to consider opportunities for interactivity. While the spectrum aspires to be comprehensive, new tools and media continually reshape the interactivity landscape, and edge cases undoubtedly exist. We consider such cases to be good fodder for discussion about new forms of interactivity. Further, this research does not endeavor to describe interactivity from the perspective of the performer or to describe audience characteristics (e.g., culture, size, and location). Such perspectives may have unique characteristics that may affect interactivity.

Future work will validate the clarity, precision, and effectiveness of the spectrum by interviewing experts in a range of domains. To help practitioners learn from other domains, we plan to use our taxonomy to survey a range of audiences, performers, and creators who participate in interactive audience experiences, allowing designers to compare diverse interaction experiences and identify patterns that emerge across domains. This will enable designers to actively consider the novelty and practicality of their interactivity designs, identifying patterns, and anticipate challenges that may arise in experimental designs.

Acknowledgements. Thank you to Jessica Hammer and Theresa Tanenbaum for their generous feedback and support.

References

1. Allen, W.: The Kugelmass Episode. New Yorker, Braunschweig (1977)
2. Anderson, D., Gosselin, V.: Private and public memories of expo 67: a case study of recollections of montreal's world's fair, 40 years after the event. Mus. Soc. **6**(1), 1–21 (2008)
3. Andersson, D., Brigante, R.: Impressive peter pan's flight interactive queue debuts dazzling pixie dust at Walt Disney World, January 2015. http://goo.gl/5hddCa
4. Azad, S., Saldanha, C., Gan, C.H., Riedl, M.O.: Mixed reality meets procedural content generation in video games. In: AAAI Conference on Artificial Intelligence and Interactive Digital Entertainment. AAAI Press (2016)
5. Azad, S., Saldanha, C., Gan, C.H., Riedl, M.O.: Procedural level generation for augmented reality games. In: Twelfth Artificial Intelligence and Interactive Digital Entertainment Conference (2016)
6. Azad, S., Xu, J., Yu, H., Li, B.: Scheduling live interactive narratives with mixed-integer linear programming. In: AAAI Conference on Artificial Intelligence and Interactive Digital Entertainment (2017)
7. Bartle, R.A.: Designing Virtual Worlds. New Riders, San Francisco (2004)
8. Bell, C.: Ritual: Perspectives and Dimensions-Revised Edition. Oxford University Press, Oxford (1997)
9. Benford, S., et al.: The frame of the game: blurring the boundary between fiction and reality in mobile experiences. In: Proceedings of the SIGCHI Conference on Human Factors in Computing Systems, pp. 427–436. ACM (2006)
10. Bernardo, F.: Music video games in live performance: catachresis or an emergent approach? In: Videojogos 2014-Conferência de Ciências E Artes Dos Videojogos (2014)
11. Boal, A.: Theater of the Oppressed. Pluto Press, London (2000)
12. Bradford, T.W., Sherry Jr., J.F.: Domesticating public space through ritual: tailgating as vestaval. J. Consum. Res. **42**(1), 130–151 (2015)
13. Brignull, H., Rogers, Y.: Enticing people to interact with large public displays in public spaces. In: Proceedings of INTERACT, vol. 3, pp. 17–24 (2003)
14. Brock, T.C., Livingston, S.D.: The need for entertainment scale. In: The Psychology of Entertainment Media, pp. 259–278. Erlbaum Psych Press (2003)
15. Brockmyer, J.H., Fox, C.M., Curtiss, K.A., McBroom, E., Burkhart, K.M., Pidruzny, J.N.: The development of the game engagement questionnaire: a measure of engagement in video game-playing. J. Exp. Soc. Psychol. **45**(4), 624–634 (2009)
16. Brooker, W.: Conclusion: overflow and audience. In: Brooker, W., Jermyn, D. (eds.) The Audience Studies Reader. Routledge (2003)

17. Bukatman, S.: There's always Tomorrowland: Disney and the hypercinematic experience. October **57**, 55–78 (1991)
18. Burn, A.: Potter-literacy: from book to game and back again; literature, film, game and cross-media literacy. Pap. Explor. Child. Lit. **14**(2), 5–17 (2004)
19. Cavazza, M., Charles, F., Mead, S.J.: Character-based interactive storytelling. IEEE Intell. Syst. **17**(4), 17–24 (2002)
20. Cavazza, M., Lugrin, J.L., Pizzi, D., Charles, F.: Madame bovary on the holodeck: immersive interactive storytelling. In: Proceedings of the 15th ACM International Conference on Multimedia, pp. 651–660. ACM (2007)
21. Cordova, D.I., Lepper, M.R.: Intrinsic motivation and the process of learning: beneficial effects of contextualization, personalization, and choice. J. Educ. Psychol. **88**(4), 715 (1996)
22. Cover, R., et al.: Interactivity: reconceiving the audience in the struggle for textual 'control' of narrative and distribution. Aust. J. Commun. **31**(1), 107 (2004)
23. Coverage, B.S.: In her own words: Sarah horn shares inspirational story of singing with Kristin Chenoweth at the hollywood bowl and going viral! August 2013. https://goo.gl/Afa6jE
24. Cross, G., Walton, J.K.: The Playful Crowd: Pleasure Places in the Twentieth Century. Columbia University Press, New York (2005)
25. Csikszentmihalyi, M.: Flow: the psychology of optimal performance (1990)
26. Cummings, J.J., Bailenson, J.N.: How immersive is enough? A meta-analysis of the effect of immersive technology on user presence. Med. Psychol. **19**(2), 272–309 (2016)
27. DeMartino, N.: Why transmedia is catching on (part 1). Accessed 2011
28. Druin, A.: Cooperative inquiry: developing new technologies for children with children. In: Proceedings of the SIGCHI Conference on Human Factors in Computing Systems, pp. 592–599. ACM (1999)
29. Durrant, A., Kirk, D.S., Benford, S., Rodden, T.: Pursuing leisure: reflections on theme park visiting. Comput. Support. Coop. Work (CSCW) **21**(1), 43–79 (2012)
30. Eicher, J.B.: Influence of changing resources on clothing-textiles and quality of life. In: Combined Proceedings, Easter, Central, and Western Regional Meetings of Association of College Professors of Textiles and Clothing. Association of College Professors of Textiles and Clothing (1981)
31. Engeser, S., Rheinberg, F.: Flow, performance and moderators of challenge-skill balance. Motiv. Emot. **32**(3), 158–172 (2008)
32. Ermi, L., Mäyrä, F.: Fundamental components of the gameplay experience: analysing immersion. Worlds Play Int. Perspect. Digit. Games Res. **37**(2), 37–53 (2005)
33. Everett, R.: Communication technology: the new media in society (1986)
34. Farbood, M.M., Pasztor, E., Jennings, K.: Hyperscore: a graphical sketchpad for novice composers. IEEE Comput. Graph. Appl. **24**(1), 50–54 (2004)
35. Fechtmann, T.J.V.: The best queues in Walt Disney World (2015). http://blog.touringplans.com/2015/07/01/best-queues-walt-disney-world/
36. Fine, G.A.: Shared Fantasy: Role Playing Games as Social Worlds. University of Chicago Press, Chicago (2002)
37. Forlizzi, J., Battarbee, K.: Understanding experience in interactive systems. In: Proceedings of the 5th Conference on Designing Interactive Systems: Processes, Practices, Methods, and Techniques, DIS 2004, pp. 261–268. ACM, New York (2004). https://doi.org/10.1145/1013115.1013152

38. Freeman, J.: Extreme sight-reading, mediated expression, and audience participation: Real-time music notation in live performance. Comput. Music J. **32**(3), 25–41 (2008)
39. Fron, J., Fullerton, T., Morie, J.F., Pearce, C.: Playing dress-up: costumes, role-play and imagination. Philos. Comput. Games, 24–27 (2007)
40. Gahr, S.: The art of dance, February 2017. https://www.warhol.org/the-art-of-dance/
41. Garris, R., Ahlers, R., Driskell, J.E.: Games, motivation, and learning: a research and practice model. Simul. Gaming **33**(4), 441–467 (2002)
42. Gilbert, L., Moore, D.R.: Building interactivity into web courses: tools for social and instructional interaction. Educ. Technol. **38**(3), 29–35 (1998)
43. Gilroy, S., Porteous, J., Charles, F., Cavazza, M.: Exploring passive user interaction for adaptive narratives. In: Proceedings of the 2012 ACM International Conference on Intelligent User Interfaces, pp. 119–128. ACM (2012)
44. Giovagnoli, M.: Transmedia Storytelling: Imagery, Shapes and Techniques. Etc Press (2011)
45. Goertz, L.: Wie interaktiv sind Medien? na (1995)
46. Goffman, E.: Interaction Ritual: Essays in Face to Face Behavior. Aldine Transaction, Piscataway (2005)
47. Goldman, A.: Predicting and motivating achievement in self-paced learning: a formative design, study and evaluation. Ph.D. thesis, University of Maryland, College Park (2014)
48. Green, M.C., Brock, T.C., Kaufman, G.F.: Understanding media enjoyment: the role of transportation into narrative worlds. Commun. Theor. **14**(4), 311–327 (2004)
49. Green, M.C., Garst, J., Brock, T.C.: The power of fiction: determinants and boundaries. Psychol. Entertainment Media Blurring Lines Between Entertainment Persuasion, 161–176 (2004)
50. Guha, M.L., Druin, A., Fails, J.A.: Cooperative inquiry revisited: reflections of the past and guidelines for the future of intergenerational co-design. Int. J. Child-Comput. Interac. **1**(1), 14–23 (2013)
51. Gupta, R., Shah, P., George, L., Pramer, E.: Harry Pottar. http://etv.gatech.edu/2016/05/16/harry-pottar-2/
52. Hoffman, E., Slotnick, S.: Design for the 21st century: media lab style. Des. Manag. Rev. **26**(1), 32–39 (2015)
53. Ito, M.: Intertextual enterprises: writing alternative places and meanings in the media mixed networks of Yugioh. ET Cult. Anthropol. Outerspaces, 180–199 (2005)
54. Jacob, M., Magerko, B.: Viewpoints AI. In: Proceedings of the 2015 ACM SIGCHI Conference on Creativity and Cognition, pp. 361–362. ACM (2015)
55. Jensen, J.F.: Interactivity: tracking a new concept in media and communication studies. Nordicom Rev. **12**(1) (1998)
56. Kershaw, B.: Oh for unruly audiences! Or, patterns of participation. In: Twentieth-century Theatre. Modern Drama XLIV.2, pp. 133–154 (2001)
57. Khut, G.P.: Interactive art as embodied inquiry: working with audience experience. In: Engage: Interaction, Art and Audience Experience (2007)
58. Kiili, K., Lainema, T., de Freitas, S., Arnab, S.: Flow framework for analyzing the quality of educational games. Entertainment Comput. **5**(4), 367–377 (2014)
59. Kronzek, A.Z., Kronzek, E.: The Sorcerer's Companion: A Guide to the Magical World of Harry Potter. Broadway (2010)

60. Lancaster, K.: When spectators become performers: contemporary performance-entertainments meet the needs of an "unsettled" audience. J. Popular Cult. **30**(4), 75–88 (1997)
61. Laurel, B.: Interface as mimesis, In: Norman, D.A., Draper, S.W. (eds.) User Centred System Design: New Perspectives on Human-computer Interaction (1986)
62. Laurel, B.: Computers as Theatre. Addison-Wesley, Reading (1991)
63. Laurel, B.: Interface agents: metaphors with character. In: Human Values and the Design of Computer Technology, pp. 207–219 (1997)
64. Lindley, C.: The semiotics of time structure in ludic space as a foundation for analysis and design. Game Stud. **5**(1), 2005 (2005)
65. Long, D., McKlin, T., Weisling, A., Martin, W., Guthrie, H., Magerko, B.: Trajectories of physical engagement and expression in a co-creative museum installation. In: Proceedings of the 2019 on Creativity and Cognition, pp. 246–257. ACM (2019)
66. Lv, Z., Halawani, A., Feng, S., Ur Réhman, S., Li, H.: Touch-less interactive augmented reality game on vision-based wearable device. Pers. Ubiquit. Comput. **19**(3–4), 551–567 (2015)
67. Machado, I., Martinho, C., Paiva, A.: Once upon a time. In: Published in Fall Symposium on Narrative Intelligence of AAAI (1999)
68. Marshall, M., Fiore, Q., Agel, J.: The Medium is the Massage: An Inventory of Effects (1967)
69. Mateas, M., Stern, A.: Façade: an experiment in building a fully-realized interactive drama. In: Game Developers Conference, vol. 2 (2003)
70. Mateas, M., Stern, A.: Interaction and narrative. Game Des. Reader Rules Play Anthol. **1**, 642–669 (2006)
71. McAllister, G., Alcorn, M., Strain, P.: Interactive performance with wireless PDAs. In: International Computer Music Conference (2004)
72. McCool, S.F., Moisey, R.N., Nickerson, N.P.: What should tourism sustain? The disconnect with industry perceptions of useful indicators. J. Travel Res. **40**(2), 124–131 (2001)
73. McDuff, D., El Kaliouby, R., Picard, R.W.: Crowdsourcing facial responses to online videos. In: 2015 International Conference on Affective Computing and Intelligent Interaction (ACII), pp. 512–518. IEEE (2015)
74. McMahan, A.: Immersion, engagement and presence. Video Game Theor. Reader **67**, 86 (2003)
75. McMillan, S.J.: A four-part model of cyber-interactivity: some cyber-places are more interactive than others. New Media Soc. **4**(2), 271–291 (2002)
76. Medianet: Teambuilding through improvisation. http://medianet-ny.com/TeamBuilding.pdf
77. Michelis, D., Müller, J.: The audience funnel: observations of gesture based interaction with multiple large displays in a city center. Int. J. Hum.-Comput. Interac. **27**(6), 562–579 (2011)
78. Miller, J.H., Lentricchia, F., McLaughlin, T.: Critical Terms for Literary Study. University of Chicago Press, Chicago (1990)
79. Milman, A.: 13 theme park tourism and management strategy. In: Tourism Management: Analysis, Behaviour, and Strategy, p. 218 (2007)
80. Monson, I.T.: Forced migration, asymmetrical power relations and african-american music: reformulation of cultural meaning and musical form. World Music **32**(3), 22–47 (1990)
81. Murray, J.H.: Hamlet on the Holodeck: The Future of Narrative in Cyberspace. MIT Press, Cambridge (2017)

82. Nelson, T.J.: Sacrifice of praise: emotion and collective participation in an African-American worship service. Sociol. Relig. **57**(4), 379–396 (1996)
83. Nettl, B., Russell, M.: In the Course of Performance: Studies in the World of Musical Improvisation. University of Chicago Press, Chicago (1998)
84. O'Neill, B., Piplica, A., Fuller, D., Magerko, B.: A knowledge-based framework for the collaborative improvisation of scene introductions. In: Si, M., Thue, D., André, E., Lester, J.C., Tanenbaum, J., Zammitto, V. (eds.) ICIDS 2011. LNCS, vol. 7069, pp. 85–96. Springer, Heidelberg (2011). https://doi.org/10.1007/978-3-642-25289-1_10
85. Palmer, C.T., Coe, K.: Parenting, courtship, disneyland and the human brain. Int. J. Tourism Anthropol. **1**(1), 1–14 (2010)
86. Pavlik, J.V., Bridges, F.: The emergence of Augmented Reality (AR) as a storytelling medium in journalism. Journalism Commun. Monogr. **15**(1), 4–59 (2013)
87. Peltonen, P., et al.: It's mine, don't touch! Interactions at a large multi-touch display in a city centre. In: Proceedings of the SIGCHI Conference on Human Factors in Computing Systems, pp. 1285–1294. ACM (2008)
88. Pohjola, M.: Autonomous Identities: Immersion as a Tool for Exploring. Empowering and (2004)
89. Pointer, M.: Charles Dickens on the Screen: The Film, Television, and Video Adaptations. Scarecrow Press, Lanham (1996)
90. Rafaeli, S.: From new media to communication. Sage Annu. Rev. Commun. Res. Advancing Commun. Sci. **16**, 110–134 (1988)
91. Rand, A.: The Night of January 16th. Penguin, London (1971)
92. Reeves, S., Benford, S., O'Malley, C., Fraser, M.: Designing the spectator experience. In: Proceedings of the SIGCHI Conference on Human Factors in Computing Systems, pp. 741–750. ACM (2005)
93. Rickman, B.: The Dr. k-project. In: Advances in Consciousness Research, vol. 46, pp. 131–142 (2002)
94. Salen, K., Zimmerman, E.: Rules of Play: Game Design Fundamentals. MIT Press, Cambridge (2004)
95. Schell, J., Shochet, J.: Designing interactive theme park rides lessons learned creating Disney's Pirates of the Caribbean-Battle for the Buccaneer Gold. In: Proceedings of the 2001 Game Developers Conference, pp. 723–731 (2001)
96. Schmitt, N.C.: Casting the audience. TDR (1988-) **37**(4), 143–156 (1993)
97. Shaker, N., Yannakakis, G.N., Togelius, J.: Towards automatic personalized content generation for platform games. In: AIIDE (2010)
98. Shani, A., Pizam, A.: The role of animal-based attractions in ecological sustainability: current issues and controversies. Worldwide Hospitality Tourism Themes **2**(3), 281–298 (2010)
99. Shernoff, D.J., Csikszentmihalyi, M.: Cultivating engaged learners and optimal learning environments. In: Handbook of Positive Psychology in Schools, pp. 131–145 (2009)
100. Shipman III, F.M.: Blending the real and virtual: activity and spectatorship in fantasy sports. In: Proceedings from DAC 2001: The Conference on Digital Arts and Culture (2001)
101. Shneiderman, B.: Designing the User Interface: Strategies for Effective Human-Computer Interaction. Pearson Education India, Bengaluru (2010)
102. Simkins, D.: The Arts of Larp: Design, Literacy, Learning and Community in Live-action Role Play. McFarland, Jefferson (2015)
103. Sit, J.K., Birch, D.: Entertainment events in shopping malls–profiling passive and active participation behaviors. J. Consum. Behav. **13**(6), 383–392 (2014)

104. Smuts, A.: Are video games art? Contemp. Aesthetics **3**, 6 (2005)
105. Squinkifer, D.: Coffee! A misunderstanding (2014). http://squinky.me/my-games/coffee-a-misunderstanding/
106. Stapleton, C.B., Hughes, C.E.: Mixed reality and experiential movie trailers: combining emotions and immersion to innovate entertainment marketing. In: Proceedings of 2005 International Conference on Human-Computer Interface Advances in Modeling and Simulation (SIMCHI 2005), pp. 23–27. Citeseer (2005)
107. Steuer, J.: Defining virtual reality: dimensions determining telepresence. J. Commun. **42**(4), 73–93 (1992)
108. Striner, A., McNally, B.: Transitioning between audience and performer: co-designing interactive music performances with children. In: Proceedings of the 2017 CHI Conference Extended Abstracts on Human Factors in Computing Systems, CHI EA 2017, pp. 2115–2122. ACM, New York (2017). http://doi.acm.org/10.1145/3027063.3053171
109. Strutner, S.: This guy quit his job to play piano around the world in a beautifully unplugged life, July 2015. http://www.huffingtonpost.com/entry/dotan-negrin-piano-around-the-world_us_559fd8c0e4b096729155ecf8
110. Summerville, A., Guzdial, M., Mateas, M., Riedl, M.: Learning player tailored content from observation: platformer level generation from video traces using LSTMs. In: AAAI Conference on Artificial Intelligence and Interactive Digital Entertainment (2016)
111. Sylvester, T.: Designing Games: A Guide to Engineering Experiences. O'Reilly Media, Inc., Newton (2013)
112. Taylor, T.L., Witkowski, E.: This is how we play it: what a mega-LAN can teach us about games. In: Proceedings of the Fifth International Conference on the Foundations of Digital Games, FDG 2010, pp. 195–202. ACM, New York (2010). https://doi.org/10.1145/1822348.1822374
113. Togelius, J., Yannakakis, G.N., Stanley, K.O., Browne, C.: Search-based procedural content generation: a taxonomy and survey. IEEE Trans. Comput. Intell. AI Games **3**(3), 172–186 (2011)
114. Toups, Z.O., Hammer, J., Hamilton, W.A., Jarrah, A., Graves, W., Garretson, O.: A framework for cooperative communication game mechanics from grounded theory. In: Proceedings of the First ACM SIGCHI Annual Symposium on Computer-Human Interaction in Play, pp. 257–266. ACM (2014)
115. van Troyer, A.: Constellation: a tool for creative dialog between audience and composer. In: 10th International Symposium on Computer Music Multidisciplinary Research (2013)
116. van Troyer, A.: Enhancing site-specific theatre experience with remote partners in sleep no more. In: Proceedings of the 2013 ACM International Workshop on Immersive Media Experiences, ImmersiveMe 2013, pp. 17–20. ACM, New York (2013). https://doi.org/10.1145/2512142.2512150
117. Unger, P., Forsberg, K., Jacobsen, J.H.: Photovote: olympic judging system. In: Extended Abstracts on Human Factors in Computing Systems, CHI 2004, pp. 1670–1674. ACM, New York (2004). https://doi.org/10.1145/985921.986184
118. Van Maanen, J., Frost, P., Moore, P., Lundberg, C., Louis, M., Martin, J.: The smile factory. In: Sociology: Exploring the Architecture of Everyday Life Readings. Pine Forge Press, Newbury Park (1991)
119. Vermeulen, I.E., Roth, C., Vorderer, P., Klimmt, C.: Measuring user responses to interactive stories: towards a standardized assessment tool. In: Aylett, R., Lim, M.Y., Louchart, S., Petta, P., Riedl, M. (eds.) ICIDS 2010. LNCS, vol. 6432, pp. 38–43. Springer, Heidelberg (2010). https://doi.org/10.1007/978-3-642-16638-9_7

120. Vorderer, P., Knobloch, S., Schramm, H.: Does entertainment suffer from inter-activity? The impact of watching an interactive tv movie on viewers' experience of entertainment. Media Psychol. **3**(4), 343–363 (2001)
121. Wardrip-Fruin, N., Harrigan, P.: First Person: New Media as Story, Performance, and Game. MIT Press, Cambridge (2004)
122. Whitacre, E.: A virtual choir 2,000 voices strong. https://www.ted.com/talks/eric_whitacre_a_virtual_choir_2_000_voices_strong
123. Winkler, T.: Composing Interactive Music: Techniques and Ideas Using Max. MIT Press, Cambridge (2001)
124. Yee, N.: Facets: 5 motivation factors for why people play MMORPG's. Terra Incognita **1**, 1708–1723 (2002)
125. Zeltzer, D.: Autonomy, interaction, and presence. Presence Teleoperators Virtual Environ. **1**(1), 127–132 (1992)
126. Zimmerman, E.: Narrative, interactivity, play, and games: four naughty concepts in need of discipline (2004)

Towards Intelligent Interactive Theatre: Drama Management as a Way of Handling Performance

Nic Velissaris[1] and Jessica Rivera-Villicana[2]

[1] Applied Artificial Intelligence Institute, Deakin University, Burwood, Australia
nic.velissaris@gmail.com
[2] Melbourne, Australia

Abstract. In this paper, we present a new modality for intelligent interactive narratives within the theatre domain. We discuss the possibilities of using an intelligent agent that serves as a drama manager and as an actor that plays a character within the live theatre experience. We pose a set of research challenges that arise from our analysis towards the implementation of such an agent, as well as potential methodologies as a starting point to bridge the gaps between current literature and the proposed modality.

Keywords: Interactive Narrative · Drama Management · AI actor · Player modelling · Believable characters · Choice-Based Narrative · Interactive theatre

1 Introduction

The concept of Interactive Narrative (IN) has been pursued for several decades in different forms with the aim of providing an experience where the player feels that their decisions have an effect on the storys development [7]. Examples of INs are the Choose Your Own Adventure (CYOA) books [1], text adventures, video games like Detroit: Become Human [12] and interactive films such as Black Mirror: Bandersnatch [8].

In this paper, we propose a novel approach to INs that consists of having an intelligent agent acting as a character in a theatre play and perform Drama Management (DM) tasks as a response to the human performers. To the best of our knowledge, such theatre modality has not yet been proposed or attempted in existing works [10,16]. We propose to implement such modality using The Melete Effect by Velissaris [20], an IN written as a theatre play.

The novelty of the proposed approach lies in its use of principles from both traditional INs and theatre. While INs allow for diversity in the possible stories resulting from the actions of the user experiencing them, they require the user's input as a participant within said story (usually as the protagonist). In theatre, the narrative typically flows linearly, with all the performers following a predefined script. As opposed to traditional INs, in our approach the user (in this case

R. E. Cardona-Rivera et al. (Eds.): ICIDS 2019, LNCS 11869, pp. 233–238, 2019.
https://doi.org/10.1007/978-3-030-33894-7_24

the audience) is an observer rather than a participant in the construction of the narrative. This involves tackling new challenges, such as the intelligent agent's improvisation/acting skills, behaviour in accordance with character archetypes, and by the performance of DM for multiple inputs. The benefit for the audience in the creation of more sophisticated interactive experiences is a more satisfying and unpredictable narrative that can continue to change and evolve. Interactive experiences which offer genuine surprises in their outcome encourage the audience to return to the experience, leading to deeper and more satisfying engagement with the IN [18]. This means that the IN has a longer lifespan and can be returned to more often.

2 Background

Interactive Narratives: This phrase is used because it is broadly understood to mean narrative experiences that change through the player's interaction. The mechanisms that influence interaction can vary widely from simple choices to complicated role-playing systems. Typically INs are focused exclusively on audience/player choice [19]. Velissaris defines this form as Choice-Based Narrative in which choice is the central mechanic that facilitates interaction [20].

The Melete Effect: This IN was developed as a part of Velissaris doctoral research work on establishing a poetics for choice-based narratives [20]. It tells the fictional story of a journalist Mary Melete in the 1970s and 80s. It has three distinct narratives and it will be utilised as there are no restrictions on its use.

Drama Management: From the AI perspective, a drama manager is an intelligent system which makes use of computational models of the narrative and the player in order to make choices within the environment to (attempt to) solve the boundary problem (i.e., the conflict between player agency and authorial intent) [6,14,17,22].

Player Modelling: Consists of studying the interaction between a player and (usually) a game with the aim to create representations that capture desired features [21,23]. Besides accounting for player freedom, a drama manager may be able to personalise player experience by considering the best narrative arc depending on each players preferences [14].

Adaptability as a Performance Trait: One of the skills an actor is taught is the ability to adapt to any situation. This adaptability is inherent to the actors job and any AI actor or Drama Manager will (1) need to be able to handle situations in which the experience as performed is not as was expected, and (2) adapt to these changes and ensure that experience continues on without interruption.

3 The Challenges/Research Goals

We now discuss the main challenges we have identified towards the realisation of this approach, and the solutions we propose.

3.1   Exhibit Believable (or up to Some Standard) Acting Skills

Successful characterisation in a narrative experience is a result of balancing compelling actions with good performance. What a character does is measured by how it is enacted by the actor playing the role. Most of the existing work in believable characters focuses on Non Player Characters (NPCs) in games [3]. The focus on NPC believability, however, is different than ours in that believability refers to their acceptance by the player as a human-like behaving entity rather than an agent able to portray emotions or behaviour in accordance with their character archetype [9,11]. In this regard, acting skills are related to character archetype behaviour, discussed later as a separate research goal.

The approach we propose towards achieving this objective is to have the agent learn the behaviour from human players. This could be achieved via techniques such as supervised learning [5]. We can then apply generative models to create different courses of action for achieving similar goals that do not seem artificial (i.e, not human). The advantage of supervised learning methods is that by having a target well defined by a human, the data and training time can be reduced, while a disadvantage is the subjectivity introduced by the expert.

Another possibility is to use unsupervised learning methods, such as Apprenticeship Learning (AL) to have the agent learn a more general behavioural pattern throughout the whole story [4]. A benefit of unsupervised learning is that there is less reliance on a human expert to dictate behaviour, but a disadvantage is that the resulting behaviour may not be of the same quality as that generated by a supervised learning method.

3.2   Behave According to the Character Its Playing

Another challenge is to make the agent behave in character. This would require a strong modelling technique for each character tied to the computational model of the story and its constraints. We propose to build a model for each character with a representative set of traits (e.g, scales ranging from lawful to evil, specific tastes, overall role in the story, etc.) and any specific constraints regarding their behaviour (e.g, a boss that is only intolerant with their employees, when at work). This representation can be used to determine a characters behaviour in certain scenes [9,11].

3.3   Adapt to Performers Behaviour Not Necessarily Observed in the Past or Planned by the Author in the Script

Theatre plays are dynamic (or uncertain) to some extent. This uncertainty is expected to increase with the implementation of an IN. An AI actor will need to be able to adapt and change the narrative in ways that do not destroy the overall narrative experience. However, these changes must be in keeping with the overall narrative and be facilitated by the Drama Manager. This believable and adaptable AI actor cannot introduce plot or character details that will radically change the character in a way that threatens the coherency of the narrative.

As opposed to games, the fact that performers do not have limitations regarding the actions they can perform increases the complexity of this problem. For example, in text-based games, commands not recognised are simply not processed by the system, prompting the player to try with a different command. A factor that helps mitigate this challenge is that a scene is bounded by space and time, limiting the number of possible actions for the agent and the performers.

The approach we propose aims to have an agent whose behaviour can generalise to different situations by (1) selecting a diverse recruitment base to learn behaviour that captures a variety of possible responses to specific events, (2) implement goal/plan/action recognition to map novel events to event types that have been observed by the agent during training, and (3) encode some predefined behaviour for events that may not have been covered by the previous steps [15].

3.4 Perform Drama Management for More Than One Subject

Existing literature focuses on managing the experience and choices of a single player. In our case, the agent needs to manage the choices of as many performers present in a scene, while the general experience is being managed for the audience.

Having multiple subjects to manage is expected to increase the complexity of the DM problem [2], however, the fact that the performers possess knowledge regarding the expected outcomes of the story, and are expected to cooperate towards reaching them, may reduce the dynamism compared to traditional DM, where the players lack of knowledge, as well as their own preferences contribute to deviations from the author's intended narrative. As, in our opinion, this is the most challenging goal at this time. We aim to observe Riedl et al.'s approach and evaluate its performance to find avenues for improvement [13].

4 Conclusion and Future Work

The steps we propose towards achieving this proposed modality are as follows:

1. Using the existing script for The Melete Effect as the basis of the drama manager to develop multiple possible permutations of the narrative.
2. Learning character behaviour from actors and/or players using player modelling techniques.
3. Introducing an AI Actor in different roles to see how it responds to different story possibilities.
4. Combining the previous steps into a single system.

In closing, we believe that this evolution of INs and AI is similar to the evolution seen in genre storytelling in other mediums. There will be many permutations and evolutionary leaps that will be required before we can establish definitively how INs and AI can work in live theatre environments. Similar to Murray's view of the creation of Hamlet on the holodeck [7], our aspirations are to bridge the barriers of technology and performance in a way that can revolutionise the live experience of storytelling for an audience.

References

1. Chooseco: Choose Your Own Adventure books (2005). https://www.cyoa.com/
2. Fairclough, C.R., Cunningham, P.: A multiplayer case based story engine. In: 4th International Conference on Intelligent Games and Simulation (GAME-ON), pp. 41–46 (2003). http://citeseerx.ist.psu.edu/viewdoc/summary?doi=10.1.1.391.3720
3. Guimaraes, M., Santos, P., Jhala, A.: CiF-CK: An architecture for social NPCS in commercial games. In: 2017 IEEE Conference on Computational Intelligence and Games, CIG 2017, pp. 126–133 (2017). https://doi.org/10.1109/CIG.2017.8080425, http://www.creationkit.com/index.php?title=Category:Packages
4. Lee, G., Luo, M., Zambetta, F., Li, X.: Learning a Super Mario controller from examples of human play. In: 2014 IEEE Congress on Evolutionary Computation (CEC), pp. 1–8. IEEE (2014)
5. Lee, S.Y., Rowe, J.P., Mott, B.W., Lester, J.C.: A supervised learning framework for modeling director agent strategies in educational interactive narrative. IEEE Trans. Comput. Intell. AI Games 6(2), 203–215 (2014)
6. Magerko, B.S.: Player modeling in the interactive drama architecture. Ph.D. thesis, Ann Arbor, MI, USA (2006)
7. Murray, J.H.: Hamlet on the Holodeck: The Future of Narrative in Cyberspace. The Free Press, New York (1997)
8. Netflix: Black Mirror: Bandersnatch (2018)
9. Peinado, F., Cavazza, M., Pizzi, D.: Revisiting character-based affective storytelling under a narrative BDI framework. In: Spierling, U., Szilas, N. (eds.) ICIDS 2008. LNCS, vol. 5334, pp. 83–88. Springer, Heidelberg (2008). https://doi.org/10.1007/978-3-540-89454-4_13
10. Pinhanez, C., Bobick, A.: It/I: A theater play featuring an autonomous computer graphics character. In: Proceedings of the ACM Multimedia 1998 Workshop on Technologies for Interactive Movies, pp. 22–29 (1998)
11. Pizzi, D., Charles, F., Lugrin, J.-L., Cavazza, M.: Interactive storytelling with literary feelings. In: Paiva, A.C.R., Prada, R., Picard, R.W. (eds.) ACII 2007. LNCS, vol. 4738, pp. 630–641. Springer, Heidelberg (2007). https://doi.org/10.1007/978-3-540-74889-2_55
12. Quantic Dream: Detroit: Become Human (2018)
13. Riedl, M., Li, B., Ai, H., Ram, A.: Robust and authorable multiplayer storytelling experiences. In: Seventh Artificial Intelligence and Interactive Digital Entertainment Conference, October 2011. https://www.aaai.org/ocs/index.php/AIIDE/AIIDE11/paper/viewPaper/4068
14. Riedl, M.O., Bulitko, V.: Interactive narrative: an intelligent systems approach. AI Mag. 34(1), 67–77 (2013)
15. Rivera-Villicana, J., Zambetta, F., Harland, J., Berry, M.: Informing a BDI player model for an interactive narrative. In: Annual Symposium on Computer-Human Interaction in Play. ACM, Melbourne, Australia (2018)
16. Rousseau, D., Hayes-Roth, B.: Improvisational synthetic actors with flexible personalities. Knowledge Systems Laboratory TR KSL97 10 (1997)
17. Sharma, M., Ontanon, S., Mehta, M., Ram, A.: Drama management and player modeling for interactive fiction games. Comput. Intell. 26(2), 183–211 (2010)
18. Szilas, N.: Interactive drama on computer: beyond linear narrative. In: AAAI Fall Symposium on Narrative Intelligence, vol. 144, pp. 150–156 (1999)
19. Szilas, N.: IDtension : A narrative engine for interactive drama. In: 1st International Conference on Technologies for Interactive Digital Storytelling and Entertainment 2003 (2003). http://ci.nii.ac.jp/naid/10026187402/en/

20. Velissaris, N.: Making a choice: the Melete effect and establishing a poetics for choice-based narratives. Ph.D. thesis (2017). https://researchbank.rmit.edu.au/view/rmit:162342
21. Wang, P., et al.: Simulating player behavior for data-driven interactive narrative personalization. In: Proceedings of the Thirteenth Annual AAAI Conference on Artificial Intelligence and Interactive Digital Entertainment, pp. 255–261 (2017)
22. Weyhrauch, P., Bates, J.: Guiding Interactive Drama. Carnegie Mellon University, Pittsburgh (1997)
23. Yannakakis, G.N., Spronck, P., Loiacono, D., André, E.: Player modeling. Dagstuhl Follow-Ups **6**, 59 (2013). https://doi.org/10.4230/DFU.Vol6.12191.45, http://drops.dagstuhl.de/opus/volltexte/2013/4335/

Technologies

Towards Procedural Generation of Narrative Puzzles for Adventure Games

Barbara De Kegel[1] and Mads Haahr[2]

[1] University College Dublin, Dublin, Ireland
[2] Trinity College Dublin, Dublin, Ireland
mads.haahr@tcd.ie

Abstract. Narrative puzzles involve exploration, logical thinking and progressing a story. This paper presents a narrative design innovation in the form of a system for the procedural generation of such puzzles for use in story-rich games or games with large open worlds. The approach uses an extended type of context-free grammar as the basis for both the generation algorithm and the puzzle solving. Each designer-defined rule in the grammar defines a possible behavior of item types in the game world. Puzzles are generated at runtime on a per area basis, through recursive generation of inputs for outputs. Given a valid grammar, the system guarantees that its puzzles are solvable.

Keywords: Procedural content generation · Puzzles · Interactive narrative · Authoring tools

1 Introduction

Narrative puzzles can be defined as puzzles that form part of the progression of a narrative, whose solutions involve exploration and logical as well as creative thinking. They are a key component of adventure and story-driven games, and often feature in large open world games, including RPGs. Narrative puzzles can be viewed as temporary obstacles to the story's advancement; though they do not always have to be solved in a precise order, certain puzzle sequences generally need to be solved before proceeding to others. Typically, good narrative puzzles involve making logical connections, which may not be immediately obvious, but which ultimately comprise a satisfying solution. Puzzlers typically find solutions by exploring the environment and investigating ways in which objects can be manipulated. Examples of narrative puzzle patterns identified by Fernández-Vara et al. [3] are: (a) Figuring out which item a character desires, usually leading to a reward in exchange; (b) Logically combining two objects to change their properties, or to create a new object; (c) Disassembling an object into useful components; (d) Saying 'the right thing' to convince a character to provide aid; and (e) Acquiring a key to open a new area.

Due to space constraints, we are not able to present a detailed review of related work here, but we refer the reader to our recent survey of procedural

© Springer Nature Switzerland AG 2019
R. E. Cardona-Rivera et al. (Eds.): ICIDS 2019, LNCS 11869, pp. 241–249, 2019.
https://doi.org/10.1007/978-3-030-33894-7_25

generation of puzzles [2], which contains a section on narrative puzzles, including Puzzle-Dice [3], as well as work by Dart and Nelson [1] and van der Linden *et al.* [4].

2   Design

Our system aims to improve replayability of smaller story-driven games as well as offer way to improve the narrative engagement of games with large open worlds and a high degree of procedural content. Our approach is inspired by (and improves upon) Puzzle-Dice [3], specifically in terms of expressivity, usability and scalability, while maintaining the guarantee of solvability.

2.1   Core Concepts

The approach is based on a context-free grammar that defines possible behaviors of game items. The puzzle generator integrates with a game world to create puzzles on the fly based on the current state of the world. There are three components that feed into the generator: a database of all items that can be used in puzzles, a set of grammar rules that describe the space of all possible puzzles, and a list of the game areas. Several core concepts form the basis of these components:

- **Items:** Conceptual game objects which are defined by their type(s) and properties.
- **Properties:** Named characteristics of Items, which have a value of specific value type.
- **Rules:** Possible in-game actions, composed of an output Term, a set of by-product Terms, an Action and a set of input Terms (see Fig. 1).
- **Terms:** The main units out of which Rules are composed, each is defined by a single type and an optional list of properties.
- **Action:** The unit of a Rule that described the player's action in carrying out a rule.
- **Area:** A single connected space that forms part of the game world; used to compartmentalize the puzzle generation.

The definition of the components is flexible in terms of the designer-defined content they can support, allowing the generator to be applied to a range of different types of games.

Fig. 1. Abstract representation of the general structure of a rule.

The generator uses the set of production rules that constitute the grammar in a left to right direction to generate a puzzle backwards from an end goal. The backwards process ensures the puzzle is solvable. In a game that incorporates the generated puzzles, the same rules—but used in the right to left direction—function as game logic.

2.2   The Puzzle Items

A puzzle item is a conceptual representation of a tangible object that can be used as part of a generated puzzle. Each puzzle item has a unique name, an optional list of properties, and an associated visual representation, e.g., a Unity prefab. There may be more than one puzzle item for an object that has multiple states, e.g., a tree in summer and that same tree in autumn. These specificities in item definitions are left open to the game designer.

Items' properties are defined by their name and type; the type—string, boolean or integer—determines the legal values for the property. Properties are freely defined by the game designer and can be tailored to the needs of the puzzle game. There are no required properties; if a property is not defined for an item, the generator assumes it does not have this property, or for boolean properties, assumes the value is *False*. For example, not specifying the *carryable* property is equivalent to marking an item as 'not carryable.'

There are several special properties which have explicit logic attached to them. One is the *carryable* property; an item is queried in-game for this specific property to determine whether it can be added to a player's inventory.

Another special property is the *isa* property, which can be used to define all the categories (i.e., super classes) a certain item belongs to; e.g., a *PineTree* might have the *isa* properties *Tree* and *Plant*. The value associated with an *isa* property may or may not be the name of another item in the puzzle items database. The name of an item is automatically considered an *isa* property of that item—it defines the most specific category the item belongs to. In addition, every puzzle item is automatically considered to be a sub-type of the type *Item*. The *isa* property allows for hierarchies among the types of puzzle items, which is central to the functioning of the grammar rules discussed in Sect. 2.3.

The *contains* property is also a special case—though it is a string property, its value is interpreted as a puzzle item. As will be discussed in Sect. 2.3, this property is particularly important in the definition of rules, which can refer to transient item states.

Finally there are two special properties that can be used to restrict the possible locations of puzzle items. The *notSpawnable* property, indicates that a puzzle item can only be used if it is already part of the game world, and will not be instantiated as a rule output, e.g., a large lake. The *area* property can be used to specify the legal areas for spawning and/or using an item, allowing the game designer to control which items may be included as part of a puzzle on a per-area basis.

2.3   The Grammar

The grammar, which comprises of a set of production rules, describes the space of all possible puzzles. Each rule describes a relationship between a set of inputs and a set of outputs, in a format that is loosely based on the format of rules that make up a context-free grammar. The rules serve a dual purpose: they are used by the generator to create puzzles and as game logic. The general format of a rule is as follows:

$$itemType[properties_{0...n}]_{1...n} ::= action\ itemType[properties_{0...n}]_{1...n} \qquad (1)$$

In a context-free grammar, all the productions are one-to-one, one-to-many or one-to-none. The rules that comprise the puzzle grammar fall under the first two categories. Production rules are read from left to right and can be interpreted as breaking down an output into its input(s), or replacing an output with one or more inputs. A puzzle, in the form of a tree structure, is created by iteratively (recursively) decomposing outputs, starting from an end goal.

In practice, the rules can (and often do) have multiple outputs because the right and left hand sides of the rule describe which items exist in the gameworld, and in what state, before and after the rule is applied. For generating a puzzle only the first output is important, and the others are considered by-products. For example, in rule 2, which expresses chopping down a tree, the axe is not an outcome, but it is important to account for the fact that it was not consumed as part of the execution of the rule. Each input (right-hand side term), is considered to be destroyed if it does not appear as an output (left-hand side term). The exception to this is an input that appear as the value of the *contains* property for an output—these are also not considered destroyed. Rule 3 shows an example of this type of behavior.

$$TreeStump\ Axe ::= ChopDown\ Tree\ Axe \qquad (2)$$

$$Container[contains : Eggs] ::= Gather\ Eggs\ Container \qquad (3)$$

The output of each rule is thus one or more terms, while the input is composed of at least one term, as shown in Fig. 1. Terms represent the non-terminals of the grammar while the puzzle items represent the terminals. There are implicit rules for replacing terms with specific puzzle items—terms can be seen as boxes with descriptions of what kind of puzzle item could be placed inside.

The terminals (puzzle items) are not directly used in the authoring of the grammar rules; a designer only looks at linking terms (non-terminals) to other terms. Internally, the puzzle generation system contains logic for determining which non-terminals could be replaced with terminals from the item database. The grammar is only valid if each input term can be matched to at least one output term in a different rule, or at least one puzzle item. Designers should be conscious of this when authoring the puzzle rules.

Terms have an item type and an optional list of properties. The item type corresponds to the previously described *isa* property and can be specific (e.g.,

PineTree) or general (e.g., *Plant*). The more general the type, the more puzzle items have the potential to be matched to a term. The special type *Item* can be used for terms that are allowed to be replaced by any puzzle item.

The properties associated with a term are fundamentally the same as those for a puzzle item. For a puzzle item to match a term it must be of the same type or a sub-type as the term's type, and it must include all properties of the term (though it can have many more properties than those required by the term).

Besides inputs and outputs, each rule must also have an action, which can be considered a terminal. This action is only used as part of the second purpose of the rules, i.e., as game logic, and has no bearing on the puzzle generation. The action is associated with the first input term, and as such, it is important to consider the order of the input terms; for example in rule 2, the action *ChopDown* should appear attached to the *Tree* term, rather than the *Axe* term.

2.4   The Puzzle Areas

Each puzzle area corresponds to a connected area in the game world and must have an associated goal. The goal is used by the generator as the starting point for generating a puzzle for that area. A designer can associate multiple possible goals with each area in order to increase the possibility space of puzzles that can be generated for that area. The format of an area goal is the same as that of a single term in a rule of the grammar. Each goal specifies a type of puzzle item that must be obtained, and an optional list of properties that must be fulfilled for that item. The generator checks that the goal cannot be satisfied by any intermediate items that are chosen as part of the puzzle, as this would result in a player completing a puzzle prematurely.

Besides a goal, a puzzle area has a unique name, a list of connected areas, and maximum puzzle depth. The maximum depth refers to the depth of the tree structure representation of the puzzle that is created by the generator. Puzzle areas can be predefined, or in the case of a procedurally generated game, they could also be automatically defined at run-time based on environmental attributes. The player's current in-game area is tracked by the generator and used to spawn puzzle items pick area appropriate rules.

2.5   Puzzle Generation

The puzzle generator works by recursively generating inputs for outputs using the set of rules that make up the puzzle grammar. The rules are used in the left to right direction as production rules and do not take into account the by-product terms. Puzzle generation is done live, i.e., while the game is being played, on the basis of currently accessible areas and items. At a high level (between areas), generation is running forwards throughout the game, but at a low level (within each area), generation runs backwards. This forward-backwards combination ensures solvability, quality and lack of repetition for the generated puzzles.

At the start of the game, a puzzle is generated for the area that has been designated as the start area. Finishing a puzzle for one area, (i.e., achieving the area's goal), causes all its connected areas to become unlocked, and triggers the generation of puzzles for those newly available areas. This forwards part of the algorithm can branch off into different tracks depending on the specified connections between areas. The system maintains each of the available areas independently, so multiple puzzles can be in progress at the same time. The overall forward direction of the algorithm allows for scenarios in which an item that is needed to solve a puzzle for one area must be retrieved from another area.

When generating a puzzle for an area, the algorithm begins by finding a rule with a left hand side term that matches the current area's goal. The area goal is analogous to the grammar's start symbol. From that starting rule, the generator continues trying to substitute right hand side terms for other terms until no suitable rule can be found to perform such a substitution, or the area's depth limit is reached. At that point, the generator adds the puzzle item (terminal) that matches the last term to the game world. The rules used for the substitutions are recursively chained together into a tree structure that defines the entirety of the created puzzle. The items spawned in the world correspond to the input terms for the rules that make up the leaves of that tree.

An example of a generated puzzle is shown in Fig. 2, followed by the rules that would be chained together to create that puzzle. In reality, it is the rules that make up the nodes of the tree, rather than the terms, but the terms make for a clearer representation of the structure. The narrative solution to this puzzle is as follows: first the player must assemble a disguise out of glasses and a fake moustache and set of a car alarm to distract the security guard; these events can happen in either order. Then the player can steal the distracted security guard's badge, and proceed to unlock the safe with it. Finally, once the safe is unlocked, the player can open it and access the gold (the goal of the puzzle).

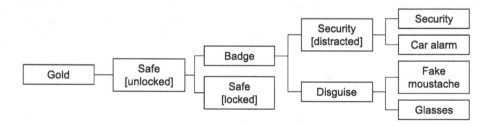

Fig. 2. An example puzzle tree.

$$Gold\ Safe ::= Open\ Safe[locked : False] \qquad (4)$$

$$Safe[locked : False]\ Badge ::= Unlock\ Safe[locked : True]\ Badge \qquad (5)$$

$$Badge\ Security ::= Steal\ Security[distracted : True]\ Disguise \qquad (6)$$

$$Security[distracted : True] ::= Trigger\ CarAlarm\ Security[distracted : False] \qquad (7)$$

$$Disguise ::= CreateDisguise\ Glasses\ FakeMoustache \qquad (8)$$

Matching Terms. Terms can be matched to other terms according to their types and properties. The properties must be an exact match, but the type of the output term can be the same or more general than the type of the input term. For example, an input term of type *Tree* could be replaced by a rule with an output term of type *Tree* or *Plant* but not by one of type *PineTree*.

Notably, the generation algorithm does not wait until it reaches a terminal to pick a matching puzzle items for a term but rather attempts to find one as early as possible. The reason is that this allows for the use of more specific rules, widening the scope of possible puzzles. Terms become more specific as a result of an associated puzzle item, and can then be matched to a wider variety of output terms in other rules. For example, a rule with an input term with type *Tree*, as in the previous example, might pick a *PineTree* item as the matching puzzle item and change its type accordingly.

When an item replacement is found for a term, that item is passed up the tree to previously visited rules, and attached to corresponding terms. In this way, each term in each rule in the puzzle tree structure will have an associated puzzle item when generation completes, for use during the solving of the puzzle.

Generation per Game Area. The game areas are modular but conscious of their context. New puzzles are created on a per area basis, with the generation algorithm taking into account all currently accessible areas, all items currently in the world, and all items in the player's inventory. The generator ensures that puzzle items chosen for a term are accessible and appropriate, making use of the items' *area* and *notSpawnable* properties. Additionally, generation will terminate upon reaching an intermediate puzzle item that already exists in the world to prevent recreating a puzzle that the player has already solved, or creating a puzzle that is trivial, because the player already has the goal item.

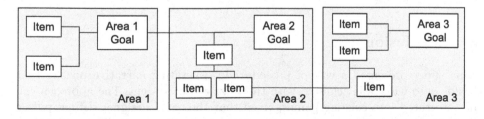

Fig. 3. A layout of how puzzles in different game areas can be interconnected.

Figure 3 shows how puzzles in each area can re-use items from previously visited areas. For example, the goal for area 1 is re-used as one of the input items needed to acquire the goal for area 2, and one of the items from area 2 can be re-used as an input to a puzzle in area 3. Puzzles are generated per area in a linear order for this example, e.g., the puzzles for area 2 are created after the goal for area 1 has been achieved.

We do not make the assumption that the world is empty at the start— existing objects in the scene can be included in the puzzles, if they are identified as puzzle items. This is an important design choice for integrating puzzles into an environment. Puzzle items could correspond to environmental features, such as a lake, or large static structures, which are more easily placed in the game world as part of scene design, allowing for freedom in the construction of the game world. One reason for this choice is the potential use of this puzzle generator in a game with a procedurally generated environment, such as *Minecraft* or *No Man's Sky*. In these games, the puzzle generator could run as a separate layer on top of the existing generator and construct puzzles featuring already spawned game objects, environmental features and NPCs.

The puzzle generator also tracks the depth of the tree that represents the current puzzle, allowing for a designer specified puzzle length. The number of actions needed to solve a puzzle is also determined by the breadth of the tree but due to a low average branching factor (most rules will have one or two inputs), depth influences the length of the solution sequence more than breadth.

2.6 Puzzle Solving

Next to puzzle generation, the grammar rules also provide the in-game logic that allows a player to solve a generated puzzle. For this purpose the rules are used from right to left; the inputs on the right hand side must be satisfied in order to produce the output(s) on the left hand side. Inputs are satisfied when they are co-located, which could be through use of an inventory system, and have all of the required properties. When the inputs for a rule are satisfied, the action to execute that rule is provided to the player. Only when the player chooses that action is the rule actually executed, i.e., are its inputs replaced by its outputs. While the generator only looked at the first (main) output, each output is important in-game because they indicate which items should be created and/or destroyed.

3   Conclusion

This paper presented a way of procedurally generating narrative puzzles that builds onto what was achieved with the Puzzle-Dice system. The approach can be integrated into existing games, given that the game designer defines puzzle items, rules and game areas as they pertain to his/her game. The difficulty of the puzzles is determined by the designer. As a preliminary evaluation, we have developed a small proof-of-concept game in Unity using the narrative puzzle generator. The game was made with free 3D assets and set in an environment with two areas; a grass field, and a river bank. The areas contained game objects designated as puzzle items, including trees, corn stalks and a well. On a given playthrough, each of these may or may not be used in the puzzle (depending on the puzzle created), but it is always possible to interact with the items. This adds consistency to the world, and can throw the player off in terms of what items he/she needs to complete the puzzles for an area. In future work, we plan to create a bigger game and evaluate the approach through a user study.

References

1. Dart, I., Nelson, M.J.: Smart terrain causality chains for adventure-game puzzle generation. In: 2012 IEEE Conference on Computational Intelligence and Games (CIG), pp. 328–334. IEEE (2012)
2. De Kegel, B., Haahr, M.: Procedural puzzle generation: a survey. IEEE Trans. Games (2019). https://ieeexplore.ieee.org/abstract/document/8718565
3. Fernández-Vara, C., Thomson, A.: Procedural generation of narrative puzzles in adventure games: the puzzle-dice system. In: Proceedings of the Third Workshop on Procedural Content Generation in Games, p. 12. ACM (2012)
4. van der Linden, R., Lopes, R., Bidarra, R.: Procedural generation of dungeons. IEEE Trans. Comput. Intell. AI Games 6(1), 78–89 (2014)

JUNGLE: An Interactive Visual Platform for Collaborative Creation and Consumption of Nonlinear Transmedia Stories

Mubasir Kapadia[1]([✉]), Carlos Manuel Muniz[1], Samuel S. Sohn[1], Ye Pan[2],
Sasha Schriber[2], Kenny Mitchell[2,3], and Markus Gross[2,4]

[1] Rutgers University, Newark, USA
mubbasir.kapadia@rutgers.edu
[2] Disney Research, Pittsburgh, USA
[3] Edinburgh Napier University, Edinburgh, UK
[4] ETH Zurich, Zürich, Switzerland

Abstract. JUNGLE is an interactive, visual platform for the collaborative manipulation and consumption of nonlinear transmedia stories. Intuitive visual interfaces encourage JUNGLE users to explore vast libraries of story worlds, expand existing stories, or conceive of entirely original story worlds. JUNGLE stories utilize multiple media forms including videos, images, and text, and accommodate branching narrative outcomes. We extensively evaluate Jungle using a focused small-scale study and free-form large-scale study with careful protection of study participant privacy. In the small-scale study, users found JUNGLE's features to be versatile, engaging, and intuitive for discovering new content. In the large-scale study, 354 subjects tested JUNGLE in a realistic 45-day scenario. We find that users collaborated on story worlds incorporating various forms of media in multiple (on average two) possible story paths. In particular, we find through initial observations that JUNGLE can evoke creativity: traditionally passive consumers gradually transition into active content creators. Supplementary videos showcasing the JUNGLE system and hypothetical example stories authored using JUNGLE independently hosted here and here.

Keywords: Storytelling · Story authoring · Nonlinear transmedia stories

1 Introduction

As the patterns of consuming and creating story content evolve, stories are increasingly generated by many authors working together to create rich, immersive, often interactive, and engaging experiences that are told across multiple media formats. Traditionally passive consumers are now dynamic prosumers, who like to be actively engaged in influencing the outcome of narratives. Existing

© Springer Nature Switzerland AG 2019
R. E. Cardona-Rivera et al. (Eds.): ICIDS 2019, LNCS 11869, pp. 250–266, 2019.
https://doi.org/10.1007/978-3-030-33894-7_26

online platforms and communication systems provide isolated support for collaboration, nonlinearity, or transmedial stories. However, there exists no accessible platform for collaborative authoring and consumption of nonlinear transmedia stories.

There are four key requirements towards meeting this goal. (1) *Exploration*: It should be intuitive to explore vast libraries of complex, nonlinear, transmedial stories in an effort to find new stories to consume and contribute to. (2) *Consumption*: The system should facilitate the discourse of nonlinear and transmedial story content, with stories told using multiple media forms, and branching in different directions. (3) *Collaborative Creation*: It should be easy to add new content (text, images, video, etc.) while working with others. (4) *Seamless Interfaces:* A seamless transition between exploration, consumption, and creation should simplify the process of finding new stories to consume and identifying points in the story to build upon, effectively empowering even traditionally passive content consumers to become prosumers.

Fig. 1. Visual interfaces in JUNGLE: (a) A planet-based metaphor for exploring large collections of story worlds. (b) Selecting a story planet allows the user to explore stories (visualized as continents) in that particular story world. (c) A traditional list-style interface for story exploration. (d) Interface for story consumption with left panel visualizing the story graph. (e) User selects an alternate branch of the story to consume. (f) Sketchboard interface for collaborative editing of story bits. (g) Story bits can be easily integrated into existing story. (h) Resulting story. Camera images sourced from Wikimedia under either Creative Commons license or from the Public Domain.

In this paper, we present JUNGLE, an interactive visual platform for the collaborative authoring and consumption of nonlinear, transmedia stories. JUNGLE was iteratively designed to make exploration intuitive, collaboration on ideas straightforward, addition to existing nonlinear and transmedial story content easy, and transitions between exploration and consumption unobtrusive. We introduce a general representation of a story which is visually encoded at different levels of abstraction, each of which caters to a particular interaction task. We explore the benefits and trade-offs of a traditional side-scrolling interface and a planet-based metaphor for exploring stories among multiple story worlds. Stories are consumed using a bi-directional scrolling interface with support for branching. A sketchboard interface is introduced to promote collaboration on individual media elements (story bits), which can then be integrated into a story to fork it into new and exciting directions. In addition, we provide a comprehensive evaluation with two studies: first, a small-scale study to focus on the usability of JUNGLE and next, a large-scale study to demonstrate that long-term engagement in this platform results in (a) collaborative efforts to produce new story worlds, (b) a diverse assortment of linear and branching narratives told through multimedia, and (c) a trend of users transitioning from consumers to prosumers. The primary purpose of JUNGLE and study is to facilitate the collaborative content ideation and creation process. The study scope has been for evaluation of the JUNGLE system as a means of research on enhanced cooperative creation tools, without intent of productization or commercial outcome. The concepts of ownership, access rights, audience adaption, prosumer migration of franchise cannon and wider prosumer media scenarios (e.g. video games) could potentially be developed in the JUNGLE platform, however, these emerging and complex topics are explicitly beyond the scope of this paper.

2   Related Work

Storytelling has been explored from a wide variety of perspectives (both academically and commercially) toward the development of platforms for collaborative user-generation of interactive stories using different media. *Storied Navigation* [26] provides an intuitive video editing interface to piece video clips from a text annotated corpus to create compelling video stories. *GameBridge* [22] presents a nonlinear transmedia story concept within the "Game Of Thrones" story world that combines plot points from the TV show and books. Shwirtz and colleagues [27] explore the impact of social media as a storytelling medium, and its potential for innovative creators to push the boundaries and invent new genres of content and means of connection with audiences. Sadauskas *et al.* [24] present a prewriting support tool to prepare meaningful writing topics from social media. Balabanović *et al.* [6] presents a physical interface for local photo sharing, analogous to a conventional photo album, as well as recording of stories that can be sent to distant friends and relatives. The Graphic StoryWriter (GSW) [30] enables users to create stories through the manipulation of graphic objects in a simulated storybook, relying on a rule-based story engine to guide story development and generate text. CANVAS [16] provides a visual storyboard metaphor for authors to rapidly prototype and visualize 3D animated stories.

Interactive stories [12] strive to transform traditional passive experiences into immersive, engaging experiences where the user can influence the outcome of the narrative. Andrews *et al.* [5] presents an interactive branching comic for consuming interactive digital narratives. More generally, interactivity is important for exploring new content. Utilizing the Space-Time Continuum creates Adaptive Storyworlds [25] that inspire a framework completely controlled and organized while yet still available to free and open exploration. Mauro and Ardissono [21] developed a co-occurrence graph for the exploration of complex information spaces such as those managed by Geographical Information Systems. Games are also a popular medium of interactive storytelling with extensive research in computational intelligence [15,23] to help authors create compelling freeform interactive narratives. Non-linear choice driven narrative creation systems with procedural generative methods are also emerging for story-centric video games [14]. Lessel *et al.* [19] investigated how an interacting collaborative audience could influence the course of action in gaming live-streams such as in "Twitch Plays Pokemon".

Some frameworks focus on collaboration. Storeys [11] is a graph-based visualization tool for collaborative story writing that represents stories in a branching tree of individual text sentences. Motif [18] uses storytelling patterns extracted from expert-authored stories to guide novice users. Liu *et al.* [20] proposed a hypermedia approach to collaborative storytelling activities in social media environments to enable students to integrate the episodes of others to develop different branches of stories into a coherent story. *Ensemble,* [17] a collaborative writing platform, presents an approach to guiding the diverse perspectives of a creative crowd by using a leader with a high-level vision for a story that articulates constraints. Basaraba proposes a framework to facilitate the collaborative authorship of non-fiction interactive digital narratives [8]. StoryMINE [28] is a platform for creating and consuming multiplayer interactive narrative experiences, in which players experience different narratives. Capturing player interactions in multi-player games [29] brings forth a Multi-Participant Interactive Narrative Framework for games.

Among commercial platforms, Interlude [1] provides a web-platform for creating interactive video stories. Likewise, Storycanvas [2] facilitates the authoring of interactive stories with a storyboarding tool, and Storyverse [3] hosts professionally created 3D interactive narratives. Existing online platforms and communication systems provide isolated support for collaboration, nonlinearity, or transmedial stories. JUNGLE aims to provide a unified solution for the collaborative creation and consumption of nonlinear transmedia stories that is accessible to everyone.

3   JUNGLE Platform

We describe the various capabilities of the JUNGLE platform and the theoretical motivations that influenced them. The careful user studies described in later sections explain the empirical motivations behind this research on data-driven collaboration enhancement.

Story Representation. Stories created, explored, and consumed in JUNGLE are nonlinear and transmedial; each story may be composed of a combination of text, images, audio, video, and other media formats, and may branch in different directions, depending on the viewer's preference. Formally, a *story* is represented as a directed acyclic graph. This ensures that it is not possible to experience repetitions unless the story is specifically authored in that way. Each node in the story is a *story bit*: a story atom which corresponds to a single scene in the progression of a story and is composed of text, image, audio, or video. JUNGLE also supports story bits that are an image sequence, or a combination of text and image (e.g., a panel in a comic). Entry and exit nodes indicate the beginning and end of a story, though story graphs can contain multiple entry and exit nodes. Edges represent plausible transitions between story bits. Branching nodes contain multiple outgoing edges to split the story into different directions. A path traversal from any entry node to any exit node represents one plausible linear story. A *story world* is a collection of stories (multiple, disconnected story graphs) that share a common theme.

Visual Story Metaphors. The general representation of a story described above is visually encoded at different levels of abstraction and presented to the user, catering to particular interaction tasks: exploration, consumption, or collaborative creation. We explore the trade-offs between a traditional scrolling-style exploration interface and a planet-based metaphor for exploring stories among multiple story worlds. Stories are consumed by scrolling in

Fig. 2. Planet visualizations of different hypothetical story worlds authored using JUNGLE. (a) A simple linear story for Alice in Wonderland. (b) A branching story in Leila. (c, d) A complex story world comprising many disconnected, nonlinear stories called Once Upon A Time.

a manner similar to current web-based consumption experiences, with the possibility to move horizontally at decision points. A sketchboard (i.e., virtual whiteboard) is proposed for users to collaborate on individual story bits, which can be introduced into the story graph to branch the story into exciting new directions. Engaging users in rich collaborative interactive entertainment environments to facilitate narrative world creation is beginning to develop for video games [4]. In addition to providing an interesting and engaging user experience, for example, our planet visualization serves a few careful purposes in prosumer collaborative creation. The use of spherical story graph layout provides a form of focus+context graph visualization (similar to Du *et al.*'s iSphere [13]) whilst remaining in 3D with familiar spatial reasoning, and the pictorial terraforming style is aimed at enhancing recall of story forms among collaborators (after observations of Borkin *et al.* [9]).

Story Exploration. Beyond the managed studies of this research we foresee, JUNGLE could contain a plethora of user-generated and professionally curated story worlds, each with a collection of nonlinear, transmedial stories. Navigation and unique visualization systems tailored by task facilitate the exploration of such a large, complex, and heterogeneous dataset. We first provide a traditional flat approach that displays a list of available story worlds. Clicking on a specific story world expands a drop-down menu with title cards for each available story in that world. The user can then browse through the list of title cards by scrolling horizontally, as illustrated in Fig. 1(c). We then introduce a planet metaphor for visualizing and exploring stories in JUNGLE. Each story world maps to a planet in the JUNGLE story ecosystem, whose continents refer to disconnected story graphs. Continents are overlaid with graphs to visualize the structures of the corresponding stories. Their shapes are procedurally generated based on their story graphs, but the relative size of a continent is decided based on its rank within the story world (Fig. 2). Entry points to these continents are represented by images projected out from the planet and grouped together according to number of story bits shared.

Different visual attributes of the planet metaphor can be mapped to semantics in the underlying stories. For example, story worlds can be ranked in a way that determines their planets' locations between the foreground and the background. Higher ranked planets are pulled towards the foreground, making them appear large than planets in the background (Fig. 1(a)). There are several measurements which users may find useful for this work's purpose of enhanced collaborative creation processes, e.g., number of likes, user-creation activity, number of branching story bits, longest path length, and total number of story bits. As the JUNGLE story ecosystem evolves with new content and consumption patterns, the planets dynamically adapt to meet the trends of the users and the continents dynamically reshape themselves to match the structures of the stories. In future, the visualizations could further support the user's preferences, allowing them to control personalized views of their preferred content.

Comparison. Although list-based visualization is pre-established and minimal, there are a couple of limitations that do not suit JUNGLE's usage. First, lists effectively have one monotonic degree of freedom for navigating. A list ordered by measured engagement takes more effort to find stories with lower activity, which in turn may make active stories become increasingly active and therefore potentially isolate other stories. This discourages exploration of new and unknown stories and story worlds. On the other hand, the planet-based visualization does not share this potential limitation. The most popular story (that a list would start at) is the first visible continent on the planet. From this initial view, the user is able to navigate with two and three unrestricted degrees of freedom. Also, although the planet is initially focused on the continent with highest activity measures, the other continents are not arranged by engagement as they would be in a list. This facilitates the unbiased exploration of the story ecosystem.

Another limitation of the list-based visualization is its inability to compare elements. In the planet-based visualization, the relationship between a given continent and every other continent can be embedded in its position. For a list to encode the same information, each continent must explicitly store similar continents, leading to redundancy. While the planet metaphor inherently takes more effort to learn than the ubiquitous list representation (in part, due to its novelty), it can potentially encourage more exploration and introduce users to new stories that match preferences under their full control.

Story Consumption Interface. The user selects a story to consume (or add to) using one of the two exploration modalities described above. This transitions the user to the consumption interface by default. A unique challenge is to consume stories that contain a combination of media forms, and have multiple branching points. To meet these requirements, the user is presented with two visual representations of the story, as shown in Fig. 1(d). The left panel contains a traditional story graph representation which provides a complete perspective of the entire story structure at a glance. The main panel provides a full-size view of each story bit. Scrolling vertically allows the user to proceed down the current story path, consuming story bits (text, images, audio, or videos) in accordance to the progression of the narrative. This is similar to current consumption interfaces which present users with linearly ordered media atoms. In order to support non-linearity in the story structure, the user has the option to scroll horizontally at any decision point in the story graph, where the user may choose to continue along the current story path, or take the story in a new direction. While consuming stories, users may post comments associated with specific story bits for other users to read.

Story Creation. A *sketchboard*, akin to a virtual whiteboard, is provided for users to work together to create story bits – transmedial atoms of a story. The creation of a story bit entails two simple steps. First, the user may either upload media elements or directly type text, and then the user can drag the tile onto the sketchboard. This serves as a visual representation for that particular story bit. Multiple users may

Fig. 3. A hypothetical story using JUNGLE set within a "Once Upon a Time" story world. This simple story contains media composed of text, images, and video, and has two possible outcomes (image source see acknowledgements).

simultaneously access the same sketchboard and collaborate in real-time, either through interaction with the story bits, such as adding comments, or by directly communicating with other active users through a traditional chat interface. When a user is editing a story bit in the sketchboard, it is locked, preventing others from simultaneously editing the same story bit. When a user edits a story by adding or removing story bits, a new story branch is created in the story graph, at the junction where the user diverges from the current story. This leaves previously authored stories untouched and mitigates any conflicts and merging issues from arising during story creation. Story bits created in the sketchboard are integrated into a story through a preview version of the consumption interface. Users can simply drag the selected story bit to the corresponding position in the story, thereby creating a new node in the story graph, and possibly introducing a new branching point. Users can preview new content and rapidly iterate through a seamless and collaborative creation-consumption cycle. In cases of alternative views among collaborators, a conflict of ideas can be remedied by branching the story graph (and perhaps rejoining at a future story bit). This particular use captures the potential of branching in stories, allowing for both small-scale changes (e.g., in a single character's actions) and large-scale change (e.g., the theme of the narrative). A basic hypothetical story with single branch is shown in Fig. 3.

4   Usability Analysis

We conducted a small-scale structured user study to evaluate the usability of the different parts of JUNGLE, and the system as a whole. In addition, we performed a comparative analysis of the two interfaces.

Participants. 15 subjects were recruited as part of this study (9 male, 6 female) aged between 19 and 34 years ($\mu = 24.54, \sigma = 5.67$). Subjects had computer proficiency and were all novice users with no creative or artistic background.

Table 1. User study questions.

Q1	I found it difficult to locate a specific story
Q2	I enjoyed browsing through the story selection
Q3	It was easy to find new content to explore
Q4	It was easy to explore different paths of the same story
Q5	It was easy to consume different types of media
Q6	It was difficult to branch into new continuations of the same story
Q7	It was easy to create stories together with other users
Q8	It was difficult to add different types of media to a story
Q9	It was easy to create stories with different continuations

Experiment Procedure and Task. Each subject was first given a brief introduction to JUNGLE and then asked to perform the following tasks in sequence: (a) Exploration task using Interface A, (b) Exploration task using Interface B, (c) Consumption task, and (d) Creation task. The exploration task required the user to find a specific story within a pre-existing collection of user-generated stories from a previously conducted large-scale study (see description below). The two exploration interfaces (traditional flat interface and planet interface) were randomly ordered for each user to mitigate the effect of learning over successive exploration tasks. For each exploration task, the user was asked to find a different story. Upon selecting a story, the consumption task required the user to use the consumption interface to go through the story while viewing the different transmedial story bits, and exploring the different branching options within the same story. The creation task involved uploading an image to create a new story bit using the sketchboard interface and creating a new branch by integrating them into the story.

After each task, the subject was asked to fill out the System Usability Study (SUS) questionnaire [10], which is a standard measure to quantify the usability of a system. The questionnaire also included a few additional questions (see Table 1) to qualitatively analyze

Table 2. Results of SUS scores

System	x̄	x̃	σ
Exploration (List)	77	77.5	4.93
Exploration (Planets)	74.83	75	5.71
Consumption	73.17	75	7.29
Creation	70.67	75	9.33
JUNGLE	72.67	75	10.10

the exploration, consumption, and creation aspects of JUNGLE. Questions were on a 5 point Likert scale (Strongly Disagree, Disagree, Neutral, Agree, Strongly Agree). Redundant questions were interspersed within the regular set of questions to ensure the responses from the users were valid and not randomly entered. Upon the completion of all 4 tasks and their respective questionnaires, the user completed the SUS form for the whole system. The study was concluded with a short oral debrief, having a total duration of less than 60 min per subject.

Table 2 shows the average, median, and standard deviation of the SUS scores for: (a) exploration using traditional flat interface, (b) exploration using planet interface, (c) story consumption, and (d) story creation. While SUS scores are particularly valuable to measure the relative improvement of the system's usability across versions, we can use guidelines [7] (SUS > 70 is considered to be "Good"), coupled with the oral feedback from the users at the end of the study, to deduce that the users were able to successfully

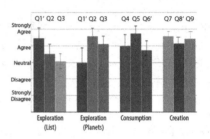

Fig. 4. User study questionnaire results. Questions marked with a prime symbol had their response results inverted for consistency ($Q' = 5-Q1$).

use all aspects of JUNGLE without hindrance and minimal supervision or training. No significant discrepancy in SUS scores between the specific aspects of JUNGLE was observed, alluding to the relative maturity of the interfaces.

Users were asked additional questions to qualitatively evaluate the various aspects of the system and to compare the two exploration interfaces. The questions are provided in Table 1. Some of the questions expected negative responses, and additional redundant questions were also included in the study for validation purposes. The aggregate statistics of the user's responses are illustrated in Fig. 4. According to the study, users find it easy to consume stories in JUNGLE with different media types, and are able to use the interface to explore the different branching points in a narrative. In addition, users find that the sketchboard provides an intuitive interface for collaboration between users and integration of new story bits into the story graph.

List vs. Planet Interface for Story Exploration. We compare the list and planet interface for exploring stories on three factors:

(a) **Q1'**: Ease of finding a specific story,

(b) **Q2**: Enjoyment in browsing,

(c) **Q3**: Discovering new and unknown story content (Table 1).

Paired t-tests were conducted to compare the list and planet interfaces for these three factors. The analysis results are

Table 3. Comparative analysis between List and Planet Interface for exploring stories in JUNGLE. The response values of **Q1** have been inverted in this analysis for consistency.

Q	List		Planet		t	df	p	95% CI	
	μ	σ	μ	σ				LB	UB
Q1'	4.47	0.74	3.00	1.0	4.56	25.85	0.0001	0.81	2.13
Q2	3.53	0.92	4.60	0.74	−3.52	26.78	0.002	−1.69	−0.44
Q3	3.07	1.16	4.13	0.63	−3.11	21.77	0.005	−1.78	−0.36

reported in Table 3, which shows a significant difference in the mean user scores for all three factors: (a) **Q1'**: $t(25.85) = 4.56, p = 0.0001$. (b) **Q2**: $t(26.78) = -3.52, p = 0.002$. (c) **Q3**: $t(21.77) = -3.11, p = 0.005$. The results suggest that the users found the traditional list interface easier to use for finding specific stories and the planet interface more engaging for browsing through a large collection of stories or for discovering new, previously unseen story content. This indicates the potential for both interfaces to accommodate different kinds of exploration tasks, as well as creative styles.

5   User Studies

In addition to the small-scale study described above, JUNGLE has been rigorously evaluated with 6 studies conducted over a period of 1.5 years, the results of which have been used to iteratively design and improve the platform. We briefly describe the results of the first set of studies, which has led to the current evolution of the JUNGLE platform.

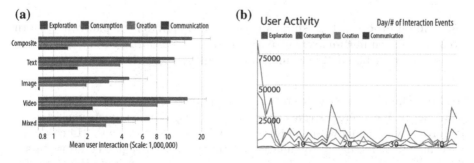

Fig. 5. (a) Average user activities for clusters of story planets with unique media signatures. (b) User activity trends.

5.1 Preliminary Studies

Five preliminary studies were completed for the purposes of validating the potential of collaborative authoring of nonlinear transmedial stories and to explore group dynamics during the creative process. In the 1st and 2nd studies, a physical one-day workshop was conducted where users (19 and 18, respectively) were asked to either write a whole story or finish a story. Users were split into groups and asked to work together to create the stories and their conclusions. They were encouraged to produce drawings, recordings, and take any material they liked from free resources on the Internet. Surveys from these workshop studies always elicited positive feedback towards the collaborative environment and the task. In the 3rd and 4th studies, individual user tests were conducted where users (5 and 6, respectively) of different nationalities were asked to interact with a preliminary version of the planet-based story exploration interface. Following a short tutorial, users found the planet metaphor intuitive and found the notion of branching stories intriguing. In the 5th study, a preliminary version of JUNGLE with exploration, consumption, and creation capabilities was released to 190 users from all over the world. Users were invited to browse through the story worlds and continue developing the stories in any way that they wished using images, text, audio, or video. Collaboration was not supported in this version, and users could not interact with each other. 80 out of 190 users developed stories, while all users explored and consumed content in JUNGLE.

5.2 Large-Scale User Study

The sixth study was conducted with 354 users, who were given free access to the JUNGLE platform over a period of six weeks. Users ranged from 16 to 71 years old ($\mu = 32, \sigma = 8.54$). 62% of the users were female, 37.7% male, and 0.3% identified as gender queer. They were asked to test the platform with no further instructions.

User Engagement. Users spent an average of 71 min on the platform with the top 30 users spending an average of 380 min on the platform. Users visited 11498 scenes and contributed 1228 comments, 243 likes, and 1021 story path ratings.

Media. There were 50 user-created story planets containing at least 1 story (the other planets were disregarded in this analysis). These planets consisted of a rich diversity of media with 439 text bits, 1033 images, 38 videos, 214 composite story bits (a combination of image and text), and 43 sequence story bits (a slide show of images). The media signatures (i.e., relative distributions of media elements) for these planets are illustrated in Fig. 6a. We cluster the 50 story worlds together into the following categories: (a) Text-centric (20), (b) Image-centric (6), (c) Video-centric (2), (d) Composite-centric (8), and (e) Mixed (14). Figure 5a provides the mean user activities for the different categories of story planets. Multiple trends stand out from the various activities of users across the

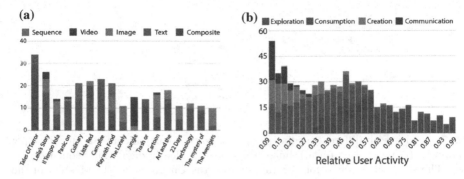

Fig. 6. (a) Media signatures of some user-authored stories. (b) Histogram of relative user activity.

planets in our research study's findings. Exploration dominates the activities of users across all planet archetypes, perhaps owing to the relative novelty of the JUNGLE research prototype. Video-centric stories were measured among study participants to have the largest consumption times, on average, but also elicit maximum consumption from participants. Video-centric planets also recorded the maximum communication between users. Figure 7 illustrates stories using different combinations of media.

Story Structure. We analyze the structure of the story graphs that were created by the users in terms of number of story nodes N, connectivity N_c (measured in terms of number of subgraphs where any two nodes in a subgraph were connected to each other through a path traversal), and maximum degree d_{max} of a story node. The relevant statistics are reported in Table 4. The largest story, "Tales of Terror" had 38 nodes (made up of text and composite story bits). Stories had a calculated average maximum degree of 2.38, with the majority of stories having between 2 and 3 story paths, and the maximum degree

Table 4. Aggregate story graph metrics across all user-authored story planets. N: number of nodes in a story graph. N_c: number of connected subgraphs in a story graph. d_{max}: Maximum degree of a story node.

Metric	N	N_c	d_{max}
Max	38	6	6
Min	2	1	1
Mean	9.78	2.06	2.38
Median	7.5	2	2

observed 6 story paths. We observe that a majority of the stories had some degree of nonlinearity ($d_{max} > 1$), with nearly 10 of the 50 planets having more than 8 decision points at various stages in the story. Figures 7 and 9 illustrate the graph structure of some stories that were created by users in JUNGLE. The structure of stories ranged from strictly linear experiences to complex branching stories with multiple decision points. More complex graph-theoretic measures may be used to glean additional insights into the structure of the stories created among users, which is beyond the scope of this study.

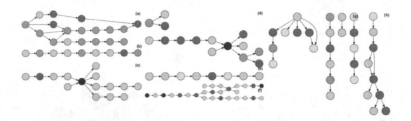

Fig. 7. Stories with different media signatures. Node color indicates the media type: Composite (orange), Text (cyan), Image (magenta), Video (indigo), and Sequence (yellow). The story titles are as follows: (a) Art and the Unconscious, (b) Mystery of the Lost Wallet, (c) Panic on Planet Parmeson, (d) Tempo Vola, (e) A Tale of Two Lovers, (f) Leila's Story, (g) Play with Food. (Color figure online)

User Activity. Within the scope of this study with careful attention to privacy, we temporarily logged the activity profiles of users according to activity type (exploration, consumption, creation, or communication) that the users were currently engaged in. The activity trends over the duration of the study are illustrated in Fig. 5b. Following an initial surge in user activity, we see a steady pattern of exploration, consumption, and creation across users, with periodic spikes that might be attributed to new story initiatives by active users. Note that no professional content was added by us for the duration of this study. All content was user-generated for this hypothetical collaborative creation study only, without any intent of formal production. A histogram of the relative user activity for all users is provided in Fig. 6b. While a large percentage of the users spend the majority of their time exploring and consuming content, a significant number of active users communicate and collaborate with one another to create new story content.

User Up-Conversion. We measure the creation to consumption ratio of all users over the study duration, and observe its trend (Fig. 8). As demonstrated by the results, users show a marked increase in creating new story content with time spent on the platform. This is indicative of *user up-conversion* where traditionally passive users who are more likely to consume content, begin to actively create new story content,

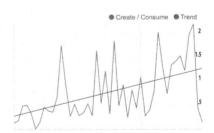

Fig. 8. Creation to consumption trend in user activity for the duration of study.

together with other users. This may in part be due to the seamless coupling of the exploration, consumption, and creation interaction tasks in the platform. JUNGLE offers the agency for users, who prefer to consume content, to actively engage with other users and create new stories.

Collaboration. JUNGLE allows users to work together on the same story by contributing new story bits and commenting on existing stories, which influences how the stories evolve over time. We use a simple measure of collaboration as the number of users who contributed story bits to a story. The number of users that worked together to create each story planet during this study ranged from 1 to 6 collaborators ($\mu = 1.476, \sigma = 1.145$). 461 users worked on 65 planets while there were 49 planets with only 1 author. Figure 9 illustrates a set of story graphs, created by multiple users, where the node color denotes a specific user. Different creation patterns are observed where users may work independently on different branches of the same story graph, or collaborate to iteratively contribute to the progression of the same story path. There are many factors that are not considered in this study. For instance, multiple users can contribute to the same story bit using the sketchboard interface. Additionally, an indirect form of collaboration occurs where users may not explicitly add new content, but influence the evolution of the story by commenting on existing stories.

6   Conclusion

JUNGLE is an interactive visual platform that allows both novice users as well as creative professionals to collaboratively create and consume branching story structures that take the form of various combinations of video, images, and text. JUNGLE has been extensively evaluated in both controlled studies and large-scale free-form experiments with hundreds of users over several weeks of activity. Our analysis shows that JUNGLE delivers users the ability to create and consume nonlinear, transmedial stories. In addition, we observe a marked increase in the creation activities of users with time spent on the platform (the longest study lasted 45 days), which is indicative of user up-conversion.

While the platform is now in a mature state that has been tested and refined across studies spanning 18 months, we will continue to improve JUNGLE based on user feedback. For example, story ownership and access rights will be integrated and studied for more perspective on the collaborative creation process. Our latest results reveal that users prefer different interfaces (a list-style interface vs. a planet metaphor) depending on the exploration task. For future versions of the

Fig. 9. Different story graphs that were authored by JUNGLE users. Node colors indicate the user who was responsible for creating the story bit. (a) Tempo Vola, (b) Leila's Story, (c) Tales of Terror, (d) Panic on Planet Parmeson. (Color figure online)

platform, we would like to consolidate both these interfaces for exploring stories into a single, unified experience.

JUNGLE opens up several exciting avenues of future research in story telling and the analysis of the creation and consumption activities of different user groups. We are interested in studying how new stories can be recommended to users (both for creation and consumption), based on their past activities. Our story representation makes it possible for existing stories to adapt dynamically and be personalized based on the viewers preferences. In future, analysing whether users from different age groups have similar or different preferences in interaction UI, content creation, and consumption behaviors. Further analysis into the media signatures of stories authored will provide insights into new genres and story archetypes of JUNGLE.

Acknowledgements. Kapadia has been funded in part by NSF IIS-1703883 and NSF S&AS-1723869. Many additional colleagues served in the development of this study, including Max Grosse, Rebekkah Laeuchi, David Sinclair, Isa Simo, Mark Miller, Soheyon Jeong, Adriano Galati, Maria Cabral, Barbara Solenthaler, Miquel Farre, Samir Mahmalat, Roberto Sousa, Nam Wook Kim, Tanja Kaser, Ancona Marco, Alesia Marra, Maggie Kosek, Maurizio Nitti, Klinger Severin, Anslem Grundhofer, Peter Kaufmann, Hanspeter Pfister, and Bob Sumner. We thank Wikimedia with images sourced as either public domain or under creative common license with attribution. Photographers include Magnus Manske, Christian Madison, Ed Yourdon, Sardaka, Puram Yun, and Pepe Robles.

References

1. Interlude (2016). https://interlude.fm
2. Storycanvas (2016). http://thetoolkitproject.com/tool/story-canvas
3. Storyverse (2016). http://www.storyversestudios.com/
4. Acharya, D., Wardrip-Fruin, N.: Building worlds together: understanding collaborative co-creation of game worlds. In: Proceedings of the 14th International Conference on the Foundations of Digital Games, FDG 2019, pp. 45:1–45:5. ACM, New York (2019). https://doi.org/10.1145/3337722.3337748, http://doi.acm.org/10.1145/3337722.3337748
5. Andrews, D., Baber, C.: Visualizing interactive narratives: employing a branching comic to tell a story and show its readings. In: Proceedings of the 32Nd Annual ACM Conference on Human Factors in Computing Systems, CHI 2014, pp. 1895–1904. ACM, New York (2014). https://doi.org/10.1145/2556288.2557296, http://doi.acm.org/10.1145/2556288.2557296
6. Balabanović, M., Chu, L.L., Wolff, G.J.: Storytelling with digital photographs. In: Proceedings of the SIGCHI Conference on Human Factors in Computing Systems, CHI 2000, pp. 564–571. ACM, New York (2000). https://doi.org/10.1145/332040.332505, http://doi.acm.org/10.1145/332040.332505
7. Bangor, A., Kortum, P., Miller, J.: Determining what individual SUS scores mean: adding an adjective rating scale. J. Usability Stud. 4(3), 114–123 (2009). http://dl.acm.org/citation.cfm?id=2835587.2835589
8. Basaraba, N.: A framework for creative teams of non-fiction interactive digital narratives. In: Rouse, R., Koenitz, H., Haahr, M. (eds.) ICIDS 2018. LNCS, vol. 11318, pp. 143–148. Springer, Cham (2018). https://doi.org/10.1007/978-3-030-04028-4_11
9. Borkin, M.A., et al.: What makes a visualization memorable? IEEE Trans. Vis. Comput. Graph. 19(12), 2306–2315 (2013)
10. Brooke, J.: SUS: A Quick and Dirty Usability Scale. Redhatch Consulting Ltd., Reading (1996)

11. Cheng, J., Kang, L., Cosley, D.: Storeys: designing collaborative storytelling interfaces. In: CHI 2013 Extended Abstracts on Human Factors in Computing Systems, CHI EA 2013, pp. 3031–3034. ACM, New York (2013). https://doi.org/10.1145/2468356.2479603, http://doi.acm.org/10.1145/2468356.2479603

12. Clanton, C., Marks, H., Murray, J., Flanagan, M., Arble, F.: Interactive narrative: stepping into our own stories. In: CHI 98 Conference Summary on Human Factors in Computing Systems, CHI 1998, pp. 88–89. ACM, New York (1998). https://doi.org/10.1145/286498.286543, http://doi.acm.org/10.1145/286498.286543

13. Du, F., Cao, N., Lin, Y.R., Xu, P., Tong, H.: iSphere: Focus+Context sphere visualization for interactive large graph exploration. In: Proceedings of the 2017 CHI Conference on Human Factors in Computing Systems, CHI 2017, pp. 2916–2927. ACM, New York (2017). https://doi.org/10.1145/3025453.3025628, http://doi.acm.org/10.1145/3025453.3025628

14. Garbe, J., Kreminski, M., Samuel, B., Wardrip-Fruin, N., Mateas, M.: StoryAssembler: an engine for generating dynamic choice-driven narratives. In: Proceedings of the 14th International Conference on the Foundations of Digital Games, FDG 2019, pp. 24:1–24:10. ACM, New York (2019). https://doi.org/10.1145/3337722.3337732, http://doi.acm.org/10.1145/3337722.3337732

15. Kapadia, M., Falk, J., Zünd, F., Marti, M., Sumner, R.W., Gross, M.: Computer-assisted authoring of interactive narratives. In: Proceedings of the 19th Symposium on Interactive 3D Graphics and Games, i3D 2015, pp. 85–92.. ACM, New York (2015). https://doi.org/10.1145/2699276.2699279, http://doi.acm.org/10.1145/2699276.2699279

16. Kapadia, M., Frey, S., Shoulson, A., Sumner, R.W., Gross, M.: CANVAS: computer-assisted narrative animation synthesis. In: ACM SIGGRAPH/Eurographics Symposium on Computer Animation, SCA 2016, Eurographics (2016)

17. Kim, J., Cheng, J., Bernstein, M.S.: Ensemble: exploring complementary strengths of leaders and crowds in creative collaboration. In: Proceedings of the 17th ACM Conference on Computer Supported Cooperative Work & #38; Social Computing, CSCW 2014, pp. 745–755. ACM, New York (2014). https://doi.org/10.1145/2531602.2531638, http://doi.acm.org/10.1145/2531602.2531638

18. Kim, J., Dontcheva, M., Li, W., Bernstein, M.S., Steinsapir, D.: Motif: supporting novice creativity through expert patterns. In: Proceedings of the 33rd Annual ACM Conference on Human Factors in Computing Systems, CHI 2015, pp. 1211–1220. ACM, New York (2015). https://doi.org/10.1145/2702123.2702507, http://doi.acm.org/10.1145/2702123.2702507

19. Lessel, P., Mauderer, M., Wolff, C., Krüger, A.: Let's play my way: investigating audience influence in user-generated gaming live-streams. In: Proceedings of the 2017 ACM International Conference on Interactive Experiences for TV and Online Video, TVX 2017, pp. 51–63. ACM, New York (2017). https://doi.org/10.1145/3077548.3077556, http://doi.acm.org/10.1145/3077548.3077556

20. Liu, C.C., Liu, K.P., Chen, W.H., Lin, C.P., Chen, G.D.: Collaborative storytelling experiences in social media: influence of peer-assistance mechanisms. **57**, 1544–1556 (2011). https://doi.org/10.1016/j.compedu.2011.02.002, http://www.sciencedirect.com/science/article/pii/S0360131511000406

21. Mauro, N., Ardissono, L.: Session-based suggestion of topics for geographic exploratory search. In: 23rd International Conference on Intelligent User Interfaces, IUI 2018, . ACM, New York (2018). https://doi.org/10.1145/3172944.3172957, http://doi.acm.org/10.1145/3172944.3172957

22. Miles, R., et al.: GameBridge: converging toward a transmedia storytelling experience through gameplay. In: Proceedings of the ACM International Conference on Interactive Experiences for TV and Online Video, TVX 2016, pp. 105–111. ACM, New York (2016). https://doi.org/10.1145/2932206.2932209, http://doi.acm.org/10.1145/2932206.2932209

23. Riedl, M.O., Young, R.M.: From linear story generation to branching story graphs. IEEE Comput. Graph. Appl. **26**(3), 23–31 (2006)

24. Sadauskas, J., Byrne, D., Atkinson, R.K.: Mining memories: designing a platform to support social media based writing. In: Proceedings of the 33rd Annual ACM Conference on Human Factors in Computing Systems, CHI 2015, pp. 3691–3700. ACM, New York (2015). https://doi.org/10.1145/2702123.2702383, http://doi.acm.org/10.1145/2702123.2702383

25. Schoenau-Fog, H.: Adaptive storyworlds. In: Schoenau-Fog, H., Bruni, L.E., Louchart, S., Baceviciute, S. (eds.) ICIDS 2015. LNCS, vol. 9445, pp. 58–65. Springer, Cham (2015). https://doi.org/10.1007/978-3-319-27036-4_6

26. Shen, E.Y.T., Lieberman, H., Davenport, G.: What's next?: Emergent storytelling from video collection. In: Proceedings of the SIGCHI Conference on Human Factors in Computing Systems, CHI 2009, pp. 809–818. ACM, New York (2009). https://doi.org/10.1145/1518701.1518825, http://doi.acm.org/10.1145/1518701.1518825

27. Shwirtz, J.: Empowering storytellers with social media. In: Proceedings of the ACM International Conference on Interactive Experiences for TV and Online Video, TVX 2015, p. 1. ACM, New York (2015). https://doi.org/10.1145/2745197.2749467, http://doi.acm.org/10.1145/2745197.2749467

28. Spawforth, C., Gibbins, N., Millard, D.E.: StoryMINE: a system for multiplayer interactive narrative experiences. In: Rouse, R., Koenitz, H., Haahr, M. (eds.) ICIDS 2018. LNCS, vol. 11318, pp. 534–543. Springer, Cham (2018). https://doi.org/10.1007/978-3-030-04028-4_62

29. Spawforth, C., Millard, D.E.: A framework for multi-participant narratives based on multiplayer game interactions. In: Nunes, N., Oakley, I., Nisi, V. (eds.) ICIDS 2017. LNCS, vol. 10690, pp. 150–162. Springer, Cham (2017). https://doi.org/10.1007/978-3-319-71027-3_13

30. Steiner, K.E., Moher, T.G.: Graphic storywriter: an interactive environment for emergent storytelling. In: Proceedings of the SIGCHI Conference on Human Factors in Computing Systems, CHI 1992, pp. 357–364. ACM, New York (1992). https://doi.org/10.1145/142750.142831, http://doi.acm.org/10.1145/142750.142831

Felt: A Simple Story Sifter

Max Kreminski(✉), Melanie Dickinson, and Noah Wardrip-Fruin

UC Santa Cruz, Santa Cruz, CA 95064, USA
{mkremins,mldickin,nwardrip}@ucsc.edu

Abstract. *Story sifting*, also known as *story recognition*, has been identified as one of the major design challenges currently facing interactive emergent narrative. However, despite continued interest in emergent narrative approaches, there has been relatively little work in the area of story sifting to date, leaving it unclear how a story sifting system might best be implemented and what challenges are likely to be encountered in the course of implementing such a system. In this paper, we present Felt, a simple query language-based story sifter and rules-based simulation engine that aims to serve as a first step toward answering these questions. We describe Felt's architecture, discuss several design case studies of interactive emergent narrative experiences that make use of Felt, reflect on what we have learned from working with Felt so far, and suggest directions for future work in the story sifting domain.

Keywords: Emergent narrative · Story sifting · Content authoring

1 Introduction

The problem of *story sifting* involves the selection of events that constitute a compelling story from a larger chronicle of events. Often this chronicle is generated through the computational simulation of a storyworld, whose output consists of a profusion of events, many of which are relatively uninteresting as narrative building blocks. The challenge, then, is to sift the wheat from the chaff, identifying event sequences that seem to be of particular narrative interest or significance and bringing them to the attention of a human player or interactor.

Ryan, who introduced the term "story sifting" [33]—as well as its predecessor, *story recognition*[1]—has identified story sifting as one of four major challenges [34] currently facing work in the domain of interactive emergent narrative. Emergent narrative, which Ryan characterizes as the approach taken by many of both the greatest successes and failures in the area of story generation, remains an area of interest for interactive narrative design [20,22] and narrative generation [1,19] communities. Despite this ongoing interest in emergent narrative approaches, however, story sifting has received relatively little attention to date.

---

[1] As distinct from the natural language understanding term "story recognition", which refers to the identification of embedded story content in natural language text.

© Springer Nature Switzerland AG 2019
R. E. Cardona-Rivera et al. (Eds.): ICIDS 2019, LNCS 11869, pp. 267–281, 2019.
https://doi.org/10.1007/978-3-030-33894-7_27

There has also been a recent wave of interest in *retellings* [8, 16, 17]—the stories players tell based on their play experiences in interactive narrative games—and in how design elements of games can facilitate and frustrate the player's creative process. From this perspective, story sifters could be viewed as mixed-initiative creativity support tools [21] that help players narrativize their play experiences by surfacing sites of potential narrative interest as they emerge.

One goal of the *Bad News* project [38] was to learn lessons about story sifting needs that could be applied to the design of a computational system that performs story sifting. Unfortunately, a computational story sifter that incorporates the learnings from *Bad News* has yet to materialize. At the same time, our own recent work has involved the design and development of several interactive emergent narrative projects, and we have increasingly found ourselves making use of approaches that resemble story sifting, especially in designing interactive narrative systems that position the human interactor as a narrative co-author. As a result, we have begun to develop a simple story sifter geared primarily toward use in a mixed-initiative context—a system that assists players in the process of narrativizing their play experiences by helping them locate sites of potential narrative interest in a larger simulated storyworld.

Our system, Felt, implements a variation of one of the approaches to story sifting discussed by Ryan, namely that involving the human specification of interesting event sequences. In order to ensure that our human-specified event sequences are generalizable, we implement them not as literal sequences that must be matched exactly, but as *sifting patterns*: queries that seek out ordered sets of events matching certain criteria, with the possibility that other events may be interspersed between the events that are matched. In the remainder of this paper, we discuss related work in story sifting and adjacent areas; elaborate on the design of Felt; present three design case studies of in-development interactive narrative projects that make use of Felt; and discuss what we have learned from the design, development and application of Felt about story sifting in general.

Many of the design decisions that went into Felt are naïve. This is by design: at each turn, we attempted to do the simplest possible thing that had a reasonable chance of realizing our design intent. It is our hope that Felt functions as a *computational caricature* [40] of a query language-based story sifter, oversimplifying where necessary to ease development while still containing fully realized versions of the key features that are needed for the system to serve as an effective argument for the value of our approach.

2   Related Work

Ryan's original paper introducing the term "story recognition" [34] provides a partial list of existing systems that do something similar to story sifting, including *The Sims 2* [25], which recognizes sequences of events that match the early steps of pre-authored "story trees" and nudges the simulation engine to promote the completion of the story tree [4, 29]. Also of note is the Playspecs [30] system, which applies regular expressions to the analysis of game play traces. Samuel et al. have made some use of Playspecs in a narrative-focused context in *Writing Buddy* [37] and in the analysis of *Prom Week* playtraces [36].

Several systems discussed in Ryan's dissertation [33] also make use of story sifting. Foremost among these is *Sheldon County*, a generative podcast set in a listener-specific simulated American county. In *Sheldon County*, a sifter called *Sheldon* operates over a chronicle produced by the *Hennepin* simulation engine to recognize, extract and narrativize (in the form of podcast episodes) sequences of events that match certain human-defined sifting patterns. These patterns are defined as chunks of procedural Python code that search for candidate events and then bind relevant aspects of these events (such as the perpetrator of a crime) to pattern-specific variables. This approach is similar to the approach we use in Felt. In *Sheldon*, however, authoring a sifting pattern requires knowledge of both the Python programming language and the specific data structures used within the *Hennepin* engine, and even simple pattern definitions are often lengthy due to the verbosity of the procedural code used to implement them.

The "wizard console" in *Bad News* [38] provides an expert human interactor (the "wizard") with a view into the underlying simulation of a small American town. Behind the scenes of the main performance, the wizard uses the console to seek out narratively potent information about the state of the storyworld, and—in real time—relays this information to a human actor who is performing as one of the town's simulated inhabitants. The wizard console is essentially a Python interpreter that enables the wizard to examine the state of the simulation data structures. As such, it provides little computational support for story sifting, although the wizard may make use of a set of helper functions intended to make common sifting tasks easier. The wizard console makes no attempt to realize sifted stories as prose, leaving it largely up to the human actor to decide how to leverage the information gathered through sifting, and—like *Sheldon*—requires familiarity with both Python programming and the particulars of the underlying *Talk of the Town* simulation engine [35] to use effectively.

Dwarf Grandpa [12], an extension to the Legends Viewer interface for browsing *Dwarf Fortress* [3] world data, makes use of story sifting to extract and narrativize the lives of certain notable characters from the game world. Dwarf Grandpa performs story sifting exclusively in a backwards-looking manner, rather than attempting to sift in real time as the simulation runs, and performs only fully automatic sifting, without a human in the loop. Unlike many existing sifters, Dwarf Grandpa also performs the natural language generation needed to automatically present sifted stories as human-readable prose.

Caves of Qud's [11] biography generation system for notable historical characters [13] also makes use of story sifting. Biographies are generated by selecting a sequence of random actions for a character to perform, then running sifting patterns over these random events to retroactively justify each action with an in-world reason. Where no pre-existing reason for an action can be located, new facts about the world are generated on the fly to produce a working rationalization. Like Dwarf Grandpa, *Qud*'s biography generator operates fully automatically and realizes sifted stories as prose.

Rules-based simulationist narrative generation systems often provide some way for events to be directly dependent on or make direct reference to past events, and therefore have some similarity to story sifting. Here we include systems such as Comme il Faut [27], the rules-based "social physics" system that underlies the social simulation game *Prom Week* [26], and Versu [10]. In both of these systems, characters may act in ways that are directly dependent on the presence or absence of a set of past events that meet a set of specified criteria—essentially a sifting pattern. This can arguably be viewed as a form of "internal story sifting": these systems recognize patterns of relevant past events, but only for internal use, and without surfacing the fact that a given pattern was recognized to the audience directly. In Ryan's terms, these systems lack *story support*: the presentation of system-recognized stories to an audience.

Prom Week in particular complicates this evaluation somewhat by presenting players with a list of all of the "social facts" that contribute to a given character's evaluation of the present social situation. Social facts are often directly tied to past events that have played out within the simulation. Arguably, the surfacing of these relevant past events to the player could be considered to be a form of story support, especially if the player is viewed as a co-author alongside the system rather than a mere experiencer of a totally system-curated story. However, in this case, narrativization of the sifted events does not occur within the system; it occurs totally within the player's head, if it occurs at all.

More generally, to describe an approach as making use of story sifting, it is arguably necessary for the underlying plot generation technique to be one that produces a profusion of events, including many mundane events about which the audience does not necessarily care. Many approaches to story generation that allow events to directly reference past events have some similarities to sifting-based approaches, but aim to exclusively produce narratively interesting events that are worthy of being surfaced to the audience. This includes many planning-based techniques [31,43]. We recognize that these approaches may have much to offer the developers of sifting-based systems, but we do not include them under the label of "story sifting" here.

3   System Description

Felt is a query language-based story sifter coupled with a rules-based simulation engine. Events that have transpired in the storyworld are stored in the database as entities, and users of the system write queries—which we, following Ryan, refer to as *sifting patterns*—to identify scenarios and sequences of past events that might make for good narrative material. A sifting pattern is defined in terms of a set of *logic variables* to bind—effectively "slots" or "roles" into which certain database entities, such as events or characters, can be substituted—and a set of relations between these logic variables, which constrain the values that each variable is allowed to take. A sifting pattern could specify, for instance, that `eventA` must be an instance of the `betray` event type; that `eventA` must have taken place before `eventB`; that both events must have the same protagonist, a character char; and that char must have the impulsive trait. The system will then consult the database and return a list of all possible combinations of variable bindings for the pattern as a whole.

In designing a Felt storyworld, users combine sifting patterns with several other features to define *actions*. The structure of actions is directly inspired by the structure of rules in Ceptre [23], a linear logic programming language for specifying interactive simulationist storyworlds. An action consists of a sifting pattern; an optional weighting function that decides how likely it is that this action should be performed, given a set of bindings for the logic variables defined in the sifting pattern; and a function that constructs an *event object* representing this action, which will be added to the database if this action is chosen to be performed. A minimal event object contains an autogenerated *timestamp*, which can be compared with the timestamps of other events to determine which happened first; a short string identifying its *event type*; and a *template string* into which the values of bound logic variables are substituted to produce a human-readable description of the event. It may also contain zero or more *effects*, which describe any other updates that must be made to the database if this event is accepted as part of the history of the storyworld, and possibly other properties on a case-by-case basis, such as the ID of an earlier event that was a direct cause of this event. Because actions are added to the database as events, Felt's story sifting features can be used to run sifting patterns over the history of everything that the simulated characters have said and done (Fig. 1).

```
(eventSequence ?eventA ?eventB)
[?eventA "eventType" "betray"] [?eventA "actor" ?char]
[?eventB "eventType" "betray"] [?eventB "actor" ?char]
[?char "trait" "impulsive"]
(not-join [?char ?eventA ?eventB]
  (eventSequence ?eventA ?eventMid ?eventB) [?eventMid "actor" ?char])
```

Fig. 1. A moderately complicated Felt sifting pattern that will match a sequence of two betrayals perpetrated by the same impulsive character, with no other actions perpetrated by the same character (but arbitrarily many other events) in between.

By convention, in the projects we describe here as case studies, actions come in two flavors. *Internal* (or *reflection*) actions describe a character reflecting on past events. These actions typically generate "intent tokens" or "motive tokens", which represent a character's intent to act on a particular interpretation of these events in the future. *External* actions describe a character acting on a previously formed intent. These actions typically consume intent tokens and update the state of the world in some outwardly visible way. This separation ensures that intent tokens can be both produced and consumed in multiple different ways: many possible actions that produce the same type of intent token can serve as the motivation for many possible actions that all consume the same type of intent token, opening up the space of possible cause/effect relationships between events. Additionally, in an emergent narrative system where actions are the player's primary window into what is happening in the simulated world, separate reflection actions help make it clear to the player that sifting patterns are at work behind the scenes, and that character behavior is meaningfully influenced by the history of past simulation events—sometimes in complex or sophisticated ways. This is one way in which we hope to address another of Ryan's four design challenges for interactive emergent narrative [34], namely that of *story support*: once a storyful sequence of events has been recognized, how should this be surfaced to the player? It also helps to ensure that we do not fall victim to the *Tale-Spin effect* [42] by failing to surface the interesting technical capabilities of our interactive narrative system to the player in a compelling way.

Internally, Felt uses the DataScript library [7] to store and query simulation state, including the history of events that have transpired within the simulated world. Felt sifting patterns translate directly into queries against a DataScript database, and are written in a minimal query language that desugars to a subset of Datalog, a simple logic programming language. DataScript provides facilities for storing, updating, and querying state as a set of simple facts of the form [e a v]; each fact represents an assertion that the database entity with integer ID e has an attribute named a with value v. A DataScript database is an immutable value: all operations that "update" the database in fact create a fresh copy of the database with the desired modifications, leaving previously stored versions of the database intact and unchanged. This property can be leveraged to snapshot the complete Felt simulation state and run queries against these snapshots while allowing the main copy of the simulation state to continue evolving, which we have found helpful during debugging. It has also enabled us to implement several features, described in Sect. 4.2, that rely on the ability to perform actions in a speculative mode and easily undo them if they lead to unwanted consequences.

DataScript also provides several other useful features that assist with the authoring of sifting patterns. not-join query clauses enable testing for the non-existence of an entity that meets a certain set of criteria; this feature is frequently used to specify sifting patterns in which two target events must not be separated by any interceding events involving the same protagonist. Rules bundle groups of query clauses that are commonly used together under a common name; for instance, an (eventSequence ?eventA ?eventB) rule may simultaneously specify that both eventA and eventB refer to event entities and mandate that eventA must precede eventB. Rules may also be recursive, allowing for the implementation of a (causalRelationship ?eventA ?eventB) rule that will match not just direct causes but also indirect causes (separated by one or more intermediate stages of causation) of eventB.

4 Case Studies

4.1 Starfreighter

Starfreighter [14] is an in-progress procedural narrative game in which the player captains a small starship in a procedurally generated galaxy, completing odd jobs to make a living while managing the needs of a small crew. The primary intent of this game was to test whether *parametrized storylets* [18]—atomic units of narrative content that, like Felt actions, are equipped with slots, preconditions, and effects—could be used to produce compelling emergent story arcs for procedurally generated characters.

It was while working alongside the developers of this game that we began to develop the earliest version of Felt. Like Felt, *Starfreighter* stores a chronicle of past events (framed as a sequence of "memories" accessible to the characters who participated in each event) and provides features for architecting storylets that refer directly to sequences of past events that meet certain criteria. As a result, *Starfreighter* storylets can contain instances of characters reflecting on sequences of past events, such as the circumstances that led them to leave their home planet or the evolution of their ongoing relationship with another character. Whenever the player completes a storylet, *Starfreighter* evaluates the sifting patterns of all other storylets to identify which ones it would currently make sense to present to the player, then chooses from this pool via simple weighted random selection—essentially using story sifting to implement a form of what Short terms *salience-based narrative* [39].

The early version of Felt used in *Starfreighter* differs significantly from the version we present in this paper. Most importantly, sifting patterns in this early version of Felt were not authored in terms of a true query language, but in terms of an ad-hoc collection of functions that retrieved entities from the game state in specific predefined ways. One notable consequence of this design decision was that, although storylets were equipped with sifting patterns that could bind a set of logic variables to appropriate values, the system would make no attempt to *unify* these variables with one another, meaning that there was no guarantee of being able to find all of the possible instantiations of a sifting pattern at any given time. Additionally, the authoring of new content became bottlenecked on the development of new functions that enabled the authors of sifting patterns to ask specific questions about the game state, forcing content authors to either learn how to write these often-complicated functions themselves (requiring deep knowledge of how the game state was structured) or else wait for the game's lead developer to implement the functions they had requested. Finally, because there was no straightforward way to get all of the possible instantiations of a sifting pattern in the context of the current game state, debugging was consistently difficult; in particular, if a sifting pattern was repeatedly failing to match a set of values for which it ought to succeed, the nondeterministic nature of sifting pattern resolution made it difficult to determine why.

Due to these issues, development of *Starfreighter* was temporarily suspended, with the intent to return to it in the future. Much of the existing *Starfreighter* content is now being rewritten using a modern version of Felt, which has helped to alleviate each of these issues.

4.2 Cozy Mystery Construction Kit

Cozy Mystery Construction Kit (*CMCK*) [15] is an in-progress AI-supported collaborative storytelling play experience (inspired by collaborative storytelling tabletop games like *Microscope* [32] and *The Quiet Year* [2]) in which two players collaborate with a computational system to write a mystery story about a small cast of simulated characters. *CMCK* uses Felt as a simulation engine for characters that sometimes perform actions autonomously and sometimes are directed to perform certain specific actions by players. It also uses Felt to help players locate and build on sites of narrative interest, such as a growing jealousy or resentment between two characters or a building conflict between two values—for instance, comfort and survival.

Of the case studies presented here, *CMCK* is the most explicitly focused on using story sifting to provide creativity support by recognizing emerging story structures as they unfold and suggesting elaborations on emergent patterns and themes. Several Felt features are especially useful in this context. Clear separation of actions that produce and consume "intent tokens" or "motivation tokens" enables players to ask the system questions about character motivation: for instance, "Who had a motive to harm this character?", or "What motives might this character currently want to act on?" This can be particularly useful when writing mystery stories. Because DataScript query evaluation is highly optimized, many Felt sifting patterns can be run over the database at once to provide players with a wide variety of suggestions as to what characters might reasonably do next. Additionally, because sifting patterns provide explicit slots for the characters and events they concern, *CMCK* can give players an interface that lets them filter action suggestions by specifying the values of one or more variables in advance. This enables players to (for instance) get a list of actions that a particular character might currently want to perform, or a list of actions that any character might want to perform in response to a particular past event.

Since the DataScript database in which Felt stores simulation state is an immutable value, *CMCK* can allow players to perform actions in a speculative mode, run queries against the updated database to decide whether they like the effects of these actions, and easily roll back to a previous database state if they do not. Immutability may also be leveraged to facilitate a sort of planning or goal-directed search over actions: because Felt actions (like planning operators) are defined in terms of preconditions and effects, search over Felt actions can be used to locate speculative future worlds where some specified set of conditions holds true. This can then be used to present users with an interface in which they specify a scenario they would like to bring about in the storyworld, and the system searches for a sequence of actions that might realize this scenario. The developers of *CMCK* plan to implement this feature in the future.

Another potential Felt-enabled feature that may be implemented in *CMCK* involves the automatic surfacing of "almost actions": dramatic actions that are *almost* possible, but currently invalid due to a small number of unmet preconditions. This is directly inspired by the feature with the same name in *Writing*

Buddy [37], and leverages Felt's per-action weighting functions to judge how dramatically significant a given action would be if performed.

CMCK is also notable for its use of story sifting to highlight character personality and subjectivity through sifting-driven reinterpretation of events. Each *CMCK* character holds several randomly selected *values* drawn from a pool of eight possible values, and these values are used in sifting patterns to influence how characters will interpret certain event sequences. Consider, for instance, a sequence of events in which a character forbids anyone from using the kitchen until a crime that took place there has been thoroughly investigated. A character who values comfort above all else may evaluate this sequence of events very differently than a character who values safety. Much as *Terminal Time* [24] narratively spins historical events to cater to the audience's ideological biases, and *Caves of Qud*'s biography generation system [13] retroactively decides how to interpret the motivations behind a character's randomly generated actions, *CMCK* characters engage in retroactive interpretation of events through the sifting of their own stories, one another's stories, and the stories of the world around them. Moreover, in *CMCK*, the differential interpretations that result from this process of sifting serve as the main driver of character conflict. In this sense, *CMCK* could be viewed as an instance of AI-based game design [9, 41] in which the AI process at the heart of the play experience is a story sifting engine.

4.3   Diarytown

Diarytown is an in-progress game in which players craft diary entries about their real life and watch as the described experiences are creatively enacted, extrapolated on, and respun through the lens of a simulated, personalized town. It is currently in active development and prototyping alongside the most recent version of Felt, and subject to design changes.

In the current version of the game, Felt is primarily used to recognize story patterns in a player's diary entries over time, allowing *Diarytown* to surface to the player different possible interpretations of things that have happened within their life. This underpins one of the project's primary design goals, of facilitating playful, generative reflection on one's life. Whenever a story pattern is recognized, *Diarytown* surfaces it to the player as a new scenery object within the simulated town. The player can then interact with this scenery object to view the recognized story, and can choose to edit the object's appearance and placement, or even to remove it from the town entirely if they reject the interpretation of their life's events that it represents. Multiple recognized story patterns that share many of the same attributes (for instance, a common focal character) might be collapsed over time into a single, larger scenery object, and these objects may thus gradually take on the role of symbols of larger patterns within the player's life (for instance, a monument to the player's ongoing relationship with a particular friend).

Players craft diary entries by composing terms from a symbolic action library consisting of actions, connectors, and modifiers designed to reflect common actions in a person's everyday life. Some are optionally parametrized with character names, places, and other reference nouns, which the player defines during play. The parametrized nature of Felt actions make it ideal for representing elements of these complex diary entries as simulation actions.

Felt is also being used to simulate autonomous town activities and background characters that are partially conditioned on player-entered actions and character definitions. This integration of player-defined and autonomous actions allows us to playfully extrapolate on a player's account of their daily life, and leverage the expressive affordances of emergent narrative (which generally requires a large number of events to sift through) even when there are relatively few player diary entries.

In the context of the *Diarytown* project, Felt was introduced to four high-school-aged research interns, three of whom had some prior programming experience (primarily in Java) and one of whom had none. At the end of a single day of instruction, all four interns were able to author new actions (including sifting patterns) on their own. Within a week, they had authored 85 new actions without expert intervention.

5   Discussion

5.1   Authoring Sifting Patterns

When adopting an approach to interactive narrative that makes integral use of story sifting, the design and development of sifting patterns becomes part of the content authoring pipeline. As such, we made it one of our design goals for Felt to make the authoring of sifting patterns as easy and approachable as possible. As a result of this focus on approachability, we initially intended to provide sifting pattern authors with a large library of preauthored functions for accessing the database in certain specific ways, and thereby to avoid creating a situation in which sifting pattern authors had to learn how to interact directly with the complicated network of relationships between game entities.

In practice, however, we soon found that it was very difficult to anticipate in advance the full range of questions that a sifting pattern author might want to be able to ask about the game state. This made it near-impossible for us to create an adequate library of preauthored functions. As a result, we found ourselves turning instead toward the path of giving sifting pattern authors access to a "real" query language. Query languages are designed for flexibility, enabling the user to ask a wide variety of questions about the game state on an as-needed basis—including questions that no one specifically anticipated ahead of time.

It may, at first glance, seem counterintuitive that authoring can be made more approachable by presenting content authors with a query language they must learn. However, as argued by Nardi [28] and evidenced by the widespread success of the Tracery language [6] among users with little or no prior programming experience, people are generally quite good at learning simple formal languages when the language is tied to a task they want to perform. This is especially the case when a gentle on-ramp to query authoring is available: novice content authors may start off using pre-composed sifting patterns without modification, graduate to making slight modifications of these pre-composed patterns, and eventually gain sufficient facility with the query language to author their own sifting patterns from scratch. Our success with having high-school-aged research interns on the *Diarytown* project write sifting patterns with little training supports the hypothesis that users can learn to write sifting patterns in a simple query language fairly quickly when they are provided with a robust library of examples to copy, paste, and modify.

5.2   Debugging Story Sifters

Another advantage of using a database with a full query language to store game state is that it greatly simplifies the process of debugging, enabling developers and content authors to write and run queries against the live database at any point. This stands in sharp contrast to the debugging experience in *Starfreighter*, where the opacity of the ad-hoc game state data structures made it difficult to explore the game state when trying to track down the reason for a sifting pattern's failure or misbehavior—especially for content authors, who had particular difficulty learning how different parts of the game state related to one another.

DataScript query evaluation is computationally inexpensive. This makes it tractable to get a list of all sifting patterns that are currently succeeding, including all possible sets of variable bindings that they could use, simply by running all of the available sifting patterns against the database in quick succession. This can significantly speed up debugging by making it visible at a glance whether or not a particular instantiation of a sifting pattern is currently possible, saving a substantial amount of time that a developer might otherwise have to spend manually testing sifting patterns they are attempting to debug.

Moreover, the DataScript queries that underlie Felt sifting patterns are partitioned into distinct clauses, which can be evaluated against the database individually or in subgroups as well as in the context of a complete query. We took advantage of the structured nature of our sifting patterns to implement a debugging helper function we refer to as `whyNot`. This function takes a sifting pattern as an argument, and can optionally also be supplied with a partial set of variable bindings for the pattern's logic variables. It then tests each clause of the sifting pattern in isolation, then each subgroup of clauses, until it identifies the set of clauses that are currently causing the pattern to fail. This information can then be reported to the pattern's developer, potentially saving them the work of manually stepping through the pattern line by line to identify why it is not succeeding when it ought to be.

5.3   Coupling Sifting and Simulation

Felt is a sifting engine coupled with a simulation engine. Strictly speaking, it is possible to make full use of Felt's story sifting features without making any use of its simulation engine. Sequences of events can be generated by an external process and then added to the database in a Felt-compatible form, enabling the authoring of sifting patterns that operate over these externally generated events. However, in practice, it is often desirable to make use of sifting patterns within the definition of simulation actions, as this enables the straightforward authoring of character actions that involve characters reflecting on, interpreting, and responding to events that have transpired in the past. Therefore, in every project to date that has made use of Felt's story sifting features, Felt's simulation features have also been employed.

6   Conclusions and Future Work

One top priority for future work on Felt involves the design and development of a more sophisticated domain-specific query language for story sifting, with features that enable more concise expression of common concepts within sifting patterns. Currently, complicated Felt sifting patterns can be quite long and unwieldy. A more sophisticated query language could help ameliorate this, ideally without adding so much additional complexity that content authoring becomes bottlenecked on the development of expertise as a user of the query language.

Felt already makes extensive use of sifting patterns, but we have as of yet made no attempt to implement what Ryan refers to as *sifting heuristics*: nonspecific, high-level computational models of an event sequence's storyfulness, which may be used to guide a story sifting system to prefer some event sequences over others. For this, we may be able to draw on general-purpose models of event relatedness, including Indexter [5]: a computational model of event relatedness based on event recall in human memory. Of the five major contributing factors to perceived event relatedness that the Indexter model describes, many existing Felt sifting patterns make use of at least three (namely searching for sequences of events that share a common protagonist, causal relatedness, and common intentionality), and Felt's explicit modeling of causality and intentionality may make it a good testbed for an Indexter-inspired set of sifting heuristics.

More generally, it is our hope that, by presenting this system, we will encourage the development of a wide variety of approaches to story sifting. The query language-based approach we explore here is only one of many possible approaches, and we have only presented a first step toward the realization of our own preferred approach. We also hope that the existence of a "reference" story sifter will inspire the design of new kinds of interactive narrative experiences based on story sifting technology—particularly experiences that use sifting to provide creativity support for the human interactor in a collaborative storytelling context.

Acknowledgements. The authors would like to thank Megna Anand, Anish Kashyap, Daniel Man, and Akhil Vemuri for their assistance in testing, debugging, and authoring content for Felt and *Diarytown*.

References

1. Adams, T.: Emergent narrative in *Dwarf Fortress*. In: Procedural Storytelling in Game Design, pp. 149–158 (2019)
2. Alder, A.: The Quiet Year. https://buriedwithoutceremony.com/the-quiet-year. Accessed 17 Jul 2019
3. Bay 12 Games: Slaves to Armok: God of Blood Chapter II: Dwarf Fortress (2006)
4. Brown, M.: The power of projection and mass hallucination: practical AI in the Sims 2 and beyond. Presented at AIIDE (2006)
5. Cardona-Rivera, R.E., Cassell, B.A., Ware, S.G., Young, R.M.: Indexter: a computational model of the event-indexing situation model for characterizing narratives. In: Proceedings Computational Models of Narrative, pp. 34–43 (2012)
6. Compton, K., Kybartas, B., Mateas, M.: Tracery: an author-focused generative text tool. In: Schoenau-Fog, H., Bruni, L.E., Louchart, S., Baceviciute, S. (eds.) ICIDS 2015. LNCS, vol. 9445, pp. 154–161. Springer, Cham (2015). https://doi.org/10.1007/978-3-319-27036-4_14
7. DataScript. https://github.com/tonsky/datascript. Accessed 15 Jul 2019
8. Eladhari, M.P.: Re-tellings: the fourth layer of narrative as an instrument for critique. In: Rouse, R., Koenitz, H., Haahr, M. (eds.) ICIDS 2018. LNCS, vol. 11318, pp. 65–78. Springer, Cham (2018). https://doi.org/10.1007/978-3-030-04028-4_5
9. Eladhari, M.P., Sullivan, A., Smith, G., McCoy, J.: AI-based game design: enabling new playable experiences. UC Santa Cruz Baskin School of Engineering (2011)
10. Evans, R., Short, E.: Versu: a simulationist storytelling system. IEEE Trans. Comput. Intell. AI Games **6**(2), 113–130 (2014)
11. Freehold Games: Caves of Qud (2020)
12. Garbe, J.: Simulation of history and recursive narrative scaffolding. http://project.jacobgarbe.com/simulation-of-history-and-recursive-narrative-scaffolding. Accessed 15 Jul 2019
13. Grinblat, J., Bucklew, C.B.: Subverting historical cause & effect: generation of mythic biographies in *Caves of Qud*. In: Proceedings FDG (2017)
14. Kreminski, M.: Procedural narrative design with parametrized storylets. Presented at GDC (2019)
15. Kreminski, M., et al.: Cozy mystery construction kit: prototyping toward an AI-assisted collaborative storytelling mystery game. In: Proceedings of the FDG (2019)
16. Kreminski, M., Samuel, B., Melcer, E., Wardrip-Fruin, N.: Evaluating AI-based games through retellings. In: Proceedings AIIDE (2019)
17. Kreminski, M., Wardrip-Fruin, N.: Generative games as storytelling partners. In: Proceedings of the FDG (2019)
18. Kreminski, M., Wardrip-Fruin, N.: Sketching a map of the storylets design space. In: Rouse, R., Koenitz, H., Haahr, M. (eds.) ICIDS 2018. LNCS, vol. 11318, pp. 160–164. Springer, Cham (2018). https://doi.org/10.1007/978-3-030-04028-4_14
19. Kybartas, B., Bidarra, R.: A survey on story generation techniques for authoring computational narratives. IEEE Trans. Comput. Intell. AI Games **9**(3), 239–253 (2017)
20. Kybartas, B., Verbrugge, C., Lessard, J.: Expressive range analysis of a possible worlds driven emergent narrative system. In: Rouse, R., Koenitz, H., Haahr, M. (eds.) ICIDS 2018. LNCS, vol. 11318, pp. 473–477. Springer, Cham (2018). https://doi.org/10.1007/978-3-030-04028-4_54
21. Liapis, A., Yannakakis, G.N., Alexopoulos, C., Lopes, P.: Can computers foster human users' creativity? Theory and praxis of mixed-initiative co-creativity. Digital Culture Educ. **8**(2), 136–153 (2016)

22. Louchart, S., Truesdale, J., Suttie, N., Aylett, R.: Emergent narrative: past, present and future of an interactive storytelling approach. In: Interactive Digital Narrative: History, Theory and Practice, pp. 185–199 (2015)
23. Martens, C.: Ceptre: a language for modeling generative interactive systems. In: Proceedings of the AIIDE (2015)
24. Mateas, M., Domike, S., Vanouse, P.: Terminal time: an ideologically-biased history machine. AISB Q. Spec. Issue Creativity Arts Sci. **102**, 36–43 (1999)
25. Maxis: The Sims 2. Electronic Arts (2004)
26. McCoy, J., Treanor, M., Reed, A.A., Mateas, M., Wardrip-Fruin, N.: Prom week: designing past the game/story dilemma. In: Proceedings of the FDG (2013)
27. McCoy, J., Treanor, M., Samuel, B., Reed, A.A., Mateas, M., Wardrip-Fruin, N.: Social story worlds with Comme il Faut. IEEE Trans. Comput. Intell. AI Games **6**(2), 97–112 (2014)
28. Nardi, B.A.: A Small Matter of Programming: Perspectives on End User Computing, 1st edn. MIT Press, Cambridge (1995)
29. Nelson, M.J.: Emergent narrative in The Sims 2. http://www.kmjn.org/notes/sims2_ai.html. Accessed 18 Jul 2019
30. Osborn, J.C., Samuel, B., Mateas, M., Wardrip-Fruin, N.: Playspecs: regular expressions for game play traces. In: Proceedings of the AIIDE (2015)
31. Porteous, J.: Planning technologies for interactive storytelling. In: Nakatsu, R., Rauterberg, M., Ciancarini, P. (eds.) Handbook of Digital Games and Entertainment Technologies, pp. 393–413. Springer, Singapore (2017). https://doi.org/10.1007/978-981-4560-50-4_71
32. Robbins, B.: Microscope. http://www.lamemage.com/microscope. Accessed 17 Jul 2019
33. Ryan, J.: Curating Simulated Storyworlds. University of California, Santa Cruz (2018)
34. Ryan, J.O., Mateas, M., Wardrip-Fruin, N.: Open design challenges for interactive emergent narrative. In: Schoenau-Fog, H., Bruni, L.E., Louchart, S., Baceviciute, S. (eds.) ICIDS 2015. LNCS, vol. 9445, pp. 14–26. Springer, Cham (2015). https://doi.org/10.1007/978-3-319-27036-4_2
35. Ryan, J.O., Summerville, A., Mateas, M., Wardrip-Fruin, N.: Toward characters who observe, tell, misremember, and lie. In: Proceedings of the AIIDE (2015)
36. Samuel, B.: Crafting Stories Through Play. University of California, Santa Cruz (2016)
37. Samuel, B., Mateas, M., Wardrip-Fruin, N.: The design of *Writing Buddy*: a mixed-initiative approach towards computational story collaboration. In: Nack, F., Gordon, A.S. (eds.) ICIDS 2016. LNCS, vol. 10045, pp. 388–396. Springer, Cham (2016). https://doi.org/10.1007/978-3-319-48279-8_34
38. Samuel, B., Ryan, J., Summerville, A.J., Mateas, M., Wardrip-Fruin, N.: *Bad News*: an experiment in computationally assisted performance. In: Nack, F., Gordon, A.S. (eds.) ICIDS 2016. LNCS, vol. 10045, pp. 108–120. Springer, Cham (2016). https://doi.org/10.1007/978-3-319-48279-8_10
39. Short, E.: Beyond branching: quality-based, salience-based, and waypoint narrative structures. https://emshort.blog/2016/04/12/beyond-branching-quality-based-and-salience-based-narrative-structures. Accessed 17 July 2019
40. Smith, A.M., Mateas, M.: Computational caricatures: probing the game design process with AI. In: Proceedings of the AIIDE (2011)
41. Treanor, M., et al.: AI-based game design patterns. In: Proceedings of the FDG (2015)

42. Wardrip-Fruin, N.: Expressive Processing: Digital Fictions, Computer Games, and Software Studies, 1st edn. MIT Press, Cambridge (2009)

43. Young, R.M., Ware, S., Cassell, B., Robertson, J.: Plans and planning in narrative generation: a review of plan-based approaches to the generation of story, discourse and interactivity in narratives. Sprache und Datenverarbeitung, Spec. Issue Formal Comput. Models Narrat. **37**(1–2), 41–64 (2013)

Toolkit for the Creation
of a Drama Dataset

Vincenzo Lombardo[1(✉)], Rossana Damiano[1], and Antonio Pizzo[2]

[1] CIRMA and Department of Informatics, University of Torino, Torino, Italy
{vincenzo.lombardo,rossana.damiano}@unito.it
[2] CIRMA and Department of Humanities, University of Torino, Torino, Italy
antonio.pizzo@unito.it

Abstract. This paper presents a novel prototype service that concerns the creation of a drama dataset. The approach relies on an ontological representation of the dramatic qualities, the characterizing elements of a drama that abstract from the linguistic or media expression. A toolkit for the friendly encoding of the dramatic qualities overcomes the difficulties of the formal representation.

Keywords: Ontology drammar · Dramatic qualities · Drama dataset

1 Introduction

In recent years, the massive availability of drama in digital form has triggered a few projects that, on the one hand, aim at the annotation of metadata for the dramatic texts for scholarly purposes, and, on the other hand, aim at exploiting the knowledge about drama, in terms of characters' personalities and events, in further production deployments, such as, e.g., edutainment and fan–fiction. These initiatives can be exemplified through, e.g., the OntoMedia and StorySpace ontologies, respectively, and in the generic context of the digital humanities by the Text Encoding Initiative[1]. The OntoMedia ontology has been exploited across different projects to annotate the narrative content of different media objects (e.g., BBC series "Doctor Who" [1]). Major concepts are the notions of character and event, respectively, and the order in which events are exposed in media for cross-media comparison. In the field of cultural heritage dissemination, the StorySpace ontology [2] supports museum curators in linking the content of artworks through stories, with the ultimate goal of enabling the generation of user tailored content retrieval [3]. More recently, as part of the more general effort of constructing resources for the automation of language processing and generation, Elson has proposed a template based language for describing the narrative content of text documents, with the goal of creating a corpus of annotated narrative texts, called DramaBank [4]. DramaBank consists of 110 encodings, limited to short stories, such as, e.g., Aesop's fables. Multi-layer annotation of narratives

---

[1] http://www.tei-c.org/index.xml, visited on 19 July 2019.

© Springer Nature Switzerland AG 2019
R. E. Cardona-Rivera et al. (Eds.): ICIDS 2019, LNCS 11869, pp. 282–289, 2019.
https://doi.org/10.1007/978-3-030-33894-7_28

is the goal of the Story Workbench tool [5], while minimal schemata are targeted at grasping the regularities of written and oral narratives at the discourse level [6].

These initiatives, rooted in narrative theories, tend to focus on the realization of narratives though a specific medium, e.g., text, neglecting the universal elements of dramatic narration that go behind the expressive characteristics of each medium. Following the tenets of the Semantic Web paradigm, in previous works, we have proposed the formal representation of the dramatic qualities in the ontology Drammar [7] and we have argued on the notion of drama as a form of intangible cultural heritage [8]. *Dramatic qualities* are those elements that are necessary for the existence of a drama, avoiding references to style and artistic issues; they can be retrieved in several drama analyses, e.g. [9–12] and have been reported thoroughly in a wiki [2]. Preliminary releases of the Drammar ontology have been validated and employed in a number of tasks: the illustration of the dramatic qualities through schematic charts, for teaching and analysis purposes [13], the implementation of emotional character models, for systems of automatic storytelling [14], the encoding of Stanislavsky's Action Analysis, useful for supporting actor rehearsals and drama staging [15]. We have also designed and implemented a web-based toolkit, named POP-ODE (POPulating Ontology Drammar Encodings), for the task of metadata annotation of specific dramas, through the creation of RDF (Resource Description Framework) graphs, aligned with drama texts [16]. The individual graphs instantiate the general classes, properties, and axioms of Drammar and are archived as OWL (Ontology Web Language) files. These drama heritage items are abstractions from the specific medium to safeguard the underlying dramatic qualities [17]. In this paper, we present the POP-ODE toolkit and how it can be used for the creation of a drama dataset.

2   Dramatic Qualities

The dramatic qualities abstract from the location, duration, form and function of a drama, which does not reduce to its discrete manifestations that are documented in many different media (see [8], which applies the criteria in [18, 146–148] for drama as a form of intangible cultural heritage). Given a number of dramatic qualities, a *drama heritage item* is an instantiation of the dramatic qualities for a specific drama. The structure of drama is recursive; so, we can identify the dramatic qualities for a whole drama as well as for some fragment of a drama. We can say that a dramatic heritage item *maps onto* a delimited fragment of a drama text or a whole drama text, and in particular the fragment boundaries are defined through the persistence of some dramatic qualities.

We take, for example, the dramatic qualities on a fragment taken from the "nunnery" scene in Shakespeare's *Hamlet*. In this scene, situated in the Third Act, Ophelia is sent to Hamlet by Polonius (her father) and Claudius (Hamlet's uncle, the king) to confirm the assumption that Hamlet's madness is caused

---

[2] https://www.di.unito.it/wikidrammar, visited on 19 July 2019.

by his rejected love. According to the two conspirators, Ophelia should induce him to talk about his inner feelings. At the same time, Hamlet tries to convince Ophelia that the court is corrupted and that she should go to a nunnery. In the middle of the scene, Hamlet puts Ophelia to a test to prove her honesty: guessing (correctly) that the two conspirators are hidden behind the curtain, he asks the girl to reveal where her father Polonius is. She decides to lie, by replying that he is at home. Hamlet realizes from the answer that also Ophelia is corrupted and consequently becomes very angry, realizing that there is no hope to redeem the court. The climax incident in the scene consists of a question-answer pair:

- Hamlet: "Where is your father?"
- Ophelia: "At home, my Lord!"

This is a (very relevant) fragment: boundaries are decided through the detection of a specific goal pursuit, distinct from the goals pursued previously. Given the classes and properties provided by the Drammar ontology [7], we have the following dramatic qualities, displayed, for the sake of space, in a table format:

```
// hierarchical structure of scenes
- Scene (Level 0): Hamlet revenge on his father's assassin
  - Scene (Level 1): Hamlet madness for proving Claudius guilt
    - Scene (Level 2): Polonius proves Hamlet madness for love
      - Scene (Level 3): "nunnery scene"
        - Unit (Position 7): Hamlet tests Ophelia for honesty

- Agents
  - Hamlet
    - Mental states
      - values at stake: honesty
      - beliefs: Polonius is in the room, Ophelia knows Polonius is in the room
      - goals: prove Ophelia honesty
      - emotions: Distress, Reproach, Anger
    - Intentions // hierarchical
      - plan: learn Ophelia honesty through question (NOT ACCOMPLISHED)
        - action: saying ''Where is your father?''
  - Ophelia
    - Mental states
      - values at stake: father's authority, honesty
      - beliefs: Polonius is in the room
      - goals: respect father's authority
      - emotions: Disappointment, Joy, Shame
    - Intentions // hierarchical
      - plan: making Hamlet talk about feelings (NOT ACCOMPLISHED)
        - plan: lying about Polonius in the room (ACCOMPLISHED)
          - action: saying ''At home, my lord.''

- Conflicts:
  - Goal/Plan conflict: Hamlet's proof for honesty VS. Ophelia's respect for father's authority
  - Value conflict: honesty VS. father's authority
```

The agents are Hamlet and Ophelia. Agents are characterized by their mental states and intentions they plan to undertake, respectively. Values at stake and beliefs of the agents determine the formulation of goals. Actions are undertaken through planning (sometimes, only hardwired reactions, such as, e.g., "lying") to achieve the goals. Planning is hierarchical, with long term plans ("making Hamlet talk about feelings") and short term plans ("learn Ophelia honesty through a question"). Actions can be accomplished or not.

Conflicts, the core of Hegel's drama analysis (collision between circumstances, passions and characters), are between the opposing actions of Hamlet and Ophelia as well as between the two values at stake of Ophelia. The conflicts at hand, as well as success/failure of the actions, determine the emotions felt by the agents. So, Hamlet feels Distress because his plan fails, feels Reproach because Ophelia is putting at stake honesty (an important value for him), and Anger as a consequence of both Distress and Reproach. Ophelia, though feeling Joy because she achieved her goal to respect her father's authority, is disappointed because her hope to convince Hamlet to talk about his feelings failed and is ashamed because she put at stake another value of hers, namely honesty.

Going formally, such dramatic qualities are described through semantic web languages and technologies, which also support sharing and access. A drama heritage item is an instantiated ontology, where the instances of the dramatic qualities provided by some specific drama are classified according to the Drammar classes (see below); the item is a digital object in the form of an OWL file. The axioms of the Drammar ontology encode each drama quality through a pattern of classes and properties, resorting to Artificial Intelligence theories and models. Ontology Drammar is available at the url http://purl.org/drammar, under the license Attribution 4.0 International (CC BY 4.0).

3 Toolkit POP-ODE

Since the use of ontology editors and reasoning tools is challenging for the scholars in the humanities [19], we provide annotators with a friendly environment that abstracts from the details of the ontology representation. The POP-ODE toolkit realizes a pipeline and a system for the creation of encoded dramas. It consists of a web-based interface, a series of intermediate modules, and a visual tool; the details of the pipeline and the system can be found in [16].

Referring to Fig. 1, an annotator (left) works through a web-based interface to fill a data base built according to the tenets of ontology Drammar, which encodes the elements mentioned above, namely story units, agents, actions, intentions or plans, goals, conflicts, values at stake (emotions are calculated automatically from these data). Through the web-based interface (bottom left of the figure), the annotator can select the text chunk for a unit from the .txt file, displayed on the top left in white background (the selected text will appear on the right, in yellow). In our example, the annotator selects the excerpt above (Hamlet: "Where is your father?". Ophelia: "At home, my Lord"). The middle of the interface shows the unit annotation (e.g., Unit_10_III_1); on the left and the right are the previous and the following units in the story timeline, respectively (in our example, Unit_9_III_1 and Unit_11_III_1), with the values that are at stake or at balance before and after the current unit. The lower part of the interface concerns the agents' intentions for this unit, and their possible accomplishments: from left to right, the agent (e.g., Ophelia), her/his goal (e.g., "respect father's authority"), her/his plan for achieving it (e.g., "lie about her father"s position"), possible conflicts (e.g., with Hamlet's plan to learn about Ophelia's honesty).

Going back to the pipeline (upper part), the annotation introduced through the interface, is encoded according to the Drammar ontology axioms (stored in a conceptual model, an OWL file) through the mapper module DB2OWL, which converts the data base tables into an Drammar Instantiated Ontology file (OWL DIO file). Automated reasoning processes derive further knowledge from the annotation (e.g., emotions felt by the agents). This file is later converted in RDF format and made available via HTTP from a triple store. A further software module, OWL2CHART, extracts the individuals and properties in a XML Drammar Chart file, which is then visualized by the interactive chart module [13], developed as a teaching device and an immediate validation of the produced encoding. The interactive chart (lower right of the figure) includes a timeline of the story units (middle part of the schema, black boxes), the hierarchical structure of scenes, each with its span on the units (upper part, grey boxes) agents' individual tracks, where intentions are horizontally aligned with units (lower part, colored boxes, colors identify agents – see headers on the leftmost column). Abandoned/failed plans are represented by incomplete arcs and marked by a cross. Also, notice the hierarchical representation of the intentions of the characters, with more complex intentions encompassing simpler intentions, the simplest ones spanning only one unit. In the figure, complex intentions of Hamlet and Ophelia alternate from left to right, to accumulate for the final conflict at the far right of the scene.

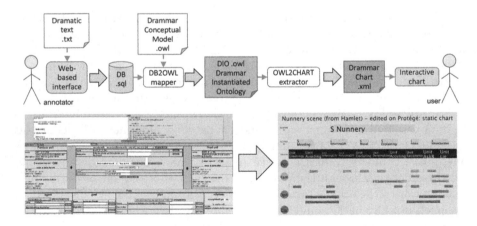

Fig. 1. The PopODE annotation pipeline: the general method (upper row) and sample thumbnails (lower row). (Color figure online)

4   The Prototype Dataset: Drammar Corpus

The purpose of the Drammar corpus is the encoding of dramas from classic repertoires, used in theatre, cinema and media teaching programmes. The POP-ODE toolkit is available for scholars and students to provide encodings. Here we briefly sketch a few encodings carried out in the last couple of years, while the toolkit was in development.

Students, about fifty per year, receive a focussed short training in formal representation (generic approach to logic languages, the Drammar ontology representation, the goals of the encoding); then, they are assigned either a unit from a classical drama for encoding (short term project), or a whole scene for segmentation and encoding (long term project). They fill the forms concerning the unit and agents' intentions; they also annotate conflicts over plans and values at stake. Inter-annotator agreement is managed by a supervisor, who is an expert in drama studies. The intervention of the supervisor is necessary to understand whether some annotation is a paraphrase of another and whether the two annotations can be reduced to one. A typical case that has occurred is the segmentation of a scene into units: some students only find a single unit, other students find several units, and sometimes with partial overlaps. The policy of the supervisor has been to identify the minimal units, and build minimal scenes from them. Although the task looks very challenging, students with many kinds of backgrounds (psychology, media studies, philosophy, linguistics) were able to perform the task. The tool has proven to be effective in inferring a number of classes and relations of the ontology that are syntactically important for the coherence of the representation but are cumbersome and error-prone for the task of a manual (or semi-manual) annotator. For example, when an annotator states that some unit follows another unit, the tool automatically creates an object timeline in the encoding. We are going to make a vast and effective test of the annotation tool over several student classes, together with questionnaires and ethnographic observations, to evaluate the functioning of the tool and create a large corpus for studies in the digital humanities.

Once uploaded into a triple store server, the annotations can be retrieved via the specific RDF query language, SPARQL, through an apposite endpoint. For example, to investigate the intentions of agent Polonius we can formulate a SPARQL query, which returns all the plans that annotators have attributed to Polonius (36):

```
SELECT ?agent ?plan
  WHERE {?plan drammar:isIntendedBy drammar:Polonius}
```

Currenty the Drammar corpus[3] is a collection of items that include a variety of dramatic artworks across media, selected to demonstrate the validity of the Drammar approach to encode the dramatic qualities. The corpus is composed by whole drama samples (*Hamlet* from Shakespeare, *Mother Courage* from Brecht, and *L'Arialda* from Testori), dramatic movie fragments (*Ride of valkyries (helicopter attack)* from *Apocalypse now - Coppola, Are you talkin' me?'* from *Taxi driver - Scorsese, Bullet time scene* from *Matrix - Wachowski, Trevi fountain scene* from *La Dolce Vita - Fellini, Flat Block Marina scene* from *The Clockwork Orange - Kubrick*, "*I've seen things ...*" scene from *Blade Runner - Scott, Russian roulette* from *The deer hunter - Cimino, Sollozzo omicide* from *The Godfather -*

---

[3] Available at the url http://www.cirma.unito.it/drammar/corpus/drammar_corpus. zip.

Coppola, dog VS. rabbit scene from *The Snatch - Ritchie, "losing the other eye"
scene* from *Kill Bill - Vol. 2 - Tarantino*), one musical drama fragment (*measures 122–174* from *Le nozze di Figaro - Mozart*), a musical video clip (3-min
video *Taylor Swift's "You belong with me" - White*), an animation short (2007
Oscar winner 2:30-min *Oktapodi - Bocabeille, Chanioux, Delabarre, Marchand,
Marmier, Mokhberi*).

The Drammar ontology encoding is able to address both the episodic nature
of the Brechtian epic narrative of the whole text of "Mother Courage" and
the dramatic climax of the two-character dialogue scene in the "Blade Runner"
movie, at different scales.

5   Conclusion

In this paper, we have presented a method, a pipeline, and a current dataset of
encoded dramas. The method relies upon the instantiation of a computational
ontology named Drammar on a drama or a fragment of it; the POP-ODE toolkit
implements a pipeline with a friendly interface that abstracts from the details
of the representation. The current dataset contains a number of dramas and
fragments of dramas, abstracting from their epoch, medium, and duration. Also,
we have seen how the dataset can be queried for information.

We are going to extend the corpus with the contributions of scholars and students and make a vast and effective validation. Also we will extend the encoding
to trace different interpretations and to allow the comparisons over scholarly
theories. Finally, software tools should be designed and implemented to address
the wider area of studies beyond the digital humanities.

Acknowledgments. We thank Giacomo Albert and Carmi Terzulli for their contribution to the development of the Drammar encoding and the POP-ODE toolkit.

References

1. Rissen, P., Lawrence, K.F.: Re-imagining the creative and cultural output of the
   bbc with the semantic web. Digit. Humanit. **2010** (2010). http://dh2010.cch.kcl.
   ac.uk/academic-programme/abstracts/papers/html/ab-878.html$#$d760e1214
2. Wolff, A., Mulholland, P., Collins, T.: Storyspace: a story-driven approach for creating museum narratives. In: Proceedings of the 23rd ACM Conference on Hypertext and Social Media, pp. 89–98 (2012)
3. Mulholland, P., Collins, T.: Using digital narratives to support the collaborative
   learning and exploration of cultural heritage. In: Proceedings of the 13th International Workshop on Database and Expert Systems Applications (2002)
4. Elson, D.K.: Dramabank: annotating agency in narrative discourse. In: Proceedings
   of the Eighth International Conference on Language Resources and Evaluation
   (LREC 2012), Istanbul, Turkey (2012)
5. Finlayson, M.A.: The story workbench: an extensible semi-automatic text annotation tool. In: Workshops at the Seventh Artificial Intelligence and Interactive
   Digital Entertainment Conference. AAAI Publications (2011)

6. Rahimtoroghi, E., Corcoran, T., Swanson, R., Walker, M.A., Sagae, K., Gordon, A.: Minimal narrative annotation schemes and their applications. In: Seventh Intelligent Narrative Technologies Workshop. AAAI Publications (2014)
7. Damiano, R., Lombardo, V., Pizzo, A.: The ontology of drama. Appl. Ontol. **14**(1), 79–118 (2019). https://doi.org/10.3233/AO-190204
8. Lombardo, V., Pizzo, A., Damiano, R.: Safeguarding and accessing drama as intangible cultural heritage. ACM J. Comput. Cult. Herit. **9**(1), 1–26 (2016)
9. Lavandier, Y.: La dramaturgie. Le clown et l'enfant, Cergy (1994)
10. Ryngaert, J.: Introduction à l'analyse du théâtre, ser Collection Cursus. Série Littérature. Armand Colin, Paris (2008)
11. Hatcher, J.: The Art and Craft of Playwriting. Story Press, Cincinnati (1996)
12. Spencer, S.: The Playwright's Guidebook: An Insightful Primer on the Art of Dramatic Writing. Farrar, Straus and Giroux, New York (2002)
13. Lombardo, V., Pizzo, A., Damiano, R., Terzulli, C., Albert, G.: Interactive chart of story characters' intentions. In: Nack, F., Gordon, A.S. (eds.) ICIDS 2016. LNCS, vol. 10045, pp. 415–418. Springer, Cham (2016). https://doi.org/10.1007/978-3-319-48279-8_39
14. Lombardo, V., Battaglino, C., Pizzo, A., Damiano, R., Lieto, A.: Coupling conceptual modeling and rules for the annotation of dramatic media. Semant. Web J. **6**(5), 503–534 (2015)
15. Albert, G., Pizzo, A., Lombardo, V., Damiano, R., Terzulli, C.: Bringing authoritative models to computational drama (encoding Knebel's action analysis). In: Nack, F., Gordon, A.S. (eds.) ICIDS 2016. LNCS, vol. 10045, pp. 285–297. Springer, Cham (2016). https://doi.org/10.1007/978-3-319-48279-8_25
16. Lombardo, V., et al.: Annotation of metadata for dramatic texts: the POP-ODE initiative. In: NL4AI@AI*IA, ser. CEUR Workshop Proceedings, CEUR-WS.org, vol. 1983, pp. 30–42 (2017)
17. Lombardo, V., Damiano, R., Pizzo, A., Terzulli, C.: The intangible nature of drama documents: an frbr view. In: Proceedings of the 2017 ACM Symposium on Document Engineering, pp. 173–182. ACM (2017)
18. Smeets, R.: Intangible cultural heritage and its link to tangible cultural and natural heritage. In: Yamamoto, M., Fujimoto, M. (eds.) Okinawa International Forum: UTAKI in Okinawa and Sacred Spaces in Asia: Community Development and Cultural Heritage, The Japan Foundation, pp. 137–150 (2004)
19. Varela, M.E.: Interoperable performance research promises and perils of the semantic web. Drama Rev. **60**(3), 136–147 (2016)

Villanelle: An Authoring Tool for Autonomous Characters in Interactive Fiction

Chris Martens[✉] and Owais Iqbal

North Carolina State University, Raleigh, NC, USA
martens@csc.ncsu.edu, omiqbal@ncsu.edu
https://go.ncsu.edu/poem

Abstract. Our goal is to discover tool and language design principles that enable powerful, usable autonomous character authorship for diverse audiences of storytellers. This paper describes the Villanelle project, an approach to interactive narrative authoring that supports seamless integration of autonomous characters into choice-based storytelling. We present our computational model based on behavior trees uniformly for scripting agent interaction, user interaction, and narrative events; our stand-alone authoring tool, which provides an integrated development and testing environment for authoring with this model; and our JavaScript API for web-based development, demonstrating the expressiveness and simplicity of our approach through two case studies.

1 Introduction

The rise in popularity of interactive narratives has led to the introduction of authoring tools that aim to bridge the gap between two different skill-sets required for creating an interactive narrative: narrative design (for authoring the narrative, world and characters) and programming (for realizing the narrative and the different mechanisms the author has in mind). Tools like Twine [11] have gained wide user bases among underrepresented storytellers and game makers due to their usability without programming experience [5]. These tools allow an author to quickly write and test the narrative ideas that they have in mind without focusing the majority of their attention on implementation details.

Meanwhile, there is active and growing interest in creating *procedural* play systems that promote player interest through worlds that continue to change and grow without player intervention, yet respond to player input [27]. One way to achieve this effect is through *autonomous NPCs* (non-player characters) who act according to their own plans and goals and create emergent interactions among themselves. The intelligent narrative research community has made significant advances in storytelling with autonomous NPCs, including reactive systems such as ABL [14] underlying the landmark interactive drama Facade [15], planning-based systems that regenerate narrative arcs based on player decisions [1,22,23], and the social practice systems encoded in CiF and Versu [4,17].

© Springer Nature Switzerland AG 2019
R. E. Cardona-Rivera et al. (Eds.): ICIDS 2019, LNCS 11869, pp. 290–303, 2019.
https://doi.org/10.1007/978-3-030-33894-7_29

However, there is a significant gap between the potential expressiveness afforded by autonomous characters in interactive narrative and the availability of authoring tools that make these techniques approachable and usable in the same way that Twine and Inform have made hypertext and parser-based storytelling authorable. Current tools lie at different ends of the approachability-expressiveness scale when it comes to intelligent character authoring, which is to say that if a tool has the capability to encode a complex behavior for an autonomous character, then it generally also has a steep learning curve.

This paper presents *Villanelle*, a framework and tool for authoring NPC behavior in interactive narrative works, which aims to bridge this gap. Our goal is to enable creators in the interactive fiction authoring community to incorporate autonomous NPCs into their work. Villanelle adopts *behavior trees* (BTs) as a computational foundation for authoring character behaviors and player interactions. Behavior trees have shown effective for scripting AI characters and proven by wide adoption in AAA games [19] and game creation frameworks like Unity 3D and Unreal Engine. Behavior tree proponents cite how easy they are to create, maintain, and scale, allowing designers to quickly be able to create the behavior they want in autonomous characters without getting lost in minute implementation details. Designers can craft reusable subtrees of behavior to be used for different characters or repeated multiple times in the same tree. Behavior trees allow authors to focus on the overall agent behavior they want to achieve.

Villanelle uses behavior trees not only for scripting NPCs in interactive narrative, but also for writing choice frames, game rules, and the outcomes of player actions in the interactive narrative. This choice demonstrates our philosophy of *language minimalism*, presenting a minimal basis of programming constructs that, once learned, can be composed to fulfill a wide range of authoring needs. We hypothesize that once an author grasps the basics of implementing a behavior tree, they will be able to author new, experimental narrative experiences that rely on believable and responsive virtual characters. In the long run, a successful execution of this concept will offer a healthy balance of expressiveness and approachability.

Our key contributions in this paper are as follows: (a) a reproducible description of how BTs can be used to author story characters and branching choice structures in the context of text-based interactive fiction (Sect. 3); (b) a system description of the Villanelle authoring tool (Sect. 4) and application programming interface (API) (Sect. 5); (c) a demonstration of Villanelle's capabilities through two case studies, one using the stand-alone authoring tool (Sect. 4) and one using the underlying API (Sect. 5).

2 Related Work

There is an extensive body of research on authoring tools for developing interactive narrative, across a wide variety of goals for the resulting narrative works. Grow et al. [7] compare three tools specifically for authoring interactive virtual agents: Bryson et al. BOD/POSH [2], Dias et al. FAtiMA [3], and Mateas and

Stern's ABL [14]. These authoring tools were evaluated on an example referred to as the "Lost Interpreter" scenario in which the player, as an armed soldier in occupied territory, must show a photograph to locals in order to find their lost interpreter. Green et al. [6] compare a broader range of contemporary authoring tools such as Twine, Inform, and Ren'Py, primarily for their user interface affordances for learning, editing, and debugging. However, this work has not evaluated tools in terms of their ability to express *autonomous* behavior, i.e. actions taken by NPCs that are *not* in direct reaction to player actions. Villanelle's adoption of BTs targets this mode of use in particular, and suggests the need for a wider range of case study scenarios with which to evaluate interactive narrative technology.

A number of other tools for interactive narrative authoring have been developed and described in academic literature, such as Scribe [18], IDTension [29], Narratoria [30], and Mimmisbrunnur [28]. These tools place varying levels of emphasis on NPC autonomy. Among these, Versu [4], CiF [17] (and its successor Ensemble [25]), and the Spirit AI Character Engine demoed at AIIDE 2018 [24]) are probably the closest in their goals to Villanelle; however, all of these tools have more of a focus on imparting characters with believable emotional and social intelligence. In contrast, Villanelle is agnostic to the particular set of actions that characters can carry out (whether they be related to mood changes, logistics like moving between locations and manipulating items, or insulting or befriending other characters) and is more concerned with the mechanics of authoring; i.e. on evaluating BTs as a computational model for coordinating NPC behaviors.

Behavior trees have seen widespread adoption in the mainstream gaming industry, particularly for NPC AI in real-time strategy and first-person shooter games [9], and efforts have been made to make them easy for designers to author through tools like BehaviorShop [8] and Unity3D's Behavior Designer. In the IN context more specifically, Kapadia et al. conducted an evaluation of behavior trees for narrative authoring and user interaction [10], comparing them to a story graph approach. This study was done using the Unity3D engine and an existing story framework created by the authors. However, their user study found that expert programmers still took multiple hours to develop a relatively minimal example. Our approach to handling user interaction with BTs requires less authoring overhead, and we anticipate that a similar example would take much less time to author.

3   Villanelle's Behavior Trees

The Villanelle project takes a "language-based" approach to authoring, which means we distinguish between the computational model afforded to authors and its implementation as an authoring tool, which included syntactic sugar and integrated editing environment support. Villanelle's computational model uses behavior trees (BTs) to represent branching narrative structures as well as NPC AI. We chose BTs based on their wide adoption in the games industry by designers [9], who vouch for their ease of development as well as reusability for encoding different characters with the same behavior. To minimize the learning curve, Villanelle chooses to implement only the minimal basic constructs of behavior trees: sequencing, selection, conditions, and actions, using the formalism described in previous work [13]. We recapitulate this formalism in this section.

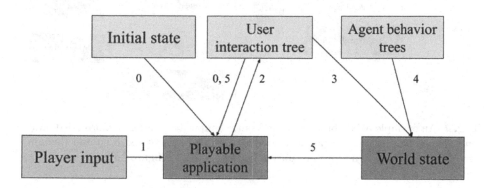

Fig. 1. A diagram of the game loop architecture in Villanelle. Yellow nodes are authored constructs, and blue nodes are run-time artifacts. The two edges labeled 0 represent configuring the initial story world for the player using the authored user interaction tree and initial state. Edge 1 indicates the player making a choice. Edge 2 propagates this choice to the user interaction tree, which updates the world through edge 3. Edge 4 represents BTs for each agent collectively taking their "turns" and modifying the world state. Finally, the to edges labeled 5 indicate rendering the updated world state to the player, potentially offering different choices based on conditions in the user interaction tree.(Color figure online)

Villanelle was designed for interactive fiction, which traditionally works in a turn-based manner. Therefore, the actions and subsequent changes to the state of the world occur over discrete time steps. Upon selection of an action to perform by the player, Villanelle executes the behavior tree mapped to that action as well as the next step of each behavior for each agent in the game (see Fig. 1).

Villanelle uses behavior trees (BTs) as its underlying computational model. We next describe the specific BT constructs that make up this computational model using the example in Fig. 2. The types of nodes that Villanelle uses are primitive *actions*, which appear at the leaves of the tree, *sequence* and *selector* nodes consisting of two or more children, and *guards*, which have a single child node. Every node type is implemented as a function that returns a Status of SUCCESS, FAILURE or a RUNNING upon execution, which sometimes depends on the status returned by its children.

3.1 Primitive Actions

Action nodes are responsible for mutating the world state. Actions need to specify their preconditions and effects. A precondition is a function that will inspect

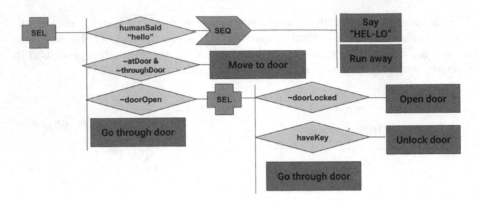

Fig. 2. An example behavior tree for an agent. Composite nodes are color-coded orange and shaped as plus signs or arrows, condition guards are colored blue and diamond-shaped, and primitive actions are purple rectangles (Color figure online)

certain variables in the world state and return a boolean value. If it is true, the effects parameter gets executed and if it is false, the Tick returns a status of **FAILURE**. Effects are responsible for all observable changes, including printing text that the player will see or changing variables that other agents may react to.

As an example, the following code specifies an action node with a precondition that checks whether a door is unlocked, and if it is, opens the door. This code implements the condition and action seen in the middle-right of Fig. 2.

```
condition: not doorLocked
effects: doorOpen := true
```

3.2   Composite and Guard Nodes

A 'Composite' is any node with two or more children. The two types of composites currently implemented in Villanelle are *sequences* and *selectors*. A sequence node executes its children sequentially until one of them returns a FAILURE. This node returns a SUCCESS on successful execution of all children. If a child node is in the RUNNING status, this node will return a RUNNING status as well. A selector node is the inverse of the sequence: it executes children sequentially until one of them returns a SUCCESS and hence the name (it 'selects' a successful node from its children). The node fails if it doesn't find a single successful node. The case for when a child returns RUNNING is the same as for the sequence node.

Finally, Villanelle also provides a Guard node, which allows the author to couple a composite node with a precondition. If the precondition fails, this node would fail else it would return whichever status the Composite node returns.

The following example represents a subtree of Fig. 2 and uses conditions, sequences, and selectors in combination.

```
selector:
    condition: humanSaid  "hello"
        sequence:
            - print "'HEL-LO,' says the robot."
            - atDoor := false
    condition: not atDoor and not throughDoor
        - atDoor := true
```

3.3   Agents

An agent is a structural entity that consists of a behavior tree and variables specific to the agent. Variables are still written to the blackboard, but they are scoped to the agent. Agents provide an easy to understand way to label behavior trees, as the typical use case would be to attach a different behavior tree for each major character in the narrative. It is not limited to only characters though, as the author could also provide a behavior tree for major narrative events in the game with a "Director" agent.

3.4   Player Interaction with the Agents and the World

Villanelle supports the use of BTs for specifying player interactions predicated on the state of the world. The author does this by defining *user interaction trees* that the framework runs after all the agent trees have run. See Fig. 3 for an example. There are two authorable components of player interaction: what the player sees, and the set of choices available to the player (coupled with their effects). *What the player sees* may contain a description of the current scene and the current state of some of the game's variables. *Player choices* consist of a list of actions the player can perform given the current state, as well as the effects of each choice and the text description of the action having been carried out.

4   Standalone Authoring Tool

In prior work on usable authoring tools [18], researchers advocate for "one centralized tool in which [all] authoring functions take place." Accordingly, we developed a standalone cross-platform desktop tool for writing and debugging interactive narrative works, available for download on the web.[1] This tool includes live visualization of all behavior trees created by the author and live rendering of the game. Our goal is to allow authors to quickly prototype their ideas with the built-in editor and play the game immediately after making their changes without requiring additional steps. With live visualization of the trees, the authors can graphically understand the structures that they are building and use the live error reporting to help fix syntax and semantic issues instantly. If compilation

---

[1] https://sites.google.com/a/ncsu.edu/villanelle/.

```
User Interaction:
   - condition: botAtDoor
     sequence:
        - description: "There is a little robot here."
        - user action:
            action text: "Say hello"
            effect tree:
                effects:
                    - sayHello := true
   - user action:
       action text: "Wait"
       effect tree:
           effects:
               - none := true
```

Fig. 3. This example presents the user with two possible choices, "Say hello" and "Wait", where the former is only active when the Robot agent is at the door. The effects of saying hello set a variable that the Robot can respond to in its next turn.

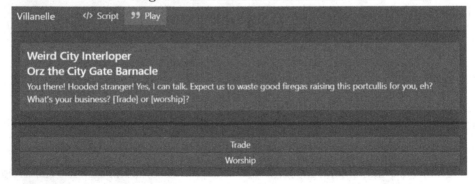

Fig. 4. A screenshot of the Editor tab.

Fig. 5. A screenshot of the Play tab corresponding to the code in Fig. 4.

succeeds, the author can play their game in the tool and see the statuses of the different nodes of the behavior trees as the game progresses. We implemented the tool using the Electron framework for creating a cross-platform desktop application, the JavaScript React framework to handle rendering the application, and Palantir's Blueprints for the user interface.

4.1 Case Study: Weird City Interloper (Port)

Every new feature in the standalone tool was tested by developing a playable experience that uses it. We have created and tested several playable experiences with the tool, two of which we highlight here to demonstrate practicality and breadth. We will explain the features of the editor using a case study based on *Weird City Interloper*, a text adventure game by C.E.J. Pacian released in 2014. On the Interactive Fiction Database, it has 32 ratings, averaging 4.5 star reviews [21]. We chose to port this game to Villanelle to evaluate its usability for developing a choice-based exploratory game centering around conversation with NPCs. Each NPC's dialogue interface is controlled by a separate behavior tree; see Fig. 6 for an example.

The Villanelle editor has two tabs, Script and Play (see Figs. 4 and 5 for screenshots). On every change to the Script input, the game is rendered immediately in the Play tab. If there are any errors in the input, the compilation fails and an error message is displayed instead. The rendered game has two components: the text display and the player choices. The text display consists of the title of the game and scene, the scene description as given by the user interaction tree, and the effect text provided for any agent actions that run, if any. In the choice input pane, we render each choice authored in the user interaction tree as a button that will execute the associated behavior tree when clicked.

4.2 Editing Support

The script tab primarily consists of the editor, seen in Fig. 4. The editor was realized using an open source embeddable code editor called Ace Editor. We used the built-in language mode for YAML, the syntax upon which we developed the Villanelle surface syntax. The Ace Editor also provides general features like a powerful search/replace functionality (which has regular expression support), highlighting other same tokens when one is highlighted and line numbers.

In a side panel next to the editor, a tree is rendered live with every change the user makes to the YAML in the editor. This tree is also responsible for highlighting the errors in the code structure if there are any. Every individual node which has children is expandable and collapsible. The following is how the different components are shown graphically (see Fig. 6).

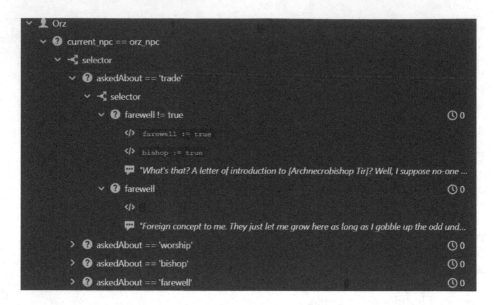

Fig. 6. The behavior tree of an agent NPC, visualized.

4.3   Debugging Support

We use *json-schema* and *ajv* libraries to perform error checks. We also run the condition and assignment expressions against the ANTLR4 grammar. Any errors in these checks are reported in a bottom bar with a dot indicating failure. If the error checks succeed, the bar turns green and includes a checkmark. Every change to the YAML input in the editor causes the error checks to be run again.

If the input is an invalid YAML schema, i.e. it violates any of the general YAML rules, the tree isn't rendered and a message is shown.

Tree Visualization. Behavior trees for agent nodes are rendered under each agent. The visual structure of the behavior trees matches node for node the structure in the YAML input. However, the conditions in actions, sequence or selectors are represented as individual nodes themselves, with the associated behavior tree node rendered as a child. This was done to visually create a sense of 'gate-keeping' the conditions provide in terms of their coupling with nodes of a behavior tree.

The number of ticks an action node takes is displayed as a clock symbol on the right hand side of the corresponding condition node (if the action has no explicit condition node, a 'true' condition node is rendered).

Nodes which have errors with types or with the Villanelle YAML schema are reported as red nodes and their children are not rendered. The error message is displayed on hovering over the erroneous node.

All ancestors of the erroneous node are automatically expanded so the author does not have to search on their own (Fig. 7).

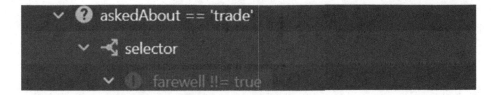

Fig. 7. The condition expression is syntactically incorrect

Tree Execution Visualization. We support debugging by rendering the live execution of behavior trees during gameplay. As the author plays through the game, the tree nodes are highlighted based on how they were processed: green means SUCCESS, red means FAILURE, and orange means RUNNING. Every time the user takes an action, the statuses of the nodes change and the tree is refreshed showing the changes, giving the author live feedback (Fig. 8).

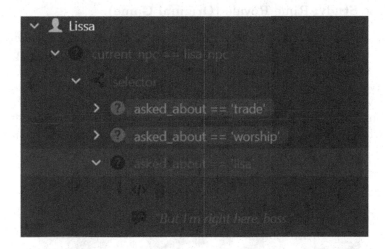

Fig. 8. The different statuses for the nodes show up as you play the game

5   Application Programming Interface

To support development of web-based interactive narrative experiences, we released an open-source web application programming interface (API) for Villanelle. This API gives authors the ability to create BTs, register initial world states, and execute the world engine, by calling JavaScript functions. The main game loop is called `worldTick()`, whose code is shown in Fig. 9.

While the stand-alone editor provides minimal language features, such as variables that can hold strings, numbers, and boolean values, the API is more flexible and intended for advanced users. It supports modularity, behaviors that take parameters (as in [26]), and arbitrary data structures supported by TypeScript (e.g. arrays and dictionaries).

```
export function worldTick() {
    // Execute each agent's behavior tree
    for (var i = 0; i < agents.length; i++) {
        var tree = agentTrees[agents[i]];
        if (!isUndefined(tree)) {
            setVariable("executingAgent", agents[i]);
            execute(tree);
        }
    }
    // Execute the user interaction tree
    runUserInteractionTrees();
}
```

Fig. 9. Code for a function provided by the API to execute all behavior trees defined by the author for agents and user interaction.

5.1   Case Study: Rime Royale (Original Game)

We showcase the expressiveness of Villanelle's API through *Rime Royale*, an original, browser-playable game developed by our lab. Rime Royale implements a guildmaster roleplaying mechanic in which the player must assign NPCs with various strengths to missions that can succeed or fail; (see a screenshot in Fig. 10). Villanelle is used to implement the behavior of NPCs not assigned to missions, which act autonomously according to their personalities and preferences while other characters attempt the missions. Rime Royale was accepted

Fig. 10. A Screenshot of *Rime Royale*

for presentation in the AIIDE 2019 Playable Experience track [12], which shows evidence of the strength of its gameplay.

Rime Royale was developed over the course of one Spring semester by two undergraduate students, one responsible for art and narrative direction and one responsible for AI and gameplay programming. Their success provides evidence of Villanelle's support for innovative forms of gameplay.

6   Conclusion and Future Work

In this paper we presented Villanelle, an API framework and a standalone tool to use behavior trees not only to author character behaviors but every other part of an interactive narrative experience as well. Although we have not yet conducted a formal user evaluation, we have found through internal testing that Villanelle enables painless development of a wide range of reusable behaviors for autonomous characters. In future work, we would like to investigate scalability to large groups of NPCs in a social simulation akin to Prom Week [16] and formally compare Villanelle to other authoring tools using benchmarks in previous tool evaluations [7,10].

Our long-term goal is to support current and future interactive fiction authors in their creative goals, and we have begun a process of soliciting feedback from this audience. Initial feedback suggests that a number of additional features would be useful, some of which (like behavior parameterization and composite data structures) exist in the API but not the standalone tool. Other more foundational features include an extension to the behavior tree language that supports a stronger notion of reactivity through continuously monitored nodes (as in Unity's Behavior Designer implementation). We also plan to investigate the feasibility and utility of behavior generation through planning: BTs lend themselves very well to Hierarchical Task Network planning [20]. We could use this technique to automatically compose trees using from the available trees created by the author. Finally, in accordance with the evidence that debugging and reasoning are key usability principles, we plan to investigate reasoning principles for multi-agent systems authored with behavior trees. This includes debugging support for stepping, jumping, and rewinding (to analyze unexpected NPC interactions) as well as behavior model checking to validate (un)reachability of story states.

References

1. Aylett, R.: Narrative in virtual environments - towards emergent narrative. In: Working Notes of the Narrative Intelligence Symposium (1999)
2. Bryson, J.J., Stein, L.A.: Modularity and design in reactive intelligence. In: International Joint Conference on Artificial Intelligence. vol. 17, pp. 1115–1120. LAWRENCE ERLBAUM ASSOCIATES LTD. (2001)
3. Dias, J., Mascarenhas, S., Paiva, A.: FAtiMA modular: towards an agent architecture with a generic appraisal framework. In: Bosse, T., Broekens, J., Dias, J., van der Zwaan, J. (eds.) Emotion Modeling. LNCS (LNAI), vol. 8750, pp. 44–56. Springer, Cham (2014). https://doi.org/10.1007/978-3-319-12973-0_3

4. Evans, R., Short, E.: Versu: a simulationist storytelling system. IEEE Trans. Comput. Intell. AI Games **6**(2), 113–130 (2014)
5. Friedhoff, J.: Untangling twine: a platform study. In: DiGRA conference (2013)
6. Green, D., Hargood, C., Charles, F.: Contemporary Issues in Interactive Storytelling Authoring Systems. In: Rouse, R., Koenitz, H., Haahr, M. (eds.) ICIDS 2018. LNCS, vol. 11318, pp. 501–513. Springer, Cham (2018). https://doi.org/10. 1007/978-3-030-04028-4_59
7. Grow, A., Gaudl, S.E., Gomes, P., Mateas, M., Wardrip-Fruin, N.: A methodology for requirements analysis of AI architecture authoring tools. In: Foundations of Digital Games (2014)
8. Heckel, F.W.P., Youngblood, G.M., Hale, D.H.: Behaviorshop: an intuitive interface for interactive character design. In: AIIDE (2009)
9. Isla, D.: Handling complexity in halo 2 ai (2005). http://www.gamasutra.com/view/feature/130663/gdc_2005_proceeding_handling_.php
10. Kapadia, M., Zünd, F., Falk, J., Marti, M., Sumner, R.W., Gross, M.: Evaluating the authoring complexity of interactive narratives with interactive behaviour trees. Foundations of Digital Games (2015)
11. Klimas, C.: Twine (2009). http://www.twinery.org
12. Liu, R., Christopher, C., Martens, C.: Rime royale: a guildmaster simulator. In: Fifteenth Artificial Intelligence and Interactive Digital Entertainment Conference (Playable Experiences) (2018)
13. Martens, C., et al.: Villanelle: towards authorable autonomous characters in interactive narrative. In: Proceedings of the Joint Workshop on Intelligent Narrative Technologies and Workshop on Intelligent Cinematography and Editing (2018)
14. Mateas, M., Stern, A.: A behavior language for story-based believable agents. IEEE Intell. Syst. **17**(4), 39–47 (2002)
15. Mateas, M., Stern, A.: Façade: An experiment in building a fully-realized interactive drama. In: Game Developers Conference, vol. 2, pp. 4–8 (2003)
16. McCoy, J., Treanor, M., Samuel, B., Reed, A.A., Wardrip-Fruin, N., Mateas, M.: Prom week. In: Proceedings of the International Conference on the Foundations of Digital Games, pp. 235–237. ACM (2012)
17. McCoy, J., Treanor, M., Samuel, B., Tearse, B., Mateas, M., Wardrip-Fruin, N.: Authoring game-based interactive narrative using social games and comme il faut. In: Proceedings of the 4th International Conference & Festival of the Electronic Literature Organization: Archive & Innovate, pp. 1–8. Citeseer (2010)
18. Medler, B., Magerko, B.: Scribe: a tool for authoring event driven interactive drama. In: Göbel, S., Malkewitz, R., Iurgel, I. (eds.) TIDSE 2006. LNCS, vol. 4326, pp. 139–150. Springer, Heidelberg (2006). https://doi.org/10.1007/11944577_14
19. Millington, I., Funge, J.: Artificial Intelligence for Games. CRC Press, Boco Raton (2009)
20. Neufeld, X., Mostaghim, S., Brand, S.: A hybrid approach to planning and execution in dynamic environments through hierarchical task networks and behavior trees. In: Fourteenth Artificial Intelligence and Interactive Digital Entertainment Conference (2018)
21. Pacian, C.: Weird city interloper. The Interactive Fiction Database (2014). (https://ifdb.tads.org/viewgame?id=wrt29d4nlm71udll)
22. Porteous, J., Cavazza, M., Charles, F.: Applying planning to interactive storytelling: narrative control using state constraints. ACM Trans. Intell. Syst. Technol. (TIST) **1**(2), 10 (2010)
23. Riedl, M.O., Young, R.M.: Narrative planning: balancing plot and character. J. Artif. Intell. Res. **39**, 217–268 (2010)

24. Samuel, B., et al.: Playable experiences at AIIDE 2018. In: Fourteenth Artificial Intelligence and Interactive Digital Entertainment Conference (2018)
25. Samuel, B., Reed, A.A., Maddaloni, P., Mateas, M., Wardrip-Fruin, N.: The ensemble engine: next-generation social physics. In: Proceedings of the Tenth International Conference on the Foundations of Digital Games (FDG 2015), pp. 22–25 (2015)
26. Shoulson, A., Garcia, F.M., Jones, M., Mead, R., Badler, N.I.: Parameterizing behavior trees. In: Allbeck, J.M., Faloutsos, P. (eds.) MIG 2011. LNCS, vol. 7060, pp. 144–155. Springer, Heidelberg (2011). https://doi.org/10.1007/978-3-642-25090-3_13
27. Smith, A.: Living worlds: the joy of NPC schedules. Rock Paper Shotgun (2016)
28. Stefnisson, I.S., Thue, D.: Mimisbrunnur: ai-assisted authoring for interactive storytelling. In: Fourteenth Artificial Intelligence and Interactive Digital Entertainment Conference (2018)
29. Szilas, N., Marty, O., Réty, J.-H.: Authoring highly generative interactive drama. In: Balet, O., Subsol, G., Torguet, P. (eds.) ICVS 2003. LNCS, vol. 2897, pp. 37–46. Springer, Heidelberg (2003). https://doi.org/10.1007/978-3-540-40014-1_5
30. Van Velsen, M.: Narratoria, an authoring suite for digital interactive narrative. In: FLAIRS Conference, pp. 394–395 (2008)

A Hierarchical Approach for Visual Storytelling Using Image Description

Md. Sultan Al Nahian[✉], Tasmia Tasrin, Sagar Gandhi, Ryan Gaines,
and Brent Harrison

Department of Computer Science, University of Kentucky, Lexington, USA
{sa.nahian,tasmia.tasrin,sga267,ryan.gaines,brent.harrison}@uky.edu

Abstract. One of the primary challenges of visual storytelling is developing techniques that can maintain the context of the story over long event sequences to generate human-like stories. In this paper, we propose a hierarchical deep learning architecture based on encoder-decoder networks to address this problem. To better help our network maintain this context while also generating long and diverse sentences, we incorporate natural language image descriptions along with the images themselves to generate each story sentence. We evaluate our system on the Visual Storytelling (VIST) dataset [7] and show that our method outperforms state-of-the-art techniques on a suite of different automatic evaluation metrics. The empirical results from this evaluation demonstrate the necessities of different components of our proposed architecture and shows the effectiveness of the architecture for visual storytelling.

Keywords: Visual storytelling · Deep learning · Natural language processing

1 Introduction

Computational storytelling is the task of automatically generating cohesive language that describes a sequence of correlated events or actions. Prior work on computational storytelling has mainly focused on plan-based approaches for generating narratives [21]. Planning based approaches often rely on complex domain models that outline the rules of the world, the actors involved, and the actions that each actor can take. This type of story generation, often called closed-world storytelling, is able to generate coherent stories, but are restricted in the types of stories they can generate by the domain model.

Recently there has been an increased interest in *open-world story generation*. Open-world story generation refers to generating stories about any domain without prior knowledge engineering and planing [13]. With the increased effectiveness and sophistication of deep learning techniques, deep neural networks, such as sequence-to-sequence networks, have been shown to be effective in open-world story generation. The primary advantage that these techniques have over

© Springer Nature Switzerland AG 2019
R. E. Cardona-Rivera et al. (Eds.): ICIDS 2019, LNCS 11869, pp. 304–317, 2019.
https://doi.org/10.1007/978-3-030-33894-7_30

planning systems is that they do not require extensive domain modeling to be effective. This makes them an effective tool for open-world story generation.

Visual storytelling is an extension to the computational storytelling problem in which a system learns to generate coherent stories based on a sequence of images. Visual storytelling is a more challenging problem because the sentences need to be not only cohesive, but also need to consider both the local context of images and the global context of whole image sequence. There have been recent successes in generating natural language that is conditioned on images. These successes are primary in tasks such as image captioning [8,10,18]. Visual storytelling presents a different challenge from image captioning in that the language generated is often more abstract, evaluative, and conversational [7]. In addition, techniques need to identify and understand the relations among the scenes of the images and describe them through logically ordered sentences. The task also needs to consider the completeness of the story.

There have been successes in visual storytelling, however. Approaches utilizing deep learning have proven, overall, to be effective at this task [3,22]. Though these approaches have achieved competitive results, the stories they produce are often comprised of short sentences with repeated phrases. In some cases, the generated sentences fail to tell a coherent story and in some cases they fail to capture image contexts.

One of the primary challenges in both computational storytelling and visual storytelling is determining how to maintain story context for long event sequences. In this paper, we address this challenge with techniques inspired by how humans usually form stories. To construct a story, a human needs to form a plot for the story at first. In visual storytelling, this can be done by going through all the images and extracting the key context from them to form the premise of the story. After that, the sentences are made by going through the images one by one. In order to ensure the coherency in the story, we need to articulate the temporal dependencies among the events of the images. This can be achieved by summarizing the events generated in the previous sentences and considering the summary during making the current sentences of the story. For instance, [16] use the sentence generated for the previous image to generate the sentence for the current image. This approach can have a cascading error effect in which errors can compound if the quality of the previously generated sentences is bad. As a result, over time the context of the story can drift from the original context.

To emphasize logical order among the generated sentences and to help our network architecture better maintain context over time, we have passed image descriptions into the network along with the images themselves. This helps to minimize the effect of cascading error as mentioned above. The descriptions are more specific and literal statements about the content of the images. The intuition behind adding these descriptions is that they can aid the network in understanding the context of the image and help the network to extract the flow of the events from the subsequent images.

To evaluate our system, we examine its performance on the Visual Storytelling (VIST) dataset using automatic evaluation metrics BLEU, CIDEr, METEOR and, ROUGE_L. Using these evaluation metrics, we have demonstrated how well our proposed architecture can learn description and image context and combine both of them to create human-like coherent visual narratives.

The major contributions of our work can be summarized as follows:

- An end-to-end hierarchical deep neural network to generate open story from visual content.
- Exploration into the use of natural language image descriptions in visual storytelling.
- An evaluation of our architecture on a large corpus of visual storytelling data against state-of-the-art deep learning techniques.

2   Related Work

Research on computational story generation has been explored in two ways: Closed-world story generation and open-world story generation. Closed-world story generation typically involves the use of predefined domain models that enable techniques such as planning to be used to generate the story. Open-world story generation involves automatically learning a domain model and using it to generate stories without the need for relearning or retraining the model [4]. Due to their ability to reason over sequences of textual input, sequence-to-sequence networks are typically used to perform open-world story generation. To better help these networks maintain context over long story sequences, many researchers have chosen to make use of event representations that distill essential information from natural language sentences [4,13,20]. These *event representations* make story generation easier in that the network only needs to focus on generating essential information. In our work, we perform the more complex task of reasoning over both story information as well as visual information. In addition, we do not make use of event representations, choosing instead to generate full text sentences.

Visual narrative has been explored previously, primarily utilizing planning-based approaches [2]. With the release of the first large-scale, publicly available dataset for visual storytelling [7], approaches based on machine learning have become more viable for the task. In [7], they propose a sequence-to-sequence network to generate story from image sequence which has been being used as a strong baseline for the visual storytelling task. [12] has proposed a visual storytelling pipeline for task modules which can serve as a preliminary design for building a creative visual storyteller. [16] has proposed a visual storytelling system where previous sentence is used to generate current sentence. [9] and [19] are the two winners from the VIST challenge in 2018. GLAC Net [9] generates visual stories by combining global-local attention and provides coherency to the stories by cascading the information of the previous sentence to the next sentence serially. In [19], an adversarial reward learning scheme has been proposed by enforcing a policy model and a reward model. One common limitation of these approaches is that the models often generate short sentences and are prone to repeating certain phrases in their story sentences. We believe that by utilizing image descriptions we are bootstrapping the language learning process. This enables our method to produce more diverse, human-like sentences that are longer than the ones generated by previous approaches while still maintaining coherence.

3 Methodology

In this work, we propose a hierarchical encoder-decoder architecture which we call a *Hierarchical Context-based Network (**HCBNet**)* to generate coherent stories from a sequence of images. Figure 1 shows the overview of our architecture. The network has two main components: 1. A hierarchical encoder network that consists of two levels and 2. A sentence decoder network. The first level of the hierarchical encoder, referred to as the *Image Sequence Encoder (ISE)*, is used to encode all the images of the sequence and create a single encoded vector of the image sequence. In the next level, there is a composite encoder, referred to as the *Image-Description Encoder (IDE)*. It takes in two inputs: an image and description of that image. The IDE consists of two encoders: an *Image Encoder* that is used to encode the individual image and a *Description Encoder* that is used to encode the description of the image in each time step. After each iteration, the decoder network generates one sentence, word by word, of the story as output. The initial state of the first time step of the Description Encoder comes from the Image Sequence Encoder as shown by the grey arrow in Fig. 1. Each of the components of our proposed architecture will be discussed further below.

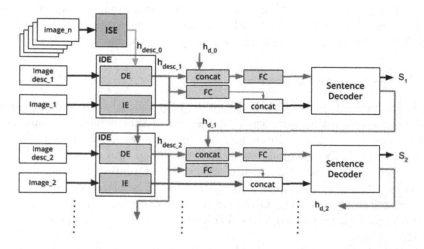

Fig. 1. The proposed hierarchical context based network. Image Sequence Encoder (ISE) takes all the images and encode them to create a vector. Image-Description Encoder (IDE) is composed of two components: Description Encoder (DE) to encode the description and Image Encoder (IE) to encode the image. In each iteration, the sentence decoder (SD) generates a sentence, word by word, conditioned on the vectors coming from DE and IE. In the figure, two iterations have been shown.

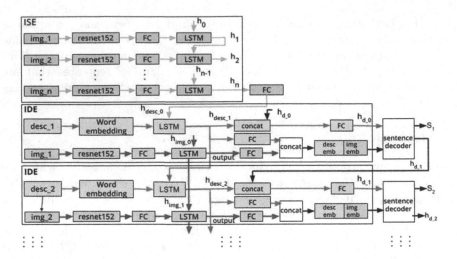

Fig. 2. Detailed architecture of the encoder. ISE (represented by grey color) generates sequence embedding vector which is used as the initial hidden vector of DE in the first iteration of IDE. IDE produces two vectors: initial hidden vector and input of the sentence decoder. Blue color represents the DE network and red color represents the IE network. (Color figure online)

3.1   Hierarchical Encoder Network

As mentioned earlier, the Hierarchical Encoder of our architecture is composed of two levels of encoder: the Image Sequence Encoder (ISE) and the Image-Description Encoder (IDE). The IDE is, itself, composed of two different encoders that are tasked with identifying different types of context in our input. Figure 2 presents a detailed representation of the hierarchical encoder.

3.2   Image Sequence Encoder

This is the first encoder which is meant to help the network understand the high-level context of the story based on the images that it has seen thus far. It takes an image sequence as input and in each time step, uses a convolutional neural network (CNN) to embed each individual image into a single vector. This vector is passed to an additional fully connected (FC) layer and then to LSTM network [6]. The output hidden state of the LSTM is forwarded to the LSTM of the next iteration. For the CNN, we have used pretrained model. We have experimented with pretrained VGG19 [15] and resnet152 [5] to extract features from the images.

After the iteration has been finished for each of the images in the sequence, we take the final hidden state of the LSTM unit and pass it to a FC layer. The output vector of the FC layer, referred to as the sequence embedding vector, represents the global context of the image sequence which works as the premise of the story. This sequence embedding vector is used as the initial hidden vector of the Description Encoder (shown in Fig. 2). Therefore the global context of the story passes through the network through time. This helps the network to better understand and maintain the theme of the story throughout the entire sequence.

Image-Description Encoder. The Image-Description Encoder (IDE) takes an image and corresponding description as input in each time step. In the first time step, it takes the sequence embedding vector from the ISE as initial hidden state as mentioned above. The IDE is a composite encoder with two modules: The first is the *Image Encoder (IE)*, which is used to extract the context vector from an individual image. The second module is the *Description Encoder (DE)*, which is used to extract the context vector from the corresponding image description.

Image Encoder. This component is used to deduce the context of the current image given additional information about the previous images in the sequence. The current image is sent to a Convolutional Neural Network (CNN) pretrained using the resnet152 model for feature extraction. The extracted image feature vector is passed through to a FC layer and a recurrent neural network. Figure 2 outlines the overview of the encoder with red arrows. It shows that the LSTM network takes a hidden state as input as well. This is the feature vector from the Image Encoder of the previous time step. The LSTM of current time step also generates a hidden state and an output vector. We pass the hidden state to the Image Encoder of the next step and pass the output to an FC layer to form the image embedding vector. The hidden states of Image Encoder propagate the local image context from one time step to the next.

Description Encoder. The Description Encoder is used to extract information about the current description and to reason over information contained in previous image descriptions. We use the image description to help maintain temporal dependencies between the sentences. Before passing the description into the RNN (LSTM), we preprocess the description and pass it through to an embedding layer. The final hidden state of the LSTM contains contextual information about the image description. This can be thought of as *theme* type information that is used to condition the output of our network. It is passed to the Description Encoder of the next iteration where it will be used as the initial state for the LSTM (shown as the blue connection in Fig. 2). By doing this, we help ensure that the context of the current sentence is passed to the next iteration.

The hidden state of the DE is also passed to a FC layer to form a vector referred as the description embedding. The description embedding and image embedding are concatenated and forwarded to the Sentence Decoder. The hidden state of the DE is concatenated with the final hidden state of the decoder of previous time step as well. A FC layer is applied on the concatenated vector and forwarded to the decoder to form the initial hidden state of the Sentence Decoder (SD). The relations are demonstrated in Eq. 1:

$$decod\_hid_{s,0} = FC(concat(desc\_hid_s, decod\_hid_{s-1,t})) \tag{1}$$

$$decod\_hid_{s,t} = decod\_hid_{s,t-1} \tag{2}$$

From the hidden state of the previous sentence decoder, the network receives information about what has been generated before and the hidden state of the description provides the theme of the current sentence. This information enables the network to construct an image specific sentence while maintaining the flow of the events across the sentences.

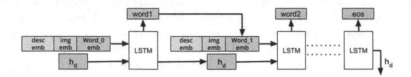

Fig. 3. Sentence Decoder

Sentence Decoder. The Sentence Decoder (SD) uses a LSTM to generate the text of the visual narrative (seen in Fig. 3). This LSTM network uses the contexts generated by the IDE to construct a story events word by word. In the beginning of a sentence, the initial hidden state of the sentence decoder is formed by Eq. 1. Then it propagates the hidden state of current time step to next time step of a sequence (represented in Eq. 2). Input of the SD is formed by concatenating the description embedding, image embedding, and word embedding of the previous word (Eq. 4). This process is repeated in every word generation step of a sentence. It works as "hard attention" on image and description context. From the image embedding vector, the decoder gets information on the local features of the current image, while the description embedding provides both the overall story context and image specific context to the decoder.

$$desc\_embed_s = FC(desc\_encoder\_hidden\_state_s) \tag{3}$$

$$sent\_decod\_input_{s,w} = concat(desc\_embed_s, img\_embed_s, word\_embed_{s,w-1}) \tag{4}$$

4   Experimental Setup

In this section, we give the details about our experimental methodology and the implementation that we used for testing. First, we describe the dataset used in the experiment followed by how we chose to preprocess the data. Then we will discuss information about the network parameters used during testing. Finally, We give an overview about the baseline architectures against which the proposed architecture has been compared. Afterward, we discuss about the evaluation metric and evaluation criteria.

4.1   Dataset

To evaluate our architectures, we have used the Visual Storytelling Dataset (VIST) [7] which is a sequential vision-to-language dataset. This dataset consists of image sequences and associated stories for each sequence. Each image sequence consists of 5 images and, therefore, five story sentences. In addition to this information, some images have an image description associated with them which is referred as "Descriptions of images-in-isolation" in the VIST paper. In this paper, we choose to use the term "image description" instead of "Descriptions of images-in-isolation". The dataset, in total, contains 40155 stories in the training set, 4990 stories in the validation set and, 5055 stories in the test set. It contains 154430 unique images in the training set, 21048 images in the validation set and 30000 images in the testing set.

Recall that our approach makes use of image descriptions to help generate narratives. Some images, however, do not have an associated description. Images that did not have an associated description were discarded, as were any stories that contained images that did not have an associated description. This process has reduced the total number of training stories to 26905, validation stories to 3354 and, test stories to 3385.

4.2   Preprocessing

In the preprocessing step, we have corrected the misspellings from the image descriptions and story texts. Stop words have been removed from the image descriptions, but not from the story texts. To build the vocabulary, we have taken all the words which have been appeared at least three times in the story text, which results in a vocabulary of size 12985. Words that appear below this threshold are replaced with a symbol representing an unknown word. We have used pretrained resnet152 and VGG19 models to encode the images. As these two models take input of size 224 × 224, we have resized all of the training, validation and test images to the required size.

4.3   Experimented Architectures

We have evaluated our proposed method, HCBNet, against two of the state-of-the-art architectures for visual storytelling: AREL [19] and GLAC Net [9]. We have trained these two networks from scratch with the same dataset used to train our proposed model. To evaluate the need for different aspects of HCBNet, we also perform an ablation study. In this ablation study, we test four different versions of HCBNet. They are:

- **HCBNet:** This is the standard HCBNet demonstrated in Fig. 1.
- **HCBNet without previous sentence attention:** In this version, the final hidden state of an iteration of the sentence decoder is not used to form the initial hidden state of the next iteration of the sentence decoder. The hidden state of the description encoder is used as the initial hidden state of the sentence decoder. The sentence decoder gets the context of the previous sentence from the hidden state of the description encoder.

- **HCBNet without description attention:** In this version, previous sentence attention is used in the sentence decoder, but the description embedding is not passed to form the input of the sentence decoder. Here, the sentence decoder does not use attention on the image description during each step of an iteration. It gets the description information from the hidden state of the description encoder in the beginning of an iteration.
- **HCBNet using VGG19:** In all of our experiments, we have used pretrained resnet152 as the CNN. Here, we have experimented the HCBNet with pretrained VGG19 model to check if there is any significant performance difference when using a different pretrained CNN.

4.4   Network Parameters

All of the networks in the experiment have been trained using same parameters. The learning rate is 0.001 with learning rate decay 1e-5. The batch size is 36, and the vocabulary size is 12985. The size of the LSTM units are 1024 which is same for all of the versions of HCBNet. We have used a multilayer LSTM with 2 layers. To prevent the overfitting, we have used batch normalization and dropout layers. Batch normalization has been applied on each FC layer that is followed by an LSTM cell in both the ISE and IE module. Another batch normalization has been used on the final output vector (FC layer) of the ISE module. We have applied dropout at a rate of 0.5 on each LSTM cell as well as the output vector of the LSTM cell of the SD. The training process is stopped when the validation loss no longer improves for 5 consecutive epochs (25 to 32 epochs in these experiments). We have used Adam optimizer to optimize the loss.

Table 1. Automatic evaluation metrics results from the experiments

	BLEU-1	BLEU-2	BLEU-3	BLEU-4	CIDEr	METEOR	ROUGE_L
AREL (baseline)	0.536	0.315	0.173	0.099	0.038	0.33	**0.286**
GLAC Net (baseline)	0.568	0.321	0.171	0.091	0.041	0.329	0.264
HCBNet	0.593	**0.348**	0.191	0.105	0.051	**0.34**	**0.274**
HCBNet (without prev. sent. attention)	**0.598**	0.338	0.180	0.097	**0.057**	0.332	0.271
HCBNet (without description attention)	0.584	0.345	**0.194**	**0.108**	0.043	0.337	0.271
HCBNet (VGG19)	0.591	0.34	0.186	0.104	0.051	0.334	0.269

4.5   Evaluation Metrics

In order to evaluate our proposed architecture, we have used the following automatic evaluation metrics: BLEU [14], METEOR [1], ROUGE_L [11] and

CIDEr [17]. BLEU and METEOR are machine translation evaluation metrics that are widely used to evaluate story generation systems. To use BLEU, one must specify an n-gram size to measure. In this paper, we report results for 1-grams, 2-grams, 3-grams, and 4-grams. ROUGE_L is a recall based evaluation metric primarily used for summarization evaluation. CIDEr is different from translation metrics in that it is a consensus based evaluation metric. It is capable of capturing consensus and is, therefore, able to better to evaluate "human-likeness" in the story than metrics such as BLEU, METEOR or ROUGE_L.

5   Results and Discussion

We evaluate the performance of our proposed method HCBNet against the baseline networks AREL and GLAC Net by using the automated evaluation metrics BLEU, CIDEr, METEOR and ROUGE_L. The scores are shown in the Table 1. These results demonstrate that HCBNet outperforms the GLAC Net on all of the metrics and AREL on all of the metrics except for ROUGE_L. Though AREL performs better than HCBNet in ROUGE_L, inspection of the stories generated by each network indicates that the quality of the stories generated by HCBNet are higher than those generated by AREL.

It is important to note that these metrics on their own do not necessarily indicate that our method produces interesting, or even coherent, stories. Recall that we claimed earlier that the stories produced by GLAC Net and AREL often suffer from having short sentences with repeated phrases. One of our hypotheses in this paper is that utilizing image description information should enable us to generate stories with longer and more diverse sentences. We perform an analysis to provide some intuition on whether this is the case. Specifically, we compare the average number of words per sentence and the number of unique 1, 2, 3, and 4-grams generated by each network. From Table 2, we can see that the average number of words per sentence is highest for AREL among the three networks. But number of unique 1-grams is only 357 for AREL, where HCBNet has 1034 unique 1-grams. This behavior is consistent across all n-grams tested. This provides support to our claim that these baselines tend to generate repetitive phrases and provides support to our claim that HCBNet can produce more diverse sentences. Interestingly enough, this also could explain why AREL performed well on ROUGE_L. ROUGE_L is meant to measure a model's recall on a reference sentence, which is likely to be high if one produces short sentences.

As shown in the Table 1, the CIDEr score of HCBNet is higher than GLAC Net and AREL. This indicates that our model has a greater ability to generate "human-like" stories than compared to AREL and GLAC Net. It is also notable that we see the greatest difference between our network and our baselines through this metric. We feel that this, especially when combined with the results outlined in Table 2, further indicate that our network produces stories that are more diverse and, potentially, human-like while still maintaining story context.

As mentioned in Sect. 4.3, we have also experimented with three other versions of HCBNet to see the effectiveness of different components of the network.

Table 2. Experiment results based on word properties

	Avg. no. of words per story	Avg. no of words per sent.	1-gram	2-gram	3-gram	4-gram
AREL	29.893	7.03	357	924	1526	1979
GLAC Net	29.826	5.996	837	2586	4069	4628
HCBNet	**30.7**	**6.141**	**1034**	**3324**	**5292**	**5966**

HCBNet without previous sentence attention gives higher score in CIDEr and slightly better score in BLEU-1, but adding the same component into the network significantly increases the score of other metrics. HCBNet without using description attention performs poorly for CIDEr. Incorporating the description embedding into the input of sentence decoder not only improves the score of CIDEr remarkably but also METEOR, ROUGE_L, BLEU-1 and BLEU-2 scores. We believe that this indicates that the description attention helps the network resist context drift and helps keep the story cohesive.

Table 3. Comparison of the stories among the networks

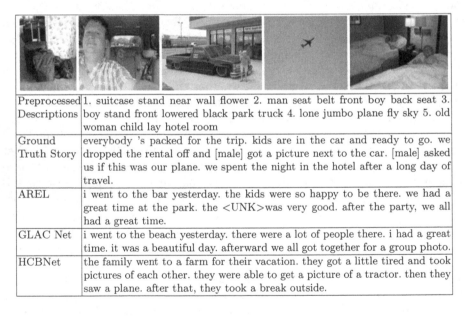

Preprocessed Descriptions	1. suitcase stand near wall flower 2. man seat belt front boy back seat 3. boy stand front lowered black park truck 4. lone jumbo plane fly sky 5. old woman child lay hotel room
Ground Truth Story	everybody 's packed for the trip. kids are in the car and ready to go. we dropped the rental off and [male] got a picture next to the car. [male] asked us if this was our plane. we spent the night in the hotel after a long day of travel.
AREL	i went to the bar yesterday. the kids were so happy to be there. we had a great time at the park. the <UNK>was very good. after the party, we all had a great time.
GLAC Net	i went to the beach yesterday. there were a lot of people there. i had a great time. it was a beautiful day. afterward we all got together for a group photo.
HCBNet	the family went to a farm for their vacation. they got a little tired and took pictures of each other. they were able to get a picture of a tractor. then they saw a plane. after that, they took a break outside.

To provide a better understand and highlight the differences between the stories generated by our network and by our baselines, we have provided some illustrative examples of stories generated by each network. Table 3 shows a comparison between the story generated by our network and the baseline networks.

Table 4. Example stories generated by HCBNet

the family gathered for a special dinner. they had a lot of food and drinks. there was also a lobster dish. [female] was happy to be there. she was so excited to see her friends.

the family went on a hike to the mountains. we saw a beautiful waterfall. it was a nice day for a walk. he was very excited. after that we took a picture of him.

The first thing to note is that the stories generated by the baseline networks are relatively vague and rely on general phrases about having a great time. In addition, they often disregard the context that each image provides. If we examine the story generated by HCBNet, we can see that our network correctly interprets the theme of the story as "vacation". The corresponding generated sentence of image 3 is interesting, though. In the image, though the vehicle is a truck, HCBNet describes it as a tractor. We believe this is because the network correctly identifies a vehicle, but wants to remain consistent with the fact that it says the family is visiting a farm in the first sentence. We feel that this type of behavior shows our network is able to balance maintaining story context along with maintaining image context. In the last sentence, though it believes the people to be outside, it understands that people are taking a break. We have also provided more examples of the stories that our network can generate in Table 4. We feel that these results combined with the results achieved on our automatic evaluation metrics provide significant evidence for our claim that HCBNet can produce high quality visual narratives.

6   Conclusion and Future Work

In this paper, we introduce HCBNet, a hierarchical, context-based neural network that incorporates image description data for performing visual storytelling. In addition, we evaluate our approach using a variety of automatic evaluation metrics and show that HCBNet outperforms two state-of-the-art baselines. Our results indicate that our proposed architecture is able to learn the expected flow of events conditioned on the input images and use this knowledge to produce a cohesive story. As our future work, we plan to expand our evaluation to include a human subjects study so that we can explore how humans perceive the stories generated by our system.

References

1. Banerjee, S., Lavie, A.: METEOR: an automatic metric for MT evaluation with improved correlation with human judgments. In: Proceedings of the ACL Workshop on Intrinsic and Extrinsic Evaluation Measures for Machine Translation and/or Summarization, pp. 65–72 (2005)
2. Cardona-Rivera, R.E., Li, B.: PLOTSHOT: generating discourse-constrained stories around photos. In: AIIDE (2016)
3. Gonzalez-Rico, D., Fuentes-Pineda, G.: Contextualize, show and tell: a neural visual storyteller. arXiv preprint. arXiv:1806.00738 (2018)
4. Harrison, B., Purdy, C., Riedl, M.O.: Toward automated story generation with Markov chain Monte Carlo methods and deep neural networks. In: Thirteenth Artificial Intelligence and Interactive Digital Entertainment Conference (2017)
5. He, K., Zhang, X., Ren, S., Sun, J.: Deep residual learning for image recognition. In: Proceedings of the IEEE Conference on Computer Vision and Pattern Recognition, pp. 770–778 (2016)
6. Hochreiter, S., Schmidhuber, J.: Long short-term memory. Neural Comput. 9(8), 1735–1780 (1997)
7. Huang, T.H.K., et al.: Visual storytelling. In: Proceedings of the 2016 Conference of the North American Chapter of the Association for Computational Linguistics: Human Language Technologies, pp. 1233–1239 (2016)
8. Johnson, J., Karpathy, A., Fei-Fei, L.: Densecap: fully convolutional localization networks for dense captioning. In: Proceedings of the IEEE Conference on Computer Vision and Pattern Recognition, pp. 4565–4574 (2016)
9. Kim, T., Heo, M.O., Son, S., Park, K.W., Zhang, B.T.: GLAC Net: glocal attention cascading networks for multi-image cued story generation. arXiv preprint. arXiv:1805.10973 (2018)
10. Krause, J., Johnson, J., Krishna, R., Fei-Fei, L.: A hierarchical approach for generating descriptive image paragraphs. In: Proceedings of the IEEE Conference on Computer Vision and Pattern Recognition, pp. 317–325 (2017)
11. Lin, C.Y.: ROUGE: a package for automatic evaluation of summaries. In: Text Summarization Branches Out, pp. 74–81 (2004)
12. Lukin, S.M., Hobbs, R., Voss, C.R.: A pipeline for creative visual storytelling. arXiv preprint. arXiv:1807.08077 (2018)
13. Martin, L.J., et al.: Event representations for automated story generation with deep neural nets. In: Thirty-Second AAAI Conference on Artificial Intelligence (2018)
14. Papineni, K., Roukos, S., Ward, T., Zhu, W.J.: BLEU: a method for automatic evaluation of machine translation. In: Proceedings of the 40th Annual Meeting on Association for Computational Linguistics, pp. 311–318. Association for Computational Linguistics (2002)
15. Simonyan, K., Zisserman, A.: Very deep convolutional networks for large-scale image recognition. arXiv preprint. arXiv:1409.1556 (2014)
16. Smilevski, M., Lalkovski, I., Madjarov, G.: Stories for images-in-sequence by using visual and narrative components. In: Kalajdziski, S., Ackovska, N. (eds.) ICT 2018. CCIS, vol. 940, pp. 148–159. Springer, Cham (2018). https://doi.org/10.1007/978-3-030-00825-3_13
17. Vedantam, R., Lawrence Zitnick, C., Parikh, D.: CIDEr: consensus-based image description evaluation. In: Proceedings of the IEEE Conference on Computer Vision and Pattern Recognition, pp. 4566–4575 (2015)

18. Vinyals, O., Toshev, A., Bengio, S., Erhan, D.: Show and tell: a neural image caption generator. In: Proceedings of the IEEE Conference on Computer Vision and Pattern Recognition, pp. 3156–3164 (2015)
19. Wang, X., Chen, W., Wang, Y.F., Wang, W.Y.: No metrics are perfect: adversarial reward learning for visual storytelling. arXiv preprint. arXiv:1804.09160 (2018)
20. Yao, L., Peng, N., Weischedel, R.M., Knight, K., Zhao, D., Yan, R.: Plan-and-write: towards better automatic storytelling. In: CoRR. abs/1811.05701 (2018)
21. Young, R.M., Ware, S.G., Cassell, B.A., Robertson, J.: Plans and planning in narrative generation: a review of plan-based approaches to the generation of story, discourse and interactivity in narratives. Sprache und Datenverarbeitung Spec. Issue Formal Comput. Models Narrative **37**(1–2), 41–64 (2013)
22. Yu, L., Bansal, M., Berg, T.L.: Hierarchically-attentive rnn for album summarization and storytelling. arXiv preprint. arXiv:1708.02977 (2017)

A Knowledge Representation
for Planning-Based Story Generation
Applied to the Manual and Automatic
Encoding of Plot

Rushit Sanghrajka and R. Michael Young$^{(\boxtimes)}$

University of Utah, Salt Lake City, UT, USA
rush.sanghrajka@utah.edu, young@eae.utah.edu

Abstract. There have been a range of coding schemes to code story structure. However, few of these coding schemes map directly to expressive formal models of story that also characterize character beliefs or the complexities that arise when mistaken beliefs lead to action failure. We describe HEADCODE, a coding scheme motivated by recent work in plan-based story generation.

Keywords: Story generation · Coding schemes · Intentional planning

1 Introduction and Background

In stories, characters commonly attempt to perform actions that fail. Sequences with action failure are designed in narratives specifically to prompt explanatory and anticipatory inferences on the part of story consumers. Because story consumers act as problem-solvers [4], anticipating the progression of characters' plans and their ultimate success or failure, the design feature of stories where characters perform actions that fail are critical to the experience of a reader.

Thorne and Young [15,16], developed a knowledge representation, called HEADSPACE, that has been used in a generative context to produce story lines that contain these anticipation-prompting elements. In this document, we isolate the knowledge representation (KR) that Thorne and Young developed and describe a methodology for human analysts to employ the KR to encode characters' intentional structures from sample narratives. We call the resulting coding scheme and coding methodology HEADCODE.

The motivation for this work comes from a necessity in the current domain: to be able to seamlessly transpose between human-authored narratives and computational narratives. There is an existing corpora of real world stories in various media, and this work is intended to provide a capability for their translation into a representation compatible for computational study.

A number of approaches involving narrative have sought to develop coding schemes for naturally occurring or artificial narratives. For example, work

© Springer Nature Switzerland AG 2019
R. E. Cardona-Rivera et al. (Eds.): ICIDS 2019, LNCS 11869, pp. 318–322, 2019.
https://doi.org/10.1007/978-3-030-33894-7_31

by social scientists exploring interpersonal relationships and health have used talk-aloud protocols to solicit insight into ill patients' perspectives on their own health [14], and coding schemes were developed to obtain structured knowledge from subject-generated personal narratives.

There is narrative psychological research that explores how people represent their lives through telling stories [10]. Narrative psychologists study people's personal stories in a range of contexts (e.g., [6–8,12,13]). These researchers typically use distinct coding schemes that address idiosyncratic questions specific to each research project.

There have been approaches to encode narratives towards generating computational representations as well. Cardona Rivera and his collaborators [1] introduce a computational model to capture information from narratives using the event indexing situation model, a cognitive model of human narrative understanding [17]. Metafor is a system which attempts to create programming constructs for stories [9] and visualize stories as constructs of object-oriented programs. Harmon's work on a narrative encoding framework is aimed at promoting analysis and comparison of narratives with each other [5]. Elson and his collaborators [2] also constructed a tool that supports an encoding process for narratives to be used for acquiring world knowledge in a narrative generation and understanding.

The HEADCODE knowledge representation borrows and adapts many of its formal definitions from the HEADSPACE planning data structures. For use by annotators, the HEADCODE knowledge representation models the actions present in a narrative sequence, the conditions in the world relevant to the actions' success, the set of characters in the world capable of executing actions, and the beliefs, desires and intentions of these characters over time. Formal definitions for all the elements of a HEADSPACE plan are provided by Thorne and Young in their original paper [15]. We provide an informal characterization of the HEADSPACE elements that are relevant for HEADCODE below. Readers should refer to Thorne and Young's work for the complete characterization.

2 Coding Cinematic Plotlines Using HeadCode

The coding process using HEADCODE requires three passes through the cinematic sequence. Each pass involves the annotator watching the sequence in temporal order from start to finish. With each pass the annotator populates the knowledge representation making reference to elements added in the preceding passes. For brevity, in the remainder of this paper we refer to the human annotator as *Ann*.

First Pass. During the first pass, Ann records the following aspects:

1. Characters. Ann adds unique character identifiers to a *Character List* just when Ann sees an as yet unrecorded character perform an action that *contributes causally* to the cinematic sequence. For example, a background character which is performing a random action in the background would not

be added to the Character List unless at least one their actions contributes causally to the plot sequence.

2. Objects. Ann adds a unique object identifier to an *Object List* just when Ann sees an as-yet-unrecorded object that plays some role in an action, either in the action's preconditions or effects.
3. Locations. Ann adds a unique location identifier to a *Locations List* just when Ann sees a distinct as yet unrecorded location where an action takes place.
4. Literals. Ann records a ground literal in the world in a *Literals List* just when Ann sees a condition in the world that plays a role in a precondition to some observed story action. Care must be taken that the literals recorded in the Literals List are consistent in their semantics. That is, Ann should not create two different literals in the Literals list denoting the same condition or its negation. For instance, Ann should not record both (unloaded gun1) and (not (loaded gun1)).

At the end of the first pass, Ann must check their list to ensure that the list is consistent and has no duplicates. Ann can choose to remove certain elements if they feel at the end of the sequence that they were not necessary for the plot, or add more elements if they seem to have contributed to the plot. Then Ann can move on to the second pass.

Second Pass. During the second pass, Ann re-watches the cinematic sequence, observing the actions performed and their relationship to world states over time. The second pass focuses on the following aspects:

1. Operators. Ann records an operator definition for an action in an *Operators List* just when Ann observes an action being executed that is (a) of an as yet unrecorded action type and (b) dependent upon or changes the state of some literal in the Literals List.
2. World States. Ann creates a world state record that describes the state of the world currently being viewed just when Ann observes an action occur in the world that changes the truth value or character belief value of a literal in the Literal List. This world state record is added to a *World States List*. A world state record consists of the enumeration of truth values of the literals in the Literal List for each character and the ground truth value for the world and the identifier of the world state record that immediately precedes it in the cinematic sequence.
3. Actions. Ann records a unique action identifier in an *Actions List* just when Ann observes an action that is dependent upon on changes the state of some literal in the Literals List. Part of this recording includes the operator of the action as well as the specification of how elements from the Characters, Objects and Locations Lists play roles in the action's arguments. Finally, the recording indicates which world state record occurs immediately prior to the action.

Third Pass. In the third pass, Ann encodes aspects of the cinematic sequence by building upon the information encoded using the first two passes. Specifically, Ann reasons about *why* characters perform those actions. This involves the following type of annotation:

1. Intention Plans. As the cinematic progresses through each world state noted in the World State List, Ann creates an intention record for each character. The intention record lists Ann's estimation of the character's current goals as well as a partial description of the plans that the character intends to pursue to achieve those goals. Goals are drawn from the Literals List and plans are composed of a partial order of actions instantiated from the Operators List using literals, locations and characters from their respective lists as arguments.

   When creating a new intention record for a new world state, Ann modifies the intention record for the preceding state by (a) updating any plans containing the most recently executed action, to indicate that action's successful execution, (b) adding any plans and goals that Ann perceives result from a character adopting a new set of intentions and (c) removing any plans and associated goals that Ann perceives have just been abandoned by a character due to the character's changing beliefs.

3   Conclusion

Because the HEADCODE coding language was designed based on the HEADSPACE planning data structures, there is a direct, one-to-one mapping between story plans produced by the HEADSPACE planner and the language elements of HEADCODE that would be used to code a sample story produced by the HEADSPACE planner. In fact, the mapping is so direct that a straightforward process can be followed that produces the mappings without human intervention. Specifically, the mapping takes each element of a HEADSPACE plan and produces the identical element in HEADCODE. It parallels much of the structure found in the HEADSPACE planning system, which itself extends the widely-used STRIPS model of action [3]. Further, HEADCODE provides a process by which output from narrative planners can be automatically translated into coding model and by which human annotators can create data from naturally occurring narratives in the same format.

References

1. Cardona-Rivera, R.E., Cassell, B.A., Ware, S.G., Young, R.M.: Indexter: a computational model of the event-indexing situation model for characterizing narratives. In: Proceedings of the 3rd Workshop on Computational Models of Narrative, pp. 34–43 (2012)
2. Elson, D.K., McKeown, K.R.. A platform for symbolically encoding human narratives. In: AAAI Fall Symposium: Intelligent Narrative Technologies, pp. 29–36 (2007)

3. Fikes, R., Nilsson, N.: Strips: a new approach to the application of theorem proving to problem solving. In: Allen, J., Hendler, J., Tate, A. (eds.) Readings in Planning. Morgan Kaufmann, Burlington (1990)
4. Gerrig, R.: Experiencing Narrative Worlds: On the Psychological Activities of Reading. Yale University Press, New Haven (1993)
5. Harmon, S.: Narrative encoding for computational reasoning and adaptation. Ph.D. thesis, UC Santa Cruz (2017)
6. Josselson, R.: The present of the past: dialogues with memory over time. J. Pers. **77**(3), 647–668 (2009)
7. Korobov, N.: 'he's got no game': young men's stories about failed romantic and sexual experiences. J. Gend. Stud. **18**(2), 99–114 (2009)
8. Lilgendahl, J.P., McLean, K.C., Mansfield, C.D.: When is meaning making unhealthy for the self? the roles of neuroticism, implicit theories, and memory telling in trauma and transgression memories. Memory **21**(1), 79–96 (2013)
9. Liu, H., Lieberman, H.: Metafor: visualizing stories as code. In: Proceedings of the 10th international conference on Intelligent user interfaces, pp. 305–307. ACM (2005)
10. McAdams, D.P., McLean, K.C.: Narrative identity. Curr. Dir. Psychol. Sci. **22**(3), 233–238 (2013)
11. Niehaus, J., Young, R.M.: Cognitive models of discourse comprehension for narrative generation. Literary Linguistic Comput. **29**(4), 561–582 (2014)
12. Pasupathi, M., Rich, B.: Inattentive listening undermines self-verification in personal storytelling. J. Pers. **73**(4), 1051–1086 (2005)
13. Schachter, E.P.: Identity configurations: a new perspective on identity formation in contemporary society. J. Pers. **72**(1), 167–200 (2004)
14. Stern, L., Kirmayer, L.J.: Knowledge structures in illness narratives: development and reliability of a coding scheme. Transcult. Psychiatry **41**(1), 130–142 (2004). https://doi.org/10.1177/1363461504041358. pMID: 15171211
15. Thorne, B., Young, R.M.: Generating stories that include failed actions by modeling false character beliefs. In: Working Notes of the AIIDE Workshop on Intelligent Narrative Technologies (2017)
16. Young, R.: Sketching a generative model of intention management for characters in stories: adding intention management to a belief-driven story planning algorithms. In: Working Notes of the AIIDE Workshop on Intelligent Narrative Technologies (2017)
17. Zwaan, R.A., Langston, M.C., Graesser, A.C.: The construction of situation models in narrative comprehension: an event-indexing model. Psychol. Sci. **6**(5), 292–297 (1995)

SHOWRUNNER: A Tool for Storyline Execution/Visualization in 3D Game Environments

Rushit Sanghrajka, R. Michael Young(✉), Brian Salisbury, and Eric W. Lang

University of Utah, Salt Lake City, Utah, USA
rush.sanghrajka@utah.edu, {young,salisbury}@eae.utah.edu,
ewlang@cs.utah.edu

Abstract. We introduce SHOWRUNNER, a tool for visualizing story world execution within a 3D game environment. SHOWRUNNER takes as input an abstract, declarative specification of a story script and a set of mappings between terms in the story and data elements in the game engine and executes the story's actions, using virtual cameras to film and present the action to a user. The implementation details on the working of the tool, as well as instructions on how users with various design and API constraints can utilize the tool are discussed in this paper.

Keywords: Story execution · Game environments · Cinematic visualization of stories

1 Introduction

The domain of computational narrative is growing steadily, using algorithmic approaches to construct plot and narrative. An important capability for systems that synthesize stories is to be able to present the output of a story's action sequences to human users in some conventional narrative medium. We have developed a tool called SHOWRUNNER that allows story action sequences generated by external systems (e.g., narrative planners, screenwriting graphical user interfaces, or human editors) to be automatically executed within a 3D virtual world, creating a machinima-based visualization for the action sequence.

SHOWRUNNER provides a specific story world built within a commercial 3D game engine (i.e., Unity) and a means for reading in a story line and a mapping used to translate from some external naming of story entities and the internal game engine entities in the game engine's data model. In this sense, SHOWRUNNER abstracts away the details of the game engine's execution of story actions and allows some exogenous system or a human author to specify the dynamics of a story in a declarative language appropriate for the external model's representational needs. Our intent in building SHOWRUNNER is to increase the accessibility of a 3D game engine as a resource for visualization for intelligent story generators, although the interface SHOWRUNNER provides can be used by any external

© Springer Nature Switzerland AG 2019
R. E. Cardona-Rivera et al. (Eds.): ICIDS 2019, LNCS 11869, pp. 323–327, 2019.
https://doi.org/10.1007/978-3-030-33894-7_32

source capable of creating story specifications. Further, SHOWRUNNER is extensible, in that developers wishing to add new scenes, set elements, objects, actions and animations can create and incorporate that content via Unity's development tools.

This paper details the design and functionality of the SHOWRUNNER system, and provides information about how SHOWRUNNER can be used by researchers in order to visualize story execution from a variety of input sources.

2   Related Work

A number of previous projects have developed the capability to execute story lines within 3D game engines. Many of these explicitly provided a tight coupling between an AI system generating the story and the game engine used to execute the story line. Pollack and Ringuette's Tileworld [8] was one of the first systems to build a game-like environment for executing the output of experimental agent architectures controlling agents in unpredictable and dynamic worlds. Laird [5] created one of the initial systems to connect an external AI controller – the SOAR Architecture [6] – to a commercial 3D game engine. Young developed a system, *Mimesis*, which created virtual world narratives using a bipartite approach of a story-world planner and discourse planner [14]. Cavazza and his collaborators [1,2] also built a number of systems that were driven by AI planning systems executing in game engines. Thuene et al. built the Virtual Storyteller system [11], which is a framework for creating plot, narrative and presentation of the narrative. Kapadia and his collaborators [4] developed a framework for authoring multi-agent environments with behaviors. Screenwriting software (e.g. [3,7] allow for features like tracking character trajectories, conflict, emotions, and even provide for previsualizations of stories.

SHOWRUNNER expands the capabilities of related work by acting as a test-bed where one could connect story input from a range of input sources: human authored, computationally generated or computer-assisted. SHOWRUNNER hopes to provide one common environment for execution of these experiences and provide one automated pipeline towards that end.

3   System Overview

SHOWRUNNER provides a layer of abstraction over action execution in pre-defined Unity game environments. These pre-defined game environments contain a set of data structures and code that hold assets corresponding to the characters and their action animations, objects, locations, and the code used to perform the actions of the story world. Extending a SHOWRUNNER level is discussed briefly in Sect. 4.

SHOWRUNNER takes as inputs three elements: a specification of the actions in a story, a (possibly empty) specification of a custom starting state for the story, and a data dictionary that maps descriptors in the start state and action descriptions to corresponding descriptors in the Unity game environment. The system first creates an internal database used to map the input story references to game engine-internal objects. Next, it modifies the starting state of the story world according to any customizations detailed in the input files. Finally, it begins executing the actions enumerated in the story script, ensuring that each one executes correctly. During execution, a camera system automatically films the unfolding action, visualizing it for the user.

We have built and tested a Western cowboy-themed story world. We are developing similarly instrumented story worlds for feudal Japan, medieval Europe and a dungeon-focused fantasy world.

The SHOWRUNNER system is built using C# and its code and art assets exist within a collection of scenes within the Unity game engine [13]. The system consists of a number of customizable, modular components, described in more detail below.

Input and Output. SHOWRUNNER input consists of two required elements and one optional element:

1. A Story Script. A story script is a file containing a declarative representation of the actions in a story along with ordering dependencies between those actions.
2. A Mapping Definition. A mapping definition is a file containing associations between the symbols used as identifiers in the story script (i.e., action types, characters, locations and objects) and the unique IDs provided by SHOWRUN-NER to the corresponding Unity GameObjects in the story world scene.
3. An optional Initial State Description. An initial state description is used to specify any ground literals whose truth value is required to be different than their truth values in the default start configuration of the story world's scene.

Output from SHOWRUNNER is a 3D visualization of the execution of the actions in the story plan running within the virtual set of the story world. These actions are filmed by virtual cameras pre-placed within the Unity scene. Dynamic camera selection is managed automatically by Unity's Cinemachine [12] camera control system, which optimizes camera selection based on visibility of target characters, user-defined weights, and other cinematic factors.

The Story World's Scene. The process of executing stories runs entirely within a Unity scene. The scene specifies the virtual world of the story, the art and code assets for the entities in the story as well as the code to manage the system's behavior.

Each SHOWRUNNER Unity scene contains the following elements:

1. The *virtual set*. This set includes the 3D space of the story world, including buildings, exterior landscape and any objects in the story world that have no dynamic state properties associated with them.
2. The *world objects*. World objects in SHOWRUNNER are Unity GameObjects that have a physical representation in the story world and are distinguished from elements of the virtual set because characters can interact with them.

3. The *character models.* In our current implementation, the characters are human figures, but future implementations may extend our character model set to include horses, fantastical beasts, or other entities with agency. These are represented within the game engine as Unity GameObjects with specific components.
4. The *animations.* Animations capture the movement of the elements of the 3D models of characters or the dynamics of other animated objects.
5. The *animlocations.* Animlocations are specially designated Unity GameObjects that are placed within the virtual set. Each animlocation is associated with one or more animations and designates a physical location and orientation that any character model performing the associated animation must be placed in. These locator objects serve a role similar to location vectors originally used by the Steve virtual agent [9].
6. The *action classes.* Action Classes are C# classes that define the processes for running an individual story action in the story world. Each action class defines a set of methods for checking that the action's preconditions hold in the game world state, performing the animations and game state changes that form the body of the action, and confirming that the action has successfully established its effects in-game. Action class methods are written as co-routines, allowing a form of concurrent execution between actions that are not temporally ordered with respect to one another.
7. The world's *virtual cameras.* Virtual cameras are placed throughout the virtual set and are accessed by the execution manager to provide the visualization of the story world action as it unfolds.
8. The Execution Manager. The SHOWRUNNER Execution Manager is the main control point for the story's execution in Unity. SHOWRUNNER is, in effect, a scheduler responsible for initiating actions for execution and tracking the success/completion of the methods used by each action's action class instance.

Execution Manager. The Execution Manager operates in two phases: Start Up and Running. In the start-up phase, the Execution Manager reads in the input files and first creates a MapDB database that translates from story entity references to SHOWRUNNER -internal object references. Next, it reviews the content of the Initial State Revision file, making any modifications to the game world the file specifies. Finally, it creates a directed acyclic graph (DAG), where each node in the graph is one of the actions listed in the input script. Orderings between nodes are created based on the partial ordering over story actions specified in the script.

Once this execution DAG has been created, the Execution Manager switches to Running Mode. The Execution Manager iterates in Running Mode by (a) checking to see if the DAG is empty, in which case SHOWRUNNER halts, and (b) selecting the minimal elements in the DAG and constructing a method call for each from the action specifics in the node and Unity method names and GameObject references provided via look-up in the MapDB. This method is then invoked with the identified parameters. As the code for each action terminates, the code removes its corresponding node from the DAG.

4   Discussion

SHOWRUNNER provides a useful level of abstraction away from the details of a game engine's coding and operation. SHOWRUNNER is designed to support at least two distinct use cases. One is its use essentially as an off-the-shelf story visualization tool. In this use case, story scripts are built using references just to SHOWRUNNER 's default virtual set, characters and actions. In a power user use case, a user can create new actions by adding new action classes, animations, etc, within the SHOWRUNNER Unity project. The code for the system is available in the project's Gitlab repository [10].

References

1. Cavazza, M., Charles, F., Mead, S.J.: Character-based interactive storytelling. IEEE Intell. Syst. **17**(4), 17–24 (2002)
2. Cavazza, M., Lugrin, J.L., Pizzi, D., Charles, F.: Madame bovary on the holodeck: immersive interactive storytelling. In: Proceedings of the 15th ACM International Conference on Multimedia, pp. 651–660. ACM (2007)
3. Hollywood Camera Work: Causality story sequencer. https://www.hollywoodcamerawork.com/causality.html
4. Kapadia, M., Singh, S., Reinman, G., Faloutsos, P.: A behavior-authoring framework for multiactor simulations. IEEE Comput. Graph. Appl. **31**(6), 45–55 (2011)
5. Laird, J.E.: It knows what you're going to do: adding anticipation to a Quakebot. In: Proceedings of the fifth International Conference on Autonomous Agents, pp. 385–392. ACM (2001)
6. Laird, J.E., Newell, A., Rosenbloom, P.S.: Soar: an architecture for general intelligence. Artif. Intell. **33**(1), 1–64 (1987)
7. Marti, M., et al.: Cardinal: computer assisted authoring of movie scripts. In: 23rd International Conference on Intelligent User Interfaces, pp. 509–519. ACM (2018)
8. Pollack, M.E., Ringuette, M.: Introducing the tileworld: experimentally evaluating agent architectures. AAAI **90**, p183–189 (1990)
9. Rickel, J., Johnson, L.: Integrating pedagogical capabilities in a virtual environment agent. In: Proceedings of the First International Conference on Autonomous Agents, pp. 30–38 (1997)
10. Sanghrajka, R., Young, R.M., Salisbury, B., Lang, E.W.: SHOWRUNNER GitLab Repo. GitLab (2019). https://eae-git.eng.utah.edu/01221789/utahpia2
11. Theune, M., Faas, S., Nijholt, A., Heylen, D.: The virtual storyteller: story creation by intelligent agents. In: Proceedings of the Technologies for Interactive Digital Storytelling and Entertainment (TIDSE) Conference, vol. 204215 (2003)
12. Unity Technologies: Cinemachine. https://learn.unity.com/tutorial/cinemachine
13. Unity Technologies: Unity. https://unity3d.com
14. Young, R.M.: Story and discourse: a bipartite model of narrative generation in virtual worlds. Interact. Stud. **8**(2), 177–208 (2007)

Using VR to Simulate Interactable AR Storytelling

Torbjörn Svensson[✉]

University of Skövde, Skövde, Sweden
torbjorn.svensson@his.se

Abstract. This paper describes a system that simulates location based AR storytelling in a VR environment and explores how VR simulation might be used as a prototyping and user-testing tool. The system is currently developed and used for testing possible future versions of local news distribution with AR devices- However it can be used as a more general tool for testing what, where and how to augment reality in other contexts.

Keywords: VR simulation of AR storytelling · Production pipeline · Prototyping AR content · User testing

1 VR Simulation of Augmented Reality (AR) Storytelling

1.1 Seeing Things That Are Not There!

AR, as a technology, has been around for a number of decades, one of the early uses being the aircraft manufacturer Boeings' 1990s experiments using a head mounted display for "revealing" hidden wiring and plumbing in an aircraft by adding a graphic overlay on the airplanes inner panels [1]. Other early applications of AR technology were driven by military research; for example trying to complement or substitute the Head Up Displays in fighter planes with helmet-mounted displays [2]. In recent years, and not least with the launch of Pokémon Go [3] in 2016, AR has entered many smartphone users' daily lives. Important to note about Pokémon Go however, is that even though it is regularly referred to as an Augmented Reality game, usually it is played with the AR feature (showing Pokémons as overlays on the camera view) turned off because of its excessive energy consumption. A general definition of AR is presented by Bekele et al. [4]; Augmented Reality: aims at enhancing our perception and understanding of the real world by superimposing virtual information on our view of the real world. In their oft-cited study, further modified by others, Milgram and Kishino offer a view of AR, as well as Mixed Reality (MR) and Virtual Reality (VR) as part of a model along a linear spectrum of immersion drawing an interdependent relationship between physical and virtual worlds [5]. Augmenting the real world also offers a possibility to extend and re-locate our digital interactions, from the screen and out into the world around us. In this paper I will suggest using a VR simulation of location based AR storytelling as a pre-production and experimentation tool for production of location-based AR interactions.

R. E. Cardona-Rivera et al. (Eds.): ICIDS 2019, LNCS 11869, pp. 328–332, 2019.
https://doi.org/10.1007/978-3-030-33894-7_33

1.2   Adding VR Simulation to the Production of AR Storytelling Pipeline?

Game studios spend a lot of effort in creating a production sequence that has an effective flow from ideation, via game design, production of the game assets trough to user testing and quality assurance [11–13]. Also smaller independent developers often have a well-functioning production pipeline. There are lessons to be learned from these kinds of production processes applicable to the production of location-based interactive storytelling, not least with a focus on user testing and an iterative development steps.

A simulation tool makes it easier to construct and test interactive location-based storytelling in connection to a real life site, foremost in that one does not have to test every iteration on location, as it can instead be done in the VR environment. This is of course even more valuable if the location for the AR storytelling is remote and hard to get to. Another benefit of using a simulation tool before implementation is being able to test instances of AR storytelling regarding order, content and not least the geo-location of augmented content with groups of users without having to bring equipment and test subjects to the actual location. In this way user testing can be done in a controlled environment with identical conditions between test groups/subjects. One benefit of having the accurate geographic profile of a site right in ones 'office' is also that one can test and decide how to route users and what can be seen from where on the proposed location. The producers can discover what is the natural route to follow, for example, and explore what 'catches the user's eye' at different locations.

The validity of using VR to simulate AR interactions has found merit in experiments by for example Ragan, et al., which were later successfully replicated by Lee, et al. [14, 15].

2   System for VR Simulation of AR Storytelling

2.1   Simulation of Augmented Reality Local News

Originally the VR simulation of AR system that forms the basis of this paper was intended for testing possible ways for presenting local news content to break free from the small screens and limited affordances of handheld devices. In the news simulation, the user move around in a simulated city by walking and using a teleportation system. Users can then "enter into", and interact with, news objects represented by pink spheres. There are a few ways to interact within the news object sphere, where the primary one is to leave a voice comment. By grabbing a virtual microphone, the user activates a speech to text routine and adds a comment in the shape of a comic text bubble. Besides commenting with voice, the user can react with four different emojis (interchangeable to other symbols). The user is of course free to choose the order of story-items to visit. The plans for the next iteration of the system include adding more dynamic reactions to a user's chosen path or time spent in certain story items, to further personalize content. Version 1.0 of the system was evaluated by 8 Master's level students, which led to several key development steps in the current 2.0 version. Features added are for example, a distant preview system that can be used to peek at a story item and see the first lines of the story and how many comments it has gotten from a distance, which is probably a very useful feature in real world location-based AR.

Another advancement is the possibility to select content that seems especially interesting in a list before entering the world. The selected story items are then given a locator beam in the simulation, that guides the user toward the selected items.

Fig. 1. The fully interchangeable map layout of the virtual city used in the VR simulation of AR news service. The story item sphere in the world, and the view from inside a sphere.

2.2 VR Simulation in Production of AR at Cultural Heritage Sites

One other possible use of a VR simulation of interactive AR storytelling is as a pre-production tool for location-based storytelling at cultural heritage sites. Using AR technology at cultural heritage sites is not a new phenomenon and several very technically advanced systems have been tested over time [6, 7]. Before the extensive spread of smart-devices, using AR at heritage sites often entailed using some more or less primitive HMDs (Head Mounted Displays) and customized tracking/positioning system. With the introduction of smart devices it became far easier to handle AR content as accelerometers, cameras for tracking and GPS system for geo-locating were already built in to smart phone systems from the start. What is gained in the simplicity of development with these devices is possibly lost, however, when it comes to immersion and with a user's interaction with virtual content. The smart devices also suffer from a limited field of vision, as the screen sizes are relatively small and the devices are often held at arms length distance from the eyes. Because the HMD see-through technology, where one adds an information layer on the real world visible through the HMD visor or display, is still in its early stages, most of the Cultural Heritage sites that uses AR are doing so via hand held devices (HHD) [4]. In their survey of Augmented, Virtual and Mixed Reality for Cultural Heritage, Bekele et al. categorize handheld AR through a mobile device as at best semi-immersive [4]. To be truly immersive AR content will likely have to be presented in some kind of HMD device and thus stay in the user's field of vision. Today's State of the Art HMDs for AR use have difficulty handling brightly lit and highly dynamic environments. These kinds of limitations can also be incorporated in the VR simulation, but in its current version it simulates an ideal future version of a wearable AR device that can be used outdoors in bright lighting conditions and that works well in dynamic environments such as in inner city traffic or crowded museums/heritage sites. Considering that the technical level of AR in general and at heritage sites in particular are still at relatively early stages, both the research on augmentation independent of the techniques used and the more hands-on testing and evaluation of AR systems looks promising enough to continue development work with AR as a tool to encourage location-based and experiential storytelling for Cultural Heritage sites [8–10]. An increased use of AR in this research suggests a simulation in VR would find its place as a low-cost rapid prototyping tool where more specific and nuanced ideas about what, how and where to augment reality can be tested.

2.3   Future Work and Research

Version 2.0 of the VR simulation of AR storytelling is just finished and will be used in my dissertation work in the Level Up Project (see below) to study users' reactions to a possible AR-based local news service. To be able to better understand the production process for AR in location-based AR application, and how the VR simulation of AR storytelling system can fit in the production cycle, an overview of how the objective production cycle has worked in a group of launched AR projects is valuable. Further, it is interesting to compare those processes to how games or other technically intense storytelling projects are being developed, not least to find out what, if any, role could be played by VR simulations of AR.

Acknowledgements. The production of the VR simulation of AR is a joint effort of the Level Up project which is focused on new ways to deliver local news to young readers, (funded by the Ann-Marie and Gustaf Ander Foundation for Media Research) and the MTEC (Media, Technology and Culture) Research Group, led by Assoc. Prof. Lissa Holloway-Attaway, at the Department for Game Development at the University of Skövde, Sweden. Programmers in the project were Etienne Beroldy, Bastien Chupin and Damien Chevaleri, students of Polytech Nantes, France, during their internships at University of Skövde.

References

1. Caudell, T.P., Mizell, D.W.: Augmented reality: an application of heads-up display technology to manual manufacturing processes. In: Proceedings of the Twenty-Fifth Hawaii International Conference on System Sciences. IEEE (1992)
2. Newman, R.L., Haworth, L.A.: Helmet-mounted display requirements: just another head-up display (HUD) or a different animal altogether? In: SPIE's International Symposium on Optical Engineering and Photonics in Aerospace Sensing, SPIE, vol. 2218 (1994)
3. Niantic, Pokémon Go. Niantic. p. Game for mobile platforms that lets you capture and train Pokémons (2016)

4. Bekele, M.K., et al.: A survey of augmented, virtual, and mixed reality for cultural heritage. J. Comput. Cult. Herit. (JOCCH) **11**(2), 7 (2018)
5. Milgram, P., Kishino, F.: A taxonomy of mixed reality visual displays. IEICE Trans. Inf. Syst. **77**(12), 1321–1329 (1994)
6. Noh, Z., Sunar, M.S., Pan, Z.: A review on augmented reality for virtual heritage system. Springer, Berlin (2009). https://doi.org/10.1007/978-3-642-03364-3_7
7. Angelopoulou, A., et al.: Mobile Augmented Reality for Cultural Heritage. In: Venkatasubramanian, N., Getov, V., Steglich, S. (eds.) MOBILWARE 2011. LNICST, vol. 93, pp. 15–22. Springer, Heidelberg (2012). https://doi.org/10.1007/978-3-642-30607-5_2
8. Manovich, L.: The poetics of augmented space. Vis. Commun. **5**(2), 219–240 (2006)
9. Chang, K.-E., et al.: Development and behavioral pattern analysis of a mobile guide system with augmented reality for painting appreciation instruction in an art museum. Comput. Educ. **71**, 185–197 (2014)
10. Clini, P., et al.: Augmented reality experience: from high-resolution acquisition to real time augmented contents. Adv. Multimedia **2014**, 18 (2014)
11. Chandler, H.M.: The Game Production Handbook. Jones & Bartlett Publishers, Burlington (2009)
12. Zoeller, G.: Game development telemetry in production. In: Game Analytics, pp. 111–135. Springer, London (2013). https://doi.org/10.1007/978-1-4471-4769-5_7
13. Dunlop, R.: Production Pipeline Fundamentals for Film and Games. Routledge, Abingdon (2014)
14. Ragan, E., et al.: Simulation of augmented reality systems in purely virtual environments. In: 2009 IEEE Virtual Reality Conference VR 2009. IEEE (2009)
15. Lee, C., et al.: A replication study testing the validity of AR simulation in VR for controlled experiments. In: 2009 8th IEEE International Symposium on Mixed and Augmented Reality (ISMAR). IEEE (2009)

Firebolt: A System for Automated Low-Level Cinematic Narrative Realization

Brandon R. Thorne[1], David R. Winer[2], Camille Barot[3],
and R. Michael Young[2]([✉])

[1] North Carolina State University, Raleigh, NC, USA
brthorne@ncsu.edu
[2] University of Utah, Salt Lake City, UT, USA
drwiner@cs.utah.edu, young@eae.utah.edu
[3] Raleigh, NC, USA
camille.barot@gmail.com

Abstract. Creation of machine generated cinematics currently requires a significant amount of human author time or manually coding domain operators such that they may be realized by a rendering system. We present FireBolt, an automated cinematic realization system based on a declarative knowledge representation that supports both human and machine authoring of cinematics with reduced authorship and engineering task loads.

Keywords: Intelligent cinematography · Machinima · Tools and systems

1 Introduction

Machinima is a burgeoning field within cinematography, expanding from in-game replays to pre-rendered cinematics in recent years. To support their customers, game studios and other software vendors have created increasingly expressive tools for using game engine technology to orchestrate and render scenes. These cinematic sequencers, such as Valve's Source Filmmaker [19], offer a rich graphical user interface for the construction of virtual scenes, coordination of the actions of virtual actors, and control of virtual cameras used to film the scene. Because all aspects of the production a cinematic – timing, animation, and filming – require human specification and authoring, using these cinematic sequencers is a labor intensive process, potentially requiring many hours of a user's time to be spent in the generation of a single minute of rendered cinematic.

One limitation of typical cinematic sequencers is a design that requires a user to specify low-level details of all story action and camera shot specifications. From a narrative theoretic perspective, a user must specify all aspects of both story and discourse [6], where story consists of the events of a narrative and all

R. E. Cardona-Rivera et al. (Eds.): ICIDS 2019, LNCS 11869, pp. 333–342, 2019.
https://doi.org/10.1007/978-3-030-33894-7_34

the settings, objects and characters involved in their occurrence, and discourse consists of all medium-specific resources used to convey story elements to a viewer. In the approach of conventional cinematic sequencers, story and discourse are conflated, as the user must work to manage their own design in the filming environment. Further, every aspect of story-world behavior must be provided by hand. Similarly, every aspect of the shots that film the world must also be specified by a human.

In contrast, we present a cinematic sequencer that provides an API and uses a well-defined declarative approach to the specification of cinematic narrative that allows systems to decouple the means of production of a sequence from the realization of the sequence. We also design our API to support a range of use cases, including (a) human-driven tools that support lower expertise levels than other approaches, and (b) the potential for integration with intelligent story and discourse generation tools, to support both automatic production and mixed-initiative interaction. The work presented here is motivated by the lack of declaratively driven realization/rendering engines. We wish to enable authors to easily script story and camera sequences without writing custom code for the rendering engine. A declarative representation that parses the story world and setting from the plan of narration would benefit narrative systems with different underlying structural representation of story, and enables reuse of authored content.

2   Related Work

We will review four categories of research related to the work presented here. First, there are narrative generation systems whose rendering capabilities are tightly coupled to those of generation [11,15,17]. Though the thrust of these works is on the determination of content and organization for cinematics, because there was no suitable system available for rendering at the time these tools were built, each employs custom code for rendering. Second, there is a class of systems focusing on geometric camera placement [8]. There are a host of issues addressed in this area of the literature from simple camera placement and target acquisition [5] to computational application of compositional techniques [1]. Our system incorporates simple and serviceable placement techniques in favor of real-time rendering but allows for future extension into more intricate placement algorithms. Third, there are a number of systems supporting cinematography-friendly declarative representation (e.g., [3,7,13]). This declarative format will benefit development of training tools for cinematography, allowing users to easily employ visual techniques recommended by such studies as [18]. Experimental design will benefit from a concisely expressive way to analyze existing films which can then be recapitulated in a controlled manner for testing the effects of film editing on comprehension. Finally, there are works which attempt to provide computationally-amenable representations for narrative-based filmmaking such as [14] and MSML [20], whose EventSync architecture we incorporate here.

3   The FireBolt System

The FireBolt System is a fully scriptable cinematic realization system for rendering cinematic visualization in a virtual environment. The system receives input data from a set of declarative representations specifying (1) available actor/object models and animations, (2) a story consisting of actor/object positioning and animations to play at specific time points, and (3) a camera plan consisting of camera shots described using cinematography-based properties and actors/objects in the story.

FireBolt's *Cinematic Model* is a declarative representation for specifying two major narrative units for cinematic generation: actors and domain actions.

3.1   Actors

FireBolt distinguishes an *actor*, which is a role in a story, from a *character model* which is a specific asset used to render the character, including the character's skeleton, mesh, textures, body motions, face, etc. The Cinematic Model is the declarative specifications for the mappings between actor names and character models.

An animation describes a file and a set of animation indices (i.e. temporal offsets relative to the beginning of the clip that are notable time points in the animation). When defining operations to perform in FireBolt when a particular story action has occurred, multiple operations may be coordinated in time using the animation indices. This coordination strategy is similar to that used in the EventSync model in MovieScript Markup Language [20].

Definition 1 (Timepoint). *A timepoint is a whole number corresponding to a time in milliseconds.*

Definition 2 (Animation Indices). *An animation·index is a tuple $\langle \lambda, \omega \rangle$ where λ is an index label and ω is a timepoint.*

Definition 3 (Animation Clip). *An animation is a tuple $\langle \eta, \Lambda \rangle$ where η is a file containing an animation trace, and Λ is a set of animation indices.*

Definition 4 (Animation Mapping). *An animation mapping is a tuple $\langle \nu, \kappa \rangle$ where ν is a label and κ is an animation clip.*

Definition 5 (Actor). *An actor is a tuple $\langle n, h, \zeta \rangle$ where n is an actor name (used in the story), h is a character model, and ζ is a set of animation mappings.*

Domain Operator. A domain operator is a template of behavior for driving an actor in a virtual world in a time-sensitive manner. Domain actions are used by the story to easily chunk the story into meaningful units, similar to STRIPS style operators [12] but without commitments to preconditions and effects.

Each domain action consists of a set of parameters (e.g. variables for actors and locations), a set of animations for an actor with relevant temporal offsets, and a set of engine-based mechanics such as creating, deleting, rotating, and translating objects/actors in the virtual world.

Definition 6 (Engine Action). *An engine-action is a predicate with n-ary terms describing a temporally indexed instruction for the virtual environment engine. It is a tuple $\langle \alpha, \upsilon, \circ \rangle$ where α is an actor, υ is an instruction for α and $\circ$ is an animation index specifying temporal parameters for υ.*

Definition 7 (Animation Action). *An animation-action is a tuple $\langle \alpha, k, \circ \rangle$ where $\alpha = \langle n, h, \langle \nu, \langle \eta, \Lambda \rangle \rangle \rangle$ is an actor, $k \in \nu$ is an animation clip label, and $\circ \in \Lambda$ is an animation index.*

Definition 8 (Domain Action). *A domain action is a tuple $\langle P, A, E \rangle$ where P is a set of parameters, A is a set of animation-actions, and E is a set of engine-actions.*

Definition 9 (Cinematic Model). *A cinematic model is a tuple $\langle C, A \rangle$ where C is a set of characters and A is a set of domain actions.*

4   Story

The declarative representation of story is expressed in Impulse [10], a formal language for narrative. Impulse augments a STRIPS-style plan representation [12] with the ability to reason over temporal intervals [2] and model a BDI agent architecture [9].

The story is divided into actions that drive the actors and objects in a time-sensitive manner. Though Impulse is capable of representing intervals of arbitrary types, FireBolt makes the restriction that interval endpoints be defined in whole numbers. This allows FireBolt to make judgments about the implicit relations of time intervals whose endpoint specifications are not identical. The templates for these actions are described below.

Definition 10 (Story Action). *A story action is a tuple $\langle D, V, \tau \rangle$ where $D = \langle P, A, E \rangle$ is a domain operator, V is a set of values for parameters in P, and $\tau = [s, e]$ is an interval bounded by two timepoints s, e such that $s < e$.*

Definition 11 (Story Timeline). *The story timeline is a function $T_s : K \mapsto A$ mapping timepoints in K to sets of actions containing the animation-actions and engine-actions to initialize or update at the timepoint.*

Definition 12 (Story Model). *The story model is a tuple $\langle T_s, A_S \rangle$ where T_s is a story timeline and A_S is a set of story actions.*

5   Camera Plan

The declarative representation of the camera shots adopts a novel cinematography-friendly shot-description language, *Oshmirto Shot Fragment Language* (OSFL), to specify an expressive but concise array of properties for a shot. The Camera Model packages OSFL descriptions into the discourse structure by defining a total-ordering of shots and their durations, including what story time they should film over.

5.1 Shot Representation

A single shot in cinematography is defined as the film from one cut to the next [4]. However, the camera may take several movements at different times throughout a shot. We wish to both enable a continuation of one movement as well as the initiation of a different movement during a shot. To capture this, we incorporate the notion of a *shot fragment* [7], a temporal interval of a shot in which cinematographic properties are defined. No two shot fragments in the same shot can be overlapping. FireBolt will attempt to film two consecutive shot fragments defined within the same shot without moving the camera between the end of the first and the beginning of the second. If there is only one shot fragment, then that shot fragment constitutes an entire shot.

Algorithm 1. Parse Impulse in Story Model to Timeline T_S

1: **for** each $s_A = \langle D = \langle P, A, E \rangle, V, \tau = [s,e] \rangle$ **do**
2:     **for** each timepoint i in T_s from s to e **do**
3:         **for** each $a_a = \langle \alpha, k, \langle \lambda, \omega \rangle \rangle \in A$ **do**
4:             **if** $s + \omega \le i < e$ **then**
5:                 Let $T_s[i] = T_s[i] \cup \{a_a\}$
6:             **end if**
7:         **end for**
8:         **for** each $e_a = \langle \alpha, v, \langle \lambda, \omega \rangle \rangle \in E$ **do**
9:             **if** $s + \omega \le i < e$ **then**
10:                 Let $T_s[i] = T_s[i] \cup \{e_a\}$
11:             **end if**
12:         **end for**
13:     **end for**
14: **end for**

5.2 Oshmirto Label Specifications

OSFL utilizes a number of label types to convey which of a set of enumerated values each property of camera control is assigned in a given shot fragment. The table below lists the values for each label type. The operationalization for each label type is discussed subsequently.

Additionally, each actor/object in the virtual world, including the camera, has a three dimensional vector corresponding to its position and a three dimensional vector corresponding to its orientation. In some cases, we define the labels in terms of coordinate axes for the sake of expedience. These definitions are relative to a left-handed, y-up, three dimensional Cartesian coordinate system.

Camera Angle : Θ. A camera angle refers to the angle of inclination of the camera on its x axis. Generally the camera is also translated along the y axis relative to the subject in order to acquire the subject in frame. A medium angle indicates that the camera is at the same height of the actor, with no tilt to the camera. A high angle indicates a 30° downward angle of the camera oriented towards the actor. A low angle indicates a 30° angle upward angle of the camera.

Framing : $\mathcal{F}$. Each actor has a bounding volume about its location that represents an upper bound on the volume occluded by that actor.

Definition 13 *Bounding volume A bounding volume b is a polyhedron which circumscribes an actor.*

The framing of an actor indicates a range of acceptable proportions of the height of the bounding volume, b_h, to the height of the screen viewport, v_h.

Direction : $\mathcal{D}$. Direction indicates a range of positions about an actor within which the camera must be placed. This range is based upon the orientation of the actor about the y axis. We enumerate four such ranges: toward, left, right, and away. In effect, the direction specifies the facing of the actor in viewport.

Movement : $\mathcal{M}$. Whenever a change of camera attributes is required during an exposure, a set of movements is used to describe that change. They are *dolly* (translate the camera in the x-z plane), *crane* (translate the camera along the y axis), *pan* (rotate the camera about the y axis), *tilt* (rotate the camera about the x axis), and *focus* (set distance at which the camera should focus).

Directive : $\mathcal{X}$. Each movement is associated with a directive, to either move *to* a position, or to move *with* some actor that may be moving in the world. The *to* directive indicates that the argument associated with the movement should be treated as an absolute position or rotation value in world coordinates. For a *pan* movement and a *to* directive, this means that the supplied argument is a heading given by a number of degrees about the y axis. For a *dolly* movement and a *to* directive, the supplied argument is treated as a position where the camera should be at the end of the movement.

The *with* directive indicates that the argument associated with the movement is an object with which the camera should maintain a static relationship. For a *pan* movement using a *with* directive, the camera should rotate about the y axis to keep the argument framed. For a *dolly* movement using a *with* directive, the camera should translate on the x-z plane so that it maintains a fixed distance to the given argument.

Focal Length : $\mathcal{L}$ Focal length is a measure of the optical power of a lens, that is, the distance over which parallel light rays converge as they are brought into focus within the lens. There are several effects of this natural phenomenon, two of which we operationalize in FireBolt. First the focal length affects the expansiveness of the view through the lens. We model this directly as the vertical field of view angle (VFoV) on our virtual camera and use a table of equivalences to relate vertical field of view to commonly available lens focal lengths. Second, the focal length affects the rate at which objects not at the point of focus lose the appearance of focus. This is closely related to aperture, and the calculations are described below.

Aperture : $\mathcal{A}$. Aperture refers to the space through which light enters the camera, which affects both the circle of confusion, used to determine the depth of field (DOF), and luminance of the image. We adopt the canonical f-number aperture labels, but currently only support the DOF effects associated with aperture.

Several optional specifications can be made about a shot fragment. These specifications are formally defined, building up to a formal definition of a shot.

Definition 14 (Duration). *A shot fragment duration is a timepoint specifying the amount of story time over which to map the image captured by a virtual camera to the viewport. It is a pair (s, e) where s, e are timepoints and $s < e$.*

Definition 15 (Anchor). *An anchor is a position derived from the location of actor dictating an exact world position to place the camera.*

Definition 16 (Angle). *An angle is a tuple $\langle \theta, \alpha \rangle \mid \theta \in \Theta$ and α is an actor*

Definition 17 (Direction). *A direction is a tuple $\langle d, \alpha \rangle \mid d \in \mathcal{D}$ and α is an actor*

Definition 18 (Framing). *A framing is a tuple $\langle f, \alpha \rangle \mid f \in \mathcal{F}$ and α is an actor*

Definition 19 (Static Specification). *A static specification is a grouping of properties defining the positioning of a camera, relative to subjects, at an unspecified timepoint. It is a tuple $\langle c, \beta, \times, \Upsilon \rangle$ where c is an anchor, β is an angle, $\times$ is a direction, and Υ is a set of framings with unique actors.*

The actor specifications in anchors, directions, and framings may all take unique actors as arguments; however, no two framings can be made on the same actor.

Definition 20 (Movement Specifications). *A movement specification defines an axis with which to translate or rotate the camera, a directive for the movement's target location, and a subject that specifies the target. It is a tuple $\langle \mu, x, \alpha \rangle$ where $\mu \in \mathcal{M}$, $x \in \chi$, and α is an actor.*

Definition 21 (Depth of Field). *A depth of field is a tuple $\langle a, \alpha \rangle \mid a \in \mathcal{A}$ and α is an actor.*

Definition 22 (Shot Fragment). *A shot fragment is a tuple $\langle \psi, \Phi, \pi, \ell, \Delta \rangle$ where ψ is a static specification, Φ is a set of movement specifications, π is a depth of field, $\ell \in \mathcal{L}$ is a focal length, and Δ is a duration.*

Definition 23 (Shot). *A shot is a tuple $\langle s, R, \aleph \rangle$ where s is a story time, R is set of shot fragments, and $\aleph$ is a bijection function $\aleph : R \mapsto [1...n] \in \mathbb{N}$ such that $n = |R|$.*

For $r_1, r_2 \in R$, if $\aleph(r_1) = \aleph(r_2) - 1$, then r_1 is filmed immediately before fragment r_2.

Definition 24 (Camera Plan). *A camera plan is a tuple $\langle \mathcal{S}, \Gamma \rangle$ where $\mathcal{S}$ is a set of shots, and Γ is a bijection function $\Gamma : \mathcal{S} \mapsto [1...n] \in \mathbb{N}$ such that $n = |\mathcal{S}|$.*

For $s_1, s_2 \in \mathcal{S}$ if $\Gamma(s_1) = \Gamma(s_2) - 1$, then s_1 is filmed immediately before s_2.

6   Execution

In keeping with the adopted bipartite view of narrative, execution of a set of inputs in FireBolt is performed in two phases: sequencing story actions and filming them. In narratological terms, the sequenced story actions form the story and the filming creates a discourse. Algorithm 1 describes the process for sequencing the story into a form that is executable in the virtual environment. Algorithm 2 describes the process for placing the camera in the virtual world relative to the provided Oshmirto instructions and the story actions to which they relate. The result is a real-time rendered visualization of the specified story through the supplied camera view.

Algorithm 1 begins by iterating over all of the story actions s_A. At each timepoint i in the story timeline T_s which falls between the start and end times $\tau = [s, e]$ of the story action, the animation and engine actions are appended to the set of actions to be invoked at i. The inclusion of the animation and engine actions for a given i is also dependent upon any animation index $\langle \lambda, \omega \rangle$ that may be associated with beginning that action $s + \omega \leq i$, meaning that if this action with its "normal start time", s, and its offset amount, ω, should already have begun by timepoint i, then add the action to the actions that should be executed at i $(T_s[i] \cup a)$.

Algorithm 2. FireBolt Oshmirto Execution Algorithm

1: **for** each $\langle s, R, \aleph \rangle$ in $\Gamma(\mathcal{S})$ of Camera Plan $\langle \mathcal{S}, \Gamma \rangle$ **do**
2:     Let $\delta = s$
3:     **for** each $r = \langle \psi, \Phi, \pi, \ell, \Delta \rangle$ in $\aleph(R)$ **do**
4:         **for** each i in T_s from δ to $\delta + \Delta$ **do**
5:             **for** each $a = \langle \alpha, \diamond, \circ \rangle \in T_s[i]$ **do** update a
6:             **end for**
7:             **if** $i = \delta$ **then** execute ψ
8:             **else** update all $\phi \in \Phi$
9:             **end if**
10:         **end for**
11:         Let $\delta \mathrel{+}= \Delta$
12:         Apply intra-shot transition rules
13:     **end for**
14:     Inter-shot transition rules
15: **end for**

In Algorithm 2 we iterate over each shot $\langle s, R, \aleph \rangle$ in the order given by $\Gamma(S)$ in the camera plan $\langle S, \Gamma \rangle$. For each of the shots, we set the current story time in the virtual world δ to the story time indicated for the beginning of the shot filming. This causes the story world to be updated to the state effected by the story actions of $T_s[\delta]$. Then for each fragment r in the ordering of shot fragments within the begun shot $\aleph(R)$, step along the timeline $T_s[i]$ from the current story time δ until the end of the shot fragment duration $\delta + \Delta$ is reached. Within each step, update all the story actions within $T_s[i]$, then if this is the first timepoint wherein r is executed, realize the static constraints ψ described in r, otherwise update the movements Φ in r. Once the shot fragment is completed $i = \delta + \Delta$, we move δ to point at the beginning of the next shot fragment. At this point we apply intra-shot transition rules, such as not allowing a new position to be calculated for the camera. Once all the fragments in a given shot have been executed, we move on to the next shot in $\Gamma(S)$ and apply higher level, inter-shot rules such as the 180° rule [16].

7 Summary and Potential Future Work

FireBolt is a declaratively-driven cinematic sequencer employing a bipartite model of narrative to inform its execution. It is suitable for use as a rendering system for a range of machinima-producing enterprises from fully generative narrative systems to direct human authorship. In these contexts, FireBolt supports real-time cinematic render performance using commodity hardware.

References

1. Abdullah, R., Christie, M., Schofield, G., Lino, C., Olivier, P.: Advanced composition in virtual camera control. In: Dickmann, L., Volkmann, G., Malaka, R., Boll, S., Krüger, A., Olivier, P. (eds.) SG 2011. LNCS, vol. 6815, pp. 13–24. Springer, Heidelberg (2011). https://doi.org/10.1007/978-3-642-22571-0_2
2. Allen, J.F., Ferguson, G.: Actions and events in interval temporal logic. J. Logic Comput. **4**(5), 531–579 (1994)
3. Amerson, D., Kime, S., Young, R.M.: Cinematic camera control for interactive narratives. In: Proceedings of the ACM International Conference on Advances in Computer Entertainment, pp. 365–370 (2005)
4. Arijon, D.: Grammar of the Film Language. Focal Press, London (1976)
5. Blinn, J.: Where am i? What am i looking at? (cinematography). IEEE Comput. Graph. Appl. **8**(4), 76–81 (1988)
6. Chatman, S.B.: Story and Discourse: Narrative Structure in Fiction and Film. Cornell University Press, Ithaca (1980)
7. Christianson, D.B., Anderson, S.E., He, L.W., Salesin, D.H., Weld, D.S., Cohen, M.F.: Declarative camera control for automatic cinematography. In: Proceedings of the American Association for Artificial Intelligent, pp. 148–155 (1996)
8. Christie, M., Machap, R., Normand, J.-M., Olivier, P., Pickering, J.: Virtual camera planning: a survey. In: Butz, A., Fisher, B., Krüger, A., Olivier, P. (eds.) SG 2005. LNCS, vol. 3638, pp. 40–52. Springer, Heidelberg (2005). https://doi.org/10.1007/11536482_4
9. Cohen, P.R., Levesque, H.J.: Intention is choice with commitment. Artif. Intell. **42**(2), 213–261 (1990)
10. Eger, M., Barot, C., Young, R.M.: Impulse: a formal characterization of story. In: The Sixth Workshop on Computational Models of Narrative, pp. 45–53 (2015)
11. Elson, D.K., Riedl, M.O.: A lightweight intelligent virtual cinematography system for machinima production. In: Proceedings of the International Conference on AI and Interactive Digital Entertainment, pp. 8–13 (2007)

12. Fikes, R.E., Nilsson, N.J.: STRIPS: a new approach to the application of theorem proving to problem solving. Artif. Intell. **2**(3), 189–208 (1972)
13. Halper, N., Olivier, P.: CamPlan: a camera planning agent. In: Smart Graphics 2000 AAAI Spring Symposium, pp. 92–100 (2000)
14. Jhala, A.: Exploiting structure and conventions of movie scripts for information retrieval and text mining. In: Spierling, U., Szilas, N. (eds.) ICIDS 2008. LNCS, vol. 5334, pp. 210–213. Springer, Heidelberg (2008). https://doi.org/10.1007/978-3-540-89454-4_27
15. Jhala, A., Young, R.M.: Cinematic visual discourse: representation, generation, and evaluation. IEEE Trans. Comput. Intell. AI Games **2**(2), 69–81 (2010)
16. Monaco, J.: How to Read a Film: Movies. Oxford University Press, Cambridge (2009). Media and Beyond
17. Porteous, J., Cavazza, M., Charles, F.: Applying planning to interactive storytelling: narrative control using state constraints. ACM Trans. Intell. Syst. Technol. **1**(2), 10:1–10:21 (2010). https://doi.org/10.1145/1869397.1869399
18. Swanson, R., Escoffery, D., Jhala, A.: Learning visual composition preferences from an annotated corpus generated through gameplay. In: IEEE Conference on Computational Intelligence and Games (CIG), pp. 363–370. IEEE (2012)
19. Valve Software: Source FilmMaker (2000–2017). http://www.sourcefilmmaker.com/
20. Van Rijsselbergen, D., Van De Keer, B., Verwaest, M., Mannens, E., Van de Walle, R.: Movie script markup language. In: Proceedings of the 9th ACM Symposium on Document Engineering, pp. 161–170. ACM (2009)

Interactive Narrative Generation Using Location and Genre Specific Context

Jon Womack(ID) and William Freeman(⊠)(ID)

Georgia Institute of Technology, Atlanta, GA 30332, USA
{jwomack30, freemanw7}@gatech.edu

Abstract. In this paper, we present a novel method of creating interactive narratives. Location-based narrative sentences are mapped to their real-world location using GPS. A corpus of genre-based sentences is aggregated to train a neural network. New narratives are created by selecting a sentence from the network's "Sentence Space" that corresponds to contextual information from the user's physical location. Each narrative is explored using GPS location tracking and WebGL based augmented reality in mobile web browsers.

Keywords: Augmented Reality · AR cloud · Machine learning · Locative narrative · Sentence Space

1 Introduction

The pervasiveness of geolocation in mobile devices has led to a wealth of technologies capable of associating interactive content with locations in the real world. Augmented reality (AR) has emerged as a potential medium for presenting digital content. Interactive narrative applications are starting to explore AR's effectiveness as narrative medium experienced over multiple locations [1–3, 13, 16]. Most narrative AR applications are anchored to objects at one location or within one environment. Most AR narratives are not read while moving between multiple locations. The concept of how a distributed narrative works across multiple locations and the poetics of narratives which rely on contextual data in the real world is an active area of research for digital narratives [4, 7, 14]. We approach narrative generation from several perspectives which relate to poetics in the form of genre and semantics as well as location-based context.

The literary theory supporting our approach is that narratives which occur across space have a different structure than narratives tied to a singular location, which usually require less context to anchor them to the real world [4–7]. We believe these narrative structures most often resemble the traditional hero's journey trope, but they may contain other narrative structures and tropes. Second, because the narrative structure is anchored to various locations it becomes difficult to ensure the content of the narrative and the reader's location context match each other. Our approach involves parsing narrative nodes with location context and uses machine learning to compare those nodes to a database of genre specific narratives. Words, phrases and sentences with local context can be transposed to a genre specific equivalent. This location-genre driven perspective on narratology allows us to isolate and address genre and

R. E. Cardona-Rivera et al. (Eds.): ICIDS 2019, LNCS 11869, pp. 343–347, 2019.
https://doi.org/10.1007/978-3-030-33894-7_35

location-based narrative structures independently. Given a large body of user generated location content, genre specific narratives can be generated to contextually match a dynamic narrative to multiple real-world locations.

Each narrative could be read by walking between the location nodes of the story which are displayed in a browser using a mobile device's GPS sensor. This database of narrative nodes serves as a repository of prototypical location-based narratives. These 'prototypes' provide contextual meaning related to their locations as well as story arc examples designed to be experienced over multiple locations. Once narratives exist in the database for a given set of locations, they provide a sandbox of story elements connected to their respective locations. From these elements we can parse for local contextual data, and syntactic structures; each of these provides information for remapping location sentences to genre sentences. We created a tool which uses context from location-based story nodes and generates a genre specific narrative, both of which are relevant to the user's current location. We named the tool StoryRemapper (Fig. 1).

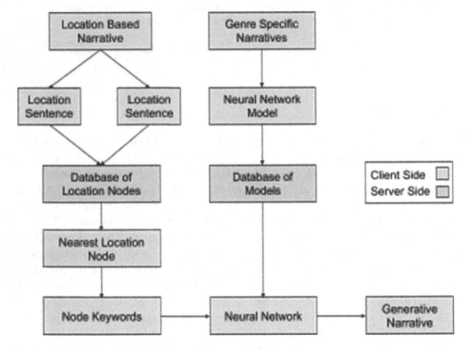

Fig. 1. Graphic illustrating the flow of data used by StoryRemapperto create new narratives.

2   StoryRemapper

2.1   StoryRemapper Overview

While there has been extensive research on creating interactive narratives with computers, our story generation is dependent on location specific information mapped to previously existing genre narratives [10–12]. These narratives could be stories written about specific locations like 'Little Red Riding Hood' and James Joyce's 'Ulysses'. They could even come from alternative sources such as guided tours, heritage sites, or other location-based content. The critical attribute for these narrative sources is that their structure and content maps to some path through multiple real-world locations or fictional scenes similar to the user's current location. Once an archive of local information is established, it is possible to generate narratives that are customized to a reader's location.

When a user walks to a real-world location, StoryRemapper finds the sentence nearest to their current location, and parses it for keywords. Those keywords are then used as inputs to a machine learning model that was trained to match keyword inputs with genre specific sentence outputs. We use location information to search a latent sentence space for the most relevant sentence.

2.2   The Sentence Space

A simple way of representing a sentence mathematically is by recording word frequency [8]. For example, the phrase "To be or not to be" would be represented as: "to": 2, "be": 2, "not": 1, "or": 1. Each word having its own dimension. Every sentence with different frequencies of words has a unique position in what we call the "Sentence Space". This reductionist model applied to language leaves out important information contained in punctuation and the ordering of words. However, punctuation and ordering could be included as extra dimensions. With word frequency, punctuation, and word ordering represented in separate dimensions, most of the information in a sentence is represented within the Sentence Space.

This model could be used to represent the set, S, of all possible sentences. However, such a set is too large to store and navigate easily. To reduce the size of our Sentence Space, we include only sentences with unique meanings. The set S is vastly greater than the set of sentences with unique meanings, S'. Additionally, removing sentences from S can integrate theme, genre, and tone into generated stories [15]. We choose sentences only from specific genres for narrative generation. Genres, like locations, contain special context related to the narrative's setting. By limiting the subset of sentences to genre, we avoid training the machine learning model on sentences that would not match a location's context.

We trained separate neural networks for each genre. The purpose of separating the neural networks was for each network to represent a subspace of the Sentence Space containing sentences related to a specific genre. We trained these networks to associate keywords with sentences. The sentences were sourced from narratives of the genre associated with their respective network. Having a separate network for each genre makes narrative generation genre specific, as the possible output sentences can only be of the network's genre. This type of reduction in training data imposes bias on the networks output. This biased output can be considered a feature and a flaw depending on the location it is mapped to.

2.3 Passing Local Information

In order to start the process, a user's location is determined by GPS. The GPS coordinates are used to find a local sentence written about that location using a location narrative authoring tool called StoryTracker. Our model parses the local sentence for keywords. Parsing the keywords from the sentence closest to the user retains the local context. The network's output is a sentence which most closely matches the location-based sentence's Sentence Space. This output would contain genre information matched to local information. Different genres may have problems in how they remap to the user's location. However, if the genre location and user location context are ill fitted, we can create functions which semantically filter narrative options for better context matching.

3 Conclusions and Future Work

Our work on this problem illustrates that locations contain meaning which can be translated into metadata. The mining and manipulation of this data can be a rich playground for creative applications in the fields of interactive narrative and digital media. In the near future, it may be possible to create an AR Cloud infrastructure of digital metadata about locations worldwide. This cloud of information would enable users to explore and experience the world through the lens of their own preferences and interests. We believe the ability to construct narratives from location-based metadata and remap the context of that data to new media is one possible application for this type of infrastructure.

We break the work that can be done to improve the process down into the following areas of improvement:

- Deriving sentence meaning from more than just keywords i.e. sentiment, punctuation.
- Generating narratives from a sentence-event level model that considers past sentences and previous story information at a higher level of abstraction [12].
- Adding reinforcement learning to neural networks to account for location context that is not represented in the sentence space.
- Processing the images used in AR to gather more scene context using real-time Semantic Segmentation models [9].

References

1. MacIntyre, B., Bolter, J.D., Moreno, E., Hannigan, B.: Augmented reality as a new media experience. In: Proceedings IEEE and ACM International Symposium on Augmented Reality 2001, pp. 197–206. IEEE, New York (2001)
2. MacIntyre, B., et al.: Three angry men: Dramatizing point-of-view using augmented reality. In: ACM SIGGRAPH 2002, San Antonio, TX, pp. 21–26 (2002)
3. Dow, S., Lee, J., Oezbek, C., MacIntyre, B., Bolter, J.D., Gandy, M.: Exploring spatial narratives and mixed reality experiences in Oakland Cemetery. In: Proceedings of the 2005

ACM SIGCHI International Conference on Advances in computer entertainment technology (ACE 2005), pp. 51–60. ACM, New York (2005)

4. Azuma, R.: Location-based mixed and augmented reality storytelling. In: Barfield, W. (ed.) Fundamentals of wearable computers and augmented reality, 2nd edn, pp. 259–276. CRC Press, Boca Raton, FL (2015)
5. Millard, D.E., Hargood, C.: Location location location: experiences of authoring an interactive location-based narrative. In: Nack, F., Gordon, A.S. (eds.) ICIDS 2016. LNCS, vol. 10045, pp. 419–422. Springer, Cham (2016). https://doi.org/10.1007/978-3-319-48279-8_40
6. Kampa, A.: Ulrike spierling: smart authoring for location-based augmented reality storytelling applications. GI-Jahrestagung (2017)
7. Gustafsson, A., Bichard, J., Brunnberg, L., Juhlin, O., Combetto, M.: Believable environments: generating interactive storytelling in vast location-based pervasive games. In: Proceedings of the 2006 ACM SIGCHI international conference on Advances in computer entertainment technology (ACE 2006), Article 24. ACM, New York (2006)
8. Mu, J., Bhat, S., Viswanath, P.: Representing sentences as low-rank subspaces. In: Proceedings of the 55th Annual Meeting of the Association for Computational Linguistics, vol. 2 Short Papers, pp. 629–634. ACL, Vancouver (2017)
9. Zhang, H., et al.: Context Encoding for Semantic Segmentation. In: 2018 IEEE/CVF Conference on Computer Vision and Pattern Recognition, pp. 7151–7160 (2018)
10. Mateas, M., Stern, A.: Structuring content in the façade interactive drama architecture. In: proceedings of the First AAAI Conference on Artificial Intelligence and Interactive Digital Entertainment, pp. 93–98. AAAI Press, Marina del Rey (2005)
11. Riedl, M.O.: Computational narrative intelligence: a human-centered goal for artificial intelligence. ArXiv (2016)
12. Martin, L.J., et al.: Event representations for automated story generation with deep neural nets. AAAI (2018)
13. Spawforth, C., Millard, D.E.: A framework for multi-participant narratives based on multiplayer game interactions. In: Nunes, N., Oakley, I., Nisi, V. (eds.) ICIDS 2017. LNCS, vol. 10690, pp. 150–162. Springer, Cham (2017). https://doi.org/10.1007/978-3-319-71027-3_13
14. Packer, H.S., Hargood, C., Howard, Y., Papadopoulos, P., Millard, D.E.: Developing a writer's toolkit for interactive locative storytelling. In: Nunes, N., Oakley, I., Nisi, V. (eds.) ICIDS 2017. LNCS, vol. 10690, pp. 63–74. Springer, Cham (2017). https://doi.org/10.1007/978-3-319-71027-3_6
15. Hargood, C., Millard, D., Weal, M.J.: A thematic approach to emerging narrative structure. In: Proceedings of the hypertext 2008 workshop on Collaboration and collective intelligence (WebScience 2008), pp. 41–45. ACM, New York (2008)
16. Rickman, J., Tanenbaum, J.: GeoPoetry: designing location-based combinatorial electronic literature soundtracks for roadtrips. In: Nack, F., Gordon, A.S. (eds.) ICIDS 2016. LNCS, vol. 10045, pp. 85–96. Springer, Cham (2016). https://doi.org/10.1007/978-3-319-48279-8_8

Emotion-Based Story Event Clustering

Hye-Yeon Yu[1], Seohui Park[2], Yun-Gyung Cheong[3], Moon-Hyun Kim[3],
and Byung-Chull Bae[4(✉)]

[1] Department of Electrical and Computer Engineering,
Sungkyunkwan University, Suwon, Korea
yu0529@skku.edu
[2] Department of Applied Data Science, Sungkyunkwan University, Suwon, Korea
huidea95@skku.edu
[3] College of Software, Sungkyunkwan University, Suwon, Korea
aimecca@skku.edu, mhkim@skku.edu
[4] School of Games, Hongik University, Sejong, Korea
byuc@hongik.ac.kr

Abstract. In this paper we explore how events can be represented and
extracted from text stories, and describe the results from our simple
experiment on extracting and clustering events. We applied k-means
clustering algorithm and NLTK-VADER sentiment analyzer based on
Plutchik's 8 basic emotion model. When compared with human raters,
some emotions show low accuracy while other emotion types, such as joy
and sadness, show relatively high accuracy using our method.

Keywords: Event representation · Event extraction · Event clustering

1 Introduction and Background

Text story comprehension requires various types of high-level intelligence, as the
reader needs to reconstruct a perceived story from a given text using a mental
model [17]. Characters and plots, in particular, are two key elements for story
comprehension which are often intertwined, constructing a series of (either major
or minor) events in the story. In this paper we posit that identification of events
and recognition of the relations among them are crucial in building a reader's
mental model for story understanding.

While there are a number of ways for the representation of events extracted
from a text story, they can be roughly divided into two categories - tuple representation and 5W (what, who, why, where, when) representation.

In the tuple event representations, core sentence components are extracted
from normalized sentences. In early studies, only subjects and verbs with the
description of the relationship (dependency) between the two were extracted.
This approach is simple and efficient, but has a disadvantage of having difficulty in detecting the connections between multiple characters. To resolve this
problem, richer event representation is proposed containing more components
- such as V(s, o, p), where V: Verb, s: subject, o: object, and p: prepositional

© Springer Nature Switzerland AG 2019
R. E. Cardona-Rivera et al. (Eds.): ICIDS 2019, LNCS 11869, pp. 348–353, 2019.
https://doi.org/10.1007/978-3-030-33894-7_36

[11]. With this proposed event representation, events between two characters can be represented such as "call (Anthony, Laura, ∅)", "help (Laura, Anthony, ∅)", describing the relevant information between the two characters. For this reason $V(s, o, p)$ is one of the most commonly used forms among other tuple event representations. Furthermore, depending on the research directions, event tuples can contain information other than the grammatical components. In Martin et al. [8], for example, event is represented as $V(s,o,p,g)$ which includes story genre (g).

5W event representation, on the other hand, summarizes the information about What, Who, Why, Where and When in a text story. This event extraction method is applied more frequently to news data than a text story because 5W1H is the usual structure of a news story [14].

In this paper we explore how events can be extracted and represented from text stories, and present our method of clustering extracted events as a way of abstraction with similar emotions.

2   Experiment

2.1   Dataset

There are a wide variety of text story corpora made available to the public - ranging from movie plot summaries collected from Wikipedia [1] and movie scene descriptions/dialogues collected from the IMSDB (Internet Movie Script Database) [6,15] to ROCStories, a text story dataset collected from crowdsourcing [10]. Each corpus has its own feature and can be used differently depending on the research purpose: plot summaries dataset is helpful to identify high-level abstract story structure relating to characters and events; scene descriptions and dialogues from movie scripts are useful for extracting low-level/primitive actions and conversations among characters.

Among the text story corpora, we utilized ROCStories dataset [10], which is convenient at several practical levels - (1) each story consists of exactly 5 sentences; (2) each sentence in the story uses indirect speech without dialogues; (3) each story maintains a coherent dramatic structure of beginning - "something happens" - ending; (4) most events in the story can also occur in our everyday life.

2.2   Event Modeling and Extraction

We employ 4-tuple event representation (v, e_s, e_o, pp) based on the method by Pichotta and Mooney [11], where v: verb, e_s: subject, e_o: object, and pp: prepositional phrase. Here we simply define an event as a verb possibly being attached with subjects, objects, or prepositional phrases.

Each story in ROCStories dataset consists of five sentences, where many sentences have either compound or complex sentence structure that can have multiple number of events. Thus we converted all compound and complex sentences into multiple simple sentences based on the dependency information using

Stanford CoreNLP [3]. In total, 397,200 events are extracted from 263,325 sentences in ROCStories, where 6,419 events are classified based only on the verbs.

While converting verbs to events, stop words are excluded by using NLTK stop word list. Excluding the verbs in the NLTK stopwords list (e.g., have, be, do), several interesting verbs such as decide, want, love, and feel are included in the top 20 verb list. Although some general verbs (e.g., get, take) need to be classified further in detail by including matching propositions (e.g., get on/off, take on/off), we did not consider it in this paper.

2.3   Emotion-Based Event Clustering

The ultimate goal of our work is to understand a text story by identifying events using a formatted structure. However, event extraction based only on verb extraction results in a large number of events. This requires abstraction or clustering of the extracted events for text story understanding. While there will be various ways of events abstraction or clustering, including narrative summarization [7], this paper focuses on a way of emotion-based clustering, since emotion is a key element for understanding narrative events.

We selected a relatively straightforward approach using NLTK-VADER sentiment analyzer to cluster the extracted events into eight basic emotion types in Plutchik's wheel of emotions model. The 8 basic emotions are trust, anger, anticipation, disgust, joy, fear, sadness, and surprise [12]. Plutchik's emotions model is chosen over other emotion models (such as the basic emotion model [4] or the circumplex model of emotion [13]) because it can easily extend the 8 basic emotions into 24 compound/complex emotions. For this paper, however, we focused only on the 8 basic emotions. The output of NLTK-VADER sentiment analyzer shows a corresponding sentiment value to an input (an event structure in this paper) with indication of polarity (positive, neutral, negative). Utilizing the compound values in the return value, we first excluded events that are identified as either neutral (neu: 1.0) or zero compound value (com: 0), based on the method proposed in [2,16]. With the compound values returned from NLTK-VADER sentiment analyzer, all the events with non-neutral sentiment value were clustered using a simple k-Means algorithm based on Weka [5]. Finally, we analyzed 138,216 events that are identified as emotional and listed them according to Plutchik's wheel of emotions model.

Figure 1 shows the distribution of emotions by cluster, where different colors refer to different clusters classified into Plutchik's 8 basic emotions. For example, a total of 20,673 events are classified as cluster 0, where *sadness* is the representative emotion using the color yellow. Each cluster (0 to 7) has a representative emotion - 0: Sadness, 1: Fear, 2: Anticipation, 3: Joy, 4: Surprise, 5: Disgust, 6: Joy, 7: Trust. Note that *Joy* emotion represents two clusters (cluster 3 and cluster 6) and *Anger* emotion represents none. We assume that it is because emotional events are not evenly distributed in the dataset. Among all emotional events, events associated with Joy emotion occupy 30% and the events associated with Anger emotion occupy just 2%.

To evaluate the results of the emotion clustering, a total of 40 sentences (5 sentences each for 8 emotion types) were randomly selected and assessed by 4 volunteer participants (2 females and 2 males). The participants were asked to select one primary emotion among 10 choices (including neutral and other as an open answer in addition to the 8 basic emotions). The agreement rate among the human participants was evaluated by Fleiss' kappa [9], where the kappa score was as low as 0.36. Among the 8 basic emotions, trust is the most agreed (kappa = .6581), while anticipation is the least agreed (kappa = .0056) emotion.

As the agreement among the 4 raters is low, it is hard to directly compare the results of our proposed method with the results of the human raters. Among the 8 basic emotions, joy and sadness emotions are the most accurately represented (60%); fear emotion is the least accurately represented (0%), under the naive assumption that the emotion clustering is considered to be *accurate* as long as at least one human rater agrees with the system. There would be several reasons for this low accuracy. One reason would be that the NLTK-VADER sentiment values are similar for several emotion pairs – e.g., joy (0.59) and trust (0.51), sadness (−0.44) and fear(−0.49), anger (−0.57) and disgust (−0.6). There could be many other reasons – such as possible inaccuracy during the event structure conversion or failure of recognition of either compound nouns (e.g., hot dog) or proper nouns (e.g., Star Wars).

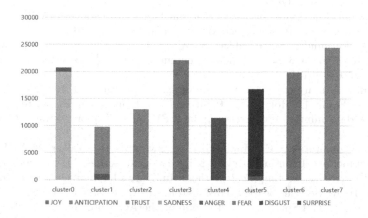

Fig. 1. Distribution of emotions by clustering

3   Conclusion

In this paper we conducted a simple experiment on extracting and clustering events from ROCStories text dataset. After converting sentences to tuple-formatted events, we applied the NLTK-VADER sentiment analyzer and k-means clustering algorithm to check whether similar events can be clustered into emotional groups using the 8 basic emotions in Plutchik's wheel of emotions model. However, there exist a variety of complex emotions in a narrative - including love, jealousy, envy, remorse, etc. In further studies we plan to explore the more complex emotions in Plutchik's wheel of emotion model. In addition, we also plan to utilize our results to generate stories with specific emotions.

Acknowledgments. This work was supported by Institute for Information communications Technology Promotion (IITP) grant funded by the Korea government (MSIT) (No. 2017-0-01772, Development of QA systems for Video Story Understanding to pass the Video Turing Test) and Basic Science Research Program through the National Research Foundation of Korea (NRF) funded by the Ministry of Science and ICT (2017R1A2B4010499). This research was also supported by MSIT (Ministry of Science and ICT), Korea, under the ITRC (Information Technology Research Center) support program (IITP-2017-0-01642) supervised by the IITP (Institute for Information communications Technology Promotion).

References

1. Bamman, D., O'Connor, B., Smith, N.A.: Learning latent personas of film characters. In: Proceedings of the 51st Annual Meeting of the Association for Computational Linguistics (Volume 1: Long Papers), pp. 352–361. Association for Computational Linguistics (2013)
2. Caluza, L.J.B.: Deciphering West Philippine Sea: a Plutchik and VADER algorithm sentiment analysis. Indian J. Sci. Technol. **11**(47), 1–12 (2018)
3. Das, B., Majumder, M., Phadikar, S.: A novel system for generating simple sentences from complex and compound sentences. Int. J. Mod. Educ. Comput. Sci. **11**(1), 57–64 (2018)
4. Ekman, P.: An argument for basic emotions. Cogn. Emot. **6**, 169–200 (1992)
5. Hall, M., Frank, E., Holmes, G., Pfahringer, B., Reutemann, P., Witten, I.H.: The WEKA data mining software: an update. SIGKDD Explor. Newsl. **11**(1), 10–18 (2009)
6. Hu, Z., Rahimtoroghi, E., Munishkina, L., Swanson, R., Walker, M.A.: Unsupervised induction of contingent event pairs from film scenes. In: Proceedings of the 2013 Conference on Empirical Methods in Natural Language Processing 2013, Grand Hyatt Seattle, Seattle, Washington, USA, 18–21 October 2013. A Meeting of SIGDAT, a Special Interest Group of the ACL, pp. 369–379 (2013)
7. Lehnert, W.G.: Plot units and narrative summarization. Cogn. Sci. **5**(4), 293–331 (1981)
8. Martin, L.J., et al.: Event representations for automated story generation with deep neural nets. In: Proceedings of the Thirty-Second AAAI Conference on Artificial Intelligence, New Orleans, Louisiana, USA, 2–7 February 2018 (2018)
9. McHugh, M.L.: Interrater reliability: the kappa statistic. Biochem. Med. **22**(3), 276–282 (2012)
10. Mostafazadeh, N., et al.: A corpus and cloze evaluation for deeper understanding of commonsense stories. In: Proceedings of the 2016 Conference of the North American Chapter of the Association for Computational Linguistics: Human Language Technologies, pp. 839–849. Association for Computational Linguistics, San Diego, June 2016

11. Pichotta, K., Mooney, R.: Statistical script learning with multi-argument events. In: Proceedings of the 14th Conference of the European Chapter of the Association for Computational Linguistics, pp. 220–229. Association for Computational Linguistics, Gothenburg, April 2014
12. Plutchik, R.: The nature of emotions. Am. Sci. **89**(4), 344–350 (2001)
13. Russell, J.: A circumplex model of affect. J. Pers. Soc. Psychol. **39**(6), 1161–1178 (1980)
14. Tozzo, A., Jovanovic, D., Amer, M.: Neural event extraction from movies description. In: Proceedings of the First Workshop on Storytelling, pp. 60–66. Association for Computational Linguistics, New Orleans, June 2018
15. Walker, M., Lin, G., Sawyer, J.: An annotated corpus of film dialogue for learning and characterizing character style. In: Proceedings of the Eighth International Conference on Language Resources and Evaluation (LREC-2012), pp. 1373–1378. European Language Resources Association (ELRA), Istanbul, May 2012
16. Yu, H.Y., Kim, M.H., Bae, B.C.: Emotion and sentiment analysis from a film script: a case study. J. Digit. Contents Soc. **18**(8), 1537–1542 (2017)
17. Zwaan, R.A., Langston, M.C., Graesser, A.C.: The construction of situation models in narrative comprehension: an event-indexing model. Psychol. Sci. **6**(5), 292–297 (1995)

Human Factors

Embodying Cognitive Processes
in Storytelling Interfaces for Children

Sarah Anne Brown[1]([⊠]) [iD], Sharon Lynn Chu[1] [iD], and Trystan Loustau[2] [iD]

[1] University of Florida, Gainesville, FL 32611, USA
sarah.brown@ufl.edu
[2] Florida State University, Tallahassee, FL 32306, USA

Abstract. This paper explores the effects of story creation interfaces for children that embody different types of psychologically-grounded cognitive approaches. Two versions of a story creation interface for children were created: one leads the user to focus on a macro-level structure of their story before furnishing scene details, while the other leads the user to focus initially on individual scene details before moving on to determine the macro-level structure of the story. A study was conducted to compare the use of the two types of story creation interfaces by children between the ages of 7 and 12. Findings indicate that different cognitive models can have differing effects on children's storytelling. In our case, a micro-first model resulted both in greater ease of use as measured by flow and usability, and in richer stories produced.

Keywords: Digital storytelling interfaces · Cognitive structures · Children's storytelling

1   Introduction

Our research investigates the design of digital storytelling interfaces for children, and how these may be grounded in relevant psychological theories of how people think and create meaning. We estimate that nearly a hundred storytelling interfaces for children have been proposed in the literature in the past two decades, yet few applied principles from psychological literature about children's storytelling processes. However, most of them appear to follow at best, only general design principles. Especially at the cusp of abstract thought development [19], children are still learning to piece together their thoughts and ideas, and may benefit from extra support as they go through the complex task of composing a story. With the goal of deriving more specific theoretically-grounded design implications for the design of storytelling interfaces for children, we developed and evaluated two storytelling interfaces that embody two different cognitive sensemaking models. Our research question was: *Does a story creation interface*

Supported by National Science Foundation Grant #1736225 *To Enact, To Tell, To Write: A Bridge to Expressive Writing through Digital Enactment.*

R. E. Cardona-Rivera et al. (Eds.): ICIDS 2019, LNCS 11869, pp. 357–363, 2019.
https://doi.org/10.1007/978-3-030-33894-7_37

that embody a macro-first approach engage children in storytelling differently from a story creation interface that embody a micro-first approach, and if so, how?

2   Related Work

Many different design concepts have been investigated with regards to storytelling interfaces for children in prior literature. Many apply and explore the concept of Tangible User Interfaces (TUIs) (e.g., [1–3,5,6,8,9,12,15,18,20,25, 26,28–30,34–36]), the potential of incorporating children's natural play processes (e.g., [17,23,25,27,32,33]), or specific features such as playback (e.g., [30,32]).

A good number of storytelling systems are founded upon learning theories, the most commonly cited one being constructionism (e.g., [2,4,9,12–14,18,24–26,31,33,35]). While it is helpful to contextualize story creation as something to be learned, such theories cannot adequately guide the design of children's storytelling interfaces. In order to fully understand how children tell and create stories, researchers must turn to psychological theories.

In this work, we explored a model proposed by Kintsch [21] that distinguishes two distinct structures of thinking. At the macro level, we process things globally, looking at the overall discourse. At the micro level, the discourse is processed locally, and parsed in individual, unique units. When applied to a process such as story creation, one can think of the micro level as the details of a story. Individual scenes, events, actions and descriptions of characters or environments are all considered micro-level details. On the other hand, the macro level would exist as the story's overall structure and flow - the way in which those details are sequenced and come together to form a complete story.

3   Interface Design

We created two different but comparable storytelling interfaces for children that embodied two distinct models based on Kintsch's levels of thinking. The two models support children's storytelling by manipulating the user's focus to be on either the macro-level of thinking or the micro-level of thinking first. In the model that we call 'macro-first', the interface emphasizes planning a concrete structure before proceeding to the story's details. In the model that we call 'micro-first', individual ideas/details are created before story structure is determined.

Base Story Creation System. The two interface variants were developed off of a base storytelling system. The base storytelling system portrays story organization as a timeline, consisting of units referred to as scenes. Three sections following the basic narrative arc are delineated in the timeline: beginning, middle and end (see Fig. 1). Details are added to story scenes through an enactment-based method, whereby the user performs voice enactment using selected characters, props and backgrounds (see Fig. 1). Story review is provided with a playback screen, allowing the user to play their entire story at once completed.

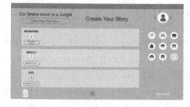

Fig. 1. Our interface time line (shown left) and enactment screen (shown right).

Interface Variants. We conceptualized the user engaging with the enactment screen to determine the actual details of a scene as thinking at a micro level. The user interacting with the story organization screen to manipulate/prepare scenes on the timeline engages with macro level thinking. The two interface models (macro-first and micro-first) were implemented by enforcing carefully-designed constraints in each interface variant (see Table 1).

Table 1. Differences in interactions between the two interface variants

Interaction	Macro-first model	Micro-first model
Enacting a Scene	Only after all scenes were prepared, and user acknowledged they were done planning their story	Enforced after each scene was added
Editing a Scene's Details	Scene details can only be changed before the user exits the planning stage	Scene details must be filled in after adding a scene, and are locked after a new scene is added
Moving or Deleting Scenes	Scenes can only be moved around or deleted before the user exits the planning stage	Scenes can be moved around or deleted even after they have been locked from content editing

4   Study Description

We conducted a between-subjects study with one independent variable: interface model. Eleven participants have participated in the study so far, 6 girls and 5 boys, ages 7 to 12. Participants were recruited through university e-mail lists, and the study took place in an on-campus lab space.

Our study protocol began with a video tutorial of the assigned interface, followed by a baseline questionnaire and interview. Participants then practiced using their assigned interface. A prompt was given, and participants had 45 min to create a story with the interface. This was followed by asking the participants to write out the story they had just created on paper. Finally, participants filled in a post-questionnaire and were administered an interview during which the interviewer went through the screen recording of them creating their story with the assigned interface.

The measures gathered included *intrinsic motivation for storytelling* using SIMS [16]); *interface usability* using an adapted version of the PSSUQ [22]); *engagement* using the GEQ [7]). All measures used a 7-point likert scale.

5   Data Analysis and Initial Results

From the interviews, the designs of our two interface variants appeared to successfully lead children to think using a macro-first or micro-first approach during storytelling. In the micro-first condition, we observed comments from participants such as *"...it helped me focus on one part...working on one scene at a time really helps"*, which implied they adapted well to the micro-level focus intent of that interface model. Similarly, in the macro-first condition, statements such as *"I added a lot of slides at once and then figured out how many I would need"* or *"...first I had to do my slots(scenes acted as'slots' for characters, props, and backgrounds), so I got each line(story section) to have a slot"* also showed adaptation to our presented mode of thinking, such that participants using that interface focused on story structure first by adding multiple scenes at a time.

The largest differences in the questionnaire ratings were seen in the *flow* sub-construct of the GEQ. The micro-first interface had a higher mean flow rating ($M = 4.11$, $SD = 1.26$) than the macro-first condition ($M = 3.70$, $SD = 0.67$). Micro-first also scored higher in usability ($M = 6.57$, $SD = 0.47$) than the macro-first interface ($M = 5.67$, $SD = 1.51$).

We analyzed the participants' stories for story richness by counting how many 5Ws+1H's (Who, What, When, Where, Why, How) were present in each story [10]. Story richness scores were standardized by number of singular idea units in the written story to account for its overall length. The micro-first interface produced richer stories ($M = 2.52$, $SD = 0.91$) than the macro-first interface ($M = 2.48$, $SD = 0.61$).

6   Conclusion

Our initial results suggest that while participants did tend to adapt to either interface's cognitive model through the use of the specific interface, the micro-first model resulted in higher flow, usability, and richer stories. An explanation could be that in the micro-first interface, the child's focus was led to be on individual story units first, and thus these units were richer than those in the macro-first condition, as shown by our analysis. Though we can only draw limited conclusions about the effects of these two specific interfaces at this time, this attests to the strong mediator role that interfaces can play in manipulating children's storytelling processes. Others have recognized that mediator role in prior work (e.g., [11]) but our results provide direct evidence of it by comparing two psychologically-grounded interfaces, and show promise for further investigation.

This exploratory study has begun a much needed investigation into the application of psychological theory in digital interactive storytelling interfaces for children. It is our hope that future work would expand on the theories that could be applied to these interfaces, with the goal of prioritizing the support of a child's story creation process over individual features and interactivity concepts.

Acknowledgements. This research was supported by NSF Grant #1736225 *To Enact, To Tell, To Write: A Bridge to Expressive Writing through Digital Enactment.* We also thank Lexi Mitchell for contributing to the design and development of the interfaces.

References

1. Åkerman, P., Puikkonen, A.: Prochinima: using pico projector to tell situated stories. In: Proceedings of the 13th International Conference on Human Computer Interaction with Mobile Devices and Services, pp. 337–346. ACM (2011)
2. Alborzi, H., et al.: Designing storyrooms: interactive storytelling spaces for children. Technical report (2000)
3. Alves, A., Lopes, R., Matos, P., Velho, L., Silva, D.: Reactoon: storytelling in a tangible environment. In: 2010 Third IEEE International Conference on Digital Game and Intelligent Toy Enhanced Learning, pp. 161–165. IEEE (2010)
4. Barnes, C., et al.: Video puppetry: a performative interface for cutout animation. In: ACM Transactions on Graphics (TOG), vol. 27, p. 124. ACM (2008)
5. Bayon, V., Wilson, J.R., Stanton, D., Boltman, A.: Mixed reality storytelling environments. Virtual Reality **7**(1), 54–63 (2003)
6. Bobick, A.F., et al.: The kidsroom: a perceptually-based interactive and immersive story environment. Presence **8**(4), 369–393 (1999)
7. Brockmyer, J.H., Fox, C.M., Curtiss, K.A., McBroom, E., Burkhart, K.M., Pidruzny, J.N.: The development of the game engagement questionnaire: a measure of engagement in video game-playing. J. Exp. Soc. Psychol. **45**(4), 624–634 (2009). https://doi.org/10.1016/j.jesp.2009.02.016
8. Budd, J., Madej, K., Stephens-Wells, J., de Jong, J., Katzur, E., Mulligan, L.: PageCraft: learning in context a tangible interactive storytelling platform to support early narrative development for young children. In: Proceedings of the 6th International Conference on Interaction Design and Children, pp. 97–100. ACM (2007)
9. Cao, X., Lindley, S.E., Helmes, J., Sellen, A.: Telling the whole story: anticipation, inspiration and reputation in a field deployment of TellTable. In: Proceedings of the 2010 ACM Conference on Computer Supported Cooperative Work, pp. 251–260. ACM (2010)
10. Chu, S.L., Quek, F., Tanenbaum, J.: *Performative Authoring*: nurturing storytelling in children through imaginative enactment. In: Koenitz, H., Sezen, T.I., Ferri, G., Haahr, M., Sezen, D., Ç atak, G. (eds.) ICIDS 2013. LNCS, vol. 8230, pp. 144–155. Springer, Cham (2013). https://doi.org/10.1007/978-3-319-02756-2_18
11. Chu Yew Yee, S.L., Quek, F.K., Xiao, L.: Studying medium effects on children's creative processes. In: Proceedings of the 8th ACM Conference on Creativity and Cognition, pp. 3–12. ACM (2011)
12. Decortis, F., Rizzo, A.: New active tools for supporting narrative structures. Pers. Ubiquit. Comput. **6**(5–6), 416–429 (2002)
13. Di Blas, N., Boretti, B.: Interactive storytelling in pre-school: a case-study. In: Proceedings of the 8th International Conference on Interaction Design and Children, pp. 44–51. ACM (2009)
14. Druin, A., Stewart, J., Proft, D., Bederson, B., Hollan, J.: KidPad: a design collaboration between children, technologists, and educators. In: CHI 1997, pp. 463–470 (1997)

15. Follmer, S., Ishii, H.: KidCAD: digitally remixing toys through tangible tools. In: Proceedings of the SIGCHI Conference on Human Factors in Computing Systems, pp. 2401–2410. ACM (2012)
16. Guay, F., Vallerand, R.J., Blanchard, C.: On the assessment of situational intrinsic and extrinsic motivation: the situational motivation scale (SIMS). Motiv. Emot. **24**(3), 175–213 (2000). https://doi.org/10.1023/A:1005614228250
17. Hayes-Roth, B., Van Gent, R.: Story-making with improvisational puppets and actors. Technical report, Technical Report KSL-96-05, Knowledge Systems Laboratory, Stanford University (1996)
18. Hourcade, J.P., Perry, K.B., Moore, J.L.: Vuelta: creating animated characters and props using real-world objects. In: CHI 2007 Extended Abstracts on Human Factors in Computing Systems, pp. 2429–2434. ACM (2007)
19. Huitt, W., Hummel, J.: Piaget's theory of cognitive development. Educ. Psychol. Interact. **3**(2), 1–5 (2003)
20. Hunter, S., Kalanithi, J., Merrill, D.: Make a Riddle and Telestory: designing children's applications for the siftables platform. In: Proceedings of the 9th International Conference on Interaction Design and Children, pp. 206–209. ACM (2010)
21. Kintsch, W., Van Dijk, T.A.: Toward a model of text comprehension and production. Psychol. Rev. **85**(5), 363 (1978)
22. Lewis, J.: IBM computer usability satisfaction questionnaires: psychometric evaluation and instructions for use. Post-study system usability questionnaire (PSSUQ). Technical report, Technical Report 54.786 (1993)
23. Lu, F., et al.: ShadowStory: creative and collaborative digital storytelling inspired by cultural heritage. In: Proceedings of the SIGCHI Conference on Human Factors in Computing Systems, pp. 1919–1928. ACM (2011)
24. Russell, A.: ToonTastic: a global storytelling network for kids, by kids. In: Proceedings of the Fourth International Conference on Tangible, Embedded, and Embodied Interaction, pp. 271–274. ACM (2010)
25. Ryokai, K., Cassell, J.: StoryMat: a play space for collaborative storytelling. In: CHI 1999 Extended Abstracts on Human Factors in Computing Systems, pp. 272–273. Citeseer (1999)
26. Ryokai, K., Lee, M.J., Breitbart, J.M.: Children's storytelling and programming with robotic characters. In: Proceedings of the Seventh ACM Conference on Creativity and Cognition, pp. 19–28. ACM (2009)
27. Shen, Y.T., Mazalek, A.: Puzzletale: a tangible puzzle game for interactive storytelling. Comput. Entertain. (CIE) **8**(2), 11 (2010)
28. Soleimani, A., Herro, D., Green, K.E.: Cyberplayce–a tangible, interactive learning tool fostering children's computational thinking through storytelling. Int. J. Child-Comput. Interact. **20**, 9–23 (2019)
29. Sugimoto, M., Ito, T., Nguyen, T.N., Inagaki, S.: GENTORO: a system for supporting children's storytelling using handheld projectors and a robot. In: Proceedings of the 8th International Conference on Interaction Design and Children, pp. 214–217. ACM (2009)
30. Sylla, C., Branco, P., Coutinho, C., Coquet, E., Skaroupka, D.: TOK: a tangible interface for storytelling. In: CHI 2011 Extended Abstracts on Human Factors in Computing Systems, pp. 1363–1368. ACM (2011)
31. Sylla, C., Pereira, Í.S.P., Brooks, E., Zagalo, N.: t-books: a block interface for young children's narrative construction. Int. J. Child-Comput. Interact. **18**, 59–66 (2018)
32. Vaucelle, C., Jehan, T.: Dolltalk: a computational toy to enhance children's creativity. In: CHI 2002 Extended Abstracts on Human Factors in Computing Systems, pp. 776–777. ACM (2002)

33. Vaucelle, C., Ishii, H.: Picture this!: film assembly using toy gestures. In: Proceedings of the 10th International Conference on Ubiquitous Computing, pp. 350–359. ACM (2008)
34. Wang, D., He, L., Dou, K.: Storycube: supporting children's storytelling with a tangible tool. J. Supercomput. **70**(1), 269–283 (2014)
35. Wistort, R., Breazeal, C.: Tofudraw: a mixed-reality choreography tool for authoring robot character performance. In: Proceedings of the 10th International Conference on Interaction Design and Children, pp. 213–216. ACM (2011)
36. Yilmaz, R.M., Goktas, Y.: Using augmented reality technology in storytelling activities: examining elementary students' narrative skill and creativity. Virtual Reality **21**(2), 75–89 (2017)

Towards a Gesture-Based Story Authoring System: Design Implications from Feature Analysis of Iconic Gestures During Storytelling

Sarah Anne Brown[1]([envelope]) [iD], Sharon Lynn Chu[1] [iD], Francis Quek[2],
Pomaikai Canaday[3] [iD], Qing Li[4] [iD], Trystan Loustau[5] [iD], Sindy Wu[1] [iD],
and Lina Zhang[2] [iD]

[1] University of Florida, Gainesville, FL 32611, USA
sarah.brown@ufl.edu
[2] Texas A&M University, College Station, Uvalde, TX 77843, USA
[3] Georgetown University, Washington DC 20057, USA
[4] Santa Fe College, Gainesville, FL 32606, USA
[5] Florida State University, Tallahassee, FL 32306, USA

Abstract. Current systems that use gestures to enable storytelling tend to mostly rely on a pre-scripted set of gestures or the use of manipulative gestures with respect to tangibles. Our research aims to inform the design of gesture recognition systems for storytelling with implications derived from a feature-based analysis of iconic gestures that occur during naturalistic oral storytelling. We collected story retellings of a collection of cartoon stimuli from 20 study participants, and a gesture analysis was performed on videos of the story retellings focusing on iconic gestures. Iconic gestures are a type of representational gesture that provides information about objects such as their shape, location, or movement. The form features of the iconic gestures were analyzed with respect to the concepts that they portrayed. Patterns between the two were identified and used to create recommendations for patterns in gesture form a system could be primed to recognize.

Keywords: Gesture analysis · Gesture-based storytelling systems · Iconic gestures · Machine learning · Human-computer interaction

1 Introduction

Today's gesture recognition systems are limited in the kinds of applications they can be applied to. When applied to storytelling, gesture systems have been mostly limited to the use of gestures to provide commands to the system (e.g., [8]) or to manipulate tangible objects related to the story (e.g., [11]). Following

Research supported by National Science Foundation Grant #1736225 *To Enact, To Tell, To Write: A Bridge to Expressive Writing through Digital Enactment.*

R. E. Cardona-Rivera et al. (Eds.): ICIDS 2019, LNCS 11869, pp. 364–373, 2019.
https://doi.org/10.1007/978-3-030-33894-7_38

Quek's taxonomy [17], the former are *semaphoric gestures* that define sets of pre-defined whole static or dynamic hand poses, and the latter are *manipulative* uses of hand movement whose purpose is typically to generate a control signal. This paper is concerned with conversational gestures that are performed in conjunction with speech. More specifically, we are interested in how gesture systems can be designed to support story authoring through the feature analysis of free gestures produced in naturalistic conversational/storytelling contexts. Such gestures are termed *gesticulation*: gestures that are constructed, typically unwittingly, at the moment of speech [16]. Gesticulation is creatively produced, and is normally impermeable to 'whole gesture' recognition techniques typically used in machine learning approaches that recognize exact repeated performances. For example, one does not always produce the stylized 'turning steering wheel' gesture when one says the word 'car'. Research has shown that gesticulation carry their meaning in gestural aspects or features that carry the mental image of the multimodal discourse utterance (e.g., [18]). With the availability of technologies that can capture and detect the movements of the hand in relatively high fidelity such as the Leap Motion and Kinect systems [14], there are increasing opportunities to enable the creation of story products (e.g., a comic) to be driven by storytelling gesticulations and speech.

Our research in this paper addresses specifically iconic gestures, which provide representational information about objects, such as their shape, location, or movement. This initial focus is because iconic gestures are critical to storytelling: of the existing gesture types, iconic gestures are frequently used to aid in visual depictions of concrete objects [16]. We conducted a study whereby 20 participants (including 3 pilot participants) were video recorded while retelling stories from various cartoon stimuli. Our analysis involved a feature-based analysis of iconic gestures extracted from these recordings.

2 Background and Related Work

2.1 Gesture-Based Storytelling Systems

The use of gestures in storytelling applications can be classified into three categories. In the first category, users are asked to perform certain gestures during the consumption of stories so as to increase their engagement in the experience. For example, in Kistler et al.'s work [8], players are asked to perform gestures indicated on screen during quick time events (QTE) during their engagement in the choose-your-own-adventure story 'Sugarcane Island'. In the second category, users use gestures to control a tangible object related to the story being told or created. For instance, in Liang et al.'s *Puppet Narrator* system [10, 11], children use specific hand gestures to control a puppet avatar to perform basic movements like 'move right' or 'stretch'.

In the third category, users can perform free gestures to contribute to storytelling scenarios. For example, Kistler et al. [7] conducted a study asking participants explicitly to perform full-body gestures for a set of given in-game actions (e.g., ask permission, approach supervisor, sit at a bar) in a story-based scenario.

They performed an analysis of the participants' full-body gestures using a high-level scheme, coding for 'form', 'gesture type', and '(involved) body parts'. An example of their results is that most participants gestured "talking to a supervisor" using a metaphoric gesture, while an iconic gesture was mostly used to indicate "sitting at a bar and waiting". They subsequently built a recognizer for the specific gestures identified in their study. Our study, in contrast, focuses on gesticulations produced in naturalistic storytelling contexts.

2.2   Gesture Recognition Systems and Approaches

As outlined in Rautaray and Agrawal [20] and Al-Shamaylehk et al. [1], hand gesture recognition, typically accomplished through machine learning algorithms [21], consists of three steps - **Detection:** Detecting the hands and extracting necessary features from them for recognition and/or tracking (tracking only necessary when the application is dynamic in nature, as opposed to static gesture recognition); **Tracking:** Maintaining detection of the hands from frame to frame; and **Recognition:** The final interpretation of what the hands semantically express in the context of a given application.

The features typically used in gesture machine learning algorithms include specific pixel values, whole three-dimensional hand models, or two-dimensional hand shapes [20]. A main focus in the literature has been on the segmentation of whole gestures for interpretation [4,6,12]. However, as can be observed during natural discourse, gestures flow in and out of each other near seamlessly at times. Our work looks at gesture features at a much lower level by using grounding from psycholinguistic research [9,16] with a goal to inform the development of gesture recognition systems for storytelling.

We note as well that few gesture recognition systems currently deal with completely naturalistic settings. The closest application of gesture recognition systems for natural, conversational gestures is to recognize sign language gestures. In that case, the gestures can be argued to be conversational, but not necessarily natural, as they stem from a predefined vocabulary.

2.3   The Semantics of Gestures and Their Features

While variations exist between different gesture taxonomies proposed in the literature [13,20], iconic gestures tend to be a common category across many of them. As defined by McNeill, iconic gestures "bear a close formal relationship to the semantic content of speech" [16], furnishing imagistic information about their referents such as their shape, location, or movement. McNeill emphasizes the need to interpret the meaning of an iconic gesture in combination with its associated spoken utterance. An example of an iconic gesture is a speaker spreading his hands out wide while describing a tree. In this case, the iconic gesture is representing the width of the tree. As such, iconic gestures aid speech by depicting a visual representation in the mind of the speaker from which both gesture and speech proceeds.

At this point, it is useful to note that the information provided by iconic gestures may either be redundant (e.g., "she is really tall" [gesture with raised hand with palm facing down indicating height]), or complementary (e.g., "he went through the entrance" [gesture with two inward facing hands close together signifying that the entrance is narrow]).

Kopp, Tepper, and Cassell [9] conducted a study that analyzed the features of iconic gestures by detailing their shapes and spatial properties/relationships (that they called *image description features*) and their morphologies or forms. They hypothesized that there exists an observable relationship between the physical forms of an iconic gesture's features and the image-describing meanings that can be derived from them. Their research primarily resulted in the framework with which they propose to continue their analysis, and a limited variety of gestures their conversational agent can utilize in to providing users with directions. Thus, their gesture research was not done for storytelling. They studied discourse in the context of direction-giving, with the intent of informing conversational agents that could describe an environment or give travel directions to a user.

A critical reason for why the analysis of gesture features is important to inform gesture-based storytelling systems is that within a discourse, gesture features tend to repeat themselves to convey similar meanings. Quek et al. [19] called such recurrences *catchments*. A catchment is "recognized when gesture features recur in two or more (not necessarily consecutive) gestures". For example, within a discourse session, a speaker may always perform a gesture of moving the right hand, palm faced down, to indicate horizontal surfaces. Research on the Catchment Feature Model has showed that addressing gestures as a whole often limits gesture recognition to a set vocabulary [18]. However, Quek et al. studied recurrent gesture features as they occur within individual speakers. We hypothesize that it is possible to find gesture patterns across speakers if the feature analysis is taken to a level that is abstracted enough.

3   Data Collection

The goal of our research was to find the commonalities between iconic gestures that are produced during naturalistic storytelling in terms of form features and the concepts they portray, such that design implications for gesture-based storytelling systems can be derived. We had a total of 17 adult participants in our final study, 15 male and 2 female, between the ages of 18 and 34. Before the final study, we also conducted a pilot study with 1 male and 2 female participants within that same age range to test our protocol. Participant recruitment took place both via e-mail and via an online recruitment system which offered course credit to enrolled students.

Our study protocol was similar to that used in previous gesture studies by McNeill [16]. After presenting participants with a cartoon stimulus, we asked them to retell the story of the cartoon from start to finish to the researcher in a conversational context. The researcher primarily remained as a listener. We video recorded the exchange from two angles - one close and one angled from slightly farther away. Participants were not informed that we were looking at gestures specifically, but rather that we were investigating how people tell stories to prevent them from being self-aware of their gestures during the retelling tasks.

Our study stimuli consisted of a combination of short scenes and full short films: 2 full cartoon shorts (a 5-minute Loony Tunes cartoon, *Box Office Bunny* [22] produced by Warner Bros. Animation, a 8-minute short film titled *Alike* produced by Pepe School Land [15]), and 5 cartoon scenes, each under a minute in length, extracted from 2 additional shorts (Pixar's *La Luna* [3] and *Alarm*, produced by MESAI [5]). The cartoon shorts were selected for being non-abstract in nature (having concrete objects and environments, even if they are fantastical or stylized), and having a clear sequence of events. Each participant watched and retold the same set of cartoons, enabling us to compare gestures across participants. In total, including the pilot study, 37 retellings of full cartoon shorts were collected, and 85 retellings of cartoon scenes.

4   Data Analysis

The analysis in this paper focuses on the retellings of only the Loony Tune's short *Box Office Bunny* [22]. The coding was done by 6 coders, who first underwent basic training sessions in gesture analysis.

Extracting Iconic Gestures. Since the identification of iconic gestures can sometimes be subjective, 2 to 3 coders were assigned to code the same retellings. Coders were also asked to give a 'confidence of iconicity' score (on a scale of 1–5) with each iconic gesture identified, as suggested by the coding scheme outlined in McNeill [16]. Once an iconic gesture was identified, a gesture was coded as describing an Object, Action, or Position (or some combination of the three, in certain cases). After the lists of iconic gestures across all coders were synthesized, a total of 161 iconic gestures were found across all the cartoon retellings. The confidence scores were averaged for each gesture across its coders. This resulted in 65 iconic gestures with confidence averages above the median (2.667). These made up the final dataset that we used for further analysis.

Identifying Gesture Concepts. From the first round of analysis, 43 iconic gesture instances were classified as referencing an Action, 15 an Object, 8 a Position. A second round of analysis was done classifying the gesture referents:

Actions were divided into: *Movement* (32 gesture instances across 11 participants): the movement of an object(s) or character(s) from one location to another; *Character Action* (10 gesture instances across 6 participants): an action performed by a character(s); and *Object Action* (1 gesture across 1 participant): an action in relation to an object(s), e.g., bombs exploding.

Objects were divided into: *Dimension* (6 gestures across 4 participants): defining the dimensions of an object, e.g., width or height; *Explicit Shape* (4 gestures across 3 participants): describing the shape of an object; Followed by *Volume* (3 gestures across 2 participants): defining the general volume in which an object would exist. Ex - cupping hands around a loose area regardless of object shape; and *Implicit Shape* (2 gestures across 2 participants): describing an implied feature of the shape of an object through the gesture, e.g., forming flat palms to imply the ground is flat.

Positions were divided into: *Relative* (7 gestures across 5 participants): position of an object from an external perspective, in relation to another object, e.g., the movie theater was on top of Bugs Bunny's home; and *Internal* (1 gestures across 1 participants): position of an object from the perspective of oneself or a character, e.g., pointing at the top of one's head to show where Bugs Bunny's ears would be.

Coding Gesture Form Features. We used the coding scheme proposed by Church and recommended by McNeill [16]. The scheme involves the coding of hand shape, handedness, space in which the gesture was performed, view, and motion direction, and meaning of the gesture (what the motion and the hands represent). For coding hand shape, the proposed method was to match the shape to an existing table of American Sign Language signs [2]. However, we found that the iconic gestures aligned with only a limited number of signs in our dataset. We thus reduced the coding scheme to three sets of form features: (i) Flat palms and fingers; (ii) Curled fingers; and (iii) One or more Pointed fingers. Coding of the other aspects of the gesture was relatively unchanged from the original coding scheme.

5 Results

We considered only concepts that had a minimum of 4 gesture instances across at least 4 participants in our results. Furthermore, we excluded entirely divergent and entirely convergent gesture features since both provide little discriminatory potential. The relevant results are shown in Fig. 1, and clear visual examples of each analyzed concept can be found in Fig. 2.

Concept	N Values		Features				
Action	N Partic.	N Gest.	Handedness	Motion Represents	Direction	Hand(s) Represent	Hand Shape(s)
Movement	11	32	Two Hands - 40.6%; One Hand - 59.4%;	Simple Motion - 96.9%; Complex Motion - 3.1%;	Uni - 62.5%; Mirrored - 15.6%; Bi-Directional - 3.1%; Different by Hand - 18.8%;	Actor(s) - 87.5%; Nothing - 12.5%;	Flat - 56.3%; Curled - 25%; Pointed - 12.5%; Etc. - 6.3%;
Character Action	6	10	Two Hands - 60%; One Hand - 40%;	Action - 70%; Nothing - 30%;	Uni - 60%; Mirrored - 30%; Bi-Directional - 10%;	Chara Hand(s) - 40%; Chara Feet - 40%; Nothing - 20%;	Flat - 60%; Curled - 40%;
Object							
Dimension	4	6	Two Hands - 100%;	Nothing - 100%	Mirrored - 83.3 %; Different by Hand - 16.7%;	Bounds - 100%;	Flat - 83.3 %; Pointed - 16.7%;
Position							
Relative Position	5	7	Two Hands - 42.9%; One Hand - 57.1%;	Obj Above Obj - 100%	Uni - 85.7%; Mirrored - 14.3%;	Object - 85.7%; Nothing - 14.3%;	Flat - 71.4%; Curled - 14.3%; Etc. - 14.3%;

Fig. 1. Results (%s reflect counts of each code within a given sub-concept)

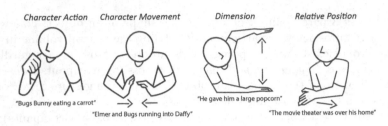

Fig. 2. Visual Examples of Concepts as Gestures (representative, but not directly reflective of participant gestures)

6   Discussion and Design Implications

As described in our Background section, gestures echo or add to information presented in speech. From the uncovered gesture feature patterns, we discuss below implications of how a gesture-based system can take advantage of storytellers' gesticulations to adjust visual story output.

For gestures referencing *Movement*, motions of the hand always depicted the imagined movement of the object referenced - these movements were split into the two codes under the feature depicting what "Motion Represents" (see Fig. 1). Within this feature, "Simple Motion" detailed movements of an object(s) or character(s) from one location to another, and "Complex Motion" detailed those that by comparison included a secondary motion, e.g., characters spinning together when they collide in a cartoonish fashion, as oppose to one character pursuing another with no further motions described. Thus, detecting hand motions in a gesture-based storytelling system could hypothetically reliably help to trace out objects' movements.

Gestures representing *Character Actions* provide a unique challenge, as their features appear to be highly tied to the specific actions being referenced, e.g., Bugs Bunny eating a carrot in our given cartoon represented all of gestures where the "Hand(s) Represent" the hand(s) of the character, Bugs Bunny. We are limited in a true analysis of this sub-concept, because the only two actions were described with any regularity from the given cartoon was the aforementioned Bugs Bunny eating a carrot, or the starring characters dancing on a gum-covered carpet (4 of either, for a total of 8 of the 10 identified *Character Actions*). However, much like *Movement*, there was a majority of hand motion directions were uni-directional, and motions of the hand tended to represent the action (comparable to the same feature, "Motion Represents" coded solely as different types of movement in *Movement*).

Gestures representing *Dimension* was one of the most promising concepts with distinguishable form features - the hands consistently (83.3% or above) represented two separate bounds of a given dimension (under the feature "Hand(s) Represent"), moved in mirrored directions (under "Directions") and, and with the exception of one example, were always both flat ("Hand Shape(s)"). These are set features a system could be built to detect so as to adjust a visualized object's dimension (with the object being determined from speech), and is reliable in that the other concepts do not replicate this set of form features.

Finally, gestures for *Relative Position* consisted largely of uni-directional motions (with larger percentages than in both *Movement* and *Character Action*), paired with a flat hand shape. We are limited by our chosen stimulus, *Box Office Bunny* [22], in that gestures produced for this sub-concept solely described objects that existed above or on top of another object. A common example was descriptions of the movie theater sitting upon Bugs Bunny's home. It is hard to say without a broader range of relative relationships, but it could be that other potential relationships share the same commonalities in form features. In which case, a system would look for a uni-directional motion paired with a flat hand to determine a positional relationship between one object and another. And perhaps, in the absence of a flat hand shape, the system could move on to explore the possibility that a *Movement* or *Character Action* is being portrayed, as they were the next concepts to have majorities in uni-directional hand motions, going down by highest percentages within those concepts. Thus, what we are describing is a system going through potential concepts by the probability that the detected form features match trends discovered through this analysis; filtering-down through an emerging taxonomy to determine in the end, what concept is likely being gestured, if any.

7 Conclusion

In this paper we presented an analysis of iconic gestures during naturalistic storytelling as investigated through specific concepts they portray and their form features. We coded iconic gestures as extracted from retellings of a cartoon stimulus, and our findings suggest that across gestured concepts, patterns can be found for specific form features. Though certain sub-concepts from our initial overarching concepts provided mixed results, there were notable patterns within the sub-concepts of Dimension and Relative Position. Our results provide a starting point to develop gesture-based systems that can recognize free gestures during naturalistic storytelling to produce concrete story outputs such as a cartoon animation or a comic.

As a limitation of our analysis, the sample size for each category of gesture concepts are unequal because in naturalistic contexts, we had no control over what content participants decided to include in their story retelling and what the gestured about. Moreover, we were limited to just one cartoon stimulus in the work presented. Many more storytelling gesture stimuli need to be analyzed.

References

1. Al-Shamayleh, A.S., Ahmad, R., Abushariah, M.A., Alam, K.A., Jomhari, N.: A systematic literature review on vision based gesture recognition techniques. Multimedia Tools Appl. **77**(21), 28121–28184 (2018)
2. Baker, C., Friedman, L.: On the Other Hand: New Perspectives on American Sign Language. Language, Thought and Culture, pp. 215–236. Academic Press, New York (1977)
3. Casarosa, E.: La luna (2011)
4. Chambers, G.S., Venkatesh, S., West, G.A.W., Bui, H.H.: Segmentation of intentional human gestures for sports video annotation. In: 2004 Proceedings of 10th International Multimedia Modelling Conference, pp. 124–129, January 2004. https://doi.org/10.1109/MULMM.2004.1264976
5. Jang, M.H.: Alarm (2009)
6. Joshi, A., Monnier, C., Betke, M., Sclaroff, S.: A random forest approach to segmenting and classifying gestures. In: 2015 11th IEEE International Conference and Workshops on Automatic Face and Gesture Recognition (FG), vol. 1, pp. 1–7, May 2015. https://doi.org/10.1109/FG.2015.7163126
7. Kistler, F., André, E.: User-defined body gestures for an interactive storytelling scenario. In: Kotzé, P., Marsden, G., Lindgaard, G., Wesson, J., Winckler, M. (eds.) INTERACT 2013. LNCS, vol. 8118, pp. 264–281. Springer, Heidelberg (2013). https://doi.org/10.1007/978-3-642-40480-1_17
8. Kistler, F., Sollfrank, D., Bee, N., André, E.: Full body gestures enhancing a game book for interactive story telling. In: Si, M., Thue, D., André, E., Lester, J.C., Tanenbaum, J., Zammitto, V. (eds.) ICIDS 2011. LNCS, vol. 7069, pp. 207–218. Springer, Heidelberg (2011). https://doi.org/10.1007/978-3-642-25289-1_23
9. Kopp, S., Tepper, P., Cassell, J.: Towards integrated microplanning of language and iconic gesture for multimodal output. In: Proceedings of the 6th International Conference on Multimodal Interfaces, pp. 97–104. ACM (2004)
10. Liang, H., Chang, J., Kazmi, I.K., Zhang, J.J., Jiao, P.: Hand gesture-based interactive puppetry system to assist storytelling for children. Vis. Comput. **33**(4), 517–531 (2017)
11. Liang, H., Chang, J., Kazmi, I.K., Zhang, J.J., Jiao, P.: Puppet narrator: utilizing motion sensing technology in storytelling for young children. In: 2015 7th International Conference on Games and Virtual Worlds for Serious Applications (VS-Games), pp. 1–8. IEEE (2015)
12. Madeo, R.C.B., Lima, C.A.M., Peres, S.M.: Gesture unit segmentation using support vector machines: segmenting gestures from rest positions. In: Proceedings of the 28th Annual ACM Symposium on Applied Computing, SAC 2013, pp. 46–52. ACM, New York (2013). https://doi.org/10.1145/2480362.2480373
13. Maricchiolo, F., Gnisci, A., Bonaiuto, M.: Coding hand gestures: a reliable taxonomy and a multi-media support. In: Esposito, A., Esposito, A.M., Vinciarelli, A., Hoffmann, R., Müller, V.C. (eds.) Cognitive Behavioural Systems. LNCS, vol. 7403, pp. 405–416. Springer, Heidelberg (2012). https://doi.org/10.1007/978-3-642-34584-5_36
14. Marin, G., Dominio, F., Zanuttigh, P.: Hand gesture recognition with leap motion and kinect devices. In: 2014 IEEE International Conference on Image Processing (ICIP), pp. 1565–1569, October 2014. https://doi.org/10.1109/ICIP.2014.7025313
15. Martínez Lara, D., Cano Méndez, R.: Alike (2015)

16. McNeill, D.: Hand and Mind: What Gestures Reveal About Thought. University of Chicago Press, Chicago (1992)
17. Quek, F.: Gesture and interaction. In: Encyclopedia of Human-Computer Interaction, vol. 54, pp. 288–292 (2004)
18. Quek, F.: The catchment feature model for multimodal language analysis. In: null, p. 540. IEEE (2003)
19. Quek, F., et al.: Multimodal human discourse: gesture and speech. ACM Trans. Comput.-Hum. Interact. **9**(3), 171–193 (2002). https://doi.org/10.1145/568513. 568514
20. Rautaray, S.S., Agrawal, A.: Vision based hand gesture recognition for human computer interaction: a survey. Artif. Intell. Rev. **43**(1), 1–54 (2015)
21. Trigueiros, P., Ribeiro, F., Reis, L.P.: A comparison of machine learning algorithms applied to hand gesture recognition. In: 7th Iberian Conference on Information Systems and Technologies (CISTI 2012), pp. 1–6, June 2012
22. Van Citters, D.: Box office bunny (1991)

When Did I Lose Them? Using Process Mining to Study User Engagement in Interactive Digital Narratives

Sergio Estupiñán[(✉)] and Nicolas Szilas

TECFA, FPSE, University of Geneva, 1211 Geneva 4, Switzerland
{Sergio.Estupinan,Nicolas.Szilas}@unige.ch

Abstract. This work aims at capitalizing advances in the field of Process Mining applied to the domain of Interactive Digital Narratives (IDN), towards the understanding of user engagement, particularly, spotting when and what happened when engagement dropped. An online IDN system was adapted to implement an engagement sampling protocol, probing 74 users for Continuation Desire during runtime. The playtest dataset was coupled with the engagement reports and analyzed using Process Mining. We identified a subset of User-Initiated Actions associated with higher engagement trajectories, as well as actionable feedback for improving the system. We consider Process Mining as an asset for the evaluation of IDN systems and the characterization of the Interactive Narrative Experience.

Keywords: Continuation Desire · Engagement · Process Mining · Interactive Narrative Experience · User Research

1 Introduction

Interactive Digital Narrative (IDN) is a computer-based media that empowers users to causally influence the course of the unfolding narrative events in a story world, mediated by a storytelling engine [3, 4]. This intentional influence, known as effectance [5], would allow users to experience interactive stories in a more personal and engaging way as a result of their direct participation.

IDN systems generally rely on Drama Manager or equivalent subsystem(s) [6] employing Artificial Intelligence techniques to balance user actions and author-defined constraints. Such subsystems should be capable to provide users not only a coherent but also an appealing Interactive Narrative Experience (INE)—the user experience particular to IDN. Despite progress in the field, notably in narrative generation, the call for more research in the systematic evaluation of IDN systems and the INE is still in force [7]. We consider that the relatively novel discipline of Process Mining, whose strength lies in the generation of actual models of human-computer interaction could be an asset to the evaluation of IDN systems.

Process Mining could use playtesting datasets to automatically build Process Maps that help cross-check the expected (or theoretical) capacities of a narrative engine with real usage data, granted it is properly timestamped. Given the generative nature of IDN

© Springer Nature Switzerland AG 2019
R. E. Cardona-Rivera et al. (Eds.): ICIDS 2019, LNCS 11869, pp. 374–378, 2019.
https://doi.org/10.1007/978-3-030-33894-7_39

systems and the multiplicity of created storylines, employing automatic analysis tools could be particularly interesting to the field. In this article, we present an experimental study focused on understanding the drops of user engagement, and briefly discussion the potentialities of Process Mining for doing User Research of IDN systems.

1.1   When Did I Lose Them?

The ability to understand how users interact in actuality with a system poses challenges and interests multiple stakeholders. 'When did I lose them?', the question that motivates this article is twofold and aims at pinpointing what happened and when during the interaction with an IDN system, that led users to a decrease in their level of engagement. By spotting and studying these drops, designers could obtain actual contextual feedback on how users interact with their systems and actionable insights.

2   Related Works

Continuation Desire [2] posits that even though engagement is a far-reaching term often related to motivation, enjoyment, engrossment, etc., all the previous concepts share a 'volitional' trait. Continuation Desire is understood as the determination, a transversal indicator encompassing the Objectives, Activities, Achievements, and Affect that drive the desire to continue making part of an interactive media experience. To sample engagement at a given point, an intrusive protocol was proposed and validated consisting of briefly pausing the execution of the experience a predefined number of times, and asking users to quantify via a Likert scale, to which extent they want to continue playing, why do they want to continue, and what they plan to do next in the game. An elevated level of Continuation Desire could then be interpreted as an indicator of the presence of engagement despite the existence of negative-valenced emotions such as frustration and anger.

Process Mining bridges Business Process Management, a discipline that deals with the modeling of the design space of business processes, (use cases and scenarios users are confronted to), and Data Mining, a discipline that treats large datasets to find patterns. Process Mining is a powerful analysis technique that goes beyond summative metrics by allowing the discovering of processes and instantiating paths of execution [1]. In Process Mining, we can distinguish Variants or unique sequences of activities, instantiations of each Variant (called Cases), and visual representations of the discovered processes (Process Maps).

3   Experimental Approach

A study was set up online using Prolific[1], a scientific crowdsourcing platform. The requirements for participating in the study were: (a) age between 18 and 40, (b) English as native language or equivalent, (c) having completed at least secondary education.

---

[1] Prolific. https://prolific.ac.

A payment of £1.50 was proposed in exchange for their 20-minutes participation. We modified the existing IDN system Nothing for Dinner to sample for Continuation Desire at three stages according to a dynamic triggering algorithm using a game-coherent look-and-feel interface that we presented in [8].

3.1 Engagement Trajectories

We defined Engagement Trajectories as paths representing the fluctuation of the self-reported level of Continuation Desire over time. We defined that user engagement at a certain point could be one of three possible Likert-scale values: High (5, 6, 7), Neutral (4), or Low (1, 2, 3). Three in-game interruptions provided us 27 possible Engagement Trajectories, from which we selected five of our interest: **Hooked** (High, High, High): Users under this trajectory experienced the highly-engaging path, **Deflated** (High, High, Neutral) featuring a gentle drop towards neutral engagement during the last part, **Betrayed** (High, High, Low) with a sharp drop in the engagement level towards the end, **Disappointed** (High, Low, Low) a strong initial desire to continue followed 'unattached' during the second and third interruption, and **Unattached** (Low, Low, Low), the opposite of 'Hooked'.

3.2 Process Mining Analysis

Disco[2], a Process Mining software, used the resulting dataset from merging data from the narrative engine, the interruption manager, and the crowdsourcing service, as input for generating the process maps and analysis of Variants. To do so, it was necessary to do a mapping of the dataset to the corresponding process mining dimensions. Once the data loaded, we selected the User-Initiated Actions by filtering by Resource *Selector* containing *Player* as value, and we filtered per interruption and engagement values. Disco employed discovery algorithms for detecting the variants and subjacent cases that ran through it.

4   Results and Analysis

A total of 90 participants (50 males, 40 females) aged between 18 and 39 years old took part in the study ($M = 27.86$, $SD = 6.24$). From this participant pool, we removed those who did not go through one of the engagement trajectories, which resulted in a final sample of 74 participants (82% of the pool), which for the most part belonged to the *Hooked* (n = 40) and *Unattached* (n = 17) trajectories.

We used Disco to automatically identify Variants of User-Initiated Actions per engagement trajectory. Variants are each of the paths of execution in a process, which contains a certain number of Cases. Process Mining analysis on the traces was performed based on segments corresponding to each of the three interruptions, allowing us to 'zoom in' into the gameplay traces.

---

[2] Disco. https://fluxicon.com/disco/.

We only found Variants for the *Hooked* and *Unattached* trajectories, which may be explained since these two trajectories have most of the participants (n = 57). By inspecting in detail each Variant segment, a series of interesting observations arise from which we instantiate the following three: First, the User-Initiated Action `Informs Wish dinner_solution`, which by design helps moving forward in the story, was strongly present in the Interruption 1 of the *Hooked* trajectory but not in the *Unattached*. Second, participants in the *Unattached* trajectory, for the most part, triggered performative activities that did not involve any other character. Finally, not finding any Variants in *Hooked*'s Interruption 3 puzzles us, since it indicates that there is no a sequence of actions that could be linked to a High Engagement. Analyzing what occurred during this interruption would require a different approach and/or additional techniques.

5 Conclusion

The nature of the AI-based systems issued in the field of Interactive Digital Narratives (IDN) affords a great multiplicity of story paths as a result of the direct intervention of the users. Such a diversity poses problems in terms of analysis of the systems and the Interactive Narrative Experience since not all the generated storylines might be interesting and engaging to the user.

We were interested in discovering when and why the user engagement had dropped during runtime in the Interactive Digital Narrative work "Nothing for Dinner" (NFD). We set up a study in which we collected telemetry data and self-reports of engagement of 74 participants during runtime, and then we employed Process Mining (PM) to discover the models and paths of interaction in the light of a set of engagement trajectories that we defined. To our knowledge, PM has not been used before for analyzing IDN systems.

Process Mining proved to be a valuable technique to discover the diverse paths in which users interact with the IDN system. Moreover, it was useful for spotting the elements of a *hooked* narrative path (high engagement), which in the case of the tested story seemed to be mostly linked to seeking the involvement of other characters in the achievement of certain activities. These leads for improvement could be implemented and further tested to validate if there is a diminishing in the number of users that exhibit drops in their engagement.

We believe that Process Mining is a new and promising approach for the automatic evaluation of different IDN systems and the advancement of the understanding of the Interactive Narrative Experience. It can provide authors and designers with powerful bird-eye analytic tools and insights on the actual interactions of the users with a complex system.

Future work may include employing Process Mining to study raises in engagement, narrative evaluation, as well as the influence of certain activities in the overall re-playability, objective metrics [9], and the emotional dynamics over time using psychophysiological measurements.

References

1. van der Aalst, W.M.P.: Process Mining. (2016). https://doi.org/10.1007/978-3-642-19345-3
2. Schoenau-Fog, H.: Hooked! – evaluating engagement as continuation desire in interactive narratives. In: Si, M., Thue, D., André, E., Lester, J.C., Tanenbaum, J., Zammitto, V. (eds.) ICIDS 2011. LNCS, vol. 7069, pp. 219–230. Springer, Heidelberg (2011). https://doi.org/10.1007/978-3-642-25289-1_24
3. Murray, J.H.: Hamlet on the Holodeck: The Future of Narrative in Cyberspace. MIT Press, Cambridge (1997)
4. Roth, C.: Experiencing Interactive Storytelling (2016)
5. Klimmt, C., Hartmann, T., Frey, A.: Effectance and control as determinants of video game enjoyment. CyberPsychol. Behav. **10**, 845–848 (2007). https://doi.org/10.1089/cpb.2007.9942
6. Arinbjarnar, M., Barber, H., Kudenko, D.: A critical review of interactive drama systems. In: AISB 2009 Symposium AI Games, pp. 15–25 (2009)
7. Louchart, S., Zagalo, N.: The Challenges with Evaluating Interactive Narratives, pp. 2–3 (2012)
8. Estupiñán, S., Andkjaer, K.I., Szilas, N.: Engagement in interactive digital storytelling: sampling without spoiling. In: Clua, E., Roque, L., Lugmayr, A., Tuomi, P. (eds.) ICEC 2018. LNCS, vol. 11112, pp. 248–253. Springer, Cham (2018). https://doi.org/10.1007/978-3-319-99426-0_25
9. Szilas, N., Ilea, I.: Objective metrics for interactive narrative. In: Mitchell, A., Fernández-Vara, C., Thue, D. (eds.) ICIDS 2014. LNCS, vol. 8832, pp. 91–102. Springer, Cham (2014). https://doi.org/10.1007/978-3-319-12337-0_9

Effects of Higher Interactivity on the Interactive Narrative Experience: An Experimental Study

Liudmyla Gapiuk, Sergio Estupiñán, and Nicolas Szilas[✉]

TECFA, FPSE, University of Geneva, 1211 Genève 4, Switzerland
{Sergio.Estupinan,Nicolas.Szilas}@unige.ch

Abstract. This article reports a study with the purpose of analyzing the Interactive Narrative Experience under different levels of interactivity: a "classic" Interactive Narrative constructed with a branching story structure, and a "generative" Interactive Narrative built on a narrative engine that integrates techniques of Artificial Intelligence. Three elements of the user experience, namely control, curiosity, and frustration were compared and examined based on the experiment with 30 participants who played one of two versions of the narrative.

Keywords: Highly interactive storytelling · User experience · Interactive Narrative Experience · Control · Curiosity · Frustration

1 Introduction

Interactive Storytelling changes the role of the user: from the observer, she becomes the active player who can influence the course of the story through her interactions with the system [1–3]. This is classically achieved by using a branching story structure [4, 5], for which the author must write all scenarios, which inherently limits the number of scenarios and the agency [1]. However, techniques based on Artificial Intelligence (AI) make it possible to generate narrative events and create a story dynamically according to user choices. The event in a generative narrative is calculated and created by the program, considering the elements and constraints specified by the author. This gives the user even more freedom of choice and the possibility to influence how the story unfolds or ends. Such *"Highly Interactive Narrative"* contains at least one event that in its occurrence (if and when it happens), its content and its formulation, is the result of a calculation [3]. It includes works such as "Façade" [6, 7], "Crystal Island" [8, 9] or "Nothing For Dinner" (NFD) [3, 10]. The latter, based on the *IDension* narrative engine allows to generate a series of narrative events and to offer in average 23 possibilities of action each time the user had to interact [12].

Currently, despite the numerous discussions on agency and freedom in Interactive Storytelling, there is a lack of research on the effective impact of this freedom of action and interactivity on the Interactive Narrative Experience. Roth et al. [13] compared the user experience in "Façade" with the adventure game "Fahrenheit" that is characterized by the relatively low degree of user freedom. Results showed that dimensions of user

R. E. Cardona-Rivera et al. (Eds.): ICIDS 2019, LNCS 11869, pp. 379–388, 2019.
https://doi.org/10.1007/978-3-030-33894-7_40

experience such as system usability, character believability, presence, and emotional state were rated much higher in "Façade" than in "Fahrenheit". They also compared each of these interactive systems with their non-interactive counterpart—watching someone play, and concluded that for "Fahrenheit", the addition of interactivity does not change many dimensions of the Interactive Narrative Experience while a strong impact of interactivity on user experience was observed in "Façade" with more favorable experience in the interactive condition. Despite these interesting finding, no research has been conducted to determine how the different *levels* of interactivity impact user experience within the *same* story world.

In this study, we aim at analyzing the effect of the higher level of interactivity on the Interactive Narrative Experience by comparing two different versions of the same story world with different degrees of interactivity. The first one, the Highly Interactive version, integrates techniques from AI, while the second one, the 'weakly' interactive version, is based on branching story structure, offering a low level of interaction. More precisely, we examine the feeling of control, curiosity and frustration resulting from the user's emotional experience in the narrative. We hypothesized that these components of the Interactive Narrative Experience would be particularly affected by the degree of interactivity in the narrative.

Control

The feeling of control over the story word is one of the important elements that can determine user engagement [4] and sense of presence [14]. But in a branching story structure, this feeling is limited by the number of possible paths of story offered to users [4]. Their experience in the narrative is likely to be homogeneous if they are prompted to make the same choices over and over, which could lead the user with an impression of loss of control over the story. We suppose that the freedom of interaction and strong autonomy in the Highly Interactive version will offer the users a stronger perception of control over their actions, compared to the weakly interactive version that does not offer enough freedom of choice.

Curiosity

Inducing curiosity in the users is important to make the IS system interesting and enjoyable to use [15]. The user can be "curious" about story progress, *"What will happen next?"*, and the consequences of her decisions on interactive story, *"What will happen if I choose this option?"*. Roth et al. [16] noted that when curiosity appears, users experience a temporary uncertainty which lead to a particular physiological state, enjoyable for most users. And when uncertainty is reduced, for example with the discovery of the dénouement of the story, the user experiences positive and pleasant emotions. For Roth et al. [16] such a repetition of increased and reduced curiosity *"create a chain of pleasant affective dynamics"*. We estimate that in the Highly Interactive version of narrative, the sense of curiosity will be more important than in the weakly interactive version because more options could mean more possible outcomes, and therefore more curiosity about these outcomes.

Frustration

Although frustration, for most people, is associated with a negative emotion, it could also be a positive element in the Interactive Narrative Experience [17]. Nylund and Landfors [18] made a distinction between bad and good frustration. According to them, bad frustration is related to technical problems while good frustration is caused by the emotional state in the game and which allows a deeper sense of immersion and engagement. The authors consider that with a good frustration, a game can offer the player a higher level of emotional engagement and she becomes thus more involved and focused. In the frame of this study, the term "frustration" refers to good frustration. In *Façade*, the user's frustration towards the personality of characters was considered as a positive element of the narrative which confirms character plausibility and player engagement [6]. Allison et al. [19] found that players of *DayZ* considered the permanent death of their character as frustrating but also a necessary component to make the game enjoyable. In *Nothing For Dinner* some users identified frustration as a positive element of user experience [10]: By embodying the role of the protagonist the user can feel the frustration that comes from the inability to change the family situation despite effort in that sense, and from the difficulties of managing daily life with a person who suffered a Traumatic Brain Injury.

Extending these examples, we hypothesize that the frustration resulting from the user emotions in the game is not only a positive aspect of user experience but also can be a fundamental characteristic of Interactive Narrative based on social context. In the version using branching story structure, users would feel mainly empathy for the characters, while in the highly interactive version, the emotions could be stronger because the high degree of freedom to interact with the story characters allows the player to simulate human relationships in a virtual world, and as a result to establish an *emotional connection* with story characters. We assume thus that in the Highly Interactive version of the narrative, the feeling of frustration is higher than in the narrative with a low level of interactivity.

2 Method

Two versions of the existing Interactive Narrative (IN) *Nothing For Dinner* (NFD), were used with different levels of interactivity: a Highly Interactive version and a weakly interactive version. These two versions are rendered in the form of a narrative hypertext. The experiment was conducted with 30 participants with the objective to compare the Interactive Narrative Experience in both versions. The independent variable was the level of interactivity in the IN (high, low) and the dependent variables were feelings of control, curiosity, and frustration.

2.1 Research Design

Both versions of the IN were written in French and based on the same story: the user plays the role of Frank, a 16-year-old teenager whose father Paul suffered a Traumatic Brain Injury and has problems with memory and behavior [10]. The IN shows the daily difficulties of Frank and his family. The experience begins with a scenario where Paul forgot to go shopping and Frank has to prepare something to eat for dinner because his mother is away. The user reaches the end of the narrative when all the family members (Paul—the father, Olivia—the grandmother, and Lili—the younger sister) are seated at the table.

Fig. 1. (Left) Screenshot of the 3D version of NFD. (Right) Screenshot of the Highly Interactive hypertext version of NFD.

Highly Interactive Hypertext Version: For this experiment, we adapted the 3D version of NFD into a dynamic hypertext version. We removed all the 3D graphics and interaction and we created a new user interface in hypertext form on top of the ID tension narrative engine [11]. We thus used the same narrative engine as in the original 3D version. Figures 1 shows the difference between the 3D version and the highly interactive hypertext version.

In the Highly Interactive hypertext version of NFD (Fig. 2), the characters and objects of the narrative are presented in the form of an interactive row at the top of the screen. The screen is divided into two parts: one part with character dialogues and the other part with possible choices. The choice list is modified according to the character with whom the player is currently interacting with and changes dynamically considering previous actions, as calculated by the Narrative Engine. The button "Next" appears as the interaction progresses to show the continuation of the undertaken action and moves forward in the story.

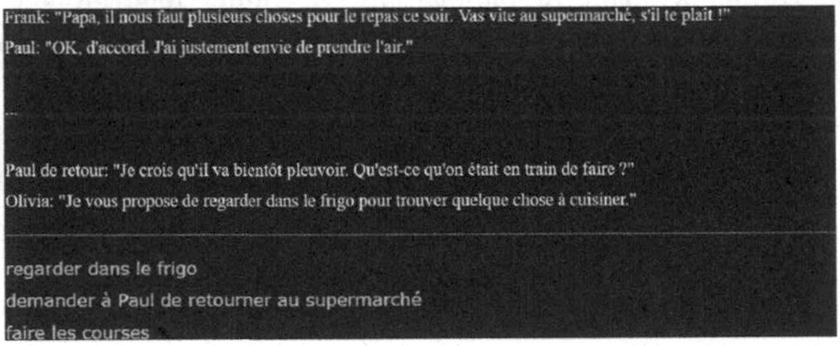

Fig. 2. Screenshot of the weakly interactive hypertext version of NFD

Weakly Interactive Hypertext Version: The weakly interactive hypertext version was built in Twine[1], a software that allows to create branching-based Interactive Narratives. All narrative actions are presented sequentially: each event that occurs depends on the

---

[1] https://twinery.org/.

previous choice. We have reduced the long list of choices proposed in the Highly Interactive version by leaving in each scene only 1 to 3 essential choices to achieve the objectives of the scenario and move forward in the story (see Fig. 2).

2.2 Participants

30 participants took part in this study, 16 males and 14 females aged between 18 and 40 years. French was their mother tongue, or they were bilingual, had no prior knowledge on Traumatic Brain Injury and had never played *NFD*. They were randomly assigned to one of the two experimental groups, one with the Highly Interactive version, the other one with the Weakly Interactive version (15 participants per group).

2.3 Measures

Feeling of control was measured using the scale Control (Cronbach's $\alpha = .80$) proposed in the Core Elements of the Gaming Experience Questionnaire (CEGEQ) [20]. 6 statements were chosen and used to evaluate the feeling of control: "I was in control of the game", "I was able to see in the screen everything I needed during the game", "I felt what was happening in the game was my own doing", "There was time when I was doing nothing in the game", "I knew how to manipulate the game to move forward", "I knew all the actions that could be performed in the game" on a 5-point Likert scale from 1 (strongly disagree) to 5 (strongly agree).

Curiosity was measured using a curiosity evaluation questionnaire in serious games (Cronbach's $\alpha = .71$) developed by Wouters et al. [21]. To make the questionnaire relevant to our theme, "cancer" was replaced by "traumatic brain injury". The questionnaire was composed of 6 items: "The game motivated me to learn more about traumatic brain injury", "I wanted to continue playing because I wanted to see more of the game world", "I was curious to the next event in the game", "I sought explanations for what I encountered in the game", "Playing the game raised questions regarding traumatic brain injury", "I wanted to continue playing because I wanted to know more about traumatic brain injury". Participants were asked to rate these statements on a 5-point Likert scale ranging from 1 (strongly disagree) to 5 (strongly agree).

Not having found an existing scale to measure frustration that results from the user's emotional experience, we established ourselves the items that could evaluate this type of frustration. Five statements were therefore issued: "I lived with Frank the difficulties of his daily life", "I can understand why Frank gets angry because of his father's attitude", "I felt Frank's frustration when he was managing relationships with his father", "I was upset by Paul's unpredictable reactions" and "I wanted to help Frank but I felt powerless in the situation". As for the two previous variables, participants estimated these statements on a 5-point Likert scale from 1 (strongly disagree) to 5 (strongly agree). All questions were translated in French.

2.4 Procedure

The experimental procedure went on in two steps: first, the selection of participants and second the participation to the experiment. In order to assess whether potential participants fulfill the selection criteria (see Sect. 2.2 above), a questionnaire was sent by e-mail. This e-mail also included the context of the research, the purpose of the questionnaire and the unfolding of the future experiment. Then, the accepted persons were contacted to come on-site for the study.

The experimental procedures were identical for both groups of participants except the time of interaction with the narrative: 30 minutes for the highly interactive group and 20 min for the weakly interactive group. This is due to the fact that the former offers more possibilities of actions (23 in average vs 1–3), which requires more time for selecting an action. The experiment took place in a quiet room with groups of two to five participants. It started with a briefing after which participants were asked to sign a consent form. Each participant had at their disposal the tutorial in paper form "How to play" explaining elements of the IN's interface and possible interactions in the game. Immediately after playing, participants were asked to complete a computer-based questionnaire to measure their feeling of control, curiosity, frustration. The questionnaire also included one open question: "How was your experience in this study?". They were also requested to fill out a computer-based questionnaire that included the 12 questions to analyze participants' learning outcomes in both interactive versions of the narrative. In this article, we do not tackle learning outcomes.

The whole duration of the experiment was 40 min for the highly interactive group and 30 min for the weakly interactive group. At the end of the experiment, participants received a remuneration of 10 Swiss Francs.

3   Results

A significance level of $p = 0.05$ was used for all statistical tests.

Table 1 presents the means and standard deviations obtained for the answers on a five-point Likert scale to the questions related to the feeling of control, curiosity, and frustration, in two experimental conditions. It indicates that in the weakly interactive condition, the level of control and curiosity is higher than in the highly interactive condition. The level of frustration is slightly higher in the highly interactive version.

Table 1. Descriptive statistics for all dependent variables in two experimental conditions

		N	Mean	Std. Dev.
Control	Highly interactive version	15	3.45	.55
	Weakly interactive version	15	3.76	.90
Curiosity	Highly interactive version	15	3.65	.72
	Weakly interactive version	15	3.94	.91
Frustration	Highly interactive version	15	3.82	.47
	Weakly interactive version	15	3.61	.69

An ANOVA analysis was conducted to examine the effect of interactivity on feeling of control, curiosity, and frustration.

Table 2. Effect of higher interactivity on all dependent variables (ANOVA)

		Sum of squares	df	Mean square	F	Sig.
Control	Between groups	.73	1	.73	1.28	.27
	Within groups	15.90	28	.57		
	Total	16.63	29			
Curiosity	Between groups	.63	1	.63	.92	.35
	Within groups	19.12	28	.68		
	Total	19.74	29			
Frustration	Between groups	.34	1	.34	.98	.33
	Within groups	9.79	28	.35		
	Total	10.13	29			

Inferential statistics (Table 2) show that the effect of interactivity was not statistically significant on our 3 dependent variables: feeling of control $F(1,28) = 1,28$, $p = .27$, curiosity $F(1,28) = .92$, $p = .35$ and frustration $F(1,28) = .98$, $p = .33$. Contrary to our hypothesis, the level of interactivity does not influence the user's feeling of control, curiosity, and frustration.

4 Analysis and Interpretation

The absence of effect of the degree of interactivity on the feeling of control (and even a tendency towards an inverse effect) may be explained by the difficulties of interacting with the system which offers too many choices. This surfaces in some answers to the open question "How was your experience in this experiment?": "*Sometimes there were too many options*" and "*It was difficult to interact correctly with characters without getting lost in the different options.*" Another interpretation could be that repetitive choices presented in the Highly Interactive version decreased the sense of control. Some participants who used this version noted that "*Obsolete options should be removed once they have already been made*" and "*Repetitive options give the impression that you are in a loop and you lose the motivation to continue.*" Also, two participants who used the high interactive version noted "*I enjoyed playing the game... you feel like you have an influence on the unfolding of the story*" and "*Interesting and enriching experience. My perception has really evolved with (this) simulation game where we see the consequences of the actions.*" These two participants effectively scored 4 for the control scale, it might be plausible that they experienced a feeling of agency [1]. Therefore, two phenomena may compensate each other: on the one hand, more interactivity, therefore more choices, led to a feeling of getting lost in the space of possibilities, thus a lack of control, while on the other hand, more interactivity was appreciated as a gain in agency. Therefore, in order to fully benefit from the increase in interactivity, it appears essential to also solve critical issues that are collateral with the increase of choices: optimize the display of many choices from a usability point of view, present enough new options in each turn, make sure that options that appear repetitive would produce a distinctive effect on the story world.

As for curiosity, one interpretation of the non-significance of the results could be related to the participants' initial interest in the subject of the narrative. The scale that was used was related to the domain of the story (Traumatic Brain Injury), while participants had no special interest in the domain. Note also that one of the Highly Interactive version users noted "I want to repeat this experience to know the other possible situations." It might be interesting to raise the question of how the higher interactivity in IN can affect the desire to replay the game to discover other scenarios of the story.

Regarding frustration, when the user plays the role of a teenager who must carry out duties of his father which suffered TBI, it is so emotionally strong in itself, that this caused a similar emotional state in the two versions and a similar level of frustration. We consider that this feeling of frustration can be used by IN authors in the design phase of narratives that attempt to make understand certain human relationships and behavior.

Regarding participants' answers to the open question, role adoption and immersion in the story world were also relevant in combination with frustration. In the highly interactive version, the participants mentioned: "(The) *Experience made me feel frustrated when you can't always help a person with this disorder*", "A beautiful experience that immersed me in the world of a person helping relative with TBI to provide for his daily needs." And in the weakly interactive version, they noted: "*I felt helpless in front of the situation, but I really felt what Frank* (story' protagonist) *was feeling*", "*I lived this experience with a lot of compassion for Frank's family.*"

Based on the analysis of participants' answers, interactivity seems to have impacted enjoyment in the narrative. In the highly interactive version, two participants noted: "*I enjoyed playing the game, interactive things are always fun*", "*I enjoyed the experience... It made me want to help Paul* (person with TBI)." Previous research showed that enjoyment in games was increased by interactivity [22, 23].

We consider it interesting that even the narrative with a low level of interactivity can cause important immersion and emotional effects, including (positive) frustration. This can be explained again by the strong emotional theme of NFD and it would be useful to analyze what effect the level of interactivity will have on these dimensions in a narrative not based on the social context. This result also suggests that creating frustration by giving more choices is certainly more complex than only considering the quantitative aspect of choice (number and frequency of choices). What these choices are, how they affect or not the success of the player's quest needs to be tackled in more detail, both theoretically and practically.

5   Conclusion

In this study, we experimentally compared two different versions of the same Interactive Narrative, each featuring a different degree of interactivity, to analyze the effect the higher interactivity on the Interactive Narrative Experience. The results indicated that the level of interactivity did not impact the user's feeling of control, curiosity, and frustration. These results challenge the idea that generative interactive narrative is necessary better than branching narrative. At the same time, this study provided hints on dimensions of improvements of generative systems, mostly related to the ergonomics of choices. It also suggests to build more relevant indicators than the number of choices, to predict the feelings of control, curiosity and frustration, based on a deeper analysis of the structure of choices in IN [24, 25].

References

1. Murray, J.H.: Hamlet on the Holodeck: The Future of Narrative in Cyberspace. The Free Press, New York (1997)
2. Laurel, B.: Toward the design of a computer-based interactive fantasy system. The Ohio State University (1986)
3. Szilas, N.: Apprendre par le récit fortement interactif: potentialités et premiers constats. In: Narrative Matters 2014: Narrative Knowing/Récit et Savoir (2014)
4. Riedl, M.O., Young, R.M.: From linear story generation to branching story graphs. IEEE Comput. Graph. Appl. **26**, 23–31 (2006)
5. Gordon, A., van Lent, M., Van Velsen, M., Carpenter, P., Jhala, A.: Branching storylines in virtual reality environments for leadership development. In: Proceedings of the National Conference on Artificial Intelligence, pp. 844–851. AAAI Press, MIT Press, Menlo Park, Cambridge, London (2004, 1999)
6. Knickmeyer, R.L., Mateas, M.: Preliminary evaluation of the interactive drama facade. In: CHI 2005 Extended Abstracts on Human Factors in Computing Systems, pp. 1549–1552. ACM (2005)
7. Mateas, M., Stern, A.: Procedural authorship: a case-study of the interactive drama Façade. Digital Arts Cult. (DAC) **27**, 1–8 (2005)
8. Linssen, J.: A discussion of interactive storytelling techniques for use in a serious game. CTIT Technical Report Series (2012)
9. Mott, B.W., Lester, J.C.: U-director: a decision-theoretic narrative planning architecture for storytelling environments. In: Proceedings of the Fifth International Joint Conference on Autonomous Agents and Multiagent Systems, pp. 977–984. ACM (2006)
10. Szilas, N., Dumas, J., Richle, U., Habonneau, N.: Apports d'une simulation narrative pour l'acquisition de compétences sociales. Sticef **24**, 123–151 (2017)
11. Szilas, N.: IDtension: a narrative engine for interactive drama. In: Proceedings of the Technologies for Interactive Digital Storytelling and Entertainment (TIDSE) Conference, pp. 1–11 (2003)
12. Szilas, N., Ilea, I.: Objective metrics for interactive narrative. In: Mitchell, A., Fernández-Vara, C., Thue, D. (eds.) ICIDS 2014. LNCS, vol. 8832, pp. 91–102. Springer, Cham (2014). https://doi.org/10.1007/978-3-319-12337-0_9
13. Roth, C., Klimmt, C., Vermeulen, I.E., Vorderer, P.: The Experience of interactive storytelling: comparing "Fahrenheit" with "Façade". In: Anacleto, J.C., Fels, S., Graham, N., Kapralos, B., Saif El-Nasr, M., Stanley, K. (eds.) ICEC 2011. LNCS, vol. 6972, pp. 13–21. Springer, Heidelberg (2011). https://doi.org/10.1007/978-3-642-24500-8_2
14. Lombard, M., Ditton, T.: At the heart of it all: the concept of presence. J. Comput.-Mediat. Commun. **3**, JCMC321 (1997)
15. Malone, T.W.: Heuristics for designing enjoyable user interfaces: lessons from computer games. In: Proceedings of the 1982 Conference on Human Factors in Computing Systems, pp. 63–68. ACM (1982)

16. Roth, C., Vorderer, P., Klimmt, C.: The motivational appeal of interactive storytelling: towards a dimensional model of the user experience. In: Iurgel, Ido A., Zagalo, N., Petta, P. (eds.) ICIDS 2009. LNCS, vol. 5915, pp. 38–43. Springer, Heidelberg (2009). https://doi.org/10.1007/978-3-642-10643-9_7

17. Bopp, J.A., Mekler, E.D., Opwis, K.: Negative emotion, positive experience?: emotionally moving moments in digital games. In: Proceedings of the 2016 CHI Conference on Human Factors in Computing Systems, pp. 2996–3006. ACM (2016)

18. Nylund, A., Landfors, O.: Frustration and its effect on immersion in games: a developer viewpoint on the good and bad aspects of frustration (2015)

19. Allison, F., Carter, M., Gibbs, M.: Good frustrations: the paradoxical pleasure of fearing death in DayZ. In: Proceedings of the Annual Meeting of the Australian Special Interest Group for Computer Human Interaction, pp. 119–123. ACM (2015)

20. Calvillo-Gámez, E.H., Cairns, P., Cox, A.L.: Assessing the core elements of the gaming experience. In: Bernhaupt, R. (ed.) Game User Experience Evaluation. HIS, pp. 37–62. Springer, Cham (2015). https://doi.org/10.1007/978-3-319-15985-0_3

21. Wouters, P., Van Oostendorp, H., Boonekamp, R., Van der Spek, E.: The role of game discourse analysis and curiosity in creating engaging and effective serious games by implementing a back story and foreshadowing. Interact. Comput. 23, 329–336 (2011)

22. Steinemann, S.T., Mekler, E.D., Opwis, K.: Increasing donating behavior through a game for change: the role of interactivity and appreciation. In: Proceedings of the 2015 Annual Symposium on Computer-Human Interaction in Play, pp. 319–329. ACM (2015)

23. Wong, W.L., et al.: Serious video game effectiveness. In: Proceedings of the International Conference on Advances in Computer Entertainment Technology, pp. 49–55. ACM (2007)

24. Mawhorter, P., Mateas, M., Wardrip-Fruin, N., Jhala, A.: Towards a theory of choice poetics (2014)

25. Estupiñán, S., Maret, B., Andkjaer, K., Szilas, N.: A multidimensional classification of choice presentation in interactive narrative. In: Rouse, R., Koenitz, H., Haahr, M. (eds.) ICIDS 2018. LNCS, vol. 11318, pp. 149–153. Springer, Cham (2018). https://doi.org/10.1007/978-3-030-04028-4_12

Towards a Quality Framework
for Immersive Media Experiences:
A Holistic Approach

Asim Hameed, Shafaq Irshad(✉) ⓘⅅ, and Andrew Perkis ⓘⅅ

Department of Electronic Systems,
Faculty of Information Technology and Electrical Engineering,
Norwegian University of Science and Technology, Trondheim, Norway
{asim.hameed,shafaq.irshad,andrew.perkis}@ntnu.no

Abstract. Immersive Media Technologies have emerged as popular media form. Their captivating nature makes them a powerful tool for participation and storytelling in a variety of domains attracting multidisciplinary interest. Existing frameworks for user-perceived quality in immersive media experiences are limited due to their exclusion of narrative dimensions. This research expands upon the current system-centered Quality of Experience framework by including Content Influence Factors based on learnings from IDN. Hence proposing a conceptual framework for measuring immersive media experiences, which comprise of four constructs: Form, Content, User, and Context. These components are interrelated through their overlapping dimensions, which is discussed through the course of this paper.

Keywords: Interactive Digital Narrative · Immersive Media Experiences · Quality of Experience · Virtual reality

1 Introduction

Over the years, immersive technologies have become inherently interactive and their dependence on narrative has gradually increased [7]. When the end user experiences these technologies it results in Immersive Media Experiences (IME). Underlying concepts and dimensions of IME have been developed from a technological perspective [10,12,21] however, quality measures are still rudimentary. Current Quality of Experience (QoE) frameworks limit their definition of content to its type (depth, texture, etc.) and reliability. Thereby, excluding the information and experiences it delivers. In turn, also excluding any narrative-based and/or task-based influences of the content on user-perceived quality. Hence, we believe that assessing quality in Immersive Media Experiences can benefit from the rich scholarship of Interactive Digital Narratives (IDN). It is not clear which factors of an IME are responsible for a user's emotion, involvement, and degree of interest for user-perceived quality. However, immersive media is widely

© Springer Nature Switzerland AG 2019
R. E. Cardona-Rivera et al. (Eds.): ICIDS 2019, LNCS 11869, pp. 389–394, 2019.
https://doi.org/10.1007/978-3-030-33894-7_41

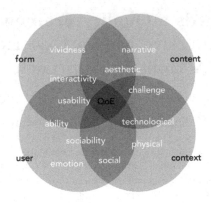

Fig. 1. Quality framework for Immersive Media Experiences (IME)

understood from an experiential perspective as a user's "sense of presence". This framework encapsulates physical, symbolic and psychological dimensions that must be considered for user perceived quality inside IMEs. Given the richness and complexity of emerging media environments, it is important to understand the dynamism of these contemporary media forms before developing quality frameworks. QoE measures are subject to a range of complex and strongly inter-related factors that fall into three categories of **Human**, **System** and **Context Influence Factors (IFs)** [13,18]. Despite their interest around user experience, existing frameworks are predominantly system-centric. With our work we want to focus on a human-centric paradigm by taking into account all those factors that reflect on the user's experience. For this, we accept the important of the above mentioned influence factors for our framework but also include *Content Influence Factors* for their role in overall user satisfaction, and QoE.

2   QoE Framework for Immersive Media Experiences

This research understands IME as a union of immersive, interactive and narrative. This section discusses our quality framework (Fig. 1) in terms of its four constructs: *Form*, *Content*, *User*, and *Context*, considering different dimensions and variables.

2.1   Form

We consider form to be the foundation upon which the entirety of IME is built. It comprises of a system-generated world that affords interaction to its users. Appropriating from Steuer, we denote form by its *vividness* and *interactivity*. One is the system's ability *"to produce a sensory rich mediated environment"*, and the latter is degree to which users can *"influence the form or content of the mediated environment"* [26]. To achieve flow inside any system the experience dimensions and quality dimensions needs to be measured.

1. Experience Dimension (Spatial Presence) is a sense of physical presence, specifically *Spatial Presence*, in the "immersive virtual environment" [26] referred as *Place Illusion* [24]. Ryan [20] refers to it as a new dimension of *Spatial Immersion* that comes from technology not narrative. System immersion is level of immersion (high or low) directly experienced by the user [16,25].

2. Quality Dimension (Vividness) is the sensorial encapsulation of the user is ensured by a distinct quality of technology, *vividness* [25,26]. It is the *"representational richness of a mediated environment ... that is, the way in which an environment presents information to the senses"* [26]. In this research, we consider vividness (extent and fidelity of sensory information) as a user-perceived quality of IVEs that depends on quantifiable system factors of tracking, latency, display persistence, resolution, optics (fov), and spatial audio.

Interaction is derived when a user responds to the *affordances* (action possibilities presented by digital elements, artifacts, and objects) inside a simulated environment [5]. It is a stimulus-driven variable that depends upon the technological formation of the IVE and is quantified under three factors: *speed of interaction* (system response time to user action), *range of interactivity* and *mapping* (system ability to map user input to changes in IVE). The degree to which the interactivity of an IVE, its controller, and feedback mechanisms match the real world has an affect on user's ability in applying natural navigation and manipulation techniques in IVEs.

2.2 Content

We introduce content as a new influence factor in our quality framework for IME. A user removed from their immediate context is immersed into *a reality represented by the medium*, i.e. the broad category objects, actors and events. We argue that an IVE with its inherent interactive qualities is a *live box of action possibilities* produced by the system. Content, on the other hand, is its *"meaning"*. It is the flow of events, inclusion of social elements, nature of task/activities performed. The overall meaningfulness of the content determines various kinds of presence [9,14,22]. Meaning, for the user, is derived from a combination of the content and the context within which the content exists [6]. We divide content into diegetic, non-diegetic, and aesthetic classes of information or experience. For our holistic framework, we have discussed the dimensions of two content factors in specific, i.e. narrative-based and task-based.

Narrative-Based: What storytellers achieved through expression, improvisation, theatrics, and exaggeration are now readily available to users as immersive environments produced by computers. Ryan [20] calls it Spatial Immersion (in her triad of spatial, temporal and emotional immersion). IVE is only a *presentation context* whereas its *narrative context* is the diegetic space of the story that takes place within it [2]. These dimensions are symmetrical to the four narrative-centric factors hypothesized by Rowe et al. [19]. These are *narrative consistency* (believability), *plot coherence* (logical order), *drama* (setup-conflict-resolution), and *predictability* (real-world authenticity). The result of which is a *Plausibility Illusion* - an acknowledgement of the truth of the environment [24].

Task-Based: Flow arises when perceived challenges correspond to perceived skills via *experience of flow* [4]. On the contrary, a mismatch between ability and challenge can lead to feelings of frustration and displeasure. A task inside a VE is determined by its nature and level of challenge (cognitive/motor). Additionally, tasks are also affected by context (e.g. temporal) and depend on the kind of interaction they require, i.e. navigation, selection or manipulation. Task performance improves when a user's ability is matched by the usability of a system. Another important factor is the introduction of aesthetic features (e.g. interface graphics, gamification, etc.) to enhance user performance. It can be hypothesized that tasks performed in IVEs influence the emotional state of the users and is directly influenced by the user's ability to use system [1,23,28].

2.3   User

User, or human, influence factors are deemed influential for the formation of quality [3]. User characteristics, their learning ability and assumed agency play a significant role in shaping the overall perceived quality of IME. *Characteristics* are demographic attributes as well as perceptual, cognitive and motor abilities of users [11]. Prior experiences of IVEs affect a willful suspension of disbelief as well as allocation of attentional resources [11] in turn, affecting presence. Other works [8,15,29] have identified the effects of age, gender, cultural background, and emotional state on user-perceived quality. Due to their characteristic similarity to the real-world, users have a higher chance of learning IVEs [17,27].

2.4   Context

Context factors are relevant situational properties that can be broken down into physical, temporal, social, economic, task and technical characteristics [18]. They have considerable effect on the quality levels of any media experience. But since fully immersive media (such as VR) occlude the real-world, we arrive at an inside and an outside. Simulated contextual changes inside virtual environments can affect user characteristics. IMEs are powerful because of the agency they give the end user. They are not mere simulations but entirely new spaces of signification as well. User do not just experience high-fidelity geometries with real-time responsiveness but the meanings those interactions deliver. This is why they require new inclusive measures for quality assessment. Hence, evaluating all the dimensions discussed above can depict the overall QoE of IMEs.

3   Conclusion

This research paper presents a modified quality framework of IMEs. In addition to immersivity and interactivity, the framework draws from theories and approaches in IDN to include narrativity as an important facet. The paper presents a four constructs i.e. Form, Content, Context and User, that determine quality in IMEs. For its practical use, the framework emphasizes on the importance of signification (the meaning delivered) aspects of these experiences for the user. We believe that any user-perceived experience evaluation is incomplete without considering narrative-related and task-related dimensions inside content.

References

1. Allcoat, D., von Mühlenen, A.: Learning in virtual reality: effects on performance, emotion and engagement. Res. Learn. Technol. **26**, 2140 (2018)
2. Brooks, K.: There is nothing virtual about immersion: narrative immersion for VR and other interfaces (2003). http://alumni.media.mit.edu/~brooks/storybiz/immersiveNotVirtual.pdf. Accessed May 2007
3. Brunnström, K., et al.: Qualinet white paper on definitions of quality of experience (2013)
4. Csikszentmihalyi, M.: Flow: The Psychology of Happiness. Random House, New York (2013)
5. Gibson, J.J.: The theory of affordances, Hilldale, USA, vol. 1, no. 2 (1977)
6. Gigliotti, C.: Aesthetics of a virtual world. Leonardo **28**(4), 289–295 (1995)
7. Gomes, R.: The design of narrative as an immersive simulation, Vancouver, CA (2005)
8. Guntuku, S.C., Lin, W., Scott, M.J., Ghinea, G.: Modelling the influence of personality and culture on affect and enjoyment in multimedia. In: 2015 International Conference on Affective Computing and Intelligent Interaction (ACII), pp. 236–242. IEEE (2015)
9. Heeter, C.: Being there: the subjective experience of presence. Presence: Teleoperators Virtual Environ. **1**(2), 262–271 (1992)
10. Hupont, I., Gracia, J., Sanagustin, L., Gracia, M.A.: How do new visual immersive systems influence gaming QoE? A use case of serious gaming with Oculus Rift. In: 2015 Seventh International Workshop on Quality of Multimedia Experience (QoMEX), pp. 1–6. IEEE (2015)
11. IJsselsteijn, W.A., De Ridder, H., Freeman, J., Avons, S.E.: Presence: concept, determinants, and measurement. In: Human vision and electronic imaging V, vol. 3959, pp. 520–529. International Society for Optics and Photonics (2000)
12. Keighrey, C., Flynn, R., Murray, S., Murray, N.: A QoE evaluation of immersive augmented and virtual reality speech & language assessment applications. In: 2017 Ninth International Conference on Quality of Multimedia Experience (QoMEX), pp. 1–6. IEEE (2017)
13. Le Callet, P., Möller, S., Perkis, A., et al.: Qualinet white paper on definitions of quality of experience. In: European Network on Quality of Experience in Multimedia Systems and Services (COST Action IC 1003), vol. 3, no. 2012 (2012)
14. Lee, K.M.: Presence, explicated. Commun. Theory **14**(1), 27–50 (2004)
15. Murray, N., Qiao, Y., Lee, B., Muntean, G.M., Karunakar, A.: Age and gender influence on perceived olfactory & visual media synchronization. In: 2013 IEEE International Conference on Multimedia and Expo (ICME), pp. 1–6. IEEE (2013)
16. Nilsson, N.C., Nordahl, R., Serafin, S.: Immersion revisited: a review of existing definitions of immersion and their relation to different theories of presence. Hum. Technol. **12**, 108–134 (2016)
17. Pedroli, E., et al.: Characteristics, usability, and users experience of a system combining cognitive and physical therapy in a virtual environment: positive bike. Sensors **18**(7), 2343 (2018)

18. Reiter, U., et al.: Factors influencing quality of experience. In: Möller, S., Raake, A. (eds.) Quality of Experience. TSTS, pp. 55–72. Springer, Cham (2014). https://doi.org/10.1007/978-3-319-02681-7_4

19. Rowe, J.P., McQuiggan, S.W., Lester, J.C.: Narrative presence in intelligent learning environments. In: AAAI Fall Symposium: Intelligent Narrative Technologies, pp. 127–134 (2007)

20. Ryan, M.L.: Narrative as Virtual Reality 2: Revisiting Immersion and Interactivity in Literature and Electronic Media, vol. 2. JHU Press, Baltimore (2015)

21. Schatz, R., Sackl, A., Timmerer, C., Gardlo, B.: Towards subjective quality of experience assessment for omnidirectional video streaming. In: 2017 Ninth International Conference on Quality of Multimedia Experience (QoMEX), pp. 1–6. IEEE (2017)

22. Sheridan, T.B.: Musings on telepresence and virtual presence. Presence: Teleoperators Virtual Environ. 1(1), 120–126 (1992)

23. Shin, N.: Online learner's 'flow'experience: an empirical study. Br. J. Educ. Technol. 37(5), 705–720 (2006)

24. Slater, M.: A note on presence terminology. Presence Connect 3(3), 1–5 (2003)

25. Slater, M.: Place illusion and plausibility can lead to realistic behaviour in immersive virtual environments. Philos. Trans. Royal Soc. B: Biol. Sci. 364(1535), 3549–3557 (2009)

26. Steuer, J.: Defining virtual reality: dimensions determining telepresence. J. Commun. 42(4), 73–93 (1992)

27. Tyndiuk, F., Lespinet-Najib, V., Thomas, G., Schlick, C.: Impact of tasks and users' characteristics on virtual reality performance. Cyberpsychol. Behav. 10(3), 444–452 (2007)

28. Tyng, C.M., Amin, H.U., Saad, M.N., Malik, A.S.: The influences of emotion on learning and memory. Front. Psychol. 8, 1454 (2017)

29. Zhu, Y., Heynderickx, I., Redi, J.A.: Understanding the role of social context and user factors in video quality of experience. Comput. Hum. Behav. 49, 412–426 (2015)

The Effects of Interactive Emotional Priming on Storytelling: An Exploratory Study

Nanjie Rao[(⊠)], Sharon Lynn Chu, Randi Weitzen Faris, and Daniel Ospina

University of Florida, Gainesville, FL 32611, USA
raon@ufl.edu

Abstract. We propose that emotional priming may be an effective approach to scaffold the creation of rich stories. There are relatively few emotion-based approaches to support users to create, instead of consume, rich stories. Emotional priming is the technique of using emotion-related stimuli to affect human's executive control and affective processing. It has been researched mostly in terms of human's behaviors and decision making. We conducted a within-subjects study with 12 participants to investigate the effects of emotional priming induced through an interactive application on storytelling quality. Two conditions of priming were compared to a baseline condition of no priming. In the first condition, the application primes participants by having asking them to perceive and recognize varying emotional stimuli (perception-based priming). In the second condition, the application primes participants by having them produce varying emotional facial expressions (production-based priming). Analyses show that emotional priming resulted in richer storytelling than no emotional priming, and that the production-based emotional priming condition resulted in statistically richer stories being told by participants. We discuss the possibility of integrating interactive emotional priming into storytelling applications.

Keywords: Storytelling · Emotional priming · Facial recognition

1 Introduction

Emotions are central to the experience of engaging in storytelling, not just during storytelling but also before and after engagement [19]. Products that can deliver more emotionally rich story experiences are more fascinating because audiences or consumers become emotionally attached to the artifacts [8, 24]. There is quite some research that use users' emotions to enable computers to be effective storytelling agents, e.g., emotional storytelling robots can observe their listeners

Supported by National Science Foundation Grant #1736225 *To Enact, To Tell, To Write: A Bridge to Expressive Writing through Digital Enactment.*

© Springer Nature Switzerland AG 2019
R. E. Cardona-Rivera et al. (Eds.): ICIDS 2019, LNCS 11869, pp. 395–404, 2019.
https://doi.org/10.1007/978-3-030-33894-7_42

and adapt their style in order to maximize their effectiveness [7], AI experience managers can predict the player's emotional response to a narrative event and use such predictions to shape the narrative to keep the player on an author-defined emotional curve [15]. Generally in previous work, storytellers' emotions have been used as input to modify features of the story plot, or as an element of character models, e.g., to adjust story characters' behaviors based on users' emotions recognized from linguistic expression [4], or changing the overall narrative according to users' captured emotions [18].

Surprisingly, we found fewer emotion-based approaches to support users to create, instead of consume, rich stories. In this paper, we propose that emotional priming may be an effective approach to scaffold the creation of rich stories. This paper presents a within-subjects study that investigates the effects of emotional priming, enabled through interactive means, on users' storytelling ability, and wraps up with a discussion of the design implications for interactive digital storytelling support interfaces.

2   Background and Related Work

2.1   Emotions and Story Authoring Applications

Emotion plays a substantial role in guiding our behaviors and decision making [16,25]. Many applications use various emotion-sensing technologies to analyze users' mental states and adjust system states accordingly. These often use facial expressions as an index of affective arousal [10], or attempt to understand expressions to determine adaptive activities [22]. For example in *StoryFaces*, the tool invites children to capture their facial expressions and combine them with drawings and animations to create dynamic stories [21].

Emotions have also been integrated in interactive story authoring applications using technologies besides facial recognition. *SenToy* [11], for instance, is a doll-like tangible interface that allows the users to manipulate it in order to express emotions while engaged in storytelling. Results showed that the emotions that were expressed with SenToy generally aligned with the users' self-report of their emotions during storytelling after the creative process. In Cavazza et al.'s work [4], the storytelling system allowed the user to participate in dialogue with virtual actors without constraints on style or expressivity to create a story. Advanced speech recognition was used to determine the user's emotions. The system mapped the recognized emotional categories to narrative situations and virtual characters' feelings, thereby driving the characters' behaviors in the story.

In prior work such as the above and references [3,12,13,23], emotions were captured and recognized during the process of storytelling in order to guide storytelling in the final story output. This is conceptualized in Fig. 1.

2.2   Emotional Priming Theory

Inspired by emotional priming theory, we propose that instead of emotions acting as a modifier of story output (in real-time or post-hoc), as shown in Fig. 1,

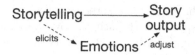

Fig. 1. Role of emotions in existing story authoring applications

emotions may play a different role by framing the user in a more active state of mind in preparation for storytelling. This allows the storytelling process itself to be unhindered by the need for intensive monitoring (e.g., facial recognition while the user is telling her story), with potentially similar benefits in terms of more emotionally rich stories.

Emotional priming is the act of modifying someone's behavior and actions through subliminal stimuli. Essentially, subliminal emotional stimuli are used to alter moods and therefore trigger a particular response [9,27], for example, to affect affective judgments. Emotional priming is considered fundamental evidence for unconscious perception and its strength is predicted by perceptual awareness levels [17]. Specifically, valenced emotional concepts can be nonconsciously activated, remain inaccessible to conscious awareness, and still affect behavior in an emotion-specific fashion [28]. fMRI studies suggest that emotional priming effects trigger specific regions of the brain that handles emotions [14].

Prior work on emotional priming typically prime participants for specific moods (e.g., showing sad pictures to prime for sadness). In our work, we are interested in priming participants for attention to emotions in general (i.e., not specific emotions per se). Our proposed process is illustrated in Fig. 2, which can be contrasted to the process in Fig. 1. Users are primed to be in an emotionally attentive state *before* the act of storytelling or story creation. In the bulk of literature on emotional priming, participants are primed by requiring them to watch a series of emotionally-specific stimuli (e.g., pictures of happy moments). We posited that emotional priming can also be achieved through the act of producing and embodying emotions rather than simply perceiving them, thus warranting interactive support systems.

Emotional
priming → Storytelling → Story
output

Fig. 2. Proposed approach with emotional priming

3 System Description

To investigate the promise of our proposed approach of emotional priming, we implemented a gamified emotional priming system that is similar to a typical rhythm game like *Guitar Hero*. The system visually presents participants with stimuli that fall from the top of the screen to the bottom of the screen. The participant needs to respond to the stimuli by the time the text reaches the bottom of the screen (pink area in Fig. 3). Three variations of the system were created for three study conditions: (1) emotional priming through emotion perception: users perceive and recognize existing emotions; (2) emotional priming through emotion production: users generate facial expressions matching specific emotions; and (3) no emotional priming.

In the system for condition A, the stimuli consist of emojis (facial expressions) and the response required from the participant is to press a key corresponding to the specific emoji emotion (see Fig. 3 right). In the system for condition C, the stimuli consist only of directional arrows, and the participant's response is to press the corresponding arrow key on the keyboard (see Fig. 3 left).

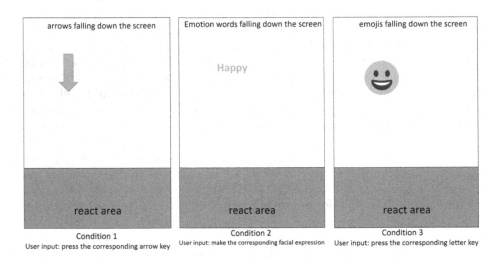

Fig. 3. Gamified interfaces used for each condition (Color figure online)

In the system for condition B, the stimuli consist of words indicating emotional states (e.g., "happy"), and the participant's required response is to produce the indicated facial expression (see Figs. 3 middle and 4). The system then recognizes the participant's facial expressions and maps it to an emotion. The facial expression recognition component of our system used convolutional neural networks to classify emotion/facial expressions based on the FER2013 dataset. We achieved real-time detection using visual-based methods [1]. Four emotions can be identified by the system: happy, angry, sad, and surprise.

In all the 3 system variations, points were awarded if the correct response was given in time. The game component was designed as a Java Standalone application, with graphics developed using AWT and Swing libraries. We also developed a sub-component for components-communication, allowing the video-game component to gather the user's input through the system clipboard which contained the recognized facial expression.

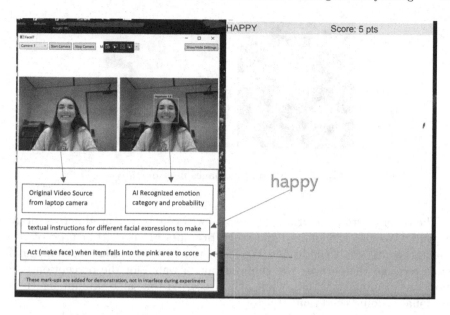

Fig. 4. Emotional priming interface - researcher's view

4   Study Description

Using the three system variations, we addressed the following research questions:

RQ1: Are there significant differences in storytelling quality after emotional priming?

RQ2: Are there significant differences in storytelling quality after perception-based emotional priming as opposed to production-based emotional priming?

The study was carried out in the lab, and used a within-subjects design with emotional priming as the single independent variable (3 levels: perception-based emotional priming; production-based emotional priming; no emotional priming). We had a total of 12 study participants, 5 males, and 7 females. All were university students. They were recruited through university listservs. They were compensated with course credit. A participant participated in only one study session during which he/she engaged in 3 conditions.

Two types of storytelling tasks were given to participants: (i) one prompted by pictures, and (ii) the other prompted by a text phrase. For the picture-prompted storytelling task, 6 paintings (Fig. 5) by the American artist Norman Rockwell were used. These were selected for their potential emotional content and because they were unlikely to be known by participants, thereby eliminating preconceived biases about the paintings. For the text-prompted storytelling task, the following phrases were used: "a child and an animal in the woods"; "an adult and a child and a lake"; and "two children take a walk". The phrases were purposefully left to be ambiguous so that participants can have freedom to create a story.

Fig. 5. Two example images used in study

The order of study/interface conditions was counterbalanced across all participants. We also randomized the story prompts given (within type of story prompts) across study conditions. E.g., for the text-based prompts, some participants received the phrase "two children take a walk" for the perception-based emotional priming condition, while other received the same prompt for the no emotional priming condition, etc.

For each study condition: (1) The participant used the designated system for two minutes; (2) The participant was shown a first image selected randomly out of the 6 paintings chosen for the study, and given 30 s to think up a story about that picture; (3) The participant was asked to tell the story to the researcher immediately after. Research has shown that priming effects tend to fade after 5 mins [2]; (4) Steps 2 and 3 were repeated with a second randomly selected image from the set (excluding the images already presented to the participant before); (5) The participant was given a randomly selected text prompt out of the 3 text prompts, provided 30 s to think about a story relating to that prompt; and (6) The participant was asked to tell that story.

In-between conditions, the participant was given a 3-minute break to reset their state of mind. After all 3 conditions, the participant was asked to fill out a questionnaire and underwent an interview about the overall experience. The study took about an hour per participant. The full protocol can be found here: https://drive.google.com/file/d/1FgzvrfWUX9hC0AbdxJcZJ-upMxaAy3YT.

5   Data Collection and Analysis

Participants were video recorded throughout all the three conditions. We transcribed the stories that the participants told in each condition. To analyze the quality of the stories, each story was first broken down into an 'idea digest' [20]. The idea digest deconstructs a story into individual units of thought or essence of meaning, and has been used as a method of story analysis in previous storytelling research (e.g., [6]). The meaning deconstruction can even occur within sentences. For example, a story sentence reading "She ate it and felt really special and found out she could fly!" would be broken down into 3 ideas: "She ate it", "and felt really special", "and found out she could fly!".

After an idea digest had been extracted for each story, it was coded for *richness descriptors*, which we operationalized as adjectives, nouns used as adjectives, adverbs, and descriptive verbs. This generated a 'story quality score'. A similar process to generate a story quality score was used in Chu et al. [5]. We standardized the value of the story quality scores in two ways: by word count and by the total number of ideas identified in the story. Thus, even if a story was significantly shorter than another, we could still comparatively gauge a sense of its richness. Paired-samples t-tests were run on the story quality scores standardized by word count and standardized by the number of ideas to see if there were statistically significant differences between the quality of the stories being told after using different interfaces.

6   Results

Since each participant had 9 stories, 108 stories were collected in total for 12 participants. ANOVA showed that means differed statistically significantly between the quality of the stories being told after 3 levels of emotional priming stimuli (when standardized by word count, $F(2, 70) = 35.31$, $P < .001$; when standardized by the number of ideas, $F(2, 70) = 45.66$, $P < .001$). Post hoc tests using the Bonferroni correction revealed that pairwise differences exist among all 3 comparisons for all 3 levels of emotional priming stimuli.

When standardized by word count, participants told richer stories after production-based emotional priming ($M = .11$, $SD = .036$) as opposed to perception-based emotional priming ($M = .089$, $SD = .028$); $t(35) = 4.10$, $p < .001$. The difference was even larger between production-based emotional priming and no emotional priming ($M = .064$, $SD = .021$); $t(35) = 6.90$, $p < .001$.

When standardized by the number of ideas, participants told richer stories after production-based emotional priming ($M = 1.25$, $SD = .40$) as opposed to perception-based emotional priming ($M = .91$, $SD = .18$); $t(35) = 4.95$, $p < .001$. The difference was even larger between production-based emotional priming and no emotional priming ($M = .63$, $SD = .21$); $t(35) = 7.88$, $p<.001$.

On average across the two standardization methods, the average story quality score told after production-based emotional priming was 1.32 times higher than for perception-based priming, and 1.88 times

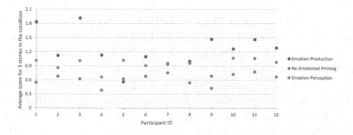

Fig. 6. The story quality scores standardized by the number of ideas

higher than no emotional priming. An example scatter plot is shown in Fig. 6. The full results can be found here: https://drive.google.com/open?id=1XObOjdEkOfjGgHaUdTSpQ7mMbwYoAAZ6.

7   Discussion and Conclusion

Based on emotional priming theory, we proposed a new approach to support users to create rich stories. In our study, emotional priming was achieved through a gamified emotional priming system that prompts users to constantly produce or perceive certain emotions. We found that emotional priming in general led to participants creating statistically significantly richer stories as opposed to no emotional priming (answering RQ1), and that production-based emotional priming produces richer stories than perception-based priming (answering RQ2).

To the best of our knowledge, our study results are the first to show that storytelling quality can be improved through subliminal emotional priming.

This warrants future research into how emotional priming can be integrated into IDN authoring systems. Emotional priming can be a pre-activity before storytelling to prepare storytellers for producing richer stories. A 2-minute emotional priming process is neither exhausting nor time-consuming, and can be fashioned in different ways. For the sake of clarity in the study procedures, we utilized a gamified application separate from the storytelling process but other means more integrated with the story authoring application can be envisioned. In fact, in the interview at the end of our study, many participants told us that the gamified experience was interesting and fun, and that they did not suspect its connection with the storytelling activity.

Another of our findings is that producing the emotions are more powerful than perceiving the emotions in terms of emotional priming. This result aligns with previous perception research, specifically attention and multiple resource theory [26]. The production-based emotional priming application demands more cognitive resources than perception-based priming and thus has stronger priming effects. This suggests that interactive production-based emotional priming which is validated by facial expression recognition may be a useful mechanism to support rich story creation.

Some limitations of this work are that first, although 108 stories were analyzed in total, we had only 12 participants for this study. In the future, a larger sample size is needed. Second, the stimuli used in the perception-based priming application was different than in the production-based priming application. One used emojis whereas the other used words. This was necessary for us to differentiate the two types of emotional priming. And third, the storytelling activity was rather short. Only 30 seconds were given to participants to create a story. This was so that the study could be kept within a reasonable total duration that would not tire out participants. A more complex storytelling activity can be allowed in future research. Furthermore, future research should investigate whether story creation through other means than oral storytelling (that we did in our study) is affected by interactive emotional priming.

This paper demonstrated the effects of applying emotional priming on the creation of rich stories, and discussed possibilities for opening up a new avenue for IDN research.

References

1. Arriaga, O., Valdenegro-Toro, M., Plöger, P.: Real-time convolutional neural networks for emotion and gender classification. arXiv preprint arXiv:1710.07557 (2017)
2. Bargh, J.A., Gollwitzer, P.M., Lee-Chai, A., Barndollar, K., Trötschel, R.: The automated will: nonconscious activation and pursuit of behavioral goals. J. Pers. Soc. Psychol. **81**(6), 1014 (2001)
3. Bradley, M.M., Codispoti, M., Cuthbert, B.N., Lang, P.J.: Emotion and motivation I: defensive and appetitive reactions in picture processing. Emotion **1**(3), 276 (2001)
4. Cavazza, M., Pizzi, D., Charles, F., Vogt, T., André, E.: Emotional input for character-based interactive storytelling. In: Proceedings of The 8th International Conference on Autonomous Agents and Multiagent Systems-Volume 1, pp. 313–320. International Foundation for Autonomous Agents and Multiagent Systems (2009)
5. Chu, S.L., Quek, F., Tanenbaum, J.: *Performative authoring*: nurturing storytelling in children through imaginative enactment. In: Koenitz, H., Sezen, T.I., Ferri, G., Haahr, M., Sezen, D., çatak, G. (eds.) ICIDS 2013. LNCS, vol. 8230, pp. 144–155. Springer, Cham (2013). https://doi.org/10.1007/978-3-319-02756-2_18
6. Chu Yew Yee, S.L., Quek, F.K., Xiao, L.: Studying medium effects on children's creative processes. In: Proceedings of the 8th ACM Conference on Creativity and Cognition, pp. 3–12. ACM (2011)
7. Costa, S., Brunete, A., Bae, B.C., Mavridis, N.: Emotional storytelling using virtual and robotic agents. Int. J. Humanoid Rob. **15**(03), 1850006 (2018)
8. Demirbilek, O., Sener, B.: Emotionally rich products: the effect of childhood heroes, comics and cartoon characters. In: Design and Emotion, pp. 318–325. Taylor & Francis, London (2004)
9. Dijksterhuis, A., Smith, P.K.: Affective habituation: subliminal exposure to extreme stimuli decreases their extremity. Emotion **2**(3), 203 (2002)
10. Ekman, P., Oster, H.: Facial expressions of emotion. Annu. Rev. Psychol. **30**(1), 527–554 (1979)
11. Figueiredo, R., Paiva, A.: Watch and feel: an affective interface in a virtual storytelling environment. In: Tao, J., Tan, T., Picard, R.W. (eds.) ACII 2005. LNCS, vol. 3784, pp. 915–922. Springer, Heidelberg (2005). https://doi.org/10.1007/11573548_117
12. Garner, T.A.: From sinewaves to physiologically-adaptive soundscapes: the evolving relationship between sound and emotion in video games. In: Karpouzis, K., Yannakakis, G.N. (eds.) Emotion in Games. SC, vol. 4, pp. 197–214. Springer, Cham (2016). https://doi.org/10.1007/978-3-319-41316-7_12
13. Gilroy, S., Porteous, J., Charles, F., Cavazza, M.: Exploring passive user interaction for adaptive narratives. In: Proceedings of the 2012 ACM International Conference on Intelligent User Interfaces, pp. 119–128. ACM (2012)
14. Hart, S.J., Green, S.R., Casp, M., Belger, A.: Emotional priming effects during stroop task performance. Neuroimage **49**(3), 2662–2670 (2010)

15. Hernandez, S.P., Bulitko, V., Spetch, M.: Keeping the player on an emotional trajectory in interactive storytelling. In: Eleventh Artificial Intelligence and Interactive Digital Entertainment Conference (2015)

16. Lerner, J.S., Li, Y., Valdesolo, P., Kassam, K.S.: Emotion and decision making. Annu. Rev. Psychol. **66**, 799–823 (2015)

17. Lohse, M., Overgaard, M.: Emotional priming depends on the degree of conscious experience. Neuropsychologia **128**, 96–102 (2017)

18. Mangione, G.R., Pierri, A., Capuano, N.: Emotion-based digital storytelling for risk education: empirical evidences from the ALICE project. Int. J. Contin. Eng. Educ. Life Long Learn. **24**(2), 184–211 (2014)

19. Mar, R.A., Oatley, K., Djikic, M., Mullin, J.: Emotion and narrative fiction: interactive influences before, during, and after reading. Cogn. Emot. **25**(5), 818–833 (2011)

20. Register, L.M., Henley, T.B.: The phenomenology of intimacy. J. Soc. Pers. Relat. **9**(4), 467–481 (1992)

21. Ryokai, K., Raffle, H., Kowalski, R.: StoryFaces: pretend-play with ebooks to support social-emotional storytelling. In: Proceedings of the 11th International Conference on Interaction Design and Children, pp. 125–133. ACM (2012)

22. Shahid, S., Krahmer, E., Swerts, M., Melder, W.A., Neerincx, M.A.: You make me happy: using an adaptive affective interface to investigate the effect of social presence on positive emotion induction. In: 2009 3rd International Conference on Affective Computing and Intelligent Interaction and Workshops, pp. 1–6. IEEE (2009)

23. Smith, G.M.: Film Structure and the Emotion System. Cambridge University Press, Cambridge (2003)

24. Solarski, C.: Interactive Stories and Video Game Art: A Storytelling Framework for Game Design. AK Peters/CRC Press, Natick (2017)

25. Tamir, M., Bigman, Y.E., Rhodes, E., Salerno, J., Schreier, J.: An expectancy-value model of emotion regulation: Implications for motivation, emotional experience, and decision making. Emotion **15**(1), 90 (2015)

26. Wickens, C.D.: Multiple resources and performance prediction. Theor. Issues Ergon. Sci. **3**(2), 159–177 (2002)

27. Winkielman, P., Berridge, K.C.: Unconscious emotion. Curr. Dir. Psychol. Sci. **13**(3), 120–123 (2004)

28. Zemack-Rugar, Y., Bettman, J.R., Fitzsimons, G.J.: The effects of nonconsciously priming emotion concepts on behavior. J. Pers. Soc. Psychol. **93**(6), 927 (2007)

Cognitive Training for Older Adults with a Dialogue-Based, Robot-Facilitated Storytelling System

Seiki Tokunaga[✉], Katie Seaborn, Kazuhiro Tamura,
and Mihoko Otake-Matsuura[✉]

Center for Advanced Intelligence Project (AIP), RIKEN, Nihonbashi 1-chome
Mitsui Building, 15th floor, 1-4-1 Nihonbashi, Chuo-ku, Tokyo 103-0027, Japan
{seiki.tokunaga, katie.seaborn, kazuhiro.tamura,
mihoko.otake}@riken.jp

Abstract. Early detection programs for mild cognitive impairment have recently been developed. However, there is no standard method of daily training to build resilience against cognitive decline. We propose a dialogue-based method for healthy older adults. This involves collecting stories from older adults to generate datasets of question-and-answer pairs for each story in a dialogue format. We then provide these datasets through an interactive storytelling experience facilitated by a robot. Here we report on and discuss initial findings on the attitudes of elderly users towards the robot, the robot's accuracy as a facilitator, and the ability of elders to remember story information provided by the robot.

Keywords: Cognitive Function · Storytelling · Dialogue system · Older adults

1 Introduction

In the wake of rapid and global societal aging, maintaining the quality of life (QoL) of elderly people has become an important concern worldwide. Social isolation and loneliness are major QoL problems affecting older adult populations. To stay mentally and emotionally fit ensuring positive social interactions and communication in the daily life of elders is key [1, 2]. Additionally, there appears to be a relationship between these social activities and cognitive functions, suggesting that they have the potential to prevent cognitive decline. For instance, research has found that communication with others balances sympathetic nerve activity, leading to more emotional support [5]. Such findings reveal the potential value of exploring the role of the social environment in protecting against cognitive decline at an older age.

To ensure that the QoL in older adults is being maintained, knowing the status of various cognitive functions and the rate of cognitive decline over time are of key

This research was partially supported by JSPS KAKENHI Grant Numbers JP19H01138.

R. E. Cardona-Rivera et al. (Eds.): ICIDS 2019, LNCS 11869, pp. 405–409, 2019.
https://doi.org/10.1007/978-3-030-33894-7_43

importance. So far, several testing methods, such as the Wechsler Memory Scale-Revised (WMS-R) and the Japanese version of the Montreal Cognitive Assessment (MoCA-J), have been successfully applied to understand the cognitive status of healthy older adults. For instance, Suzuki et al. [6] were able to detect the presence of delayed verbal memory through a randomized controlled trial. However, these testing methods are designed for experimental settings and are thus difficult to use in daily life. Moreover, such testing is aimed at assessing the current status at one moment in time; because we would like to perform cognitive training in a proactive and sustainable way, we may need a method that can be used easily on a daily basis by older adults and caregivers.

To this end, we propose a dialogue-based system that aims to provide cognitive training for healthy older adults on a daily basis. Our system consists of five steps. First, we collect stories from older adults using voice records taken during participation in an existing group conversation system [4]. We then generate a dataset of question-and-answer (QA) pairs for each story in a dialogue format. We also create a storyteller persona to further structure the experience of each story. The story datasets are then provided in an interactive way through a storytelling and QA experience, which is facilitated by an original robot that we developed (Bono-06). This robot takes on the storyteller persona of each story. To evaluate the current datasets, user experience, and feasibility of the dialogue system and robot-based facilitation, we conducted a user study with 21 elderly participants. We report on the results of this evaluation here.

2 System Design

We describe each component of our dialogue-based, robot-facilitated storytelling system in detail below, going step-by-step through the process of preparation and use, with the case evaluated later in this paper (see Sect. 3.) as a representative example:

Step 1. Story Collection: We first collect stories from elderly participants using an original conversation-based system introduced by Otake-Matsuura [4]. In this instance, we collected 36 stories from two older adults whose stories caused other participants to laugh the most, based on Kikuchi's analysis of laughter responses for these stories [3]. The number of stories is designed to provide one story each day fora long-term experiment situation. For instance, if three stories are provided per week, it will take three months for all of the stories to be experienced. In this case, we chose one to evaluate.

Step 2. Transformation of Original Stories: In this step, we anonymize the original stories to protect the privacy of the storyteller. We also condense the content so as to allow other listeners to understand the stories more easily. This is required because sometimes too much detail, such as specific location names, can distract or confuse those not familiar with the details. In general, we revise the length of each story to be between 30 and 40 s long, in line with one of the tasks of the WMS-R [8]. Moreover, the names of people are replaced with more generic words, e.g., Mr. Tanaka is converted to he/him. The following sentences provide an example extracted from the story we evaluated here: "About twenty years ago, I bought a tray at an overseas airfield. I think it was about a hundred dollars. It's not a big deal, but it's lacquered…"

Step 3. Development of the Storyteller Persona: In this step, we develop a story-teller persona to be used in the dialogue system by the robot facilitator. Because our goal is to develop a dialogue system for daily use by older adult users, we decided that the storyteller should have a personality and speak naturally. Moreover, after gener-ating and reviewing the initial sets of QA pairs, we realized that a personality would be useful for the content format and the storyteller. We thus developed a persona that was based on the elderly people mentioned in Step 1. Specifically, a persona called BONO, aged 70 years old, male, with the hobbies fishing, piano, healthy food, and golf.

Step 4. Generation of QA Pairs: Next, towards creating a daily system, we generate pairs of questions and answers to be used in the interactive QA-type dialogue system with the robot. In this case, we use done of the 36 stories that were collected to generate a dataset. We then create a fixed number of QAs pairs using crowdsourcing via a company. In this case, we used a local company to generate about 65 QA pairs.

Step 5. Transformation of Generated QA Pairs: Finally, we thoroughly check the QA pairs for grammar, syntax (e.g., punctuation), and other formatting issues. We also modify the story text for robot processing by replacing words written in logographic Chinese characters with the phonetic alphabet equivalents for pronunciation accuracy. For example: "What is attracts you to this plate?" with the answer being "I think the best point is I can put something on it. I always use it in daily use. I also like the appearance of it."

Robot Facilitation and an Example Use Case: Figure 1 illustrates how the robot (Bono-06) is integrated into the dialogue system through a general use case. The robot has a microphone and a physical button for operation, designed with elderly users in mind [7]. Once the user pushes the button on the robot, speech recognition starts (1). The user then asks the robot a question, with their speech data transcribed via the tablet and forwarded to the dialogue system (2.askToSystem). Next, the dialogue system replies to the tablet with an answer and the confidence level for this answer (3.re-plyFromSystem). Finally, the robot vocalizes the answer it receives from the dialogue system. Its face turns yellow if the dialogue system has an answer to the question.

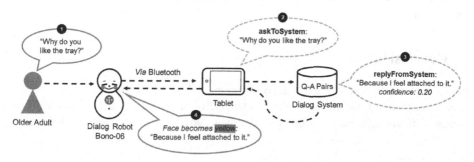

Fig. 1. Use case of the dialogue system integrated with the robot Bono-06 (Color figure online)

3 User Study

We conducted a user study that revealed the attitudes of older adults towards the robot, their ability to remember the stories they experienced, and some technical difficulties with the QA system and robot.[1] 21 healthy older adults (12 men, 9 women) aged 65 and above participated individually in one session with one human operator. We began each session by explaining the user study and how to use the robot. First, Bono-06 relayed one story to the participant, and then the participant experienced a 3-minute QA period. After this, the participant filled out an original self-report questionnaire (see Table 1). Each item used a 5-point Likert scale. In items 1 to 3, we asked about the robot's appearance, such as size and facial expression. Items 4 to 6 (marked with a † symbol) tested how much the participant remembered of the robot's original story and are relevant to cognitive function tests.

Table 1. Questionnaire about the story, robot, and QA task

Number	Item of the questionnaire	Score
(1)	What do you think of the volume of the robot?	2.38
(2)	What do you think of the size of the robot?	2.28
(3)	What do you think of the facial expression of the robot?	2.33
(4)†	Where did the robot buy the plate?	0.52
(5)†	How much was the plate?	0.43
(6)†	Where did the robot put the plate?	0.43

Questionnaire results are summarized in Table 1 under the "Score" column. Results from items 1 to 3 suggest that the robot's appearance was acceptable, with all scores higher than the mean value. However, results from items 4 to 6 indicate that participants had difficulty remembering the story, with the rate of correct answers at about 50% or lower. Additionally, our observations and video analysis show that the system often did not reply with a valid answer. Reasons include: speech recognition failure; lack of QA pairs datasets; some of the answers including too much information (despite our efforts to reduce detail); and the user's answer not being in the form of a question. We plan to correct these technical issues and smooth over the UX in the next version of the system.

4 Conclusion

In this paper, we present a novel dialogue-based, robot-facilitated system that aims to provide cognitive training for healthy older adults on a daily basis. To evaluate the current datasets, UX, and feasibility of the dialogue system and robot facilitation, we

---

[1] This study has been approved by the research ethics committee of RIKEN (No. W2018-058). Written informed consent was obtained from participants.

conducted a user study with 21 elderly participants using one story crowdsourced from elders. We confirmed that most participants could use the system with little difficulty and that the appearance of the robot is acceptable. However, we found several technical and design factors that lead to human error and poor UX in some cases. After improving these, we plan to conduct a long-term randomized controlled experiment (RCT) to confirm the effects on and experience of elders using our system on a daily basis.

References

1. Arnetz, B.B., Eyre, M., Theorell, T.: Social activation of the elderly: A social experiment. Soc. Sci. Med. **16**(19), 1685–1690 (1982). https://doi.org/10.1016/0277-9536(82)90093-4
2. Golden, J., et al.: Loneliness, social support networks, mood and wellbeing in community-dwelling elderly. Geriatr. Psychiatry **24**, 694–700 (2009)
3. Kikuchi, I.: Development of the extraction and reuse method of interesting topics based on analysis of laughter in coimagination method. Master's thesis, Chiba University (2017). (Japanese)
4. Otake-Matsuura, M.: Conversation assistive technology for maintaining cognitive health. J. Korean Gerontol. Nurs. **20**, 154–159 (2018)
5. Seeman, T.E., Lusignolo, T.M., Albert, M., Berkman, L.: Social relationships, social support, and patterns of cognitive aging in healthy, high-functioning older adults: MacArthur studies of successful aging. Health Psychol. **20**, 243–255 (2001)
6. Suzuki, H., et al.: Cognitive intervention through a training program for picture book reading in community-dwelling older adults: a randomized controlled trial. BMC Geriatr. **14**(1), 122 (2014)
7. Tokunaga, S., Otake-Matsuura, M.: Development of Dialogue Robot Bono-06. The Robotics Society of Japan (2019, to appear)
8. Wechsler, D.: Wechsler Memory Scale-Revised. Harcourt Brace Jovanovich, San Antonio (1987). https://ci.nii.ac.jp/naid/10013355821/en/

Doctoral Consortium

Companionship Games: A Framework for Emotionally Engaging and Empathetic Interactive Characters

Alice Bowman(✉)

Abertay University, Bell Street, Dundee DD1 1HG, UK
1704646@uad.ac.uk

Abstract. 1 in 2 people are diagnosed with cancer in their lifetime, and for those living with cancer loneliness and isolation are significant problems. This paper discusses the development of a virtual cancer support group, using the support group format to offer a companionship game to breast cancer patients. Seven characters populate this support group, designed as empathetic virtual agents. Interviews and playtests will assess the effectiveness of the design practice developed, and these learnings will be used to create a design framework for emotionally engaging and empathetic interactive characters.

Keywords: Interactive Storytelling · Serious games · Cancer support · Narrative design · Character design

1 Introduction

Most of us will be affected by cancer to some extent over the course of our lifetimes. The lifetime risk of receiving a cancer diagnosis for people in the UK born after 1960 has risen to 1 in 2 according to Cancer Research UK [1]. Even those who are not affected directly are likely to see friends or family diagnosed with cancer.

As the likelihood of diagnosis increases and the average lifespan of cancer patients lengthens due to developing treatment options, we must also increase the soft services offered to accommodate the growing population living with cancer. People live with technology, smartphone ownership in the UK has risen to 78% [2], games and apps have become a part of daily life for many people. Individuals living with cancer are perhaps even more invested in this outlet - a smartphone or tablet could be a lifeline to the outside world to someone who is bedridden, or a doorway into escapism for someone suffering through chemotherapy. With this in mind, I am undertaking the challenge of creating a game to offer additional support to cancer patients.

Specifically, I have chosen to design a virtual cancer support group for breast cancer patients. Loneliness and isolation are significant problems for people living with cancer [3], and when severe can be detrimental to patient prognosis. Accessing a support group can be difficult for a range of reasons, and virtual cancer support group would provide a supplement or replacement to patients who might not be able to access these services.

R. E. Cardona-Rivera et al. (Eds.): ICIDS 2019, LNCS 11869, pp. 413–417, 2019.
https://doi.org/10.1007/978-3-030-33894-7_44

This project is not the first to employ game design practice in an attempt to solve a problem, or otherwise offer a service other than entertainment through the format of games. Serious games are a genre made up of games that aim to engage their players beyond fun or entertainment [6], and a sub-genre of serious games deal with topics relating to healthcare and wellbeing. Some of these games have specifically addressed issues around cancer - That Dragon Cancer [7] is a biographical game made by a developer to depict his young child's experience of terminal cancer and the impact on his family. Beyond this, other games such as Re-Mission [8] and The Cancer Game [9] allow players to play out actions of fighting cancer and destroying cancerous cells - these games can be cathartic for players of any age, and can be used to help younger patients frame the often traumatising treatment in positive terms. The area of companionship games is less explored, but the greater context of serious games and the topic of cancer in gaming provides some insight in the form of critical play with which to prime this research.

2   Research Aims

Previous studies and literature indicate that players can develop meaningful attachments to game characters and games themselves [4]. The driving question behind this research is how can characters be designed to foster these emotions in the context of a serious game? Previous papers have examined the potential for emotional authenticity in virtual agents [5]. This research seeks to test the extent to which emotional authenticity and feelings of empathy and companionship can be generated using characters designed to be empathetic virtual agents.

The prototype developed for this project aims to use a fictional simulation of a support group to provide companionship to breast cancer patients and alleviate loneliness. For patients who are unable to access support groups, the app will offer an alternative that can provide some of the emotional support that patients can derive from support groups. For patients who can access support groups, the app might be supplementary allowing them to access emotional support when their group is not runningor might also serve as a transitional tool for patients who are tentative about accessing a group.

Ultimately this research will enable the development of a design framework identifying the core qualities of the empathetic virtual agents required for companionship games, as well as defining what a companionship game is. This style of game might be used in any scenario where a user group could benefit from emotional support that empathetic virtual agents can provide. Additionally, it could be used to educate users about the emotions and reality of living with cancer and might provide empathy training.

3 Methodology and Process

A preliminary literature review of comparable work and relevant research was carried out at the start of this work to prime the early stages of planning this research. This literature review acts as a foundation for the research being undertaken and has also been used to build a case as to the value of the research and reasoning for the hypothesis of players benefiting from emotional attachment with virtual characters.

A thematic analysis of patient forums and online communities of people living with cancer was carried out. This was the first step in developing an awareness of the experiences of cancer patients, and an understanding of what it can be like to live with cancer. This knowledge has been important to the project as it has facilitated the accurate representation of patients and their experiences, and was a good preparatory step prior to carrying out further research with patients.

Following this early research, I began working on designs for a virtual support group prototype, designing the game flow and some potential characters. This design work was done in parallel to other continued streams of research and allowed me to explore the project through practice and prototyping. This practice as research has been the core of the project and has continued throughout the development of this work, drawing on my background in game design and working within a framework of design literature that discusses emotional bonds between players and characters.

A series of 1-1 interviews with breast cancer patients are currently being carried out. These interviews are semi-structured, focusing on topics such as loneliness, isolation and emotional wellbeing. These interviews are hosted by Dundee's Maggie's Centre, the local branch of a UK-wide cancer charity. These interviews are being used to inform the narrative and character design, enriching the stories with realistic detail and ensuring that they are accurate representations of the patient experience. The narrative and characters do not directly depict any of the individuals interviewed or their experiences, but the qualitative data gathered has informed the design practice.

A co-design session with breast cancer patients will then be used to examine the prototype and gather feedback that can be used to iterate on the game's design and hone the narrative and characters. Patients will be asked to list the topics they would be likely to discuss at a support group, and will be asked about who they would most want to discuss each topic with. The character designs will be broken into components (i.e. individual personality traits, age, background, appearance) so participants can create their own variations on characters. This session will be used to explore player preference in identifying companions and to better understand what makes a player recognise a fictional character as an empathetic confidant.

Through this research, the prototype will be iterated on to account for design learnings and insights that the character design framework provides as it develops. The final prototype of the game will be playtested at breast cancer support groups in brief half-hour play sessions to capture initial player reactions. A small sample of breast cancer patients will be asked to participate in an extended study of engaging with the game over a longer period of time and playing the content in full. This extended playtest will be followed by individual interviews to gather feedback on the player's experience and feelings towards the game and characters.

4 Prototype

The prototype is currently in development, and this practice is a key component of the research being undertaken. It is being made in Unity using the Fungus plug-in, which gives developers a series of flow-chart based scripts to direct dialogue and branching narrative. Seven characters have been designed as fictional breast cancer patients to populate the support group. The first iteration of these character designs has been based on a combination of early research and practice-based experimentation ideating through multiple concepts. These character designs will evolve as the research progresses and provides more material to inform the design. At present, the characters have been written to encourage a close and empathetic bond with the player, and their backgrounds have been designed so as to represent an array of different types of patient.

At present the working framework (see Fig. 1) is built off of practice-based research, a literature review of relevant work and the other types of research undertaken so far, as discussed in the above section. This framework will likely evolve as the research continues, the current iteration of the character designs have been developed using the framework, and their dialogue, character arcs and interactions with the player all reflect the impact of this framework. These aspects of the prototype can all be iterated to accommodate changes to the framework based on new findings.

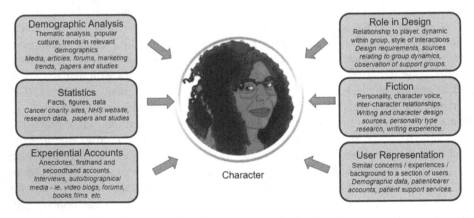

Fig. 1. The working framework for designing empathetic virtual agents in companionship games

5 Next Steps

Patient interviews are still ongoing, and they will be followed by the co-design session, and later playtesting of the prototype. The prototype is currently in development, with the first iteration almost complete, and will continue to evolve to reflect the new learnings uncovered by the ongoing research. In presenting this research to the ICIDS Doctoral Consortium I would like to gather feedback specifically on the research methods employed and the development of the character design framework. These two components of the project both have a significant impact on the validity of the research being undertaken, and it will be crucial in the dissemination of this research that the reasoning behind the methods and the output of the framework can be explained clearly and compellingly.

References

1. Cancer Research UK: Cancer Statistics for the UK. https://www.cancerresearchuk.org/health-professional/cancer-statistics-for-the-uk. Accessed 1 Aug 2019
2. Ofcom: Ofcom Communications Market Report 2018. https://www.ofcom.org.uk/__data/assets/pdf_file/0022/117256/CMR-2018-narrative-report.pdf. Accessed 1 Aug 2019
3. Macmillan: Isolation among cancer patients (2013). https://www.macmillan.org.uk/documents/aboutus/newsroom/isolated_cancer_patients_media_report.pdf. Accessed 1 Aug 2019
4. Mallon, B., Lynch, R.: Stimulating psychological attachments in narrative games: engaging players with game characters. In: Simulation & Gaming (2014)
5. Turkle, S.: Authenticity in the age of digital companions. In: Interaction Studies - Social Behaviour and Communication in Biological and Artificial Systems (2007)
6. Chen, S., Michael, D.: Serious Games: Games That Educate, Train and Inform. Course Technology PTR, Boston (2005)
7. Numinous Games: That Dragon Cancer, Unity (2016)
8. Realtime Associates: Re-Mission, Hopelab (2006)
9. Oda, Y., Kristual, D.: The Cancer Game, Albright College (2014)

Towards Design Principles for Fashion in Interactive Emergent Narrative

Kenneth Chen[✉]

Drexel University, Philadelphia, PA 19104, USA
kc666@drexel.edu

Abstract. In this paper, we explore the concept of fashion and its relevance to interactive emergent narrative. This relationship has been understudied, despite fashion's prevalence in other narrative mediums. We discuss some of the potential ways in which fashion can enhance or drive a narrative, and argue that it can help to solve the issue of compositional representation.

Keywords: Fashion · Interactivity · Emergence · Narrative

1 Introduction

The field of interactive emergent narrative rallies around the concept of "Hamlet on the Holodeck," the dream of a story where the user can interact and watch the world react accordingly [9]. However, a story generation algorithm naturally lacks the artistic touch of a human author, and so many aspects of narrative must be distilled into functions and logic that can be enacted by a nonhuman. Such work has already been conducted on various areas such as timing [10], analogies [16], and backstories [12]. In this paper, we will discuss the area of fashion in interactive emergent narrative.

Fashion is a vital component of linear visual mediums of storytelling: it may be called "character design" in video games or "costume design" in films. It is comparatively unexplored in the field of interactive emergent narrative, seemingly relegated to an afterthought. Two of the most influential projects in interactive emergent narrative, "Facade" [7] and "Prom Week" [8], use manually authored character designs which deliver emergent narrative. What would it mean for fashion to be a part of the generation process, and what could be gained from such an undertaking?

2 Fashion as Story or Discourse

We can begin by looking for ways to categorize fashion in the overall experience of a narrative experience, using Chatman's framework of story and discourse

R. E. Cardona-Rivera et al. (Eds.): ICIDS 2019, LNCS 11869, pp. 418–421, 2019.
https://doi.org/10.1007/978-3-030-33894-7_45

[2]. Story refers to elements that affect the content, whereas discourse refers to elements that affect the way such content is told.

At first glance, it may seem that fashion falls squarely in the realm of discourse, following the logic that a character's outfit does not significantly change their role in the plot. An outfit may help the reader quickly understand a character's emotional state, such as a depressed character wearing black. The depressed character could feasibly be wearing anything, but the designer/author chooses to make them wear black in order to communicate this knowledge to the reader. This approach is deeply explored by character design as a way for the author to tell the reader how to feel about a character upon their first impression [15].

Chatman also makes a distinction between "kernels" and "satellites," two types of story events with varying levels of importance. A kernel is vitally important to a story, but a satellite is a nonessential luxury. This is similar to the concept of "hair complexity" explored by Tynan Sylvester, designer of "Rimworld" [14]. He references the example of dwarves having randomized appearances in "Dwarf Fortress," which have no functional purpose but help players develop a mental image of their characters. They may imagine a backstory to justify this appearance, developing an emotional bond with the character. The act of imagining draws upon the power of apophenia, the human tendency to make connections that don't exist.

However, there are also plenty of examples of fashion as a driving force behind a narrative's story. "Hamlet" itself provides such an example in scene 2.1, as Ophelia confesses her shock at a late-night visit:

My lord, as I was sewing in my closet, Lord Hamlet, with his doublet all unbraced; No hat upon his head; his stockings foul'd, Ungarter'd, and down-gyved to his ancle; Pale as his shirt; his knees knocking each other; And with a look so piteous in purport As if he had been loosed out of hell To speak of horrors,–he comes before me.

This scene is a pivotal moment in recognizing not only Hamlet's descent into madness, but also the ways in which that descent affects the characters around him. Imagine if "Hamlet" was not prewritten, but had all the freedom of interactive emergent narrative that the Holodeck affords. If the user were able to convince Hamlet to put on his clothes properly, this would drastically change the rest of the story. Ophelia might have accepted his advances that night and become his ally.

The tension between fashion as story or discourse becomes even more strained when we look at "Middle Earth: Shadow of Mordor" (and its sequel, "Shadow of War") [11]. These are triple-A games that implement interactive emergent narrative through the Nemesis System, which creates enemies that interact with each other and the player over long periods of time [5]. Enemies remember their past encounters and adapt accordingly, creating epic rivalries over the course of the game. If you defeat an enemy by shooting him in the head with an arrow, he may be wearing a helmet the next time you face him. His helmet is an element of discourse (communicating the enemy's defensive nature) which references an element of story (the fact that you defeated this enemy with a headshot in the past) which affects the current story (the player can no longer use headshots against this enemy). This creates a complex interweaving between story and discourse, past and present, and authored and generated content.

Stepping away from Chatman's work, we can also see conceptualizations of fashion as personal storytelling. In real life, fashion companies use branding to create personal stories that consumers can opt-into, to join a story or build their own [4]. This stretches the concept of "story" away from manual authoring and towards personal expression and growth. Strangely enough, this reconceptualization from the field of fashion branding also mirrors a reconceptualization from the field of game design. Game designers have distinguished the differences between an explicit story (manually authored by the writer) and a player story (emergent experience from the user) [6]. Each of these approaches mirrors the goal of interactive emergent narrative as a user-driven experience.

3   Purposes of Fashion in Interactive Emergent Narrative

We can see that fashion serves various purposes in various different mediums. Which purposes are particularly relevant to interactive emergent narrative? Where should future work focus its efforts? So far, we have looked at fashion as first impressions, fashion as fuel for imagination, fashion as a driving force, fashion as a reference to past events, and fashion as personal branding. However, there are many more applications: fashion for functional usage, fashion as foreshadowing, or fashion as cultural identity.

Fashion can also be seen as an analogous effort to several other areas. For example, fashion can be similar to environmental storytelling [3], where the environment is just a single person. The classic example of environmental storytelling might be walking into a room with bloodstains on the wall, and wondering what happened there. Likewise, a character could have bloodstains on their clothes. Procedural animation also explores visual presentation as a potential plot device [1].

In interactive emergent narrative, fashion can be a component of how characters express themselves and perceive the expressions of others. Characters in stories (and people in real life) do not understand each other immediately, but rather develop an understanding through implicit measurements such as body language, facial expressions, and fashion. Ryan et al. issue the idea of "compositional representational strategies" as an open design challenge for interactive emergent narrative, arguing that the field needs better ways to indicate abstract concepts such as a character's internal state [13]. It seems that fashion would be a worthwhile approach.

Fashion in interactive emergent narrative is an unexplored area that could potentially yield fruitful results. Some of our oldest stories, from Adam and Eve covering themselves with leaves, explore the relationship between fashion and the human experience. By studying fashion, we can bring interactive emergent narrative to a greater level by improving the quality of character-to-character behaviors.

References

1. Cavazza, M., Charles, F., Mead, S.J.: AI-based animation for interactive storytelling. In: Proceedings Computer Animation 2001, Fourteenth Conference on Computer Animation (Cat. No. 01TH8596), pp. 113–120. IEEE (2001)
2. Chatman, S.: Story and Discourse: Narrative Structure in Fiction and Film. Cornell University Press (1978)
3. Fernández-Vara, C.: Game spaces speak volumes: indexical storytelling (2011)
4. Hancock, J.: Brand/Story: Cases and Explorations in Fashion Branding. Fairchild Books (2016)
5. Hoge, C.: Helping players hate (or love) their nemesis. In: GDC (2018)
6. Lee, T.: Designing game narrative (2013). https://hitboxteam.com/designing-game-narrative
7. Mateas, M., Stern, A.: Façade: an experiment in building a fully-realized interactive drama. In: Game Developer's Conference (2003)
8. McCoy, J., Treanor, M., Samuel, B., Waldrip-Fruin, N., Mateas, M.: Comme il faut: a system for authoring playable social models. In: Proceedings of the Seventh AAAI Conference on Artificial Intelligence and Interactive Digital Entertainment (2011)
9. Murray, J.: Hamlet on the Holodeck: The Future of Narrative in Cyberspace. MIT Press (1998)
10. Porteous, J., Teutenberg, J., Charles, F., Cavazza, M.: Controlling narrative time in interactive storytelling. In: The 10th International Conference on Autonomous Agents and Multiagent Systems, vol. 2, pp. 449–456, May 2011
11. Productions, M.: Middle earth: shadow of war (2017)
12. Rank, S., Petta, P.: Backstory authoring for affective agents. In: Oyarzun, D., Peinado, F., Young, R.M., Elizalde, A., Méndez, G. (eds.) ICIDS 2012. LNCS, vol. 7648, pp. 144–149. Springer, Heidelberg (2012). https://doi.org/10.1007/978-3-642-34851-8_14
13. Ryan, J.O., Mateas, M., Wardrip-Fruin, N.: Open design challenges for interactive emergent narrative. In: Schoenau-Fog, H., Bruni, L.E., Louchart, S., Baceviciute, S. (eds.) ICIDS 2015. LNCS, vol. 9445, pp. 14–26. Springer, Cham (2015). https://doi.org/10.1007/978-3-319-27036-4_2
14. Sylvester, T.: The simulation dream, Blog (2013)
15. Tran, V.: Why fashion in (most) games sucks, and why you should care. In: GDC (2019)
16. Zhu, J., Ontanon, S.: Shall i compare thee to another story? – an empirical study of analogy-based story generation. IEEE Trans. Comput. Intell. AI Games **6**, 216–227 (2014)

A Design Framework for Learning About Representation in Video Games Through Modification of Narrative and Gameplay

Kenton Taylor Howard[(✉)]

University of Central Florida, Orlando, FL 32816, USA
khowarl2@knights.ucf.edu

Abstract. In this paper, I provide an overview of a dissertation project that examines gameplay modification as a method for exploring queer representation in video games. First, I offer an overview of my research goals and the project itself. I then provide a brief outline of the game that is a major component of my dissertation. Next, I discuss the theoretical framework that informs the narrative design of the game to highlight sources that are important to my approach. Finally, I outline my current results, status, and the next steps I will take in the project. The goal of my dissertation is to find out whether players can effectively explore queer representation in video games by playing and modifying a game I built in the Ink scripting language called Life in the Megapocalypse. Overall, I argue that gameplay modification is an effective framework for exploring critical concepts because it allows players to model solutions to issues like problematic portrayals of queerness in gaming by implementing those solutions within the game's code.

Keywords: Games and Education · Queerness in Games · Game Modification

1 Research Goals and Brief Project Overview

While research on education and games is relatively common, there has been less work that examines modification of games as a method for exploring critical concepts like problems with queer representation in video games. This dissertation focuses on expanding the field of research on learning and games by answering the following research question:

RQ: Can players effectively explore queer representation in video games through playing and modifying the video game I design, Life In The Megapocalypse?

I answer this question by providing a model for using video games to help players learn about queer representation in games. This model takes the form of two projects that inform one another: 1. a written portion that lays out a method for using modification of video games to explore queer representation in games and 2. an easily modifiable web-based video game built in the Ink scripting language that provides a framework that users can build upon through modification. This game, Life in the Megapocalypse, is a choice-based interactive fiction game that features a narrative focused on queer representation in a hostile setting. The game is designed for use as a

© Springer Nature Switzerland AG 2019
R. E. Cardona-Rivera et al. (Eds.): ICIDS 2019, LNCS 11869, pp. 422–426, 2019.
https://doi.org/10.1007/978-3-030-33894-7_46

general learning tool that could also be used in educational settings, especially in the context of modification-based assignments in game design courses.

The main objectives of the two projects described above build upon and reinforce one another: one goal is to create a written framework for educational game design focused on using modification for learning about queer representation in video games, and the other is to create a playable example of what a game based on that framework might look like that others can easily modify. Overall, I argue that by carefully designing the narrative and gameplay of a game, it is possibly to create an easily modifiable video game that can be used as a method to explore critical concepts like queer representation in video game culture. I suggest that video games are an effective avenue for such an approach because they can create a variety of different narratives through procedural content generation and because players can model critical responses to issues like problems with queer representation in gaming through modification of a video game.

2   Brief Outline of Game

Life in the Megapocalypse is an interactive fiction game developed in Ink, a free, open-source scripting language developed by Inkle Studios to build choice-based stories. The game depicts the lives of five different characters in a "megapocalypse" setting: a world in which many of the common tropes in post-apocalyptic video games have all played out, leaving few survivors. The team is mostly composed of queer characters who are trying to reach a nearby refuge after the previous one they were living in fell, and the player, an inhabitant of that safe haven, follows the team's journey via text chat and gives them advice about how to resolve the situations they encounter. The goal of the game is for the player to help as many characters survive as possible and it is designed to be short, replayable, and easily modifiable. This game design allows the player to experience different narratives over the course of multiple playthroughs and to also modify the game to fit their own interests.

Life in the Megapocalypse's narrative approaches the characters and setting from a critical perspective that focuses on problems with queer representation in video games. The game aims to subvert many common stereotypes seen in mainstream games through empowering portrayals of queer characters. As such, most of the player's team members are not the typical violence-prone straight males who are common in post-apocalyptic stories and the game's queer characters resolve situations through methods that are not violent. Like much of post-apocalyptic fiction, however, there is a hypermasculine, straight "savior" character on the team who solves his problems through violence, though relying on his skills causes the player to lose the game as the rest of the team quickly abandons him to fend for himself.

The goal of Life in the Megapocalypse is to provide a narrative and gameplay framework that users can easily modify to explore queer representation in video games. Since Ink is not difficult to learn and could be used in a variety of educational contexts, I provide sample assignments in my dissertation focused on modifying the game that are based on users with different skill levels. This design allows the game to be used as a learning method in a variety of environments both in and out of the classroom.

3 Narrative Design

Life in the Megapocalypse relies on generating randomized story content to create an overall narrative for each playthrough of the game, so I used a procedural narrative framework to design it. Authors such as Bogost [1] suggest that many kinds of media can be approached from systematic perspective that examines how media are composed of discrete units of information. I expand upon that approach by designing Life in the Megapocalypse so that the individual narratives of the game's characters are constructed by systems that users can easily modify with the Inky editor. Modification of the game is useful as a learning exercise because Squire [2] suggests that games are "ideological worlds;" as such, modification allows players to directly change the ideological world of the game. Life in the Megapocalypse also relies on procedural rhetoric as a method of persuasion through systematically generated representation, a notion developed by Bogost [3]. I suggest that modification of such representations is an effective method of learning about the rule systems that govern portrayals of queerness in video games. The ability of video games to create a procedurally generated narrative that presents different scenarios is key to my approach because that ability can encourage a diversity of perspectives on issues like queer representation and can also be used to suggest ways that players could modify the game's systems. Overall, I argue that procedural story generation in Life in the Megapocalypse encourages players to explore solutions to in-game problems through the game's queer characters with the aim of placing a focus on narratives that are not told as often through video games.

I also designed *Life in the Megapocalypse* from a critical perspective by relying on sources that discuss critical game design. Costikyan [4] discusses a critical vocabulary for game narrative and suggests that players will treat almost any decision in a game's story as a puzzle by trying to find the best solution to it. I considered this issue in the design of my game narrative: in *Life in the Megapocalypse*, optimal solutions to in-game problems involve anything other than the typical violence-prone approaches usually found in post-apocalyptic video games. Squire [2] suggests a similar idea when he argues that all games enable learning because they place a focus on problem-solving: as such, my game design focuses on queer representation to help players consider ways to solve problems with that kind of representation in video games. In addition, Ryan [5] looks at game narratives in a design context to distinguish between "narrative games" that focus primarily on gameplay and "playable stories" that mostly rely on storytelling elements. In such terms, *Life in the Megapocalypse* might be described as a playable story, since much of the focus is on story that emerges over the course of a playthrough. The game also has clearly defined victory and loss states, however, so it could be considered a narrative game as well. Exploring the tension between these two kinds of games is useful in the context of *Life in the Megapocalypse* because playing and beating it helps players learn about queer representation in games but also focuses their attention on observing the evolution of a story about queer characters in a hostile environment.

Finally, I used critical sources related to queer representation to inform the design of *Life in the Megapocalypse.* The concept of queer game design was coined by Ruberg [6] to describe game design practices that challenge the traditional ways of presenting sexuality and queerness in video games. I employ queer game design in *Life in the Megapocalypse* by primarily relying on LGBTQ characters and narratives in the game itself. More importantly, my suggestions for modifying the game focus on both changing elements related to the game's queer narratives and on changing the game's mechanics, allowing players to queer the game's story as well as the logic of the game's mechanics. I also rely on game design advice from sources such as Queerly Represent Me [7], who provide a flowchart model to help answer common questions that designers have about creating game narratives that focus on queer representation. In particular, their advice that designers avoid stories of trauma and focus on empowering portrayals of queerness informs the design of the narrative and gameplay in *Life in the Megapocalypse:* the main focus of the narrative and gameplay is on empowering the game's queer characters. Furthermore, within the game's code I encourage players to explore those concepts by providing suggestions in code comments for how a player might modify the game to change its portrayal of queerness.

4 Results, Status, and Next Steps

I have written a draft of my introductory chapter at this point, as well as a draft of my game design focused chapter, which much of this content comes from. That chapter also presents a game design document for the game I am building. It also contains a short discussion of potential classroom applications for my approach and refers to some sample assignments that I provide in the appendix of my dissertation. I have focused on writing that chapter at the same time as I designed my game so that I could document my design process as I went instead of trying to do so after the game was developed.

At this point in my research I have also built a prototype of the game described in this document and submitted it to my dissertation committee for feedback. I am currently working on incorporating my committee's feedback and designing the final version of the game. The game should be fully developed by the time of this conference, and I plan on soliciting additional feedback on my narrative and game design at the doctoral consortium. I will also make a prototype available on my website for my doctoral consortium mentor.

While I do not plan to conduct a full-scale research study as part of this project, I will conduct user testing next year that will help me demonstrate preliminary effectiveness of my approach. This user testing will be conducted with game design students and will use gameplay logging and interviews to find out what kinds of content people create when modifying my game and why they created such content. I will solicit feedback on the design of my user testing as part of my doctoral consortium presentation.

References

1. Bogost, I.: Unit Operations: An Approach to Video Game Criticism. MIT Press, Boston (2006)
2. Squire, K.: Video Games and Learning: Teaching and Participatory Culture in the Digital Age. Teacher's College Press, New York (2011)
3. Bogost, I.: Persuasive Games: The Expressive Power of Videogames. The MIT Press, Cambridge (2007)
4. Costikyan, G.: I have no words and i must design. In: International Proceedings on Computer Games and Digital Cultures Conference, pp. 9–33, Tampere, Finland (2002)
5. Ryan, M.: From narrative games to playable stories: towards a poetics of interactive narrative. Storyworlds: J. Narrative Stud. 1(1), 433–460 (2009)
6. Ruberg, B.: Video Games Have Always Been Queer. New York University Press, New York (2019)
7. Queerly Represent Me: So, You've Decided You Want to Make a Diverse Game Now What?. https://queerlyrepresent.me/resources/articles/making-diverse-games. Accessed 8 Jan 2019

Demonstrations

The Book of Endless History: Authorial Use of GPT2 for Interactive Storytelling

John Austin[✉]

A Stranger Gravity, San Francisco, CA 94107, USA
kleptine@gmail.com
http://astrangergravity.com

Abstract. We present *The Book of Endless History*, an infinite Wikipedia of fantasy stories written in the style of Borges and Calvino, exploring the use of structural conditioning on GPT2 to generate text with explicit subjects and embedded web-links. Users are presented with a Wikipedia-like interface, containing a short fantasy description of the topic and containing embedded web-links to other related subjects. Users may click on links to learn more about different topics, following an endless trail of generated pages. The GPT2 architecture is a text completion model – it has no explicit understanding of structure and it can be a challenge to integrate it with authorial intent. Nevertheless, through this work we show that it can be conditioned to learn to write *about* a subject and additionally to generate the topology for an encyclopedia. We refer to this technique as subject conditioning, or more generally, *structural conditioning*.

Keywords: Structural conditioning · GPT2 · Interactive storytelling

1 Introduction

The GPT2 deep learning architecture, released in February 2019 [3], has made massive strides in the fields of general text generation and analysis. GPT2 is text-completion model, able to generate long-form, complex blocks of text given only a sample prefix. Recently, news articles generated from the largest GPT2 models were found to be at least as believable as equivalent human-written articles, and in some cases, *more* believable [4]. Further, and of interest in the narrative generation domain, the model architecture is able to recall information about the dataset it is trained on. As the primary dataset was taken from a random walk of Reddit, the model is able to generate stories about figures such as Luke Skywalker, Hillary Clinton, Gandalf, and even pull in related concepts such as The Shire without additional prompting.

A primary strength of GPT2 is the generality of the approach: the model is trained simply to produce the most probable next word, given a sequence of tokens. Because of this, GPT2 can even be formulated to perform *non-generative* text analysis tasks such as question-answering, translation, and summarization.

© Springer Nature Switzerland AG 2019
R. E. Cardona-Rivera et al. (Eds.): ICIDS 2019, LNCS 11869, pp. 429–432, 2019.
https://doi.org/10.1007/978-3-030-33894-7_47

The trick is to formulate these tasks as text completion tasks, providing them in "Question: Answer" format. Although the performance of GPT2 on these tasks compared to other specialized approaches is not state of the art, the generality of the system is staggering.

In the narrative generative domain, traditionally the properties of GPT2 are difficult to control. It generates incredibly realistic text, but because it is primarily a text-completion system, it lacks any degree of authorship beyond allowing the user to provide a prefix. Even when prompted with a clear prefix, it can be challenging to compel the model to talk *about* the intended subject, rather than completing valid but unrelated text.

With *The Book of Endless History*, we present an approach we refer to as subject conditioning, or more generally *structural conditioning*, making use of the unique non-generative flexibility noted above. By transforming a raw text dataset of books into a "{subject}\n text" representation (see Approach), we are able to condition the model to expect all text following a line containing the "{subject}" syntax to discuss that subject. We use an off-the-shelf POS tagger and Python to perform this transformation.

Additionally, we layer another structure into our generator: links out. By surrounding *all* named entities in our dataset with square brackets, GPT2 learns generally to place brackets around subjects. After training, all returned text contains a variety of phrases and words 'linked' by GPT2 (see Fig. 2). In the book, we show these as clickable web-links, which query the book recursively for the linked page.

With the combination of these two techniques we are able to create an infinite fantasy Wikipedia of sorts: one where every page is generated, and the topology of the encyclopedia is generated as well. Clicking on a link within the encyclopedia takes a user to a generated page for that topic, and presents them with another set of links to choose from. The result of a random walk through the pages of the book is a bit like a deep-dream [2] experience, where the result of the generator is fed back into the generator itself.

2   Approach

Our approach consists of two steps: link conditioning and subject conditioning. To create a model that generates text with links, we first collect the complete works of Jorge Luis Borges and Italo Calvino in text format and transform this dataset using the off-the-shelf tool, SpaCy [1], to identify named entities and surround them with square brackets. We fine-tune the 345 million parameter version of GPT2[1] on this data[2]. This results in a model that generates fairly

---

[1] As of the writing of this paper, GPT2 comes in two sizes: 345m and 117m, both distilled from an unreleased 1558M model trained by OpenAI. The 345 m model, while slower and larger, is much more robust than the 117m.

[2] The training took approximately 4–6 hours on an NVidia T4, provided for free by Google Colab.

interesting prose in the style of Borges and Calvino, and additionally one that surrounds subjects within the text with brackets.

At this point we perform the subject transformation and training, but on a much smaller selection of books, selected for their focus on short, descriptive stories: *Invisible Cities, Book of Imaginary Beings, A Universal History of Infamy*, and *Labyrinths*. Again, we use SpaCy, selecting the first named entity in each line, and inserting it in curly braces on a new line above.[3] A sample of this final transformation can be see in Fig. 1.

We take this two pronged approach, because while we would like to copy the style of Borges and Calvino from their full body of works, many of their books are first person stories. Performing the subject conditioning on the full collection results in the model generating quite a bit of dialogue (which is undesirable for an encyclopedia), because the primary place of named entities in these stories occur in lines such as:

```
''The next time I kill you'', replied [Scharlach].
```

On the other hand, four books is not nearly enough data to create a compelling and varied generator. The two-phase training allows us the best of both worlds. By training first on a large corpus we get improved style and generality. Then, by confining our subject conditioning to just the works that are written in a non-fiction or third person style, we push the generator to generate non-fiction as well.

A sample query on the final generated text can be seen below in Fig. 2

```
{Zora}
BEYOND SIX RIVERS and three mountain ranges rises [Zora], a city that ...
```

Fig. 1. A sample line of text in the final training dataset.

```
Query:     {Einstein}
Completes: The most significant incident in Einstein's life occurred on
           a summer's day in 1869. He was riding his bicycle along the
           avenues of [Munich] when suddenly, in front of him, was a
           figure which he could never forget.  ...
```

Fig. 2. A sample result querying the book for "Einstein".

The Book of Endless History is presented online[4] in the format of an encyclopedia of the present day found by a hypothetical future society - one which

---

[3] As you may notice, this causes our text to be double spaced, with subjects in between real lines. However, GPT2 manages to learn to ignore this structure incredibly quickly.

[4] http://bookofendlesshistory.com.

ruminates on the nature of truth and history. As we move into an age where false text becomes easier to create than the real, there is somewhat of a dark irony to the nature of the book.

3   Conclusion

We hope that this project will inspire further research into the usage and authorial control of GPT2 and other deep learning architectures for storytelling. While GPT2 may lack in consistency and structure, it makes up for it in creativity and prose. Correspondingly, structured approaches such as grammars and planners can be powerful tools for authorship, but are limited in their ability to generate eloquent text (or require unreasonable amounts of labor to do so). We believe that there is an ideal hybrid system: one in which an author may generate the high level structure with a planning system, and provide these 'structural hints' to a deep learning model which fills in the textual discourse. While this project applies this concept simplistically, we are eager to see similar results with more provided structure and larger models. With the recent acceleration of research on GPT2, we are excited to see the how the landscape of tools available to interactive story generators transforms over the next few years.

References

1. Honnibal, M., Montani, I.: spaCy 2: natural language understanding with bloom embeddings, convolutional neural networks and incremental parsing (2017, to appear)
2. Mordvintsev, A., Olah, C., Tyka, M.: Inceptionism: going deeper into neural networks, Blog (2015). https://ai.googleblog.com/2015/06/inceptionism-going-deeper-into-neural.html
3. Radford, A., Wu, J., Child, R., Luan, D., Amodei, D., Sutskever, I.: Language models are unsupervised multitask learners. OpenAI (2019)
4. Zellers, R., et al.: Defending against neural fake news. CoRR abs/1905.12616 (2019). http://arxiv.org/abs/1905.12616

Author Index

Printed in the United States
By Bookmasters